A History of German

This book provides a detailed but accessible introduction to the development of the German language from the earliest reconstructible prehistory to the present day. Joe Salmons explores a range of topics in the history of the language, offering answers to questions such as: How did German come to have so many different dialects and close linguistic cousins like Dutch and Plattdeutsch? Why does German have 'umlaut' vowels, and why do they play so many different roles in the grammar? Why are noun plurals so complicated? Are dialects dying out today? Does English, with all the words it loans to German, pose a threat to the language?

This second edition has been extensively expanded and revised to include extended coverage of syntactic and pragmatic change throughout, expanded discussion of sociolinguistic aspects, language variation, and language contact, and more on the position of German in the Germanic family. The book is supported by a companion website and is suitable for language learners, teachers, and students of linguistics from undergraduate level upward. The new edition also offers more detailed background information, which is designed to make it more accessible to beginners.

About the author

Joseph Salmons is the Lester W. J. 'Smoky' Seifert Professor of Language Sciences at the University of Wisconsin-Madison, where he is also co-founder and director of the Center for the Study of Upper Midwestern Cultures. His work focuses on language change in the context of linguistic theory, especially speech sounds. He serves as editor of *Diachronica: International Journal for Historical Linguistics*, and his main publications include *The Oxford Handbook of Historical Phonology* (co-edited with Patrick Honeybone; OUP, 2015) and *Germanic Heritage Languages in North America: Acquisition, Attrition, and Change* (co-edited with Janne Bondi Johannessen; Benjamins, 2015).

A History of German

What the Past Reveals about Today's Language

Second Edition

JOSEPH SALMONS

OXFORD
UNIVERSITY PRESS

OXFORD
UNIVERSITY PRESS

Great Clarendon Street, Oxford, OX2 6DP,
United Kingdom

Oxford University Press is a department of the University of Oxford.
It furthers the University's objective of excellence in research, scholarship,
and education by publishing worldwide. Oxford is a registered trade mark of
Oxford University Press in the UK and in certain other countries

© Joseph Salmons 2012, 2018

The moral rights of the author have been asserted

First Edition published in 2012
Second Edition published in 2018

Impression: 1

Published in the United States of America by Oxford University Press
198 Madison Avenue, New York, NY 10016, United States of America

British Library Cataloguing in Publication Data
Data available

Library of Congress Control Number: 2018937075

ISBN 978-0-19-872302-8

Printed in Great Britain by
Bell & Bain Ltd., Glasgow

Short contents

Detailed contents

Preface to the second edition

Only with a couple of years' distance can I now see the extent to which WRITING *A History of German* was exciting and the extent to which PUBLISHING it was terrifying, and mostly for the same reasons: I decided to approach the book in a way very different from how most introductions to language history have been done, in tone and style and in content and argument. Getting so personally invested in a book makes you nervous about how readers, including students and reviewers, will react to it.

Producing this second edition has been a vastly different experience, thanks to the extremely generous feedback and reviews from so many of my best colleagues in the field, writing in so many good journals (some of the kind words are quoted, under 'reviews', at http://ukcatalogue.oup.com/product/9780199697946.do). Playing off an old cliché about bad publicity, I said at the time that I'd be happy if reviewers got my name right (which all these people did):

- Schlücker, Barbara. 2013. *Morphology* 23.91–93.
- Pichigun, Alexander E. 2013. *Unterrichtspraxis* 46.284–286.
- Durrell, Martin. 2014. *The Modern Language Review* 109.522–523.
- Fertig, David. 2014. *Language* 90.548–551.
- Quak, Arend. 2014. *Amsterdamer Beiträge zur älteren Germanistik* 72.307–308.
- Sundquist, John. 2015. *Journal of Germanic Linguistics* 27.194–200.
- Dewey, Tonya Kim. 2015. *Beiträge zur Geschichte der deutschen Sprache und Literatur* 127.328–331.

In addition, I have received really valuable and detailed comments from some of those reviewers and other colleagues, especially Joshua Bousquette, David Connelly, Martin Durrell, Stephan Elspaß, Matt Hamann, Mike Putnam, Artūras Ratkus, Paul Roberge, Markus Schiegg, John te Velde, and Freek van de Velde (see the website for a fuller set of names; and please forgive me for all the names I've neglected to include). All this has reshaped the book in many ways and helped my own thinking tremendously. Joshua Bousquette went beyond any reasonable expectation of collegial help in providing detailed comments on the new material in this edition. Saranya Jayakumar, Manuela Tecusan and Michael Janes were extremely helpful during production and Sam Litty provided huge help on the indexing.

As nice as it was to read positive assessments, I'm even more grateful for the many constructive suggestions for how to make this second edition much stronger than the first. There has been real progress on many fronts in the research since I wrote (see the sketch just below) and, between that and input from colleagues and reviewers, a set of topics have been reworked in this version of the book. Of course now I'm already worrying about what I have missed this time round and thinking about the things I knew I wanted to include but didn't manage to squeeze into a manuscript without going well over the agreed word count.

One basic point in the first edition (picked up on by some reviewers, especially David Fertig) is that this is an exciting time to be doing language history because there is massive progress on virtually every front. As I'm finishing this new preface, the revised version of the manuscript has about eighty references to work published since I finished the first edition, and dozens more new references to work published before 2012. If I had unlimited space for lengthening the second edition, there would be twice as many. (Here's hoping for a third edition, I suppose.) A lot of the new things I knew I would want to develop in another edition, if I had the privilege; but there have been some surprises, like the idea, from Seiler (2014), of thinking of our writing cultures and written materials in terms of 'media', which makes the advent of writing a real media revolution. And while I knew that there was excellent work coming on early glosses, I had no idea that so much would be available.

A few things have not changed, even with recommendations from people to make changes. For instance, a number of people suggested giving more attention to vocabulary, in terms of lists of borrowings and stylistic layers. With limited space, that just doesn't feel like a high priority by comparison to other structural and social issues at hand. Along with updating discussions in line with the last few years of research, here are some of the ways in which this edition differs from the first:

1. Perhaps the most common thing that reviewers noted was that the book was heavier on phonology and morphology than on syntax. That was completely true, and the balance has shifted with various additions on syntax in several chapters.
2. Several reviewers noted a need for greater accessibility for real beginners, including definitions and more detailed background. I have expanded the definitions and the background within the text to an extent. I have opted against a glossary, since online glossaries of linguistic terms are already available, linked on historyofgerman.net. This edition has considerably more cross-referencing to help the reader follow key threads throughout the book.
3. Even since the publication of the first edition, there has been great progress in understanding European linguistic prehistory, including work in population genetics, language contact, and issues of Germanic subgrouping. I've added some discussion of key new and emerging issues.

4. Perhaps against all odds, philology is suddenly cool, very cool. There's a lot of progress coming in our fundamental data sources, especially for early German and across Germanic; and I have tried to show that.

5. I have expanded the sociolinguistic discussions for the early periods, for example with regard to the relationship of early German to Latin and to how German came to be written and who did the writing.

6. Language histories in general typically give little attention to derivational morphology (aside from issues like the creation of weak verbs) and compounding. New research is now beginning to allow some expansion of the discussion on those fronts.

7. I have built up a thread of discussion of templatic structure throughout the book; it includes morphological, prosodic, and syntactic templates.

8. There is a long overdue explosion of work on language variation and change in contemporary German, especially in exploring the role of media in language change, but also in areas like sociophonetics.

9. Where I could, I have also built up the later periods in the history of German, recognizing another imbalance in the first edition, although that is hardly fully resolved (in part for good reason, I think).

10. In the last chapter I have expanded discussion of how German fits and does not fit with the rest of Germanic and with languages beyond. Just as the past reveals much about how German works and how German and English compare, it can also open up a broader view of the family. And I have built up comparative angles throughout the book... yes, this is a history of German, but it benefits from being fully embedded in its Germanic context.

In short, this second edition contains a number of extended stretches of new prose and a few sections of significantly revised prose, but you will see, if you compare the two closely, that the real substance of the revision is woven more deeply into the fabric of the book. The table of contents is only minimally changed, but this is a pretty different work if you scratch the surface. Still, at the end of writing, I'm left with an overwhelming feeling of what is not here that needs to be here. Alas, that would be a couple more volumes.

The website, very sparse when the book was first published, is now large, with well over 100 files, including practice sheets, answer keys, homework assignments, sample tests, and more. But please help me keep the website up to date by sending ideas and improvements for a third edition.

I again owe profound thanks to so many colleagues and students for ongoing discussions on the history of German. And, once again, the staff at Oxford University Press have been a real and consistent pleasure to work with. Thank you, Julia Steer and Vicki Sunter.

Preface

In 1979, I was a first-year graduate student in Germanic Languages at the University of Texas, working to get proficient in German and then return to my real interest—philosophy—when I took a required class on the History of the German Language, taught by Edgar Charles Polomé. That course fundamentally changed how I thought about language: after years of wondering about and bothering instructors with questions about why certain things in German are the way they are, in every class hour I was suddenly seeing clear and compelling answers, including to questions I had not thought to ask. I was unexpectedly coming to understand how German worked in a far more basic way than I had even hoped for until then.

That course literally (in the old sense of the word *literally*) changed the direction of my life—I never returned to the academic field of philosophy, but instead became a linguist, initially specializing in historical Germanic linguistics, then general historical linguistics and later expanding into other areas. Edgar became my mentor from that point forward, though I didn't realize it until later; he directed my dissertation and guided me through my early career. While my own primary research and teaching interests have expanded over the decades, what I learned in that one semester is with me in every single thing that I do professionally. That course, the History of the German Language, still feels like the cornerstone of training in Germanic linguistics to me, and just putting these materials together therefore brings some sense of resolution with it.

All of us who teach a course repeatedly accumulate sets of handouts, worksheets, and so on. In the fall of 2007, as I prepared to teach the History of the German Language at the University of Wisconsin, I decided to turn my own materials for the course into a book, initially simply as a textbook but then increasingly as a general introduction to the history of the language. The group of students in that course was an outstanding one—a broad mix of undergraduates, new graduate students, and second-year graduates, most from German but some from Linguistics, and with wildly varying backgrounds. They were patient enough to be the guinea pigs in this experiment, reading a rough first version of this book as their course text, albeit incomplete and often written and posted to the course website only days before they read it. Their response was encouraging enough to develop this into a 'real' book. More importantly, members of that class gave good feedback on the earliest version. In the fall of 2009, I again taught the course, and developed the manuscript further, thanks again to the active assistance of another excellent group of students. Since its inception, this project has moved from being heavily anchored in phonology and morphology, the core areas of traditional Germanic historical linguistics and my own research interests, to include more sociolinguistics and more recently more syntax and pragmatics. That transition remains incomplete, but I hope the current version has enough balance to cover the field adequately and, as in so many ways, I hope to have the chance to improve things in a future edition.

It is simply impossible to acknowledge all the people who were central to this manuscript. As will be clear from the above, Edgar Polomé is all but a co-author of this book. The same holds for Rob Howell, in a very different way, for sharing various homeworks and handouts. Who knows how many points made in this book come from comments Rob has made 'zwischen Tür und Angel' as we've talked about the history of German. A number of colleagues have provided page upon page of detailed commentary and critique. For that extraordinary help, I thank Katerina Somers (who read two different versions), Elly van Gelderen, Nils Langer, Monica Macaulay, Marc Pierce, and Rob Robinson, as well as Chris Sapp and Paul Roberge, who both read a near-final draft with a careful eye. Many other people have provided comments and suggestions to improve the manuscript, including Andy Kraiss, Andrea Menz, and Tom Purnell. Colleagues like Neil Jacobs have given me much guidance along the way. Horst-Dieter Rönsch, in the course of a truly entertaining cycle ride through the countryside, stopped to show me the *Fachwerk* building that is shown on the cover of this book and then provided the photograph. I have struggled throughout to give the fullest credit to sources, but have doubtless failed on some data or the source of some arguments, for which I apologize in advance. I only hope that the book might reach a second edition to allow for correction of such blunders.

For those who work with the linguistics of German, the maps in König et al. (2015 and going back to the first edition) have become iconic. Inspired in part by that work and the long tradition of German linguistic cartography it is part of, this book contains many maps, created by Mark Livengood. Mark has worked with me to make the maps simple and clean, with the aim of conveying quickly to beginners what the geographical picture can tell us. I'm extremely grateful to Mark for what I've learned from him, on this and other projects. Additional graphic material and maps are available on the project website, at http://www.historyofgerman.net (see below).

This book came to Oxford University Press thanks to conversations initiated by John Davey, and more recently Julia Steer has guided me through the later stages of the process. Working with such reliable and competent individuals is a true pleasure. The original two readers for Oxford University

Press provided important feedback on many topics, for which I am grateful. Julia Steer was kind enough to arrange an additional third review of a near-final version of the manuscript, and that reader made extremely useful suggestions, especially in terms of increasing the amount of research covered in the areas of semantics and pragmatics—not just the suggestion to do that, but ways to do it productively. Jenny Lunsford, Vicki Hart, and Lesley Rhodes led me through the production process smoothly, for which I'm grateful. I owe special debts to former professors besides Edgar Polomé (especially W. P. Lehmann, Hubert Heinen, John Weinstock), former fellow graduate students (especially Julie Bonner, Fred Schwink, Ken Todd), Wisconsin and other colleagues (especially Tom Purnell, Mark Louden, B. Venkat Mani, Andrew Sihler, Paul Roberge, John te Velde), graduate students past and present (Dan Nützel, Jennifer Delahanty, Joshua Bousquette, Mike Olson, and especially Dave Holsinger, Laura Catharine Smith, and Andrea Menz), and Monica Macaulay. Students like Alex Kramer, Kelsey White, Kat Thomas, Alicia Groh, Debby Oakes, Joel Stark, Emily Heidrich, Matt Boutilier, and many others really stepped up in searching for typographical and other errors. Matt also did important work helping me collate images, find material, and other work on the final version. Many of these people not only provided concrete comments and help, but also equally important encouragement on the project. This list is missing many important names and I apologize for those gaps.

List of maps

Guide to symbols

Symbols provide a particular challenge for a book like this: practicing specialists have to be familiar with a range of traditions, while newcomers benefit from a simple and consistent system. As with many similar challenges, I try to strike a balance, keeping things as simple as possible but reflecting the key range of uses in the field.

Full guides to the full International Phonetic Alphabet are available online, of course. These websites are particularly useful since they include sound files, so that you can actually hear the sound in question, listen to contrasting sounds, forms of sounds from different living languages, etc.:

- http://www2.arts.gla.ac.uk/IPA/ipa.html
- http://www.phonetics.ucla.edu/course/contents.html

These are the best references for understanding special symbols. Below are a few notes on particularly salient or potentially difficult points, as well as points particular to historical linguistics or Germanic linguistics.

Some particularly important or common symbols, things you should take good note of now:

- > simply means that some earlier form turns into some later form; so, if a 'z' sound becomes an 'r' sound, we can write 'z > r'. If we compare the archaic English plural form *kine* with the new form *cows*, we can write it *kine > cows*.
- * = a reconstructed form, rather than a directly attested one. Reconstructed forms are, in other words, basically made up and therefore should be treated with great caution. Linguistic examples are normally italicized (including in this book), but reconstructed forms are not, to emphasize that they are not attested. While I do not use it, note also that '+', a raised plus sign, is used by some scholars for this.
- In syntax, '*' is used to indicate an ungrammatical sentence, one that native speakers do not accept as acceptable. (Context virtually always disambiguates the two.)
- Square brackets—[]—indicate PHONETIC transcription, a way of capturing the actual pronunciation of a sound, typically with some detail. (See next entry.)
- Slashes—//—indicate PHONEMIC transcription, a more abstract way of representing sounds. We think of the *t* sound in *top* and *stop* as the same, and both are indeed /t/ but the first is aspirated [tʰ] and the second is unaspirated [t].

- Angle brackets—<>—reflect spelling, so German <sch> = [ʃ].
- A hyphen, '-', will typically indicate a morpheme boundary, the seam between meaningful elements within a word, such as in *un-mög-lich*, with the negative prefix *un-* and the adjective-forming suffix *-lich*.

For sounds:

- The symbol 'h' usually represents the first sound in *house,* but after stops is used for sounds like *bh, dh, gh* = the 'voiced aspirates' of Indo-European, today regarded as having been 'breathy' or 'murmured' stops. You can hear samples from Hindi here: http://www.phonetics.ucla.edu/course/chapter6/hindi/hindi.html
- superscript '^{w}': k^w, g^w, h^w = labialized (produced with rounded lips, as in *queen* or *Gwen, whether* (for those who distinguish this word from *weather*)). For the voiceless labiovelar h^w, IPA [ʍ], Gothic has a special letter: ƕ.
- $\acute{k}$, $\acute{g}$, '$^\prime$' over *k, g,* etc.: palatal (not velar), pronounced with the tongue body farther forward in the mouth, so a *k* as in *Kiel* not *cool,* etc., IPA = c, ɟ.
- *n̩, m̩, l̩, r̩,* or 'syllabicity mark', under consonant symbols is used for syllabic consonants, that is, consonants that function like vowels, as in rapid speech forms of *sittin'*, *habe<u>n</u>, bott<u>le</u>,* and so on. Some traditions use an 'underdot' (*ṇ, ṃ, ḷ, ṛ,*) or circle.
- ə: 'schwa', 'reduced' vowel, as at the end of *bitte.*
- ɐ: 'turned *a*', as at the end of Standard German *bitter.*
- ŋ: velar nasal, as in the last sound of English *ring*/German *Ring.*
- ̃: over a vowel, indicating that the vowel is nasalized, so that speakers allow air to flow through the nasal passages, like the last vowel in *Restaurant* [rɛstorã].
- š: the sound of English *sh* / German *sch*, IPA = ʃ.
- ž: the middle consonant in English *measure*, IPA = ʒ.
- H: Indo-European laryngeal sounds (see Chapter 2).

Note that different traditions in historical linguistics have two ways of marking vowel length:

- ō (a 'macron', traditional).
- o: ('colon', IPA).

Both are widely used and will be used here, a macron typically for texts that used this or where the normal transcription does (as for Old High German), and the latter especially for discussions tied to phonetics or phonology. It is important not to confuse these with an accent, which usually indicates or stresses high pitch rather than length (in many languages, accented vowels can be long or short):

- ó

Here is a brief **overview** of the most important differences between traditional spellings in Germanic historical linguistics and the IPA, using 'vd' for 'voiced' and 'vl' for voiceless:[1]

	Traditional	IPA	
Consonants			
Fricatives			
Labial, vd	ƀ	β	like Spanish *b* in *haber* (Gothic uses *b*)
Dental, vl	þ	θ	like English *th* in *think, thumb, throw*
Dental, vd	đ	ð	like English *th* in *the, this, them* (Gothic *d*)
Alveopalatal, vl	š	ʃ	the first sound in German *scharf*
Alveopalatal, vd	ž	ʒ	the first sound in (Standard) German *Journalist*
Velar, vl	h/ch	x	like German *ach*; note potential confusion with [h] (see above)
Velar, vd	g	ɣ	like Dutch *g* in *goed*, used for *r* by some, esp. in the Rhineland. (Gothic *g*)
Stops			
Aspirate, vd	bh, dh, gh	bʰ, dʰ, gʰ	
Vowels			
Long	ī, ā, ō, etc.	iː, aː, oː, etc.	
Short	ĭ, ă, ŏ, etc.[2]	i, a, o, etc.	
Lax		ɪ, ɛ, ʊ, etc.	Usually not specifically marked in traditional treatments
Diphthongs[3]	ei, au, etc.	ej, aw, etc.	
Front rounded vowels	ü, ö	y, ø	
Lax		ʏ, œ	Usually not specifically marked in traditional treatments

---

[1] In the German tradition, 'fortis' and 'lenis' are used instead of 'voiceless' and 'voiced'. 'Fortis' means that a consonant is produced with greater muscular exertion, 'lenis' with less. Fortis stops are typically aspirated. Lenis may be phonetically voiced or not.

[2] Usually only used to disambiguate, to highlight the short status: even in traditional treatments, short vowels are not marked with a diacritic.

[3] In other words: traditionally (and often today), diphthongs are written as two vowels, while in IPA they are sequences of vowel plus glide.

The **fricatives** are perhaps the big challenge for early Germanic, because the traditional transcriptions differ systematically from the International Phonetic Alphabet. The traditional symbols for the voiced are called 'stung', so that <ƀ> is referred to as a 'stung *b*'. The IPA terms are known by the names for the corresponding Greek letter, e.g. <ɣ> is *gamma* and <β> is *beta*. The <ð> is called *eth* (using the voiced sound for the 'th'!), and the Germanic symbol <þ> is called 'thorn'. The diacritic on <š> is called a *hachek*.

Anyone working in the area needs to be able to recognize both the traditional form and the IPA. In professional work, people tend to use the traditional symbols if they are tied to philological research or Indo-European studies, while those who are aiming to reach more theoretical audiences or audiences working in different language families tend to use IPA. For many purposes, either system is fine, but consistency is obviously extremely valuable.

Abbreviations

Technical terms will be defined as they are introduced. The most useful dictionary for general linguistics in English is Crystal 2008 and specifically for historical linguistics both Campbell & Mixco 2007 and the older Trask 2000 are easily usable.

Note that CE and BCE (i.e. Common Era and Before the Common Era) are used instead of AD and BC.

A	adjective, also Adj
A or Acc	accusative case
AP	adjective phrase
Aux	auxiliary, helping verb
C	in phonology, consonant, usually obstruent (stop or fricative)
C	in syntax, complementizer, subordinating conjunctions that mark an embedded sentence, also Comp
D or Dat	dative case
Det	determiner, usually meaning 'article'
DP	determiner phrase
Du	dual, number specifically for two of something
EFranc	East Franconian
ENHG	Early New High German
Fem	feminine gender
FU	Finno-Ugric, language family including Finnish, Estonian, Hungarian, and other languages
G or Gen	genitive case
Gmc	Germanic
Goth	Gothic
IE	Indo-European
Imp	imperative
Ind	indicative
Infin	infinitive
Instr	instrumental case
IPA	International Phonetic Alphabet
L	liquid consonant, *r* or *l* sound
Langob	Langobardian
LG	Low German, or *Plattdeutsch*
Masc	masculine gender
MFranc	Middle Franconian
MHG	Middle High German
N	in phonology, nasal consonant

N	in syntax, noun
Neut	neuter gender
NHG	New High German
N or Nom	nominative case
NP	noun phrase
O	object, generally direct object, in syntax
OHG	Old High German
ON	Old Norse
Opt	optative
OS	Old Saxon (the ancestor of Low German or *Plattdeutsch*)
Part	participle
Pass	passive
PGmc	Proto-Germanic
Pl	plural
PP	prepositional phrase
PPart	past participle
Prep	preposition
Pres	present tense
Pret	preterit or past tense
Pro	pronoun
Refl	reflexive
RhFranc	Rhenish Franconian
S	sentence
Sg	singular
SRhFranc	South Rhenish Franconian
Subj	subjunctive mood
V	in phonology, any vowel, V: = long vowel
V	in syntax, verb
V2	verb second
VP	verb phrase
X	any/unspecified element, as in XP, indicating any kind of phrase in syntax

1

Introduction

Aims and scope

History is the interpretation of the significance that the past has for us.

Johan Huizinga

A study by a team of economists (Falck et al. 2010) shows that contemporary movements of population in German-speaking Europe correlate closely with areas where particular dialects have been spoken historically. That is, people who move tend to stay within the same traditional dialect region. The authors conclude that:

[German] dialects were shaped by past interactions, prior mass migration waves, religious and political divisions, ancient routes and transportation networks, and so forth. Dialects act as a sort of regional memory that comprehensively stores such information. Consequently, language variation is probably the best measurable indicator of cultural differences that one can come up with.

Understanding how these dialects formed and where is critical to understanding contemporary cultural differences across regions. We will see this same pattern time and again through this book: the history of German can inform and improve how we understand many seemingly unrelated topics.

Contemporary geographical evidence about the past can reach amazingly deep into history, such as the many Slavic placenames in especially eastern Germany and Austria or Roman placenames especially in the Rhineland. The former is exemplified by *Berlin*, usually traced to a Slavic root meaning 'swampy place' plus a placename suffix *-lin*, counter to folk etymological connections to *Bär*. The second is illustrated by *Köln* < Lat. *colōnia*, from *Colonia Claudia Ara Agrippinensium*. In fact, this approach has often been pushed, always controversially, back to prehistory, in an effort to understand who lived in German lands before the ancestors of the Indo-Europeans.

Most recently, Vennemann (e.g. 2003) has sought Basque-like structures in placenames across much of Europe.[1]

In this same spirit of looking at how the past remains visible today, this book aims to provide a concise linguistic introduction to the history of German as specialists understand it today. The subtitle should suggest a focus on how the past can help us better understand the contemporary German language structurally and in its social context. Not every point is directly tied to the present, of course, but this is an organizing principle of much of the discussion. To the extent possible, I assume only basic knowledge of German and virtually no background in linguistics.

The field of linguistics is growing today and in particular many foreign language departments in North America are currently enjoying a groundswell of interest in linguistics.[2] Students beginning graduate work in a foreign language, even those already interested in linguistics, are often first introduced to the subject through a course on the history of the language. That is, the core audience for such classes typically includes some students ultimately interested in theoretical linguistics, some who are interested in second-language acquisition, and probably more still who are interested in more distantly related fields, such as area studies, cultural history, and literature.

In reality, the audience this book aims for is broader, and the obligation for accessibility greater: learners, second-language users, and teachers of the language can all benefit from understanding how German has unfolded over time. In particular this book is intended to reach those in classes dedicated to the history of German, and beyond to engage language learners who want to begin to understand how the language came to be the way it is and how it works. Mark Twain famously expressed what all language learners have felt in 'The Awful German Language' (an appendix to *A Tramp Abroad*, 1880, readily available online):

A person who has not studied German can form no idea of what a perplexing language it is. Surely there is not another language that is so slipshod and systemless, and so slippery and elusive to the grasp. One is washed about in it, hither and thither, in the most helpless way.

The healthy curiosity of most learners, beginning and advanced alike, naturally leads us to ask about seemingly odd and often difficult patterns in the language,

---

[1] The linguistic study of names is something we will not deal with here in any detail, but Eichler et al. 1995 provide a tremendously detailed introduction, with ample attention to the German-speaking world.

[2] Some see this as a part of a more general move to re-expand *Germanistik* beyond narrowly literary studies. Such a reorientation of undergraduate and graduate study in foreign languages has been, in fact, actively encouraged by the Modern Language Association in a report available here: http://www.mla.org/flreport.

if not with Twain's wit and mock despair. (The essay actually reveals a good understanding of how German works.) These questions range from what seem to be minor patterns of 'exceptions', such as why the so-called modal verbs have unusual inflections like *ich darf* and *sie muss*, where other verbs require endings in the present tense like *ich gehe*, *sie arbeitet*. Other issues have broader ramifications, such as why German has 'umlaut' vowels and why they show up in so many different functions scattered across the grammar—certain inflected verb forms (*schlafen ~ schläft*), noun plurals (*Mantel ~ Mäntel*), comparative adjectives (*stark ~ stärker*), and in word formation (*rot ~ rötlich*). In each instance just given and many more, knowing the history of German can pull back the curtain on particular narrow questions while revealing more broadly how language works, whether with regard to sound changes, the nature of verb inflection in ancestral languages, or how principles of assigning gender to nouns have changed throughout history. A major focus of this book is on just such architectural aspects of the language, and how history can help us understand the blueprints of the grammar in new ways. The cover photograph reminds us that the language also harbors countless smaller points about understanding the history and culture of its speakers. The exposed panel in the center of the *Fachwerk* wall—on a building which stands near the border between Nordrhein-Westfalen and Niedersachsen—reminds us directly of the history of the word *Wand*. From *wandu 'Flechtwerk' or 'wattle and daub', it reflects a historical link to *winden* (as explained in the entry in Kluge's *Etymologisches Wörterbuch*), reflecting ancient underlying wickerwork construction techniques, which were then covered with clay. The other usual translation of 'wall' into German, *Mauer*, has a distinct meaning and history: it comes from Latin *mūrus*, first attested in the 8th century (though surely borrowed earlier), and used specifically for stone walls, a construction technique foreign to the early Germanic peoples. Another term, *Wall*, is cognate with English *wall*, both borrowed forms of Latin *vāllum*, for fortifications originally including (wooden) palisades. In English this one generalized in meaning to become the broadest term for walls, while in German it has retained the narrower meaning of 'earthwork, rampart, embankment'.

Crucially, examples like the ones just given cover all periods of the language and all parts of the language. For example, the story of the endings of modal verbs, a matter of word structure or morphology, goes back to Indo-European, ultimately, while the development of umlaut, part of sound structure or phonetics and phonology, unfolded in large part during the early medieval period.

History provides no magic key to automatically decoding the complexities of the language or to learning it, but knowledge of the history of any language reveals deep regularities and patterns. For German, these are of the sort Twain pretended not to see. Knowing this can naturally help us explain contemporary grammar and usage to others. A basic knowledge of German's historical development even gives access to generalizations that many native speakers are unaware of. For instance, gender assignment—whether a given German noun is masculine, feminine, or neuter—is far more regular than most even linguistically aware native speakers realize. The answers to such questions are almost always deeply rooted in history. (And in this case, the development spans many centuries and is undergoing active change today.)

English speakers who know German are well aware of many similarities and differences between the two languages, and knowing the history of German can deepen their knowledge of English in surprising ways. It can even give a new perspective on oddities of English, such as why we have a written *s* (pronounced with a *z* sound) in *was* but an *r* in *were*, to give a mundane example. Likewise, dialect differences come into new focus, since the most salient regional patterns are direct continuations of historical patterns visible since the earliest texts we have, and the history of the language opens new ways of understanding regional variation.

While a newcomer to the topic might think that language history consists of changes in pronunciation, sentence structure, and so on, 'the German language' consists only in part of grammatical structures and dictionary entries: it is defined by the forms of language in real use by many millions of speakers over generations and across communities. Those people have lived and moved across vast expanses of time and space, and they have come into often intimate contact with speakers of many other languages and dialects. By definition, if you want to understand earlier texts written in German—whether that means Kant and Hegel, Martin Luther and Bismarck, or the *Nibelungenlied* and Schiller—you soon find yourself digging in the rich, dark soil of language history. Less obvious may be the value of language history for understanding the nature and sources of differences between 'formal' and 'informal' styles. We'll deal with all of these in the coming pages.

Our understanding of how German has unfolded over time is drawn from the evidence of all those kinds of texts, filtered and pressed through the fine mesh of historical transmission, and those relatively few texts which have come down to us limit what we can know about earlier periods. We will draw heavily on such documents as are available for a given time and in their social, cultural, and historical context to the extent we know it. Those texts, of course, provide our foundational evidence for language history. That is, we have to use and will use all information available to us, an approach Janda & Joseph (2003) call 'informational maximalism', discussed further in Chapter 8. As the reader will see, this situation improves over time, with richer documents and clearer cultural and other contexts.

The setting of medieval Europe has, unsurprisingly, left us with written documents mostly from the social and political elite, and only from the early modern period do we have documents from a broader range of society. In reading such texts, it is not simply the linguistic structures that are relevant to us. Political, religious, and other elites clearly encode their attitudes in what and how they wrote. Authorities, often self-proclaimed, have repeatedly tried to stipulate how people spoke and wrote, even what languages they used. Our views of and attitudes toward 'proper German', 'bad German', and 'mere dialect' have been shaped by such forces. In fact, our ATTITUDES have generally been shaped in this way far more than actual USAGE in speech or writing.[3] All of these matters related to questions such as who speaks a particular kind of language, who they come into contact with, what attitudes they have about 'correct' and 'incorrect' language, and so on are often called 'external' aspects of language history, in contrast to the structural or 'internal' aspects noted so far. So, the texts we have reveal something about not only linguistic structures such as the genitive case or dual pronouns, but also attitudes about usage, toward languages and dialects, and so on.

Where does the present book fit into this field? Most specialists in Germanic historical linguistics own a shelf full of histories of German, from Super 1893, Wright 1907 through Young & Gloning 2004, Besch & Wolf 2009, Sanders 2010, and Nübling et al. 2013. Yet not one has felt fully comfortable for me to use as a textbook for a course on the subject today. Many of these books provide only limited coverage of the language, some treating just the development of sounds, but more often including word forms and sometimes vocabulary. This is typical for older books, for example Frey, Kienle, Schweikle, Szulc in German. Few works, for all intents and purposes, treat sentence structure (syntax) systematically, though Keller and Wells both make significant nods in that direction. One, Sanders (2010), provides a kind of cultural studies discourse on the history of the language and barely deals with core structural issues at all. A few works are simply too sparse to give a full picture of developments (Stedje, Wolff, Schmidt et al., and most recently Ernst). An admirable effort to exploit Flash technology for teaching this material is Donhauser et al.'s CD-ROM (2007) and the graphics are often stunningly smart, but it too lacks the deep and broad exposition that students need to be prepared for advanced study. (Sadly, the CD-ROM no longer works on current Mac operating systems.) A further whole set of compendia are aimed at

---

[3] Still, odd prescriptions do occasionally win out, as for example we will see in why standard pronunciation mandates that *König* be pronounced with final -*ich* but *königlich* has an -*ik* for the same pair of letters. Here, and in many other cases, we will see how artificial the modern 'standard' is and how crazy its development has been; see Chapter 7.

advanced researchers, such as the tomes edited by Besch and others, and von Polenz's multi-volume project. The closest to the present work is, in some sense, Nübling et al. (2013), now in its fourth edition, though it is organized around modules of grammar rather than chronology. (The less obvious but more substantial differences may be in the theoretical perspectives presented and the balance of topics and level of detail across topics.)

As the field progresses, we see a steady flow of new data and fresh insights, and one aim of this book is to incorporate those. Just consider two examples for a moment: new data from ancient Germanic languages and the over-turning of long-held standard views. First, it stuns non-specialists to learn how often new data are being discovered from the earliest Germanic languages. Since the first edition of this book, we have a couple of pages of new Biblical Gothic (described in detail already by Auer & de Vaan 2016), new pages from the oldest known book in German, the Abrogans (visit http://www.ksta.de/panorama/kloster-in-oesterreich-forscher-entdecken-aeltestes-schriftstueck-auf-deutsch-26892578, and see Schuhmann 2017), and some possible new attestations of Crimean Gothic (presented at http://www.hse.ru/pubs/share/direct/document/169329298, especially at pp. 64–65, with commentary in English at http://altgermanistik.blogspot.com/2016/01/neue-gotische-graffiti-von-der-krim.html?spref=fb). This leaves aside the steadily growing sets of Runic inscriptions and glosses in Old High German and other languages. Second, by comparison to textbooks that were in use when I took the course (and still today, to an extent), late 20th-century histories typically make clear that there was not a 'standard' Middle High German in any real sense, and Martin Luther is no longer taken to be 'the father of the Modern German language' in most modern texts (all points Polomé insisted on!).[4]

Let us take now another example from the very beginning of the history of Germanic—one widely believed to have had vast consequences. Many textbooks say that Indo-European possessed a 'mobile' accent marked by 'pitch', which became a 'fixed', 'stress' accent in Germanic. This assertion is usually accompanied by strong claims about the eventual effects of this change on unstressed syllables. I was so baffled by such descriptions that it helped inspire me to write a dissertation on the subject. None of these textbooks, as far as I can see, gives readers much real sense of what a 'pitch accent' is. In fact, as you'll see in Chapter 3, specialists in phonetics and phonology are increasingly concluding that there is no such accentual type. And while the connection between 'stress accent' and reduction is tantalizing, we really do not yet understand how these can be causally related. In a real sense, then, those

---

[4] See Chapter 6 for discussion.

histories are simply outdated. In recent years we have witnessed significant advances in every aspect of the field: a better developed understanding of the sound system of early Germanic, groundbreaking work on Germanic and German historical syntax, fundamentally new insights into the standardization of German, and patterns of change in usage over the 19th and 20th centuries beyond the confines of 'Standard German'. It is surely no longer reasonable to treat the history of German as if advances in these areas didn't matter to students of the subject. And in the interest of truly understanding material rather than learning it by rote, even beginning students need to see how and why things happen. While I strive here to be up to date on these matters, I aim to make the presentation as theory-neutral as possible. I intend this specifically in terms of current linguistic theories, such as particular forms of generative or 'functional' grammar. That is, a reader does not need any background in Optimality Theory, the Minimalist Program, or other research programs to gain entry into this volume. If we interpret analyses of particular phenomena as 'theories', such as 'a theory of umlaut', this text is pretty much anything but 'theory-neutral'. Throughout, for example, I unapologetically follow the views of what some call 'the Wisconsin School' on the unfolding of umlaut and on the socio-historical treatment of how a standard language arose. The concluding chapter will revisit how theory, understood in this sense, has and has not been used in the volume.

Still, all textbooks on the history of German are trips down basically the same path. This one too uses some familiar examples and hits on familiar themes—I haven't tried to reinvent the wheel when handbooks or even other histories of the language have developed good accounts that we can draw on. But the present work differs from those previous ones in important ways. To begin with, I focus on showing how history has shaped the present-day state of the language and how understanding that history can help us understand the contemporary language, structurally and sociolinguistically. As already noted, the present approach relies relatively heavily on textual evidence as an organizing thread and devotes fuller attention to the whole spectrum of linguistic subfields, including syntax. At the same time, my treatment of the subject is obviously brief, and I do not cover certain topics that seem de rigueur in most textbooks. For example, many (like Lockwood, Stedje, and Priebsch & Collinson) include a brief treatment of Yiddish, and sometimes other related West Germanic languages. Many specialists in Germanic have never been comfortable with that decision, especially given the long history of attitudes relegating Yiddish to the status of 'corrupt German': Yiddish is a language whose history must be treated on its own terms, not as a footnote to a history of German. Happily, Jacobs (2005) provides an excellent introduction to 'Yiddish *qua* Yiddish' (p. 5) and Max Weinreich's seminal history of the language is available in English translation (Weinreich 2008). Like a number of earlier histories of German, the book you are reading now seeks to balance and even integrate the structural and the social. More than most texts, it also treats the language as changing steadily down to the present, in contrast to the common implicit (and sometimes explicit) assumption that nothing much of interest has happened to German structurally since the early modern period.

This work is organized chronologically,[5] and it is divided into chapters around traditional 'periods' of German linguistic history. Those period boundaries are essentially all illusory for our purposes, and the dynamics and trajectories of change prove more interesting and important. This book aims to present the history of German, in other words, in primarily diachronic terms rather than as a set of discrete language stages. As a result, some discussions of particular points will stretch far beyond the period at hand. With that, there are clear threads running across the chapters. In the sound system, regional and later social variation in pronunciation is a theme. In morphology, gender and plurality play a role throughout the nominal inflectional sections, and *Fugenelemente* is one of the still few derivational morphological topics treated. In syntax, periphrasis is obviously a topic of ongoing concern, and negation will be touched on several times. The broader sociolinguistic concern of most interest is who was writing (or speaking, once we have sound recording) and what the social parameters of variation are.

In the early part of the book, I have kept a relatively tight focus on German, with enough references for those who want the broader context of West Germanic, Germanic, and Indo-European languages. You will notice considerable differences in length across chapters. This comes in part from an effort to introduce concepts, terms, and ways of arguing in historical linguistics to readers new to the field. While many language histories are rigidly parallel from one period to the next, this one is not. The early foundations in morphology allow briefer treatments in later chapters, for example, while the necessary data for rigorous syntactic analysis become available as we progress later in time. The same holds yet truer for pragmatics and sociolinguistics, where reasonable data are available at relatively shallow time depths.

---

[5] Virtually all histories of languages are arranged this way, including this one, but this has always struck me as backwards: we start from the least familiar, least known material and move steadily to the familiar. Usual pedagogical practice, of course, starts from the most familiar material and moves to the unfamiliar. Perhaps our preference against going backwards through history is ranked higher than our preference against beginning a journey on unfamiliar territory. The other viable organizational principle is that already noted for Nübling et al. (2013): a book organized which is primarily around subfields of linguistics rather than chronology. The extensive subject index to the present volume and the section organization gives the reader an opportunity to do this here to a degree.

At times over the years, I have felt frustrated by the gap between texts presenting basic facts stripped of meaty, theoretically informed explanation and texts that are 'inside baseball', only really accessible to those already well prepared in general linguistics or conversant in the secret code of Indo-Europeanists. Part of the goal of this book is to bridge that chasm. I aim to walk the line of making the work accessible to real newcomers to the field, but also to avoid any hint of 'dumbing down' anything or sidestepping difficult topics. In fact, those using this book as early reading in the study of German and Germanic linguistics should find the state of the art presented here, and more attention to how we know what we know about the history of German rather than a mere recitation of presumed facts and received wisdom. As a result, though, readers with more background may skip some paragraphs here and there or perhaps a section, while raw beginners reading without the help of an instructor may find a few stretches challenging. In the conclusion, I will step back to highlight and draw together a few of the major themes of the book with an eye to how they fit into current theoretical linguistic discussion.

After this Introduction, Chapter 2 treats the earliest recoverable information about prehistory. Here we rely on reconstructed forms of the hypothetical ancestor language, Indo-European, of which the Germanic languages form a branch. In Chapter 3, we begin to trace structural changes, up to the earliest period of direct attestation, where our texts are figurative and sometimes literal shards—Runic inscriptions and names and words used in Latin and other classical documents. Chapter 4 focuses on the period where we find an array of longer texts from a broad range of dialects (and closely related languages), from the 8th century CE on. By the High Middle Ages, around which Chapter 5 is built, we see a greater quantity and diversity of materials, allowing us to track changes more closely and provide more social and geographical context for the linguistic structures at hand. In early modern times, the subject of Chapter 6, the amount of surviving textual material explodes, both due to the invention of the printing press and to increasing literacy. Here, for the first time, we can read the words of large numbers of ordinary people written in their own hands, and often we have good knowledge of their lives—their social networks and families, education, line of work, and social status in their communities. Chapter 7 brings us up to the present, where contemporary variation and sometimes rapidly spreading changes make clear that German today continues to evolve structurally and socially.

Given the immensity of the topic, this book treats a select fraction of the material that could be covered. Throughout, I've kept treatment of vocabulary to a minimum. While public interest in the topic is intense, orthography is simply not relevant enough to actual language to warrant discussion (and the topic is well covered in Nübling et al. 2013). While work on historical pragmatics is burgeoning, I have focused discussion of it on later chapters, where the database for such work is larger and it is better understood. I would very much have liked to include discussion of sociophonetics, change in progress, and related issues in language variation and change (especially since much of my own research now falls in that area, for English and German in the United States), but that tradition is simply not yet developed in the German-speaking countries in the way it is for research on English, French, Spanish, and Nordic languages. The treatment of syntax has increased steadily over the development of the project, but I passed the contractual word count for the book before finding a place for coverage of current work on information structure and change, to give one example. (As noted above, this second edition brings, to an extent, an opportunity to improve that imbalance.) The focus changes steadily over these chapters: in early chapters, our knowledge of sound patterns and word forms is better, in part because they are more easily reconstructed than syntax and our knowledge of the social setting of language change is limited. In later chapters, we have vastly better information on those topics, and there is a natural shift toward them.

Each chapter contains elements that are identifiable as internally oriented and externally oriented sections but, as already noted, that is often an organizational exigency rather than a point of principle or substance. The further breakdown varies according to available data and my own choices of topics. For example, syntactic information is especially obscure for the earliest periods: the applicability of comparative reconstruction to syntax has long been questioned and many of our earliest Germanic texts (early Runic inscriptions, for the most part) are typically too short to allow any serious analysis, while others are translated from Greek or Latin texts, leading to long debates about possible influence from the originals on word order, use of pronouns, and so on.

For those using this as a textbook, practice sheets, homework assignments, additional graphics, and so on are available online, at http://www.historyofgerman.net. For instructors, answers to those problems, along with a larger set of exercises, practices, sample texts, and other materials are also available. I beg that readers send suggestions, errata, references to work that should be cited to jsalmons@wisc.edu, so that important updates can be listed on the site.

The crucial internet resource for the history of German in coming years seems likely to be *DeutschDigitalDiachron*: http://www.deutschdiachrondigital.de/. For a recent general survey of internet resources for especially German historical linguistics, see Masalon 2010.

In the end, then, this book is one big effort to weave together many disparate threads, spun over millennia, within unsettlingly few pages. While it is easy enough to be more current than older introductions and to provide meatier and more detailed discussion than the briefer ones, presenting the state of the art in this complex and rapidly changing field is a daunting task. Throughout, the goal is really just to elucidate the significance that the past has for us as speakers, teachers, and learners of German. There are many points that I have missed (or not laid out clearly, even or especially) in this second edition, but I do hope this book represents progress for some readers.

2

The depths of prehistory

Up to Indo-European

2.0 Introduction

We need to begin with some background on how to think about language change and language history. This chapter will focus primarily on general principles to provide a foundation for the detailed discussion of Indo-European and Germanic linguistics that follows in the next chapter. More concretely, the goals are to introduce some key concepts of historical linguistics, such as reconstruction, cognates, the family tree model, and the rudiments of sound structure. You should also gain a basic overview of the Indo-European languages—membership of the family, timeline and geography, and some basic structures. Finally, the chapter lays out how the Germanic languages are historically connected to one another and to neighboring languages, genetically and by contact. While this provides less obvious material for understanding today's language, even here you will find relevance.

A fundamental question about the history of any language is what other languages it is related to. Anyone who knows some German and English recognizes many similarities in words and structures, and clear parallels exist between these cousins and the Romance and Slavic languages, and so on. But how do we show relatedness, and just which languages is German genetically related to? We begin by exploring these questions, in a way that will set up discussions in Chapter 3.

Our knowledge of the earliest prehistory of languages is built around figuring out kinship—which languages are related to which. To frame an introduction to German's genetic relationships, let us begin with a simple introduction to how linguists determine family relations among languages, which will lead us into an example of how German and English sounds correspond in a systematic way to sounds in some other related languages. From there, we will turn to the broader family that the Germanic branch is part of, Indo-European. There, we focus on what we can deduce about the prehistory of the Germanic peoples and languages after the Indo-European period, especially about contacts to other groups, both Indo-European and non-Indo-European, before recorded history.

Before we pursue these matters, let us raise yet more basic questions: how and why does language change? In the coming chapters, we'll see a number of aspects of an answer and how they are intertwined. Language acquisition is clearly crucial to language change whatever our stance on the innateness of grammar. Children build grammars from the linguistic input they are given and if they are exposed to different input than earlier generations were, or if they make different analyses of ambiguous input, they will build a different grammar. Our minds are remarkably good at recognizing and even creating patterns, and learners and speakers 'adjust' things, yielding cleaner patterns. People choose, to some extent, who they associate and identify with and we normally come to talk (and act generally) like those people and often set ourselves apart linguistically or otherwise from those we do not associate or identify with. As we grow older, we become less able to change how we speak and to acquire new languages. This is true of certain bedrock aspects of language but not of all aspects, and we readily pick up new vocabulary, for example. And we all have control of various ways of saying things, different pronunciations or grammatical constructions. As we age, we may come to favor some variants over others. And exposure to other languages or dialects certainly plays a major role in change as well. All of these factors, cognitive and social, are at play in language change. And all will play roles in the coming chapters. Beyond that, we'll think about the origins of a change—how something is introduced into the speech of a community—and how it is transmitted or diffused through the community.

2.1 How do we know that languages are related?

Languages show similarities for only a handful of reasons. Much modern work in linguistic theory is built around the characteristics ALL human languages share, 'UNIVERSALS'—every language has consonants and vowels, nouns and verbs, and so on.[1] When speakers come into contact with speakers of other languages, they of course often BORROW words and even end up with structural similarities of various sorts. To a limited extent, onomatopoeic words, like *meow*, *hiss*, and *buzz*, can create cross-linguistic similarities, since people imitating the sound of a cat or a bee naturally tend to create similar-sounding forms. And a few 'children's words' like *mama*, *papa*, *caca* may fit a related pattern—as children are learning to talk, they tend to produce some similar sounds and put them together similarly, like syllables consisting of a

---

[1] This has implications beyond historical linguistics. Perhaps the most fundamental question in linguistic theory is why such similarities exist, from some particular language competence or deriving from general cognitive abilities.

consonant and a vowel, often with repetition, and so on. As a result similar forms can arise independently in different languages. Less frequent but more surprising are real accidental similarities: language has a limited set of sounds and basic words are often only a few sounds long, so that by pure chance, we find 'look-alikes'. The word for 'dog' in Chalcatongo Mixtec, an indigenous language of Oaxaca in southern Mexico, is *inà*. That closely resembles Japanese *inu* 'dog'. Given the extraordinary unlikelihood of relevant contact between these languages, we treat this as obvious coincidence. Usually, when linguists talk about relatedness, we are talking about languages thought to be GENETICALLY related, languages that appear to have descended from a common ancestor earlier in time.[2]

For many pairs of languages, anyone who knows both of them can easily recognize that they are related, like Spanish and French, Finnish and Estonian, Menominee and Potawatomi. Similarly, the connections among the Germanic languages are readily clear.[3] If we want to identify more distant relatives of German, as the natural starting point for our historical survey, we are faced with a problem: it is far from obvious exactly which languages in, say, western Europe are related. In early historical linguistics, for instance, scholars debated whether Irish was an Indo-European language and even today a small army of mostly amateur linguists is laboring to show that Basque is related to some other language or family. A major accomplishment of linguists in the 18th and 19th centuries was in developing a method for establishing genetic relationships, that is, for determining which languages share a historical ancestor.

When non-linguists think about 'language', including language change, they often focus on words, which for present purposes we can think of as just some string of sounds corresponding to some meaning. Words make a reasonable starting point for talking about relatedness, as well: if languages have particular words that sound similar and have similar meanings, people have long reasoned, it suggests that the languages are related. This has been widely believed to be particularly true for basic vocabulary—common words for kinship, body parts, major features of the natural world, and so on.

Of course, things are actually more complicated, since there is yet another way that languages can acquire those matches. Notably, given the slippery nature of meaning over time and the fact that all human languages work with a surprisingly small set of sounds, we can have ACCIDENTAL similarities, like between

---

[2] Campbell & Poser (2008) provide the best current introduction to language classification.

[3] You can go here to see some data: http://en.wiktionary.org/wiki/Appendix:Swadesh_lists_for_Germanic_languages. The list in this link is adequate for our purposes, but please note that I am not endorsing Wikipedia as a source for linguistic information. For example, at this writing, it gives data for SOME Germanic languages only, leaving out some other important and interesting data.

English *bad* and Farsi (Persian) *bad*.[4] Or take German *Mann*, which looks amazingly like *man* 'husband' in Guajajara (an indigenous language of Brazil). In fact, the Guajajara meaning matches one meaning of the German word perfectly and the strings of sounds are basically identical. But we can pretty easily show that this is an accident, rather than a sign of inheritance: given the limited number of sounds human languages use and a large set of meanings that we find in all languages, some meanings are bound to be encoded with similar strings of sounds. It is a good party game to find such look-alikes, but nothing more.

An approach called 'mass comparison', which relies heavily on these surface resemblances (Greenberg 1987), has been developed with the remarkable goal of establishing 'Proto-World', a common ancestor to all human languages. Some of the strongest data for the strongest example of this ambitious enterprise are given in Table 2.1.

TABLE 2.1 **A claimed 'global etymology': *tik 'finger, one'**

Phylum/language	Form(s)	Meaning
Nilo-Saharan	tok ~ tek ~ dik	'one'
(South) Caucasian	tit-i	'finger'
	tito	'single'
Indo-European	*d(e)ik	'to point'
Uralic	ik ~ odik ~ γtik	'one'
Ainu	tek	'hand'
Japanese	te	'hand'
Eskimo-Aleut	tik-(eq) (Esk.)	'index finger'
	tik-(laq) (Aleut)	'middle finger'
Sino-Tibetan	*tik	'one'
Yeniseian	*tok	'finger'
Austro-Tai	*diaŋ	'finger, point'
Indo-Pacific	tong~tang~teng	'finger, hand, arm'
Na-Dene	t'ek ~ tikhi ~ ɬaq, (ka-)tleek	'one'
	tɬeq ~ (ka-)tliki	'finger'

Source: Ruhlen (1987: 261), assembled and supplemented in Salmons (1992e); recall the list of symbols and links to the International Phonetic Alphabet on pp. xxi–xxiv.

Looking at contemporary word forms in this way might suggest that some sets of languages are worth examining in more depth, but it cannot show them to be related. The point here is that we cannot assume any relationship between languages based on general similarities between a few words or other superficial characteristics.

---

[4] In fact, the Persian–English example here is instructive precisely because these languages ARE clearly related. The histories of both these languages are well enough known and understood that we can say with certainty that these are indeed an accidental match.

If this is not a reliable way to establish relationships, then how can we do it? Early comparative linguists cataloged extensive sets of similarities of varying quality across many groups of languages. The key step came in the late 19th century with the recognition that SYSTEMATIC CORRESPONDENCES exist between sounds in related languages. This is closely tied to the notion that sound changes are regular, something we will talk about in what follows. So, keeping in mind our Mixtec–Japanese examples from earlier on in the chapter, if Guajajara and German are related, the test is whether particular sounds regularly match up in the same words, like the *m* and *n* of *Mann ~ man*. It turns out that if we check some basic terms, we find no matches: *Magen ~ herie, Messer ~ takihe, Mutter ~ hɨ* (Guajajara data from here: www.sil.org/acpub/repository/11416.pdf). If you check just some Guajajara words starting with *m*, they likewise do not normally match German *m*. When we have checked a set of such possible correspondences across enough words, we conclude that there are no systematic correspondences and that we cannot currently show that Guajajara and German are genetically related.

Let us take an example closer to home, where you know or suspect the languages are related. A set of basic words in Romance languages such as Spanish or French begin with *p*, and match German and English words starting with *f* (ignore spelling, of course, since initial 'v' in German = [f]):

Spanish	French	German
padre	père	Vater
pie	pied	Fuß
pescar	pêcher	fischen

These examples could, of course, easily be multiplied, and with Romance and Germanic languages, we have old written records, so that we can go back and compare parallel data from many centuries earlier. If you look back at Latin, instead of the modern Romance languages, and Old High German instead of Modern German, we find similar patterns:

Latin	Old High German	German
pecus	fehu	'Vieh'
plenus	fol	'voll'[5]
nepōs	nefo	'Neffe'

In short, it looks like the real historical match between Germanic languages and Romance is that our *f* corresponds regularly to Romance *p*. Secure family relationships, such as Germanic and Romance, do not rest on raw SIMILARITY of

---

[5] These may not look related at first glance, but they are. The connection will be clearer when we get to the notion of 'zero-grade' in §3.5.

forms, nor on isolated words that look similar. Indeed, where we do find *p* matching with *p*, or *f* with *f*, across these families, there is some other explanation, such as German *pur* and Spanish *puro*, where German borrowed the word from Romance in the 14th century. In fact, a whole set of *p*-initial words in German were borrowed from Romance at various points, from *Pilger*, first borrowed from Latin into Old High German over a thousand years ago, to 19th-century words like *Pikkolo* from Italian and more recent examples. This simple principle of SYSTEMATIC CORRESPONDENCE is a powerful tool, central to comparative linguistics.[6] This approach is the heart of the Comparative Method (see Campbell & Poser 2008).

Establishing a set of such correspondences—aiming to cover all sounds in the languages—sets the stage for RECONSTRUCTION of the sounds found in the earlier language, called a proto-language.[7] This is more art than science, but one principle often used is what we know about the direction of sound change. In many languages of the world, *p* sounds have turned into *f* sounds, but changes of *f* to *p* are rare, at best. In fact, the broader trend is that stops—such as *p*, *t*, *k*—regularly become fricatives—such as *f*, *θ*, *h*. Thus, the Romance–Germanic correspondence is not surprising and we would have good justification for hypothesizing that German may have changed its old *p* sounds into *f* sounds, while Romance may have maintained them. In fact, comparative linguists make a working assumption that sound change is regular, that is, if one *p* becomes an *f* in some language or dialect, all of them will. As we will see in the next chapter and beyond, this has some complexities and limits, for example that the phonetic context, like certain neighboring sound(s), may prevent a change.

2.2 Germanic's extended family: Indo-European

Most of the languages spoken in Europe turn out to be related to each other and to a string of languages stretching through the Middle East and far into the Indian subcontinent. (A fairly detailed clickable map is available here: http://titus.uni-frankfurt.de/didact/karten/euro/europam.htm; good introductions to the family include Beekes 2011, Clackson 2007, and Kapović 2017.)

A particularly difficult area for Indo-European is etymological resources: many scholars have reconstructed large sets of IE vocabulary, but the differences in what is reconstructed and how are bewildering to many newcomers and annoying or unsettling to many experienced people. Basic IE forms are given

---

[6] In practice, linguists do not rely solely on systematic sound correspondences to establish relationships. In certain settings, shared morphological irregularities also play some role, for example.

[7] Fox (1995) and Campbell & Poser (2008) provide excellent introductions to linguistic reconstruction.

in Watkins (2011), in Mallory & Adams (1997; 2006), and in online materials from the Linguistics Research Center at the University of Texas at Austin (https://lrc.la.utexas.edu/lex), though none of these sources is a technical one. Rix et al. (2001) provides the most valuable single source; it is focused on verbs and gives the fullest accounting. A similar book for IE nouns, Wodtko et al. (2008), provides analyses that not all specialists always accept. The still widely cited dictionary by Pokorny (1959) is flawed and dated to the point of no longer being usable.

Already in the 19th century, most of these languages were recognized as being related. Aside from Germanic, working roughly from southeast to northwest, IE is usually divided into these subgroups:

- Indo-Iranian, further divided into:
  - Indic languages, such as Hindi, Marathi, Nepali, attested early in Sanskrit
  - Iranian languages, such as Farsi and Pashto, attested early in Avestan
- Armenian
- Greek
- Albanian
- Balto-Slavic languages, such as Russian and Polish among the Slavic languages and Latvian and Lithuanian for Baltic, attested early in Old Church Slavonic and Old Prussian
- Italic languages, which include the familiar Romance languages—such as French, Spanish, Romanian, attested early in Latin, along with non-Romance languages such as Oscan
- Celtic languages, such as Welsh and Irish, attested early in Old Irish.

Indo-Iranian languages have written traditions going back thousands of years. Today, they cover much of South Asia and reach far into the Middle East, but Iranian languages were once spoken in southeastern Europe, in the Persian Empire. Armenian is now spoken primarily in an area between the Black Sea and the Caspian Sea. Its position within the IE family is unclear, but some scholars have suggested a close relationship with Greek. Like Indic and Iranian, Greek has a long written history and these all played critical roles in early work on Indo-European. Albanian, spoken in Albania and some other areas of the Balkan peninsula as well as in Italy, represents its own branch of the family. An ancient language of the same area, Illyrian, is often regarded as its ancestor. The remaining groups—Balto-Slavic, Italic, and Celtic—are all western European neighbors of Germanic and will be dealt with in a little more detail later.

During archeological excavations in the early 20th century, texts were uncovered in two different parts of the world which have since been deciphered and identified as being written in Indo-European languages comprising two more branches:

- Anatolian, found in modern Turkey, represented most famously by Hittite, and other languages, including Luvian. It is written, often on clay tablets, in a cuneiform syllabary (syllable-based writing system), but surviving texts include hieroglyphs from other ancient Middle Eastern languages.
- Tocharian, found in Chinese Turkestan. Its preservation is even more remarkable, with texts written on leaves and paper and other fragile materials. It was also written in a syllabary, based on a Brahmi script (see Figure 2.1).

If the Germanic family is related to the bigger and more ancient Indo-European family, could Indo-European itself be related yet more distantly to other languages? That seems highly likely on various grounds, but our current evidence and methods do not allow us to demonstrate it rigorously. Certainly there were early connections of some sort between Indo-European and Uralic languages,

FIGURE 2.1 A Tocharian text. Note the fragility of the text and consider the philological challenge such texts offer.

Image courtesy of the Depositum der Berlin-Brandenburgischen Akademie der Wissenschaften in der Staatsbibliotek zu Berlin—Preussischer Kulturbesitz Orientabteilung, THT 001A, Toch B 1, T III So 96 Udanalankara brahmi.

and also with the Afro-Asiatic languages (the broader family to which Semitic belongs). Indo-European and Uralic, in particular, share a few basic vocabulary items, more than seem to be attributable to accident. Contact and borrowing may account for such shared vocabulary, but a dedicated group of scholars has for more than a century posited a macro-family usually called 'Nostratic', which typically includes Indo-European, Uralic and Afro-Asiatic, and various other families. Nostratic remains highly controversial. A key concern is that the time depth is so great that sufficiently rigorous and systematic correspondences have not been established. (See Joseph & Salmons 1998, Campbell & Poser 2008, and other work for detailed discussion from various perspectives on the question.) Still, careful work, new evidence, and new methods could provide progress here, and we may someday learn that IE has siblings.

Homeland and chronology. The correspondences that have been established in vocabulary, sound systems, and grammar leave no serious doubt that the IE languages are related, but the geography and chronology of their shared ancestor remain far more obscure. As Ringe (2006: 4) puts it:

we can't say with certainty where and when [Proto-Indo-European] was spoken; a reasonable guess would be the river valleys of Ukraine in the centuries around 4,000 BC, though one can't absolutely exclude a somewhat earlier date, nor a place somewhat further east.

This Black Sea (or 'Pontic') homeland is associated with pastoralism. The culture is often called 'Kurgan', after the Russian name for their distinctive burial mounds, and dated to roughly 6,000 years ago (Anthony 2007). The most likely alternative view is one of an Anatolian homeland, associated with agriculture, and dated to roughly 9,000 years before the present (Renfrew 1987 and his followers—a dating supported by Gray & Atkinson 2003; see Map 1).

The recent support for an Anatolian homeland and for an earlier dating of the proto-language has come especially from quantitative methods adapted from biology, in particular from phylogenetics, though Chang et al. (2015) use related methods to argue for the steppe hypothesis and for a more recent dating. A very different kind of evidence comes from Haak et al. (2015), who build on earlier studies of DNA from remains of prehistoric Europeans to support the argument that at least one critical wave of migrants to central Europe came from the steppes, but as part of a more complex set of migration: 7,000 or 8,000 years ago, groups of (related) farmers appear in modern-day Germany and other areas and, around 5,000 years ago, farmers had more ancestry from the earlier hunter-gatherer populations than from these migrants. About 4,500 years ago, people associated with the 'corded ware' culture (on which more to follow) appear in Germany. Those people's DNA relates them very strongly to early steppe populations with more distant

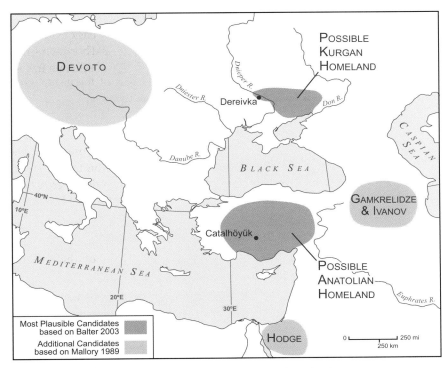

MAP 1 Some current candidates for the Indo-European homeland.

Compiled from maps in Balter (2003) and Mallory (1989: 144).

connections to the Near East. Important here and in other similar work is the evidence for complex patterns of migration—there was not one single indigenous population that was simply invaded at one point in prehistory—and potentially even more complex patterns of integration of populations over time.

Returning directly to language, most importantly, even if this reconstructed language was at some remote point in time a single entity, its relevant history was as a set of languages that evolved over millennia as speakers moved over vast distances to end up from northern- and westernmost Europe to China to central and northeastern India. In keeping with the notion of genetic or family relationships, constructing a family tree has long been a topic for many Indo-Europeanists. The branches in trees such as the ones here (pp. 22–23) are implicitly based on an assumption that languages split away from the original community at some relatively definable point in time—much like American English split from British English in the colonial period, or Pennsylvania German from European dialects.[8]

---

[8] Those points are only relatively definable, of course, since immigration did not happen instantaneously and contacts between hearth culture and colony continued for some time in both cases.

Simply speaking, if all languages in a family but one or some subset show a distinctive innovation, this suggests that the one language broke away before that feature arose. (In the next chapter we'll explore this notion of 'shared innovation' in more detail with regard to the Germanic family tree.) A tree, then, gives part of the picture of how long particular languages remained part of the group. One plausible current tree looks like this, adapted from Ringe (2006: 5):[9]

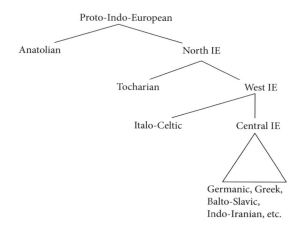

Various aspects of this tree are controversial, including the position of Anatolian, but the relevant point for our purposes is that, in this view, Germanic forms a part of the 'central' group, which includes Indo-Iranian, Greek, Balto-Slavic, etc. Italo-Celtic is a separate branch but its daughters have had long and intense contact with Germanic for millennia. Mallory & Adams (2006: ch. 5) provide a set of different trees that have been proposed for IE while Campbell & Poser (2008) provide extensive discussion of how such trees are constructed.

Still, this tree is probably the most standard, although occasional doubts are expressed about whether Balto-Slavic went through a common stage of development and, as we just noted, some see Italic and Celtic as a single group. A laundry list of other languages, mostly found in the Mediterranean, are represented by mere fragments and are by and large ill understood. Among the best known of those are Phrygian, Illyrian, and Thracian. Various as yet undeciphered scripts could turn out to provide even more evidence for reconstructing Indo-European—and other texts are being uncovered regularly.

---

[9] Ringe and his colleagues have played a central role in developing new family trees using cladistics, an approach from biology. A new generation of computer scientists, (evolutionary) biologists, and mathematically oriented scholars is bringing this and other new tools to this old problem. Most are based simply on shared vocabulary, but Ringe and others have begun including grammatical information. In coming years, we can look forward to progress on this front.

Our understanding of some languages, such as varieties of Celtic spoken on the European continent, have advanced considerably in recent years through discoveries of new texts and ongoing analysis.[10]

A more detailed tree is presented below, from Ringe et al. (2002), reflecting the results of a computational approach to the problem based on data from individual languages. This tree also includes a dotted arrow added by Labov (2007) to reflect contacts between Germanic and Celtic, a point to be picked up again later (pp. 26–27).

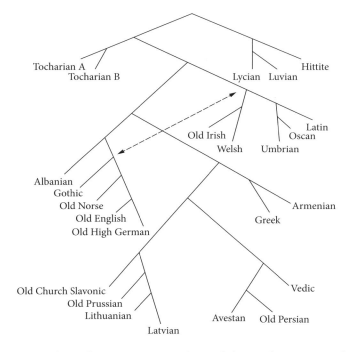

Turning now to the Indo-European peoples and their cultures, a vast literature has grown up using vocabulary and the just-mentioned notions of determining groupings and splits to suggest something about Indo-European culture, an approach known as 'linguistic paleontology'. Since IE languages virtually all share common words meaning 'salmon' and 'beech', it was proposed that their speakers must have lived in a place where these were familiar items during the time of IE unity. Unfortunately, as people move, they can readily apply old names to new species, just as a 'robin' in American English refers to a set of birds in England but not to the same one—a 'thrush' in the former case

[10] Fortson 2010 gives far more detailed sketches of each branch.

(*Turdus migratorius*) and birds that include the Old World 'flycatcher' (*Erithacus rubecula*) and the one called a 'chat' in the latter. English speakers in North America applied the old name to a new bird: the birds differ considerably in size and color, and so on.

Even in recent times the application of linguistic paleontology has led to dubious conclusions (drawing examples here from Salmons 2015). For instance, Gamkrelidze & Ivanov (1995: 763–764) favor a mountainous IE homeland west of the Caspian Sea. They base this, in part, on words like these:

*neb^hes- 'cloud, thundercloud, sky'
*Hwent^h- 'wind'
*seu-/*su- 'rain'

They continue: 'Another set of words connected with climatic phenomena precludes locating the Indo-European proto-homeland in the northern regions of Eurasia: *g^hoer-m- and *t^hep^h- "heat, warmth".' Of course, all human cultures know such things and notions, and all languages have words for them.

Tracing the spread of cultural artifacts in archeological digs over time and space has likewise been widely used, such as the 'corded ware' or *Schnurkeramik* pottery in Figure 2.2. But shards of pottery clearly do not tell us who made or used the vessels.

If linguistic paleontology is critically applied to culture, though, some patterns may emerge, if the case involves matches between archeological and linguistic evidence, and is built not on single etymologies but rather on

FIGURE 2.2 Corded ware pottery.
Photo courtesy of Jan Turek.

broader patterns of connected evidence.[11] To draw a couple of quick examples from material culture, IE has a word for 'metal', cognate with English *ore*, and usually reconstructed as something like *Heyes-, found in Gothic *aiz* 'money, metal coin' and related to Latin *aes* 'copper, bronze', Old Indic *áyas-* copper, iron', and so on.[12] (In this context, 'cognate' simply means words that share a single ancestral form at some earlier historical stage.) In contrast, archeological evidence for iron-working is not present until about 2,000 BCE, well after the period of supposed IE unity, but the metal and presumably the term spread to the northwestern corner of Europe by about 500 BCE. Cognates of *yoke* and *Joch* are found in virtually every branch, and several old words for 'wheel' are reconstructed, including ancestors of *Rad*, which are especially associated with chariots. Many conclude from this that during the period of IE unity, there was technology such as yokes and wheels, although even this is less than certain.

In the case of weaving, a whole set of terms go back to IE, including words for wool and other fibers, sewing and weaving, and more, making clear that textiles were known. House vocabulary varies considerably, but evidence points to wooden frames, and all branches share a word for 'door jamb' and many words for 'pin' etc. that would suggest how doors were kept closed. The word from which *door* and *Tür* come is itself likewise widespread, and generally used in the earliest languages in the plural or dual (an inflectional category indicating that a noun refers to exactly two of something). The usual conclusion is that early Indo-Europeans had framed doors, typically double doors.

2.3 The breakup of IE: the road to Germanic

Let us now move on to what this shared vocabulary approach might suggest about the prehistoric evolution from Indo-European to Germanic. While the TREE MODEL exemplified here (pp. 22–23) nicely captures 'clean breaks' such as when whole populations move away from a common homeland, another common historical relationship is better captured by what is called the 'wave model': cultural and linguistic (especially vocabulary) innovations can spread over an area, even where the majority of the population remains in one area. This has long happened and still is happening today in Europe with 'international' vocabulary items: people continue to speak German, Dutch, French, and so on, but using clearly related words

---

[11] Fortson (2010) offers a readable contemporary introduction to what this approach tells us about social classes and family structure, economics, law, and so on. See Mallory & Adams (2006) for detailed discussion of IE vocabulary. The present examples draw also on Mallory & Adams (1997).

[12] German has a cognate form, *ehern* literally 'bronze' and now used mostly in a figurative meaning, 'firm, unshakable'.

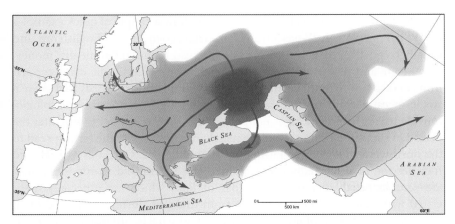

MAP 2 Geographical expansions of the Indo-European peoples.

for the financial institution we call a *bank*, ultimately borrowed from Italian. Map 2 shows one view of the geographical expansions of the Indo-European peoples, associated with the Steppes and 'Kurgan' culture.

Three different kinds of possible wave-like situations are relevant for the prehistory of German: (1) contact with their known IE neighbors, (2) contact with unknown IE or non-IE populations in central Europe, and (3) contact with their known non-IE neighbors, notably Finno-Ugric speakers.

'The vocabulary of the Northwest'.[13] Many traditional views treat the IE languages now found in western and central Europe as a subgroup: Celtic, Italic, Germanic, and Balto-Slavic. If Ringe's family tree given on p. 22 is right, the languages we find in this area today did NOT break off from IE as a group and come to their known homelands together as a cohesive community—perhaps Italo-Celtic split off earlier, while what we now think of as Germanic and Balto-Slavic populations arrived later. Either way, it appears that changes diffused throughout the region after all these groups were present. In comparing data from the European languages, Antoine Meillet proposed a 'vocabulary of the Northwest', a set of lexical connections among these northwestern-most branches of IE, vocabulary which might reflect areal diffusion rather than common inheritance. As should already be clear from the discussion so far, any claims about prehistory at this depth are controversial and difficult, but the lexical items that have been cited as northwestern include these, drawing on the natural environment:

[13] This section draws on Salmons 1992c.

Plants: 'apple', 'dwarf elder', 'grain', 'hazel'
Animals: 'thrush', '(wild) boar', 'bee', 'snake' < 'to slither'
Other environment: '(free) land, heath', 'sea', 'lightning'

Many other lexical correspondences appear to be uniquely shared by Germanic and Celtic. More than the early northwestern vocabulary, these often point to a certain degree of technological and cultural sophistication. This is relatively speaking, of course—no common word for *iPhone* can be reconstructed, and this book may someday perhaps be read by someone unaware of what that ancient piece of technology was. Consider some words that can be roughly grouped as technical and social vocabulary:

1. **Technical vocabulary**
   Metal: lead, iron, wire, oven
   Weapons: spear, sword
   Medicine: doctor, herb/drug, soap, leprosy
   Clothing: tunic, breeches, leather
   Agriculture: fork, harrow, goad
   Transportation: harbor, to ride, to drive, vehicle, fathom
   Horses: mare, male horse/stallion, mane

2. **Social vocabulary**
   Language (or meta-language): poet/story, rune, language, talk
   Social roles and institutions: servant, oath, free, bond, debt, to lend, ruler, town, village, troop, inheritance/heir, right/law, hostage, fight

For example, the Old Irish and Welsh words for 'iron', *ïarn* and *haearn* respectively, are related to Old Norse *ísarn* and Old High German *īsarn*, but quite different from Latin *ferrum* (which some think was borrowed from a Semitic language) and the Slavic forms, like Old Church Slavonic *želězo*, perhaps another loanword. Iron-working was known in Anatolia from about 4,000 years ago and slowly made its way into western Europe by about 800 BCE and Britain by 500 BCE. These shared words and others are usually interpreted as evidence of contact, as reflecting words borrowed by one group from the other. On the assumption that less powerful or 'prestigious' groups borrow cultural terms from more powerful or 'prestigious' groups, the 19th and 20th centuries witnessed nationalistic debates between those arguing for and against 'Celtic domination' over the Germanic peoples. Today, the suggestion that Celts were more technologically advanced is regarded as very plausible, but we can reckon with 'mutual linguistic influence', in the words of Hickey (forthcoming).

Early contacts with Finno-Ugric. The non-Indo-European languages spoken closest to modern Germanic languages are Finno-Ugric (FU): Finnish, Estonian, Hungarian, and so on. Hundreds of early IE (often specifically early Germanic) words were loaned into Finno-Ugric, especially the group known as Baltic-Finnic languages. Here are a few examples, using Old Norse forms. Norse/Scandinavian has, of course, continued to be in contact with these languages, so that we find many more recent loans as well.[14]

Old Norse	Finnish
á < *ahwu-	-ava in river names
barmr 'lap, womb'	parma
barn 'child'	paarna
blot 'sacrifice'	luode 'magic etc.'
borð 'table'	porras
hringr 'ring'	rengas
konungr 'king'	kuningas
land 'land'	lannas 'beach' (GEN.SG. lantaan)
ormr 'worm'	urme' 'worm under the skin of a reindeer'

The Finnish words look not just like Old Norse forms (provided here), but often almost exactly like what we reckon to be Proto-Germanic forms of these words, as they would have been adapted into Finnish. For example, our word *ring* would have once been something like *hrengaz*. The loss of *h* would have been necessary to make it pronounceable for early Finnish speakers, but the ending, not preserved even in Old Norse, is still visible there. It is then unsurprising that these words have been the topic of massive discussion, recently especially from specialists in Finno-Ugric languages. Recent work pushes the dating of important IE loanwords into FU back to the turn of the second to first millennium BCE or even into the second millennium, much of this work done by Jorma Koivulehto. Based on a range of arguments and evidence beyond our immediate concern, he places the earliest Germanic loans into the first half of the first millennium BCE. These etymologies and dates would fit not only with Germanic and IE, but he argues also with what we know about the history of the Finno-Ugric languages of the Baltic region. Koivulehto (1999, 2001, and other work; see more recently Kallio 2012) brings additional non-linguistic support, especially from archeology, for this absolute chronology of FU contacts with northwestern Indo-European dialects.

---

[14] Pioneering work in lexical borrowing between IE and Finno-Ugric was done by Koivulehto, and many of his key papers have been collected into his 1999 volume. A multi-volume dictionary of such terms has been produced by Kylstra and others. De Vries, in his etymological dictionary, lists seven pages of five columns per page of clear or possible loans into Finno-Ugric. These examples come from the latter, and the Finnish forms do not always correspond to Modern Standard Finnish.

Proponents of this view often push the dating of Germanic settlement in Scandinavia back to at least the late second or early first millennium. This general view of the chronology of FU has gained some support over the years.

To conclude, it should be clear that our knowledge of early European prehistory is fragmentary and fragile, for language and generally, but we can see broad, plausible outlines of where Germanic fits within the larger IE family, and even identify important contacts with neighbors. Moving forward in time, our evidence improves, happily, and the next chapter, on developments from IE to Germanic, is built on more secure foundations.

Possible pre-IE vocabulary? We know there were people in the areas where the (pre-)Germanic people settled, but we know nothing of any substance about them or what languages they spoke. In some instances, these would have been other IE languages and Finno-Ugric languages, but they naturally may have included languages of which no direct traces are left today. Speakers of such languages presumably interacted, and probably intermarried, with the newcomers, and if so, that surely had some impact on the formation of Germanic and other languages in the area. Those original languages form a kind of 'layer underneath', what historical linguists often call a 'substrate'. As English spread across England, various Celtic placenames remained, along with a few words. Algonquian languages in the northeastern United States are not widely spoken across the region today, but words such as *moose* have carried over to English. Vocabulary would be the obvious place to look. Polomé (1989: 54–55, see also Salmons 2004) provided some guidelines for teasing out likely substrate vocabulary:

(a) Is it culturally plausible; does it reflect likely substrate semantic domains and/or basic vocabulary?

(b) Does it lack a clear Indo-European etymology?

(c) Is it a borrowing from neighbors or a *Wanderwort*, similar to what we would today call an 'internationalism'?

(d) Does it show discrepant phonological or morphological features vis-à-vis Indo-European?

A look at the Native American words in American English gives some idea of what domains we might look to: new technology (*canoe, wigwam, moccasin*), flora and fauna (*tobacco, maize, tomato, skunk, moose*), placenames, river names, geographical features, and so on.

The most intriguing criterion is (d), especially since some semantically plausible words show oddities. Recall the *p*-initial words from Romance. Most varieties of German, as we will see in the coming chapters, are not expected to ever have words starting with *p*-. In those instances, we were able to find an identifiable source, the Romance languages, with which German has long and intense connections. Consider how difficult the problem becomes in prehistory. First, in some supposed substrate vocabulary, the vowels *a* and *o* show confusion, rather than clean and systematic correspondences, as illustrated briefly with a few words in Table 2.2. These words appear restricted to this region and show odd variation between those two vowels. If the indigenous population spoke a language lacking such a distinction (much like Americans who pronounce *cot* ~ *caught, don* ~ *dawn, rot* ~ *wrought* the same), the newcomers might have varied in their interpretation of the sound.

TABLE 2.2 **a ~ o in the Northwest**

*òblu	'apple'	Slavic, Celtic, Italic, possibly Baltic
loch, lago	'lake'	Celtic, Italic
*mari/mori	'sea'	Germanic, Celtic, Italic
*badjos	'bay' (color)	Celtic, Italic

Second, in IE, the sound *b was rare. Also, the language did not have the simplest forms of words where two stop sounds were voiced—that is, you could not have two *b, d, g* sounds within a single root, like *bad* or *dog*. But within this region, a number of words seem to show just such a pattern:

*badjos 'bay' (color, of horses) Celtic, Latin
*dub- 'drop' Gmc
*dud- 'shake' Gmc
*gedu- 'meat, cut' Celtic, Gmc

Here again, then, we see patterns in Northwestern IE languages that look as if they do not fit more general IE patterns comfortably.

These kinds of patterns may be the best guides we have to guessing what vocabulary may have come from pre-IE or pre-Germanic substrates, but they remain mere guesses. If we apply the same standard to modern English, we would be misled sometimes. For example, for simple historical reasons (the kinds of syllables that were possible in the language), English used to have no words with long vowels followed by the *sh* sound (written phonetically as *š* here). Over time, that gap has been filled with borrowed words, especially from French, as shown in Table 2.3, but also from Arabic, Japanese, and elsewhere.

TABLE 2.3 **o:š (with date of first known attestations)**

gauche	1751	(< French 'left, maladroit')
brioche	1826	(< French 'pastry roll')
guilloche	1842	(< French 'interwoven design')
hashish	1598	(< Arabic 'dry herb, hay, hemp')
skosh	1942	(< Japanese *sukoshi* 'a little bit')

Yet another set of words shows the same pattern (Table 2.4):

TABLE 2.4 **Affective, onomatopoeic words with tense vowel plus /š/**

swoosh	1885	(Oxford English Dictionary)
whoosh	1899	(OED)
squoosh	1942	(Merriam–Webster)
sheesh	1959	(OED)
smoosh	unknown	
moosh	unknown	
koosh	unknown	a kind of ball

According to the criteria given here for Indo-European by Polomé, these items would look like ideal candidates for substrate status:

- Each one lacks anything resembling a solid etymology within the well-documented history of modern English, likewise in Germanic and IE.
- Each belongs to a domain where borrowing would be unsurprising—affective vocabulary etc.
- These do not reflect known borrowings and at least a couple are attested in other languages, thus making them *Wanderwörter* of a sort.
- Each violates sound structures of contemporary American English.

Where does that leave us? It seems highly likely that some vocabulary does indeed trace back to earlier, non-IE languages, but even with broad patterns of such words, we can draw no firm conclusions about earlier languages and their impact. Maybe precisely because it is so intractable, that problem has proven irresistible to many, including some of the brightest minds in our field.[15]

But let us now turn from the depths of prehistory to an era from which we have considerably better evidence, and much more obvious connections to understanding today's language. In the next chapter, we will cover the reconstructed ancestor of Germanic, namely Indo-European, and then reconstructed Germanic, reaching eventually the earliest written texts in Germanic.

---

[15] In particular, Vennemann (2003, elsewhere) has explored the possibilities of Semitic influences and of Basque or 'Vasconic' substrates in Europe. Those views have met with strong reactions, as reviewed by Baldi & Page (2006), and a new volume helps synthesize discussion, namely Olsen et al. (2015).

3

The dawn of history

Germanic up to the earliest direct attestation

3.0 Introduction

While Indo-European is a reconstructed language, 'made-up data' for a hard-bitten but hardly irrational skeptic, two centuries of intense work have yielded a lot of good clues to what the language was like. (Of course, this leaves aside real issues of exactly how reliable our contemporary attested data may be for various purposes!) In practice, historical linguists work backward from known data to reconstructed forms, such as medieval German texts, back to prehistory. Still, we will pursue the traditional exercise of edging forward in time, from the unknown to the earliest known direct evidence in Germanic.

We focus on several key goals, starting with structural features that characterize what we understand as Indo-European (IE) and how they develop into German. We first treat the ways that IE and Germanic used to emphasize particular syllables within a word, then consonants (especially Grimm's Law and Verner's Law), and finally vowels. Related to that is the aim of learning to trace simple IE forms to Germanic by applying those sound changes. Moving beyond sounds, the chapter should give you an understanding of the foundations of the IE nominal and verbal systems, including case and the basics of noun classes, as well as the verb system. We will then trace key changes in nouns and verbs from IE into Germanic, where even 1,200 years ago, many patterns are recognizable from Modern German. Finally, we will introduce what we know and suspect about the unfolding of Germanic, how the languages in the family are more and less closely connected to one another, by common heritage and contact. The last section brings us to the beginning of the direct attestations, our first written texts.[1] Drawing on that data, we'll explore basic

---

[1] We not only draw on our earliest texts, but also contemporary languages, where we have actual pronunciations to help us decipher sound patterns. You can get a good picture of how

issues in sentence structure, within the limits of the available material. At this time depth, we're still setting the table for understanding the modern language, but you'll see many clear reflections in contemporary German.

3.1 Indo-European accent and the Germanic accent shift

When speakers of English and German think about speech sounds, we tend to focus on particular segments of speech, vowels and consonants. We have started out with that perspective in Chapter 2 and will continue to give them a lot of attention throughout the book. But larger chunks of sound are systematically organized, and they change systematically over the history of German. While we'll soon talk about syllables and groups of syllables, let us begin with how some syllables are made more prominent within a whole word or phrase than others, that is, with the accentual system.

An accent shift is one of the key features that define Germanic as a distinct branch of Indo-European. The change itself can be straightforwardly described, but for later discussions it will be helpful to understand some of the broader context.

The basics of 'stress' and 'accent'. Languages can emphasize a syllable within a word by using one or more from a set of phonetic cues to signal prominence (for more, see Hyman 2006):[2]

1. pitch (in the usual, musical sense)
2. duration (length)
3. intensity (loudness)

In English and German, we use all three to some extent, in contrasting pairs such as (Standard American English) *a pérmit* versus *to permít, an ínsult* versus *to insúlt*. In each case, the stressed syllable is 'louder, longer, and often marked by a pitch excursion' (*Handbook of the IPA* on English stress, 1999: 43).[3]

In traditional terms, linguists distinguish the following different ways that languages exploit these phonetic cues in speech:

diverse that evidence is from this project: http://www.languagesandpeoples.com/Germanic, the Germanic part of the 'Languages and "Dialects" of Europe' project. They provide pronunciations of a set of words in modern varieties as well as our best guesses about past pronunciations.

[2] Not all languages do emphasize syllables in this sense, employing stress or tone on words in this way. French is often argued to lack stress or tone in this sense. Words are typically stressed on the final syllable, taken to be a kind of default or non-rule.

[3] The spectrograms given here come from the IPA's sound files, which you can listen to and download here: http://web.uvic.ca/ling/resources/ipa/handbook_downloads.htm. The pictures come from opening the files in the free phonetics software package called Praat, available here: http://www.fon.hum.uva.nl/praat/. You can record your own speech in Praat or other similar programs, and compare your own pronunciation of forms like those discussed here.

- **Tone systems.** Pitch is relevant on every syllable, as in Chinese or Yoruba. That is, a particular pitch doesn't signal a prominent syllable relative to less prominent ones, but is an inherent part of that syllable.
- **Stress systems.** Some syllables are pronounced louder and/or last longer than others, such as in English or German, so that we can think about stressed versus unstressed syllables. The placement of stress sometimes correlates with edges of words (initial or final syllables).
- **Pitch accent systems.**[4] Pitch is used to mark a syllable as more prominent, but usually only on one syllable in the word, not every syllable, a type of system found in Japanese and Serbian/Croatian/Bosnian. Instead of seeing this as a distinct type, it is becoming more common to simply think of pitch accent as a system that combines elements of tone and stress. Notably, one syllable is marked by tone rather than all syllables as in tone languages proper.

English and German use pitch as well, as part of marking stressed syllables but more importantly in intonation—you can utter the following sentence as a statement or question (etc.) by varying the pitch contour you use: 'Das soll man ernst nehmen.'

Consider the picture in Figure 3.1—a spectrogram, showing spectral characteristics of speech over time—of the pronunciation of the German word *Schornsteinfeger* (with a rough indication of where which sounds come).

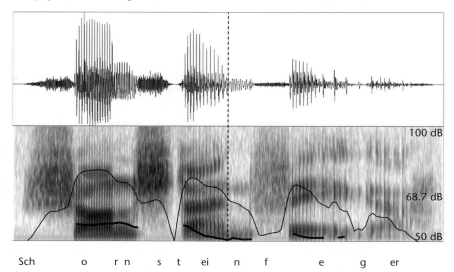

FIGURE 3.1 Spectrogram of *Schornsteinfeger*.

---

[4] Not all specialists in the study of accentual systems accept 'pitch accent' as a type, or even these general types as a whole (see Hyman 2006).

This shows all the above-mentioned characteristics of the word (with lines added by Praat). The thin line tracks intensity, or loudness, and, as you can see, it moves dramatically up and down—going up on vowels, highest on the vowel with main stress, and disappearing on the 't' sound, where this speaker, a man, isn't allowing any air to pass through his vocal tract for that moment. The thick line measures pitch (what phoneticians call fundamental frequency or f0), and it appears only on the parts of the picture corresponding to the

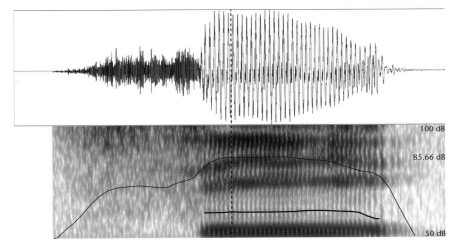

FIGURE 3.2 Cantonese 'silk'.

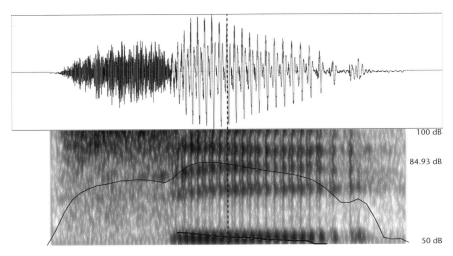

FIGURE 3.3 Cantonese 'time'.

vowels. You should be able to see that pitch is higher on the first syllable than on the others. Compare this to two words pronounced in Cantonese (Hong Kong), a tone language. The words for 'silk' (Figure 3.2) and 'time' (Figure 3.3) both consist of the sound segments *si*, but with different tones:

In the first picture, we see a level tone, where the tone (again, the heavier line) starts high and stays steady. In the second word, where we have a mid-low to low falling tone, you see that the line begins much lower and drops from there, compared to the first picture.

Stress can be FIXED—i.e. it can always come on one particular syllable within the word, such as the first or last in a word—Finnish regularly stresses initial syllables and Turkish stresses final syllables, for example. (This can help listeners recognize where words begin and end.) In some other languages, stress has traditionally been called 'free' or 'mobile'. This does NOT mean that speakers just put an accent wherever they happen to feel like it (there are no libertarian stress systems), but rather that accent does not always fall on the same syllable. Instead, as we'll see shortly, accent varies in IE morphologically, so that certain verb forms (particular tense and person forms) have accent on the first syllable and others on a later syllable. We find a trace of this kind of system, for example, in the few English pairs where initial stress is associated with nouns such as *permit* and final with verbs such as *to permit*. Mobility is more robust and systematic in Spanish, where you can contrast three different positions marking different word forms (I've added an accent mark in the middle form, where Spanish spelling would not have one.):

término   '[the] end'
termíno   'I finish'
terminó   'he/she/it finished'

In yet other languages, such as Russian and Serbian/Croatian/Bosnian within Indo-European, or Japanese outside the family, stress/accent not only varies by grammatical category but also by word, so that in the extreme case it must be learned for each word.

In these terms, the nature of Indo-European accent is relatively well understood, and the accent shift to Germanic is largely agreed upon:

- IE used pitch to mark accent (as in the third type described on p. 34); specifically, it had a high tone associated with the accented syllable. This became chiefly a stress accent in Germanic. That is, IE had an accentual system that was more like Serbian while English and German continue the presumed type of early Germanic.
- IE had mobile accent, which became fixed on the initial syllable in Germanic. So, Greek (nominative) *patér* contrasts with Old English *fǽder* ('´' indicates accent).

How can we know this with considerable confidence? Most scholars, like Kiparsky (1973), reconstruct IE inflectional accent based on three dialects or dialect groups: Sanskrit, Greek, and Balto-Slavic. These languages all have mobile pitch accent, and they show parallels that suggest that they have retained an old system: when accent is reconstructed for IE, the results match the position of accent in these languages, as in the example in Table 3.1:

TABLE 3.1 **Sample Sanskrit forms for 'foot'[5]**

Sanskrit	Case/number	IE
pā́d	NOM.SG.	*pḗs
pā́dam	ACC.SG.	*pédm̥
padás	GEN.SG.	*pedós
padí	LOC.SG.	*pedí
pā́das	NOM.PL.	*pédes
etc.		

This is a simple example of one noun type in one daughter, and accent placement involved intricate conditions of various sorts: IE verb and noun classes show a variety of different accentual patterns. Much work (recently Kim 2002) has been invested in tracing the complexities of where accent came in each particular form.

A number of factors could have motivated this change from an IE mobile pitch to a Germanic stress system, and similar changes have taken place in a number of other Indo-European daughter languages. Halle (1997) argues that the IE system was such that when languages lost mobile accent, the default was initial stress, just what we find in Germanic, Celtic, and probably an early stage of Italic. Languages such as Serbian/Croatian/Bosnian that use pitch heavily often have 'demarcative' stress as well. That just means that other cues (loudness, length) are used to signal the beginnings or ends of words. In other words, if an IE language lost the designation of pitch on some particular syllable, it almost automatically had a Germanic-like system. This is understandable: it is simpler for learners and speakers to know that words are stressed on the first syllable than to master the intricate system of accent placement that IE had.

At the same time, accentual systems are prone to change when speakers are in contact with other languages, especially when there is widespread bilingualism. There seems to be a particular tendency for pitch accents (and tone systems) to be lost with the result often being a stress system (Salmons 1992a). In fact, language contact often leads to simplifications of particular sorts.

---

[5] Recall that there is a simple guide to the phonetic symbols on pp. xxi–xxiv. Cases, including the locative, are discussed later in this chapter. The forms here are from Szemerényi (1996: 164) and they obscure some issues beyond our immediate concerns. One, the difference between the Sanskrit *a* vowel versus the IE *e, is something we'll return to later.

In the case at hand, these two motivations—simplification driven by structural considerations and by language contact—likely pushed in the same direction.

In some languages weak syllables are REDUCED, while in other languages they are not. Finnish is an example of the latter type, while Germanic fits the former. The Finnish word for 'ice cream', for example, is *jäätelö*, and none of the vowels is reduced. In Germanic, the tendency is perhaps most readily apparent in the strong tendency to reduce vowels to schwa ([ə]) when they are unstressed. This characteristic of Germanic stress appears to have massive historical consequences, as we will explore in more detail before long in our discussion of the Laws of Finals.

Next, we turn our attention to the consonant system and Grimm's Law. There, we will find that Germanic retains traces of the earlier IE placement of accent, so that our understanding of accent will be put to use.

3.2 Consonants: Indo-European to Germanic

> If non-specialists know anything about historical linguistics, it is Grimm's Law.
>
> W. P. Lehmann (1967: 46)

In Chapter 2, in introducing the comparative method, the cornerstone of determining linguistic relatedness, we have already drawn on the classic example of it, the correspondences between the consonant system of Germanic compared to many other Indo-European languages: Latin voiceless stops (that is, sounds like *p, t, k*) normally correspond to voiceless fricatives (sounds like *f, θ, h*) in the Germanic languages, and so on. This set of relationships is the traditional defining phonological characteristic of Germanic as a branch of Indo-European. This section explores this change and an intimately connected one, in more detail, while also introducing some basics about speech sounds.

The Danish linguist Rasmus Kristian Rask is usually credited with having first reported these correspondences in 1818, in an essay called 'Undersøgelse om det gamle Nordiske eller Islandske Sprogs Oprindelse' (the work is available in several versions online; quotes come from the annotated translation here: http://www.utexas.edu/cola/centers/lrc/books/read03.html).[6] Comparing an assumed ancestor of Latin and Greek with Icelandic, he observed the systematic correspondences between voiceless stops and fricatives at the beginning of words, assuming that stops had changed to fricatives. The examples below come from the just-mentioned translation (keeping the

---

[6] In fact, Edward Lhuyd had sketched many of the correspondences already in 1707; see Morpurgo Davies (1975).

original spellings), with the assumed ancestral (Latin-Greek-like) forms on the left and Old Norse/Icelandic on the right:

Correspondence	'Ancestral' examples	Old Norse/Icelandic
p to *f*, e.g.:	*platus* (broad) *patēr* (father)	*flatur* (flat) *fadir* (= [ð])
t to *þ*, e.g.:	*treis* (three) *tego* (roof) *tu* (you)	*þrír* *þek* *þu*
k to *h*, e.g.:	*kreas* (meat) *cornu* (horn) *cutis* (skin)	*hræ* (dead body) *horn* *hud*

That is, *ps* in the words for 'broad' and 'father' correspond to *fs* in Old Norse, not just in a particular word, but across whole sets, showing how systematic sound change is. Not only does one sound regularly change into another, but they follow broader generalizations: these three sets actually reflect one single change at a certain level.

Sounds can be divided into MANNER and PLACE of articulation. In manner, the consonants under discussion, for example, are stops (or plosives) and fricatives. In the former, like 'p', 't', and 'k', you completely cease air flow for a short period of time, often less than a 1/10 of a second. In the latter, you don't halt air flow, but create a constriction with your speech organs enough that it produces noisy friction. The three boxes with ancestral forms all contain stops, but with different places of articulation, the first produced with the lips (labial), the second with the tongue tip at or behind the teeth, or at the alveolar ridge (alveolar or coronal), and the last with the body of the tongue at the soft palate (velar). In each case, they become fricatives—*f*, *þ*, and *h* in Rask's spelling, but [f, θ, x] in modern phonetic notation.

Another key distinction involves laryngeal features, especially whether our vocal folds vibrate during production of the sound (voiced) or not (voiceless). Many languages have aspirated stops, produced with a puff of air (as in the 't' of German *Tonne*, English *tunnel*). Indo-European also had, and many modern languages of South Asia have, another kind of stop, called 'voiced aspirates' traditionally, but known as 'breathy' or 'murmured' in phonetics (here are Hindi examples: http://www.phonetics.ucla.edu/course/chapter6/hindi/hindi.html). All of the examples in the ancestor presented above are voiceless stops (though we pronounce them as aspirated now in German or English). A single generalization can now capture this set of changes: voiceless stops become voiceless fricatives.

Below you'll find some data from a broad set of IE languages (though still hardly complete). You should be able to see the basic relationship of Germanic (represented in Table 3.2 by Gothic) to IE as a whole:[7]

TABLE 3.2 **Indo-European**

	*p	*t	*k
Sanskrit	pitár-	tráyas	hŕd
Latin	pater	trēs	cor (GEN. cordis)
Greek	patēr	treîs	kardíā
Old Irish	athair	tri	cride
OCSlav.		trije/tri	srŭdĭce
Gothic	fadar	þreis	haírtō
Armenian	hayr	erek'	sirt
Hittite		tēri	kir-
Toch.	pācar	trai/tarya	
	'father'	'three'	'heart'

	*b[8]	*d	*g
Skt	bála-m	dásamá	jā́nu
Lat	dē-bilis	decimus	genū
Grk	bélteros	dékatos	gónu
OIr		dechmad	glūn
OCS	bolĭjĭ	desętĭ	kolěno
Goth		taíhunda	kniu
Arm		tasn	cunr
Hitt			gēnu
Toch		śkänt	kenī(ne)
	'strong'	'ten, tenth'	'knee'

	*bh	*dh	*gh
Skt	bhrā́tā	dvā́ras	ghn-ánti (pl.)
Lat	frāter	foris	dē-fendō 'ward off'
Grk	phrātēr	thýrā	theíno
OIr	brāthair	dorus	gonaid
OCS	bratrŭ	dvĭrĭ	ženǫ
Goth	brōþar	daur	gūþ (Old Eng., no Goth. cognate)
Arm	ełbayr	duŕn	ganem
Hitt		an-durza	kuēnzi
Toch	pracar	twere	käsk
	'brother'	'door, gate'	'strike' etc.

---

[7] With minor changes, this set of data follows the forms given in Mallory & Adams (1997).

[8] As noted in the last chapter and discussed a little more in what follows, *b is very rare in IE. This is probably the strongest single etymology with initial *b and the gaps in distribution are notable compared to the other terms given here.

Until just now, we have talked about CORRESPONDENCES between sounds in similar-looking words in different languages, thus making reference only to directly attested data. From there, historical linguists—including Rask—have taken the additional step of RECONSTRUCTING a PROTO-FORM, of positing a specific form that they regard as the ancestor form. Consider the *p~f* correspondences we dealt with in this chapter. In historical sound change, as noted, it appears relatively common for stops to become fricatives but relatively uncommon for fricatives to become stops, suggesting that *p* is the older form. A variety of other tests point in the same direction, such as the simple observation that many of the attested forms have *p* (Sanskrit, Latin, Greek, Tocharian), while *f* is less common. And it's common to assume that fewer languages changed, while more stayed closer to the original system. There are other considerations, but we will not dwell further here on how to reconstruct proto-forms, but note again that these are in essence invented forms, albeit invented with care, sophistication, and knowledge. Some comparative linguists assume a 'realist' position, figuring that their reconstructions reflect actual historical usage—often down to details of pronunciation; others take an 'abstractionist' position—seeing reconstructions as convenient ways to represent the correspondences we have discussed so far, while remaining far more agnostic about how these forms sounded. The latter, algebraic, approach is far safer, even if you lose the joy of believing you're able to pronounce sounds as people did millennia ago.

In fact, once we venture beyond the safe confines of actual correspondences, little can be taken for granted. Even the stop system of IE, surely the most basic element of the sound system of the most intensely studied proto-language, has areas of great controversy. In recent decades, a profound revision of the traditional reconstruction has been proposed, based on a range of concerns about the plausibility of the details of the traditional reconstruction. In particular, what we call 'voiced stops' turn out to be strikingly uncommon across the vocabulary of IE—few IE words contain voiced stops, while voiced stops usually occur widely in languages that have them (not all do). Voiced stops are not found in inflectional endings, and roots that have two stops never have two voiced ones, it appears, so that words such as *dog*, *dude*, and *bug* would have been impossible. And the *b* sound is so rare that some claim it did not exist at all (that rarity is captured by putting the symbol in parentheses in Table 3.3). The 'Glottalic Theory' proposed that the voiced stops were actually implosive (a kind of stop illustrated in the top row here: http://www.phonetics.ucla.edu/course/chapter6/sindhi/sinhi.html) or ejective stops (here: http://www.phonetics.ucla.edu/course/chapter6/lakhota/lakhota.html). Sounds such as voiceless ejective [p'] are produced by closing the glottis and opening it after the lips open. I argued long ago (1992c) that the problems raised by this new view about the traditional system are serious ones, but that the new proposals suffer an array of serious problems themselves. Debate has died down in the last few years, but without any fundamental resolution, either by addressing the issues with the traditional reconstruction or by adopting a new proposal. What has changed over the last few years is that more Indo-Europeanists, even in introductions and hand-books, are willing to acknowledge the debate. This often includes admitting problems with traditional reconstructions, and sometimes even going so far as to accept a glottalic reconstruction (e.g. Clackson 2007: 45–48; Beekes 2011: 128–129; and Kümmel 2015, with further discussion in Salmons forthcoming).

The key for our purpose is merely that our reconstructions at this time depth are profoundly fragile and uncertain. With that in mind, one widely accepted consonant system of IE is given in Table 3.3:

TABLE 3.3 **The Indo-European Consonant Inventory**

	labial	coronal	palatal	velar	labiovelar
Stops					
voiceless	p	t	ḱ	k	k^w
voiced	(b)	d	ǵ	g	g^w
murmured	bh	dh	ǵh	gh	g^wh
Fricative		s			
Sonorants					
liquids		l, r			
nasals	m	n			
glides	w		j		
Laryngeals	H_1, H_2, H_3				

From Howell et al. (forthcoming).

In our first example of sound correspondences, we've already been introduced to some of these categories. Palatal stops are simply produced with the body of the tongue (dorsum) hitting the hard palate, farther forward in the mouth from the soft palate or velum. In German, the difference between *ich*-Laut and *ach*-Laut illustrates the difference: *ich* is produced with the tongue body held close to the hard palate, *ach* with it close to the velum. Also, we automatically produce a palatal stop in German or English when *k* or *g* comes before an *i* sound in a syllable—so palatal *Kiel* as opposed to velar *Kuh*. While we hear and interpret these two *k*s as the 'same' sounds in German and English, the two

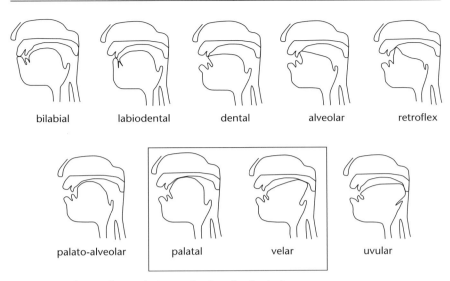

FIGURE 3.4 Places of articulation, palatal and velar in box.
Adapted from http://www.hc-sc.gc.ca/dhp-mps/brgtherap/images/g_kondrak_3-eng.gif.

types are distinct in many languages. We usually illustrate place of articulation with a graphic showing a cross-section of the vocal tract from the mouth facing toward the left, as in Figure 3.4, and showing how especially the position of the tongue (the blob dominating the middle of each image) position changes (images from here: http://www.hc-sc.gc.ca/dhp-mps/brgtherap/images/g_kon-drak_3-eng.gif). The sounds just mentioned are illustrated by the middle two on the second row.

The status of palatal stops in IE is not uncontroversial, and they had merged with the plain velars before Grimm's Law took place, so that both *ḱ and *k yield Germanic *h.

Labiovelar stops are simply velar stops with a following *w* sound as part of them, such as English *quit* or *Gwen*. There is good reason to believe that they were single sounds in IE, though, not two sounds as in contemporary English. These leave clearer traces in Germanic, such as the *wh* spelling in words like *whether, why, which*, which trace back to *k^w. For many older speakers and speakers of some dialects (some Southerners in the US, or Scottish speakers in the UK), this correlates with a distinct pronunciation—people who differenti-ate *whether ~ weather, why ~ Y, which ~ witch*.

While stops involve total cessation of air flow and fricatives involve enough narrowing to create friction, SONORANTS are those sounds with yet less restriction of air flow. The *w is the first sound of *way* and the *j of *yet*. Otherwise, these sounds offer no particular challenges, except for how *r was pronounced, which we will

FIGURE 3.5 Ferdinand de Saussure.

revisit in §6.7 and §7.1. In the meantime, interested readers can consult Howell (1991), Catford (2001), and Denton (2003) for the best discussions.

Finally, IE had mysterious sounds called 'laryngeals', which clearly disappeared well before Germanic came into existence.[9] They are, though, important as a reminder of how uncertain reconstructions are, and the genius employed in solving such problems. The Swiss linguist Ferdinand de Saussure, then the age of a typical undergraduate (and pictured in Figure 3.5), proposed them based on oddities he saw in IE reconstructions: almost all roots consisted of a consonant followed by a vowel and another consonant, thus described as 'CVC' roots. A few, such as *ed- 'to eat', lacked one or the other consonant. Based on this and other patterns, he argued that these roots had once had an additional sound in them, to make them match the three-segment pattern of most IE roots. The proposal was not widely accepted at the time, but when Hittite texts were deciphered in the early 20th century, it turned out to have a sound, often apparently an *h*-like sound, in these positions. So, the word for 'white, silver' is vowel-initial in many languages, such as Latin *argentum* 'silver', while the Hittite cognate is *harkis* 'white'. Current scholars still debate how many laryngeals IE had—most specialists believe three. It is likewise not settled whether these were consonants or vowels—beyond the *h* example already presented, most traces of laryngeals are changes in vowels.

---

[9] Lindeman (1987) provides a succinct technical introduction to the topic, if no longer current. Note that in IE linguistics, 'laryngeal' refers to these sounds and does not have the usual phonetic meaning, namely sounds produced with the larynx. For a traditional take specifically on Germanic, see Ringe (2006).

3.2.1 Grimm's Law

Even though the correspondences between Germanic and other IE languages had been recognized for a long time, the fuller picture was most famously worked out by Jacob Grimm, and the whole network of correspondences has, rightly or wrongly, come to be known as Grimm's Law.[10] (The celebration of Grimm as a linguist is a long tradition and it often has the feel of the Romantic era about it, as in the drawing by his brother shown in Figure 3.6.) Indeed, the impressive systematicity of the changes sketched so far leans heavily on insights from Grimm himself, particularly that the changes involve the same features (e.g. of a voiceless stop to a fricative) regardless of place of articulation, and that the whole complex set of changes preserves the overall set of 'slots' in the consonant system. Collinge (1985: 64) sees the special features of Grimm's presentation as these (adapting and paraphrasing here):

- Grimm does not focus overly on phonetic detail, but reaches for 'systemic exploration'.
- He states his 'rules' as correspondences, but by using them as a *Prüfstein* he implies the testing of a law.
- He connects these changes to closely parallel changes found in High German. (See §4.1, in this volume.)
- 'Fuzziness is freely admitted', due to borrowing and other causes.

At a time when speech sounds were poorly understood—Grimm himself talked about *Buchstaben*, not *Laute*—these are significant steps toward capturing this process as a coherent set of changes. It clarifies the relationship of Germanic languages to IE, and underscores the systematic nature of sounds and sound correspondences. This helped later scholars establish the regularity of sound change, *die Ausnahmslosigkeit der Lautgesetze*, which in many ways marks the beginning of historical linguistics as a modern scientific enterprise.

Now that you've seen the kinds of data scholars drew on and the kinds of generalizations Grimm and others made, a full set of the correspondences known together as Grimm's Law are presented in Table 3.4 in simple form.

TABLE 3.4 **Grimm's Law: simple correspondences**

	IE	Germanic
Spirantization	Voiceless stop	Voiceless fricative
Labial	*p	*f
Alveolar	*t	*θ
Velar	*k	*x ('ach-Laut')

---

[10] It is also known as the Germanic Consonant Shift or the First Sound Shift and, even in English, as the *Lautverschiebung*. Note that Grimm's name is not used in the German appellations, where it is known generally as the *erste Lautverschiebung* or the *germanische Lautverschiebung*.

Labiovelar	*k^w	*x^w
Devoicing	Voiced stop	Voiceless
Labial	*b	*p
Alveolar	*d	*t
Velar	*g	*k
Labiovelar	*g^w	*k^w
Deaspiration	Voiced aspirate	Voiced
Labial	*bh	*b
Alveolar	*dh	*d
Velar	*gh	*g
Labiovelar	*g^{w}h	*g^w

The whole set of changes is then simple, as we saw in discussing Rask, illustrated with labials but holding across other places of articulation:

- IE voiceless stops (like *p, t, k*) become fricatives: *p > f.*
- IE voiced stops (like *b, d, g*) become voiceless: *b > p.*
- IE voiced aspirate stops (like *bh, dh, gh*) become voiced: *bh > b.*

The connectedness of these elements is clear and they are often described as a CHAIN. In this (widely used) ordering, it might be thought of as a chain where each shift drags along the one after it: the change of *p > *f leaves no *p in the system. Voiceless stops are found in almost all of the world's languages (maybe all, depending on the analysis), so that if a change removed these stops, a language might create new ones, in this case by devoicing the voiced stops, *b> *p. Once again, the voiced aspirates have been seen by some as prone to simplify, giving us *bh > *b. If we think of the shift beginning with p > f, as below on the left, it creates the system shown on the right, which some think of as having a 'gap' in the plain voiceless stops now. The figures below show the system of stops at a given stage (with place of articulation on the horizontal and type of stop on the vertical), while the offset line shows the change.

First stage of 'drag chain'   Resulting system

bh   dh   gh   g^{w}h   bh   dh   gh   g^{w}h

b   d   g   g^w b   d   g   g^w

p   t   k   k^w

f   θ   x   x^w f   θ   x   x^w

From there, the dominos fall as the voiced stops shift to fill the voiceless stop gap (left) and the voiced aspirates deaspirate to become plain voiced (right).

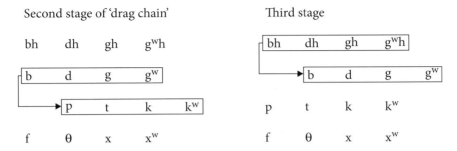

Second stage of 'drag chain'   Third stage

The result is a shift of each series one link along the chain.

Another view of the shift, one that some may find a useful mnemonic in learning the connectedness of the steps of Grimm's Law, treats the shift as having links connected by pushing rather than pulling, with each element moving one step, illustrated by the labials:

*bh > *b > *p > *f

This view is perhaps best motivated by the 'markedness' of the voiced aspirates. Some linguists argue that sounds that are complex phonetically (requiring a configuration of the vocal folds that many languages don't have) and phonologically (marked by two features, voice and aspiration) are more readily lost over time. On this view, in an effort to rid themselves of *bh, *dh, and the rest of the series, speakers began to simplify them to *b, *d, etc.

Which direction this game of musical chairs went in is somewhat controversial, but from early on, the systematic nature of these changes—along with other ones known from Germanic and other languages—has been captured graphically as below. This figure shows one form of a 'Kreislauf' or rotation of consonants, following a tradition dating back at least to Streitberg (1896: 104, see Schrodt 1974: 207):

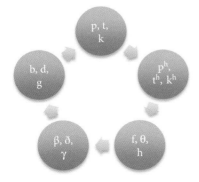

That is, starting from the top, a 'plain' *t* (unaspirated, as in Spanish, Dutch, French, Polish) can become aspirated, then become a voiceless fricative (as in *think*) become voiced (as in *then*), become a stop again, lose its voicing, and so on. Today, with a vastly larger set of sound changes to consider, we know that changes do not rotate in such a simple way, but this is a striking early effort at finding bigger patterns in sound change.

The figures above make explicit the interlocking, chain-like character of Grimm's Law that scholars have been aware of since the beginning: the IE voiceless stops change into fricatives, but new voiceless stops arise from the old voiced stops. The complexity of this shift appears to be without close parallel in known histories of consonant systems in the languages of the world, rivaled perhaps only by the (in some sense presumably related) Second Sound Shift, which we will discuss in Chapter 4.

A note on the voiced aspirates. In the technical literature we find disagreements about the fate of the IE voiced aspirates (*bh etc.) in Germanic. Above I presented the voiced aspirates as becoming voiced stops in Germanic (*b etc.), in traditional fashion, but others have argued that these sounds

FIGURE 3.6 'Im Kolleg bei Jacob Grimm', by his brother Ludwig Emil Grimm, 1830.

became voiced fricatives (*β etc.). In traditional sources, these are often written *ƀ, *đ, *g, but more often in modern sources given in IPA,*β, *ð, *ɣ, as I just did. Both types of sound appear in various places in German daughter languages. In many languages (Spanish, Danish, Hebrew (with additional complexities), some German dialects), voiced stops and voiced fricatives vary systematically according to the sounds around them. Take these examples from one Hessian dialect (Schirmunski 1962: 304, following his orthography), where we have *b* at the beginning and end of words (with *Auslautverhärtung* or final 'devoicing' at the end), but *w* (phonetically a bilabial fricative, [β], like the Spanish *b* in words such as *haber*) between vowels:

Hessian	German
blaiwə	bleiben
blaibst	bleibst
grāwə	graben
grāb	Grab

This kind of weakening or 'lenition' is triggered here by the presence of vowels immediately before and after, though similar processes in German dialects and around the world differ in their precise conditioning. In some High German dialects, we can find this where a following unstressed pronoun 'leans on' the end of a verb (forms like these pronouns are called 'clitics' and we'll discuss them in detail later):

iç hab 'ich habe'   but   *haw-iç* 'habe ich'
                              haw-ən 'habe ihn'

An easy way to resolve the question of the voiced aspirates is similar: early Germanic worked like this dialect: the sounds that developed from *bh, *dh, and *gh could be voiced stops (*b, *d, *g) or voiced fricatives (*β, *ð, *ɣ) depending on the sounds that surrounded them, their phonetic/phonological environment. Further changes have taken place in most languages and dialects over the millennia, complicating the picture.

This provides the last bit of detail we need on the change itself, a refinement to what was dubbed Stage Three:

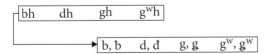

The full correspondence set, then, can be summarized like this, leaving aside only the *s*-clusters and double-stop clusters of Indo-European, where the second elements don't shift:

Indo-European				Germanic			
bh	dh	gh	gʷh	b, ƀ	d, đ	g, g	gʷ, gʷ
b	d	g	gʷ	p	t	k	kʷ
p	t	k	kʷ	f	θ [=þ]	x, h	xʷ, hʷ

'Causes' of the shift. How and why could something like this have happened? Even for changes underway in languages today, those questions are maddeningly difficult (and incredibly exciting—we are making progress now, as you'll see). For such ancient changes, speculations have run rampant (see Schrodt 1974: 200–216). Infamous wild ideas from famous scholars include Grimm's own suggestion that it was 'an expression of the impetuous character of the Germanic tribes' (as Prokosch 1938: 55 describes Grimm's view), Meyer-Benfey's (1901) attempt to connect increased aspiration—the often-assumed underlying phonetic motivation of the shift—caused by huffing and puffing due to life in high mountains, to Julius Pokorny's theory that a climatic disaster triggered the shift, as an articulatory reaction to cold, damp air. Given that moving air is blamed for so much in German-speaking culture (from the *Föhn* to *es zieht*—see http://german-way.com/blog/2009/02/13/german-phobia-killer-draft/), why not the Sound Shift?

Somewhat more serious discussion has often focused on possible pre-Indo-European roots of the shift. In that spirit, Prokosch (1917, 1939: 56–57) suggests that the shift correlates with the upheavals of the *Völkerwanderung*. While this is in some sense plausible—second-language learners of Germanic could certainly have reinterpreted the complex stop system of (Northwest) Indo-European into the Germanic system, and passed that on to their children—it is utterly unknowable and I have to concur with Schrodt (1974: 186) that this is 'ein totes Kapitel, mit dem sich vorläufig nichts anfangen läßt' (see also Iverson & Salmons 2008).

3.2.2 Fricative + stop clusters

It was recognized from early on that a systematic group of sounds failed to conform to the expectations of regularity in Grimm's Law:

If a fricative comes before an IE stop, that stop does not shift.

IE had only one fricative, *s, and we find it only before voiceless *p, *t, *k. In cases where they occur after *s, the stop is unchanged:

IE	Germanic	
*spreg-	*sprek-/*spek-	'to speak'
*stel-	*stel-	'to put'
*skel-	*skel-	'to cut'
*pisk-	*fisk-	'fish'

There's a broader pattern: IE allowed two stops together, just as we find in German *Abt* (pronounced [apt]), or English *apt*. Here the first stop shifts but the second does not.

IE	Germanic	
*kapt	*haft-	'captive, etc.'
*nokʷt-	*naxt-	'night'

This group also includes a few forms that would have had *zd in IE, such as *Nest*. It was built from *ni 'down' plus a form of 'to sit': *ni-zd-, which became *nist- in Proto-Germanic. (We use a hyphen, '-', to mark morpheme boundaries, and they do not typically interfere with sound changes.)

This restriction on the shift is likely linked to the trigger of the Sound Shift: almost all modern Germanic languages aspirate stops word-initially, that is, we produce them with an audible puff of air. Aspiration, as we'll discuss in the next chapter, often leads stops to become fricatives, partly through how they can be produced but also due to how they are perceived by listeners. When an [s] precedes, though, there is no aspiration, no puff of air. That is, you may think of the second sound in *Stadt* and the first in *Tat* as being the same, but the second is aspirated while the first isn't. Evidence suggests that this pattern of not aspirating stops after a fricative is ancient. If aspiration helped turn stops into fricatives, and aspiration did not occur on stops after fricatives, that yields exactly the pattern we find (Iverson & Salmons 2005, elsewhere).

These clusters (as groups of consonants are called) remain from IE down to the present, as is clear from many of the examples, and only in a few places do other changes obscure this, notably in old *sk* becoming German [ʃ] <sch>.

3.2.3 Verner's Law[11]

We have just seen that in the course of the First Sound Shift, IE *t (like the first sound in *Tat*) develops into Germanic voiceless *θ (as in e*th*er). But in some cases what should turn out in Germanic as voiceless fricatives actually became voiced, so IE *t becomes *ð (as in ei*th*er): the sounds in the words for 'brother' and 'father' both surely trace to an IE *t (*bhréH₂ter, *pH₂ter).[12] In fact the attested forms differ, like Gothic *broþar* vs. *fadar* (pronounced [faðar]) and Modern German *Bruder* vs. *Vater*.[13]

---

[11] This section draws on material developed with Dave Holsinger during a teaching practicum, extensively updated and revised, in collaborative work with him and Greg Iverson.
[12] Recall that 'H' stands for an IE laryngeal.
[13] Later developments obscure this distinction in English.

In what looks like a sporadic process, this voicing happens with words involving all IE voiceless stops, as well as the fricative *s* vs. *z*, as shown in the words for 'rabbit': German *Hase*, Old Frisian *hasa* show a different development from English *hare*, Old Norse *heri* (as we'll see in the next chapter, this *r* comes from *z). Because of this example, the difference is sometimes called the 'Bunny Conundrum', the conundrum in finding different outcomes in the same context in the same word.[14] This is more traditionally called *grammatischer Wechsel*, a 'change in letters' that happens in different inflected forms of the same word:

	'I become'	'I became'	'we became'	participle
PIE	*wérto	*wewórta	*wewr̥təmé	*wr̥tonós
Skt.	vártāmi	va-várta	vavr̥timá	vr̥tānáḥ
PGmc.	*werþō	*warþa	*wurðum	*wurðan(a)z
OHG	wirdu	ward	wurtum	wortan
Ger.	werde	wurde (ward)	wurden	geworden

	infinitive	'I freeze'	'we froze'	participle
PGmc	*friusana(n)	*fraus	*fruzum	*gafruzan(a)s
OE	freosan	fréas	fruron	gefroren
Ger.	frieren	fror	froren	gefroren
Eng.	freeze	froze	froze	frozen

Grimm couldn't explain these alternations, and the 'Bunny Conundrum' shows that different daughters can have different forms of what must have once been one and the same sound in one and the same word. Grimm figured that there must have been some sort of grammatical explanation. But this was no ordinary scholarly problem: the status of linguistics as a science was under intense discussion, with debate raging about whether there were LAUTGESETZE—rules that ALL sound change follows, like the laws of nature— or whether there could be exceptions, e.g. that 'each word has its own history'. The former position would give (historical) linguistics exceptionless laws, thus real rigor and scientific status. These data, the apparent exceptions to Grimm's Law, became a key battleground: the correspondences were over-whelmingly regular, but had this large set of unexplained exceptions. This problem was solved in Karl Verner's 1877 essay, 'Eine ausnahme der ersten

---

[14] German has the variant too, in the obsolete form *hehr* 'noble, sublime', originally meaning 'gray[-haired]', related to English *hoary*.

lautverschiebung'. This paper changes the game in favor of sound laws. As a result, as Lehmann (1967) wrote, it 'may be the single most influential publication in linguistics.'[15]

In studying the accentual patterns of Sanskrit, Verner observed a correlation between where accent stood in Sanskrit forms and whether Germanic had a voiced or voiceless fricative from Grimm's Law from an inherited IE voiceless stop: 'When the accent in Sanskrit rests on the root syllable, we have the voiceless fricative for the root final in Germanic; on the other hand, when the accent in Sanskrit falls on the ending, the Germanic forms show a voiced stop for the root final.'

An easy formulation of Verner's Law for our purposes is:

Verner's Law

(1) In sounds: when IE *p, *t, *k, *s follow an UNstressed vowel (and come before another vowel or sonorant consonant or at the end of a word), they become Germanic *β, *ð, *ɣ, *z.[16]

(2) A little more abstractly: when an IE voiceless stop/GERMANIC voiceless fricative directly follows an UNstressed vowel, it becomes voiced in Germanic.

This formulation quietly indicates that voiceless stops in initial position (at the beginnings of words) will follow Grimm's Law but not Verner's. In fact, Verner's Law is often negatively formulated: voiceless fricatives become voiced except initially and after a stressed vowel. Also clear is that in words of several syllables, the only position that really matters is whether the immediately preceding vowel is accented in IE. That said, the data here are stunningly complicated and this sketch is truly only a sketch; the interested reader is referred to Schaffner's (2001) encyclopedic, blow-by-blow presentation of the data on this subject.

Part of what's remarkable here is how Verner (pictured in Figure 3.7) connects placement of accent with voicing. These must have seemed to be unrelated facts about the language, but he made the connection based on close examination of the data before him, rather than preconceptions about what might condition voicing.

We can see the contrast in examples from the vocabulary of kinship terminology:

---

[15] Verner's lucid presentation of data and tight argument surely helped. Lehmann's introduction and Verner's essay are available here: http://www.utexas.edu/cola/centers/lrc/books/read11.html. His fame reaches now beyond historical linguistics, with a set of brilliant YouTube videos by Ari Hoptman, here: http://www.youtube.com/watch?v=aal9VSPkf5s&noredirect=1.

[16] Recall the relationship between voiced fricatives and voiced stops. A consonant at the beginning of a word doesn't follow anything, so it escapes this rule—only Grimm's Law applies.

Figure 3.7 Karl Verner.
Image courtesy of The Royal Library, Copenhagen, Department of Maps, Prints, and Photographs.

/t/	Gk. patḗr 'father'	Gmc. *fáðar (OE fæder)	Verner
	but Skt. bhrā́tar 'brother'	Gmc. *brṓþar (OE brṓðor)	Grimm
/k/	PIE *swek̯rúh 'mother-in-law'	Gmc. *swé ur (OHG swigar)	Verner
	but *swék̯uros 'father-in-law'	Gmc. *swéxur (OHG swehur)	Grimm

Now, with Grimm's Law and Verner's Law together, we're in a position to account for a yet broader set of connections. The flowchart below gives a full overview. In the case of *s, a new sound SPLITS off, *z, but in the case of the fricatives created by Grimm's Law, the voiced fricatives MERGE with existing sounds. (Keep in mind that the products of the voiced aspirates, written here as voiced fricatives, alternate with voiced stops, as already described.)

Flowchart of Grimm and Verner

PIE	Grimm's Law	Verner's Law

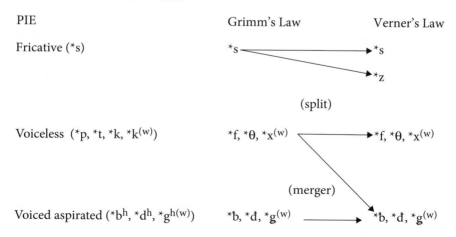

If we return to a chain-shifting view of Grimm's Law (§3.2.1), Verner's Law creates a new set of sounds, voiced fricatives (including *s in the picture since it's involved now), when IE accent did not precede the Germanic fricative:

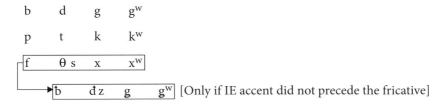

While the alternations of Verner's may seem exotic, we have some striking parallels in English and German, although few people are aware of them and not all speakers have these patterns in their speech. Examples of this phenomenon, sometimes called Jespersen's Rule, are given below with added accent marks:

	'voiceless'	'voiced'
German		
[f] ~ [v]	Hannóver[f]	Hannoveráner [v]
	Nérven [f]	nervös[17] [v]
English		
[ks] ~ [gz]	éxit [ks]	exért [gz]
	Álex [ks]	Alexánder [gz]
[s] ~ [z]	póssible [s]	posséss [z]

Much remains to be understood about Verner's Law, but producing high pitch, which IE used to mark accent (§3.1), involves configuring the vocal folds in a way that conflicts with the position they need to be in in order to vibrate, to create voicing. So, there may be in part a physiological reason for this effect, that high pitch inhibits voicing (see Iverson & Salmons 2003a).

For newcomers to linguistics, Grimm's Law at first may look complicated, and Verner's Law on first encounter even daunting, but grasping the generalizations that underpin them is a big step toward understanding language change.

---

[17] This pair reflects the pronunciation of some speakers. English speakers likewise show variation in what pairs they have of this type.

3.3 IE > Germanic vowel changes

As with consonants, generations of scholars have pieced together a tremendous amount about Indo-European vowels, even though their reconstruction has provided challenges. Recent reconstructions posit a vowel system for IE that looks like those of many languages, with five long and five short vowels (using IPA ':' to mark length):

	Short			**Long**	
	front	**back**		**front**	**back**
high	i	u		i:	u:
mid	e	o		e:	o:
low	a			a:	

First, for those who are not familiar with how linguists think about vowels, let's give a quick explanation of these vowel charts: the symbols correspond to German-like pronunciations, roughly, and thus approximately to the vowels in these words:

bitte	Butter	bieten	Bude
besser	Bock	Beet	Boot
Back		Bad	

The vowels are arranged according to where they are produced in the mouth (front = left). So, *i* and *u* are 'high' vowels, *e* and *o* 'mid', and *a* low. You can track this by saying *eeeeeeee* and gradually turning it into *aaaaaahhhhh*; your jaw (and tongue) will lower noticeably, reflecting the lower position of *a*. The vowels on the left, *i* and *e*, are 'front' vowels, while *u* and *o* are 'back'. You can track these positions by saying *eeeeeeee* and gradually turning it into *uuuuuuuuuu*; the body of your tongue will move back in your mouth noticeably, reflecting the difference in position. The vowel *a* varies by language and dialect but is typically less far back than *u* and *o*.

Figure 3.8 shows x-rays of these vowels (with the same left-facing orientation we saw before), plus [ɑ] a low back vowel, marking the high part of the tongue: *i* is pronounced with lips spread wide apart, while German *u* involves

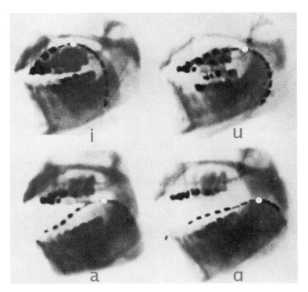

FIGURE 3.8 X-rays of cardinal vowels, from Daniel Jones.

the corners of the lips drawn together much more. This is called 'rounding', and we'll discuss it later.[18]

Pieces of the IE vowel picture remain controversial for certain scholars. *a is relatively uncommon and some reject its existence. Nonetheless, the charts presented so far provide a relatively clean starting point for our discussion of Germanic. And the changes from this reconstructed system to that of Germanic are relatively simple.

Most vowels remain unchanged in most positions. Compare Germanic with Latin vowels, which were also stable in the relevant ways:

Lat piscis	fisks, Goth.	'Fisch', 'fish'
Lat super	ubir, OHG	'über', 'over' (The Latin is from *ex + uper*.)
Lat edo	ezzan, OHG	'essen', 'eat'
Lat suīnus	swīn, OHG	'Schwein', 'swine'
Lat mūs	mūs, OHG	'Maus', 'mouse'
Lat fēcī	dēd, OE	'Tat', 'deed'

This is a simple vowel system, similar to many others in languages around the world.

One traditional observation about language change is that we often see simplification or loss of complexity over time. Indeed, we've just seen some

---

[18] A nice animated model of the articulatory apparatus is available here: http://homes.chass. utoronto.ca/~danhall/phonetics/sammy.html.

simplification in the large system of stops and will soon see reduction in case distinctions in nouns, for instance. At the same time as some structures have simplified, others have become far more complex. As we'll see in later chapters, the vowel system is a shining example of increasing complexity: this five-vowel system yields a vastly more complex one in Modern German.

3.3.1 Vowel merger

One common kind of sound change is MERGER, where the distinction between two sounds is obliterated—where two sounds once existed, speakers have only one. American English is experiencing several similar changes at present. For instance, vast numbers of speakers in the West, lower Midwest, and elsewhere have merged the vowels /a, ɔ/ in *cot* and *caught*, *Don* and *Dawn*, *rot* and *wrought*.

In the evolution from IE to Germanic, *a* and *o* merge differently according to whether they're long or short.

	IE	attested Germanic	
*a = *a	*ghans	gans, OHG	'Gans'
*o > *a	*orbho	arbi, OHG	'Erbe'
*ā > *ō	*bhrātēr	brōþar, Goth.	'Bruder'
*ō = *ō	*plō	flōdus, Goth.	'Flut'

IE had four different vowels here, long and short *a*, as well as long and short *o*. In Germanic, these have reduced to two vowels, namely short *a* (from old *a* and *o*) and long o: (from old *a*: and *o*:), in this way:

This pair of changes leaves a less 'balanced'-looking system between the long- and short-vowel systems, with boxes showing the gaps that emerge:

Short		**Long**	
i	u	i:	u:
e	□	e:	o:
a		□	

This is an 'unconditioned' merger, that is, a change that happens regardless of the surrounding sounds. Other changes, you'll notice, are strictly conditioned, especially by FOLLOWING sounds.

3.3.2 Nasalschwund mit Ersatzdehnung

This German term is so mellifluous that some use it in English rather than 'nasal loss with compensatory lengthening'. We have mostly been looking at unconditioned changes so far, but sometimes a sound change happens only in narrow circumstances, and so here: a nasal is lost before /x/, and the vowel lengthens to fill that gap, keeping the word the same length. In an intermediate stage, the vowel was probably long and nasalized. (As we'll see later in this chapter and beyond, nasal loss with compensatory lengthening has happened independently several times in Germanic, often before other fricatives or sets of fricatives.)

As illustrated here, this happens within the Germanic period, after Grimm's Law, and some modern oddities of German and English verb forms go directly back to the process.[19]

IE	early Germanic	later Germanic	Old High German	
*tn̥k-tō	*þuŋx-tō	> *þūx-tō	> dūhta	'seemed'

We start from an IE verbal form, here with a suffix that comes to indicate past tense. The first *t and the *k undergo Grimm's Law, but the second does not because it follows another stop (see §3.2.2). The resulting string of sounds contains three consonants in a row, *ŋxt, and the first of those, the nasal, disappears. This has an important consequence for the vowel system: if the vowel in the word happens to be /a/, the lengthening creates a long /a:/ which fills the gap created by the merger of old ā with ō:

IE	pre-Germanic	later Germanic	OHG	
*bhroŋk-tō	*braŋx-tō	> *brāxtō	> brāhta	'brachte'
*toŋk-tō	*þaŋx-tō	> *þāx-tō	> dāhta	'dachte'

That is, the system now only has one gap, at short /o/.

Short		**Long**	
i	u	i:	u:
e	☐	e:	o:
a		a:	

In the change from *braŋxtō to brāhta, we lose a sound, the nasal, but we keep the overall length of the word as a whole, thanks to the vowel lengthening. For that reason, this process is called COMPENSATORY LENGTHENING. Each speech sound takes some time.[20] If we represent such 'timing slots' with an

---

[19] Recall that [ŋ] is a velar nasal, the last sound in *Ring*.
[20] If we control for stress and intonation etc., the timing tends to be strikingly consistent.

X and use two Xs for a long vowel, we still have the same number of Xs after
the change, despite losing a sound—the loss is 'compensated' for by the
lengthened vowel. We can represent the change this way:

Earlier

X   X   X
V   C   C
a   n   x

Later

X   X   X
V   V   C
a   a   x

Understanding speech sounds isn't merely about consonants and vowels,
but about strings of sound, such as syllables and other units.[21] In this change,
the vowel extends to take over the slot where the consonant was. Again,
modern languages give us suggestions of how this might have happened:
when a vowel is followed by a nasal consonant in English or German, that
vowel takes on a nasal quality—that is, some air escapes through the nasal
passage, represented phonetically as '˜' over the vowel. Many English speakers
pronounce nt at the ends of words with just that nasalization on the vowel and
no actual n sound, so that can't can be and often is pronounced almost like cat,
EXCEPT that it has nasalization on the vowel: in careful speech, we might
produce don't as [dõnt] (note that the vowel is still nasalized), most of us
often or usually say [dõ:t]. That is traditionally seen as a path toward the loss
of the nasalization, so that future American English speakers might say [do:t]
for 'don't'.

At the most mundane level, this discussion shows you how we have pairs
of verb forms like denken ~ dachte, bringen ~ brachte, and English think ~
thought, bring ~ brought, along with Dutch brengen ~ bracht, denken ~ dacht
and other forms. More importantly, you should see another way in which
sounds function systematically, where particular segments can and do go,
but the 'slots' they held stay on. This abstract, i.e. phonological, pattern is
tied to a very concrete, or phonetic, pattern, namely how vowel nasalization
works. That is, a contemporary morphological pattern is tightly connected to a
set of sound patterns going back millennia.

---

[21] The notion of the 'syllable' is intuitively simple but has proven extremely difficult to define
rigorously. See Vennemann (1988) for a classic treatment of the role of the syllable in sound
change. Cairns & Raimy (2011) gives a current overview of synchronic issues in syllable theory.

3.3.3 Anaptyxis[22]

IE had SYLLABIC sonorants, consonants which act like a vowel. German has these, especially in informal speech, using common spellings: *haben* > *habm*, *hatten* > *hattn*, etc., or English *fightin'*, *bird*, or *bottle* in rapid or informal speech. They are usually indicated phonetically with a small mark under the sound. Some IE languages have these as an ordinary part of the grammar, like Serbian/Croatian/Bosnian *brzo* 'fast'. These IE syllabic consonants become sequences of *u* + consonant in early Germanic:

IE *bhr̥tis 'carrying [noun]'	OHG gi-**burt**
IE *wl̥kʷo 'wolf'	Goth. **wulfs**[23]
IE *mn̥tis 'thought'	Goth. ga-**munds**
IE *dekm̥ '10'	Goth. tai**hun** (The old final *-m* > *-n*, as we'll see.)

3.3.4 Prenasal raising

The SHORT mid vowel *e raises, or becomes *i, before any nasal consonant (*m*, *n*, *ŋ*), but only IF the nasal is in the same syllable.[24]

| IE *bhendh- | → | Gmc *bind- 'to tie' |
| IE *HweH-nt-[25] | → | Gmc *wind- 'wind' |

But when the *n* belongs to the following syllable, the *e does not raise:

| IE *tenu- | → | Gmc *þenu- 'to stretch, thin' |

We have a close modern parallel: many Southern US English speakers pronounce *pen* and *pin* the same (using *ink pen* versus *straight pin* to distinguish these two items which could otherwise be confused), likewise *Jim* and *gem*, *sinner* and *center* (where the medial consonants can also merge, so that these are homophones), and many other pairs.

When we see the same basic change happening in different historical circumstances, linguists look for structural factors that could lead to these parallels. For this change, and similar changes found in many languages, we have an excellent motive: when nasal sounds, like *m*, *n*, *ŋ*, come at the end of a syllable, they interfere with the quality of a preceding vowel, making them

---

[22] This technical term means 'vowel insertion', and it is widely used for this particular process. Another common name for inserting any sound is 'epenthesis'.
[23] Note that the *kʷ appears as *f* in Germanic, where Grimm's Law would require *hʷ*, a known but not fully understood wrinkle of *kʷ after consonants.
[24] Roughly, if the nasal ends the word or is followed by another consonant, it will count as being in the same syllable and trigger raising. If it is followed directly by a vowel (as in the third example), it will not.
[25] This is a 'deverbal' noun, from *HweH- 'to blow'.

hard to distinguish—not a difficulty in pronouncing the sounds, but one in hearing them and for children to learn.

3.3.5 Diphthongs

You may think of diphthongs as sequences of two vowels together, as in *Haus*, *Häuser*, *heiß*. In fact, the second half is in many ways better considered a glide (that is, pronounced roughly like English *y*, *w*), like [aw] in *Haus* or [aj] in *heiß*. In IE, we find the following patterns, arranged by where the first element, or onset, is located in the vowel space:

Indo-European diphthongs

ej, ew   oj, ow

               aj, aw

There is a clear pattern here, as you can see: the two glides *j and *w can appear after the three non-high vowels, that is, mid *e and *o and low *a. The absence of *ij and *uw is natural, since they would yield *ī and *ū.

Some consider these sequences of vowel plus glide in IE and in early Germanic to be independent elements rather than diphthongs in the narrow sense, that is, single units of sound. Evidence for this is that the vowels participate normally in the vowel changes we have already discussed, namely the merger of *o with *a:

    *oj-no   *ajn-   'one'
    *rowdh-   *rawd-   'red'

On the road from IE to Germanic, we find another minor change: the sequence *ei becomes a long vowel, *ī. The historical *ei sequence posited here was probably close to how many English speakers say the vowel in *bait*, as a long [e] vowel ending with gliding up toward [i] (not like German *ei* in *Zeit*). That is, this sound would have been considerably more diphthongal than German *Beet*. The dating of *ei to *ī is hard to pinpoint precisely, and it may have come later in history.

    *ei → *ī

IE	>	Gmc
*deik-	*tīh-	'show'
*steigh-	*stīg-	'climb'

Overview: the big picture

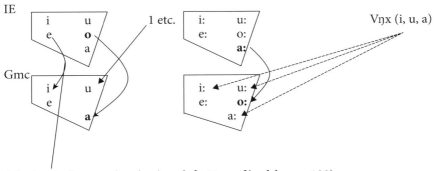

/e/ raises before nasal codas (see definition of 'coda' on p. 138)

Chronology: absolute and relative. The order in which changes happened matters. In the treatment of consonants, we noted the ordering of a 'drag chain' analysis and that others have proposed the reverse order, a 'push chain'. Verner's Law must come after Grimm's Law, and the position of IE accent must have been there since that defines Verner. We don't know the dates when these happened, or their absolute chronology—people often suggest 2,500–3,000 years ago—but we can often recover this kind of relative chronology, which happened before the other.

Consider the merger of low-back vowels, as in *bhrātēr to brōþar. This happened before nasal loss with compensatory lengthening, such as the development of Germanic *braŋx-tō to Old High German brāhta. If the order were reversed—that is, if nasal loss and vowel lengthening had happened before ā became ō—the long vowel of brāhta should have participated in the merger, which would have created *brōhta (using the asterisk here to indicate an impossible form in OHG rather than a proposed reconstruction).

Likewise, evidence suggests that the prenasal raising of *e to *i preceded nasal loss. IE *tenko- 'to fit, adapt' is regarded as the source of Germanic *þinxa- and then *þīxa-, Modern German *gedeihen*. IE *Hleng^wh-to- also appears to be the forerunner of Germanic *linxta- and then *līxta-, Modern German *leicht*, English *light* (of weight). Still, Ringe (2007: 149–150) notes that few of these particular words have 'solid PIE pedigrees', and given the vagaries of word histories, cases built on a few examples are insecure by nature.

3.4 Morphology

Let us now turn to morphology, the study of word forms, and trace those developments over the same period. The word *morphology* itself was coined by Goethe as a general term for the study of forms in nature and art, from Greek *morphḗ* 'form, shape' + *logie* 'science or study of something'.

Words come in different flavors, called 'parts of speech' traditionally and 'lexical categories' in linguistics. The most fundamental distinction, one we will build our discussions around here, is between NOUNS and VERBS. Grammar school definitions—'person, place, or thing' and 'action word', respectively—are highly problematic. More fruitful than a semantic definition is to look at the formal properties of words. That is, linguists often consider what kinds of AFFIXES (prefixes, suffixes, or infixes) they take and define them in accordance with that behavior. In German and its ancestors nouns (and adjectives) inflect for case, and verbs for tense, among other things. Nouns and verbs play different roles in clauses and sentences, nouns as subjects and objects for instance. As we explore the inflectional categories relevant to IE and Germanic, we will also touch on derivational morphology, the study of how new words are formed, where words can move from one lexical category to another. (The ability of English speakers to make more or less anything into a verb is something many are aware of, as we hear complaints about new verbs from prescriptively minded people or humorously, as in Figure 3.9.)

Consider one way morphological change can differ radically from sound change. The Neogrammarians in establishing the principle of regularity of sound change distinguished it from types of change that were not driven by sound patterns. Central is ANALOGY, where learners adjust some form to fit a larger pattern, like making strong verbs weak motivated by the vast numbers of weak verbs in German. The preterit of *backen* was until recently *buk* 'baked', but it is now generally realized as *backte*. (We'll explore this in depth later.)

3.4.1 IE > Gmc nominal morphology

So far, we have talked about regular sound changes, illustrating them with basic word forms, which we call ROOTS, word forms without any inflectional material attached.

If you compare reconstructions of fully inflected Indo-European words and Germanic words (like the myriad examples provided in Ringe 2007 or Bammesberger 1986, 1990), it is notable how well the roots follow the relatively straightforward changes we've treated above, and downright striking how often the endings fail to match in any remotely plausible way. Here are two pairs (Ringe 2007: 172, orthography adapted):

	IE	Gmc
'heavy' (adj., ACC.SG.FEM.)	$*g^w\underset{.}{r}$H-éw-iH-$\underset{.}{m}$	*kur-jōn
'putting' (noun, GEN.PL.)	*dhH-téy-oHom	*dēd-ijōn

In the first form (related to Latin *gravis*, English *grief*, etc.), the root behaves as you would expect (with wrinkles), but an especially alert student might ask how IE *-éw-iH-m̥ could become Germanic *-jōn. The answer is that we are not dealing here with regular sound change, but rather changes in the inflectional system: new endings and sets of endings have emerged and many words have been moved into new classes of inflection, old morpheme boundaries have been lost, and so on. At the same time, even in Germanic, we find first signs of erosion of endings, a tendency which still characterizes the family down to today, as we'll see. And individual forms within a PARADIGM[26] often get adjusted to iron out irregularities and oddities vis-à-vis other members of the paradigm. (This is the apparent source of the long vowel in the second example.) These are types of change, and morphological changes generally are notoriously irregular.

3.4.2 Basic structure of IE words

IE was, compared to English and German, rich in inflection. A traditional typology of morphological systems distinguishes 'synthetic' or heavily inflecting languages from 'analytic' or less inflecting ones. In those terms, the history of Germanic is the movement from a relatively synthetic system to relatively analytic systems. More than the modern languages, IE had a straightforward system for building words, 'agglutination' in the traditional typology. Here are some building blocks used for deriving nouns.

- Typical IE roots consist of CVC, representing the stripped-down core of a word. (Recall that this pattern was clear enough to Saussure that he was able to use it in arguing for the existence of IE laryngeals.)
- These roots could also have an additional final consonant, called an 'extension' or 'enlargement'. We usually have no clear idea of their meaning, though scholars have long speculated about this.

  Root (+ Extension)
  *wl̥kʷ-   'wolf'
  *wer+m   'heat' (cf. 'warm')

- Starting from a root, a suffix was added to indicate what kind of inflection the noun takes. Think about Spanish or Italian, where if a noun ends in -a or -o, you have a good idea of its gender and/or plural forms from that last vowel. In IE, the elements are called THEMES. *e and *o are the most common.

---

[26] A paradigm is simply the set of grammatically conditioned forms of a particular word—like the case forms of a German noun (*Haus, Hause, Hauses, Häuser, Häusern*) or forms of a verb (*mache, machen, machte, machtest, gemacht*, etc.).

FIGURE 3.9 Verbing weirds language.

Thematic vowel
*wl̥kʷ-o
*werm-o

In IE, nouns could be athematic, which simply means that they lack these 'thematic' suffixes and so are shorter, like *ped-/pod- 'foot' (and these involved complex accentual patterns).

While relatively few athematic nouns exist, the system of thematic suffixes is expanded by Germanic. A regular sound change discussed in §3.3 turns *o into *a, and several pre-Germanic changes help rearrange the old theme system. Other derivational suffixes could be added as well, like the collective and feminine -H_2 (e.g. Bammesberger 1990: 99 ff.).

As we will see in the coming chapters, this system provided crucial information about how nominal morphology is organized. Ultimately, modern German's complex system of plural formation has its roots here, a development we will follow through the book.

In the study of word forms generally, 'derivation' means 'word formation' as opposed to inflection—number and case forms. Derivation, in other words, creates a new word in some sense, as already noted, often changing the lexical category and dramatically changing meaning, like *a verb* versus *verbal, verbose*, or *to verb*,[27] etc. Inflection, in contrast, is about a form of a word, in the same lexical category and basic meaning: *to verb*, [she] *verbs*, [we all] *verbed*, etc.

Take a German example:

gehen
Derivation: *begehen, entgehen, vergehen, vergänglich, das Gehen, der Gang, die Vergangenheit*, etc.
Inflection: *gehe, geht, ginge, ging, gingen, gegangen*, etc.

---

[27] For the record, Merriam–Webster records *to access* as a transitive verb since 1962.

- The root together with derivational affixes is called a 'stem', forming a complete (uninflected) word.
- Finally, inflectional endings appropriate to the theme are added, like NOM.SG. *-os*, ACC.SG. *-om*, DAT.PL. *-mos*, etc.

*wl̥kʷo-s   Nom
*wermo-m   Acc

While this may seem like a complex way of building words, it is also relatively transparent in that you can identify the elements.

3.4.3 Nominal categories

Now compare the inflectional categories of the IE noun to Germanic.

Case. Traditionally, IE is said to have had eight cases, following the Indo-Iranian evidence: nominative, accusative, dative, genitive, ablative, locative, instrumental, and vocative. The first four are familiar from Modern German, and two more were attested, to some extent, in early Germanic. INSTRUMENTAL indicates that something is used as a means to something else, and VOCATIVE is used for directly addressing someone.[28] Others are not present in Germanic: ABLATIVE indicates the place from which something comes, among other things. LOCATIVE indicates the place where something is. Based on Anatolian evidence, like Hittite, some scholars posit a ninth for IE, ALLATIVE, which indicates motion toward something, but it is not directly relevant for Germanic. Even some of the better understood cases, though, were apparently not widely marked in the morphology, such as the ablative. Hittite shows fewer case distinctions overall, but is attested earlier. This may reflect the loss of some cases in Hittite, but some cases may have emerged after it had split from IE.

As noted, Germanic has the cases of Modern German plus some instrumental and vocative forms. Instrumental forms are still found in early West Germanic (including Old English and Old High German) and the vocative is maintained for some classes in Gothic, but otherwise merges into the nominative. The locative merged into the dative. Some case forms are lost with the WEAKENING OF FINAL SYLLABLES (see §4.1.3) and the distinctions in meaning come ultimately to be carried by prepositions associated with surviving cases.

Number. IE had singular, plural, and a dual, a category specifically for two of something—convenient for talking about arms, legs, couples, and the kind of doors Indo-Europeans seem to have had. A few modern languages retain

---

[28] The vocative is often glossed with 'Oh, _____!' ... in the old days, we learned to decline Latin nouns by saying things like 'Oh, wall!' This is echoed in *Alice's Adventures in Wonderland* when she addresses a mouse as 'O mouse'.

some dual forms (Lithuanian, for example). Germanic had the dual early on and has maintained numerous vestiges as we'll see later when we talk about Bavarian forms such as the second person plural *enk*, from an old dual form.

Gender. As you can see in what follows, gender correlates to some extent with the noun classes, marking relationships among the elements within a sentence or text. Almost all early IE languages show three genders, save for Anatolian, which lacks a feminine (Schwink 2004). The easiest interpretation of this evidence is that Anatolian lost a third gender. Still, some argue that IE originally had a distinction between animate and inanimate (neuter), and that the former later split into masculine and feminine.

Without pursuing too many details, note how complex this overall system becomes, based on eight cases and three numbers, without accounting for differences across noun classes. Let's consider the example of one important class, the masculine *a*-stems, the IE *o*-stems (Bammesberger 1990: 39). For clarity, our discussion focuses on key Germanic categories. Below, you see how IE has transparent elements: theme vowels *o, followed by the case/number suffix. In Germanic, the *o becomes *a by the change just described.

	IE	Gmc
Sg.		'day'
N	*o-s	*dagaz
A	*o-m	*daga(n)
G	*o-so	*dagas(a)
D	*o-ey	*dagai
I	*ō	*dagō
Pl.		
N	*o-es	*dagōzez[29]
A	*o-ns	*daganz
G	*o-ōm	*dagō(n)
D	*o-bhyos	*dagamaz
I	*ōis	*dagamiz (?)

[29] As Martin Durrell notes in correspondence, this is a 'double plural', much as English *children* contains two old plural markers (*er-n*); see Bammesberger (1990: 44).

In some instances, Germanic forms continue IE morphology with the relevant sound changes accounted for, like the instrumental singular and plural. In others, we have systematic fusion of forms or weakening, like the change from *-m to *-n.[30] In a few, the IE forms Bammesberger gives cannot match his Germanic ones, like dative and instrumental plural. These are not sound change but morphological change, which we'll treat in detail later, with rich data.

Still, while this paradigm is strikingly different from what we have in Modern German, you can recognize one similarity to the modern language, the *s* in the genitive singular. In some other cells, bearing in mind that endings have WEAKENED over time, it's not hard to surmise that the dative singular *-ai* and genitive plural *-ō* correspond to the suffixes in contemporary *dem Tage* and *der Tage*.

In this paradigm, there is no part of an ending that indicates directly that a noun is plural, or that indicates what case the noun has: no particular pluralizing element is found in all cases, and the genitive singular and plural endings have nothing in common. Endings as a whole encode case and number together. Linguists call forms that mark more than one category at once *portmanteau* morphemes, and these are an example.

Here is the bigger picture, in terms of comparing what and how many categories—case, number, gender—were marked at particular stages.

	IE	Gmc	German
Case	8–9	6	4
Number	3	3	2
Gender	3	3	3

English has traveled much farther down this path, of course, with only remnants of case (like non-nominative forms of pronouns, *me, her, them*), and no grammatical gender in the relevant sense. The key development has less to do with numbers of categories and more with how and where they are marked. In other words, it's not just how many categories are distinguished but how the whole system is organized. In IE and early Germanic, those distinctions were made basically by adding inflectional suffixes directly to the noun, while we'll see that other ways of carrying these distinctions gain importance steadily over time. (See Barðdal 2009 for a general discussion of the history of case in Germanic.)

---

[30] Sounds like *n* (and *d, t*), alveolar or coronal sounds, are often considered the 'default' place of articulation, so that a change from labial to coronal may be simplification.

3.4.4 Major nominal classes and their Germanic forms

Different IE daughters often went different directions in how they assigned nouns to classes, so we'll take a Germanic perspective here.[31] Nouns are organized around the resulting stem types. The IE *o theme, again, becomes Germanic *a, which comes to be associated with large numbers of masculine and neuter nouns, known as 'a-stems'. In another development, thematic *e was sometimes followed by the suffix -H$_2$, and this *-e H$_2$ yields Germanic *ō, which comes to be the dominant class of feminine nouns. Actual class markers like -a and -ō, are often lost already in Gothic, but leave distinct traces behind so that their developments can be followed. Even after they are gone, -a and -ō are used as the names for the classes (see Table 3.5).

TABLE 3.5 **Some key nominal classes**

IE shape	Gmc class	Gender	Examples
-o	-a	M/N	*daga-, Gothic *dags* 'day'; *fatam, OSax *fat* 'vat'
-jo	-ja	M/N	*herd-ija, Gothic *hairdeis* 'Hirt'
-wo	-wa	M/N	*snaiwa, OHG *snēo* 'snow'
-ā	-ō	F	*gebō, Goth *giba* 'Gabe'
-jā	-jō		[Largely merges with the above class]
	-n	M/N/F	'weak' nouns: *hanōn 'chicken'
-i	-i	M/N/F	*gasti, Gothic *gasts* 'guest'
-u	-u	M/F	*sunu, Gothic *sunus* 'son'
-r	-r	M/F	kinship terms: *Vater, Mutter, Schwester*, etc.
-s	-iz (> -ir)		'lamb'

Germanic *a*-stems and *ō*-stems have subclasses (see *-ja, *-wa) and together these account for a large number of nouns. The *n*-stems, source of Modern German 'weak' nouns, were also significant. Some classes were tiny, like the kinship terms in *-r. In fact, it's not always clear that a particular class existed. For example, traditional sources posit a class of Germanic *-nd nouns, which we'll discuss further on, based on participles and creating nouns like *Freund, Feind*, but Ringe regards it as 'more than a little rash' to project them into Proto-Germanic in this way (2006: 199). Still, some small classes, like the *iz-* and *i-stems*, play important roles in the later development of the language.

Knowing only the modern languages, for the moment, this may look like an odd tangle of categories. As we treat morphology in each following chapter, though, we'll see how this overall system has been sorted into the modern

---

[31] In Old Indic, for example, we find many more *-i* and *-u* stem nouns than in Germanic.

language, with clear traces of morphological heritage readily visible in contemporary German to the trained eye you will soon have.

Sometimes, the path of development from Germanic to Modern German is clear, like the old *n*-stems becoming 'weak' nouns, like *Herr, Student,* and so on, marked with an *-(e)n* suffix in forms other than the nominative singular. Many members of the old feminine *ō*- (and *jō*)-stems still have a singular *-e* in the modern language (*Gabe, Stunde, Bitte, Ehre, Farbe,* etc.). In other cases, the connection is less direct: the *i* ending of the *i*-stems caused umlaut in Old High German, which today characterizes the plural forms of many old members of that class (*Gast ~ Gäste, Apfel ~ Äpfel, Schlag ~ Schläge,* etc.).

We'll return to this topic several times, but note that the old class structure is mirrored most clearly in the genders and plural forms of nouns today, where if you know the gender, you can take a good guess at the plural form: masculine nouns in Modern German tend to take *-e*, feminine nouns tend to take *-(e)n*, etc.

3.5 The verbal system

In nominal systems, the meanings of morphological categories are often relatively straightforward—you know immediately what significance is conveyed by the difference between singular and plural, or after a semester of German, between nominative and accusative. More complex case systems can offer various wrinkles, but in verbal systems, meanings are often messier. In IE, dialectal developments vary wildly, so there's more debate about what particular categories meant, and even what inflectional categories IE actually had.

Informal ways of talking about verbs don't always match the technical terminology. For example, what is often called 'tense' includes both TENSE—the indication of the time when something occurs—and ASPECT—indication of temporal qualities of an action like duration (that the action lasts), punctuality (the action happens at a particular point in time), completion (the action is finished and done with). While laypeople talk about 'tense' in English, English uses aspect in addition to real tense distinctions more than German: German uses a simple present form for meanings that in English include both present tense and present progressive forms: *Die Katze frißt* can be rendered as *the cat eats (every morning at 8)* or *the cat is eating (right now),* causing considerable difficulties for German speakers learning English, so that they produce forms like *the cat is eating in the morning at 8.[32]

---

[32] Here, the asterisk indicates an ungrammatical form, not in the sense that grammar books forbid it, but in the sense that native speakers don't use it and find it odd.

The basic organization of Indo-European verb types differs dramatically from Modern German or English. Languages vary tremendously in how verb systems are organized, so this isn't shocking. The key IE distinction is this (Sihler 1996: 442–446):

- **Stative:** denotes states: 'know, be aware, remember', and so on.
- **Eventive:** denotes events that happen, change, etc.: 'fly, seek, find, break, kill', etc.

In IE, these were completely distinct types of verbs—they differ in endings and structure as well as meaning. At some early point, stative forms existed for verbs denoting states rather than events, while later, more verbs developed forms of this type, traditionally known as 'perfect', i.e. indicating completion. For the group of IE languages that includes Germanic, eventive stems divide into perfective (traditionally called 'aorist' by IEists) or imperfective (traditionally called 'present'). For the purposes of Germanic, the complexities of what these types meant are not directly relevant, but we should note, with Ringe (2006: 24): 'Each verb stem . . . was inherently imperfective, perfective, or stative. A basic verb did not necessarily make all three stems; some made only two or one.'

Germanic keeps a handful of STATIVE verbs, *wait- 'to know' (*wissen*), *skal- 'to be obliged' (*sollen, shall*), *mag- 'to be able' (*mögen, may*), *kann- 'to know how to' (*können, can*). These mostly become modals, and are traditionally known as 'preterit presents' since they inflect as if they were past but have present meanings. Their endings are usually seen as coming from the 'perfect' paradigms (see §3.5.6 in this chapter). and, at least in part for this reason, their origins generally have often been sought there. Randall & Jones (2015) provide a detailed account, including arguments that this small class of Germanic verbs points to the existence of a distinct type of verb in Indo-European, a 'derived stative' category. This was done by using stative inflections on eventive roots.

The forms in the modern Germanic languages still reflect their heritage as stative verbs: we use no -s in 3rd singular in English (*she may* but *she works*), and the same holds for 1st/3rd person singular forms of *wissen* and modal verbs without ending in German, for instance. *Wissen* has a somewhat different history from the modals, a present tense meaning built from an old IE verb meaning 'to see' (connected to Latin *videre* etc.). The stative form, like 'I have seen' comes to mean something like 'to know' (Lehmann 1986: 407). We already see something about Modern German and English verbs: the oddities in inflection in our 'modals' have deep historical roots (in addition to Randall & Jones 2015 and references there, see Birkmann 1987 for more).

Otherwise, the IE stative forms developed into the basis for an inflectional category in Germanic, the preterit. IE statives had the vowel *o* in the stem (*o*-grade) in the singular and no vowel (zero-grade) in the (dual and) plural. Some of them also had reduplication, about which more in a moment.[33]

3.5.1 Inflectional categories

The key categories in the IE verb system are these:

Tense and aspect. Verbs distinguished between a PRESENT (more precisely 'non-past', including 'future') and an IMPERFECT, which, for our purposes, indicated 'occurring in the past'.

Voice: active versus middle. There was no passive voice, but a 'middle' voice, for actions affecting the subject and for reflexives, meaning something like a passive. Very little of the morphology of the middle voice remains in Germanic.

Mood: indicative, subjunctive, optative, imperative. The IE optative, originally indicating a wish or desire for something, becomes our 'subjunctive'. The subjunctive (in meaning between the optative and the imperative, indicating an intermediate degree of desire/command) is gone in Germanic.

3.5.2 Inflected forms

We will not devote time and space to IE verb paradigms, but note the following about how they inflected:

- Verbs, like nouns, could be thematic or athematic.[34] Only a few remnants of the athematic verbs have survived in Germanic: *to do, go, be*. These lack a thematic element, and so tend to show SHORTER forms. (Some exceptions in Modern Dutch and some German dialects have longer forms, a pattern that goes back to Old High German, e.g. 1st sg. *ih gām* 'I go', *ih tōm* 'I do', see Braune & Reiffenstein 2004: 310–312.)
- IE had no real INFINITIVE form of the verb but most of its daughter languages created one. Germanic built on an old IE ending *-ono, found in 'verbal adjectives'. That becomes *-ana in Germanic with an additional *n used for marking the accusative. For Proto-Germanic, scholars typically reconstruct *-anan or assume that the last vowel is simply nasalized, *-anã. It eventually yields the *-en* we have on German infinitives.

---

[33] Reduplication is simply copying and repeating part of a word or even a whole word for some function. In English, we use *shm-* (from Yiddish) to dismiss something (*danger shmanger*) and reduplicate whole words to indicate genuineness—a Ph.D. is a *doctor*, but in a medical emergency, you want a *doctor doctor*.

[34] Recall from above, §3.4.2, that IE had theme vowels on most nouns.

- **Participles**, essentially equivalent to our *-ing* forms, were formed with
  *-ont/-ņt. Many nouns were formed from this construction: *Zahn* 'tooth'
  < 'eating' [thing or instrument for eating], *Feind* 'fiend' < 'hating' [person],
  Freund 'friend' < 'loving' [person]. For instance, Germanic had a verb
  *frij-ō 'to treat in a friendly way', among other meanings. The participle
  form, *frij**ond**, yields *Freund/friend*.

In English, many verbs have 'particles' associated with them that convey
crucial parts of their meaning: *to come* means something quite different
from *to come to* 'to regain consciousness'. Indo-European similarly had
preverbal particles. One in particular comes to play a major role in Germanic:
our past participle marker *ge-* developed from the IE verbal particle *kom
'together, with, collective, intensive'. This is an example of GRAMMATICALIZATION,
a description of how 'free' words become affixes. While the status of
grammaticalization is controversial, such processes often happen, and
we'll see numerous examples.[35] Alongside the change from free form to
affix, other hallmarks of the process are semantic bleaching (loss of specific
meaning) and phonetic reduction.

Originally an independent word, *kom was unstressed and leaned onto the
beginning of verbs in various forms as well as of nouns. At first, this bond was
'loose', so that prefixes or particles sometimes occur between it and the verb in
Gothic: *ga-laubeis* 'you believe' (related to German *glaubst*) occurs as *ga-u-
laubeis*, with a so-called 'question particle' *u* in the middle, so 'do you believe?'
Over time, its meaning and distribution became more and more limited,
eventually directly connected with past participles.[36]

3.5.3 The Germanic system of ablaut: 'strong verbs'

IE made extensive use of ABLAUT, stem vowel alternations, for morphological
purposes. (We'll learn soon about umlaut, a different process.) German and
English verbs still show this: *singen, sang, gesungen/sing, sang, sung*.

Ablaut is the source of stem vowel changes in 'strong' verbs in Germanic.
All ablauting verbs belong to two broad groups, the *e*-group or the *a*-group,
depending on their basic stem vowel. The former group is far larger.

In the *e*-group, infinitives and presents were marked by the *e*-grade (like in
IE eventives, presented above), the preterit singular characterized by *o*, the
preterit plural and the past participle by so-called Ø or 'zero-grade' (like in

---

[35] There are several book-length studies of grammaticalization in German, such as Diewald
(1997) and Szczepaniak (2009), as well as §8.3.
[36] As we'll see, it also plays a role in noun derivation: *Getue, Gebäude*, etc.

statives). IE *o* develops into Germanic *a*, so we had a single pattern for all such verbs:

INF.	SG. PRET.	PL. PRET.	PPART.
e	a	Ø	Ø
*help-	*halp	*hl̩p-	*hl̩p-

As noted, Indo-European roots have typical 'shapes' built around a CVC root, often with an enlargement, a fundamental pattern still visible in Germanic. If we divide consonants into stops and fricatives (C), liquids (l, r = L), nasals (N), and note that the character of the initial consonant is not relevant, the verbs in early Germanic all fit into a few types based on what consonant(s) came before the final C of the root. These root types, or what we can call TEMPLATES, are still often obvious in German, to a striking extent.[37] The keys to seeing the patterns are bolded in Table 3.6:

TABLE 3.6 **The *e*-group**

I	CejC	*schneiden, scheiden, greifen*
II	CewC	*fliegen* (< *****fleuga**), *lügen* (< *****leuga**)
III	CeLC/CeNC	*helfen, werden, binden, finden, trinken*
IV	CeL/CeN	*stehlen, gären, nehmen*
V	CeC	*geben, sehen*

To highlight the regularities, I've momentarily left aside monophthongization of *ei to *ī, in other words written the words in a relatively early form, before the change.

If you look at the root shape, you can generally tell what class it belongs to, I–V. But this algebra is more powerful: if you take the e-a-Ø-Ø pattern and apply it to a given shape, you can produce the principal parts of Proto-Germanic verbs by simple substitution. Because we have *e* in the present this set is sometimes called the E-GROUP. Since we have following glides in I and II, we get diphthongs or sequences of vowel + consonant in the *e* (present) and *a* (preterit singular) forms. Then, for the Ø-grades, the glides *j* and *w* behave like vowels (*i, u*). In classes III and IV the sonorants were originally syllabic (*r̩, *l̩, *m̩, *n̩) in IE and developed (§3.3.3) into *ur, ul*, etc. in Germanic. This gives us most strong verbs:

---

[37] We will return to this issue in Chapters 7 and 8; for now, by 'template' I simply mean a fixed structure where the segmental material within it varies. Here the fixed structure is the requirement for consonantal positions and particular consonants (shown as 'C' etc.), while the vowels vary by class and form. We will explore this notion later, in quite different contexts.

	Template	Present e-grade	Pret.sing. a-grade	Pret.plur. Ø-grade	Past participle Ø-grade	meaning
I	CejC	dreiban	draib	dribum	driban	'to drive'
		reidan	raid	ridum	ridan	'to ride'
II	CewC	leugan	laug	lugum	lugan	'to lie'
		sleupan	slaup	slupum	slupan	'to slip'
III	CeLC	helpan	halp	hulpum	hulpan	'to help'
	CeNC	drinkan	drank	drunkum	drunkan	'to drink'
IV	CeL	stelan	stal	st**ē**lum	stulan	'to steal'
		k^weman	k^wam	k^w**ē**mum	kuman	'to come'[38]
V	CeC	geban	gab	g**ē**bum	geban	'to give'
		wegan	wag	w**ē**gum	wegan	'to move'

A few wrinkles remain. Note the forms in boldface for IV and V. $\bar{e}$ in the plural preterit here may have IE sources, but that's controversial. In several classes, a zero-grade form would have created ordinary-sounding word forms: the glide (j, w) in I and II can readily become a vowel (i, u), for example. For class V participles and plural preterit, which are Ø-grades between two stops or fricatives, if you didn't add SOME vowel, we would have syllable structures like *gbum, *gbans. Many languages of the world allow such consonant clusters, but they were foreign to early Germanic.[39]

Here again, we see the long heritage of German still visible in the contemporary language. At this great time depth, you can see the simple, elegant underlying structure, made into a far less transparent, more complex system by patterns of sound change and morphological change over the millennia.

Another, much smaller group, the A-GROUP, is largely of Germanic origin, whereas e-group verbs tend of be of IE origin (van Coetsem 1994: ch. 8, elsewhere). This group is simpler in that it contrasts vowels of the present and past participle only with one vowel form characterizing the preterit, both SG and PL. Note that it involves a contrast between short and long vowels, the latter called a 'lengthened grade' (see Table 3.7).

---

[38] The sequence $*k^w u$ simplifies to *ku-.

[39] In some varieties of German, you can find such pronunciations in rapid speech or dialectal speech: the ge- participle prefix often loses its vowel in forms like geboten (or even the whole prefix).

TABLE 3.7 **The *a*-group**

	Present	Pret.sing.	Pret.plur.	Past participle	
VI	faran	fōr	fōrum	faran	'to drive'

In Gothic, and probably earlier in Proto-Germanic, some other *a*-group verbs reduplicated to form the preterit (including a handful of forms with stem vowels of *ē* or *ō*, illustrated by 'to let, allow'). In other words, they copied (part of) the first syllable and placed it at the beginning of the word, as illustrated here again (Table 3.8) with Proto-Germanic forms, and the reduplicated element boldfaced:

TABLE 3.8 **The *a*-group (continued)**

	Present	Pret.sing.	Pret.plur.	Past participle	
VII	haitan	**he**hait	**he**haitum	haitan	'to be called'
	falþan	**fe**falþ	**fe**falþum	falþan	'to fold'
	lētan	**le**lōt	**le**lōtum	lētan	'to let, allow'

These forms are typically reconstructed for Proto-Germanic (Bammesberger 1986: 64, Ringe 2006: 248–250) and may have originated from copying of the full first syllable or at least initial consonant plus vowel, such as *haihait- and *lōlōt (Niepokuj 1997), but by Gothic, the pattern has become 'fixed vowel reduplication', where we have copying of the initial consonant but always the same vowel *e. Gothic shows a further restriction that is often reconstructed as well: if the verb stem begins with a consonant plus a liquid (*l, *r), only the first is reduplicated, as with *hlaupan 'to run' > *hehlaup and *slēpan 'to sleep' > *seslēp-, *grētan 'to weep' > *gegrēt. If it begins with *s plus a stop, both are, as with *staldan 'to possess', pret. >*stestald, *skaiþan 'to separate' > *skeskaiþ (Bammesberger 1986: ch. 8, Ringe 2006: 248–250). Again, the evidence for this is found in Gothic. Reduplication is gone, virtually without traces, in West Germanic, where we find instead *e*'s in the preterit, as we'll discuss. For now, note that there was a class VII involving reduplication.

Just as the *e*-group is organized around the sound patterns of the verb root, classes VI and VII differ systematically (van Coetsem 1994: 124–129). Namely, verbs in class VI have a short vowel and also typically a single consonant after the root vowel, either obstruent or sonorant (still visible in OHG *faran*, *slahan* 'to hit', *watan* 'to wade', *graban* 'to bury', etc.), parallel to the structure of classes IV and V (eL, eC). In contrast, the earliest structure of class VII verbs paralleled the forms of classes I–III, with structures like *haita- (like I), *hlaupa- 'to run' (like II) and *halta- 'to hold' (like III). Van Coetsem provides the following table (1994: 127, adapted) to emphasize such parallels:[40]

I.	ei + C	VII.	a + RC
II.	eu + C		
III.	e + L/NC		
IV.	e + L/N	VI.	a +L/N, a + C
V.	e + C		

That is, originally reduplicating verbs (VII) originally had root structures like I–III of the e-grade, while VI were originally structured like IV and V. These patterns are steadily obscured over time, but still provide a useful guide.

If you understand these shapes and the basic ablaut patterns (*e, a, Ø, Ø* for I–V and *a, ō, ō, a* for VI), things become simple. Again, the only real ODDITIES are the preterit plurals of IV, where the *ē* is often explained by analogy, and V, where we surprisingly get *ē*, as well as the participle of V, with *e* The latter has inspired many proposals, none completely compelling.

Indo-European exploited ablaut as a morphological tool beyond the verbal system, and this accounts for differences in the vowels of 'foot' discussed in the section on accentuation (§3.1). IE had both *e and *o forms for 'foot', *ped-/*pod-, along with further wrinkles. In fact, Germanic was particularly productive in terms of ablaut, even in the nominal system, and we see remnants of nominal ablaut in Modern German, for example in various nouns related to *fliessen* 'to flow', from PGmc *fleuta- and IE *pleud- 'to flow, swim': *Floß* 'raft' (thing that floats/swims), *Fluß* 'river' (thing that flows), as well as *Flut* 'flood' and *Flotte* 'fleet' built from slightly different formations (see the final consonants). Much work remains to be done in the area, but Mailhammer (2008) shows that many Germanic nominal ablaut forms differ from what would be expected in IE, and tied to the structure of strong verb ablaut, though, he argues, without functional significance per se in Germanic nouns.

Returning now to verbal ablaut and the strong verb system, keep one rule in mind which interacts with these forms: VERNER'S LAW. And we see a specific case of morphological mobility of IE accent as it is reflected in Germanic: accent fell on the root in the first two principal parts of the verb and on a later syllable of the word in the last two. Recall these forms from §3.2.3:

---

[40] In this table the glide of the e-group—second half of the diphthongs in I and II—is represented as a resonant, R, in the a-group. As he notes, a few reduplicating verbs have different present tense vocalism and in some sense represent 'independent series' (1994: 128).

	'I become'	'I became'	'we became'	participle
PIE	*wérto	*wewórta	*wewr̥təmé	*wr̥tonós
Skt.	vártāmi	va-várta	vavr̥timá	vr̥tānáḥ

Given those facts, when we have fricatives in the root, we get voiceless ones in the first two forms and voiced in the last two. This is an opportunity to remember where IE accent fell AND what Verner's Law yields:

> werþan   warþ   wurðum   wurðan

In this example, Verner gives us an alternation between $s \sim z$ and that z later becomes r:[41]

> keusan   kaus   kurum   kuran

As we've seen, this kind of effect in the verbal system occasionally stays around in the modern languages, like English *was* vs. *were*. Here, the historical Verner alternation was between [s] ~ [z], but the [z] rhotacized, while [s] remained the same, creating variation between [s] and [r].

These alternations continue to evolve, with differences often popping up in surprising places, like (archaic) *kiesen* vs. *küren, erkoren*, etc., which also connect to words like *kosten*. Almost all the time, though, in German and English, these alternations are lost. Today, *lesen* has written *s* throughout the paradigm, whereas Old High German *lësan* 'to select, read' showed Verner effects in preterit plural *lârum* and past participle *gilëran*. Elimination of such wrinkles is called LEVELING, which we'll discuss later.

3.5.4 The dental preterit: 'weak verbs'

Many IE verbs had 'perfect' forms, the forms which developed into Germanic preterits, but other verbs lacked these forms. Some IE languages expanded the set of perfect forms to build a tense/aspect system, but Germanic developed a new way of forming preterits as it reorganized the IE system. This new pattern took root and became extremely productive, now by far the most common way to inflect new verbs. It involved not ablaut but adding a suffix including a coronal (or 'dental') consonant, the source of modern *-te* in German and *-ed* in English.

This new system has been spreading ever since and continues down to the present. At any point in time, we find widespread competition between weak and strong forms: *dragged* or *drug, sneaked* or *snuck* (an old weak verb that has become strong for many speakers) in English, or far more in today's German, like *melkte* or *molk, backte* or *buk*. That is, while early in prehistory all verbs

---

[41] *r*-like sounds are called *rhotics*, and turning something into an *r*-like sound is thus *rhotacism*.

were strong and weak verbs joined the fray before our earliest historical records, by Middle High German (during the High Middle Ages), there were 339 strong verbs, and Modern German only has 169, by one count (Wells 1985: 165, drawing on Augst 1975). They are vastly outnumbered by weak verbs.

The origin of this important innovation is a longstanding problem. Two main theories show up in the modern literature, though none of the many proposals made to date, including these, has been widely accepted:

- IE *dhē/dhō 'to put, place' could have led to the creation of the Germanic suffix *-de by grammaticalization (see pp. 172–175).
- IE had a past participial suffix *-to which might have yielded a suffix like this.

Certainly the first has cross-linguistic support: many languages around the world develop new verb tense morphology from former auxiliary ('helping') verbs which weaken and become attached to main verbs. In Romance languages, for example, future forms have developed from the verb 'to have' which becomes a suffix, e.g. French *je chanterai* 'I will sing' where we see the reflex of the Latin infinitive (*cantare*) with a reduced form of *habeo* 'I have' attached to it (Hopper & Traugott 2003).

Increasingly, some specialists believe that both played a role, 'conspiring' to create a new way of marking past tense in Germanic (Hill 2004, 2010, Ringe 2007, others). That is, Germanic could have used a past participle followed by a form of 'to do' and these two fused together to create the new preterit. In Hill's proposal (2010), for instance, the third person plural form of 'to do' was *dēd-unt and it attached to a participle. He illustrates the process with forms like these, taken from Gothic:

Infinitive	Past participle	3 Pl. preterit
waurkjan 'to work'	*waurht-* < Proto-Gmc *wurhta-	*waurhtēdun*
bugjan 'to buy'	*bauht-* < Proto-Gmc *buhta-	*bauhtēdun*
þaurban 'to need'	*þaurft-* < Proto-Gmc *þurfta-	*þaurftēdun*

These broad outlines are eminently plausible, but much work remains to be done.[42]

3.5.5 Classes

The strong verb or ablaut types given above (§3.5.3) exemplify the older verb classes, the different patterns of inflection that verbs have. Weak verbs too were organized into classes, often written with small roman numerals, while

---

[42] A vast literature deals with Germanic verbal history, particularly the relationship between strong and weak verbs. See Bittner (1996), and Mailhammer (2007a, 2007b).

upper case roman numerals are used for strong. Let's begin with how such verbs were formed, before looking at their inflection:

  i **-jan.** Usually 'causatives', some of these were built from nouns: *dauþs* 'dead' yields *dauþjan* 'to kill' ('to cause to die'). Consider, as a modern parallel, how we can add *-ize* to adjectives and nouns to create verbs meaning to cause something, like *prioritize* 'to make/create/arrange priorities'.

  In addition to formations from nouns, a second set created strong/weak pairs, where new weak verbs are formed on old strong verbs. These are typically preterit forms, like *drank* yielding *drankjan* 'tränken' ('to water' [horses]). The result is a causative verb matching a strong one: *fallen/fällen* 'to fall, to fell', *sitzen/setzen* 'to sit, to set', *essen/ätzen* 'to eat, to etch', etc.

  ii **-ōn.** Usually denominatives (from nouns), often with iterative meaning (repeated action): *salba* 'salve, unguent' yields Old High German *salbôn* 'to salve, anoint'.

  iii **-ēn.** Usually durative (referring to something that goes on for some longer period): *wonēn* 'to reside', *lebēn* 'to live', *habēn* 'to have'.

  iv **-nōn.** Usually inchoative (indicating starting something): Go. *fullnan* 'to fill up', ON *vakna* 'to wake up'. Only minor remnants are found in West Germanic, so it's not important for German.

3.5.6 Endings

Endings change for the indicative, the optative, the imperative, and the preterit and we have different sets for various types: strong and weak, old statives, etc. The key relevant split in personal endings is in the present tense forms, where the strong verbs and class i weak verbs show one pattern, and weak classes ii–iii show another. Here are examples from Old High German with notable points in boldface and personal pronouns, to help you see connections to the modern language more clearly.

	Present strong/weak class i		**Present weak ii–iii**	
	Sg	**Pl**	**Sg**	**Pl**
1	ih nim**u**	uuir nëm**umēs**	ih hab**ēm**	uuir hab**ēmēs**
2	dū nim**is**	ir nëm**et**	dū hab**ēs**	ir hab**ēt**
3	er/siu nim**it**	sie nëm**ant**	er/siu hab**ēt**	sie hab**ēnt**

	Preterit indicative strong		**Preterit weak**	
	Sg	**Pl**	**Sg**	**Pl**
1	ih starb	uuir sturbum	ih hab**ēta**	uuir hab**ētum**
2	dū st**u**rbi	ir sturbut	dū hab**ētōs**	ir hab**ētut**
3	er/siu starb	sie sturbun	er/siu hab**ēta**	sie hab**ētun**

- The variation between -*u* and -*m* in 1.SG. reflects an IE distinction between two sets of endings. In Old High German, the -*m* is found in weak classes 2–3 AND in athematic verbs: *to be* (OHG *wesan*, see §3.5 and p. 155), *do* (OHG *tuon*), *go* (OHG *gân*), *stand* (OHG *stantan*).
- The 1.PL. shows a 'long' ending, unique to Old High German—which disappears later. It may be connected to the frequent pattern, as in Modern German, of a word order where the subject pronoun *uuir* follows the inflected verb. The change from a *w* sound (usually written <uu> in Old High German) to *m* would be like Bavarian and other dialect forms of the type *hamma* 'haben wir', which likely led to the rise of the *m*-forms, *mer* or *ma*.
- 2.SG. -*s* >-*st* later on, with centuries of variation. Like the 1.PL. forms, this is widely seen as reanalysis from having a pronoun added on, as in *beristū 'you carry', where such forms occurred often enough that learners reinterpreted the *t* as part of the ending. It was also supported by the preterit present 2.SG. ending, -*st*: *þū waist* 'you know'. That is, analogy may have played a role.
- Strong verbs: the preterit indicative of 2.SG. shows a Ø-grade—*u* from an earlier syllabic *r̥*, rather than an *a* like the 1. and 3. Why this is so is an old problem without an obvious solution.

Finally, many of the most striking irregularities of Modern German are ancient. It is common for highly frequent words to show irregular patterns of some sort and 'to be' is by far the most common verb in Germanic (and other!) languages. Its paradigm is built from two IE roots, *Hes- and *bhuH-, like in many IE languages. A third verb, *Hwes- 'to be, live' contributes to this paradigm as well, seen in the Old High German infinitive, *wesan*.

Sg	Pl
bim	birum
bist	birut
ist	sint

Modern forms of 'to be' like *bin*, *bist*, *ist*, *sind*, *gewesen* have, in short, deep historical roots. See §4.3 for more.

3.6 *Die Ausgliederung*:[43] breaking up is hard to reconstruct

So far, we've been talking about a hypothetical, unified Germanic 'parent language'. The separation and independent development of the earliest

---

[43] This section draws on the work of Hans Frede Nielsen (especially 2000), Robinson (1992: 247–264), and Roberge (2010).

MAP 3 Earliest territory of the Germanic-speaking peoples.

Adapted from a map available at http://commons.wikimedia.org/wiki/File:Pre-roman_iron_age_%28map %29.PNG.

Germanic 'daughter' languages from a more or less unified 'Proto-Germanic' happened just beyond the historical horizon, not long before our first written records. This process is known in German (and sometimes in English) as the *Ausgliederung* and it has spawned a massive literature, punctuated regularly with new views and new twists on old views.

Archeological evidence is widely used to support linguistics here, and it suggests that the soon-to-be Germanic peoples probably moved into southern Scandinavia early in the 2nd millennium BCE. This is when we see a new kind of burial (single graves) and a new kind of pottery, 'corded ware', *Schnurkeramik* (Chapter 2). The probable area of habitation of the peoples who were becoming Germanic in the first millennium BCE is shown in Map 3 (from http://commons.wikimedia.org/wiki/File:Pre-roman_iron_age_(map). PNG, a site which has other historical maps).

A significant archeological record also attests to the presence of peoples in northern Europe long before the Indo-Europeans arrived. These older non-Indo-European cultures and newer invading cultures are often thought to have mixed, as sketched in Chapter 2, with this language contact speeding the creation of a new IE language and culture. Obviously, and as the literature makes clear time and again, it's impossible to say what language people spoke based just on pottery shards associated with where they lived, so this material is uncertain, but some kind of influence from a non-Indo-European language spoken earlier in the area on Germanic is quite likely. Guesses about linguistic developments after settlement in northern Europe lead people to suspect that Proto-Germanic existed about 500–1,000 BCE. Every linguistic community covering the geographical extent that we assume for Germanic shows considerable regional and social variation, so that this was probably never a single homogenous community.

3.6.1 The early Runic evidence

Scattered Germanic words and names—of people, ethnic groups, etc.—are recorded in Latin and Greek sources going back to before the beginning of the Common Era. For example, Tacitus gives names, including *Gothones*, often associated with the Gothic peoples. The first writing in a Germanic language likely written directly by its speakers are inscriptions in the Runic alphabet. Early inscriptions are often memorial stones and are interpreted as a show of wealth and power (Schulte 2013). They often include names inscribed on valuable objects, like bracteates or weapons.

Early Runic, from 200 to 500 CE, reflects a fairly uniform language over a broad geographical area, and one that looks a lot like Proto-Germanic. For example, Runic is the only directly attested form of Germanic that retains certain unstressed final vowels that are usually lost, like final -*a* and -*i*.

	IE	PGmc	Runic	Gothic	OHG
'I'	*Heg-o[44]	*eka	eka	ik	ih
'guest'	*ghosti	*gastiz	gastiz	gasts	gast

This still does not allow us to conclude that Proto-Germanic was spoken when and where these inscriptions were carved or that the written forms we find actually reflect the language of the time of carving, because they could easily have reflected a conservative writing tradition. In fact, many inscriptions have

---

[44] The IE was likely originally *Heg-, extended with an additional vowel in Germanic and some other 'daughter' languages.

a decidedly formulaic character, so the spoken language(s) may easily have had innovations when these were carved. For a modern parallel, just consider the language of gravestones: people wrote (and no doubt still sometimes write) 'Here lies Johan Michael' although that hasn't been normal word order in spoken English for quite a long time—you don't say 'Here lie my shoes by the door'. While we should take seriously the archaizing role of the medium and text types, many people think of early Runic as reflecting a later form, 'Northwest Germanic' (see §3.6.3), and it may point toward a large part of Germanic having been relatively unified around or after the turn of the Common Era (Nielsen 2000).

At the same time, recent work is tracing what appear to be spoken elements in early Runic, notably Schulte (2006). He analyzes an inscription from Blekinge which conveys a curse condemning to death anyone who breaks the monument. He argues that the inscription records reductions of unstressed vowels like those characteristic of rapid, informal speech.

3.6.2 Basic divisions: background and definitions

In the next chapters, we'll discuss languages within the Germanic family, but these connections were not linear developments. In other words, Runic does not turn into Gothic and neither becomes Old High German. The ancestor dialects that are reflected in Runic surely differed from the earliest forms of Gothic and both in turn from what became various dialects of Old High German. Ultimately, even the development from Old High German spoken in one place does not straightforwardly become the modern dialect spoken in that same place, as we'll discuss later.

Turning to the earliest differences within Germanic, the most traditional and simplest division of Germanic is, like that of Caesar's Gaul, into three parts. This view has been widespread from the early days of the field into the 1970s:

- North Germanic: Swedish, Norwegian, Danish, Faroese, Icelandic
- East Germanic (extinct): Gothic, Langobardic, and various other ill-attested languages
- West Germanic: German, Low German, Frisian (West, East, North), Dutch, English, Yiddish, Afrikaans, Pennsylvania German

Assuming a 'flat' structure, we can draw a picture to represent that view.

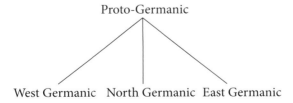

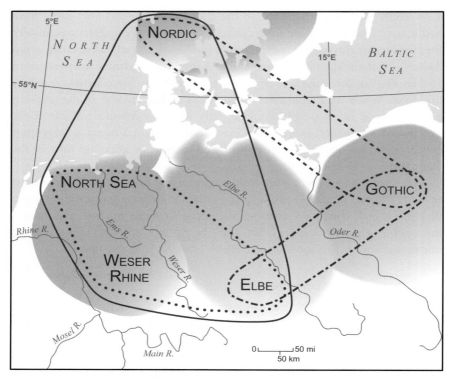

MAP 4 A wave model of Germanic.
Based on a line diagram in Kufner (1972: 74).

Just as we saw with Indo-European in Chapter 2, linguists graphically represent the language history with a family tree or *Stammbaum*, a model developed by August Schleicher in the mid 19th century.

The above formulation is 'flat' in the sense that it simply posits three
branches without any internal hierarchical relationships—it suggests that all
three branches split off at once. More modern efforts at groupings have often
focused on how the three might be interrelated, with binary branches. The
view that North and West Germanic stayed together after the departure of the
Goths is shown in this diagram.

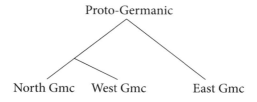

A range of evidence suggests that this view, with East Germanic splitting off first, leaving a NORTHWEST GERMANIC group, is most plausible. Schulte (2017) provides evidence that northern and western groups began to show key differences by the 1st century of our era, drawing on recent evidence from continental runes, like the Frienstedt comb, found near Erfurt, notably loss of old final *z and distinct patterns in the inflection of *n*-stem nouns (on the comb, see http://www.zbsa. eu/news/news-2015/oldest-evidence-of-westgermanic-language).

Branching trees are fine for cases of real split in communities, but do not capture so easily how contiguous areas are differentiated over time. This was recognized in the 19th century. The view that linguistic changes sweep over territories is known as the *Wellentheorie* or Wave Model. The illustration in Map 4 offers a better way of portraying contacts among groups, while dividing West Germanic into three groups.

Within West Germanic, scholars have often posited further subgroupings, as shown. The Elbe Germanic and Weser-Rhine Germanic groups were, on this view, the ancestors of later Central and Upper German speakers, while a cluster of groups on or near the North Sea are known as 'Ingvæonic', a name taken to be of a Germanic 'tribe' reported by Tacitus. North Sea Germanic is regarded by many as the ancestor of English and Frisian, with Ingvæonic traits found in Dutch and Low German.[45]

Once regarded as competing views, modern approaches integrate aspects of both tree-like and wave-like evolution for Germanic, as we'll see. The more interesting question is what kind of evidence such pictures are based on, to which we now turn.

3.6.3 How do we determine subgroups within Germanic?

While archeological and (pre)historical evidence is important, linguistic relationships are normally determined primarily on linguistic evidence, beginning with cataloging shared features across the relevant languages. Ringe & Eska write: 'shared history can be established only by demonstrating shared innovations; moreover, the innovations in question must be unusual enough that they are not likely to have occurred more than once independently' (2013: 256; there are similar statements in several chapters of Bowern & Evans 2015).

The table below (simplified from Robinson 1992: 250–251) surveys some features, most of which we will discuss in the coming chapter. Still, you can quickly see patterns. To ease that, I have bolded some forms that stand out from the group, ones that might suggest a holdover from earlier or an independent development. In some cases, like nasal loss with compensatory lengthening, we have a relatively even split. (Old Low Franconian is an ill-attested variety, ancestral to a Dutch dialect.)

---

[45] Frisian is English's closest linguistic cousin. See Bremmer (2009) for an introduction to Old Frisian, and Munske (2001) for a full handbook.

	Gothic	Old Norse	Old Saxon	Old English	Old Frisian	Old Low Franconian	Old High German
Phonology							
Vowels							
PGmc *ǣ (ē[1])	ē	ā	ā	ā > ǣ	ā > ē	ā	ā
Umlaut	**no**	yes	yes	yes	yes	yes	yes
PGmc *a, ā > o, ō bef. nasal	no	no	(no)	**yes**	**yes**	no	no
Consonants							
Verschärfung (sharpening)	**yes**	**yes**	no	no	no	no	no
Rhotacism	**no**	yes	yes	yes	yes	yes	yes
PGmc nasal loss before fricative	no	with *s*	**with *s*, *f*, *þ***	**with *s*, *f*, *þ***	**with *s*, *f*, *þ***	no	no
Consonant shift	no	no	no	no	no	no	**yes**
Morphology							
Nouns, pronouns							
PGmc masc.nom. sg. *-az	-s	-r	Ø	Ø	Ø	Ø	Ø
Masc. *a*-stem nom.pl.	-ōs	-ar	-os	-as	-ar, -a	-a	-a
Masc. 3.pers.pro., nom sg.	is	hann	hē	hē	hi	he	er
Dual pronouns	yes	yes	yes	yes	**no**	**no**	**no**
Reflexive pronouns	yes	yes	yes	no	no	(yes)	yes
Verbs							
Reduplication	**yes**	no	no	no	no	no	no
Inchoative verbs in -nan, -na	**yes**	**yes**	no	no	no	no	no
2.sg.pres.ind. of 'to be'	ist	er	is, ist	is	is	ist	ist

North Germanic and Gothic share 'sharpening' (as we shall see), have class iv weak verbs, and lack gerunds. North and West Germanic share umlaut and rhotacism, and so on. But shared similarities don't necessarily reflect genetic inheritance; they can come from language contact or be coincidental, parallel changes. As just noted, to determine what is inheritance versus contact or borrowing vs. independent innovation, we need to filter out shared features which are known to be easily borrowed and features which represent common changes across languages. So, shared words for technological innovations and so on simply do not normally deserve much weight. Consider a morphological example: where early Germanic had distinct verb endings for first, second, and third person plural forms of verbs, in North Sea Germanic languages, all three take a single ending in all forms of the present (unlike the contrasts we saw in §3.5.6) and which we will discuss again).

OE *we/ge/hie makiaþ*
Low Saxon *wi/ji/si mak(e)t*

Since this kind of reduction of contrasts is common in languages that are losing endings generally, it hardly needs to reflect inheritance, but could be an independent development or a simplification resulting from language or dialect contact.

Robinson's (1992: 250–251) list contains many features that reflect retentions from the Indo-European parent language. While he lists the existence of a shared class of weak verbs in *nan* (class iv, as already discussed) between Gothic and North Germanic, this could have been a common Germanic innovation, lost in West Germanic, and this is how it is often treated (Ringe 2006: 259). Similarly, dual pronouns presumably reflect retentions from IE, where dual was robustly marked. Other changes are common. For instance, it is unremarkable to find simplification of a cluster like *ngw > ng, as in *sengwa- > OHG *singan* 'to sing'; and, as we will see several times in this book, labiovelar consonants like *gw can readily lose their 'w'. The palatalization of *k > ts and *g > dz before i/j is famously common in the world's languages and indeed has happened in similar ways, independently, within Germanic.

For this reason, most attention is devoted to INNOVATIONS in phonology and morphology, and especially those which look like unusual developments cross-linguistically. North Germanic and Gothic share, for instance, a development of geminate (i.e. doubled) glides *j* and *w* into stops, where OHG keeps the glide. This process, the *Verschärfung*, is exemplified by the words for 'two' in three languages:

OHG	zweiio ('of two').
Gothic	twaddje
Old Norse	tveggja

OHG shows the earlier form, probably phonetically a long [j] sound. Gothic and Old Norse have turned it into [ddj] and [ggj], respectively.

While this process is now known to have some general parallels in the languages of the world (a set of them reviewed by Mortensen 2012, Hall 2014, and now by Bousquette & Salmons 2017), it is an uncommon kind of sound change, in fact predicted to be impossible on some earlier views, making it unlikely to many that two distinct languages would independently develop this way. Unfortunately, evidence of this kind of odd-looking shared innovation is scarce. Worse, this particular development does not form part of a broader pattern pointing toward a particularly close connection between North and East Germanic. Finally, this all leaves aside the fact that the specific results of the change (velar stops in Norse but coronal in Gothic) differ.

To give another example, when it was thought that Gothic forms like *þliuhan* 'to flee' reflected the older form by comparison to the presumed innovative OHG *fliohan*, that looked striking to many scholars, given the correspondence of [θ] to [f] in a small set of words. More recent IE etymologies, though, suggest connections to IE words in **p*, making Gothic the odd tongue out. But interdental fricative fronting, where th-sounds are pronounced [f] or [v], is widespread in modern English—growing numbers of British speakers say *brover* for 'brother' and *free* for 'three', for instance—and this looks like a related change, though its sociolinguistic context would be needed if we are to understand it. Honeybone (2016) explores whether a change of [f] to [θ] may actually be impossible as a regular sound change.

In fact, some problematic early Germanic etymologies may provide parallels. For example, while modern German *finster* and Middle High German *dinster* 'dark' have related meanings, they may not look directly related, but both are traced by Kluge to forms with West Germanic **þ*, assuming fronting in this particular word. Within the broader family, German *Feile* 'file' appears to correspond to Old Norse *þél*, which reflects the direction of change found in Gothic. That is, these changes, though they may look odd, have happened again and again in various ways, and so are not useful for subgrouping.

But some interconnected changes in North and West Germanic do suggest significant shared innovations, even if they are too technical to be pursued in detail here—for example the use of /ē²/ in class VII preterits and the lowering of /ē¹/ to /ā/. Moreover, these patterns fit with the chronology of migration, namely the early departure of the Goths. Like umlaut, which is first attested centuries after that departure, this pattern may simply have arisen after the Goths left Scandinavia. The real shared innovations across North and West Germanic, then, may simply have happened after the departure of Gothic and close enough to the dawn of history that we can see the geography of tree-like (East Germanic leaving) and wave-like (spread across the remaining continuum) patterns.

Beyond the earliest period, language contact becomes central, but contact effects are largely identifiable and distinct from what is traditionally treated as shared innovations. Some recent proposals see English as a 'fourth branch' of Germanic (Forster et al. 2004, Forster et al. 2006), and even as part of North rather than West Germanic (Emonds & Faarlund 2014). It would stray too far from our topic to pursue this in detail; but, from everything I can see, English is unremarkably West Germanic, though it shows significant contact effects from North Germanic, patterns that have clear parallels in modern contact settings (see Font-Santiago & Salmons 2016 and various others).

Today our understanding of sound change allows far more reliable insights into shared innovation than was possible only a couple of decades ago. Importantly, that evidence on subgrouping fits with a current understanding of external history and language contact phenomena. This leaves us with a reasonably clear picture: East Germanic speakers departed early, so that Northwest Germanic remains as a group. The remaining territory was large enough that there presumably was a dialect chain, from north the south especially. Contacts were surely robust, even aside from the migrations, as suggested by the archeological record and the consistency of runic writing. As we will see in the next chapter and beyond, interregional mixing remains a vibrant source of variation and change.

Pelkey (2015) proposes that some varieties can act as a 'cladistic hinge' in subgrouping, allowing 'blending' of innovations across distinct varieties. Cladistics is simply the name, in evolutionary biology, for connecting organisms with ancestors. Like in linguistics, this rests on use of shared unique characteristics. Pelkey defines the hinge as a situation where 'speakers of a geographically central variety mediate innovations between isolated extremes of a sub-branch, while all three daughter branches maintain evidence of their own exclusive innovation' (2015: 397). The kinds of contact in early Germanic—surely fluid and at times quite intense over an expanding space—invite an application of this notion. For now, note that this possibility further complicates Germanic sub-branching and further underscores the importance of contact.

3.6.4 The migrations: some highlights

One traditional area of disagreement about the *Ausgliederung* has been what types of evidence should be considered relevant for this question: especially important is how much weight we can place on non-linguistic evidence. In terms of ethno-historical and archeological evidence, the break-up of Germanic is tightly tied to the famous *Völkerwanderungen*, or Germanic migrations. While some recent research has challenged whether these migrations ever happened on the scale traditionally thought, Heather (2010) provides a compelling account of mass movements of Germanic speakers and others.[46] Germanic social organizations have been traditionally labeled 'tribes', but Heather provides strong evidence and arguments that suggests we would do better to think of these as political units. From loose and initially inchoate groupings, he traces a rapid development in the early centuries of the first millennium, yielding relatively complex political structures by the 4th century, of the sort social scientists would regard as 'complex chiefdoms' or 'early states'. During this period, power begins to be consolidated and labor specialized, for instance. It is, then, only over this period of time that we see the real emergence of the groups we call Goths, Franks, Vandals, Saxons, and Bavarians, and Heather argues persuasively that such groups 'can be shown to be new political units created on the march' (2010: 20).

A few notes on the migrations give you an idea how complex the movements were; understanding some of that (pre)history helps free us from the view that ancient peoples somehow tended to be geographically stable for long periods of time. In the 4th century, these movements involved tens and hundreds of thousands of individuals moving across vast territories in a few generations—from southern Scandinavia to the Black Sea or from eastern Europe to Spain and on to northern Africa.

The Goths. This group departed from the Germanic hearthland early. After that, Goths were likely relatively isolated from other Germanic languages for centuries, but in contact with Greeks and other peoples. The Goths are widely thought to have left Scandinavia about 2,000 years ago. To support this, people typically appeal to a set of placenames like Gotland, many in Sweden, and the Goths are also mentioned by the author Jordanes in a way that would be consistent with this area of origin. They are now relatively securely identified with the Wielbark culture of northern Poland (Heather 2010: 104–105). From there, over the 2nd century they spread southward and eastward. The archeological

---

[46] The real danger is likely in imagining any point in time where early Germanic speakers were geographically and socially stable, since their agricultural methods exhausted soils quickly and forced them to move often.

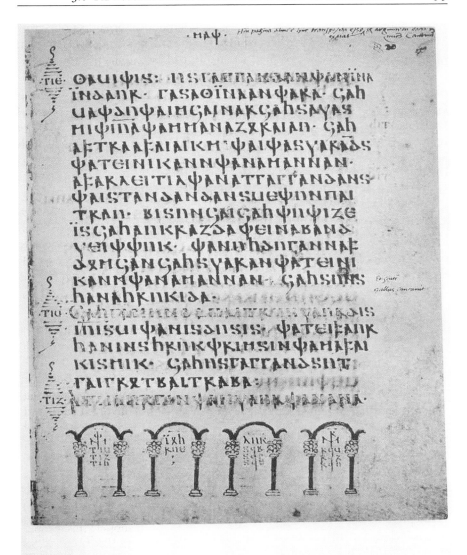

FIGURE 3.10 Codex Argenteus: the Gothic Bible.

From filologia-germanica.wikispaces.com.

record shows change over this period as Gothic political organizations grow and become better organized. They moved to the Oder–Vistula area and then on to southern Russia, where they are mentioned by 214 CE.

They had contacts with Old High German, leading to some lexical borrowings in Bavarian. Many of them end up near the Black Sea, where Crimean Gothic was spoken into the 18th century.[47] They split into the Visigoths and Osthrogoths (western and eastern, respectively, though that is not what the names mean), possibly before leaving the north. They famously fought with and then negotiated with the Romans. Over time many Visigoths converted to Christianity, and Wulfila, most likely with a group of other people (Ratkus 2018), translated most of the Christian Bible into Gothic in the 4th century. Much of this survives as our earliest extensive text in a Germanic language, and it is handed down to us in the beautiful *Codex Argenteus* (Figure 3.10). The passage is from near the end of Matthew, and the text starting after the colon on the first line reads:

> us gaggandan þan ina
> in daur gasaƕ ina anþara jah
> qaþ du þaim jainar: jas-sa was
> miþ Iesua þamma Nazoraiau . . .

In the King James version:

> And when he was gone out into the porch, another maid saw him, and said unto them that were there, this fellow was also with Jesus of Nazareth

We have only scattered bits of evidence about other East Germanic languages like those of the Vandals and Burgundians, often personal names and place-names, but not running texts.

Central and Upper Germans. These groups stayed largely in the heart of what has remained Germanic- and even specifically German-speaking territory to the present, albeit with rich patterns of language and dialect contact. These groups included many names we today identify with Modern German-speaking regions and dialects—Alemannic peoples (a name connoting alliance), Swabians, Bavarians, etc.—though the connections between these political units and dialects are vague at best and often illusory. In fact, the Franks (the 'free ones') are mentioned late (in 258 CE) and from early on represented a league of units rather than a single group, one which grew steadily as they conquered various neighbors.

---

[47] For what little is known about this story—and how we have records of Crimean Gothic—see Stearns (1978).

This applies to the Bavarians too, who are mentioned yet later. The Franks expanded their territory greatly, developed tremendous political clout, to the point that Heather (2010: 364) could rightly call them a 'superpower'. They are thought by many to have exercised considerable influence linguistically. (We will talk more about the Franks in Chapter 4.)

Anglo-Saxons. The Germanic speakers living on the coast were raiding in England long before they started moving and settling there. Immigration to the island included large numbers of Saxons, the Angles (probably from eastern Schleswig), plus Jutes, and a smattering of Frisians. Scholars have long speculated that the name 'English' (connected to 'Angle') was chosen by its speakers as more distinctive than 'Saxon', which was widely used on the continent too. After they settled in England, they slowly expanded over the island and beyond, and speakers of British Latin and Celtic languages steadily shifted to this new language (Trudgill 2010).

Non-Germanic speakers. One could too easily imagine an early central Europe populated only by speakers of the languages we associate with Europe today: Celtic, Romance, Germanic, along with Finno-Ugric, Basque, and whatever language the Huns spoke (likely Turkic). But the landscape was richer; for instance during the time of migrations, the Turkic-speaking Avars had a presence in Europe, and Iranian languages existed there as well: speakers of an ill-attested language called Alan lived along the Rhine. They allied themselves closely with the Vandals and then moved into Spain and even northern Africa with them. The presence of Iranian languages in even western Europe makes clear how different the linguistic map of Modern German-speaking territory was in the first millennium. While Germanic tribes continued to inhabit northern areas of eastern Europe long after the Goths had moved on, their presence seemed to have collapsed and the Slavs moved well into what is now again German-speaking Europe.

All these communities certainly played a role in the development of Germanic, but the role of Latin was unique. Recent work like Heather (2010) shows how Germanic social and political organization developed under pressure from Roman military and political might. And there was certainly bilingualism, to judge from various explicit comments to this effect. Adams (2003) charts what is known about contact between Latin and the languages of Europe, of the Middle East, and of North Africa. For early Germanic, that is relatively little: scattered explicit references to bilingualism. Early on, the Roman army was surely a key locus for learning Latin, since Franks and speakers of other West Germanic varieties served in it, as Adams argues (2003: 274–279). Much later, the establishment of monasteries leads to a very focused contact setting, which we will discuss in some detail in the next chapter.

A bottom line. We have some confidence that the Goths left the broader Germanic-speaking territory early and we have seen that early Runic looks surprisingly uniform across the northwestern area, extending over a long period of time. The northwestern area was large and expanded over time, in all likelihood representing a dialect continuum with increasing differences. In particular, North Sea Germanic was for a long time intermediate between what became North Germanic and what became Central/Upper German, though it is distinctly West Germanic. In short, beyond the basic breaks with people moving away (like the Goths), much of the further differentiation was likely driven by language contact with emerging differences gradually across a dialect continuum.

It has been suggested that many of the similarities in Central/Upper German territory are the result of the later prominence of the Franks in the south and that shared features in the North Sea area can be connected with the role of the Saxon confederation in the north. Leveling out of linguistic differences in closely related dialects when they are in contact is well attested and fits broadly with at least many of the changes or developments we find. The 'striking position' of Dutch (as Buccini 1992 puts it) between German and English comes from its position at a key point of North Sea Germanic-Frankish contact. We will see in later chapters that the tensions and balances between Franks and Saxons have long been and remain an ongoing topic in the history of Germanic.

Throughout, these migrations triggered myriad situations of contact among different dialects and different languages. Any emerging Germanic political group was forged from integrating members of other Germanic-speaking communities and they surely absorbed non-Germanic speakers as well, whether Celts, Romans, or Huns. And these communities as a whole dealt with both other Germanic groups and non-Germanic groups, often intensely. We are learning now how different the effects of dialect contact and language contact can be (Trudgill 2010) and work has only begun to explore how that shaped Germanic (Frey & Salmons 2012).

The core points of this discussion are these:

- Each of the three traditional branches (East, West, North) looks distinct.
- The tree model is useful—in capturing the split of Gothic, for example— but we also have to factor in language contact, so that the wave model is useful too.
- Given a set of small decentralized societies and intense language contacts, the lines would be blurry even with better data.
- Cataloging simple shared features doesn't help much, but unusual changes are valuable.

- Filtering out likely later parallel changes is another challenge, another reason to be cautious in what we assume happened during and after the break-up.

Ultimately, as Roberge (2010: 414–417) observes, early Germanic should be understood as a chain of closely related dialects which develop into discrete communities.

3.7 The earliest texts in Germanic

We have seen that the Indo-European language—its sounds and words and word forms—is a tenuous construct in many ways, aiming as it does to unify linguistic patterns found across dozens of modern and ancient languages and across vast expanses of time and space, all spoken long before our first texts. Thus, we have no texts that resemble anything remotely close to Indo-European. Here, we turn to the beginnings of writing. We'll first look at a reconstructed text which aims to depict one form of Germanic spoken language at the time of Caesar, then turn to a couple of early Runic inscriptions. Finally, having looked at our first early Germanic sentences, we'll conclude the section with a note on early Germanic syntax.

Before Runic. Despite the enormous difficulty of the undertaking, numerous specialists have yielded to the temptation to reconstruct texts in Indo-European. The tradition began with a short fable written by August Schleicher (of *Stammbaum* fame) in 1868. That text has been updated many times (see http://en.wikipedia.org/wiki/Schleicher's%27s_fable, although I cannot vouch for the quality of the material). This arcane parlor game has value largely for comparing differences in reconstruction techniques, of course, and no serious scholar believes that such texts approximate the actual speech of Indo-Europeans.

Our earliest Runic inscriptions do not, on mainstream views, represent the language common to all the Germanic peoples, but as we saw in the last section, they seem to come close. While it is far more art than science, a reconstructed text serves as a convenient heuristic, giving us a chance to illustrate some points we've discussed. Polomé (1996) pieces together a bit of Proto-Germanic text of the sort we might have expected to see if we had written eye-witness accounts. He takes a historical event as his starting point, a depiction of Germanic peoples by Caesar in his *De bello gallico* (from 55 BCE, book 4).[48] Caesar's key passage

---

[48] I have changed his text only marginally, but have added punctuation as a help to interpreting it.

reads (from this translation: http://enlightenment.narechk.net/DeBelloGallico/book_4.html):

[4.7] Having provided corn and selected his cavalry, he [Caesar] began to direct his march toward those parts in which he heard the Germans were. When he was distant from them only a few days' march, ambassadors came to him from their state, whose speech was as follows: 'That the Germans neither make war upon the Roman people first, nor do they decline, if they are provoked, to engage with them in arms; for that this was the custom of the Germans handed down to them from their forefathers, to resist whatsoever people make war upon them and not to avert it by entreaty; this, however, they confessed, that they had come hither reluctantly, having been expelled from their country. If the Romans were disposed to accept their friendship, they might be serviceable allies to them; and let them either assign them lands, or permit them to retain those which they had acquired by their arms; that they are inferior to the Suevi alone, to whom not even the immortal gods can show themselves equal; that there was none at all besides on earth whom they could not conquer.'

[4.8] To these remarks Caesar replied in such terms as he thought proper; but the conclusion of his speech was, 'That he could make no alliance with them, if they continued in Gaul; that it was not probable that they who were not able to defend their own territories, should get possession of those of others, nor were there any lands lying waste in Gaul, which could be given away, especially to so great a number of men, without doing wrong [to others]; but they might, if they were desirous, settle in the territories of the Ubii; whose ambassadors were then with him, and were complaining of the aggressions of the Suevi, and requesting assistance from him; and that he would obtain this request from them.'

Building on this foundation, Polomé assembles these comments:

Ni haðugernōz izumz,	*haðu* 'combat, war'
jaƀa itō nauðiþarfta munum	*jaƀa* 'in the case which, if', *man* 'to think'
weixamz.	*weixanan* 'to fight'
Swēƀōz hiðrē kʷēmun anði siē	
unsar landa auðja lagiðun.	*auðja lagjanan* 'to lay waste to'
Unsiz uzlauƀi hēr saljanan.	*saljanan* 'to stay, remain'
Welēmē Rōmanōnz þeuðōz	
frijōndz wesan.	

We're not aggressive, but if we think it's necessary, we will fight. The Suebians came here and they laid waste to our lands. Allow us to stay here. We want to be friends of the Roman people. (Translation adapted from Polomé 1996: 142)

The full details motivating this text are laid out in the original article, and every specialist will disagree on certain points. The precise chronology of changes is particularly difficult, for example, and in the section on verbs (§3.5.6), we gave 'fuller' first person plural verb forms, as attested in many Old High German texts, like *nëmumēs* 'we take'. For this group at this time, Polomé opted to show early vowel reduction to *-umz*. In other cases, evidence for Proto-Germanic leaves choices between possible words, as with *uzlaubjan* versus *lētanan* for 'to allow, let'.

Actual texts. The oldest preserved material in a Germanic tongue written by its speakers consists of inscriptions in the Runic alphabet, typically carved into objects. These inscriptions are, especially early on, very short, often consisting of nothing but a personal name or the name given to a weapon. Their interpretation remains difficult today, and new inscriptions are being found regularly in archeological digs across Europe, and occasionally beyond. (Here, I have mostly followed Antonsen 1975, as an accessible modern source.)

The Runic alphabet is known as the *futhark*, named after the first six letters, based on several inscriptions listing the whole alphabet in consistent order. Its early form typically contained 24 characters, sometimes written left to right and sometimes right to left. The script shows clear similarities to several other alphabets used farther south and east, and the development of Runic surely drew heavily on such models. The origins of Runic provide a source for constant discussion and speculation, as the further references indicate. The Runic alphabet itself shows considerable variability over time and space, though it is perhaps more surprising that things change so little.

The Kowel spearhead is one of the oldest known texts in a Germanic language; it was found in the Ukraine and is regarded as East Germanic in light of the migration history of the Goths and their cousins. The inscription in Figure 3.11 is on the top image, reading from right to left: *tilarids*. Runes vary a lot in how they are written or carved and the 't' here is a little unusual, but they are similar enough to our alphabet that you should be able to recognize most of the letters, certainly the last four. It's been translated as 'goal-pursuer' or *Anreiter*, with *tila* related to German *Ziel*, and *rids* '(the) one who rides (or goes)'. Since it was carved into a spearhead, it is often interpreted as encouraging the spear to hit its target.

Here is a considerably later text, and a longer one, on one of the Sjælland bracteates (Figure 3.12).[49] The inscription reads from right to left, as follows:

hariuha	haitika	farauisa	gibu	auja
Hariuha	am-called-I	travel-wise	give-1.sg.pres	luck

'Hariūha I am called, the travel-wise, [I] give good fortune.'

---

[49] A bracteate can be a piece of jewelry or a small, one-sided coin, the former often made from the latter. They were widespread in early northern Europe, presumably on Latin models, and many contain inscriptions. See the Vadstena bracteate in Figure 3.12.

The presumed name comes from compounding *harja* 'army' and *ūh-a* 'highest', but beyond that, the language is almost accessible to German speakers: the verb is one of the reduplicating members of class VII, **hētan* 'to be called'. We see the first person singular pronoun written here as *ika*. Since we would expect a verb with an *-ē* ending, like *haitē ika*, this pronoun was probably intended to 'lean' on the verb as an enclitic, as we find with Modern German postposed pronouns—*So-und-so heiße ich* often gets produced together as *heißich*. *Fara* and *uīsa* (that is, *wīsa*) are recognizable, as is *gibu*, which shows the expected first person singular ending for a present tense strong verb (see pp. 150–152, 153). The ending clearly signals the person, number and tense, so that leaving out the pronoun (found earlier in the text anyway) is no problem. The last word, *auja*, is found only in Runic, but has clear relatives especially in Old Norse. It shows the form of a *ja*-stem noun, and is sometimes interpreted specifically as 'divine luck'.

The most famous early Runic inscription is the Golden Horn of Gallehus. Two horns were dug up in the town of Gallehus in Jutland in 1639 and 1734, and the smaller one (upwards of a meter long) had a Runic inscription on it. (The larger horn has images that have sometimes also been interpreted as runes, but that's far from certain.) In 1802, the horns were stolen and apparently melted down and sold, but replicas (like in Figure 3.13) and good drawings remain. In the early 19th century, piecing together evidence from a variety of sources, scholars made headway in interpreting Runic generally using this inscription (Nielsen 2000: 42–48, 64–70, and elsewhere). From those early efforts, the language was recognized as archaic, believed by some to be close to Proto-Germanic.

Figure 3.14 shows the inscription clearly. Note that words are not generally separated but that we have sets of vertical dots marking some boundaries.

Variation in the alphabet is exemplified here by the symbol for *j*, which is above the arrow inserted in Figure 3.14. This symbol was long interpreted

FIGURE 3.11 'Tilarids', Kowel spearhead, *c.* 250 CE.

FIGURE 3.12 The Vadstena bracteate.

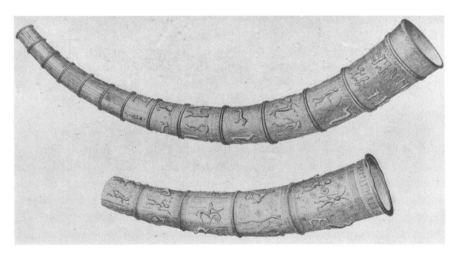

FIGURE 3.13 The Golden Horn of Gallehus.

based on an Anglo-Saxon Runic symbol for *ng* (that is, [ŋ]), leading to the name *HoltingaR* rather than *HoltijaR*. This *z* had been created from *s* by Verner's Law. It became an *r* sound, often transliterated as 'R', which was presumably distinct from the 'normal' *r* sound at this point; they later merge in the Germanic languages.

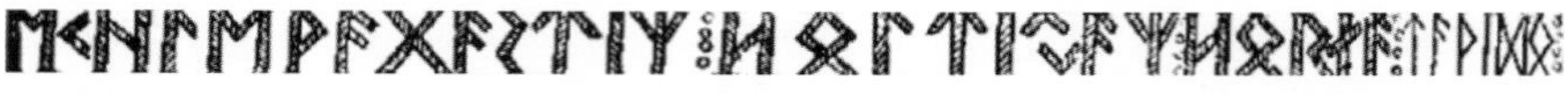

ᛖᚲᚺᛚᛖᚹᚨᚷᚨᛊᛏᛁᛉ᛬ᚺᛟᛚᛏᛁᛃᚨᚺᛟᚱᚾᚨᛏᚨᚹᛁᛞᛟ

| ek | hlewagastiz | | holtijaz | | horna | tawido. |

⇧

| 'I | Hlewagast | | [son] of Holt | | [this] horn | made, |

[famous or protected guest]   [woods?]

FIGURE 3.14 Inscription on the Golden Horn of Gallehus.

3.8 A note on early Germanic syntax

Because we have so few early inscriptions, largely short texts without broader context, and because the language is so formulaic, it is maddeningly difficult to sift much serious understanding of sentence structure from the older Futhark. Worse, the comparative method, which reveals such insight into sounds and word forms, proves problematic when applied to much of syntax, depriving us to some extent of a tool for understanding syntactic prehistory. Reconstructing syntax provides special challenges—see the vigorous exchange between Lightfoot (2002) and Campbell & Harris (2002), and Ferraresi & Goldbach (2008). For now, we will take a brief look at some of the earliest syntactic evidence and then examine efforts to reconstruct patterns that will be discussed throughout the book. Still, we have to leave substantial discussion of most syntactic phenomena to later chapters, where we have enough texts to permit rigorous analysis.

Syntax is the study of sentence structure in general. For the earliest inscriptions, word order provides a relatively tangible area to focus on with a limited dataset. The position of a verb (abbreviated with V) with regard to direct objects (O) and subjects (S) is a point about sentence structure that is obvious on even superficial examination of texts. The basic or most expected order is represented with those three letters. English, for instance, has a classic SVO order, while German shows many SOV patterns, like in subordinate clauses, where verb forms are placed at the end of sentences, or the similar placement of infinitives and participles. Antonsen (1975) starts his discussion of syntax by noting that of the 121 inscriptions his grammar treats, he can determine the position of the verb in only 34. While word order in early Germanic has traditionally been claimed to be 'free' in many respects (more like German than English), he makes some generalizations based on his data. First, imperative verb forms, of which he has only three examples, appear in initial position, just as in Modern English and German. Second, other verbs tend strongly to appear in final position, 71% of the time, though again, that reflects only 22 clauses (including Gallehus). A number of other clauses are verb-initial, sometimes where a subject pronoun is not expressed.

Work in syntactic typology has argued for broad correlations of word order patterns, where the relationship between verb and object correlates with other kinds of word order. If a language shows OV patterns, it tends to also have adjectives following nouns, genitives following the nouns they modify, pre-positions rather than postpositions (like German *gegenüber*), and so on. Lehmann (1994: 34–36) shows some traces of broad OV patterns in Gothic, though the overall picture is mixed.

Overall, for Runic, Antonsen concludes (1975: 24): 'It is clear that the normal, unmarked order in indicative sentences is S+O+V; in imperative ones, V+O, as in Proto-Germanic...'. More recent scholars often soften this position, stressing competition between OV and VO patterns. I would agree with Nielsen (2000: 174):

The word-order of Early Runic would thus appear to be in a transitional state, in which an older OV layer is being replaced by a younger one with features characteristic of VO typology.

The key point for the history of German is the tendency to have verbs in final position. It will echo down to the present.

Word order only scratches the surface of syntactic analysis, but the early Runic data allow little more. As we'll see in coming chapters, the development of negation and of definite articles have proven to be very rich areas for research in historical syntax. The early Runic corpus, though, contains only two instances of *ni* 'not' (based on Antonsen 1975), 'no obvious articles', and only three demonstrative pronouns (van Gelderen 2011: 203).

With such a sparse base of attestation in the earliest languages, how could we be able to push farther back into prehistory? As just noted, reconstructing syntax has proven extremely difficult and controversial, but people often tackle basic patterns like word order and more. At an even deeper level in prehistory, Hock (2013) tries to build a case that Proto-Indo-European had an unmarked word order of SOV alongside some verb-initial patterns, and with some unusual patterns in relative clause structures. For Germanic, this fits with a variety of other views (e.g. Dewey 2006), but bridging the gap between what is supposed for IE and what is attested in the early Germanic language is far from trivial. And treating word order in the gross terms of position of subject, verb, and object is surprisingly difficult for many living languages, even German on some views.

Let us look at two issues that we will revisit over the course of this book: the position of the inflected verb and whether a subject pronoun is required.

Walkden (2014) addresses both of these, among many other matters. (And Hinterhölzl & Petrova 2009 provide a basic introduction to many of the issues for Germanic historical syntax generally.) We will discuss both matters in detail later, but for now just note two things: (1) The inflected verb typically occurs in modern German in second position, a pattern known as 'V2' and found across Germanic, aside from English (see the next chapter for more on this). (2) Today German requires an 'overt' subject, even if that is a 'dummy' subject, as in *es wird getanzt* or *es regnet*, where the *es* is without any semantic content. In contrast, many languages like Spanish and Italian don't require subject pronouns at all in many contexts, a phenomenon called 'pro-drop'. So, in Spanish, *hablo alemán* 'I speak German' is fine, even expected, without the subject pronoun *yo* 'I', which tends to add emphasis or to play some other pragmatic role. In German(ic), V2 occurs from the earliest texts, but not rigidly, and it is subject pronouns that are often omitted; the question is how far back these patterns go historically.

To get an idea of how complex this problem is, consider Walkden's (2014: 231–232) concluding set of examples, about which he asks whether they could have really been produced by a Proto-Germanic speaker, with the basic meaning 'I slew the dragon':

a. *ek   slōh   wurmi
   I   slew   dragon

b. *ek   wurmi   slōh
   I   dragon   slew

c. *hʷat[1]   ek   wurmi   slōh
   how   I   dragon   slew
   'how (impressively) I slew the dragon'

d. *slōh   wurmi
   slew   dragon

While he reasonably finds that 'it is not very meaningful to talk about the reconstruction of sentences' (Walkden 2014: 232), there are enough similar patterns across all the early attested Germanic languages (OE, OS, ON, Gothic, and OHG) for all of the above to have been likely possible. So the structure in (a) he figures to be most likely if the dragon hasn't already been talked about, while (b) would be more likely a neutral construction, (c) would be an 'exclamative' form, and (d) would be permissible where there's no need to emphasize the subject.

Consider how Walkden comes to these conclusions. First, he is working within a theory of generative syntax (Minimalism) where variation in syntax is understood as reflecting properties that are encoded in the words themselves, which gives him a better parallel to the reconstruction of words. The details of that theory are beyond our concern, but it's worth noting that theories can profoundly shape what data we accept and how we deal with them. Second, he draws on extensive comparisons, typically quantitative and often recent (including his own, though others are 100 or more years old), of sentence patterns across the early Germanic languages.

First, with regard to word order (and keeping in mind that, like in modern German, main clauses and subordinate clauses behave quite differently), a key question is how far back in time the V2 stretches. It is widely attested in the earliest languages but, as in the examples just above, it is hardly rigidly required. OHG and its sisters allowed verb-initial forms, verb-second forms and forms with the verb later, in declarative clauses. These are some of Walkden's (2014: 70, 92) OHG examples:

V3 erino portun ih firchnussu
    iron portals I destroy
    'I destroy iron portals' (Isidor)

V1 fluog er súnnun pad
    flew he of the sun path
    'He flew the path of the sun' (Otfrid)

Verb-initial sentences occurred often in OHG poetry and in translated prose, according to Cichocsz (2010), but rarely in original prose.

V2 and V3, Walkden argues, were ancestral patterns. Yet there is more evidence to be sifted, and Somers (manuscript) shows that, within OHG, Otfrid (as we will see later, a poetic text composed in OHG rather than translated) produces more diverse V3 patterns than others have found.

Let us turn to whether subject pronouns are expected. In main clauses, all the early languages allow subject pronouns to be omitted (though not in subordinate clauses), a pattern called 'pro-drop'—again, something to be discussed in the next chapter. In addition to this, modern German also allows 'topic drop', where utterances like *habe ich schon gesagt* or *hatte er ja gesehen* are complete sentences in the spoken language, where a topic (here a grammatical object) is not realized on the surface. A related but distinct structure existed in OHG, where an object could be unexpressed, as in this sentence from the Muspilli (Walkden 2014: 188):

denne varant engilā uper dio marhā wechant deotā wīssant ze dinge

then travel angels over the lands, wake people, lead to judgment

'Then angels fly over the lands, wake the people, leading **them** to the judgment.'

The bolded pronoun in the translation is absent in the original, as you can see.

Such patterns appear across the early languages, and the two phenomena together are called 'null argument' patterns. Walkden concludes that restricted patterns of pro-drop would have been possible in Proto-Germanic. Across the world's languages, it appears that such partially null argument languages can always be traced, where evidence is available, to fully null argument patterns (2014: 226), strengthening the case of this for Proto-Germanic. Yet things have also changed, of course: the modern German situation is better seen as 'topic drop', which arose much later.

While Walkden's work (including his 2013 piece) won't pacify the waters for all, it advances discussion, I think, beyond earlier sweeping generalizations about prehistoric syntactic patterns.

3.9 Conclusion

For the time before we have extensive texts, you may not have expected to learn very much about how contemporary German works, but consider a few points we've already covered. We've seen how consonants in Romance and other IE languages match so often with those in Germanic languages, like $p \equiv f$, for instance, from Grimm's Law, and while we will fill in details, Verner has begun to show how we have alternations like *war* versus *gewesen* (and *was* versus *were*). An oddity like how *bringen* has forms like *brachte* should now make sense to you. You've seen the roots from which the German case/gender system has grown. You have begun to glimpse the systematicity of 'strong verbs' and where 'weak' verbs come from. You know why certain verbs take no suffixes for the first and third person singular—*ich darf, sie weiss, es kann*. You've learned how to think about the connections among Germanic languages and dialects.

Just as importantly, you've started to see examples of how sounds change, word forms change, and how difficult the interpretation of historical evidence about peoples and languages and even actual written texts can be. This prepares you for the next chapter, where we have vastly more texts and where patterns of regional variability yield direct connections to modern dialects.

4

From Germanic to Old High German

Early textual evidence

4.0 Introduction

You have just covered the most difficult ground in the history of German—reconstructed forms, unfamiliar kinds of data, and ways of thinking new to many readers. Only at the end of the last chapter did we have actually attested material, and that extremely sparse. Beginning here, we start to see the payoff for that effort, turning to the earliest period for which we have extensive written documents. Old High German (OHG) is the name given to this form of the language, attested since the 8th century. The Second Sound Shift is already present in this period, a change often treated as the defining characteristic of Modern German dialects. Other changes, like umlaut, trigger developments still ongoing today. The texts that have survived provide a firmer basis for understanding structural aspects of the languages and dialects at hand, but they also reveal much about language in society.

OHG is not a single language but a collection of remarkably diverse varieties. The usual distinction between 'language' and 'dialect' is whether speakers of different varieties can understand each other: if they are 'mutually intelligible', they are considered 'dialects'; if not, they are 'languages'. (Social and political considerations can override this—Norwegian and Danish are largely mutually intelligible, while Chinese includes very divergent 'languages'.) 'OHG dialects' include varieties that would not have been mutually intelligible. And from earlier discussions, you know not to think about the speakers as part of a coherent early 'German' society, but a set of emerging and constantly shifting political units, including the major groups shown in Map 5.

The map sketches the locations of key West Germanic groups up to the beginning of robust attestation of OHG. The southernmost groups, Alemannic and Bavarian, are identified with the modern dialects of the same name (though we cannot assume historical continuity), while the Thuringians and Franks

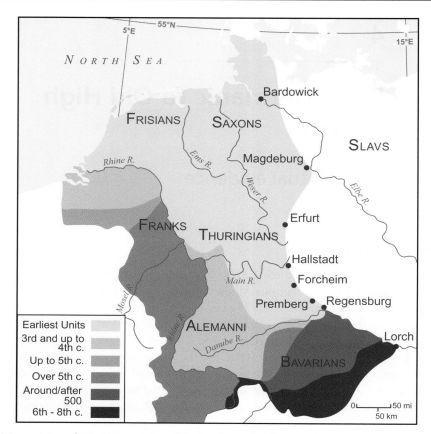

MAP 5   Map of West Germanic political units, 3rd–8th centuries.
Adapted from König et al. (2015:58).

(Franconians) are identified mostly with central dialects. The Saxons were ancestral to modern Low German dialects. Their language has been recorded since the 8th century in the Old Saxon *Hêliand*, a retelling of the New Testament adapted to a coastal Germanic audience—with Jesus presented as a forceful chief and the role of ships and sailing highlighted. 'Saxon' survives as a name for places, peoples, and languages/dialects from England (Anglo-Saxon) to southeastern Germany, underscoring the disconnect from any particular group and way of speaking. The boundary between Germanic and Slavic is much farther west here than it is today.

Map 6 gives you an idea of the movement and expansion of these political units over time, and it is important to keep in mind how dynamic the situation is. Between our earliest Runic inscriptions and the appearance of OHG documents is the so-called *Völkerwanderung*, the Germanic migrations (last

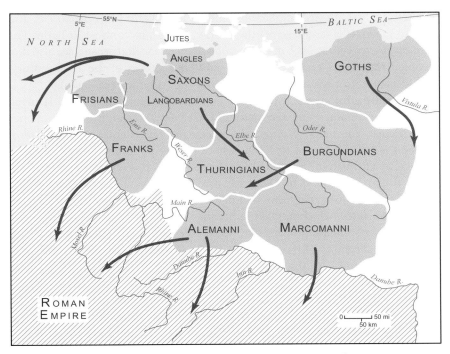

MAP 6 Key Germanic settlement areas and movements vis-à-vis the Roman Empire.
Adapted from Krüger et al. (1983: 13).

chapter) from the 3rd century on (Heather 2010). The map gives a somewhat more dynamic picture, in addition to including some smaller groups.

Even this more dynamic map fosters illusions of unity over time and space. These are small groups, constantly moving (even beyond the traditional periods of 'migration'). At the same time, there was surely some stability in population over time, as recent genetic studies across Europe support. These seemingly inconsistent bits of evidence may suggest that there was enough contact that differences over space were reduced—genetically and linguistically.

Let us take this as another easy opportunity to make a note on the history of the name of the language and people under discussion, *Deutsch*. The term *Deutsch* follows perhaps the most typical pattern for ethnonyms (names of peoples)—it just means '[the] people' in early West Germanic languages. The material below is typical etymological dictionary information (Kluge):

Proto-Germanic *þeudō 'people', Latin-German *Teutoni* (tribal name), and perhaps Gothic *þiuda* 'heathen'; cf. Old Irish *túath* 'people', Old Prussian *tauto* 'land', Hittite *tuzzi-* 'army', etc.

The term is first attested in 786, in England, in its Latin form *theodiscus*, and used to mean '(the language of) the people', that is, in contrast to Latin. The *Etymologisches Wörterbuch des Althochdeutschen* (s.v. *diutisc*; and see also *diot* 'people') reports its first use in OHG in Vergil glosses of the 10th century, considering it 'firmly established' only after the Annolied (ca. 1080).

Like many ethnonyms, it comes to apply to the language as well (Durrell 2007). Other names for German and Germans come from the names of particular Germanic groups, like *allemagne* (cf. Alemannic). Our term *German* is usually traced to Latin, where it may be attested as far back as 222 BCE, in a Roman inscription (Nielsen 2000: 325). It is often thought to be of Celtic origin, connected to Old Irish *gair* 'neighbor', and possibly a Celtic tribal name. It doesn't appear in English until the 16th century, replacing *almain* and *dutch*, which applied to broader groups of people and languages, and meaning something more like 'West Germanic on the continent'.[1] But given the malleability of these groups, often 'created on the march' and often destroyed in battle or absorbed into new groups, the significance of these names is limited.[2]

One native way of referring to the language in the OHG period reflects the dominant political group of the day, namely *frenkisg* 'Frankish'. This name is attested in 258 and means 'the free ones', known today in the phrase *frank und frei*.[3] They were in all likelihood 'a tribal league', perhaps starting as organized opposition to the Romans and others, absorbing smaller groups whose names are known from Tacitus, like the Usipi and Tencteri (Nielsen 1989: 47–50). They converted to Christianity early, and with the 'fränkische Mission' spread the religion far and wide, as shown in Map 7.

Consider the probable linguistic impact of this situation: many small, formerly independent communities become part of a larger group, with considerable population movement. In modern times, such situations lead to the formation of *koinē* dialects, leveling out differences in speech. (The term *koinē*—ancient Greek 'common'—refers today to such leveled-out varieties generally; originally it designated a dialect that came increasingly to be shared in the Greek world during and after the Hellenistic period, becoming a supraregional form of Greek.) The influence and power of the Franks is a

---

[1] Merriam–Webster includes this meaning down to the present, in fact as its first meaning, listed as 'archaic': 'any of the Germanic languages of Germany, Austria, Switzerland, and the Low Countries'.

[2] There is an entire literature on this etymology and this word. A critical starting point for further reading would be Klein (1994a, 1994b).

[3] The term was loaned into Latin before 600 and related terms are attested for France and its inhabitants only centuries later.

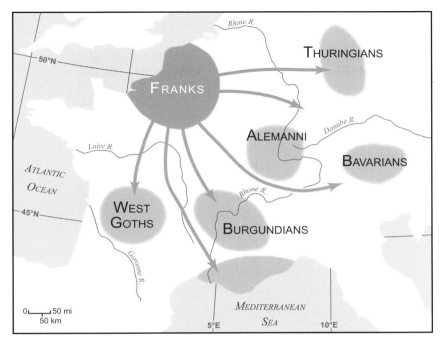

MAP 7 The 'Frankish Mission'.
Adapted from Krüger et al. (1983: 289).

theme in this period of the history of German and similar patterns of *koinē* formation run throughout the rest of our story.

Before moving on, look at some Old High German to get an initial impression of the language. Given the history of political power, access to education and literacy, much of our material is religious, or consists of glosses written on Latin texts, but we also have glimpses into something far closer to the spoken language. Among our Old High German texts are a couple intended as phrase books for non-native speakers, including the *Pariser Gespräche* (late 9th/early 10th century, see Klein 2000 for an analysis of the language) and the *Kasseler Gespräche*. Both are bilingual OHG–Latin texts, and the former set includes lots of imperatives (for ordering servants around, mostly) and rowdy insults (like the famous second example below):

- *gimer min ros* 'bring me my horse!'
- *undes ars in tine naso* 'a dog's ass in(to) your nose!'

Penzl (1984) suggests that the second sentence, like the first, is language for dealing with servants, where 'tough language is recommended' in accordance with cultural norms. We see strong suggestions that the texts were written by

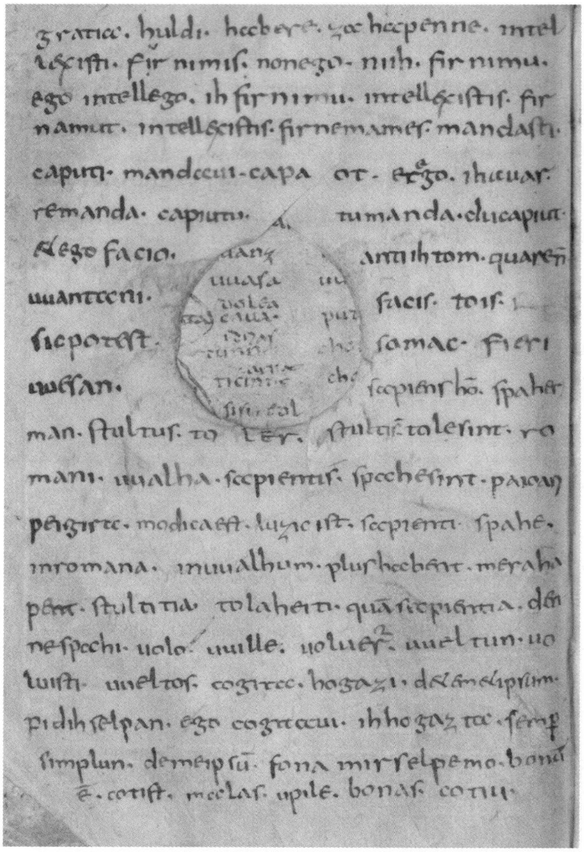

FIGURE 4.1 Kasseler Gespräche, 4 Ms. theol. 24, Seite 17 v.

Image reproduced with permission of the Universitätsbibliothek Kassel, Landesbibliothek und Murhardsche Bibliothek der Stadt Kassel.

speakers of Old French (or some other Romance language). This is suggested, for instance, by the missing *h-* at the beginning of what we would expect to be *hundes*, much like a heavy modern French accent.

The next examples are from the Kassel collection, pictured in Figure 4.1 (text from here: http://www.hs-augsburg.de/~harsch/germanica/Chronologie/ 09Jh/Kassel/kas_text.html). It was composed far earlier than the Paris material, about 810. Penzl describes the author as 'a learned, skillful native speaker of Old Bavarian' (1984: 394). With a little patience, you should be able to decipher parts of this simple material:

- Sage mir uueo namun habêt desêr man.
- Uuanna pist dû?
- Uuanna quimis?
- Fona uuelîheru lantskeffi sindôs?
- Foor, fôrun, farant.
- Quâmut?
- Quâmum.
- Firnimis?
- Ni ih firnimu.
- Ih firnimu.
- Firnâmut?
- Firnemamês.

These are classic useful tourist phrases: 'Tell me this guy's name', 'where are you from?', forms of 'to go/travel' and 'to come', and crucially: 'do you understand?', 'I don't understand', 'do you [plural] understand?', and 'we understand'. (We still have the verb *vernehmen*, though with a somewhat different meaning.) Only a few terms will be entirely new to you, like *sindôn* 'to travel', here in the second person plural.

Very old texts are endlessly amazing, even aside from looking at marks made on parchment 1,200 years ago. The first thing you notice about the manuscript is the large hole in the middle, from stretching of the parchment in preparing it as a writing surface. Parchment is made from animal skin, through a complex process of treatment and stretching. Even with a hole, this material was too valuable to discard, and ended up being put to a use that provides us with a unique piece of evidence of the early history of German.

Slips of the pen, corrections, and additions abound in our texts, and even apparently mundane Latin texts, copies of familiar works, can contain OHG or other words. These are called 'glosses' and you've no doubt seen them in used books read by people with limited command of the language—readers often write in a translation of words or phrases, along with other commentary. (For a simple overview of some aspects of this issue, see the link on p. 114.) In Figure 4.2, the darker text is the Latin with the lighter text scribbled in in OHG (image from here: http://www.e-codices.unifr.ch/de/csg/0916/19).

In some cases, glosses aren't actually written on the page with ink, but scratched in with a dry pen, so-called 'drypoint glosses' or *Griffelglossen*, which then can only be seen by holding the manuscript up against light. As we'll discuss more later, writing material was constantly reused. The discovery in May 2006 of two pages of the Old Saxon *Hêliand* in a library at the Universität Leipzig came from someone who happened to look at the binding of a much later book—pieces of the old manuscripts had been reused for binding a medieval book.

The study of glosses is a core philological undertaking and is currently an area of remarkable progress; it is readily accessible at http://www.uni-augsburg.de/glossenwiki (with interpretative essays). The best among many new works in this area may be Schiegg (2015), which showcases how philology has become hip today. Far from being just lexical help for readers with weak Latin skills, glosses—which often include scratch glosses—give phonetic or phonological and grammatical information (e.g. they mark stress or Latin case forms) and make comments about the text or give instructions (e.g. they signal passages to be committed to memory). Schiegg is able to use glosses to bring new insights to the reading and teaching culture of the early Middle Ages. An important sociolinguistic insight, for instance, is that glosses sometimes represent a form of language that is closer to oral language than most OHG writing, sometimes showing changes to be more advanced, more innovative at a given time period than they would otherwise seem to be (see also Glaser 1996). As Schiegg writes in correspondence on the topic, 'scratched glosses are the area of OHG where we can expect the most new insights'; and he notes that the list of known glosses has tripled in the last two decades. (See Bergmann & Stricker 2009 for a standard reference.)

Returning to the text we were discussing, part of the fame of the Kassel text stems from its lines mocking Romance-language speakers, called 'ethnic slurs' by Penzl:

Tole sint Uualhâ, spâhe sint Peigira;   spâhe *wise, smart*
luzîc ist spâhi in Uualhum,   luzîc *small, little*
mêra hapênt tolaheitî denne spâhi.

Stulti sunt Romani, sapienti sunt Paioari,
modica est sapientia in Romana,
plus habent stultitia quam sapientia.

Romans (Romance speakers) are stupid, Bavarians are smart;
there's little smartness in the Romans,
they've got more stupidity than smartness.

Now that you know more than you ever expected to about the language of early medieval bar fights in central Europe, let us get an overview of the present chapter and then move on to sound changes and morphology—and we will return to more texts soon.

Our basic goals in this chapter are to understand, be able to describe, and produce good examples of the key patterns and changes in the phonology, like these:

- West Germanic consonant gemination
- The Second Sound Shift (including *Medienverschiebung*)
- Umlaut (height harmony and *i*-umlaut)
- $\bar{e}^2$, monophthongization, diphthongization.

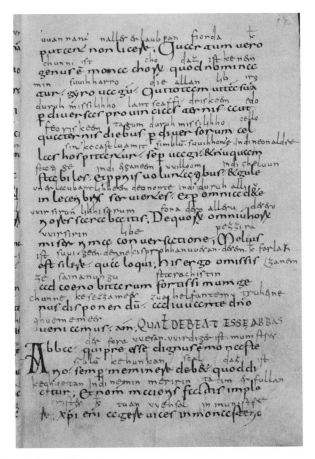

FIGURE 4.2 OHG glosses in Latin text.

Image courtesy of the Stiftsbibliothek St. Gallen.

For morphology, we'll continue to trace developments in the verbal and nominal systems:

- OHG ablaut patterns
- *Rückumlaut*
- The major stem classes of nouns, patterns of inflection
- Adjective endings.

In syntax, we now have enough data to begin examining clause and sentence structure in some detail, including these topics:

- The rise of periphrastic forms in the verb system
- Verb position, especially 'V2'

- The rise of articles and definiteness
- Patterns of negation
- Grammaticalization.

With significant texts from various regions, we can now begin to look at dialects and related matters:

- Major OHG dialects based on text samples
- Major types of texts, patterns of attestation, etc.
- Evidence of contact with other languages, patterns of lexical innovation.

Even at this early stage of the language's history, we can gain real insight into the relationship between language and society; and we will look at this in terms of the 'media revolution' that comes with writing culture.

By the end, you should also be able to give a coherent overview of these bigger topics:

- How the Second Shift unfolded, what motivated it;
- How umlaut came about and why it developed as it did;
- How the Laws of Finals operated and their impact on the broader grammar, especially morphology;
- A set of the ways basic OHG syntax differed from Modern German, including definiteness, word order, the rise of periphrastic constructions, and negation.

4.1 Sound changes from Germanic to Old High German

4.1.1 The consonant system

Starting from early Germanic, we'll treat some processes that are found throughout Northwest Germanic (like umlaut) or all of West Germanic (like gemination), but at the same time we also see the defining characteristic of the Modern German dialects, the Second or High German Consonant Shift, which is the key change in pre-OHG consonants, as umlaut is for the vowels.

Gemination: BEFORE the Second Sound Shift. Many languages, like Italian and Finnish (and some German dialects, especially Swiss) have long and short consonants, just as they may have long and short vowels. A certain set of Proto-Germanic single consonants were historically doubled or 'geminated' across West Germanic.[4] The most pervasive environment for this was between

---

[4] While contemporary spelling is far more complex, we still tend to *write* these things as double consonants in German (as a way of marking the short vowel) and English.

a short vowel and /j/, where all consonants except /r/ doubled. The Old Saxon examples illustrate forms without the Second Sound Shift.

	*bidjan	>	OS biddian	OHG bitten
	*satjan	>	OS settian	OHG setzen
	*halja	>	OS hellia	OHG hella 'Hölle'
But:	*narjan	>	OS nerian	OHG nerien 'nähren'

Three of the four examples are (class i) weak verbs or *-jan* verbs (often causatives). This class provides a good environment for gemination—by definition they had a *j*-initial suffix and many had short vowels in the stem.

Sometimes, you get gemination before liquids (*r*, *l*) rather than just *j*, but this is sporadic. Vowels appear between the stop and the liquid in typical attested forms, as you see here.

*akraz	>	OS akkara	OHG ackar 'Acker'	*acre*
*apla	>	OE æppel	OHG apful 'Apfel'	*apple*

Once in a while, you get it before *w* or nasal. With /w/, this happens only in OHG and just with /k/ or /h/:

*nakwada > OHG nakkot 'naked'
*sehwa- > OHG sehan/sehhan 'see'
*drukna- > OHG trukkan 'dry'

Denton (1998, 1999, 2002) has made strides in accounting for gemination phonetically, including these points:

(1) It presumably started with *k*, which has the longest aspiration (*h*-like noise) among stops, a phonetic effect typically exaggerated when that sound is followed by *i/j*. So, these would have automatically been pronounced somewhat longer, enough so that listeners may have noticed it. That may have led learners to interpret the sequence as having been a doubled or 'long' stop.

(2) *r* resisted the process because early Germanic *r+j* was broken up by an inserted ('epenthetic') vowel, so that we didn't usually have the right environment for the process (i.e. Cj).

In short, Denton establishes correlations between the phonetics of sounds in modern Germanic (and other) languages and where gemination happened or failed to in early Germanic.

Another approach is Murray & Vennemann's (1983), relying on abstract sound patterns. In other words, their analysis is more phonological and less phonetic, although these are connected: we've talked about the universal preference for syllables consisting of a consonant and a vowel (CV). Early Germanic had this tendency, but also another potentially conflicting preference: stressed syllables (the first syllable of unprefixed words) needed a certain amount of WEIGHT, or phonetic substance. Specifically, a syllable ending in a short vowel without a consonant after it was too 'light', and such syllables were often repaired by lengthening the vowel or moving a consonant into that syllable. One way to keep a consonant to start the second syllable and yet to get enough weight into the first, is to lengthen that consonant—so that each half counts toward the structure of a different syllable. This notion of 'syllable weight' proves important for Germanic historical phonology, and represents an exciting area of research today.

Finally, gemination was not a completely regular process. We expect, as we saw earlier, for sound change to be regular, but we find messiness in real historical data. Over the decades, people have identified particular types of change that show irregularities. Page (1999) shows that prosodic change is such a type, changes involving units of sound bigger than individual segments, like syllables or groups of syllables. While patterns involving individual segments (like Grimm's Law or *a/o* merger) are (relatively) wrinkle-free, gemination, in the view of people like Murray and Vennemann, is distinctly prosodic, concerned with boundaries of syllables where they are in contact, the weight and shape of syllables and yet larger chunks of sound.

These strands are important to current theories of sound change: the role of how we pronounce and how we hear sounds, the role of abstract (phonological) patterns and patterns of variability. Much present research focuses on how such factors work together in sound change. With a basic understanding of gemination, we are ready to tackle the most far-reaching and notable change in the period, another consonant shift.

The Second or High German Consonant Shift. Grimm's Law is often known in German as *die erste Lautverschiebung*, implying a contrast to a *zweite*. While Grimm's Law defines Germanic as whole, the High German shift affects, as the name suggests, only the geographically 'high' German dialects, that is, the central and southern ones, setting them off from the rest of West Germanic. Standard views treat the first and second shifts as completely independent changes that occurred centuries and possibly a millennium apart. Beyond the general similarity of voiceless stops turning into voiceless fricatives, another key parallel is that the 'exceptions' look similar: just as with Grimm, when you have a fricative plus a stop, the stop stays unchanged. So, IE *sp- and *st- stay unchanged to the present and *-pt, *-kt show shift of the first stop (with Grimm's Law) but then stay to the present. These parallels—and others—presumably reflect key aspects of the phonetics and phonology of Germanic, as argued by Iverson & Salmons (2005) and others.

In this second shift, Germanic voiceless stops are affricated. That is, Germanic *p*, *t*, *k* become OHG sounds consisting of a stop phase plus a fricative phase, like Modern German, where <z> (with those brackets to signal spelling) is pronounced [ts]. In many environments, they fully fricativize or spirantize, i.e. become a fricative only, much like the IE voiceless stops became Germanic fricatives in Grimm's Law.[5] If you consider the cycle of sound shifts given with Grimm's Law, the basic phonetic/phonological dynamic of the Second Sound Shift is this:

Stops become   **affricates** become   **fricatives**.

p	pf	f
t ⟶	ts ⟶	s
k	kx	x

This varied depending on the particular sound, phonological environment AND across dialects—it happens most extensively in the south and is less robust, less fully developed, as we move into central (or 'middle') German dialect areas. In Grimm's Law every stop shifted, save for a few clusters (recall the fate of *st, *pt, etc.). In the second shift, only the voiceless are directly involved and we have no shift at all in some dialects (the north, broadly) and some environments (*s*+stop again, for example). We find partial shift—stop to affricate—in other environments and dialects, e.g. with *t* becoming *z* (= [ts]) and *p* becoming *pf* word-initially in central and southern dialects, but initial *k* becoming affricated *kx*- only in the far south. The full shift from stop to fricative is found only in remaining settings, for instance for *p*, *t*, *k* between vowels.

A key concept in linguistic geography is the 'ISOGLOSS', or geographical boundary between different linguistic features. We can draw rough lines on a map between different linguistic forms, such as where Americans say 'pop' or 'soda' or 'coke' for soft drinks or where British speakers call the season when leaves fall from trees 'autumn', 'fall', or 'backend'. The isoglosses resulting from this early medieval consonant shift have been used by scholars as the basis for traditional divisions of German dialects since the 19th century: some southern dialects show the degree of shift found in or close to that found in the

---

[5] Whether affricates are phonologically single segments or sequences of two (a stop plus a fricative) is unresolved. Historically, they clearly emerged from single segments.

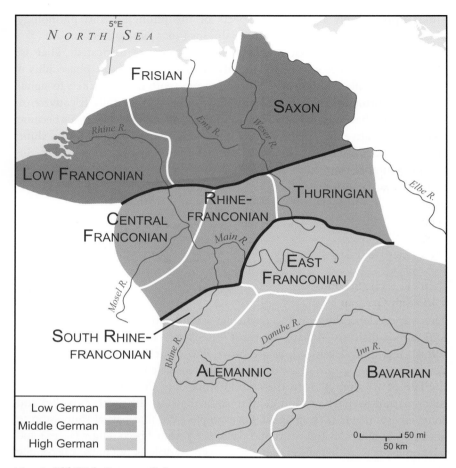

MAP 8 Old High German dialect areas.

Adapted from Meineke & Schwerdt (2001: 209).

modern standard. The far south has more shift, while the northernmost dialects and the related West Germanic languages show no shift (Low German, along with English, Dutch, and Frisian) and central dialects show partial shift. And the data are complex along other dimensions. For instance, some north-central dialects show a few unshifted forms—especially *dat* 'that', *wat* 'what', etc.—many borrowings from more northern dialects and others likely survivals from an earlier Low German-speaking population.

Table 4.1 is a detailed chart of the changes across the major dialects, modeled on material from Sonderegger. The first column shows a broad set of West Germanic dialects, starting with the northernmost Old Saxon

(OS), the ancestor of modern Low German. Like Low German is to High German, it is arguably a distinct language from Old High German. We move southward through three Central German dialects of the Rhineland area—Middle Franconian (MFranc), Rhenish Franconian (RhFranc), and South Rhenish Franconian (SRhFr)—followed by East Franconian (EFranc). (Compare these to Map 8 to see the geography.) Bavarian and Alemannic are the two major southern or Upper German dialects, while Langobardic (or Langobardian, Langob) is ill attested; it is usually classified as Upper German.

In the top row, you see the pre-OHG consonants affected by the shift. Old Saxon shows no shift, while Alemannic shows the greatest extent of shift attested. The unshaded cells show no shift, and the shaded cells show the relative shift of *p*, *t*, and *k* by context, while East Franconian is highlighted as a point of reference, since it shows a degree of shift relatively close to that of the modern standard.

TABLE 4.1 **The Second Sound Shift: distribution of Germanic fortis stops in Old High German by place and position**

	CORONAL					LABIAL						VELAR			
Pre-OHG	t-	-tt-	C+t	-t-	-t	p-	-pp-	-mp	-lp	-rp	-p(-)	k-	-kk-	C+k	-k(-)
OSaxon	t	tt	t	t	t	p	pp	mp	lp	rp	p	k	kk	k	k
MFranc	z	zz	z	33	t/3	p	pp	mp	lp	rp	f(f)	k	kk	k	ch
RhFranc	z	zz	z	33	3	p	pp	mp	lp/	rp/	f(f)	k	kk	k	ch
									lpf	rpf					
SRhFr	z	zz	z	33	3	p	pf	mpf	lpf	rpf	f(f)	k	kk	k	ch
EFranc	z	z	z	33	3	pf	pf	mpf	lpf	rpf	f(f)	k	kk	k	ch
Bavarian	z	z	z	33	3	pf	pf	mf	lf	rf	f(f)	kχ	kχ	kχ	ch
Aleman	z	z	z	33	3	pf/f	pf/ff	mf	lf	rf	f(f)	ch	kχ	ch	ch
Langob	z	z	z	s(s)	s	p	p(p)	mpf	lpf	rpf	p/f(f)	k	kk	k/kχ	ch

Adapted from Sonderegger (2003: 263).

Before we turn to examples, note the conditioning by surrounding sounds or environment: we must consistently distinguish word-initial position (*t*-) from geminate (*-tt-* geminates only appear medially for our purposes), intervocalic (*-t-*), post-consonantal (*-Ct-*), and final (*-t*) position. The spelling in part follows the usual OHG spelling: *z* is like Modern German *z*, and these become *ss* in medial position for single *t*, but remain affricates in various other positions. Many scholars use a 'long-tail z' (ʒ) or 'tailed z' (z̨) for the outputs of pre-OHG *t*. There's discussion about exactly what sound this letter represented, and it eventually merges with plain old *s* in German (Chapter 5). For labials, -C+p- differs by the particular consonant: *m*, *l*, and *r* yield different results. *ch* is the modern *ach-Laut*. *kχ* is a velar affricate, variously spelled in manuscripts, basically a *k* sound with an *ach-Laut*.

As you work through this chart, you can use East Franconian as a point of reference: this dialect matches the patterns we find in the modern standard language you know relatively well, as noted. Second, you'll see this strong correlation between place of articulation (coronal, labial, velar) and spread of the shift:

- Coronal *t* shifts to *z* far to the north.
- Labial *p* shifts to *pf*, an intermediate stage (north of the Modern German stage)
- Velar *k* shifts to *x* (<ch>) over the smallest area.

Position within the word is also directly relevant to shift by place of articulation:

- Between vowels and in final position, *p* and *k* shift much farther to the north.

With that background, let's have a closer look at data, ignoring Langobardic. For the CORONAL *t, we have a relatively straightforward situation. In word-initial position, in geminates, and after another consonant, it becomes *z* in OHG:

Old Saxon	OHG	Related English form
tand	zan(d)	tooth (with nasal loss before fricative)
smeltan	smelzen	smelt
sittian	sizzen	sit

Between vowels and finally, it becomes a long-tailed ʒ, which becomes modern *s*:

Old Saxon	OHG	Related English form
lātan	lāʒʒan	let
fat	faʒʒ	vat

As illustrated by the first example, the spelling is often inconsistent, but single -*t*- often yields double -ʒʒ-, Modern German -*ss*-, even though this is not a context for West Germanic gemination. Especially in final position, we find some unshifted forms. As already noted, these are known or likely borrowings from northern dialects, such as *fett* (cf. English *fat*).

For the LABIAL *p, Middle and Rhenish-Franconian do not generally shift except for finally and intervocalically. South Rhenish-Franconian shifts initially. After liquids, there is more variability than the table can capture.

Old Saxon	(most) Franconian	Rest of OHG	Related English form
pad	pad	pfad (phad, etc.)	path
appel	appel	apful	apple
kamp	kamp	kampf	camp (note semantic differences)
helpan	helpan/helpfan	helpfan/helfan	help
werpan	werpan/werpfan	werpfan/werfan	warp
opan	of(f)an	of(f)an	open
up	ūf	ūf	up

Again, real texts show richer variation and these should be treated as guidelines.

Finally, for VELAR *k, all dialects shift to /x/ in final position or intervocalically, an environment written as -k(-). After nasals and liquids, central dialects do not shift k, so that for instance *þanka yields Standard German *Dank*. *Alemannic* and Bavarian show more shift, changing forms that contain initial k-, geminate -kk-, or medial/final clusters like -rk(-) to affricates or even fricatives. Note that the fricative is often spelled h in manuscripts and edited texts.

Old Saxon	Central OHG	Far southern	Related English form
kind	kind	chind	child (Yes, it is related.)
stark	stark	starch	stark
makon	mahhon	mahhon	make
ik	ih	ih	I

Finally, to see how well this matches modern patterns, look at Map 9, which shows modern dialects divided in terms of the Second Sound Shift. The darkest parts have no shift in the local dialect, the lightest areas show at least as much shift as Standard German (more in the south), and intermediate areas have an intermediate level of shift. And rest assured, we'll talk more later about the modern material.

The chronology of this change is hard to pinpoint, but it is usually dated to shortly before the earliest attestations of OHG. This is suggested by the participation of loanwords from Latin borrowed before then in the change but not those borrowed later. Placenames and personal names written in Latin texts provide the best evidence for the shift. Using such evidence, Braune & Reiffenstein (2004: 86) put the earliest shortly after

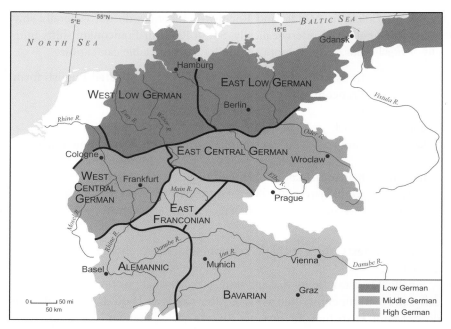

MAP 9 Modern German dialects, classified by the Second Sound Shift.
Adapted from König et al. (2015: 230–231).

550, like a member of the Alemannic elite named *Buccelenus*, presumed to include the first element from *Butto*, with the spelling thought to reflect an affricate [ts]. More famously, *Attila* is attested not much later in a shifted form, like German *Etzel*. Other aspects, most importantly how the change spread over time and space, e.g. north to south or south to north, remain poorly understood.

Another chain? Medienverschiebung.[6] Knowing Grimm's Law, where three different sets of consonants (voiceless, voiced, voiced aspirated) change in tightly linked fashion, you may wonder if we have any other related changes connected with the second shift, that is, something besides the voiceless stops. In fact, the Second Sound Shift creates a partial gap where the plain voiceless stops once were, the simplest, most basic stops, which

---

[6] Grimm discussed the First Sound Shift in terms of 'tenues' (voiceless), 'mediæ' (voiced), 'aspiratæ' (aspirates). The term here refers to the OHG voiced stops, from the IE aspirates or voiced stops which developed from the voiced fricatives of Verner's Law.

would invite a 'drag chain', to turn voiced stops into voiceless and fill that gap. In the southern dialects, where the High German Consonant Shift was most developed, we get a shift of Proto-Germanic voiced stops to voiceless ('lenis') stops. The changes follow:

/d/ is often written as <t> in Upper German, East Franconian, and partially in Rhinefranconian in geminates and finally.

/b/ merges with /p/ in Upper German, consistently in Bavarian (*be-* = *pi-*, *Glaube* = *calaupa*, etc.), initially in Alemannic (*bist* = **pist**, but *kilaubu*). In final position, we find merger (*selp* for *selb*).

/g/ behaves generally in parallel with /b/, devoicing in the far south to yield forms like: *kip* = *gib* and *cot* = *Gott*.

Recall that these sounds go back to the IE 'voiced aspirates', which show complex patterns in Germanic as fricatives and stops. As discussed in Chapter 3, Verner yields patterns like *ziehen* vs. *gezogen*.

Other consonant changes to keep in mind:

- **þ > d.** To the extent we can trust the orthography, this occurs in the south, starting medially, in the 8th century, reaching Middle Franconian by 1000. English did not undergo this change, and its obstruent system is remarkably close to West Germanic, while High German has moved far from those roots. The process goes on today, with many dialects of English showing similar patterns, e.g. in the United States from Brooklyn to Wisconsin.

- The weakening of **x > h** is often dated to OHG, although it's hard to be sure. *h* is commonly used to represent [x] as well as [h], and we lack detailed phonetic descriptions. Howell (2017) presents evidence of the weakening of this consonant already in Runic and Gothic, which suggests that a full consonant remained just long enough to condition breaking and then was lost in Old English and OHG. (For related reasons, Freek Van de Velde takes the change to be Common Germanic, as he notes in personal communication.)

- **Rhotacism—z > r:** IE *s became voiced in some circumstances in Germanic, notably from Verner's Law. This also happened finally, as we'll discuss. In Gothic, the sound stays as *s* or *z*, but elsewhere, from Old High German to Old Norse, it becomes *r*:

Gothic	OHG	
láisjan	lêren	'to teach'
huzd	hort	'hoard'
wêsun	wârun	'were'

In Old Norse, these words have an *r*, e.g. in *læra* 'to teach'. Over time, we see the elimination of Verner alternations across Germanic. That is, alternations between *s* and *r* within paradigms surely sounded odd to listeners/speakers and presumably reflected the kind of irregularity that tends to get leveled out in morphological change. Traces are still visible especially in highly frequent words. For instance, in Old Norse 'to be', earlier *vesa* later appears as *vera*, taking the *r* route on that particular word, while German has *r* with *war*, *wäre*, and so on, but keeps the fricative in *gewesen*. English also keeps the alternation in that particular word, with *was* vs. *were*.

In outline and many details, this consonant system is recognizably German, and we turn to the vowel system, where the principles at work will forge a recognizable system in later centuries.

4.1.2 The vowel system

Recall the basic structure of a simple vowel system, as treated in §3.3:

	front	back
high	i	u
mid	e	o
low	a	

We'll begin with assimilations, where sounds become more like other sounds. Assimilations are among the most common phonetic processes, phonological patterns, and sound changes. Consider this chart in terms of the distance a speaker has to adjust their articulatory apparatus between vowels. The *a* sound and the *i* sound are at essentially opposite corners of the possible space, often the longest distance between any two vowels in a system: to produce a word like *Vati* [faːti], you move from a low back tongue position on the first vowel to the highest and most front position on the second. Vocalic assimilations simply reduce such differences, making one vowel more like another one. Armed with that concept, let's tackle an important development in Germanic vowels, umlaut.

The pre-Germanic merger of *ᵒo with *ᵃa and *ā with *ō leaves gaps in the short system at *ᵒo and the long system at *ā. The latter gap is then filled by the product of nasal loss with compensatory lengthening, creating a small number of *ā forms in a tightly defined environment, notably before *-xt.

	front	back
Short		

high	i		u
mid	e		
low		a	

Long

high	ī		ū
mid	ē		ō
low		ā	

1. What's umlaut? Broadly speaking, umlaut is an assimilation of vowel features. UMLAUT—found in Germanic, Micronesian languages, etc.—is often contrasted with VOWEL HARMONY—found in languages including Menominee, Turkish, Finnish, Mixtec. In most definitions, umlaut is regressive (with a vowel feature at the end of a word, or right, spreading toward the beginning, or left), while Vowel Harmony is typically progressive, from left to right. We often see umlaut as a sound change that unfolds in a language historically, while Vowel Harmony is often an 'active' process, stable over generations. In Turkish Vowel Harmony, greatly simplified here, vowels agree in frontness and rounding. *-in* is a genitive suffix that varies according to the quality (frontness and rounding) of the vowels in the word it is added on to:

ev-[**in**]	of the house
otobüs-[**yn**]	of the bus
orman-[**ɯn**]	of the forest
vapur-[**un**]	of the steamer

If we have a front vowel in the word, the suffix is front, and if we have a back vowel, the suffix is back. The same applies to rounding.[7] Similar processes, if often less complex, are found in many Romance varieties (Calabrese 2011).

---

[7] For a detailed account of Turkish vowel harmony, see Kabak 2011, and for a broad current theoretical perspective on how such assimilatory processes do and don't happen in human languages, see Walker 2011.

2. 'Germanic umlaut'. The term 'umlaut' is used, as just indicated, for a range of vowel assimilations in different languages, and it's also used for a range of distinct, but ultimately related early Germanic phenomena. The first involves HEIGHT assimilation, which leads some of us to prefer the name 'height harmony', to avoid confusion with the more famous process of *i*-umlaut. Let's talk first about adjustments on the vertical dimension.

Height harmony: In early Germanic, after *a/o* merger, a kind of harmony develops, whereby the vowels in adjoining syllables assimilated partially in height. The first pattern, U-UMLAUT, represents the process of raising mid /e/ to /i/ before /u/ or /i, j/:

PGmc *helpu > OHG hilfu 'I help'
      *fehu > OHG fihu 'Vieh, fee' (with semantic change in English)
      *medjōn > OHG mitti 'Mitte, middle'

This does not apply to *a (yet), and there was no *o* in the grammar at this point, due to earlier merger of *o with *a. There's some evidence for a parallel early process of raising before *i*.

The natural counterpart here is a lowering, or A-UMLAUT: high vowels (*i, u*) were lowered before non-high vowels, except when N+C intervened.

IE *wiros >   PGmc *wiraz >   OHG wer   'man'
IE *nizdos >   PGmc *nistas >   OHG nest   'nest'
IE *ghḷtom >   PGmc *gulþa >   OHG gold   'gold'
IE *jugom >   PGmc *juka >   OHG joh   'yoke'

That is, *i* becomes *e* and *u* becomes *o* before *a*. This change creates a new *o*, filling the gap from the just-mentioned *a/*o merger. The *gold* example shows that this process works on the *u* that arose from anaptyxis, as described in the last chapter.

With nasal plus consonant, this process fails to occur: *zunga* 'tongue', *wunta* 'wound', perhaps because of the effects of nasal consonants on preceding vowels. Recall that *-eN- > -iN-, as in *wend > *wind*. This reflects the effects that nasals generally have on preceding vowels.

The BIG umlaut process: *i*-umlaut. Some form of *i*-umlaut occurs across all attested North and West Germanic languages, but it varies wildly in how it has unfolded. This and other evidence strongly suggests that it began in the late Northwest Germanic period, but developed at least in part after the languages had separated.

Piecing together the points just sketched, *i*-umlaut is an assimilatory effect of an *i* or *j* (a glide very much like *i* phonetically) on preceding vowels. The frontness of *i/j* spreads from that sound toward the beginning of the word—in anticipation of pronouncing that /i, j/, you already set up the articulation of the first vowel in the front of the mouth. Experimental phonetic research suggests that everyone does this in speaking—that the *o* in *Obi(-Wan Kenobi)* is more fronted than the *o* in *Opa*, driven by the differences in the place of articulation of the final vowels. The first vowel retains a key characteristic of its earlier pronunciation—namely rounding of the lips—but it ceases to be pronounced in the back of the mouth. These examples are about assimilation across syllables, but it's also easily illustrated from the interaction of consonants and vowels within a syllable. If you pronounce the German vowels in *Kiel*, *kühl*, and *cool* while paying attention to where your tongue is and whether your lips are rounded (again, that is, with the corners pulled somewhat together), you can see exactly how this works: *kühl* is produced with a palatal, not a velar stop (as discussed earlier), as a result of the following front vowel. In a more technical formulation, this is 'coarticulation', a regressive or anticipatory assimilation of back vowels to a following high front vowel or glide.

We find *i*-umlaut everywhere in Germanic except Gothic. Even there, some would try to see umlaut in one Crimean Gothic name, recorded a millennium after Biblical Gothic: *Egila*, which could possibly reflect an original *Agila*, though it's impossible to be sure.

Old Norse:	katilaR > ketilR 'kettle'[8]
Old English:	kunni > cynn (*y* like German *ü*) 'kin'
Old Frisian:	harjis > here 'army', cf. *Heer*

Note that English, Yiddish, and many German dialects have unrounded those umlaut vowels, as illustrated here with *kin*. English has only a few remnants of umlaut alternations, like *louse ~ lice*, *woman ~ women*, *tooth ~ teeth*.

OHG data. Before we consider possible explanations of umlaut, let us look at a little data from OHG, organized in the traditional way, following the traces we find of umlaut in early spellings: the process appears to have begun with short *a*, and is known as 'primary umlaut', illustrated in (a). Primary umlaut fails when certain consonants come between the target vowel, *a*, and the trigger vowel, *i/j*, as in (b). The process later expanded to those blocking environments and to long *a*, which I'll call 'secondary umlaut', as in (c), while the last stage was the changing of all back vowels in all environments before *i/j* in the following syllable, as in (d). This last stage is reflected consistently in the orthography only many centuries later, as we'll see in the following chapters.

---

[8] As already noted, the symbol *R* is used in early Norse for the special rune showing the *r*-sound created from *z by rhotacism.

a. Primary umlaut: short a → e before i/j—spelled in most OHG texts

gast ~ gesti	'guest, guests'
lamb ~ lembir	'lamb, lambs'
faru ~ feris	'I drive, you drive'
fasto ~ festi	'solid/fast', adv. and adj. (cf. German *fast* vs. *fest*)

b. Blocking: primary umlaut fails (intervening hC, LC)—written by Otfrid during OHG, otherwise later

maht~ mahti	'power, powers' (also dialectal *mehti*)
haltan ~ haltis	'to hold, you hold' (also dialectal *heltis*)
starch ~ starchiro	'strong, stronger' (also dialectal *sterchiro*)

c. 'Secondary' umlaut: ā →ǣ (long ä) before i/j—marked only after OHG

zǣhere	'tears', cf. OHG zahari
kǣsi	'cheese'
slāfet ~ slǣfet	'he/she/it sleeps'
wǣnen	'to say, mean', cf. OHG wānen < *wa:njan

d. General umlaut of ALL back vowels, including long and short *u* and *o* and in blocking environments—only marked long after OHG

Every back stem vowel that stood before an *i/j* was fronted:

OHG	Modern German
skôni	*schön*
kuchina	*Küche*
stucki	*Stück*

Scholars write the product of secondary umlaut as *ǣ* or as (long) *ä*, reflecting that it was clearly a lower vowel than the mid vowel *ē*, as found in *snēo*, German *Schnee*. We know that these vowels were distinct, e.g. because poets in Middle High German did not rhyme these two types. That is, they rhymed only the product of secondary umlaut with other products of secondary umlaut but not with earlier *ē*. The difference, in fact, is still reflected in many dialects today, especially in Upper German, where the vowel in the 'cheese' word is lower or more open than the one in 'snow' (Schirmunski 1962: 197).

This broader umlaut is generally attested much later, as we'll discuss. There are occasional suggestions of earlier marking, e.g. Notker's use of *iu* for *ü*. Gütter 2011 argues that a number of placenames recorded before 957 show efforts to write umlaut of /o, o:, u:/.

Sometimes ignored in the literature are two sets of data where umlaut is not found in modern West Germanic, one at the southern and the other at the northwestern edge of the territory:

- Southern German umlautless residues, especially before geminate *kk* or *hh* and especially with *u*: *Stuck, Muck, Kuch* (vs. German *Stück, Mücke, Küche*).
- Dutch umlautless residues, especially in western dialects showing only primary umlaut: *machtig* 'mighty', *kaas* 'cheese', *horen* 'hear', *schoon* 'clean', *groeten* 'greet' (vs. German *mächtig, Käse, hören, schön, grüßen*).

The broad sweep of the unfolding of umlaut can be summarized with a simple graphic. The prehistoric process of height harmony changes vowels vertically, raising and lowering them, while primary umlaut cuts diagonally, moving low /a/ up, like height harmony, and forward. General umlaut then simply fronts vowels.

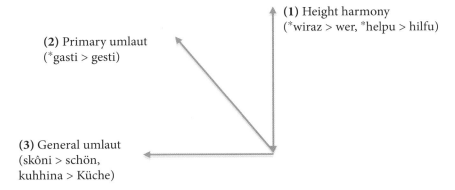

(1) Height harmony
(*wiraz > wer, *helpu > hilfu)

(2) Primary umlaut
(*gasti > gesti)

(3) General umlaut
(skôni > schön,
kuhhina > Küche)

The classic theory of Old High German umlaut grew from Twaddell's 1938 five-page paper in *Monatshefte*, but has been elaborated since. His key was phonemicization, the moment the new sounds came to contrast with un-umlauted variants, when this difference came to make a difference in meaning. Twaddell's theory has been called 'the greatest achievement of American Structuralism' (Keller 1978: 160), which was a key linguistic theory into the mid and even late 20th century. Here is a summary:

1) A normal phonological rule arose: in OHG, every back vowel before *i/j* became a front vowel ('allophonically' or conditioned by surrounding sounds, namely following *i/j*).
2) Weakening of final vowels leads to loss of endings with *i/j*, thus eliminating the earlier rule: eventually there is no front high vowel to cause this assimilation.
3) With this, the fronted vowels are no longer conditioned, but they stay front even without the *i/j* to condition them.
4) Later, umlaut comes to mark certain morphological categories, like plural nouns.

To some specialists in sound change, point (3) sounds implausible: when conditioning factors are lost, we would expect umlauted variants to 'de-umlaut'. Over the following decades, many important works explored these and other wrinkles in the development of umlaut across Germanic—such as the important contributions of Kyes 1967, Robinson 1975, 1980, and Fertig 1996, leaving aside many discussions in theoretical phonology on the topic.[9]

Today, new approaches to OHG umlaut have emerged and throughout this book I adopt one that returns in some ways to the pre-Twaddellian tradition but which, like Twaddell's work, is closely associated with the University of Wisconsin. This view has grown up in various circles, but started in many ways with Buccini 1992. It rests largely on a careful sifting of the full evidence, especially variation across dialects and other West Germanic languages. In fact, Otfrid, the first known author of a major OHG text, writes umlaut variably, but he often has it in environments where no other OHG author does.

Here is a sketch of the general approach:

A. Primary umlaut was chronologically earlier than secondary umlaut, because:
    (1) Primary umlaut is the only process to affect the entire continental West Germanic area. Secondary umlaut, including umlaut of *ā and *a in blocking environments, does not occur in western Dutch.
    (2) Non-umlaut of West Germanic *a in 'blocking environments' dialectally in OHG implies later onset of at least this part of what is commonly called secondary umlaut.
    (3) Primary and secondary umlaut result in fundamentally different vocalic mutations—it is difficult or impossible to state the two processes in one phonological rule. Primary umlaut causes the fronting AND raising of West Germanic *a, while secondary umlaut only fronts the affected vowels.
B. Umlaut blocking patterns cannot be accounted for under Twaddell's view but they make good phonological sense. Namely, where blocking took place was with intervening *h, l, r* (originally /x, l, r/) before consonant. These three sounds can and do vocalize (like Boston or British Received Pronunciation /r/ at the end of a syllable, or the 'silent' /l/ in 'talk'), disappear (like /x/), or become a glide like [w]. Blocking occurs historically in exactly the dialects where these Cs have vocalized, namely *l* in Bavarian and western Alemannic and *r* in Bavarian but not Alemannic:

---

[9] Other alternatives, like Voyles 1991, are less successful. Schulze (2010) attempts to defend a Twaddellian view against the 'Wisconsin School' approach generally. I do not find the arguments compelling.

(1) <ht>, <hs>: Blocking is pan-OHG: Franconian, Bavarian, Alemannic (but not Otfrid [= O]):

maht/mahti (O mehti); mahtig	'power' nom.sg./pl.; adj.
naht/nahti	'night' nom.sg./pl.
gislahti	'race, tribe'
wahsan/wahsit (O wehsit)	'grow' inf./3rd sg.pres.

(2) <hh>, <ch>: Blocking in Bavarian, western Alemannic, but not in Franconian (e.g. Tatian [= T]):

sachan/sahhis/sachit (T forsehhis/-sehhit)	'see' 1st/2nd/3rd sg.
gimachida	'connection'
ahir (Fr. ehir)	'ear [of grain]'
slahan/slahit (Fr. slehit)	'hit' inf./3rd sg.pres.
dwahan/dwahit	'wash' inf./3rd sg.pres.

If umlaut is restricted to short vowels, a vocalized liquid would create a diphthong-like sequence, so that blocking is expected. The explanation for *h* is more complex, as detailed in Iverson & Salmons (1996), Howell & Salmons (1997), and other work.

(3) /lC/, /rC/: Blocking only sporadically in Franconian; /lC/ blocks umlaut consistently in Bavarian, Alemannic, while /rC/ blocks normally in Bavarian, but only occasionally in Alemannic:

haltan/haltis/haltit (Fr. heltis/heltit)	'hold' 1st/2nd/3rd sg.
waltan/waltit (Fr. weltit)	'rule' inf./3rd sg.pres.
altiro (Fr. eltiro)	'older'
chalb/chalbir	'calf' nom.sg./pl.
marren/merren	'to hinder' (doublet)
warmen/wermen	'to warm' (doublet)

C. Upper German has numerous umlautless forms (Upper German *Innsbruck* vs. Central German *Saarbrücken*, or originally Southern *Rucksack* 'backpack' vs. *Rückgrat* 'backbone', an example suggested by Matt Hamann). A Twaddellian view must account for all such forms as analogical changes. The new view can explain them as regular and easily understood sound change.

Here's an overview of the chronology and unfolding of this set of changes:

- Things start with height harmony, that is, a-umlaut and u-umlaut (which includes some i-based raising effects).

- Fronting umlaut is later, but primary umlaut (short *a* to *e*), and to a lesser extent secondary umlaut in blocking environments and of long *a* to *e*, is a kind of transition, since it involves fronting AND raising.
- Fronting umlaut starts as a narrow process (just short *a*, and with blocking effects), but over time the process generalizes steadily, eventually affecting all vowels.

Other developments: ē, zweimal. In West Germanic, inherited ē > becomes ā, but this is not found in Gothic so that Classical Greek *títhēmi* 'I put' corresponds to Gothic *ga-dēþs* but OHG *tāt*. Some scholars write the vowel from which these developed as æ (the vowel of English *cat, bad*) to capture its apparent in-between status. This sound is usually called ē[1] or Proto-Germanic *ē.

After that change, a new vowel entered the same part of the vowel space, another ē, called ē[2]. Evidence from modern dialects that keep these distinct indicates that this vowel was HIGHER in the vowel space (more closed) than old ē. This vowel exists in a fairly limited set of forms, and it becomes *ia*, as seen in the OHG forms here:

- OHG *hiar*, Gothic *her* 'here'
- OHG *stiag* 'stairs', cf. *Steg*
- loanwords like Gothic *mes* 'table' or OHG *ziagal* from Latin *tēgula*.
- Class VII or 'a-class' verbs like *lassen* (OHG *liaz* 'he let') and *heißen* (*hiaz*), etc.

The origin of this new vowel is hotly disputed. The main theories are that it came from:

- IE or Proto-Germanic *ei or *ēi. The former view would represent an exception to our rule from the last chapter that *ei yields ī; and the latter has its own problems: while IE seems to have possessed some 'long diphthongs' (a long vowel plus another vowel or glide, like here), the connection to our vowel is not obvious.
- *e+V in the reduplicated (class VII) preterits. That situation of two vowels coming together in reduplication is a place where a new vowel might arise, but how this change might have spread to other environments is difficult to explain.
- *e+H (laryngeal). Almost all specialists believe that the laryngeals were long gone by Germanic, let alone West Germanic, making this highly unlikely.

None of these theories is persuasive, because we simply have too little data. You should know two things, (1) that this new vowel emerges in the places just described and (2) unless we find new evidence or methods of attack, this is not a promising research topic. The synchronic situation in OHG is, though, simple: we have an ā (from the old *ē) and a new diphthong *ia* (from the new *ē).

Diphthongal developments and monophthongization. Things start here with partial assimilation in diphthongs. That is, the initial element of the diphthong becomes more like the second element, or glide: in *au, for example, the *a raises to *o, halfway to the *u.

Original *au > ou   *augo > ougo 'eye'
Original *ai > ei   *maist > meist 'most'

Note how much this looks like harmony/umlaut processes WITHIN a diphthong: in height harmony and umlaut, vowels in adjoining syllables become more alike; here, it's the first element of a diphthong that becomes more like the second, 'glide' element.

This goes to complete monophthongization before some consonants:

- (*ai >) **ei** > ē before *r, h, w*. This is apparent in pairs of forms where one has rhotacism (again, an *r* sound created from an old *z) and the other does not: Modern German *mehr* contrasts with *meist-*, a pattern which goes back to OHG *mēr ~ meist*. Gothic, which lacks rhotacism, has the form *maiza* 'more'. Beyond explaining why German words for 'more' and 'most' have different vowels, this shows us the chronology of the change: rhotacism happened before this monophthongization took place, so that the new *r*'s are included in the change.[10]
- (*au >) ou > ō before *r, l, h* [*h* from Grimm's Law, IE *k, but not the one from the Second Sound Shift] and all alveolar consonants (*t, d, s, z, n*).

	Go	**OHG**	
'ear'	auso	ōra	following *r* triggers monophthongization
'eye'	augo	auga/ouga	following *g* does not

- *ē², as noted, yields *ia*, which becomes *ie*.
- *ō > uo, OHG *bruoder, fluot, fuor*. As we'll see later, this has monophthongized in recent times, to Modern German /uː/: *Bruder, Flut, fuhr*.
- *eu > eo > io before a low vowel in the following syllable: earlier *beuda 'to offer', *skeuta 'to shoot' yield OHG *biotan, skiotan*. This *io* then later merges with *ie* from *ē². If we have a high vowel following, we get *iu*. This splits stem vowels in verbal paradigms—*liogan* 'liegen', *liugu* '[ich] liege', and in some derivationally related words, like *deota* 'people' but *diutisk* 'in the people's language' (cf. *deutsch*).

The last-noted development yields another dialect difference, a complex but significant one.[11] In Franconian, we find *io* or *eo* before non-high

---

[10] Gothic lowers *i* to *e* in these same environments, so it's a broader pattern; see Howell (1991).
[11] Sources differ in how they analyze this pattern; I follow Braune & Reiffenstein (2004).

vowels, but *iu* before high vowels. In Upper German (the Bavarian and Alemannic dialects), you get *io* only with /h/ or alveolar before the non-high vowel, but *iu* before all labial and velar consonants except *h* regardless of the vowel. In short, Franconian has generalized more vowel lowering than Upper German. The first two examples illustrate the dialect difference, while the last two illustrate the similarities in height harmony:

	Franconian	Upper German	German	
Before labial	tiof	tiuf	*tief*	deep
Before velar	flioga	fliuga	*Fliege*	fly (noun)
Before alveolar	biotan	biotan	*bieten*	offer
Before high V	liuti	liuti	*Leute*	people

Leaving aside $\bar{e}^2$, these changes GENERALLY look like partial assimilations, where diphthongs lessen height differences between their two elements and, under some circumstances, take the process to completion with monophthongization.

Overall, OHG vowels, then, look much more foreign than the consonants do from the perspective of someone who knows Modern German. In part this has to do with the omnipresent REDUCTION OF UNSTRESSED VOWELS, to which we now turn.

4.1.3 Prosody and the Laws of Finals: IE > OHG

The weakening of final syllables is a notable trend in the development of the Germanic languages. Handbooks and textbooks often tell you without flinching that the weakening of unstressed syllables leads to the loss of inflectional morphology. As we'll see, this is a tantalizing idea, but rigorous support for it is hard to come by. The process of weakening and loss of material at the ends of words is extremely variable, as we expect for prosodically conditioned changes (as we will see in the coming pages). While German shows limited active (synchronic) reduction of this type today, English is rife with stress-conditioned reductions. *Photo* is pronounced with two full vowels, for instance, while *photograph* has reduction of the second *o* to schwa [ə]. In *photography* or *photographer*, many speakers have no vowel at all in what we would think of as the first syllable, thus beginning the words with [ft]. Reduction is also dependent on rate of speech and other considerations reaching far beyond word-internal factors. Many central and southern German speakers reduce a phrase like *haben wir es* to something like *hammas* [haməs], even [hams], for example. In contemporary English, the range of pronunciations of a string like 'Did you eat yet?' runs from full articulation of four syllables to the heavily reduced two-syllable form many people use, along the lines of [dʒitʃɛt], potentially unrecognizable out of the context of a noon-time question to a co-worker. Still, over the long term, the outcomes are surprisingly consistent, especially if we consider the role of prosodic structure explicitly.

Prosody.[12] As outlined earlier, prosody is basically how stretches of speech larger than the individual sound are organized. This has been an area of recent progress, and by looking at bigger 'chunks' of speech, we can see surprising unity across what look like different patterns at the segmental level.

First consider the 'vertical' organization of sounds into larger units, called the 'prosodic hierarchy' (Selkirk 1995). Parts of this picture are controversial and not all languages exploit all of these. We'll start with an abstract unit of weight or timing called a 'mora', of which short vowels have one and long vowels have two. Segments are organized into syllables, which in turn are organized into 'feet'. Words are made up of a foot or more than one foot. We normally use Greek letters for each of these levels, and represent them visually from the smallest at the bottom to the largest at the top, with branching trees to show relationships (writing the long vowel in *Moni*, the German short form for *Monica,* with a double *o*):

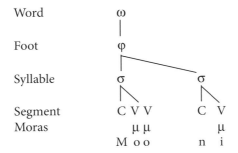

For each level, languages have some typical, often rigid patterns. 'Open' syllables end with vowels, and are found in all languages, for instance. In some languages (like Hawaiian), only open syllables are permitted, and in others, only sonorants and perhaps a few other consonants can end a syllable (like Spanish). We can call these possible or preferred shapes 'prosodic templates'.

Take a phonotactic problem, an issue in the possible sequencing of sounds. Let's assume syllables are organized this way, illustrated with several modern words. The nucleus, typically a vowel, is just the most sonorous element in the syllable, while the onset is any and all consonantal material before the nucleus, and the coda is the consonant material after:

---

[12] Parts of this section draw on my contributions to the forthcoming *Cambridge History of the Germanic Languages.*

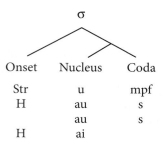

Syllable codas—the material after the vowel—have changed dramatically over time, especially where there are clusters of consonants. As noted, languages show a general bias toward open syllables, toward not having any or much material after the vowel within a syllable. West Germanic has sets of consonants in that position, like these OHG forms (keeping in mind *h* was pronounced as an *ach*-Laut):

> *bërht* 'bright'
> *forht* 'fright'

Many non-native speakers find these clusters hard to pronounce and they seem to have presented issues for OHG speakers as well: they found various ways of eliminating these patterns. Phonologists call these 'conspiracies', or 'a set of rules that serve the same purpose: to rid the surface forms of the language of certain undesirable (marked) configurations' (Baković 2000, following Kisseberth 1970). Look at some solutions:

- Epenthesis: we often find new vowels inserted to break up the cluster and create new syllables: *bëraht, foroht.* This strategy is common for clusters down to the present, including a schwa-like vowel inserted between *l* and *m* in words like *film* and *elm.* It's found in Dutch and various British dialects (Northern Irish English, Geordie) and some American dialects, cf. the Dallas, Texas neighborhood *Deep Elm*, pronounced [ɛləm], e.g. in the song title 'Deep Elm Blues'. Many Americans produce it in words like *athlete* without even realizing it: *ath*[ə]*lete* with three syllables rather than the expected two.
- Metathesis: especially with *r* and vowels, we often find reversal of sounds: Old English *beorht* and *fyrhto* have become *bright* and *fright.*
- Reduction and simplification of a cluster: many West Germanic languages vocalize *r* in codas, lose the consonantal character of the liquid, and produce it as a glide- or vowel-like sound. We find this with southern British, Boston, coastal Southern and African-American varieties of

American English. Dutch speakers do this with *l* in coda clusters: German *alt* = Dutch *oud*. Southern US speakers, among others, do this as well, and it's pervasive with *-lk* in certain words, especially before a low vowel—like in *talk, walk*—but for some speakers not in *milk*.

- Another related strategy is the outright loss of a consonant: Standard German maintains a cluster in *Nacht, Recht, Licht*, while English and some German dialects, e.g. in the Rhineland, have lost the fricative.

OHG speakers resolved the problem of complex coda clusters in a variety of ways, all of which served to create syllable structures more like those familiar from other languages.

Let's move on to the overall shapes of syllables. In Germanic, the following syllable types are typically posited (after Lass 1994 and other sources, but illustrated with OHG examples):[13]

light	V(C)	*ha.so* 'rabbit', *hol* 'cave'
heavy	VV(C)	*hrô* 'raw', *hûs* 'house'
	VCC	*hrust* 'armor, etc.' (cf. *Rüstung*)

Syllable weight is thus calculated usually without concern for the onset, just the amount of material in the nucleus and coda. You'll need to keep in mind the distinction between light syllables—short vowel alone or short vowel followed by a single consonant—and heavy syllables—long vowel with or without a consonant after it or short vowel plus two consonants. Using the notion of moras introduced earlier (see p. 137), phonologists refer to the former as monomoraic, having one mora, and the latter as bimoraic, having two moras.

Foot structure has spawned much discussion (Riad (1988), various works of Dresher & Lahiri, Page (1999), and Smith (2004 and subsequent works). The main point for our purposes is that the Germanic foot was 'left-headed', that the first syllable is the 'stronger' ('s'), typically stressed, while the other is 'weaker' ('w').

Prokosch recognized long ago that stressed syllables in early Germanic were or became heavy, that is, they had or somehow developed two moras, known now as Prokosch's Law, but also the Weight Law or Stressed Syllable Law.

---

[13] We will ignore, as we did earlier, material before the vowel which does not 'count' in the relevant sense. A period (.) indicates a syllable boundary.

Here again, different languages and dialects find a variety of ways to obey the law (as argued first by Murray & Vennemann 1984), so to speak: gemination, as shown earlier, creates a heavy initial syllable. In other situations, we have Open Syllable Lengthening, where short vowels in light initial syllables become long, as we'll find in German later.

The foot is generally important for Germanic phonological history. Dresher & Lahiri (1991) propose that a range of Germanic sound patterns, synchronic and diachronic, can be captured in terms of foot structure. They define the 'Germanic foot' as 'maximally binary, left-headed, where the head must dominate at least two moras' (1991: 251), where the head could include one or two syllables and the non-head element may contain only one mora. This includes Prokosch's insight, but also the preference for a short, weak second syllable, to which we now turn.

Why does reduction of unstressed final syllables happen? The standard story is that the fixing of stress on initial syllables, together with the rise of intensity as the main marker of stress, leads to these reductions. But some languages show initial stress without apparent reduction, such as initially-stressed but richly inflecting languages like Finnish.

A more nuanced view is that languages differ in how they arrange the timing of longer stretches of speech. Within the overall durational patterns of 'stress-timed' languages, some higher level patterns—say, the foot—remain stable, while the timing of lower level patterns—say, the syllable—are skewed by stress. By contrast, 'syllable-timed' languages (French, Spanish) are thought to have relatively stable timing of each syllable. That is, in a stress-timed language like Germanic, the building of the stressed syllable comes at the direct expense of the unstressed syllable. The claim is that we find asymmetries like these, where the boxes represent syllables and the length shows the duration:

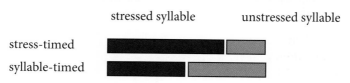

If this view is right, the shorter time for the unstressed syllable makes it hard to fully articulate the unstressed sounds, so that, for example, 'full' vowels are prone to end up being pronounced like schwas to the extent that children learning the languages would hear and learn those vowels as schwas rather than as full vowels. This relies on duration as a way of marking stress, rather than pitch or intensity, and these factors may work hand in hand.

Still, the phonetics of this type of imbalance have recently been the subject of important work. Recent research shows that speakers of languages like

English and German use much more forceful articulation (more movement of the tongue, longer holding of positions, etc.) in stressed positions, while these are more reduced in unstressed positions. That could be the seed that these changes grow from, but a tremendous amount of work remains to be done. For instance, Menz (2010) tests whether some languages which conserve more suffixal morphology actually skew duration less than closely related ones that have reduced endings more, and finds no correlation.

One pattern has been explored in detail by Smith (2004, 2007), namely that heavy-stem words (with a heavy stem syllable) show faster and clearer loss of their final syllables than short-stem words (with only a short vowel and one consonant in the stem syllable). She argues that Germanic speakers had and have a strong sense of how much phonetic material words contain where. That is, we come to expect sounds to be organized into certain patterns or templates, like the Germanic foot, which yields a nice rhythm of long-short, long-short, and so on.

The road to ruin: some patterns of reduction. Here are some key examples to help illustrate concretely the transition from IE to more German-like morphology, drawn in part from Boutkan 1995. These changes generally don't apply to MONOSYLLABIC words, only UNSTRESSED FINAL syllables.

Consonants. Germanic historical linguists traditionally distinguish 'gedeckter' vs. 'absoluter' Auslaut. In the former, the vowel of the last syllable is followed by a consonant or consonants, so the vowel is 'covered'. In the latter, the final vowel is the last sound. In gedeckter Auslaut, vowels are found longer in the historical record, because of the 'protection' of the consonant, assuming that things tend to erode from the right edge of the word toward the left. This can be seen in the development of a word like *horn*. In the last chapter, we saw that early Runic has the form *horna* (Gallehus). By OHG, we see the modern-like form without *a*.

- **-m > -n, then > Ø in polysyllabic words.**
  Lat. tum 'then' = OHG *dann* (but a controversial connection, cf. Lehmann 1986)
  IE *kloybh-om = Gmc *hlaiba* > OHG *hleib* 'bread', ACC.SG.

The word-final nasal is lost early, and then the vowel already by OHG. This particular development obviously obscures the class marking of the weak or *n*-stem nouns mentioned in Chapter 3: whereas they were clearly marked in IE by *-n, that's gone in Germanic: *zunga* (*Zunge*), *hano* (*Hahn*), etc.

- **IE final alveolar stops > Ø**
  IE *nepōt > *neffo*

- **s > Ø in the West.** IE *s became -*z/-s*, depending on Verner's Law; in final position it weakened to *z before being lost. We see this development in attested languages: *gastiz gives us Gothic *gasts* (Gothic final devoicing turned the *z* into *s*), Runic *gastiR* and Old Norse *gestr*, but OHG *gast_*, ON *dagr* vs. OHG *tag_*, etc. -*z* is lost after -*m*- or -*n*-:

PGmc   *gastimz > OHG gestim   'den Gästen'
PGmc   *beramiz > Got. berom   'wir tragen'

Vowels. As we just saw, a 'mora' is a timing unit of which short vowels have one and long vowels have two. The BASIC RULE is that final vowels in Germanic lose a mora, so that:

- short vowels > Ø,
- long vowels > short.

By the 10th and 11th centuries, all of the remaining forms come to be spelled <e>, probably pointing to normal pronunciation as a schwa.

Two further points where the 'weight' or amount of phonetic material in the stem is important to understanding the changes:

Short vowels. /a/ and /e/ are lost but /i/ and /u/ are kept in short-stem words, that is, words with short vowel followed by only one consonant. /i/ and /u/ ARE lost in long-stems (long vowel, diphthong, or short vowel + more than one consonant) or in third syllables.

*siduz	>	*situ*	Sitte, 'custom' (vowel kept in 'short-stem')
*esti	>	*ist*	ist, 'is' ('long-stem')
*nemiti	>	*nimit*	nimmt, 'takes' (third syllable)
*tageso	>	*tages*	Tages, 'day' GEN.SG. (third syllable)

Rückumlaut. The interaction between these reductions and losses and sound changes like umlaut and gemination can be rich, and they have left distinct patterns in German. Consider verbal alternations in the modern language like *kennen ~ kannte, brennen ~ brannte*, historical -*jan* verbs where the infinitive shows what must be an umlauted vowel but the preterit forms do not. These data confused early scholars and Grimm treated them as cases of umlaut reversal or de-umlauting of sorts, coining the name 'Rückumlaut'. You have the tools to understand how these patterns came about.

In present forms of weak -*jan* verbs, we can find gemination AND umlaut, both caused by the /j/, for example, in Germanic *brannjan, eventually umlauting to *brennjan*, before disappearing, yielding *brennen*. In early OHG, you have syncope (vowel loss) in many unstressed MEDIAL syllables, especially important in just these preterits of LONG-STEM-*jan* verbs. That is, three-syllable words with a heavy initial syllable were prone to lose their middle vowel. The original suffix of the 'dental preterit' was something like *-iða, and thus loses its first vowel, so that a form like *brann-iða becomes *brannða. Since this /j/ or /i/ (depending on its position relative to other vowels and consonants) is lost early in preterits, we do not have umlaut: this particular word form was no longer formed with -i/-j at the time umlaut happened. In short, -i/-j causes umlaut where it stays, on the one hand, but it gets lost in long stems on the other and so there's no umlaut in the preterits. In participles, you find variation based on these two possible formations. See Table 4.2.

TABLE 4.2 **Class i weak or *-jan* verbs in OHG**

INF.	PRET.	PAST PART.	GLOSS
brennen	*branta*	*gibrennit*	'to burn'
sterken	*starcta*	*gistarkit*	'to strengthen'
zellen	*zalta, zelita*	*gizalt, gizelit*	'to say, tell'

Sources: Braune & Eggers (1986); Holsinger & Salmons (1999).

In the Laws of Finals, vowels are lost sooner after long stems (CVVC-/CV:C or CVCC-, like *teilen*, *hôren*, or *sterken*) than short ones (CVC, like *nerien*), including in unstressed medial syllables. As noted, the weak suffix -ita (< -iða) loses its vowel in long stems, creating this pattern of umlautlessness in long-stem preterit forms.

   To make things more complicated, past participles had two forms: -it (with umlaut) and one inflected like an adjective. A masculine nominative had the dental suffix plus -er (like Modern German *ein schöner Tag*).[14] Competition between these two kinds of forms creates ambiguity in the past participle, as shown below:

Infinitive	PGmc	Preterit	Past participle	Stem type
brennen	*branjan	*branta*	*gibrennit/gibrant-*	-VCC- = long stem
lôsen 'loosen'	*lôsjan	*lôsta*	*gilôsit/gilôst-*	-V:C- = long stem
feren 'ferry'	*farjan	*ferita*	*giferit*	-VC- = short stem (no gemination), so *i* stays

---

[14] The preterit subjunctive forms had an *i* but almost never umlaut: *branti*, etc. These forms were pretty rare, though, and often involved blocking environments, such as *zalti*, *starkti*, etc. Even Otfrid, who normally umlauts at every opportunity, writes *zalti* or retains the medial vowel that is often lost, so *zeliti*.

OHG and MHG had a considerable set of such verbs, over 200, but the pattern was mostly leveled out in the modern language. We still see the effects of this in forms like:

kennen   kannte
brennen brannte.

To conclude this section, while we saw prosody shaping sounds earlier—from the CVC template for IE roots—and the beginning of reduction of unstressed final syllables even in Runic, these processes are now in full swing, so that even for Germanic, Ramat (1981: 62) could talk about a 'crisis in the inflectional system'. Whatever its ultimate causes, ongoing reduction drives much of the change from OHG to the present day, in particular the reshaping of morphological classes.

Overview of sound changes. In the last chapter, sound changes discussed were posited for reconstructed languages and thus relatively uniform—in the absence of messy attested data. With the emergence of OHG, we can see more information about the order of changes, patterns of conditioning from surrounding sounds, and especially the regional differences that we find from the earliest texts. Here's a capsule summary of sound changes here:

Consonants:

- Gemination
- The Second Sound Shift, variable across dialects and by position of the consonant
- The *Medienverschiebung*, yet more variable
- The 'stopping' of þ to *d*.

All of these are found more developed and/or earlier in the south and to a lesser extent or later moving north.

- /x/ weakening
- rhotacism, or *z to *r*.

Vowels:

- Height harmony: raising and lowering, with some blocking
- *i*-umlaut: unfolding from primary umlaut (with blocking) to a general process
- Lowering of $\bar{e}$ to $\bar{a}$, with the rise of new $\bar{e}^2$
- Partial assimilation in diphthongs (*au > *ou*, etc.) and conditioned monophthongization, variably by dialect
- The Laws of Finals begin to weaken final vowels and consonants, sensitive to syllable weight (long versus short) and syllable count (medial syllables in tri-syllabics).

4.2 Old High German dialects

Starting from a good knowledge of Modern German, it is surprisingly easy to learn to recognize the regional background of an OHG text.[15] Dialect variation is so pervasive and complex in OHG that specialists often say that each text has its own grammar, which is not much of an exaggeration—though Seiler (2014) shows far more orthographic consistency than previous scholars have generally recognized. For this reason, we will keep things pretty simple. For most purposes, it is easiest and fully adequate to divide the texts into three groups/areas:

- Northern
- Central
- Southern.

This is also the basic approach taken with Modern German dialects. Indeed, you already know the major features:

- Second Sound Shift
- *Medienverschiebung*. We can think of this extending to the related northern retention of 'th' relatively late for *d*.

A few other differences can be useful, even if they are less common in texts:

- Vowel height differences in *io/iu* before labial and velar consonants, where northern dialects have *io* and southern dialects have *iu*.
- Umlaut blocking is inconsistent in many texts, but lack of blocking quite often points to Otfrid's work, and occasionally to Franconian texts more generally.
- We find a tendency to break up clusters with *l, r, h* + C especially in the south: *perec* 'Berg', *starah* 'stark'.
- Unstressed prefixes differ regionally: northern with *i* (*zi-, fir-, gi-*) versus southern *za-, far-, ga-/ka-*.

Other features can suggest that a text is northern, often things that tend to look like English (and Low German, Dutch, Frisian):

- *he* instead of *er*
- *r* metathesized with some vowels: *Kirst* for *Krist*. This pattern is visible in the modern languages and dialects in many instances, like between English and German—*burn* vs. *brennen*, or regionally in Germany— *Paderborn* vs. *Heilbronn*, etc.
- *v* used for expected *b*: *selvo* 'self' vs. *selbo*.

---

[15] Sonderegger and Keller give detailed information on OHG dialects and works by Penzl describe the grammar of individual texts or authors.

With those tools and a little practice, you will be able to locate an OHG text within the three general regions mentioned at the beginning of this section, make good suggestions about closer regional identification for many texts, and identify examples of dialect mixing. A careful eye searching for signs of reduction of unstressed syllables (and the *th* to *d* change in some cases) may even discern something about chronology, whether texts are early or late.

The main centers of scribal activity are shown in Map 10. Each center had its own traditions, and many scribes presumably came from the surrounding areas, so tended to speak local dialects. In practice, many texts show mixed features, sometimes dramatic and impossible mixtures, of the sort that must have sounded like someone with a strong Liverpudlian accent using Southern US features like *y'all* and *might should*.

These patterns of dialectal inconsistency have various explanations, like speakers/writers of one dialect copying or interpreting a text written by someone with a different dialect. The movement of scribes and manuscripts from one monastery to the next plays a role here, something philologists sometimes call 'scribal traffic' or 'manuscript traffic'.

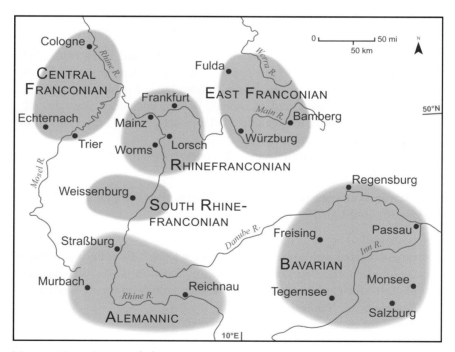

MAP 10 Major OHG scribal centers.
Adapted from König et al. (2015: 66).

Example texts. With that background, let us move on to some actual OHG texts. Look at the materials that follow and try to establish what dialect they are written in, keeping track of what features you use to make the judgment. While no translations and few glosses are provided, most of the basic meaning of the texts can be deciphered with a little work. For that, use the same strategy you would with any text in a language you don't know well: read a couple of lines, identify familiar material, use context, etc. Most of these samples come from here: http://texte.mediaevum.de/ahd.htm. (Sources like the one in that link also typically identify dialects and, if you need, often provide translations.)

Let's start with a text that is familiar to many readers (and see also a manuscript image of another version in Figure 4.3):

Pater noster (from the *Weißenburger Katechismus*).

Fater unser, thu in himilom bist,
giuuihit si namo thin. quaeme richi thin.
uuerdhe uuilleo thin, sama so in himile
endi in erthu. Broot unseraz emezzigaz*   *steadfast, cf. German *emsig*
gib uns hiutu. endi farlaz uns sculdhi unsero,
sama so uuir farlazzem scolom unserem.
endi ni gileidi unsih in costunga*.   *Cf. Gm *kosten* 'to try, taste'
auh arlosi unsih fona ubile.

Credo

Kilaubu in kot fater almahticun̥
kiskaft himiles enti erda
enti in Ihesum Christ
sun sinan ainacun
unseran truhtin*,   *lord, master
der inphangan ist fona uuihemu keiste,
kiporan fona Mariun macadi euuikeru,
kimartrot in kiuualtiu Pilates
in cruce pislacan,
tôt enti picrapan...

Spurihelti (this is an example of a charm, used to heal an animal)

Primum pater noster   (First, say the Lord's Prayer)
Visc flot aftar themo uuatare,
uerbrustun sina uetherun:
tho gihelida ina use druhtin*.   *= *truhtin*
The seluo druhtin,

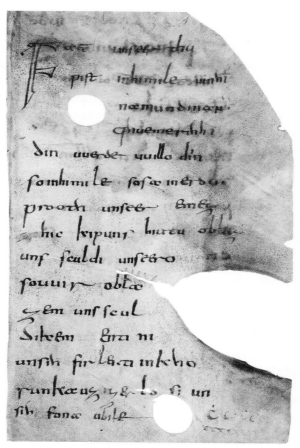

FIGURE 4.3 Lord's Prayer, from the Abrogans.

thie thena uisc gihelda,
thie gihele that hers theru spurihelti.
Amen.

Pariser Gespräche (described at the beginning of this chapter):

31. Guer is tin erro? (ubi est senior tuus?)
32. Ne guez. (nescio.)
51. Gimer min ros. (da mihi meum equum.)
52. Gimer min schelt.
53. Gimer min spera.

55. Gimer min ansco.
56. Gimer min stap.
57. Gimer min matzer.
58. Gimer cherize.
59. Guar es taz uip?
106. Trenchet cher guole in gotes mine, in aller gotes helegen

Ludwigslied (this is the beginning of a song of praise, celebrating King Ludwig for his victory over the Norse at Saucourt in 881. This is probably the hardest to decipher in the current set).

> Einan kuning uueiz ih, Heizsit her Hluduîg,
> Ther gerno gode thionôt: Ih uueiz her imos* lônôt.   *= *ihm+es*
> Kind uuarth her faterlôs, Thes uuarth imo sâr buoz:
> Holôda inan truhtîn, Magaczogo uuarth her sin.
> Gab her imo dugidi, Frônisc githigini,
> Stuol hier in Urankôn. So brûche her es lango! . . .

While we are not directly concerned with literary activity per se here, this period represented the beginning of known creative writing in German. We have seen a good range of texts—religious, historical, and some of the handful of pre-Christian charms. Bostock (1976) provides the best introduction to this body of work in English, as literary works set in their historical, social, and linguistic context. See also more recent works like Schlosser (2004) or Müller (2007), both including texts with translations. The best scholarly edition is Braune (1994).

4.3 Old High German morphology

In many basic structures, OHG stays close to the Germanic patterns you've already learned, and from there, the effects of final weakening yield many modern forms. The other big factor, which we'll deal with soon, is a trend toward ironing out irregularities, a movement toward regularization in various respects. Overall then, things look much more familiar at this stage. A few verbs change classes, move from strong to weak, but the real action comes in the effects of sound changes—the changes we've just discussed start to obscure the nice clean patterns of Proto-Germanic. Overall, as Harbert notes (2007: 270), verbs have many more inflectional categories than nouns in Germanic and they have 'in general more successfully resisted the effects of final syllable reduction.' The types of verbs are still weak versus strong, as well as preterit presents and a handful of truly irregular verbs. And the relevant categories for which verbs are inflected are familiar: the tense system is widely described as contrasting just 'present' versus 'past', leading to the old joke among linguists that 'Germanic has no future'.[16] We also distinguish indicative, imperative, and subjunctive (often called 'optative'), with inflection for the person and number of the subject.

In this period we see some familiar patterns of derivation. For instance, verbs already show the general kinds of prefixes we see today in terms of separable and inseparable. Kuroda (2007) analyzes verbal prefixes in the *Evangelienbuch* and points to patterns still visible today, where prefixing changes the argument structure of a verb, for example *bi-* (modern *be-*), makes some intransitive verbs transitive, along with some semantic changes. Such derivations accelerate and become more productive, over time, but the point for now is that OHG already has them.

Let us turn now to the main types of verbs, exemplifying their inflection in ways aimed at helping you better decipher OHG texts.

Weak verbs. We have three Germanic classes: i *-jan*, ii *-ōn*, iii *-ēn*, along with a handful of remnants that may or may not reflect Germanic weak class iv, which we can ignore.

The second and third classes are basically as we saw for Proto-Germanic in the last chapter (with lots of denominatives in ii and inchoatives or duratives in iii):

ii.	*badōn*	'bathe'	*badōta*	*gibadōt*
iii.	*fūlēn*	'become rotten'	*fūlēta*	*gifūlēt*

The personal endings are generally fairly straightforward, with a couple of notable exceptions:

- We've mentioned 'cliticization', the process of reduced forms attaching to, or glomming onto, larger chunks of sound. The 2nd singular gets a *-t* added to the old *-s* (German *-(e)st*). This was probably driven by the frequent presence of postposed pronouns. The pronoun in phrases like *zelis dū* would have cliticized onto the verb, as happens in colloquial modern forms of the sort *haste* 'hast du', eventually leading child learners to interpret the ending as *-st* rather than *-s*. Somers (2011) shows that the change began with *bis* > *bist*, and spread to other verbs, especially where the verb was or could be followed by a pronoun.

  Regionally, we find an immediate parallel development with the plural verb form in many kinds of Bavarian, i.e. *-ts*, attested in forms like *draipts* for German 'ihr treibt' or *zitsts* 'ihr sitzt' (Wiesinger 1989:42). This ending comes from the old dual pronoun *ez* added to the usual second plural verbal suffix *-et* (Schirmunski 2010: 591, Wiesinger 1989: 39).

---

[16] The joke doesn't work as well as it once did: given the tremendously thriving research programs on the languages, the field of study has a future.

This kind of reanalysis over boundaries isn't uncommon, in English for example with *an* before vowel-initial words:

○ *an apron* was once *a napron*
○ *a newt* was once *an ewt*.

Contemporary English has related phenomena, like *a whole nother*.

• The 1st plural shows lots of early forms with *-mēs*, as indicated earlier. The original form would have been simply a vowel plus *-m*. People speculate that this could have come from an IE form, but this is less than certain. At any rate, while it's well attested in OHG, this suffix was leveled out to plain *-en* even in late OHG.

Endings. Here are the key categories and the most typical variants, according to the handbooks:

	i suoch(i)en		ii salbōn		iii habēn	
	Sg	Pl	Sg	Pl	Sg	Pl
1st	suochu	suochemēs	salbōm	salbōmēs	habēm	habēmēs
2nd	suochis(t)	suochet	salbōs(t)	salbōt	habēs(t)	habēt
3rd	suochit	suochent	salbōt	salbōnt	habēt	habēnt
Pres opt	Sg	Pl	Sg	Pl	Sg	Pl
1st	suoche	suochēm	salbo	salbōm	habe	habēm
2nd	suochēs(t)	suochēt	salbōs(t)	salbōt	habēs(t)	habēt
3rd	suoche	suochēn	salbo	salbōn	habē	habēn
Pret	Sg	Pl	Sg	Pl	Sg	Pl
1st	suohta	suohtum	salbōta	salbōtun	habēta	habētun
2nd	suohtōs(t)	suohtut	salbōtos(t)	salbōtut	habētos(t)	habētut
3rd	suohta	suohtun	salbōta	salbōtun	habēta	habētun
Imp	suochi	suochet	salbo	salbōt	habe	habēt
Past part	gisuochit		gisalbōt		gihabēt	

If we step back and look at the general picture of the personal endings, things are much richer than in the modern language, where first person singular present forms are just *-e* (save for modal verbs, see pp. 154–155, 271–273), and the differences between first and third person plural endings in the present have been erased. Still, these are recognizably related to modern forms, as in these:

Pres	OHG	Modern
Sg 1st	suoch**u**	suche
2nd	suochis(t)	suchst
3rd	suochit	sucht
Pl 1st	suoche**mēs**	suchen
2nd	suochet	sucht
3rd	suoche**nt**	suchen

Strong verbs. Again, we have the same seven classes as earlier and the same basic forms. Vowel changes trigger splits in patterns, which makes them interesting:

	Infin	3sg. pres	sg. pret	pl.pret	past part	Key sound changes[17]
I	trīban	trībit	treib	tribun	gitriban	ai > ei
	zīhan	zīhit	zēh	zigun	gizigan	ai > ei > ē / __ r, l, h; Verner
II	sliofan	sliufit	slouf	slufun	gisloffan	eu > io/iu; au > ou
	siodan	siudit	sōd	sutun	gisotan	au > ou > ō before / __ r, l, h, alveolar
III	werfen	wirfit	warf	wurfun	giworfan	
	spinnan	spinnit	span	spunnun	gispunnan	**e > i / __ NC, -nC- = no lowering**
IV	stelan	stilit	stal	stālun	gistolan	ē > ā
V	geban	gibit	gab	gābun	gigeban	ē > ā
VI	tragan	tregit	truog	truogun	gitragan	**Primary umlaut, ō > uo**
VII	heizan	heizit	hiaz	hiazun	giheizan	**ai > ei; ē² > ia**
	lāzan	lāzit	liaz	liazun	gilāzan	ē > ā, ē² > ia; **ā doesn't umlaut yet.**

(*zīhan = zeihen, sliofan = schlüpfen, siodan = sieden*)

---

[17] The notation here is probably intuitively clear, but just in case it is not, '>' means 'becomes' (see Guide to Symbols) and the material after the slash indicates the environments where it happens. In the second set under class I, the change happens when the consonants given follow (in addition to Verner's Law, an independent pattern.) Height harmony effects are common throughout (§4.1.2, here) and are not marked.

You still see the effects of Verner's Law, as in the second example in class I. Verner alternations are mostly lost, but a few hang on (and see *wesan* pp. 125 and 155):

snīdan/gisnitan
friosan/gifroran
ziohan/gizogan.

All this makes it clear how the clean system of earliest (pre-)Germanic continues to unravel: a mounting pile of sound changes interferes with recognition of the simple *e a Ø Ø* ablaut as it interacted with the clear CV structure of the first five classes. Presumably as a consequence, a few verbs now fail to follow the consonant-vowel templates reconstructed for Germanic. That is, they do not belong to an ablaut series based solely on their Germanic root structures. We have three verbs with *ū* (*sūfan* 'saufen') in class II and a few verbs in class IV with stems ending in *-h(h)-* (*brehhan*, *sprehhan*). The basic system, though, is strikingly intact.

Endings. You can see that these endings are like those of the *-jan* verbs:

	faran	
Pres	**Sg**	**Pl**
1st	faru	faremēs
2nd	feris(t)	faret
3rd	ferit	farent
Pres opt	**Sg**	**Pl**
1st	fare	farēm
2nd	farēs(t)	farēt
3rd	fare	farēn
Pret	**Sg**	**Pl**
1st	fuor	fuorun
2nd	fuori	fuorut
3rd	fuor	fuorun
Imp	far	faret
Past part	gifaran	

Preterit–present verbs. In the IE system, we noted briefly that some verbs were 'stative', reflecting states of being rather than actions, generally speaking.

They look different, as the name suggests and as noted in Chapter 3, because the present tense forms look like preterit forms, for instance in the *a* vocalism they often show and the zero-suffix in 1st and 3rd person singular. Under a dozen of these verbs exist in OHG, and a couple others have faded to occasional remnants. In fact, many of the preterit presents are only partially attested—that is, we cannot piece together full paradigms for them even drawing on all OHG texts. Furthermore, a couple of old Germanic ones have been lost altogether. Finally, there is also a lot of regional variation and change over time with these—in other words, it's an unstable set.

They have the characteristic present tense inflections that look like past strong verbs and their preterit forms are formed with a dental suffix but without the initial vowel we have generally seen (-*ta*, -*da*). Like strong verbs, their ablaut forms reflect the CV structure of the stem, though the patterns are different.

INFINITIVE	3RD SG.PRES.	PRETERIT
kunnan	kan	konda, konsta
durfan	darf	dorfta
scolan	scal	scolta
magan, mugan	mag	mahta
muoʒan	muoʒ	muosa/muosta

Specialists understand most of the major complications in these forms, and they often result from a lack of a 'linking vowel' (*i*) before the preterit suffix. For example, there's an old (but rare) change whereby *t+t* became a long *s* (cf. *wissa*, on the next page). When *g* stood before a *t*, it becomes *h* (so, *mahta*), and so on.

In many ways, though, we can surely speak of these verbs as playing the role of modal verbs by this period: they still have meanings as normal 'lexical' verbs—i.e. not just auxiliaries but as stand-alone verbs. For example, *thurfan/durfan* is defined in Braune & Ebbinghaus's OHG glossary as 'Mangel haben, entbehren, bedürfen, nötig haben', while *magan/mugan* is glossed as 'vermögen, können'. Such patterns continue down to the present (cf. *sie kann Deutsch*) and we'll discuss the evolving and splitting meanings of these verbs later but note that they are already being used not as free-standing verbs but here together with infinitives (example from Schrodt 2005):

uuaz mag tougenora sin?
What may be more secret?

Not all the contemporary modals became modals at the same time (and we're developing new ones today, as we'll discuss in Chapter 7). Diewald (1999) analyzes the core OHG modal system as consisting of *mugan (mögen), skulan (sollen)*, and *wellen (wollen)*. Others, the ancestors of *müssen, können, dürfen*, were not yet fully formed modals, but more like full verbs.

Let's turn now to the forms of *wiȝȝan* 'to know'.

	Sing	**Plural**	
1	weiȝ	wiȝȝum	Opt.: wiȝȝi (3rd sg.), etc.
2	weist	wiȝȝut	Pret.: wista, wissa
3	weiȝ	wiȝȝun	

This verb does not become a modal, but retains full, lexical meaning.

Irregular verbs (athematic). Few verbs were truly irregular in OHG. The notable example is 'to be' (cf. §3.5). This is a highly frequent verb and as noted earlier highly frequent words often show irregularities. Consider a couple of brief examples, 'be', 'do', 'to want' (a 'preterit optative' verb rather than a preterit present).

'to be'		**'to do'**		**'to want'**	
bim	birum	tuon	tuomēs	willu	wellemēs
bist	birut	tuos(t)	tuot	wili	wellēt
ist	sint	tuot	tuont	wili	wellent

Optative					
sī + pers. ending:				'e' stem vocalism:	
ih/er sī		(wild variation)		ih welle	
du sīs(t), etc.				du wellēs	

Even today *sein* contains forms from three IE verbs, **Hes-* (*ist, sind*, etc.), **bheuH-* (*bin, bist*), and **Hwes-* (*war, gewesen*). The preterit forms came from a strong class V *wesan*, from an IE verb meaning 'to live, dwell, pass the night'; it keeps Verner alternations down to the present, but otherwise reflects the least odd parts of this paradigm.[18]

4.3.1 Nominal morphology

Nouns. The basic outlines of OHG noun inflection show clear connections to contemporary German, but there's been a dramatic pattern of change: in early Germanic and well into OHG, the suffix on a noun provided speakers with much of the basic grammatical information a listener needed—case, number, gender/class. Today, we do all of that overwhelmingly with articles or adjective

---

[18] These verbs have changed meanings from IE (cf. Watkins 2000): **Hes-* from 'to be, to be true' (English *sin*, German *Sünde*), **bheuH-* from 'to exist, be, grow', with *o*-grade variants yielding *bauen, booth* and the second element of *husband*.

endings, as well as by the greater use of prepositions, as we'll explore in the section on syntax.

Keep in mind that the OHG nominal suffixes don't clearly distinguish the categories of number and case individually, but are 'portmanteau' morphemes, which we introduced in the last chapter, forms where a single marker (a suffix, in this case) signals more than one piece of grammatical information. For instance, OHG speakers knew that *tago* could ONLY be the genitive plural form of *tag* 'day' but there wasn't really a distinct, unified marker of plurality at that stage. Today, German tends to make a clear singular/plural distinction. And when a case marker is added, it's added onto the plural form: *Tage* but DAT.PL. *Tagen, Bücher* but DAT.PL. *Büchern.*

FIGURE 4.4 Notker Labeo relief, from the St. Gall Monastery. Notker Labeo, also known as Notker Teutonicus, was one of several Notkers of the period, known for extensive translations into OHG.

Let us take a somewhat closer look at four key examples of noun classes: *a*-stems (the biggest masculine and neuter class), the *ō*-stems (the biggest feminine class), the *i*-stems (which show us how umlaut came to mark plurals so clearly in Modern German), and the *n*-stems (which become the modern 'weak' or 'mixed declension' nouns). Following Sonderegger's model, the paradigms are presented further down divided into the earliest attested patterns and late OHG patterns (as represented by the works of Notker, who is depicted in Figure 4.4), to highlight the changes and to make clear how close the late OHG patterns are to German.

First, here are some key examples of noun classes, with rough indications of class size and showing genders, with classes underlined and subclasses not, drawn from Braune & Reiffenstein (2004):

a-stems [huge]

    masculine: tag, berg, (h)ring, scalk 'servant', fisk, (h)leib 'bread', hals, stuol, truhtīn 'lord', himil, kuning 'king', tiufal

    neuter: wort, kind, barn 'child', fel 'Fell', jār, swert, houbit 'head', honag 'honey'

ja-stems [subclass of a]: hirti, 'shepherd', kunni 'kin', hrucki 'back'

wa-stems [subclass of a, small]: hlēo 'hill, grave', snēo 'snow', sēo 'sea', wēo 'pain', bū 'Bau, Wohnung', kneo 'knee'

iz/az stems [small but growing]: lamb, kalb, huon 'chicken', farh 'Ferkel', blat, ei

ō-stems [huge].

    feminine: geba 'gift', erda, ēra 'honor', lēra 'Lehre', zala 'Zahl', fehta 'fight', manunga 'warning', samanunga 'Versammlung'

jō-stems [subclass of and eventually collapse with ō]. sunta 'sin', kuningin 'queen', reda 'Rede', hella 'hell', brucka 'bridge', minna 'love'

i-stems

    masculine: gast, liut 'people', bah 'creek', scaft 'speer', wurm 'worm', slag 'blow'

    feminine: anst 'joy', huf, huffi 'hip', hūt 'skin, hide', stat 'place', jugund, tugund 'virtue'

u-stems [mostly gone or going to *i*-stem, some to *a*-stem]

    masculine: sunu, hugu 'Sinn', sigu 'victory' fridu 'peace'

    feminine: hant

    neuter: fihu 'Vieh'

n-stems [huge]

    masculine: hano 'chicken', haso 'rabbit', garto 'garden', bero 'bear', sterno 'star', gomo 'man', namo 'name', boto 'Bote'

    neuter [small]: herza, ōra 'ear', ouga 'eye', wanga 'cheek'

    feminine: zunga, bluoma, sunna, diorna 'girl', wituwa, kirihha 'church', frouwa 'woman'

er-stems [very small]
    masculine: fater, bruoder,
    feminine: muoter, tohter, swester

The *a*-stems are common enough that we can readily think of them as a default noun class for masculine and neuter nouns. In a sense, this is what children learning OHG did, which promoted the growth of this class. Especially in the singular, the laws of finals reduced and eliminated differences between the *a*-stems and other classes (compare the singular forms to the masculine *i*-stem singulars presented further down).

a-stems, masculine

	Oldest	Late
Sg.N	tag	tag
G	tages	tages
D	tage	tage
A	tag	tag
I	tagu	
Pl.N	taga	taga
G	tago	tago
D	tagum	tagen
A	taga	taga

a-stems, neuter

	Oldest	Late
Sg.N	wort	wort
G	wortes	wortes
D	worte	worte
A	wort	wort
I	wortu	
Pl.N	wort	wort
G	worto	worto
D	wortum	worten
A	wort	wort

Handbooks like Braune & Reiffenstein (2004: 186) declare a majority of OHG masculine nouns to follow the *tag* pattern, including *berg, weg, geist, (h)leib, hals, helm,* and *stein* (all identical to Modern German forms), and *fisk* 'fish', *stuol* 'chair', *truhtin* 'lord', and *kuning* 'king'. Neuters like *wort* include *swert* 'sword', *barn* and *kind* 'child', *honag* 'honey', and *fuir ~ fiur* 'fire'.

We have talked briefly about the instrumental case, which was present but fading in Germanic. It's still around in this class, in the singular.

During Old High German, it dies out and prepositions that once governed instrumental come to govern dative. You will see in what follows that some paradigms had no instrumental forms in even earliest OHG.

We also see effects of the Laws of Finals, e.g. in dative plural -*um* > -*en*. This shows what's to come: in numerous other cells in the paradigm, once final vowels weaken to schwa, we have the modern system. The exception, where material seems to have been added, is the zero or unmarked plural of *wort* (NOM., ACC.). This is only an illusion of sorts, which we'll discuss later, with the rise of more distinct plural marking.

Turning to feminine nouns, the largest classes are the $\bar{o}$-stems and the *n*-stems (to which we'll turn momentarily).

$\bar{o}$-stems feminine

	Oldest	Late
Sg.N	geba	geba
G	geba	gebo
D	gebu	gebo
A	geba	geba
Pl.N	gebā	geba
G	gebōno	gebōn
D	gebōm	gebōn
A	gebā	geba

Examples include *erda* 'earth', *lēra* 'teaching', *zala* 'number', *fehta* 'battle', *(h)riuwa* 'sadness' (cf. *Reue*), and *farawa* 'color'. These nouns typically come to end in schwa, spelled -*e*. Since $\bar{o}$-stems were the largest feminine class, this creates in German the association between final -*e* and feminine, which in turn take an -*n* plural (a generalization that even beginners may learn). As we will see in the next chapter, many analyses connect the development of these feminine nouns with both the old $\bar{o}$-stems and the *n*-stems.

More broadly, categories that were distinctly marked (i.e. had different suffixes) in early OHG become identical in late OHG. In the plural, three of four cases were originally clearly marked: *gebōm* could only be a dative plural, for instance. In late OHG without some further context, we can only be sure that a plural form is NOM./ACC. or GEN./DAT., and the NOM./ACC. forms are the same across the singular and the plural.

Another significant class—*i*-stem nouns—looks like the *a*-stems in the singular, but shows clearly distinct plural forms. Unlike *a*-stems, this class included masculines and feminines:

i-stems

	Masculine		Feminine *anst* = Gunst	
	Oldest	Late	Oldest	Late
Sg.N	gast	gast	anst	anst
G	gastes	gastes	ansti	ensti
D	gaste	gaste	ansti	ensti
A	gast	gast	anst	anst
I	gastu/gastiu			
Pl.N	gasti	geste	ansti	ensti
G	gasteo, -io	gesto	ansteo, -io	ensto
D	gastim	gesten	anstim	enstin
A	gasti	geste	ansti	ensti

This class of *i*-stems was relatively large among masculine and feminine nouns plus a few neuters. Here too the effects of the Laws of Finals trigger a fundamental change: the *i* which triggers umlaut weakens and is variably lost during this period, more and sooner in long stems than in short. The umlaut stays. In *gast*, by the end of this period, this process creates a good correlation: as you can see in the 'late' columns here, no umlaut means singular; umlaut means plural.

This class is important for the clear association between plurality and umlaut, something which has grown stronger over time. Wurzel (1989 and many other works) has used just such examples in arguing that morphological change tends to bring to the fore ways of organizing language that make sense to speakers. In his view, the most 'natural' way to mark a category like plurality is by the addition of new material, like *Tisch* ~ *Tische*. Umlaut for marking plural, especially together with a suffix, is far more complex.

For the moment, note that Sonderegger's 'oldest' forms aim to capture the fact that our earliest texts quite often do not show primary umlaut.

Masculine *i*-stem nouns include *ast* 'branch', *liut* 'people', *bah* 'creek', *wurm* 'worm', *apful* 'apple', while the feminine members include *hūt* 'skin', *stat* 'place', *tugund* 'virtue', as well as nouns ending in the suffixes *-skaf* ~ *-skaft* (Modern German *-schaft*) and *-heit* (still *-heit* today).

Distinct in both appearance and inflection are the *n*-stems, source of 'weak' nouns.

n-stems

	M	N	F
Sg.N	hano	hërza	zunga
GD	hanen, hanin	hërzen, hërzin	zungūn
A	hanon, hanun	hërza	zungūn
Pl.NA	hanon, hanun	herzun, herzon	zungūn
G	hanōno	herzōno	zungōno
D	hanōm	herzōm	zungōm

Masculine nouns were particularly common among the *n*-stems. Even a quick look at these paradigms and a little knowledge of the Laws of Finals could easily suggest that you'd end up with modern forms that distinguish nominative singular forms in -*e* (schwa) or nothing, with other forms ending typically in -*n*.

A handful of those nouns have remained weak or 'mixed' down until recent times or even to the present, such as *boto* 'Bote', *namo* 'Name', *herro* 'Herr', *bero* 'Bär'. Numerous others have taken on the -*n* even in the nominative singular: *Garten* (< *garto*), *Samen* (*samo*), *Schaden* (< *scado*). (We'll talk more later about this.) Neuters and feminines are less resilient, though *Herz* shows modern oddities reflecting this history.

A note on other classes. Especially with the weakening of the suffixes, some of the smaller noun classes start to lose members, as they move to bigger classes. As noted in our first section on nouns, some nouns were originally athematic, basically monosyllabic nouns lacking thematic vowels (*zand/zan* 'tooth', *fuoȝ* 'foot'). These were few and had pretty minimal endings. *Man* is such a noun:

Sg.NA	man
G	man, mannes
D	man, manne
Pl.NA	man
G	manno
D	mannum, mannun

By OHG already, words like *zand* and *fuoȝ* had moved into other classes, the *i*-stems in this case, so that they end up umlauting in the plural. This is again a morphological realignment: these small classes lose members to bigger classes over time—just as 'strong' or ablauting verbs steadily move into the 'weak' or 'regular' group in German and English.

Still, even in OHG texts, most nouns already belong to the dominant classes (*a*-stem for masculine and neuter, *ō*-stem for feminine) and many others are readily recognizable (weak nouns, or the plural of the *i*-stems).

OHG had, as noted, the same three grammatical genders as the modern language. Many nouns vacillated, showing two or even three genders for a single noun in a single meaning (Froschauer 2003). As you see in this material, nominal classes correlate with gender—*a*-stems masculine or neuter, *ō*-stems feminine, etc.—with clear (though hardly rigid) connections to earlier IE correlations. There are semantic correlations as well, such as Grimm's observation that abstract nouns are relatively rarely masculine, but often feminine (Froschauer 2007), reflected in the feminine-assigning character of various abstract suffixes, from modern -*ung* and -*heit* back to OHG -*unga* and -*ida*.

Pronouns. OHG personal pronouns are largely recognizable (forms adapted from Braune & Reiffenstein 2004: 241–243):

	1st person	2nd person	3rd person masc.	neut.	fem.
Sg.N	ih	dū, du	ër	iȝ	siu, sī, si
A	mih	dih	inan, in	iȝ	sia, sie
G	mīn	dīn	sīn	ës, is	ira, iru
D	mir	dir	imu, imo	imu, imo	iru, iro
Pl.N	uuir	ir	sie	siu	sio
A	unsih	iuwih	sie	siu	sio
G	unsēr	iuwēr	iro	iro	iro
D	uns	iu	im, in	im, in	im, in

You'll notice that OHG showed some distinction of gender in the third person plural pronouns, something which has been largely lost, and which was already shaky in OHG texts.

Adjectives. One of the biggest challenges for learners of German today lies in mastering adjective endings. Once again, knowing history doesn't instantly help you learn them, but allows you to see how the modern system came about and helps you understand the logic of some patterns.

Weak. *n*-stem noun paradigms are close to the pattern of weak adjectives. In fact, they started out the same, but the adjective system gets reorganized to an extent. This set is a Germanic innovation, not an IE inheritance.

blinto   blinta   blinta
blinten . . . (etc.)

Strong. This set continues an old IE tradition of nominal inflection, with a mix between endings from the nouns and from pronouns, including 'demonstrative pronouns' that become definite articles. That is, many strong adjective endings closely resemble third person pronominal forms, like a masculine singular nominative ending in -*er* (cf. *er*), the accusative in -*n* (cf. *in*), the feminine nominative in *iu* (cf. *siu*). Again, these are traditionally traced to demonstrative pronouns.

dër tac   earlier: guot_ tac   later: guot**er** tac
daz uuord   earlier: guot_ uuord   later: guot**az** uuord

We traditionally indicate this mix by putting the endings that come from the pronominal system in boldface:

	Masc	**Neuter**	**Fem**	**Plural** (by gender in N-A)		
N	blint (-**ēr**)	blint (-**az**)	blint (-**iu**)	blint**e**	blint	blint**o**
A	blint**an**	blint (-**az**)	blint**a**	blint**e**	blint	blint**a**
G	blint**es**	blint**es**	blint**era**		blint**ero**	
D	blint**emu**	blint**emu**	blint**eru**		blint**ēm**	

Finally, the numerals 1–3 inflect in OHG. Let us illustrate this with some forms for 'two', which differ by gender, and the neuter forms show case inflection (Braune & Reiffenstein 2004: 234–235). This pattern was robust up until Early New High German and clear traces are still found in some modern dialects, for example East Franconian, where it is now limited to the neuter:

	Masc	**Neuter**	**Fem**
NA	zwēne	zwei	zwā, zwō
G		zweio	
D		zweim, zwein	

We will return to these sets in 6.3.

A cautionary note. What you have read so far reflects handbook wisdom. As you've seen in the treatment of dialects, almost every OHG dialect has its own striking characteristics and the variability is beyond even what the most capable mind can have the full scope of just from working with the texts. Remarkably, for all of the dissertations and books written on OHG, no one has pieced together the bigger picture of what forms actually are characteristic of what periods and dialects. Specialists regularly assume that the handbooks are not accurate, but piecing together the real data has only begun. Luiten (2011) and Luiten et al. (2013) show that much reduction happens earlier and more systematically than the handbooks would suggest, that is, that the typical forms of classic OHG look more like the modern language than handbook paradigms would suggest. They find patterns beyond simple chronology as well: the reduction of dative plural -*um* to -*en* does happen largely when the handbooks say, the earlier form in the 8th century and the innovative one in the 9th onward, but two major texts of the period, *Otfrid* and *Tatian*, overwhelmingly show the advanced forms, while other texts of the same period show about half -*m* and half -*n*. In short, our understanding of OHG morphology should be sharpened greatly in coming years.

4.4 Old High German syntax

Before OHG, we had too little data to say much about syntax, so that serious discussion begins here. Even OHG texts have surprisingly little 'normal' syntax.

Many are Latin translations and others are poetic. In close translations, word order follows the original: both Latin and OHG had relatively flexible word order, so the Latin order was often possible without creating overly odd clauses. Poetry manipulates word order to create rhymes or alliteration. Within those limits, though, we can make a lot of hay with OHG syntactic data, as expressly argued for the Tatian translation by Fleischer et al. 2008.[19] Many are willing to assume, it seems, that translations generally fall within the bounds of what is grammatical for the translator. That is, translations may be different from writing or speaking in the language, but we usually expect them to obey the basic rules of the language.

Early scholars certainly made significant contributions to historical and comparative syntax (such as Delbrück 1900, Neckel 1900, or Erdmann 1886) and research never died out, but in recent years we've seen the rise of really vigorous research programs in Germanic historical syntax that parallel what we have for vocabulary, sounds, and word forms. This section illustrates how people are approaching some of the key issues: after introducing the basic notion of syntactic constituency, we'll explore some issues in the relationship between syntax and morphology. We've already talked about the movement from synthetic to analytic, or more to less heavily inflected structures. The rise of greater periphrasis illustrates this in the verb system and the rise of articles does that for the nominal system. At the same time, we see movement in the opposite direction, the creation of increasingly grammatical forms, which we'll illustrate with cliticization and changes in negation.

'Constituency' is simply what units belong together and make up bigger units. Look at this sentence from Tatian, with a loose translation under it.

In themo sehsten mânude gisentit uuard engil Gabriel fon gote in thie burg Galilee, thero namo ist Nazareth, zi thiornûn gimahaltero gommanne, themo namo uuas Ioseph, fon hûse Davides, inti namo thero thiornîn Maria.

In the sixth month, the angel Gabriel was sent by God into a city of Galilee, the name of which is Nazareth, to a maiden engaged to a man,[20] whose name was Joseph, from the House of David, and the maiden's name was Mary.

---

[19] There are a few general treatments of German historical syntax, such as the relatively extensive but traditional Admoni (1990) and the briefer Ebert (1978), along with the new textbook by Fleischer & Schallert (2011).

[20] The preceding phrase means 'to a virgin/maiden engaged to a man'. *Thiorna* is a feminine ō-stem cognate with modern *Dirne*, 'girl, maiden', while *mahalen* is a weak verb meaning 'to promise' and *gomman* 'husband' is related to the *n*-stem noun *gomo* 'man', familiar as the last element of *Bräutigam* and *bridegroom*, cognate with Latin *homo*.

Within this sentence, you will recognize coherent pieces that fit together and form clear units. First, we can recognize CLAUSES, each with a verb. The sentence is given next with brackets around each clause. A couple of clauses—like *thero namo ist Nazareth*—are contained within another clause, or 'embedded'.

[In themo sehsten mânude gisentit uuard engil Gabriel fon gote in thie burg Galilee, [thero namo ist Nazareth], zi [thiornûn gimahaltero gommanne],] [themo namo uuas Ioseph, fon hûse Davides,] [inti namo thero thiornîn Maria].

The wrinkles even in this long sentence are minor. For instance, the last clause—*inti namo thero thiornîn Maria*—doesn't actually have a verb spelled out, but the clause parallels the previous one closely enough that it can be left out, like in Modern German *sie **ging** in den Park und ich* [ ] *nach Hause.*

If we take a clause, we can identify various PHRASES within it, in the (passive voice) main clause:

[In themo sehsten mânude] gisentit uuard [engil Gabriel] [fon gote] [in thie burg Galilee] [zi thiornûn] ...

Leaving aside the verbs for the moment, the subject is a phrase, 'angel Gabriel', and we see a set of prepositional phrases which contain other phrases. This includes one for the agent of the action ('by/from God'), as well as phrases indicating the time, place, and the person the angel was sent to visit.

Constituency can change over time. Consider the question of how complex constructions, like the multi-clausal sentence just treated, arise. For the relatively recent past, like the OHG period, the assumption is that the language had roughly the same level of complexity as today, at least in terms of what could be expressed. But how meanings get expressed can change. One way is that constituent structure gets reanalyzed, that is, interpreted by new learners/speakers as having a different structure from earlier. Take a simple example (based on Harris & Campbell 1995: 287–288):

> *Joh gizalta   in   sâr   thaʒ thiu sâlida untar in uuas. (Otfrid)*
> And told.3SG them immediately this,   the fortune among them was.
> 'And he told them immediately that good fortune was among them.'

As the punctuation (not in the original!) and the translation suggest, *thaʒ* is a demonstrative pronoun, part of the first clause. Over time, it was reanalyzed as part of the second clause, namely as a conjunction that marks the following material as a complement of the main clause, an element called a 'complementizer', abbreviated C. Note that the sentence is ambiguous in this way: either interpretation is in principle possible. This C eventually came to be spelled distinctly in German (*das, daß*). Just as we use tree structures to represent relationships among languages and syllable structure, we can use them in syntax. A phrase here is simply a single structural element and it's named for its main element, like Verb Phrase (VP). ('S' just means 'clause' here.) The left structure is the earlier and the right the later structure:

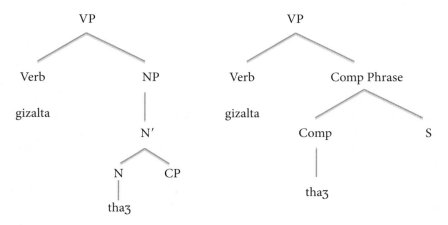

Periphrastic forms. You know that sound change interacts with word structure, or morphology, with sound changes often disturbing once-clear morphological patterns. Morphology also naturally interacts with sentence structure. We call these points of contact between parts of grammatical architecture 'interfaces'. An important example comes from the verbal system: OHG shows 'periphrastic' forms. PERIPHRASIS is simply the use of a set of words to express a grammatical category rather than an inflected form of a single word. For some Germans who use both, *die Frau arbeitete* and *die Frau hat gearbeitet* mean in practice similar or even identical things (aside from the difference in level of style). The first form is inflected and the second periphrastic: one has the inflection as part of the verb and the other uses a particular verb form (past participle) and an auxiliary (or 'helping verb', in this case *haben*) to express similar meanings. Periphrastic forms of the perfect and passive[21] are clearly found in OHG, and sources differ about whether we see the first signs of a *werden* auxiliary at this stage of the language. Otfrid writes:

| *thô* | *ward* | *mund siner* | *sâr* | *sprechhantêr* |
| then | became | mouth his | immediately | speaking |

'then his mouth at once began to speak'

---

[21] Gothic had an inflectional passive verb form, as just discussed. Even there, we find the equivalents of *werden* and *sein* passive forms.

Lockwood (1968: 111, English translation from there) interprets this use of *werden* plus a present participle as literally 'became speaking', arguing that it has an ingressive or inchoative meaning. That is, the 'become' verb was used to indicate that the meaning of another (main) verb was getting started. Schrodt (2004: 129–130) flatly rejects such interpretations, and argues that future meaning was signaled by the present tense used together with certain particles like *thane, noh, furdir, sar*, or by the use of modal verbs like *sculan* and even *wellan*.[22] German still shows widespread use of directly inflected forms for tense (like 'simple past') rather than periphrastic forms (like 'present perfect'), but we certainly see patterns of more than one verb in a clause.

habēn (or eigan) + past participle. The most discussed periphrastic construction in Europe is probably the present perfect. Early in the periphrastic construction in Europe is probably the present perfect. Early in the, and *eigan* has a similar meaning and function). Schrodt (2004: 16) argues that the past participle describes the object of *habēn*, with a sense of possession of the object.

> *phigboum*   *habeta*   *sum*   *giflanzotan*
> fig tree   had   somebody   planted
> 'somebody had planted a fig tree'.

His interpretation is that someone possessed a planted fig tree, which is true enough, but Lockwood (1968: 115) argues:

this example should only be quoted with the reservation that it can hardly have been idiomatic German at the time (ca. AD 830). It is too obviously a word-for-word rendering of the Latin sentence, which for that matter, is an equally servile calque on the Greek.

Participles, as already mentioned, were often inflected in OHG, like adjectives, and participles have similarities to adjectives more generally. I am wary of overinterpreting such data, though, since we don't have native speaker understanding of the patterns and the written data are quite sparse. Soon, we will see structures that look more like present perfects:

> *er*   *nehabet*   *irgezen*   *daz*   *uuir*   *stuppe*   *birn*
> he   not-has   forgotten   that   we   dust   are
> 'he hasn't forgotten that we are dust'.

A long tradition has speculated that because Latin (which was known and used in certain circles) had a preterit versus perfect system, OHG speakers took that as a model for creating new distinctions of their own, like the present perfect (Lockwood 1968: 114–115, elsewhere). This is highly unlikely: the community

---

[22] You'll recognize these as the source of English periphrastic future: *shall* and *will*.

of Latin–OHG bilinguals was presumably never terribly large, and it would be an unusual kind of language contact change for such a pattern to be transmitted through the whole population. In short, the development of the preterit versus perfect distinction was almost certainly an indigenous development, perhaps supported by non-native patterns. The claim of Latin influence exemplifies a pattern we'll see time and again in how the history of the language has been written: people have longed to find developments being driven by the adoption of forms used by some social and political elite (here, those fluent in Latin). In fact, relatively little change comes 'from above': the real action is almost always with 'the people', not the elite. At the same time, the geographical distribution of a periphrastic perfect formed with *have* and *be* as auxiliaries is striking. As detailed by Drinka (2004, 2015), these patterns are found in much of Europe but are rare outside of there, along with some clear structural parallels.

Periphrasis is hardly limited to the perfect. For instance, as just noted in fn. 21 on p. 166, Gothic has an inflected form of the passive, like *nimada* 'he/she/it was taken', (see Miller forthcoming), but in OHG, we find things like *wirdu gitoufit* '[I] get/come to be baptized'. Here too, then, we have the development of auxiliary verbs, called 'auxiliation'. We already find two kinds of passive in OHG, roughly parallel to Modern German: *wesan* + participle (*Zustand*) versus *werdan* + participle (*Vorgang*). These differ somewhat in meaning from the modern parallels, and their distributions vary greatly over the time and space of OHG, as detailed by Jones (2009).

In OHG, 'bare-infinitives' could appear with other 'main' verbs, as here (examples from Demske 2001b):

Táz **peginnet** si únsih nû   mit exemplis lángséimo   **lêren**. (Notker)
That begins   she us now   with examples thoroughly   to teach.
Das **beginnt** sie uns jetzt anhand von Beispielen ausführlich **zu lehren**.

As Demske's modern German translation shows, this requires a *zu* in the modern language. Constructions arise during the period with *zu (zi, ci)* + infinitive:

ih haben   thir   sihuuaz   ciquedanne
I have   to-you   something   to tell
'I have something to tell you'.

Related forms were also used nominally, as gerunds, e.g. inflected for case, as in this example:

Oba ir hiar findet iawiht thés thaz wirdig **ist des lésannes**.
Whether he here finds something which is worthy of reading
Ob er hier etwas findet, das **des Lesens** würdig **ist**

Determining which verb forms are verbal versus nominal is not always easy, and someone who wanted to argue that *zu* was always required could try to interpret the *lêren* in the Notker example above as nominal, by glossing it as 'she begins [the] teaching'. That interpretation seems unlikely here, for several reasons. First, there's already an often-used noun with that meaning, *lêra*. Second, we have an adverb form, *langseimo*, where a gerund would presumably have an adjectival forms (see the entry for *langsamî* in the *Etymologisches Wörterbuch des Althochdeutschen* 1988–). Of more interest, as we will see in later chapters, the presence or absence of *zu* is a test for modal status, as in contemporary forms like *man braucht das nicht* [zu] *Machen.*

Demske documents the broad and surprisingly complex patterns of such forms. We'll pursue further developments connected to periphrasis in later chapters, but let us turn now to a parallel set of changes in nominal morphology.

Subject pronouns and the rise of articles. Two striking characteristics of OHG syntax are the possibility of not having an expressed subject pronoun and not using what we informally call 'articles'. An example comes from one of our earlier dialect readings, the Alemannic *credo* (translation from Wipf 1992: 99):

Kilaubu in kot fater almahticun	**Ich** glaube an Gott, **den** allmächtigen Vater
kiskaft himiles enti erda	**den** Schöpfer[23] des Himmels und **der** Erde.

You see the absence of subject pronouns, and the verb form makes clear that the subject is first person singular. As already briefly introduced in the previous chapter, such deletion or omission of subject pronouns, 'pro-drop', is common in many languages, e.g. Spanish and Italian. In OHG, omission is thoroughly possible, but does not justify, in the view of many specialists, labeling OHG a 'pro-drop language' in a technical sense, since not all subject pronouns can be dropped in all contexts, a situation found only in Gothic among the Germanic languages, see Schrodt (2004: 76), Harbert (2007: 221–223). Axel (2007) presents a broad set of arguments for considering OHG a 'partial pro-drop language'.

The absence of subject pronouns is both widespread and variable across our OHG texts, as shown here for three large texts (Axel 2007: 300; this version is from work by Joshua Bousquette):

---

[23] *Kiskaft* is probably a translation error; the form would normally mean 'Schöpfung'.

	Main Clause		Subordinate Clause	
Text	Overt	Null	Overt	Null
Isidor	56% (n=61)	44% (n=48)	91% (n=85)	9% (n=8)
Monsee	36% (n=48)	64% (n=84)	85% (n=73)	15% (n=13)
Tatian	60% (n=1434)	40% (n=960)	92% (n=1180)	8% (n=95)

Isidor and Tatian use overt subject pronouns in main clauses over half the time, while the Monsee Fragments show them just over a third of the time. This variation is not simply across dialects, authors, and time, but also syntactic: overt pronouns are far more common in subordinate clauses than in main clauses.

According to Axel (2007: 321–322, also Eggenberger 1961), subject pronouns are overtly marked beginning after about 1000, so in late OHG. She argues against the common view that so-called null pronouns (as in the examples on the previous page) are connected to the richness of verbal morphology, since even modern German has relatively rich inflection and OHG had very full verbal inflection. Instead, following Sprouse & Vance (1999), she argues that this was not driven causally by any other grammatical change, but simply reflected the outcome of competition between null subject pronouns and overt ones. Briefly, clauses with subject pronouns are easier to process, biasing learners to opt for that structure.

Turning to articles, many languages do not have definite or indefinite articles, and other related elements like possessors, together called 'determiners'. Early Germanic was such a language. Their emergence in Germanic correlates with the increased use of subject pronouns, recognized since the time of Grimm as important developments. Pronominal elements (if not actual pronouns) develop first into demonstratives, like modern *dieser*, etc., and then into articles. The exact timing of these changes is somewhat controversial (see Abraham 1997 for one view).

Early Germanic patterns of not having articles and not requiring subject pronouns are common across languages, including in Europe. Early Germanic languages were like most Slavic languages in not using articles, although in OHG and in most Slavic languages, demonstratives (like *dieser*) and forms of 'one' could and still can be used in ways that resemble definite and indefinite articles, respectively.

The traditional account for the rise of articles was that they served to compensate in some sense for the case morphology being lost, and in Germanic it does appear that these changes happen at about the same time. Many people have found that connection intuitively appealing, and we find some correlations along these lines in Europe: Slavic and Finno-Ugric languages tend to have a lot of cases but lack articles, while Celtic and Romance have articles but much less case morphology. However, many languages of the world have rich case systems and articles or lack both, and not all languages which lose nominal morphology develop articles. That is, this compensatory strategy is perhaps a tendency but not a necessity.

To overcome these problems, Philippi (1997) pursues a somewhat different view, namely that all languages have strategies for marking definite versus indefinite (or specific/non-specific) noun phrases (*eine Katze, irgendwelche Katze* vs. *die Katze, diese Katze*). She argues that in early Germanic, including OHG, this was marked primarily with case while in several of the modern Germanic languages, including German, it is marked primarily with articles. She gives these kinds of examples:

> Indefinite = genitive
> skancta sinan fianton   **bitteres lides** (Ludwigslied)
> He poured his enemies **a** bitter drink.

> Definite = accusative
> Inti dir gibu   **sluzzila** himilo riches (Tatian)
> And to you I give **the** key to the kingdom of heaven.

Philippi lays out this loss of genitive and its correlation with the rise of articles. And once more, this piece of history helps us understand German. We have direct and indirect remnants of this system still in German, sometimes still marked with case:

> **Den ganzen Tag** hat sie Fußball gespielt.[24]
> **Eines Tages** ging sie einfach weg.

Old genitive forms have given rise to a set of adverbs with specifically INDEFINITE meanings: *abends, letztens, tagsüber, jederzeit*.

Philippi's core point, that case loss does not directly cause the rise of articles, is almost certainly correct. Traditional accounts have treated morphological reduction as leading to myriad changes, like fixing of word order and increase in analytic or periphrastic constructions. There may be something to these points, but they are inevitably far less direct than traditionally thought. But the underlying notion, that such losses must be compensated for structurally, is false. As Harbert puts it (2007: 107): 'When inflectional affixes are lost, the grammatical information they encoded sometimes simply ceases to be expressed, as in the case of gender distinctions in English and Afrikaans.'[25]

---

[24] Note that *Tag* is clearly not a direct object in this sentence!
[25] There's much recent work on definiteness in Germanic, e.g. Abraham 1997 and Leiss 2000 on Germanic and Mladenova 2009 for parallel work on Bulgarian, which has seen the rise of

At the same time, van Gelderen (2011: 203, elsewhere) shows how the particular grammatical information conveying definiteness has been 'renewed' many times in Germanic. (See Chapter 8 on 'linguistic cycles'.)

Grammaticalization. Even as many parts of the grammar move toward more analytic structures, some forms become more grammatical. We noted such 'grammaticalization' in Chapter 3, with IE *kom 'with': reconstructed as an independent word, it evolved into modern ge-. Let us now deepen our understanding of the topic with some OHG data (for more detail, see Leuschner et al. 2005 or Szczepaniak 2009).

Hodge (1970) observed that 'one man's morphology was an earlier man's syntax' (later Givón 1971). That is, relationships among 'free' words turn into sets of word forms. Again, this runs counter to the intuitively appealing notion that language 'simplifies' over time by losing endings: languages can acquire NEW sets of endings systematically.

If you recall the notion of 'clitics' ('weak' material that 'leans' on or gloms onto a neighboring element), we can represent the process like this:

word   >   clitic   >   affix

Crucially, people pursuing research into grammaticalization early on did not talk generally in terms of fixed categories, but tended to see 'word' status and 'affix' status as on a continuum, where some words are more word-like than others and some more affix-like. In addition to the history of ge-, other examples seem to follow this path, such as second person singular verb -(e)st from earlier -es by the frequent cliticization of the pronoun du.

Work, starting with Lehmann (1985), has developed 'grammaticalization' into a broader approach to morphosyntactic change. Many of these scholars have proposed that this 'path' of change is powerfully unidirectional. That is, it is claimed that independent words can become grammatical morphemes but not vice versa. While it is undeniable that many changes have followed this path, the history of German provides enough counterevidence to represent a cautionary note about these claims. The rest of this section will illustrate how OHG seems to have allowed structures farther to the (on the cline from word to affix) than the modern language does. That is, comparing OHG and modern German seems to contradict unidirectionality.

Today, modal particles like *doch, aber, nun, ja* are classic examples of 'particles', which are often counted as a kind of adverb (Zwicky 1985). In OHG, though, they sometimes appear written together with other words, typically

definiteness and the loss of case morphology. On the syntax of genitive constructions, Demske 2001a is the key source.

verbs, and with what may be spellings indicating reduced vowels. The particle *nu* appears in OHG texts written as a clitic leaning on imperative verbs:[26]

se**nu**	cumit	zit (Tatian: 176.3)
behold+PARTICLE	comes	time

'Behold, the time comes.'

In her description of such data, Wauchope (1992) notes that the cliticized particle is often distinguished orthographically, namely written as *no* rather than *nu*. This vowel difference could easily be regarded as a reduction in the context of Germanic phonological history, further supporting its status as leaning on a host. Most interestingly, Wauchope notes a case of double *nu*:

Truhtin,	seh**nu**	**nu**	zuei suuert	hier (Tatian: 166.4)
lord	see+PART.	PART.	two swords	here

'Lord, behold two swords here.'

This is found in Tatian and Otfrid, while similar imperative + *nu* constructions in the Isidor are not written together and often occur, according to Wauchope, with intervening adverbs. The point for us is that these are impossible today: if the path from free word to affix were inevitable, given evidence that *nu* was grammaticalizing in OHG, it should at least still be a clitic today. This in turn would predict, among various other things, that Modern German *Sieh nu!* would be realized as something like [zi:nə], rhyming with *Biene*, with a heavily reduced vowel. That does not seem to be the case, and arguments put forth in the 1970s that modal particles might behave as clitics have been forcefully rejected. Here then, a set of items have gone from being more grammatical, more closely tied to their hosts, to being less so, cf. §8.3.

Other clitic or clitic-looking forms have been lost through other means: negative *ni* grammaticalized with *wiht* 'thing' to create *nicht* and has otherwise been lost, while OHG and MHG show many occurrences of forms like *nist* < *ni-ist*.

A famous oddity of OHG illustrates a close bond between a postposed or enclitic pronoun and its host: in Otfrid's *Evangelienbuch*—and almost exclusively in this work—a pronoun starting with *i* triggered umlaut in the verb it followed:

---

[26] A clitic following its 'host' is called 'enclitic' while one that precedes it is called 'proclitic'. Wauchope (1992) finds this *nu* pattern ONLY in translation of the Latin *ecce* 'behold', which might suggest a special status for this particular phrase, like the reduced forms of *going to* we use for future meaning, e.g. *gonna head out*.

Usual OHG   **Otfrid**
drank ih 'I drank'   *drenk ih*
warf iz 'threw it'   *werf iz*

Somers Wicka shows that Otfrid in fact generally wrote cliticized subject pronouns together with the host about 87% of the time, as illustrated here with *uuolter* 'he wanted', *santer* 'he sent', and *zalter* 'he told' (Somers Wicka 2009: 109).[27] Later, MHG shows forms like *sam mir* 'so to me' or *daʒ ist* 'that is' which alternate with forms like *semmir* or *dêst* (Braune & Eggers 1987: 27).

What is striking about these cases is that separate words should not trigger a process like umlaut. In Otfrid's Old High German, the *ih* or *iz* must have formed a part of the 'phonological word' with the verb (as reflected in the orthography even; see Figure 4.5).

Ultimately, then, the Germanic languages illustrate problems with some aspects of grammaticalization that call out for additional work. That said, OHG also exemplifies 'well-behaved' developments, like negation, to which we now turn.

Negation. The particle *ni* is widely used for negation in OHG. It stands to the left of the element being negated, typically a verb:

enti	imo	hilfa	**ni**	quimit
and	to-him	help	NEG	comes

'and help does not come to him' (Muspilli)

uuolter	II 4, 14 (46r)
santer	II 7, 4 (50v)
zalter	I 25, 16 (37r)
Uuio mezih uuizzin	I 4, 55 (17r)
juuio mezih biuuânen	I 25, 8 (37r)

FIGURE 4.5 Samples of verb+pronoun spellings from Otfrid.
Manuscript images courtesy of the Österreichische Nationalbibliothek.

---

[27] See Somers Wicka (2009) for detailed discussion on Otfrid. That work is also an excellent example of how current research integrates the full spectrum from the most traditional philological research to contemporary linguistic theory in a single work.

ni	scribu	ih	nu
NEG	write	I	now

'I do not write now ...' (Otfrid)

Reduction is often visible, with the negative particle often spelled *ne* (perhaps reflecting a schwa-like pronunciation), and especially where the following word begins with a vowel, so that *ni alles* 'not everything' can be *nalles*, or *ni ist* 'is not' is often *nist*. With indefinite forms like *io*, 'ever, any', this process has continued and has led to Modern German words like this:

1. ni io wiht   > nicht
   not any thing
2. ni io   > nie
   not ever
3. ni io mêr   > nimmer (regional)
   no more

Like many dialects of modern German and English, and many standard languages (e.g. Polish), OHG allowed multiple negation, or 'negative concord'. We find this pattern with indefinite negative forms, like this:

dô	dâr	**ni**wiht	**ni**	was
then	there	no-thing	NEG	was

'then there was nothing' (Wessobrunner Gebet)

While *ni* does not always appear in all negative clauses in all texts, it is widespread (Donhauser 1998).

In OHG, we typically have only direct evidence from texts, but occasionally we get bits of metalinguistic information, comments from an author about the language. Otfrid, who has already been mentioned as the first known author in OHG, wrote Latin prefaces to his great *Evangelienbuch*, including this comment (from here: http://www.harbornet.com/folks/theedrich/hive/Medieval/Otfrid.htm, Marchand's translation):

Duo etiam negativi, dum in Latinitate rationis dicta confirmant, in hujus linguae usu paene assidue negant ...

Also, two negatives, in proper Latin, make an idea's wording affirmative, but in this language, almost always negative.

That is, Otfrid observes that 'two negatives make a positive in Latin, but not in OHG'.

V2: 'Verb second'. As introduced in the last chapter and, as you have seen, word order in early periods of the language differs from modern German word order. One striking feature of modern Germanic languages where word order is relatively fixed is the requirement that there be a verb in second position within clauses; this 'verb second', or 'V2', requirement is so famous that it's been called 'the most celebrated feature of Germanic syntax' (Kiparsky 1995: 161). English lacks this to a large extent—it has less V2 than any other modern Germanic language—but German still has it so fundamentally that it's taught as a basic rule in beginning language classes.

Historically, it was not always so. We saw that Runic tended to have verb-final constructions. All Germanic languages have a variety of periphrastic verbal constructions and they increase over time. In fact, German today has highly frequent patterns where the finite verb (the one agreeing with the subject) is in second position and a non-finite verb (infinitive or past participle) is in final position:

Unsere Leute **haben** alle hervorragende Doktorarbeiten **geschrieben**.
'Our folks have all written outstanding dissertations.'

The most common view today is that German remains a verb-final language at an abstract level, even though it shows powerful V2 patterns with finite verbs in most main clauses. Indeed, the rise of verb-second patterns alongside the retention of verb-final ones creates the highly distinctive 'verbal frame' (known as the *Satzklammer, Satzrahmen*, etc.), which we'll discuss later.

The last chapter introduced 'basic word order' in terms of the position of subject, verb, and object.[28] Germanic word order is thought to have begun as SOV, as noted in Chapter 3. In some respects (and in English), it has become generally SVO, something sometimes attributed to loss of morphology. We'll talk more later about this, but most scholars believe that as part of this, learners reanalyzed the order SVO in terms of the position of the verb. In main clauses, strict V2 is not the norm until Early Modern German. (And in coming chapters, we will discuss patterns of verb-initial or 'V1' declarative sentences.)

Old High German, Old Saxon, and Old English all tend toward V2 structures, while Old Norse shows it more consistently (Faarlund 2004: 191–192). Axel (2007) shows in great detail that OHG already possessed strong V2 properties, though quite different ones from Modern German. For instance, the traditional view is that V2 does not occur in languages with pro-drop (see pp. 169–170). If one accepts Axel's view that OHG is a partial pro-drop language, it is the first good example of this. In OHG, as you'll see exemplified in a Bible translation (p. 105), we also have verb-initial word order in declarative

---

[28] Today, instead of 'O', 'X' is often used, since any element can occupy a preverbal slot—*zu Hause ist sie, morgen fahren wir*, etc.—not just an object—*dieses Buch hat unsere Kollegin geschrieben*.

sentences, whereas in modern German, that order is more commonly reserved for a much narrower set of uses, like in imperatives (*Komm schon!*), conditional clauses (*Ist sie da, ist alles in Ordnung*), and emphasis (*Bist du aber klug!*).[29]

Before moving on, let us note one last empirical issue in syntax. One of the major issues in historical syntax has been what data we have and, for earlier periods, what material we can have. Classic generative syntax relies on grammaticality judgments: the introspective evaluation, by native speakers, of whether a particular sentence is grammatical for them in situations where not just positive evidence, but also the ability to say that a structure is ungrammatical is key. This is obviously lacking for a historical variety; but, even aside from that, for a stage like OHG we have extremely limited data, so that certain phenomena seem not to exist. Consider that last clause, where the claim is really about the existence of the phenomena, but on the surface that subject agrees with 'seem'. This used to be captured by assuming the structure below (following the structure in Crystal 2008: 401 and taking out the negation):

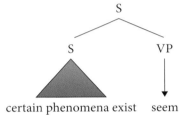

The form 'seem' belongs to another clause in modern, abstract analyses; and the subject gets 'raised' so as to be the subject of 'seem'. Modern German shows a parallel pattern with verbs like *scheinen* and *dünken*. (The analysis of such constructions has changed greatly in ways not of interest to us for the moment, but the name 'raising' is still widely used.) Earlier sources claim that these structures of such verbs with infinitives arose only in ENHG. Demske, however, shows that even in OHG we have patterns that should be analyzed as raising; this is illustrated here with an example from Notker that uses *dunchen*, the cognate of *dünken* (with her glossing and tweaking her translation):

Mír   dunch-ent ... tíu zuéi   ringen únde uuider   éin-anderén sîn
me-dat   think-3.pl ... the two.nom.pl   wrestle and against   one-another be
I think the two are wrestling and are against one another.'

For syntax, then, it is not always necessary to have new data, since we also have opportunities to sift new insights from currently readily available data.

---

[29] Önnersfors (1997) provides extensive discussion of the sets of verb-initial declaratives that do exist in the modern language.

In short, even with the current corpus, there is a lot to be learned about early German syntax.

This introduction establishes a context for discussions to come of syntax in more modern times. As we move on, keep an eye on constituency, word order, and other issues.

4.5 The sociolinguistics of writing Old High German

We have already talked about key moments in the rise of a writing culture in the German-speaking lands, from early runic inscriptions to glosses in Latin manuscripts and to the writing of Old High German. In this section let us ponder who came to write German and how we might best think about their language use. This exercise suggests some surprising things about the kind of crazy-looking dialect mixing we saw at the beginning of this chapter.

To begin with, Seiler (2014: 22–23) understands 'the adoption and adaptation of the Roman alphabet among the Germanic peoples' as nothing less than a 'media (r)evolution', and for a set of reasons:

The spread of the Roman alphabet encompassed the use of various new technologies. Wax tablets, charters, and books became the new channels of transmission of writing. The handling of these medial necessitated the development of pragmatic literacy competences since media are always instrisically tied to the performance of specific media skills—witness current debates on computer literacy, media literacy, etc.

She describes the most fundamental change in terms of the use of writing as 'a new intermediate agency or mode of communication' introduced into what had been almost entirely oral cultures. Following some previous scholars, she compares this to the introduction of printing and now of the internet.

Latin and Germanic, as we have already seen, had been in serious contact at least since Roman times, as Germanic speakers interacted with Romans and surely learned Latin as a second language (Adams 2003: 274–279). The spread of runic inscriptions centuries before has been seen as connected with social changes (Schulte 2013, among many others), and now, too, writing came to the German-speaking lands with a massive cultural change, namely the introduction of Christianity. With the 'Frankish mission' mentioned at the beginning of the chapter we have not only a new religion, but political changes, especially when Charlemagne converts to Christianity. Writing, too, comes in at first not as indigenous-language writing but as a tool for writing another language, Latin; and the system has to be adapted to spelling the forms of 'German' it was used for (see Seiler 2014 on this process of 'scripting'). Let us leave aside the Irish monks and others who first brought writing culture and concentrate on the writing of German within local communities.

Writing was heavily associated with the church, though essentially there always was secular writing for official documents and the like. McKitterick traces patterns of scribal activity for charters from the broad region around St. Gall and concludes:

The distribution of scribes over the period 700 to 920 thus shows the increasing preponderance of monastic scribes and a decreasing number of local scribes.... The general picture is one of contraction and consolidation, rather than continuing expansion, and with an increasing web of local ties and connections in the immediate vicinity of the monastery. (McKitterick 1989: 124)

In terms of the broader situation, McKitterick writes:

Most studies of Carolingian book production assume that it was an exclusively ecclesiastical affair. Undoubtedly the main centres of book production were the great monastic and cathedral scriptoria. It was they who developed their distinctive house styles of script, who trained great numbers of scribes and who built up the library resources of the institutions of which they were a part. (1989: 255)

We won't pursue this matter here, but she provides some relatively fine-grained sociolinguistic evidence, exploring a list of known scribes and raising basic questions about who they were—lay or clergy, cloistered or not.

Keeping in mind that they only represented a slice—if a thick and important slice—of the set of writers of texts that have come down to us, let us take monks living and working in monasteries as an example. What might we assume about these writers and their linguistic experience and knowledge?

- They would have typically come into monasteries as young men, six years old or so. In other words, these were people who were still developing linguistically. Indeed, preadolescence is seen as a time when children dramatically reshape their language, away from how their parents talk and toward how their peers do—a process called 'vernacular reorganization' (Labov 2001: 415–417).
- While some of these people would have been local, others came from farther away. If they came into the monastery that young, even with ongoing contacts to home communities, they surely acquired the local (i.e. monastery) variety near-natively. Still, the situation would have permitted great variability, the kind of patterns characteristic of koineization (Kerswill 2002). That is, they were primed to develop new, distinct ways of speaking.
- In a monastery, these people worked and lived at close quarters and in intense social environments, where there was a focus on order and obedience. This is the kind of social situation in which people forge new speech varieties, again, as in the *koiné*-formation processes mentioned earlier in the chapter.

- Scribes were by definition oriented toward and dedicated to language, and writing was a key focus. But that focus was, professionally at least, on Latin: they had to acquire Latin and use it. (See especially Grotans 2006 on the teaching and learning culture.)

What would we expect to find here in terms of spoken language and dialect? These young people might have smoothed off some particularly distinct features of their home varieties; and they surely adopted many features of those around them, but above all the situation would surely have led to tremendous linguistic variability. This kind of setting exposes learners and speakers to a wide range of dialects (and languages) and people learn to understand them, often speak them in some form, and even codeswitch between them.

Now think about this in the context of the dialect mixing noted in §4.2. Handbooks such as Braune (1994) treat the selected texts as showing a hodgepodge of dialect characterizations, which are given in their table of contents (with key pieces of the German text paraphrased below):

Text	Dialect description
Abrogans	alemannische Um- und Abschriften eines bairischen Originals
Monsee-Wiener Fragment	bairische Abschrift eines nichtbairischen Originals
Fränkisches Gebet	bairisch nach rhfr. Vorlage
Christus und die Samariterin	alemannisch-fränkische Sprach- und Orthographiemischung
De Heinrico	nordrheinfränkisch oder ... thüringisch
Merigarto	bairisch mit einzelnen ostfränkischen Merkmalen

These descriptions—mostly of relatively 'minor' texts—range from claims about the dialect of the original manuscript and its copy ('Bavarian copy of a non-Bavarian original') to claims of mixing ('Alemannic–Frankish linguistic and orthographic mixture') to disagreements about what dialect the text is in ('North Rhinefranconian or Thuringian'). These dramatic kinds of apparent mixing are one of the most surprising aspects of our OHG texts—for students, and even scholars. Perhaps the most common view is the one reflected in Braune & Reiffenstein (2004: 5), who note the kinds of reasons that might motivate such variation, from movement of manuscripts to the existence of monastery dialects that differed from local speech:

Auf Grund der Überlieferungslage lässt sich das Ahd. sprachgeographisch immer nur punktuell erfassen. Außerdem sind der Schreibort einer überlieferten Hs. und der Entstehungsort des Originals oft nicht identisch. Wird eine Vorlage in einem anderen Dialektgebiet oder schon in einem anderen Skriptorium des gleichen Gebietes abgeschrieben, können schreibsprachliche Mischungen entstehen, die die dialektgeographische Beurteilung weiter erschweren.... Die Schreibsprache eines Klosters muss (entsprechend der Zusammensetzung des Konvents) nicht mit dem lokalen Dialekt der Landschaft übereinstimmen. Auf der Reichnau treten zuerst rheinfrk., dann alem. und im 9. Jh. sogar ostfrk. Dialektmerkmale auf, in Murbach alem. und rheinfrk.

Given the state of attestation, we can capture only points of the linguistic geography of OHG. Moreover, where a manuscript was written and where the original came from are often not the same. If a base manuscript was copied in a different dialect area or even in a different scriptorium in the same area, orthographic mixtures can arise, which make it more difficult to determine the dialect.... The written dialect of a monastery (corresponding to the composition of the monastery) doesn't necessarily correspond to the local dialect. In Reichnau Rhinefranconian features show up first, then Alemannic and then in the 9th century even East Franconian, in Murbach [we have] Alemmanic and Rhinefranconian ones.

Sonderegger (2003: 64) has similar views:

Neben mundartlichen Denkmälern gibt es im Ahd. viele Denkmäler in Mischdialekten (Kreuzungen durch Um- oder Abschrift). Verschiedene Stufen können in den rund zwanzig ahd. Denkmälern in Mischmundarten unterschieden werden:

(a) bloße mehr oder weniger genaue Umschrift eines Denkmals von der einen in die andere Mundart, wobei eine Mundart dominiert ... [Muspilli];

(b) mehr oder weniger durchgehende gleichmäßige Mischung zweier Mundarten in sich eng verflechtender Weise... [Christus und die Samariterin];

(c) Mischung zwischen ahd. Mundarten und außerahd. germanischem Sprachgut [Hildebrand].

Alongside dialectal works, there are a lot of works in OHG written in mixed dialects (mixes by rewriting or copying). Different stages can be distinguished in the approximately 20 manuscripts written in mixed dialects:

(a) simple more or less exact rewriting of a work from one dialect into another, where one dialect dominantes [Muspilli];

(b) more or less even mixture of two dialects woven into a text throughout [Christus und die Samariterin];

(c) mixture of OHG dialects and non-OHG Germanic material [Hildebrand].

Sonderegger (2003: 65) notes the same patterns for mixing of OHG and Latin, arguing that these are about written varieties produced specifically in monasteries that employed OHG dialects in either pure or mixed form (*Schreibsprachen,... die ahd. Mundarten entweder **rein** oder vermischt verwenden*). He is most certainly right to conclude that Old High German writing culture was full of linguistic movement and exchange (2003: 65).

If we look at particular texts, the speculation can go deeper; but it often feels, to me at least, no more satisfying. Consider the Hildebrandslied, the most famous and possibly the most mixed text. In a section titled 'Was there a standardized OHG written language?', Waterman (1966: 75–77) argues that, 'whatever the influence of the Carolingian court, it would be inaccurate to suppose that there resulted at this time anything substantially resembling a standard written form of Old High German'. This is true enough, and it is a question to which we will return in coming chapters. About Hildebrand, Waterman writes that it is 'a peculiar mixture of Low German and High German, it would seem to be the result of a rather clumsy attempt to transpose an originally High German version into what the scribes (there were two of them) thought was Old Saxon' (75). This point has not fared so well. Probably the most reasonable assessment comes from Bostock (1976: 78), who writes:

It is almost universally agreed now that the manuscript version represents an attempt to convert a text from one dialect into another. It was formerly thought by many scholars that a Low German text had been incompletely converted into High German' but now the opposite view is generally held.... The efforts of scholars to devise a scheme of evolution which would afford a logical explanation of all the details have led to elaborate constructions, some of which reflect more credit on the ingenuity than on the common sense of their authors.

This is harsh, but to the point. Is there a logical explanation for such patterns? A first critical step is to get beyond the reification of 'dialect' and beyond notions and expectations of 'pure dialect'. Some (though hardly all!) 19th-century linguists established strict categories of dialects, past and present, as we have seen and will see throughout this book. In reality, that person who sounds so Swabian or has such a classic Berlin accent is behaving in more complex ways than the behavior might suggest: they may have the features we identify with those varieties, but there is no pure prototype that they match or others fail to match. Human speech is highly variable in any language or dialect; it varies by situation, interlocutor, and other factors. Since the pioneering work of Weinreich et al. (1968), variability within communities and speakers has moved steadily to the center of linguistic theorizing and can help us on this point. If you are interested in any aspect of the history; and that is a major theme of this book.

These OHG scribes and writers would have been prone to greater variability than many people of their time, given their intense exposure to lots of different ways of speaking German and extensive exposure to Latin. Scribes were familiar with a far broader range of spellings and regional (and no doubt social) structural forms than a rigid notion of dialect would suggest; and they worked with older and newer manuscripts during a period of great change in the language, maybe recognizing, 'oh, yeah, that's how my grandparents would have said that'.

This is compounded by various ways of writing, of getting speech into writing. Scriptoria established strong traditions of spelling, but even under the best circumstances these were not encoded and transmitted the way modern orthographic norms are: nobody had spellcheckers or autocorrect.

My claim is that these written text mixtures by no means reflect how anybody ever told these stories or recited these poems; the point is instead that the kinds of variation wouldn't have been as foreign as we take them to have been. Even outright switches from one dialect to another in the course of speaking must have been common to hear in the lived experience of some of these writers.

Testing the scenario sketched out here to the extent that it becomes fully testable for OHG would require at least a dissertation or two, but this is suggestive of a way in which we could get the variation we find in texts. We will return to this issue of dialect mixing much later in the book (Chapter 7), to see that strikingly similar patterns have emerged in the very recent past. I don't want to overplay the point, but maybe the 'dialect' variation in Old High German texts is not as bizarre as we have long thought. Basically, we need to think beyond 'mixed dialects' from manuscript transmission in ways that are often conceived of as somehow aberrant. The social and historical setting in which OHG was written down surely means that we are not seeing the full range of variation that was there. Almost any text we have will reflect processes of leveling, and some limited kinds of 'mixes' were inevitable and ultimately understandable.

4.6 Vocabulary

In treating various texts, we have seen many examples of vocabulary and how it differs from the modern language. Not long ago, the OHG lexicon was estimated at over 24,000 different words (lemmas, not individual word forms) found in glosses of various sorts and almost 11,000 in the literary and cultural texts we have—as laid out by Splett (2000), who estimated the total number of words in OHG at around 330,000. Current estimates exceed 650,000 words (according to http://www.deutschdiachrondigital.de). At noted earlier in this chapter, that number is growing steadily with the discovery of new (especially drypoint) glosses, and Schiegg (2015: 19) estimates that a 1,000 OHG words (with around 40,000 attestations) can be found in Latin sources.

Our sources are heavily skewed, then, toward glosses rather than prose or poetry. OHG vocabulary is a remarkably well-studied area and the changes in vocabulary naturally provide a window onto historical, political, and social developments of the period, especially Christianization and the language contacts associated with that. Below are just a few examples of how vocabulary changed during this period.

Native vocabulary. It is important to keep in mind that while a lot changes, there is tremendous stability too: most of the vocabulary is historically Germanic, or built from Germanic elements by familiar processes of word formation.

4.6.1 Loanwords into OHG

Latin. The most numerous and best known loanwords into German in this period were from Latin and are often chronologically distinct; some early ones come from the imperial era and others date from after Christianization.

For decades, much effort went into building a taxonomy of the different types of loanwords, including for Latin loans in OHG. Werner Betz (1974) provided a widely used one, illustrated briefly here:

- Lehnübersetzung (he gives ca. 25–30 for OHG): translation of the individual elements, like *Wolkenkratzer* based on 'skyscraper'.
  - com-passio mit-leid
- Lehnschöpfung [creation of new term from native elements]
  - find-unga (experimenta)
- Lehnbedeutung (ca. 300): old word takes on new meaning from cultural contact.
  - Sünde (see 156, p. 186).

While the literature on lexical borrowings into OHG is vast, Tadmor et al. (2010) show OHG as having the second lowest rates of loanwords in basic vocabulary of all languages they examined (6%), behind only Mandarin (1%). English is near the other end of the scale, with 41%.

The domains of borrowing are largely what you would expect given the nature of contacts, for example with many Latin and some Greek words in religion:

kyrikḗ (Greek) > *chilihha, kirihha, etc.* 'Kirche'
pix   > *peh* 'Pech'
poena   > *pēna* 'Pein'.

This group extends to words like *altari* 'altar', *crux* 'cross', and so on.

Education is likewise well represented: *tincta (Tinte), schōla (Schule), scribere (schreiben)*, etc., as are food and plants: *rosa (Rose), petrosilium (Peterselie), thymus (Thymian), cedrus (Zeder)*, and so on.

Technology and farming were also particularly productive areas:

mūra < *murus (Mauer)*
ziegal < *tegula (Ziegel)*
kṍla < *caulis*, meaning '*Kohl, Gemüse*'
kersa < *ceresia (Kirsche)*.

These are hardly restricted to new concepts or objects, and Latin terms often replace old native words: *fenstar* < *fenestra* replaces *ougatora* in German, while English has maintained a native term, *window*.

Latin was clearly the most important language OHG was in contact with, but other languages contributed smaller numbers of words as well:

East Germanic (Gothic) into Bavarian (ultimately from Greek)

Tuesday   *Ertag* (< Day of Arius)
Thursday   *Pfinztag* < Greek 'fifth day'.

A number of other Gothic loans (again, mostly into Bavarian, not all of OHG) were church-related, like *pfaffo* < Gothic *papa*.

Irish: *clocca* > *Glocke*
Anglo-Saxon: *Heiland*
   Geist exists in competition with a form *ātum* (cognate with German *Atem*) and a southern form *wīh*.

4.6.2 Borrowing in the other direction

Germanic borrowed vocabulary from Latin, but Romance speakers also borrowed from Germanic speakers, including Frankish into Old French and (Visi-)Gothic into Spanish. In fact, a few familiar Romance words are of Germanic origin, along with sets of words in the military sphere, for instance:

jardin   <   garto
guerre   <   *werra
blanc   <   *blanka (German *blank*)
Names
Henri   <   Heinrich   < Herrscher im Heim
Baudouin <   Baldwin   < Freund der Kühnheit.

4.6.3 Survival and adaptation of pre-Christian vocabulary

Traditional texts give glimpses into how early Germanic people saw the world—including literally the notion of 'world', where we have the famous *mittingart* ('middle world') vs. *weralt* ('age, world' < age of man) (Sonderegger 2003: 359–360).

Some old cultural vocabulary survives, but often with shift in meaning:

- truhtīn 'lord' military > religious meaning
- Ostern *Austrṓ(< goddess of spring?, Anglo-Saxon Eostrae) *aurōra* 'Morgenröte', (baptisms often took place at dawn, so OHG ōstarūn perhaps < lat. *albae* 'Tagesgrauen'). *Paschen*, etc. < *pascha* 'Ostern'

- Hölle 'realm of the dead' > 'place of punishment'; Lehmann 1986: 'hidden place' < IE *ǩel 'hide', see German *enthüllen* etc.)
- got > Gott: neutral > positive connotations; now just in the singular, plus gender change from neuter to masculine
- sundio > Sünde: 'Verhalten, dessen man sich schämt' (old legal term).

Other words get replaced with cultural change. In the Germanic forms, many of which survive today, we have ties to Germanic mythology, e.g. *donner* is connected to *Thor*.

Days of the week, 'loan translations' (*Lehnübersetzungen*)

solis dies	sonntag
lunae dies	montag
jovis dies	donnerstag
veneris dies	freitag.

bluostar > opfar (< lat. *operāri* 'to perform' [religious ceremony])
weihs, weiha, weihnan, etc. > Priester (< prēst, prēstar).

We also have some indigenous developments in the vocabulary, such as the creation of indigenous names for the months by Charlemagne (Hüpper 1988):

uuintarmānōth = January
heilagmānōth = December.

If these few examples whet your appetite for more on this topic, Green (2000) provides a good introduction to early Germanic culture and history, rooted in discussion of vocabulary, both indigenous and borrowed. Kroonen (2013) provides a contemporary etymological dictionary, available online through many libraries.

4.7 Conclusion

Every section of this chapter has shown that OHG, even over a thousand years ago, tells us something about the modern language, big or small. The outcome of the Second Sound Shift is still an excellent guideline for identifying Modern German dialects and related languages, though we have to accept—in the past and in the present—more variation than earlier scholars were willing to assume. You've seen how umlaut takes root in the language, though its present form is quite different. You now see how patterns like *kennen* ~ *kannte* have arisen, why we have an association between feminine gender and nouns ending in schwa, and how constructions like the present perfect arose.

At the same time, you now know the answers to lots of smaller puzzles about the language, from how *mehr* is connected historical to *meist* on to why words like *jederzeit* and *abends* exist. From here, things look ever more familiar.

5

Middle High German

The High Middle Ages

5.0 Introduction

Familiarity with earlier historical stages of German often begins for students with the canonical literary works of the High Middle Ages, especially poetic texts written in Middle High German (MHG). Most newcomers to the topic of this book, I imagine, did not know the OHG works discussed in the last chapter, but many more will be familiar with an epic poem like the *Nibelungenlied* or examples of *Minnesang* poetry. The scholarly tradition reflects this as well, with a major new introduction to Middle High German that shows a proper balance between the linguistic and the literary (Jones & Jones forthcoming). At the same time, the new *Referenzkorpus Mittelhochdeutsch* (1050–1350) gives us ready access to very important non-literary texts.[1]

During the Middle High period, the amount of textual material that survives to the present increases markedly, as does the diversity of that material. Importantly, it includes dramatically more non-religious texts. We also know more about the social and historical circumstances of those who wrote in many cases, and they came from a somewhat broader spectrum of society—notably less restricted to clerics, if still overwhelmingly written by people who were taught to read and write by clerics. The effect of all this is clear: while OHG texts show wild dialectal and chronological variability, MHG texts show similar variability, but with more historical context to help us piece together a picture of the language. With relatively sparse socio-historical background associated with earlier texts, we have been forced to focus heavily on structural aspects of language—sound patterns, word forms, and to a lesser extent sentence

---

[1] I should note that here the north is usually excluded from discussion more than it is for some other periods (see §8.1 on this). There's important work being done on Middle Low German, though, for instance the Corpus of Historical Low German, which includes a Middle Low German grammar project available at http://www.chlg.ac.uk/grammar.html.

structures. Now, we can begin to develop a sharper picture of the social context in which the language was used and how it varied and changed over time and space.

At the same time, even today some aspects of the language have been less intensely studied given the amount of data available, and in a sense we have more open questions for which evidence is available to answer them. For Germanic and OHG, in other words, much progress comes from new theories and methods. From MHG forward, we have mountains of data that have not been systematically sifted for the nuggets they hold about language structure and its social setting.

Our basic goals in the present chapter include these:

- We will look critically at the issue of PERIODIZATION in language history, with a focus on where MHG fits into the history of German.
- We will review the set of relatively modest sound changes in MHG, many of them building directly on patterns discussed in the last chapter, such as umlaut and weakening of endings.
- With our richer empirical base, we will discuss variability in these changes, over time and space, as well as social variation. This includes the question of whether there was, in any sense, a 'standard MHG'.
- In syntax, we'll pick up on topics that were introduced in the last chapter, from increasing periphrasis to word order and negation.
- Again building on knowledge from the last chapter, we will explore how to identify dialect features and the dialect of written texts, and now with some attention to social variation in language.

A brief textual example. One of the most famous literary monuments of this era is the *Heidelberger Liederhandschrift*, a large collection of MHG poetry. Figure 5.1 shows an example of a poem by Der von Kürenberg, with a digital version of the manuscript, with an arrow marking the first line of this poem (which is available at http://digi.ub.uni-heidelberg.de/diglit/cpg848/0122).

Ich zôch mir einen valken
mêre danne ein jâr.
Dô ich ihn gezamete
Als ich in wollte hân
Und ich im sîn gevidere
Mit golde wol bewant,
er huop sich ûf vil hôhe
und fluog in anderiu lant.

Sît sah ich den valken
Schône fliegen:
Er fuorte an sînem fuoze

Sîdîne riemen,
und was im sîn gevidere
alrôt guldîn.
Got sende si zesamene
Die gerne geliep wellen sîn!'

Der von Kürenberg um 1160

Here is, for comparison, a New High German translation (taken from http://www.saelde-und-ere.at/Hauptseite/Arbeitsgruppen/Mhdt/Falkenlied/Falke.html):

Ich zog mir einen Falken
länger als ein Jahr.
Nachdem ich ihn mir gezähmt,
wie ich ihn haben wollte,
und ihm sein Gefieder
mit Gold wohlgeschmückt,
erhob er sich hoch in die Lüfte
und entflog in fremdes Land.
Seither sah ich den Falken
schön fliegen.
er führte an seinem Fuße,
seidene Riemen,
und sein Gefieder
war ganz rotgold.
Gott sende sie zusammen,
die gerne geliebt wollen sein.

For most readers, this text will provide far less of a challenge than your first exposure to attested OHG in the last chapter: the language definitely looks more 'German'. The manuscript is ornate, but probably readable. If you look closely, you'll see some typical medieval manuscript conventions, like the use of a line over a vowel, such as *einē* in line 1. This marks a following *n* (and not vowel length). These are major changes, but others from the manuscript to the edited version of the text are more minor:

sach 'saw' is edited to *sah,*
fuosse 'foot' (dat. sg.) to *fuoze,*
gelieb 'geliebt' to *geliep.*

With this example in mind, we will soon look at sound changes in this period, beginning with the relevance of manuscript editing traditions.

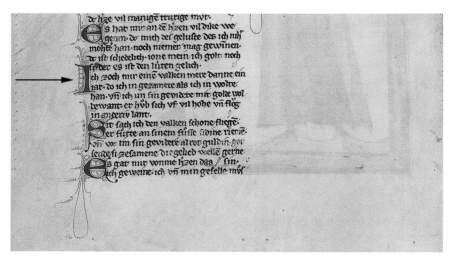

FIGURE 5.1 Der von Kürenberg (Heidelberger Handschrift).
Courtesy of the Universitätsbibliothek Heidelberg.

5.1 Periodization

Until now, we have not really needed to talk much about periodization—how (and whether) we divide the history of German into distinct historical periods. With Indo-European and prehistoric Germanic, that's a speculative enterprise, and Old High German begins basically with the earliest texts written in what appear to be direct ancestors of modern German dialects. With OHG, we covered texts up past the first millennium of the Common Era, in line with the traditional end date for OHG of 1050. One typical periodization, drawing here from Paul (2007: 10), is the following:

- (Pre-German)   5th c.–750
- Old High German   750–1050
- Middle High German   1050–1350
  - Early MHG   1050–1170
  - Classical MHG   1170–1250
  - Late MHG   1250–1350
- Early New High German   1350–1650
- New High German   1650–

Elspaß (2007) lays out the history of such classifications, with their benefits and pitfalls (and see Roelcke 1995 for a book-length treatment of the topic, as well as part II of Besch & Wolf 2009). He goes on to argue that we've now entered the next major phase of the history of German, as we'll discuss in Chapter 7. All such classifications are obviously constructs projected back onto the periods in question: while we don't have definitive evidence, I'm confident that speech of individuals and communities on December 31, 1650 did not differ appreciably from the speech of those same individuals and communities on January 1, 1651, to take a boundary within the span where the Gregorian calendar has been used. Still, dividing language history into periods is a valuable heuristic, a way of organizing things that allows us to develop better analyses. Moreover, it has become a firmly entrenched way of organizing our knowledge about the field: our grammars and dictionaries, as well as the core technical literature, are all built around describing these periods, with the necessary overlap across transitional areas and reference to other periods.

Periodization surely needs to be done with reference to both language-internal and language-external events, that is, by the timing of changes to the language structure and changes in the communities where the language is spoken. That said, there is something oddly and maybe reassuringly symmetrical about what Elspaß (2007: 2) calls 'die bisherige Einteilung in 300-Jahre-Schritte'.

Let us return to the period at hand for an example of the details of period boundaries. Of most immediate concern to us here is the just-mentioned date of 1050 as the boundary between Old and Middle High German. This number is widely used in handbooks, like Paul, and it is built around, in part, the solidification of some linguistic changes that we've already discussed:

- The weakening of final unstressed syllables, like -*um* to -*en*, becomes more consistent.
- *i*-umlaut, beyond 'primary umlaut' of short *a* to *e* (and excluding blocking environments), begins to be written more consistently.

As noted in the last chapter, and as will be exemplified in a moment, the first of these changes is actually well advanced by late OHG. That is, it is not a realistic criterion for establishing a boundary between OHG and MHG.

Far worse, neither process ever really reaches completion in MHG—umlauts are inconsistently written even in the early modern period, though it was clearly no longer a phonetically 'active' process. That is, the fronting of vowels was a morphological feature and not a simple anticipatory assimilation, as it was in earliest OHG. In short, while we'll basically follow these dates, do not lose sight of the fact that they are extremely artificial: in terms of the features just noted, what we deem relatively innovative texts from before 1000 can look 'later' than conservative ones from 1200.

There are some clear markers of boundaries between these periods, including language-external ones. We have an extensive gap in textual transmission around the end of OHG and the beginning of MHG, referred to often as a 'silent century' or 'the big gap'. While it has been variously defined, some talk about a gap from Otfrid—who probably wrote before 871—down to Ezzo, author of the eponymous *Ezzolied*—from probably before 1100. Sonderegger (2003: 229 ff.) discusses this 'große literaturgeschichtliche Lücke', and shows that it is not a gap in all attestation, but rather an era from which we have scattered small texts instead of literary monuments. The bigger point, as Sonderegger rightly stresses, is the overall increase in texts over time, though one can observe a clear drop in the number and types of texts during this period.[2]

In fact, there's a bigger problem with periodization as it has often been done in the past: for OHG, we have under 100 total manuscripts, leaving aside glosses in Latin texts and so on. Rather than tracing the line of development for a particular variety, this limited set of texts available across so many dialects and three centuries has forced scholars to jump from one dialect or other variety to another as they move from period to period, often simply because texts are available or because particularly important texts (say, from a literary perspective) are available. This adds regional and social variation on top of historical developments and so creates an illusion of change in addition to actual changes, crudely illustrated in Table 5.1:

TABLE 5.1 **A schematic of illusory change in language history**

	Period I	Period II	Period III	Period IV	Period V
Dialect A	Bits of data				The standard language; regional data often ignored.
Dialect B		Important literary text		Lots of data	
Dialect C		Some non-literary data			
Dialect D			Important literary text	Some data	
Dialect E	Ignored	Ignored	Ignored	Ignored	

If we could easily do a 3D graphic, we would have to include the fact that in one period, clerics are doing virtually all the writing, in the next poets working for the political elite, and in the next bureaucrats, before relatively ordinary people begin to write.

---

[2] Sonderegger's arguments seem to me compelling from the point of view of language history, if perhaps discussable in terms of canonical literary history. Nonetheless, recent work often continues to follow the old view, e.g. Young & Gloning (2004: 26).

That is, despite the powerful inclination to think of the history of a language in simple, linear terms, the empirical record is remarkable for its discontinuity. As we move through time, we do not have the same kinds of texts from the same kinds of writers from the same places. We have to keep in mind how multi-dimensionally different texts by a cleric from what's now Alsace (Otfrid) are from those written by a court poet who was probably Bavarian writing centuries later (Wolfram von Eschenbach). Perhaps worst, many histories portray a slow and steady march to a modern standard language. As we'll soon see, the standard is an artificial construct and structurally far less interesting than the rich sets of regional and social variants actually spoken in the world today.

Seen from this perspective, our job is in part to learn to triangulate time and space, both geographical and social. A key task, as we'll discuss in later chapters, is seeing the present endpoint not as the artificial standard but the full range of varieties of German. With MHG, we actually have a broad enough sample of original prose texts across time and space to ameliorate this problem (see http://www.mittelhochdeutsche-grammatik.de/DE/korpus_bonn.php, and also §5.5), but earlier work, including handbooks, relied heavily on the literary canon for evidence, and did not take advantage of the rich variation available. That has certainly begun to change.

In addition to these purely areal biases, as we saw in the last chapter, OHG writing was concentrated in a small number of scriptoria, which were not only obviously located in particular dialect areas but which also drew and developed their own mixes of regional speakers and even writing traditions. In the Middle High German period, activity continues in such religious centers, but at the same time, a significant amount of new activity develops in centers of political power, namely the courts, where literature in the indigenous language becomes popular. While governmental and other writing continues largely in Latin, this shifts over time toward the vernacular. This is a remarkably slow transition and in a sense, it is only now reaching completion, as the use of Latin for doctoral dissertations has steadily faded in German higher education. But even among the German texts we have, specific social varieties arose and disappeared that were unique to their times and had particular and perhaps unique relationships to the spoken language: the mix of varieties and language knowledge in a scriptorium surely differed clearly from those at a medieval court.

The social and historical developments of this era have tremendous impact on the language. Traditional treatments of the history of German focus overwhelmingly on social and political elites, often in the context of the great medieval poets and their works. And after all, they produced the kinds of texts just noted. But it is clear from modern linguistic changes that the elites have a remarkably limited role in language beyond things like spelling conventions and standardized forms, which we'll treat after this chapter.

More interesting is the speech of ordinary people. Demographic changes—
e.g. in where people live and who they have contact with—have an impact on
how they speak. These include the population growth of the Middle Ages and
movement of populations, especially eastern colonization. In the first case, we
see an explosion of urban areas within the old German-speaking areas. In the
9th century, the German-speaking lands had only about 40 cities growing to
around 3000 in the 14th, with the major growth in the 13th (Hotzan 1997: 33).
With improved agricultural techniques (*Dreifelderwirtschaft*) and technology
(iron plows), the population explodes, as Table 5.2 (translated from Hotzan
1997: 33) shows (and we'll return to this topic in Chapter 6):

TABLE 5.2 **Population development in Germany**

Year	Est. pop., millions	Event
ca. 900	2.0	
ca. 1050	5.0	
ca. 1200	10.0	
ca. 1340	16.0	Plague
ca. 1360	8.5	

In these settings, we often find people moving in from the surrounding
countryside with changes in local speech patterns resulting from such contact.[3] Recall that since Tacitus the Germanic peoples had been regarded as
rural, so that this represents a basic change in how people lived and how many
people they had contact with.

Second, the so-called *Ostkolonisation* led to the formation and development
of German settlements in Upper Saxony, Pomerania, and other areas, mostly
formerly Slavic-speaking areas. Map 11 illustrates this colonization. Movement of many speakers of diverse dialect backgrounds into new territories
correlates often with the formation of new linguistic varieties, usually called
koinē. Koinē development or the closely related process of new dialect formation is happening constantly and recent work (such as Kerswill 2002, Kerswill
& Trudgill 2005) makes clear that such varieties show leveling of differences or

---

[3] We'll see these processes of urbanization and dialect formation and leveling accelerate
dramatically in the early modern period and then down to the present.

'compromise' of divergent dialectal features, and can lead to the creation of new dialects. While adult speakers may adopt certain new features from others (within the limits of adults to acquire new features), an easier and often less conscious process is the elimination of differences that an individual or small group has that draws attention from others. That is, *koinē* development often centers on the suppression of differences more than the creation of new forms. Most people who have moved away from the area they grew up in experience this at some level, by the use of some word or pronunciation. Over generations, new dialects can crystallize from communities formed in this way, and with time we do see the rise of unique new forms of pronunciation or grammar in such settings. This can happen quickly, even over a few years. Members of the American military, for instance, often come to speak pretty differently from how they grew up speaking—they are young adults typically, who live and work in intensely close contact with others, and in a setting where group solidarity is critical. Given how language is often used to signal membership in a group—that is, we tend to talk like those we closely identify with—it is not surprising that we would find such patterns. *Koinē* formation is a topic we'll revisit several times in the rest of the book, but it is almost surely a factor in the development of the new, eastern dialects of German due to the colonization. See Map 11.

Finally, while they involved far fewer people, the Crusades create important new cultural and linguistic contacts. The really immediate linguistic effects of the Crusades were limited, largely to the introduction of new vocabulary.

In general, as noted, we have far more textual material and material of a far wider range of types than is the case for OHG, and the quantity and diversity rises steadily from this time forward. From this, we can start to see more systematic patterns of variation. The rise begins, in fact, directly within the MHG period. Consider Figure 5.2 from Bertelsmeier-Kierst (2000: 158), charting the growth of German-language manuscripts from the 11th–13th centuries (she uses light shading for texts to signal the early and late parts of periods, to avoid an all-or-nothing effect in the graph).

In other words, it is only late in the MHG period that we see an explosion of texts. She also shows that these numbers can be further increased if we include various smaller texts, sometimes written into Latin manuscripts. As Bertelsmeier-Kierst notes, the quantity increase correlates with an increased range of sources, in particular a movement away from almost exclusively clerical writers. She ultimately concludes: 'Weltliche Dichtung wird in nennenswertem Umfang erst im 13. Jahrhundert handschriftlich verbreitet.' This dating then pushes the real rise into late MHG. Still, our focus in this chapter will reflect what increased linguistic evidence shows us about variability regionally and stylistically.

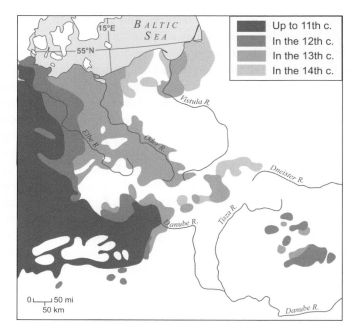

MAP 11 Eastern colonization showing eastward spread.

Adapted from a map available at http://info-poland.buffalo.edu/classroom/maps/.

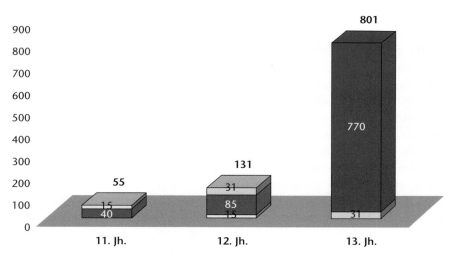

FIGURE 5.2 Vernacular manuscripts in the High Middle Ages.

5.2 Sound changes from Old High German to Middle High German

5.2.1 Introduction

The 'Middle High German' language we typically see in non-technical editions, such as literary anthologies, is often significantly different from the language of written texts with regard to how sounds are represented in writing. This goes back ultimately to the practices of 19th-century editors. In particular, following the models he learned from the editing practices of classical philology (so it's said), Karl Lachmann (pictured in Figure 5.3) produced the first major influential editions of many of the classic MHG works through the early 19th century. Unwilling to simply take the written record at face value, Lachmann worked hard to 'improve' it, following the practices of the 'best' manuscripts, and introducing spellings that are unknown from the manuscripts. Lachmann, in his work as an editor, is often credited with having created a regularized form of the language, known today as 'normalisiertes Mittelhochdeutsch' or 'Normalmittelhochdeutsch'. In eliminating the kinds of variation found in manuscripts, editing no doubt moved the texts further from natural Middle High German speech. The features of this variety include regularization of highly variable but equivalent spellings like *f* versus *v* and the introduction of a circumflex (ˆ) to mark long vowels, something known but uncommon in the actual manuscripts.

FIGURE 5.3 Karl Lachmann.
Image courtesy of the Porträtsammlung, Universitätsbibliothek, Humboldt University.

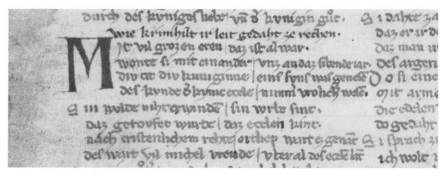

FIGURE 5.4 Das Nibelungenlied.

Image courtesy of the Bayerische Staatsbibliothek, *Nibelungenlied und die Klag*, Leithandschrift A—BSB Cgm 34.

More salient than that, Lachmann introduced a key graphic convention for umlaut (¨), a foreign diacritic in actual MHG manuscripts. In fact, umlaut generally was still typically not marked in MHG manuscripts.[4] The image from the *Nibelungenlied* in Figure 5.4 illustrates this with several occurrences of words for 'king' and 'queen', usually spelled *künig* and *künginne* in the standard edition (see the version below from de Boor 1972, strophe 1386 ff.). In OHG, Notker wrote <iu> sometimes for what would have been *ü*, around the year 1000. Only in the 12th century do we begin to find umlaut spelled (by whatever orthographic means) with any regularity, and even such spellings remain sporadic centuries later. When it is written, it is done in a wide range of ways, as we'll see later (Schneider 2009: 94–95, elsewhere).

XIII. Âventiure

Mit vil grôzen êren,	dáz ist álwár,
wónten si mít ein ander	unz an daz sibende jar.
die zît diu küneginne	eines suns wás genesen.
des kunde der künic Etzel	nimmer vrœlîcher wesen.
Sine wólde niht erwinden,	sine würbe sint.
daz getoufet würde	daz Étzélen kint
nâch kristenlîchem rehte;	ez wart Ôrtlíep genant,
des wart vil michel freude	über élliu Etzelen lant.

For those used to reading editions, where the epic is broken into *Âventiuren*, some other manuscripts are already striking in showing no real breaks—here the new chapter begins with red ink. If you compare the two versions more closely (and you can also consult an older English translation at http://books.google.

---

[4] Despite this, in traditional views, the presence of phonological (if not orthographic) umlaut is still considered criterial for the beginning of the MHG period.

com/ebooks/reader?id=FfVlAAAAMAAJ), you see consistent spelling of umlaut in the edited form, but not in the original, along with various other spelling differences. (You can find good digital editions at http://www.hs-augsburg.de/~harsch/germanica/Chronologie/12Jh/Nibelungen/nib_a_oo.html.)

The editorial practice of regularizing texts provides practical help for modern readers beginning to work with the language, but it obscures some of the most interesting patterns of language change in the period. Indeed, it is designed expressly to suppress variation, which is a central concern for the rest of this book. As discussed at length in Chinca & Young (2017, see also Stackmann 1964 for an earlier discussion), the traditional view assumes that these texts came from a single base manuscript, the editor's job being to reconstruct the original form of that manuscript. A movement known as 'new philology' or 'material philology' (see Nichols 1990) eventually sought to place the focus on manuscript culture and on the fuller context of manuscripts and manuscript transmission. This includes attention to and acknowledgment of variation rather than an effort to reconstruct some uniform proto-text. Today digital philology is coming to the fore, and this is the central focus of Chinca & Young. Let us illustrate this with examples from sound change.

With regard to understanding earlier variations, note, for example, these two related trends, with examples laid out in the rest of this section:

First, many or even most changes do not affect the whole 'German'-speaking world, so that we find some modern dialects that escaped some of these changes. That is, like with the Second Sound Shift, the spread of changes in this period are often still embodied in modern German dialects. The changes presented in the rest of this section help to define modern dialects more precisely, as you'll see.

Second, if we trace them through manuscripts, some changes look like the 'undoing' of earlier changes, or represent changes that haven't been adopted in the modern standard. This variability is surely connected to spelling conventions, dialectal differences, and so on. With careful work, we can still often tease out a lot of details, as we will illustrate in what follows. In fact, similar patterns are found generally in language history, and in a study of such of them in the history of English, Hickey (2002) has dubbed the phenomenon 'ebb and flow'.

The chronology of changes is also complex in MHG, partly because of the better documentation: many of the changes treated in this section don't fit neatly into this single period. In fact, virtually all reach back into OHG times and/or forward into the Early New High German period, and sometimes even in both directions. (This is the case with the spelling of umlaut.) Thus, the changes presented next will look strikingly familiar for the most part.

5.2.2 Consonants

In the consonant system, the MHG period is characterized in part by a string of relatively minor changes in terms of the modern standard. But the era is rich in patterns of interesting variation. We'll cover some of the more salient changes, then turn to the problem of *Auslautverhärtung*, or 'final fortition'.

Auslautgesetze continue on their way. Especially inflectional -*m*'s largely became -*n* already in OHG, and this process is completed in early MHG:

- *tagum* > *tagen*
- *bodem* > *boden*
- *bim* > *bin* (showing that this happens even in some monosyllabics)

In fact, quantitative evidence shows that these changes were far advanced already early in OHG. Consider the dative plural noun forms given here (and in Chapter 4) for OHG as -*um* and for MHG surprisingly often as -*en*. For texts that were likely written before 800, for instance, Luiten (2011) shows that forms ending in *n* are already more common than those in *m*. Table 5.3 shows all forms consisting of any vowel plus *m* ('Vm'), *m* without a preceding vowel ('m'), vowel plus *n* ('Vn') or just *n*:

TABLE 5.3 **Dative plural -*um* in the earliest OHG texts (see also Luiten 2011)**

Form	Number
-Vm	89
-m	26
-Vn	159
-n	61

While OHG handbooks give the dative plural endings in -*m*, early OHG already had predominately -*n* forms. A look across modern dialects and other West Germanic languages shows surprising retentions of final *m* in even unstressed syllables: in *Boden*, the labial is retained in English *bottom* and some German dialects, like Hessian *borəm*.

In fact, down to the present, scattered dialects keep -*m* in final position in lexical items, if not as a grammatical marker. Such dialects range from Upper Austrian in the south, through Hessian in the central areas, to some kinds of Low German. For example, Odenwald (Hessian) dialect has *farəm* 'Faden'[5] and *besəm* 'Besen' (Schirmunski 1962: 371–372). In short,

---

[5] *d* > *r* is a dialectal change, somewhat like English 'flapping' of *d/t* in *atom* but not *atomic*. It is sometimes called 'rhotacism' but is obviously historically and phonologically distinct from the change from *z* > *r*.

patterns of 'change' described in the handbooks often reflect patterns of chronic variation involving changes that began in our earliest texts and have never reached completion in some modern varieties.

Several minor changes involve consonant clusters.

1. Where in OHG we had medial *-nt-* forms, we now find the modern *-nd-*: *bintan* > *binden*. The oddity here is that this and other similar forms go back to Germanic *bind-. Even to the extent these spellings are consistent, it is difficult to be sure what was being pronounced, of course.

2. Medial *-mb-* > *-mm-*: OHG *zimber* > MHG *zimber/zimer* > modern German *Zimmer*. This *b* appears to have been inserted in prehistory to create a transition between the *m and the *r, much like we often pronounce *warmth* as *warm*[p]*th*: Germanic *temre > OHG *zimber*. Similarly, earlier *umbi* > *umbe* > modern German *um*, where the *b* is clearly historically present. Here, the *mb* became final with loss of the schwa. (And as we will see immediately, long consonants (geminates) simplify, or become short.)

3. /ng/ > ŋ. Where *n* came before a velar consonant (*g, k, x*), it was always pronounced as [ŋ]. In this period, <ng> sequences come to be pronounced with just the nasal, like in modern German *Finger* [fɪŋɐ] and not like (rhotic) English *finger* [fɪŋɡɚ].

5.2.3 'Contractions': loss of b, d, and (especially) g intervocalically

In the mid-12th century, we find the disappearance of voiced (or 'lenis') stops between vowels. This is a highly variable process, affecting numerous verb forms (like infinitives), as well as other words. Note that the forms with a consonant usually win out in the modern standard language although dialects (and regional *Umgangssprachen*) differ greatly:

OHG	MHG contracted ~ uncontracted	
sagêt	*seit ~ saget*	'says'
magadi	*meide ~ mägede*	'maiden'
habên	*hân ~ haben*	'have'

Note the similarity to changes well known from the history of English:

English		German
say	vs.	*sagen*
maid	vs.	*Magd*
nail	vs.	*Nagel*
bow	vs.	*Bogen*
hail	vs.	*Hagel*

How could we have this medial consonant loss showing up frequently (though hardly universally) in Middle High German texts but not in the modern language? It's largely illusory for both periods. First, historically, all languages, certainly those with large numbers of speakers spread over large territories, always show considerable variation. When we have written records mostly from an elite, we inevitably see only a slice of the language. In MHG, varieties allowing contraction were among those widely written. This again underscores the spottiness of our historical records: we do not have an unbroken chain of written material for a single variety of German, but a kind of historical scatterplot across time and space, as well as the third dimension of society.

In Standard German, the short forms have been lost generally, through a process of eliminating variants in the written language we'll discuss in the last two main chapters, 6 and 7. In some particular forms, they survive in the contemporary standard, such as second and third person forms of *haben*, i.e. *hast* and *hat*, which lack the *b* of the rest of the paradigm. (The process also has morphological aspects to it, beyond our immediate concern.)

These same contractions live on in a remarkable range of dialects (Schirmunski 1962: 562–571). The form *han* or *hān*, for instance, occurs as an infinitive and present tense form (1st singular, 1st and 3rd plural) across western dialects from the Cologne area down through Hessian, and related forms are even more widespread. In some Bavarian, East Franconian, and other dialects, a new grammatical distinction has apparently developed around the distinction: the short or 'contracted' forms of *haben* are used when it serves as an auxiliary verb—along the lines of *ich han* + past participle—but a full form with *b* (or *w*) is used in the meaning 'to have'—along the lines of *ich habe*.[6] In some dialects the process shows wrinkles, like in the Lorraine dialect of Falkenberg (now Falquemont), where medial /g, b/ normally become /j, β/, but the process does not apply in the modern dialect before /l/, yielding *legen* = *le*[j]*en* but *Kegel* = *ke*[g]*el* (see Glover & Hall 2009 for detailed discussion).

Sibilants. The set of *s*-like sounds undergoes a set of important changes during the MHG period:

1. OHG sk > MHG ʃ. This is traditionally dated to the mid-11th century, and the cluster is believed to have gone through a stage of [sx] before becoming a single sound. We still find this intermediate stage in Netherlandic, in initial position, where the Amsterdam airport name *Schiphol* begins with [sx].

---

[6] We've noted a near-parallel earlier: English speakers tend to use reduced forms like *gonna* for the 'going to' future (although the unreduced form is still possible), but the full lexical meaning of *to go* cannot be reduced—*I'm gonna Detroit.

scōni >   *schoene*
wascan >   *waschen*
fisk >   *visch*

We have a parallel change in English, from Old English /sk/, spelled *sc-*, to modern *sh*: *sceadu* > *shadow*, *scéotan* > *shoot*, *englisc* > *English*. In English, the change is dated to roughly 1100. This is another reminder of how language history, including sound change, really does repeat itself.

2. **'Long-tailed z',** <ʒ> > /s/. The fricative that emerged from the Second Sound Shift of *t, often spelled *ʒ*, merges with *s*, as in *eʒʒan* > *essen*, *waʒ* > *was*. This is a late change, dating from the 13th century. We know from textual evidence, where the sounds were spelled distinctly, that this was a real difference. It cannot have been one of (just) voicing, but must have been in the place or manner of articulation. The usual view (e.g. Schirmunski 1962: 356–357) is that <s> was actually closer to [ʃ] or [ʒ], while the product of Germanic *t was actually more *s*-like. Our evidence for the particular pronunciation of <s> as /ʒ/ comes from German loanwords in West Slavic, languages and dialects which have richer fricative systems than modern German—they often contrast [s, z, ʃ, ʒ]. German *Sold* 'pay' is found, for instance, in Polish as *żołd*, i.e. with initial [ʒ]. Further evidence, more direct, comes from a community of Bavarian speakers who migrated from Southern Bavaria and ultimately founded the community of Gottschee in present-day Slovenia ca. 1300. They have retained a distinction between /s/ and what is traditionally transcribed as /ʒ/. In that dialect, the cognate of modern German *Sohn* appears as [ʒy:n]. (You can hear samples here: http://gottschee.com/.)

3. **S-clusters,** [s]C > [ʃ]C. *sleht, smal, snel, swert, stein, spil* come to be pronounced as in standard pronunciation of modern German.[7] This did not take place in some northern varieties, which still pronounce [s] here, like *Stadt* as [stat] not [ʃtat]. Examining written documents from the late MHG period and beyond, Benware (1996) shows that the change began before *l*, where the strident *s* before *l* began to be spelled *schl*, and then expanded to *s* before *n*, then *m*, and finally before *w*. This is based on spelling and much is uncertain about the pronunciation, but Benware argues that the <s> was actually pronounced as a retroflex, [ʂ], and ties this to the broader changes in stridents just discussed.

   Moreover, the same or a closely related change happens in some other environments, namely post-consonantally like *-rs* becoming *-rʃ*. The

---

[7] A similar change appears to be happening in many American English dialects today, where [s] is becoming [ʃ] especially before another consonant (most often *t*) and an *r*: *street*, *strike*, etc.

Latin loanword *kerse* appears in MHG as *kirse* but becomes Early New High German *kirsche*. The process is more widespread across many regional dialects, cf. *Wurscht* for *Wurst*. (See Hall 2008 for a phonological analysis of the development of *-rs*, and see §7.5 for a little further discussion.)

A number of other changes occur late in the period:

1. Geminates, or double consonants, are simplified, although spelling is kept to indicate short vowels preceding them. You'll recall from the last chapter that stops and fricatives could be single (short) or geminate (long) in OHG, and other West Germanic dialects. The forms we write still as *offen* versus *schlafen* at that time had a long [f:] in the first word and a short [f] in the second. A few dialects still have geminates, typically far southern ones, Bavarian and Alemannic dialects of the Alps.

2. /x/, or the *ach-Laut*, develops a variant (allophone) [ç] after front vowels or after consonants, the *ich-Laut*. That is, until this period, Germanic *x (from IE *k by Grimm's Law) was pronounced like modern *ach-Laut*, in positions like at the ends of words, where it did not weaken to [h]. In late MHG, it appears, most of the German-speaking lands begin to change that velar fricative to a palatal after a front vowel. Since front vowels are in some sense palatal, this is an assimilation. This development never takes place in some areas, famously in Alemannic dialects (but also including Thuringian and Bavarian dialects), so that down to the present they have only *ach-Laut*, and words ending in *-ich* are pronounced something like [ɪx].

3. MHG *v* merges with *f(f)*: *oven* > *offen*, *vaz* > *Faß*. That is, a voicing distinction is lost in these fricatives. You'll be reminded of the earlier situation by seeing the *v* spellings in MHG texts. Related to this change, the old [w] sound becomes [β], the *b* in Spanish *abuela* 'grandmother', and it typically goes on to [v]. Numerous modern dialects, like East Franconian, retain the [β].

4. The *Medienverschiebung* gets undone, in part: in late OHG, we see in texts that <p, k> revert to <b, g>, but Bavarian *p-* stays. Around 1300, a new weakening of stops starts moving north from Vienna, which we'll discuss in the next chapter. At the same time, old initial *dw-* is written as *tw-* (MHG *twingen* 'zwingen').

Auslautverhärtung. Standard German has 'final fortition' or 'final devoicing', where [b, d, g, z, v] are pronounced like [p, t, k, s, f] at the end of words (or syllables). We see such spellings occasionally in OHG from the 8th century

(though they are sometimes difficult to distinguish clearly from those associated with the *Medienverschiebung*), but these are often represented in
spelling in MHG:

> tac   *tages*
> lip   *libes*
> leit   *leides*

The surprising thing is that this seems to disappear in the early modern
period, only to reappear in modern German, though not in all dialects, by
any means (Mihm 2004, Iverson & Salmons 2006, 2007, 2011). If fortition was
lost, one explanation for it could be schwa apocope (see p. 256 and following
pages). That is, with vowel loss, a pair like *ta*[k] ~ *ta*[g]*e* 'day NOM./ACC.SG.' vs.
'day NOM.ACC.PL.' could have been realized as *ta*[k] ~ *ta*[g], reintroducing the
laryngeal contrast in final position. Gress-Wright (2010) has studied the
spellings in later texts, from the 14th and 15th centuries, and found that in
fact words of the *ta*[k] type, where there never was a schwa, show more
frequent fortis spellings, while the *ta*[g] type more often shows a lenis spelling.
This supports then the case for loss of final fortition in ENHG, and therewith
another possible case of 'ebb and flow'.

But consider a fuller historical context: while Auslautverhärtung has been
traditionally dated to MHG, Vaught (1977) argued long ago, at great length,
that it is "clearly evident" in Old High German (1977: 179), although it is
highly variable by text, dialect, and place of articulation. On the last point, for
instance, he finds the hardening of /g/ to <k> to be the most common; he also
finds some hardening of /b/ and, least of all, of /d/, in addition to an apparent
confusion of forms that reflect *θ.

Vaught finds the most consistent patterns of fortition in Isidor, which is an
early text. Traditionally it has not been securely identified with a particular
dialect, though that is almost surely some sort of Franconian (as noted recently
by Seiler 2014: 56). More importantly, the text is written in a distinctive and
very systematic orthography (where modern *dass* is spelled *dhazs*, for
instance). Vaught identifies alternations within paradigms of individual
words, so that the 'king' word without a suffixal vowel is written *chuninc*,
while inflected forms are *chunigo* and *chunige*. Braune & Reiffenstein (2004:
106–107) are skeptical of this account, primarily because they see it as
obscured by the *Medienverschiebung* (discussed in the last chapter), though
they do acknowledge real patterns involving /g/ from early on in Old Bavarian.
The shift of medials was of course place-sensitive, though in quite different
ways, and consistent shift of velars in a Franconian dialect would be striking.
At the very least, this shows that the relationship between *Medienverschiebung*
and final fortition warrants more research.

Across the whole German-speaking territory, it is highly likely that some dialects did have final fortition at this point; and it is clear that others did not. Overall, then, the record shows depth of historical complexity and crucially suggests that the MHG patterns in edited texts probably were not as clean as they may seem to be. (Just recall the edited vs. manuscript versions of *gelieb ~ geliep* in the poem by Der von Kürenberg discussed at the beginning of this chapter.) We'll return to final fortition later, only to see continuing rich variability.

5.2.4 Vowels

Auslaut. Unstressed vowels in general reduce to schwa, [ə], written as <e>. When this happens with endings, this obviously means that numerous morphological distinctions are lost in nominal and verbal paradigms. In the forms below, the distinct forms posited for OHG are given in bold, while the MHG forms, presumed to be pronounced as schwa, are spelled as *-e*:

	OHG	MHG		OHG	MHG
DAT. SG.	**tage**	tage	PRES.	**leitis**	leites
NOM./ACC. PL.	**taga**	tage	SUBJ.	**leitês**	leites
GEN. PL.	**tago**	tage	PRET.	**leitôs**	leites

We will explore these consequences in more depth in what follows, but in terms of the importance of this as sound change, note that the same reduction happens in unstressed initial syllables:

bi-, ga-, etc. > *be-, ge-*, etc.

And a bigger step is taken in medial syllables as well, where unstressed vowels are lost altogether:

hêriro > *hêrre, sâlida* > *sælde* 'Glück, Heil' (note umlaut)

Umlaut. In OHG, only primary umlaut was clearly and (relatively) consistently spelled. In MHG, the rest come to be written in normalized texts: *ä:, ö, ü, äu*, and even short *ä* in old blocking environments. This is far less common in actual manuscripts than in edited versions of them, as already noted, and marking of umlaut remains inconsistent even into the early modern period (16th century). In this period, some dialects (notably Bavarian) already start to unround the front rounded vowels (like in the many modern central and southern dialects where *schön* is pronounced like *scheen*, almost like the English name *Shane*).

OHG	MHG
wânen	*wænen* (old *-jan* verb: **wânjan*)
turi	*tür*
lôsen	*lœsen*
skôni	*scæn*
mahti	*mähte*, etc.

Note here that <iu> is the MHG spelling for /ü:/, reflecting its origins from earlier /iu/ (OHG *biutu* 'ich biete'), umlaut of this *iu* (OHG *liuti* > *liute* 'Leute'), and umlaut of OHG *û* (OHG *hûsir* > *hiuser* 'Häuser').

The remarkable point here is that the umlaut 'triggering' *i/j* weakened to schwa or disappeared altogether far earlier, during the early OHG period in many instances. The fact that German dialects so faithfully have umlaut where there were once umlaut triggers gives us secure reason to think that umlauted vowels were produced before loss of the triggers, even though they were not consistently written for centuries.

At the same time, the generalization of umlaut from its originally specific environment—short *a* becomes *e* when *i/j* occurs in the following syllable— never reaches completion everywhere. Contemporary dialects of Upper German show some patterns of umlaut blocking. The classic example is short /u/ + geminate consonants, especially velar (examples, given in the last chapter, taken from Schirmunski 1962: 201–203):

Southern	Standard	Earlier form
muck	*Mücke*	OHG *mucka*, cf. Old Saxon *muggia*
ʃduk	*Stück*	OHG *stucki*
khuxë	*Küche*	OHG *kuchina*

So, from this period forward, dialects varied in just which words and word types had umlaut or lacked it. The process of language standardization involves choosing a particular form, even of a particular word, from among possible variants. In just such a process, a few of these forms are not umlauted in modern Standard German, like *suchen*, a class i weak verb which shows umlaut in the north, e.g. *sööken*, and even in scattered southern dialects.

We also find limited regional blocking of umlaut with intervening NASAL + CONSONANT. In such cases, the umlauted forms were overwhelmingly made the standard ones, but one important form of this sort is OHG *umbi* 'um', where the unumlauted form found its way into the modern standard, though many dialects and closely related languages show umlaut, e.g. Low German *öm* 'um'.

MHG <ie> (=[iə]). In OHG, we have seen a number of diphthongs that look unfamiliar to an eye only familiar with the modern language, including the reflexes of *eu and *ē², plus an old combination of *ai + w. Most of these conveniently now merge into MHG *ie*, still pronounced as a diphthong at this time but now spelled in a way familiar from the modern language:

*eu >   OHG eo, io, eu > ie   *biotan > bieten, ziohan > ziehen*, etc.;
*ē² >   OHG ia, ea, ie > ie   *hiar > hier, hialt > hielt*
*aiw > OHG io, eo   > ie   *io-/eoman > ieman* 'jemand' [je- < *aiw-]

Together with the development of OHG *iu* (just below), this makes the reflexes of old Height Harmony look odd in certain morphological alternations: OHG [ih] *biutu* vs. *biotan* = MHG *biute* [bü:tə] vs. *bieten*.

Two more major vowel changes start during this period, though they are usually more associated with the Early New High German period and will be further discussed in the next chapter:

Diphthongization. The long high vowels of OHG and through MHG, /iː, uː, yː/, all become diphthongs:

zît, hûs, hiute > Zeit, Haus, heute
Early: î, û, iu > BAVARIAN <ei> , <au> , <eu>

How can we know when changes like these happened? Textual evidence helps: by the early 13th century, one author, Heinrich von dem Türlîn, makes rhymes between the old monophthongs and old diphthongs which are phonetically and phonologically similar to the new diphthongs:

zît ~ geleit
hiute ~ freute

By the end of the 13th century, this process reaches north to East Franconian and by the 16th, it goes as far southward as Alemannic, where it peters out—we today find monophthongs in numerous dialects beyond that area of spread. For instance, in Alemannic dialects, the 'house' word has a long *u*, *hūs*. Map 12 shows the spread of the new diphthongs. Note also that these changes parallel, in some regards, the Great Vowel Shift of English, where *hūs > house*.

Monophthongization. In a kind of inverse process to diphthongization, we have a pattern of monophthongization, involving three high diphthongs which become modern long monophthongs.

lieb, grüen, bruoder > liep (= [liːp]), *grün, Bruder*

The reflexes of this process in the modern dialects are shown in Map 13.

The spelling conventions of the modern language keep <ie> for old [iə], so that we can still recognize words that had that old diphthong, though this spelling serves other functions as well in the modern language. The process

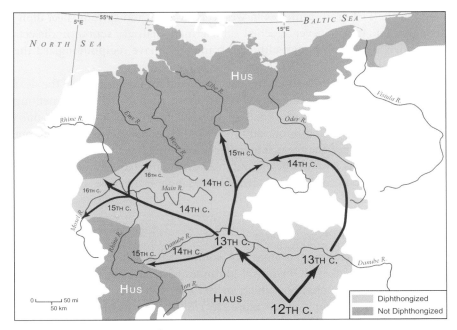

MAP 12 Diphthongization of /uː/.

Adapted from König et al. (2015: 146).

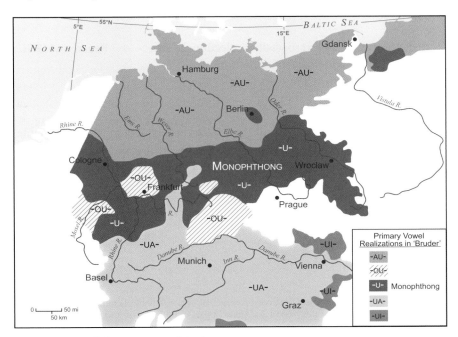

MAP 13 Monophthongization of /uo/.

Adapted from König et al. (2015: 146).

starts in the 11th–12th centuries in west central areas and spreads. Like diph-thongization, it has never reached all German dialects: southern dialects still widely have diphthongs, although some areas have rediphthongized the long vowels.[8]

While we will not talk about the rise of a standard language until the next chapters, it is worth noting already that these changes tell us something about the modern standard: Standard German today includes both mono-phthongization and diphthongization—we say *Haus* not *Hus* and *Bruder* not *Bruoder*. But neither change is found across anything like the whole German-speaking territory. Nor are they found in a particularly large number of cities, nor are they found in the areas identified today with the 'best' German, like Hannover.

5.2.5 Summary of sound changes

In the last chapter, our summary of sound changes highlighted regional differences above all. This obviously continues to be an issue in MHG, along with the ordering of changes, which we've dealt with since the beginning of the book. Now, though, we see more clear difficulties in the interpretation of the written record, but ever richer value for understanding modern regional and other variation.

Consonants

Reduction:	Final (especially inflectional) *-m* > *-n*. Began in OHG; regionally variable.
Clusters:	**-nt-** > -nd-. Variable?
	-mb > -mm
	-ng > [ŋ]
Contraction:	Medial *g, b,* and (to a lesser extent) *d* > Ø. Highly variable, later mostly lost.
Auslaut:	**Lenis (voiced) obstruents** are spelled—and presumably pronounced—as **fortis** in final position: *tage* but *tac* [tʰak]
Sibilants:	**sk** > [sx] > [ʃ], 11th c.

---

[8] Like the vowel changes just treated, processes of Open Syllable Lengthening and Closed Syllable Shortening begin in this period, but these in part unfolded later, and so will be treated in the next chapter.

| Late changes | sC > schC (= [ʃC]), late, found especially in southern dialects. ꝫ (from Germanic *t by the Second Sound Shift) **merges with s**, 13th c.
Degemination: long consonants merge with short, absent in far south.
[x] develops [ç] allophone before front vowels and before consonants, not found in far south. |

Vowels

Reduction:	Unstressed short vowels generally reduce to **schwa**, [ə], e.g. in the second syllable of disyllabic words and unstressed prefixes. Trisyllabic words often lose medial vowels. Began in OHG, progressed slowly, and was highly variable.
Umlaut:	Surely present phonologically, given the loss of umlaut 'triggers', but not reliably spelled, except in normalized texts.
Diphthongs:	The host of OHG diphthongs spelled *eo, io, eu, ia, ea, ie* all become <ie>, [iə]. Variable.
Late changes:	**Diphthongization** of *î, û, iu* (= [y:]) > *ei, au, eu* (= [aj, aw, oj]. Begins 12th c. in southeast, never reaches most of Alemannic or northern areas. **Monophthongization** of *ie, üe, uo* > long high monophthongs, spelled *i, iu, u* in normalized MHG (= [i:, y:, u:]). 11th–12th c., begins in west central areas.

5.3 Morphology: It's beginning to look a lot like German

Over the course of OHG, we already found restructuring in the morphology as endings weakened, but MHG is the period when the fundamental changes are traditionally thought to really come into sharp focus. Following on our earlier discussion, let's consider a phonological change that could have triggered simplification, then look at patterns of morphological simplification directly. As we'll see, the phonological reductions do contribute to morphological change, but in some arenas, other kinds of change took place (like analogy), or little change took place (like in the relatively stable ablaut patterns). There is also the possibility, though it has too seldom been explored in the literature, that morphological changes are the driving force.

A phonological trigger? Reduction of unstressed vowels from the Laws of Finals continues. Again, <e> here reflects schwa.

	OHG	MHG	
Reduction:	bi-, gi-, fir- →	be-, ge-, fer-	in affixes, and often complete loss in Upper German
Loss:	tuifales →	tuifels	unstressed syllables
	wirdit →	wirt	often between similar consonants
	scôni →	schœn	final position (called 'apocope')

This dramatically reshapes the appearance of many words, as shown by examples already given:

hēriro	→	hêrre, hërre	'Herr'
sālida	→	sælde	'Glück, Seligkeit'
scōnisto	→	schœnste	

Underlying this kind of analysis is the view that sound change is regular, so that, when it sweeps through morphological paradigms, it disrupts them (think about sound changes in the OHG ablaut patterns), while analogy then restores some order. This is known as 'Sturtevant's Paradox' (Sturtevant 1947: 109): 'Phonetic laws are regular but produce irregularities. Analogic creation is irregular but produces regularity.' As obvious as this scenario seems to be, and as reflexively as historical linguists tend to accept it, some now question it.

For the loss of morphology in mainland Scandinavian case distinction, Enger (2013) makes a strong case that process is not simply phonological. He describes the traditional view of inflectional changes as coming from the 'disturbance' of morphological oppositions by sound changes, so that morphology is 'reactive'. If we assume an independent morphological module, we shouldn't necessarily expect that 'phonology-first' pattern. This would also be broadly consistent with the kinds of arguments put forth by Menz 2010, and discussed in §4.1.3. This is promising turf for future work.

Whatever the ultimate cause, the big effects are in the leveling of morphological distinctions, to which we now turn.

Effects of weakening on the verbal system. Handbooks, as noted, posit full vowels for OHG and reduced vowels for MHG, contrasting pairs like OHG *nimu* 'I take' with MHG *nime*, where, again, <e> reflects [ə]. The change eliminates contrasts among certain verb forms, of course. More importantly, in OHG, preterit indicative and subjunctive forms were clearly distinguished by different vowels, with a range of different vowels in the indicative contrasting with *i* in the subjunctive. By MHG, these all weaken to schwa, obliterating the distinction.

	OHG		MHG
	indicative	subjunctive	BOTH
1/3 sg	hôrta 'I heard'	hôrti 'I would have heard'	hôrte
3 pl	hôrtun	hôrtīn	hôrten

Strong verbs: ablaut. There's remarkably little change here—the classes discussed for OHG continued the Germanic patterns well and they are still quite visible in MHG, with mostly the weakening of unstressed vowels (and using now the conventional circumflex to mark vowel length), which does not disturb ablaut:

	Infin	Sg pret	Pl pret	Past part
I	trîben	treip	triben	getriben
	zîhen	zêh	zigen	gezigen
II	biegen	bouc	bugen	gebogen
	bieten	bôt	buten	geboten
III	werfen	warf	wurfen	geworfen
	binden	bant	bunden	gebunden
IV	stelen	stal	stâlun	gestolen
V	geben	gap	gâben	gegeben
VI	tragen	truoc	truogen	getragen
VII	lâzen	liez	liezun	gelâzen

As the verb *zîhen* shows, Verner effects remain in some verbs. Of course, the regular sound changes apply here, e.g. in OHG *ia* becoming *ie* in class VII. Class VII shows some unity, in fact: it still contains many possible vowels in the infinitive (*a, â, ô, ou, uo, ei*), but the singular and plural preterit all normally have *ie* throughout, and the participle's vocalism reflects that of the infinitive, giving an A B B A pattern in the paradigm, like for class VI.

Similarly, we find little change in the forms of the preterit present verbs, as shown by forms like *kan, kunnen, konde* for modern *kann, können, konnte* and *sol, sullen, solde* for modern *soll, sollen, sollte*. The language had a few preterit presents that are not modals today, like *tugen* 'taugen' and *turren* 'wagen'.

In meaning and function the preterit presents continue to move toward the modern modals (see Paul et al. 2007: 271–274, and the next chapter).

Personal endings. The weakening of final vowels brings us close to the modern language in the verbal suffixes—though with a few wrinkles familiar from OHG:

- For the first singular present, we tend to see the modern *-e* ending, but we still do get forms with *-en* (recall OHG *salbôm* 'I salve' etc.). One place we find this pattern a lot is specifically in the construction *ich hân* 'I have'. As noted in the last section, this form remains widespread in many modern dialects, especially when the verb serves as an auxiliary.

- MHG *lâȝen* (modern German *lassen*) also has a contracted form *lân* in the first singular and in the infinitive, along with *er lât, wir lân*, and so on.
- We still usually have a schwa before the -*t* in third singular forms where it is long since gone in modern German: *er nimet* vs. modern *er nimmt*.
- The third person plural present still has -*ent* endings (*nement*), though we see modern-looking forms by late MHG, especially in central dialects. That is, during this period, the ending begins to simplify to -*en*.
- The form that may look oddest to you is that for strong verbs (but not weak ones), the second person singular preterit has not yet taken the characteristic -*s* or -*st* suffix: *du næm(e)* 'you took', still following the OHG forms (*nâmi*, but now umlauted in MHG). In central dialects, we see during this period the rise of -*st* endings, so that second person singular strong verbs come to end in -*st*, as in *names(t)*, both adopting the ending otherwise so widespread for this cell of the verb paradigm and losing umlaut.

Developments like the last one are hardly surprising, given that the -*st* suffix was already so closely associated with second singular in the present tense and for weak verbs in the preterit. This is a classic situation for analogy, or the extension of an existing pattern to new forms.

WEAK VERBS reduced from three types in OHG to only two in MHG. In OHG, the classes are distinguished by the different suffix vowels—original -*jan* (sometimes indirectly visible in gemination), -*ôn*, -*ên*; but in MHG the key difference is carried by the presence/absence of a linking vowel or *Bindevokal*, so that earlier classes ii and iii collapse:

OHG i	nerien	MHG	nern	ner(e)te	gener(e)t
	brennen	MHG	brennen	brante	gebrennet
OHG ii	lobôn	MHG	loben	lobete	gelobet
OHG iii	lëbên	MHG	lëben	lëbete	gelëbet

That is, what distinguished the three weak classes in OHG were the suffixes, but they have merged entirely in MHG, although, as Joshua Bousquette points out in correspondence, this is foreshadowed by variation in OHG. What does remain in MHG, however, is the presence of a linking vowel after a short stem (as in *lobete*) and its absence in old long stems (like *branta*) with some complexity by stem-final consonants and with loss of schwa more commonly after /l, r/ (*nerte*, 'nährte', *spilte* 'spielte') and less likely after obstruents, as in the examples above. This pattern continues to the present, with the linking vowel found only with nasal plus consonant or coronal plus consonant.

The *ge*- prefix. This is the period when the *ge*- prefix comes to be more closely associated with the past participle of verbs. Like in the modern language, this doesn't happen when there's an unstressed (inseparable) prefix, but it does appear with *-ieren* verbs (as is still the case in modern Dutch and various German dialects, though the prefix does not appear with *-ieren* in Standard German). For example, *leischieren* 'to ride with loose reins' appears in Wolfram in this line *dô kom geleischieret . . . ein ritter* 'there came a knight riding at full speed' (Lockwood 1968: 104). (The best analysis of *ge-* overall is Fertig 1998.)

The *ge-* prefix still has some perfective meaning—that is, serving to mark the completion of something. Consistent with that, some verbs that are already perfective in meaning don't usually take it on past participles in this period, creating participles like *funden, troffen, gëben, komen*, etc. So, *ge-* was used on participles except those that express completion—if you have found something or met someone or given someone something, the activity is indicated as completed by the meaning. We still have a trace of this in modern German, in fact, with *ge*-less *worden* in perfect forms of the passive (*ist gemacht worden*).

Nonetheless, the occurrence of *ge-* on verbs in MHG remains highly variable and Lockwood argues that it was commonly used in poetry or not depending on the needs of meter, rather than simply grammatical grounds.

5.3.1 An example of the effects of weakening on the case system

We saw in the last chapter that many morphological distinctions in the nominal system were encoded in final vowels, like these in the masculine *a*-stems:

Old High German

Dat. sg.	tage
Nom./acc. pl.	taga
Gen. pl.	tago

The reduction of those vowels to schwa means that each form is pronounced as [tagə], so that these distinctions must be marked by other means (articles, adjective endings, prepositions) or be lost.

TABLE 5.4 **Development of strong (vowel stem) versus weak noun (n-stem) paradigms**

		STRONG			WEAK		
		OHG		MHG	OHG		MHG
Sg	Nom	stein	>	stein	boto	>	bote
	Acc	stein	>	stein	boton/-un	>	boten
	Gen	steines	>	steins	boten/-in	>	boten
	Dat	steine	>	steine	boten/-in	>	boten
Pl	Nom/Acc	steina	>	steine	boton/-un	>	boten
	Gen	steino	>	steine	botôno	>	boten
	Dat	steinum	>	steinen	botôm	>	boten

In short, the effects of reduction of unstressed syllables on the morphology of German in this time period are massive. While in OHG we had a large class of distinct stem classes, the merger of essentially all suffixal vowels into schwa and the merger of final *n* and *m* obliterates yet more key distinctions. The old array of endings are pronounced merely as [ə] and [ən], leaving basically the modern patterns for words like those illustrated in Table 5.4. As a result, instead of the historical stem classes, we can now capture the synchronic patterns far more simply (following Paul 2007: 186–199).

As a result, the complex stem class system inherited in Germanic from Indo-European and still evident in OHG can now be reconfigured around four distinct noun categories. Historically, of course, these groups continue earlier classes, but from the perspective of a child learning to speak MHG, the organization below is likely to have been how they organized the system.

As you look through these tables of data, notice how the role of gender now grows as a way of organizing the whole nominal system, and how the distinction between singular versus plural is becoming more systematic and for learners, presumably easier to notice and acquire. Only a few forms show case directly, like DAT.PL.-*(e)n* or GEN.SG. -*(e)s* for most MASC./NEUT.

I. No umlaut in plural

	Masculine		Neuter		Feminine	
	Sg	Pl	Sg	Pl	Sg	Pl
N	tac	tage	wort	wort	tür	tür(e)
A	tac	tage	wort	wort	tür	tür(e)
G	tages	tage	wort(e)s	wort(e)	tür(e)	tür(e)
D	tage	tagen	wort(e)	wort(e)n	tür(e)	türen

These are our old *a*-stems for masculine and neuter and *ō*-stems for the feminine, and the membership of the classes remains partly stable. In the masculine nouns, we see our first signs of direct plural marking, rather than the earlier portmanteau marking. (Recall that in OHG *tago*, the -*o* simultaneously marked genitive and plural.) Namely, the schwa, written -*e*, emerges from vowel reductions—from the collapse of -*e*, -*a*, -*o*, illustrated with OHG *stein*, just above—as a unified indication of plurality.

The old *a*-stems (and -*wa* and -*ja*) and old root nouns (like *man*) merge into this group, including some old feminine root nouns (like *bluome*), and some *i*-stems with vowels that didn't umlaut, such as *zît*. Not only are the plural forms now coming to be better defined, but the role of umlaut is becoming steadily more prominent:

II. Umlaut in plural

	Masculine		Neuter		Feminine	
	Sg	Pl	Sg	Pl	Sg	Pl
N	gast	gest(e)	lamp	lember	kraft	krefte
A	gast	gest(e)	lamp	lember	kraft	krefte
G	gast(e)s	gest(e)	lamb(es)	lember	krefte	krefte
D	gast(e)	gesten	lamb(e)	lembern	krefte	kreften

These are in large part old *i*-stems, as well as the small class of old neuter *-iz* nouns (like *lamp*), where rhotacism and vowel reduction created *-er* from earlier *-iz*. This class was originally tiny, including *lamp ~ lember*, *kalp ~ kelber* 'calf ~ calves', *huon ~ hüener* 'chicken ~ chickens', and a small number of other nouns. We saw in the last chapter that the laws of finals eroded the sparser endings in the singular sometimes faster than in the plural, leaving the original class marker of the *i*-stems, for instance, associated with the plural. Here too, an original class marker becomes associated with plurality. It is the source of modern plurals with umlaut and *-er*, and already in MHG, the class was growing to include words like *dorf*, *wort*, *tal*, and others.

Here again, we see pretty clear signs of a distinct plural form emerging, although even in this kind of handbook data, the distinction is not yet unambiguous, as exemplified by the umlaut in the feminine singular genitive and dative forms, reflecting the old *-i* they had in OHG.

As observed at the outset of this section, we're seeing here the intricate interplay of sound change and morphological change. This relationship has long been contentious in historical linguistics: a traditional view is that regular sound change reshapes morphology and morphology then reacts, with leveling or analogical change ironing out the wrinkles created by sound change. That is, the question is whether sound change can be morphologically conditioned. If you recall the *i*-stem paradigm from the last chapter, *gast* had an instrumental case form, originally *gastiu*. Such a form should have umlauted, when the time came. In fact Wurzel (1984, elsewhere) argues that it did not, because in this case a morphological generalization overrode the sound change: the association between singular and umlautlessness on the one hand and plural and umlaut on the other was, in his view, established quite early. I showed in a 1994 article, though, that the OHG patterns still look phonological: umlaut tends to occur in instrumental forms when the *i* is present (*in stediu* 'on the (river) bank', Tatian), while we often find early loss of the umlaut trigger, so that one manuscript of the *Benedikterregel* shows an unumlauted *kastu* 'guest, instrumental'. The key point for us is the relationship between umlaut and plurality is established only much later, during the course of the MHG period. This hardly resolves the general theoretical issue of morphological conditioning of sound change, but it removes one often-cited case, in favor of the regularity of sound change (in the relevant sense).

III. Feminine

	Sg	Pl
N	gebe	gebe
A	gebe	gebe
G	gebe	geben
D	gebe	geben

The set continues the group of old *ô* stems, at least in the singular; but let us consider some more context, namely the weak nouns, before talking about the plurals.

In terms of the broader nominal system, classes like this show the diminished role that case plays on nouns. Of course, case distinctions are not lost, but they and the meanings they convey migrate from being marked directly on nouns to being carried on articles and adjectives, with increasing support from the system of prepositions. The fourth class contains old *n*-stem nouns, today's weak nouns:

Weak

	Masculine	Feminine
	Sg	Sg
N	bote	zunge
Other	boten	zungen

The neuters are like this except for one point, namely that the accusative patterns with the nominative.

	Sg
NA	herze
Other:	herzen

We find odd echoes of this in some modern forms, where patterns exist for some speakers with *ins Herz_* contrasting with *im Herzen* (now a lexicalized form, not truly 'inflected').

The emergence of the modern correlation of feminine singular nouns in -*e* with -*n* plurals is often seen as the product of mixing between old ō-stem singular forms and feminine *n*-stem plural forms. That is, words like *gebe* adopted an -*n* throughout the plural and words like *zunge* lost the same sound in the singular. Paul (2007: 196–197) sees the old ō-stem paradigm as surviving longer in abstract nouns (*êre, volge, güete*, etc.), while concrete nouns (*brück, strāʒe*) are more likely to get inflected like weak nouns, and also to follow some different developments regionally. Fertig (2014) cites several pieces of very good evidence for this scenario: the *n*-declension is very productive for feminines in OHG, which suggests that ō-stems were not a default class for that gender, including feminine agent nouns (*forasaga*, 'prophetess'), loans like *kirriha* 'church', and borrowed names of women (*Maria*). Also, class movement between *n*-stems and ō-stems support a mixing of the classes; and Fertig notes that movement into the *n*-stems was more common. He makes a larger point about morphological change here as well (2014: 550, drawing on Fertig 2013: 72–76):

The longstanding debate over whether analogical changes that result in greater similarity among forms within a (sub)paradigm are motivated primarily by intraparadigmatic or by interparadigmatic ('proportional') relations has usually focused on the leveling of stem alternations....This case shows that the same issues can arise with changes involving inflectional affixes.

Moving on to the general picture of nominal inflection, already in MHG, we see the beginnings of the changes to adjust this system to the modern patterns. A word like *vater*, which belonged to the always-tiny class of *r*-stems, took plurals in -*e*, but two schwas in a row (*vatere*) were a perfect environment to lose the final one. We already find in MHG forms like *veter(e)* here, which reflect a more secure singular–plural distinction. Similarly, in the neuter *a*-stems, the absence of plural marking on Nom/Acc *wort* yields to *worte*, especially in central dialects, presumably following the handy (and popular) model of the masculines with otherwise parallel inflection. Down to the present, we've continued to have movement from one class to another (and even today we see variability), e.g. weak nouns becoming strong. Most importantly, this is a key early step toward the solidification of the SINGULAR ≠ PLURAL distinction at the apparent expense of case marking on nouns (a development often known as *Pluralprofilierung*). The singulars of nouns generally become harder to distinguish by old classes, with masculines and neuters following old *a*-stem patterns and feminines the old ō-stems. At the same time, there is more diversity in the plural patterns (as shown in §5.3.1).

5.3.2 Base form versus stem inflection

Recent work has begun to look at these changes in terms of deeper changes to the morphological system and providing better data on how things have and haven't changed. In discussing how IE words were built (Chapter 3), we began with what are called 'roots', the most stripped down form of a word, to which derivational and inflectional affixes were added (along with other changes, like ablaut). We've since noted repeatedly that the transparency of the individual elements, like theme vowels, have eroded steadily and very variably over time. Each generation of new speakers has to make sense of this kind of data, and organize it into a coherent system. Without the (relatively) simple and transparent root of IE morphology, what form of the word does the speaker start from to build derivational or inflectional forms?

Compare these OHG and MHG inflectional forms, for which we just saw the full MHG paradigm:

	OHG	MHG
Nom.sg.	boto	bote
Gen.sg.	boten	boten

Wurzel (1989: 42–47, elsewhere) distinguishes two ways that words can inflect. In one, the 'base form' of a word takes inflection directly, in German called the *Grundform-Prinzip*. In the other, a 'stem', or part of the basic form of the word, takes inflection, *Stammform-Prinzip*.[9] As you can see, these OHG forms adhere to stem inflection and the MHG ones to basic word inflection: the OHG genitive singular is built from *bot-* while the MHG form comes from *bote*. Wurzel (1992: 14, and cited in Harnisch 2001: 2) generalizes about this: 'Während das Althochdeutsche noch Stammflexion hat, zeigt das Mittelhochdeutsche (wie das Neuhochdeutsche) Grundformflexion' (see also Nübling 2008: 295 for a closely related view).

Harnisch (2001) conducts a detailed study of such forms across OHG, MHG, and the modern language. He finds a far more complex situation, including outright counterexamples (2001: 47):

OHG	Modern German	
ketina	Kette	'chain'
ketinlîn	Kettlein	'chain (diminutive)', cf. also *Kettchen*
ketinôn	ketten	'to chain'

Here, OHG follows the base form principle while the modern language works from the stem form.

How can we reconcile these patterns? Harnisch finds overall that in OHG, consonants are retained (the *n* in *ketin-*) but vowels are not (the final *o* in *boto*). In MHG, the weakening of vowels to schwa introduces a kind of ambiguity: *boto ~ boten* becomes *bote ~ boten*. In the genitive, speakers would have had no way to tell whether the alternation involved the stem (*bot-e ~ bot-en*) or the base word form (*bote ~ bote-n*). That is, a more nuanced analysis can handle data that Wurzel's sweeping statement could not. In fact, Harnisch traces fine-grained patterns of differences between inflection and derivation and across words ending in liquid (*fater*), nasal (*ofan* 'oven') and vowel (*garto* 'garden', *bluoma* 'flower').

---

[9] Morphological technical terms are used differently in different theories and traditions, and *stem* is such a case: you will find it used with different meanings in the scholarly literature.

The details of those patterns go beyond our immediate interest, but there's a larger point here, one that reaches fully into the contemporary language: while there has been some movement in German along this typological parameter, there has been no wholesale shift from one type to the other. Harnisch documents rich variation between base form- and stem-oriented patterns in OHG, MHG, and modern German. In fact both patterns remain active in the language today, e.g. with loanwords. This can manifest itself as variation within the paradigm of a single word, as with *Konto* 'account', which has the genitive form *des Kontos* but the plural form *die Konten*. In other instances, we increasingly see loanwords changing. Harnisch's favorite example (and the inspiration for his book) came from being laughed at over the phone for ordering *zwei Pizzen*, when the listener clearly expected the (typically newer) form *zwei Pizzas*. The answer to our question—what form of the word does the speaker start from to build new forms from?—has been relatively stable since OHG: base forms are widely used, but stem-oriented inflection has not disappeared from the language.

5.4 Syntax

We have stressed that early texts—even reaching into OHG—all too often showed little about syntax because they were at first short inscriptions or glosses, or leaned heavily on texts they were translated from. By the MHG period, we finally start to see a substantial number of functional/secular texts (*Gebrauchsprosa*) written in the vernacular, alongside the better known literary works, to give us a clearer idea of what syntax was like in the MHG period.

The broad outlines of MHG syntax continue the patterns we introduced in the last chapter for OHG. Word order was never entirely free, for instance, but it comes more often to follow particular patterns which foreshadow the modern patterns of inflected verb in second position of main clauses and non-finite forms (infinitives and participles) in final position. The present section will lay out important patterns of MHG syntax, including increasing periphrastic forms in the verbal system, which sets up a discussion of word order, as it begins to look more like the structures of the modern language. Beyond that, we will look briefly at changes in negation, and the rich range of uses of the genitive case in the nominal system.

5.4.1 Configurationality

Relatively free word order can include, in the languages of the world, discontinuous constituents, where the actual word order does not correlate neatly with what elements belong together in an abstract sense. Behaghel long ago formulated what's now known as his first law on this point (1923–1932, see also 1909): 'Geistig eng Zusammengehöriges wird auch eng zusammengestellt', essentially that which belongs together is placed together. Patterns that follow Behaghel's 'law' are often described as 'configurational', but many languages do not follow it. Germanic and many Indo-European languages have moved clearly from being less to more configurational over the millennia. Luraghi traces these developments more broadly for Indo-European languages, and aptly describes the trend as 'how semantic constituency turned into syntactic constituency' (2010: 226). Configurational patterns are perhaps most obvious in word order, where for instance syntactic constituents can be discontinuous, that is, a constituent can have elements of other constituents interspersed within it. The phrase *of a good family* is a constituent, a prepositional phrase in traditional terms. The Latin form *bono genere*, however, appears in Cicero with a verb stuck between the two elements (Luraghi 2010: 218):

> Si tibi hoc sumis,   nisi qui patricius sit
> If you that assume,   if not who patrician is
>
> neminem **bono** esse **genere** natum
> nobody good to be **birth** born.
>
> '... if you assume that nobody is from a good family, unless he is a patrician...'

Semantically related elements are not necessarily adjacent in the form of the sentence. Such patterns have faded over time in Germanic, though Luraghi shows that this isn't a unidirectional development—some modern IE languages are losing some configurational patterns.

This kind of difference is important for understanding the relationship between German and English. As in various other ways, English has moved further from Proto-Germanic than German has. Hawkins (1985, with reference to Sapir 1921) sees the historical loss of inflectional morphology as having led to less strict mappings between meanings and surface forms, arguing that this unity underlies the 'realignment in the mapping between surface form and meaning' (1985: 215):

The morphological and syntactic structures of German are regularly in closer correspondence with their associated semantic representations than those of English. English tolerates greater collapsing of distinct meanings onto common surface forms (whence greater ambiguity and vagueness).

This is a more modest claim about the relationship between morphological loss and syntactic (and other change) than most earlier ones in the literature, but nonetheless one which is not without controversy.

5.4.2 Verbal syntax: more on periphrasis

In Middle High German, we frequently see periphrastic verb forms that weren't common or sometimes even attested in OHG, and with time periphrasis comes to be widespread in all the West Germanic languages. Before we turn our attention to actual structures, let us expand on our earlier discussion about how and why this might (not) have come to be.

As noted in the last chapter, traditional scholarship often held that the use of *haben* or *sein* plus past participle arose on the model of Latin, which had parallel constructions. Many scholars today have become skeptical of this, for a reason indicated at the beginning of this chapter: despite what you may intuitively think, the linguistic behavior of elites seldom has far-reaching impact on the speech of a whole community, certainly not in a setting without widespread common education. Only a small segment of society had direct knowledge of Latin, and those spoke it overwhelmingly as a second language. Even extensive exposure to those who might have spoken in a way reflecting some Latin influence will not have been so widespread. Nonetheless some specialists continue to hold weaker versions of the traditional view, like Wolf (2000: 1353): 'Durch den Kontakt zur Latinität nützt das Ahd. vorhandene Möglichkeiten und Tendenzen aus, um das verbale Flexionssystem durch analytische Formen zu ergänzen bzw. zu erweitern.' To support that view, strong evidence would need to be presented, and at present, internal accounts seem far more plausible. In particular, a good account would be needed of how the spread could have been successful from small, elite groups to the broad populace. Words can be and often are picked up in this way (recall the Latin borrowings into OHG, for instance), but this is not how language contact typically triggers phonological or grammatical change. Such changes are far more often the result of adults learning new languages and imposing features of their native language on the second language than from borrowing from a learned language. This includes word order changes. English speakers can topicalize (or move to the beginning of the sentence) definite forms for emphasis or contrast, as in '**that** book I like'. Some English dialects spoken by those in communities where earlier generations were heavily Yiddish- or Irish-speaking have extended this process to indefinite forms, like the complete sentence 'a hotel she lives in' (see Salmons & Purnell 2010). Such structures are found in Yiddish and Irish (and German) and survive the transition of the community to English. Similar examples of borrowing are rare. But let us now turn directly to the syntactic patterns and changes themselves.

The structural change involved in the creation of periphrasis seems more widely agreed on: participles in the languages of the world often behave like adjectives to some extent. As noted briefly in the last chapter, past participles of transitive verbs could be used in OHG adjectivally with *habên* or *eigan* (also meaning 'to have'), and the participles could be marked with adjective endings, like in this example from Otfrid (from Paul 2007: 292):

> sie **eigun**   mir   **ginomanan**   liabon druhtin minan
> they have   from me   taken   dear lord mine
> 'They have taken from me my dear lord.'

With intransitives, passives and other forms, you can find agreement of the adjective/participle with the subject (from Tatian, and again Paul 2007), a pattern known more broadly across Germanic:

> tho   argangana warun   ahtu taga
> then   passed were   eight days
> 'then eight days were past'

From there, the adjectival forms were simply reinterpreted by later generations, it is argued, as part of the verb, creating periphrastic forms, which included *werdan* + participle for the passive, and future constructions as well. These are illustrated below (examples all from Paul 2007).

   Old High German, as just illustrated, had not only preterit forms for the past tense but also structures with 'to be' or 'to have' plus a past participle. Today, the preterit or 'simple past' has receded in modern German for many speakers, replaced by the present perfect in southern areas in colloquial speech. MHG almost inevitably falls between these two situations, with growing use of perfect structures along with widespread use of the older preterit.

- *Present perfect:*
  wie stêtz iu umben grâl? **Habt** ir **geprüevet** noch sîn art?
- *Perfective use of modals:*
  der **kunde** se baz **gelobet hân**
  'er hätte sie besser loben können'

We likewise have a *periphrastic future*, but usually with a present participle rather than an infinitive:

> ier **werdent** mich ain clain zît niht **sehende**
> 'you won't be seeing me for a little while'

Occasionally, this is already found with an infinitive, as in:

> sô **wirt** er **sprechen**.
> 'so he will speak.'

This last form has a parallel in the present tense that isn't found in modern German:

mit dem der leu **varend ist**
mit dem der Löwe **fährt**

This pattern exists also with modal verbs:

daz er und sîn pfärdelin **muosen vallende** ûf die bluomen **sîn**
'that he and his horsie must be falling onto the flowers'

At the same time, while we have an increase in periphrasis, what we now see as auxiliary (or 'helping') verbs in the modern language are more flexible and variable. They are, for instance, not necessary, something we see down into the 19th century, at least:

ichn gehôrt...
I-NEG heard
'I haven't heard'

The rise of periphrasis has many consequences for modern German grammar. In §5.4.3, we look at one of the most famous characteristics of German, one made more possible by frequent periphrasis: the word order patterns used in German for inflected verbs (typically in second position) versus those of infinitives or participles (typically in final position).

5.4.3 Word order and the verbal frame

With the MHG period, we finally have enough prose texts that we can begin to track syntactic developments like word order in more detail over time, and even to an extent over dialect regions. German linguistics, historical and synchronic, has traditionally focused on word order in terms of the 'sentence frame' created by the *Satzrahmen* or *Satzklammer* (verbal or sentence frame), perhaps the classic characteristic of modern German word order, and noted in passing already in the last chapter.[10] It involves words used as 'brackets', typically a verbal element in second position (V2) and another in final. (Recall the evidence for verb-final patterns going back to earliest Germanic.) The brackets are shown in bold here:

(1) verbs within a clause separated by other elements:

Kohl **hat** in seinem ganzen Leben   kein einziges Mal an so etwas **gedacht.**
Kohl has in his whole life   not a single time about such   thought
'Kohl's never thought about such a thing in his whole life.'

---

[10] A good introduction to word order change, accessible and highly relevant to Germanic languages, can be found in Faarlund (2010).

(2) final placement of finite verbs in dependent clauses:
   Ich glaube, **daß** Kohl... gedacht **hat.**

We'll talk more about this later, but the first 'slot' in this system is called the *Vorfeld* and the material between the (typically) verbal bookends is the *Mittelfeld*, as illustrated below with brackets marking verb positions:

   Kein einziges Mal **hat** er an so etwas **gedacht.**

   Vorfeld   [Mittelfeld]   (Nachfeld)

Where the right bracket or *Klammer* is the last word (as in the examples ending with a verb form), we have what is called a full frame. Material after the right bracket is said to be 'extraposed' or known as 'leaking behind the verb'. We can still do this in modern colloquial German, with various limits:

Ich erzähle dir gleich, was ich gehört habe **bei Müllers**
(Lockwood 1968: 264; see also Hawkins 1985; Nachfeld)

The verb second (V2) order of the modern language is not yet the norm in poetry, and if your familiarity with MHG was limited to the *Nibelungenlied*, you might think it was exceptional. Even there, though, we find many examples of it, like this case of inversion, where a preposed adverb correlates with the verb coming before the subject:

dô sprach der junge Gîselher...
(Nibelungenlied)

In prose texts, though, V2 is already the norm (Klein 2007: 449), as a look through many of the MHG examples in this chapter will show. That means that the establishment of the frame depends on the position of the non-finite verb in the clause. The initial slot is often filled, just as in the modern language, with something other than the subject, as we'll discuss later.

   While the full frame—or the absence of extraposition—is the written standard today, numerous modern dialects still allow infinitives in non-clause-final position today, see for example Dubenion Smith 2010, but this order is generally widespread in MHG. Let's look now at one example in more detail, drawing from Sapp (2011a).[11] He undertakes a statistical analysis of word order in over 1,100 examples of subordinate clauses in prose texts from across the MHG period and across MHG dialects. In subordinate clauses—like those introduced in the modern language with *dass*, *weil*, relative pronouns, etc.—the modern standard language puts finite (that is, inflected) verbs at the end, of course:

---

[11] Bousquette (in preparation) surveys other differences between main and subordinate clauses in the history of German.

Sie glaubt, dass wir morgen noch eventuell Zeit haben *könnten*.
'She believes that we could possibly still have time tomorrow.'

In MHG, second position seems to be avoided in subordinate clauses, even if we don't regularly have inflected verbs in final position. If we limit ourselves to the simple relationship between finite and non-finite verbs, which we can label '1' and '2' respectively, we find two possible orders. That is, the inflected verb (1) can come before or after the infinitive or participle (2). These are illustrated next with sentences from Sapp, with the key elements in bold:

(wi er daz volk verflvchet.) daz got **gefegent het**.
how he the people cursed, REL God **blessed₂ had₁**
'(How he cursed the people) whom God had blessed.'

Buch der Könige 04va

(daz dv vnſ vergæbest) swaz wir vbelſ **heten** an dir **getan**.
that you us forgive REL we evil **had₁** to you **done₂**
'(...that you forgive us) whatever evil we have done to you.'

Buch der Könige 03va

These patterns vary, as Sapp's study shows, along a set of parameters, some perhaps surprising. The first is what kind of verbal construction we have. Inflected verbs overwhelmingly come at the end of clauses with passives formed with *sein* (often called the 'statal passive' in modern German), but far less often with modal verbs.

	2-1 (non-finite–finite)	1-2 (finite–non-finite)
sein passive	127 (90.1%)	14 (9.9%)
modal verb	272 (64.5%)	150 (35.5%)

But even morphological factors and prosodic considerations may play roles here, since verbs with stressed prefixes show finite-verb-final less often than those with unstressed prefixes.

	2-1 (non-finite–finite)	1-2 (finite–non-finite)
stressed prefix	31 (59.6%)	21 (40.4%)
unstressed	555 (76.4%)	171 (23.6%)

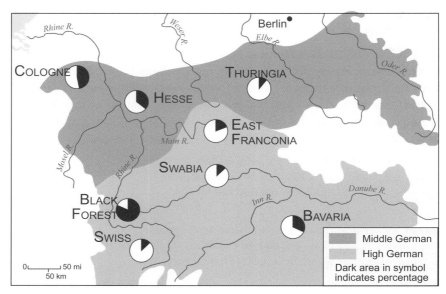

MAP 14 Percentage of 1–2 word order.
Adapted from Sapp (2011a).

Surprisingly, given the broader path of syntactic development in German, he finds no clear change in the course of MHG in his data. That is, the earliest texts he examined do not differ significantly in this regard from the latest. Nonetheless, there are powerful regional differences, as shown in Map 14 (which gives the percentage of 1–2 order).

Before leaving the topic of word order, I will mention one issue that deserves further research. We have been talking about V2; but, throughout most of its history, German has allowed V1 declarative sentences, as noted and illustrated in the previous chapter. Axel (2009) provides detailed discussion of exactly how and where these sentences are attested, but just consider these examples (2009: 28, both from Notker's *Boethius*):

Keskíhet óuh ófto dáz...
happens also often that...
it also happens often that...

lustida sie christinheidi chilaupnissa chihoran
desired them Christianity's belief to-hear
they wanted to hear the belief of Christianity

Traditional sources have seen these as disappearing in MHG, but in ENHG they are again well attested, at first following Latin models (Reichmann &

Wegera 1993: 431), especially with verbs of speaking, then spreading from there to other contexts, for instance emphatic ones; are two examples, the first from Maximilian I's chancery and the second from Dietrich:

Ist beslossen, das...
is decided that...
It is decided that...

Stehet doch im Vatter vnser nit ein wort von Christo
stands though in the Lord's Prayer not a word about Christ
But there's not a word about Christ in the Lord's Prayer

However, Coniglio (2012) shows that V1 is attested in MHG, if less frequently than in OHG and EHNG. Far more important is his conclusion that 'the syntactic and pragmatic properties of the V1-pattern have not varied during the centuries' (2012: 5).

Earlier in this chapter I touched upon Hickey's notion of 'ebb and flow', that changes seem to disappear only in order to reappear later. This example suggests that 'ebb and flow' is not limited to phonology but may be found in syntax as well. It can depend not only on spelling conventions but also on text type and on what material happens to exist for a given language stage—yet another reminder that we should be cautious about extrapolating from an absence of data. For those who think in terms of changes that arise and progress through a system and spread through a speech community to completion, such chronic or long-term variation may be sobering.

While this is a rich picture of variation compared to what is possible for OHG, too little real sociolinguistic information is available about writers— there are few texts written by women in the period, and often nothing is known about the education or occupation of writers—for even Sapp's data to yield many results. Still, he establishes a difference between clerics and non-clerics, with the former more likely to use the 1–2 order. Real sociolinguistic patterns of variation will have to wait for the next chapter.

Sapp alertly observes that whatever other changes in the history of German may be driven by morphological changes (as discussed in the previous section and previous chapters), from MHG onward, the inflectional morphology of German varieties tends to be stable. That is, word order changes of this type cannot be the result of morphological change.

5.4.4 Negation

In OHG (§4.4), we saw the particle *ni* used to negate clauses, appearing most often before an inflected (finite) verb, as in this example from Psalm 138 (with Müller's modern translation, 2007: 90–91):

Ne megih in gidanchun   fore dir giuuanchon
Not can-I in thoughts   before you turn
Ich kann nicht einmal in Gedanken mich   vor dir abwenden

This pattern is found even where verbs are clause final, at the right rather than left edge of a clause (example from Isidor, translation from Jäger 2008: 88):

dhiu sie eomaer   furi dhazs   in iro samnunghe dhar haldan **ni** mahtun
which they ever   before that   in their community there hold not could
'which they could not hold before that in their community'

This example is from the Kasseler Gespräche, given in Chapter 4, and shows a far less typical word order, with negation before the pronoun:

Ni   ih   firnimu.
not I   understand
'I don't understand.'

The particle was clearly unstressed and so the vowel reduces, yielding *ne*, and an unstressed particle can come to lean on a neighboring stressed word. This instance of grammaticalization involves a clitic attaching at the beginning of a word (procliticization). With vowel-initial verb forms, we find the negation written as a simple *n-* at the beginning of the verb, with this example pervasive:

ne ist > nist 'isn't'

With consonant-initial verbs, the particle is still often a proclitic, but written *en-*:

nu enwelle got 'God doesn't want . . .' (Iwein)

The MHG example just given continues the OHG pattern of using just the negative particle, but is exceptional: Jäger (2008: 138, elsewhere) finds that double negation is more common, especially in certain texts like the *Nibelungenlied*, from which this example comes (2008: 143):

Done chvnd im   **niht** gestriten   daz starke getwerch
Then-not could him   not fight   the strong dwarf
'The strong dwarf could not defeat him then.'

Niht can occur alone already at this period, though it's not the norm.

The simple particle forms have entirely disappeared in the modern language, but this same basic pattern leaves other traces in the modern language, creating particular lexical items rather than general patterns of cliticization. Consider *eo* 'always' or *eoman* 'somebody, anybody':

ne eo > neo > nie[12]
ne eoman > neoman > niemand

Most notable in this regard, though, is yet another lexical item created on this model. The noun *wiht* 'thing' (related to modern German *Wicht*, and English *whit*, as in 'not a whit') had an indefinite form *eowiht*. The lexicalization of the negative form of this is the source of our word *nicht*. Forms of this appear since late OHG. Like French *ne … pas*, it is common to find *ne/n-* + *nicht* in MHG. As is found down to the present in many varieties of German, the language also allowed negative concord or 'multiple negation', as in an example we've already seen:

ichn gehôrt	*bi mînen tagen*	*nie*	*selhes*	*niht gesagen* (Iwein)
I-NEG heard	in my days	never	of such	not told

As the *Mittelhochdeutsche Grammatik* discusses, modern editors of MHG texts often add the clitic forms where manuscripts have only *niht* or a similar negation, with the result that manuscripts can look more modern than editions.

In MHG, then, scholars have long seen the key transition from OHG *ni* particles for negation to the creation of the forms that are used today, though multiple negation has clearly become less common.[13]

5.4.5 Nominal syntax: case

Until now, we have talked about the particular FORMS that are used to mark case (like dative plural *-um*, modern *-(e)n*), and in Chapter 4 you saw how cases were associated with (in)definiteness. The genitive continues its association with indefiniteness—recall constructions like *eines Tages*—but we haven't talked more broadly about the FUNCTIONS of cases. The genitive provides a good illustration for the heterogeneity of functions—Paul (2007: 340) calls it 'der am stärksten polyfunktionale Kasus' in the language. MHG uses the genitive case extensively and all the more so since its use has declined down to modern German—and continues to decline.

To give you an idea of the range, let us simply give a set of examples of genitive (from Paul 2007):

- *Verbs with genitive objects* are common in MHG, including *beginnen*, *vergezzen*, *warten*, *pflegen*, and so on. In modern German, this type of usage is limited to a few forms, like 'sich erinnern' plus genitive, or fossilized expressions like *des Deutschen mächtig sein*.

---

[12] Note also the modern regional form *nimmer* 'never', and see §4.4.
[13] See Pickl (2017) for an account raising important questions and adding considerable nuance to this story.

dô erbiten sie der nahte   (Nibelungenlied)
'then they waited for the night'

swer ie dâ pflac der lande   (Parzival)
'whoever ever took care of the lands'

- *Partitive genitive*: indicates that the object of a transitive verb is only part
  of a whole, as in this example:

er az daz brôt und tranc dâ zuo **eines wazzers** daz er vant
'he ate the bread and drank with it some of the water that he found'

- *Relational genitive*: translates into modern German roughly as 'in bezug auf':

daz im **prîses** niemen glîchen mac = 'that no one will be equal to him in fame
got sol iuch bewarn **der reise** = 'may god protect you on this trip'

- Occasional *instrumental* usage, even though the instrumental itself is long
  dead and typically marked with prepositions:

des einen slags daz ors lac tôt
'(with) one blow the horse lay dead'

What about genitive with prepositions? Early Germanic had prepositions,
though few governed the genitive—only one in Gothic, *in*, which appears
with dative and accusative as well (Hewson 2006: 291). This system is developed in OHG but with some variability (described in detail by Schrodt 2004).
Even in MHG, genitive does not appear widely after prepositions, and the
prepositions that can govern genitive all appear with dative or accusative (Paul
2007: 347–348), and they are typically not genitive prepositions today: *bî* (*bei*),
hinder, *(en)zwischen*, and many others.

Prepositions that govern genitive today are later creations. *Wegen*, for instance,
was originally *von wegen*, and appears in the 14th century, according to Kluge,
while others like *während* appear only in the 18th century (*Duden Herkunftswörterbuch*, v. *währen*) and *anlässlich* in the 19th (*Duden Herkunftswörterbuch*, v.
lassen).

The genitive participates in broader and more complex changes as well,
including with regard to word order, whether the possessive element precedes
or follows the noun it is associated with. In OHG, we tend to find forms like
these (from Demske 2001a: 217), with the genitive preposed:

thaz	uuirdit	genemnit	**gotes barn**	(Tatian)
it	is	named	god's child	

'it will be named the son of God'

fona	**paradises**	**bliidhnissu**	(Isidor)
from	paradise's	joy	

'from the joy of paradise'

Steadily over time, Demske finds that animate nouns in the genitive (like in the first example, and including proper names) continue to be preposed while other nouns (like in the second example) are moved to after the noun. (We will see animacy playing other roles in nominal morphology on pp. 327–328.)

Most striking to you may be the amount and complexity of change from this situation to the present: a general retreat of the genitive forms and restrictions in the meanings conveyed, yet the rise of genitive prepositions and gradual change in word order involving genitives.

A concluding word on morphological and syntactic change. You now have seen some pieces of syntactic analysis across two traditional 'eras' in the history of German and morphological analysis reaching back into prehistory. Many of the general patterns of change we've seen—and this will be true all the way from Indo-European to modern German—have often been connected historically to the loss of inflection. In fact, Rögnvaldsson (1995) points out that modern Icelandic has lost little of the inflectional complexity of Old Norse, yet it has become more configurational, in the sense discussed at the beginning of this section (§5.4.1).

Some would argue that if the reduction of suffix vowels triggers the loss of a morphological distinction between indicative and subjunctive verb forms or between dative singular and nominative/accusative plural forms of nouns, then you need a new way to express those things. Periphrasis allows that, whether it's with new auxiliary verbs or with regard to increased use of articles and prepositions. Once again, there's no real historical necessity for a connection in some regards. Beyond Germanic, many languages lack plural noun forms altogether. And in other areas, Germanic never had an inflected form for the forms that develop in periphrasis, like a future tense. Still, the general correlation has real appeal and has been probably best argued for in modern linguistics by Hawkins (1986), using German and English as key examples.

5.5 Social and regional variation come into view

In the last chapter, we focused our discussions of variability within German on 'dialect', basically regional variation. Regional variation continues to be tremendously important, as the poet Hugo von Trimberg wrote in *Der Renner*:

Doch wil ich einz vür wâr iu* künden: *euch
Swer* tiutsche wil eben tihten,   *whoever
Der muoz sîn herze rihten
Ûf manigerleie sprâche...

Very loosely translated, that is: 'I want to tell you one thing for sure. Whoever wants to write poetry in German has to wrap their mind around some linguistic diversity.' Medieval poets, then, were acutely aware of variation, regional and social. And von Trimburg thinks like a modern linguist here: as we saw in Chapter 4 and will see throughout the rest of this book, observing and understanding those kinds of variation are at the heart of understanding language change and language itself.

But with the richer data set and (increasingly) broader set of literate people, the visible parts of the picture are more complex now socially and politically. In this section, after a brief discussion of how people came to learn to read and write in the period, we can look at the old proposal of the unified Middle High German, at least for literary purposes. After that, you'll see some regional features of the period and we close with some examples of texts. This sets up a key theme in the more recent history of the German language: down to the present day, we see interconnections and tensions between regional and social variation.

First, how did someone in this era come to be literate and what does literacy mean?[14] As in the Old High German period, monasteries were the centers of writing, but of course with a heavy focus on learning and using Latin. Children who became literate were typically sent to monastery schools around age 7 or 8 and continued until 15 or so to become a monk or nun and longer for the priesthood. While literacy was surely more common among males, nuns clearly did write from the Middle Ages onward (e.g. Schneider 2009: 21). Wittmann (1999: 44) succinctly notes that 'Sehr wenig wissen wir ... über das Lesepublikum vor 1500' and he reasonably speculates that the literacy rate is unlikely to have been over 2%.

The culture of reading and writing among lay people, including courtly people, was quite different. Weddige (2008: 49) notes that the distinction between *pfaffen unde leien* corresponds to that between *litterati et illiterati*, and gives (2008: 54) a range of descriptions of education among courtly figures in literature, from Heinrich (*ein ritter sô gelêret was / daz er an den buochen las*, 'a knight was so learned / that he read in books') to Wolfram (*ine kan decheinen buochstap*, 'I don't know a letter'). Writing among the non-clerical population picks up in the 12th century (Schneider 2009: 21), and by the late 13th century, not only clerical but also city schools were established for lay people (Schneider 2009: 70). Secular higher education in universities begins well within this period, but in places like Bologna and Paris, not in the German-speaking lands.

---

[14] There are many good sources on medieval education and literacy, with much good work going on today. Weddige (2008, especially ch. 3) provides an accessible introduction, on which I've drawn here.

There are other reasons for the rarity of written material. Parchment remains the normal writing material into the 15th century, a rare and expensive material. Even ink and writing utensils were not to be taken for granted: goose feathers cut as pens wore down quickly, and the *Federmesser*, a knife for sharpening/cutting pens was standard equipment, as Schneider (2009: 119, elsewhere) describes in some detail.

[K]eine mittelhochdeutsche Hochsprache. For decades, scholars stressed the extent to which MHG literary texts seemed not to show dialectal features in the way that OHG texts did, nor to the extent that we find in the Early New High German dialect texts or the modern dialects. The major poetry of the time shows similarities across broad regions—like from the central Rhine to Austria. This long ago led to a name for this variety, *die (höfische) Dichtersprache*, and the already discussed editorial tradition going back to Karl Lachmann (over-)emphasized similarities and played down differences in texts: Lachmann did not simply regularize written texts, he believed in a unified, spoken Middle High German. Similarly, Grimm claims (cited in Paul 2007: 12–13, emphasis added) that:

die Dichter des 13. Jahrhunderts, bis auf wenige mundartliche Einzelheiten, ein bestimmtes unwandelbares Hochdeutsch REDETEN.

Modern scholars have increasingly backed away from such extreme views, but even Paul's *Mittelhochdeutsche Grammatik* refers to this literary variety as 'eine ritterliche Kunstsprache', 'ein Literaturidiom' springing from the central Rhine area (2007: 34–35). That variety is characterized by vocabulary and spellings that surely must have shown greater uniformity than local speech patterns of the time.

But did a uniform language exist to any extent? We can tease out plenty of regional variation from manuscripts (see also §5.2), though some regional variation is suppressed, certainly. For example, we tend to find roughly the same level of Second Sound Shift. Consider these examples of textual traditions, drawing from Wells' 1985 summary:

- Heinrich van Veldeke came from the area close to the Netherlandic border, but his texts are in part transmitted only in High German form. That is, the dialect has presumably been adjusted in copying and transmission across time and space. It is also possible that he composed in a variety that was not his native tongue.
- For some other authors it's hard to be sure what dialect background they have: Walther von der Vogelweide seems like he may have been Austrian, and Hartmann von Aue perhaps Swabian, though their texts betray little evidence of this.

Keller (1978) argues that the fact that documents from remote places show more dialect features than those from the major centers is a kind of negative proof for the existence of a unifying tendency. We also have the appearance of a relative absence of regional variation in numerous northern texts, such as *schaft* for *scap*. That is, the northern areas from which these texts come still have dialects where Standard German *-schaft* would have been and would still be *-scap*, but in MHG they are rendered in this standard-like form. This may be spelling influence from the south, where people were writing the southern-looking *-schaft* but still saying *-scap*.

Some other characteristic features of modern dialects are hardly attested (from Keller 1978): Alemannic texts for instance show *uns*, not forms like *üs*, *öis*. These dialects have clear loss of nasal before fricative with compensatory lengthening, and it happened before this period. Similarly, Alemannic varieties often retained full unstressed vowels (as discussed at the beginning of this chapter), but these are often spelled <e>, reflecting a reduction not found in the dialect. These are old patterns that we still find in those areas today, and they must have been around in speech in this period.

Does this represent a 'standard' in any sense, or any process of standardization? In part the answer is about what 'standardization' means. We have some dialect mixing in the period that would have led to some leveling for people at court, and the poets of the era were often working to reach broader audiences, so shaving off some linguistic differences. Of course that is not what 'standardization' means in contemporary terms—for example with norms established and systematically used by speakers and writers. But some of the pattern is strongly reinforced by manuscript transmission, where you get further 'cleaning up' beyond how the poets actually spoke and wrote. Here as always in standardization, we need to keep in mind patterns of bottom-up developments that lead to more unified varieties—*koinē* or new dialect formation—versus top-down developments, whether through the explicit creation of norms or simply in the process of transmission of written texts.

How could this have happened? A whole set of reasons have been invoked, including these:

- The literary language and some other text types were restricted to a **social elite**, especially around the courts, so even if it was supra-regional in some ways, it was hardly a general language of the land(s). We have many more texts from this period, but still a thin slice of society is doing the writing, and a considerably different slice from the one of OHG times.
- These courtly circles drew members from various areas, creating a situation for some 'leveling' of differences or KOINEIZATION, as sketched at the beginning of this chapter. Important poets moved around—the

Alsatian Reinmar von Hagenau wrote in Vienna (Wells 1985), so that he worked in a profoundly different linguistic environment than the one he grew up in.

- We saw already in OHG texts that dialect identification can be complicated when a text was written by a speaker of one dialect, then copied or even reworked by someone from a different area. We see evidence of these effects of MANUSCRIPT TRANSMISSION in many cases. In fact, by late MHG, we start to get large collections of songs and poetic texts (probably most famously, the *Manessische* or *große Heidelberger Liederhandschrift*), bringing together the work of many poets. Not only would one normally assume that the collecting and writing processes themselves would lead to some ironing out of regional differences, but the fact that such collections are being made says something about the supra-regional character of this literature. The early reliance on canonical literature rather than the most local texts matters as well: the Heidelberg manuscript is fundamentally different from non-literary regional texts in both manuscript history and transmission.

- Given the broad and INTERNATIONAL LITERARY AND CULTURAL MOVEMENTS of the time—courtly culture, in particular—some argue that authors consciously sought to suppress regionalisms in their writing. We will see this argument made again, and powerfully, when we discuss the so-called 'printers' language' of the early modern period. The literature itself was formalized in various ways, thematically and structurally, for example. In a kind of modest parallel, all speakers of English, and most speakers of German, who can write have learned conventions that are far from their own native pronunciations. More clearly, perhaps, early British rock music was sung in a kind of English far from what the members of the Beatles and Rolling Stones grew up speaking or even used in ordinary speech. It is largely with the punk movement that British regional varieties come to be widely used in rock (Trudgill 1983). If we had recordings of English from Liverpool and London up to 1950 and after 1980 but only their records in between, we might squander considerable effort in trying to understand what happened to English for this brief period, when the speech patterns were restricted to a truly tiny group and to a highly developed and specific cultural milieu.

Together such factors account for at least much of the uniformity we find in especially the literary texts of this period. As more studies of non-literary texts become available, with their richer regional variation, this question is slowly fading from view.

Despite these arguments, some authors, like Erich Straßner, continue to believe that unifying tendencies in the language really reach back into the monastic culture of Old High German. MHG, on that view, simply continues the old tradition. The MHG literary language itself seems to fade after roughly 1250. The mystics and others continue the basic writing tradition for some time beyond this, but its influence certainly wanes. Still, there are social developments beginning in the medieval period that will eventually support the emergence of a more unified kind of German: there is significant movement of people (lots of colonization to the east and elsewhere), some early urbanization which drew people from outlying areas, and so on. Again, this is precisely the ideal seed bed for koineization or new dialect formation.

Wells (1985: 109) gets it basically right, I think, in calling Middle High German 'a convenient abstraction':

The issue [of a 'standard MHG'] is obscured by the small number of original or contemporary manuscripts surviving, by the preconceptions of editors and grammarians, who reconstruct texts and normalize spelling and language, and by the U(pper) G(erman) geographical bias of most of the literature, which was, moreover, largely composed before geographically and chronologically phased shift in German vowel phonology had become established.

But another question arises with this, one about the scholars of the 19th century: Why were people so apparently invested in positing some kind of standard language for this period? One usual answer (Wells 1985: 116–117) is, as foreshadowed earlier, that Lachmann was a classicist, used to working with Classical Latin, a language with a long literary tradition and in some sense with well-established norms.

These may play some role, certainly, but the best answer, I think, lies in what Rosina Lippi-Green calls 'standard language ideology' (1997: 64—the term comes from Jim and Lesley Milroy, but the definition is hers):

a bias toward an abstracted, idealized homogenous spoken language which is imposed and maintained by dominant bloc institutions and which names as its model the written language, but which is drawn primarily from the spoken language of the upper middle class.

While defining the 'upper middle class' is a serious sociological problem and an utter impossibility in Middle High German society, the basic point is clear: as you may be aware (and as we'll explore in the next two chapters of this book), such an ideology is a powerful one in the German-speaking lands. This was in part, some believe, because of a deep-seated linguistic insecurity about a language accorded second-class status to first Latin, then French, and now English. Whatever the psychological motivations, a number of influential scholars pushed hard to impose this ideology on the historical record of German, sometimes positing a relatively unified literary language even for OHG, as just noted. An interesting (if generally alarmingly uncritical) collection of materials on attitudes toward German over its full history can be found in Straßner (1995).

Already in the last chapter, I talked a little about the reification of linguistic varieties, the tendency to distill invariant grammars where they don't exist. The interplay of this tendency with language ideology, especially with notions of 'standard' language, runs through the rest of this book. Here's the spoiler: standard varieties are far less interesting and relevant to language history than was long believed and is still widely believed among people who do not work on the edge of our understanding of language change.

5.5.1 Sample texts[15]

Below are a few texts.

Samples of literary treatments of regional and social variation. Below are two examples of MHG texts, both of which treat language variation. These are exceptional in the meta-linguistic discussion and so widely cited. They are given here without translations, though the first has some key annotations and glosses, for you to work through on your own.

Wernher der Gärtner's MEIER HELMBRECHT pokes fun at the damaging linguistic effects of visiting the Court. The (Middle High German-speaking!) protagonist returns from a long journey, and meets his family this way—pay close attention to the material in quotes.

'Vil liebe soete kindekîn,   'Sweet' here means 'dumb', probably.
got lâte iuch immer saelec sin!'
diu swester engegen im lief,
mit den armen si in umbeswief.
do sprach er zuo der swester:
'gratia vester'.
. . .
zem vater sprach er: 'deu sal'
zuo der muoter sprach er sa
beheimisch: 'dobra ytra!'

---

[15] While online texts are widely available, it's worth also noting that audio recordings of speakers reading MHG and other earlier forms of Germanic languages are now widely available. For several MHG texts and a sample of others, see *Stimmen aus mittelalterlichen Frauenklöstern*.

The joke is that he wrecks all of these languages and dialects. As Martin Durrell points out in correspondence, language ideology is at play here, including stirrings of nationalism.

Classen (2007: 114–115, with ample references to earlier work) analyzes some of the non-German phrases as follows:

he at first resorts to Dutch or Flemish: 'vil liebe soete kindekîn' (my dear children). He then approaches his sister with the Latin phrase 'gratia vester!,' thereby assuming the role of a priest, pompously displaying his fragmentary language abilities which are supposed to provide him with the necessary attributes of another social class. But the attempts to shine as a polyglot, or as a courtly educated knight who knows how to express himself in those languages traditionally associated with high social status fail miserably. In the first place, Helmbrecht does not use the grammatically correct forms. Instead of 'gratia vester' he should have said 'gratia vestra,' and the alleged Flemish amounts to not much more than slightly changed Middle High German. The French formula 'deu sal' (726), reserved for his father, is free of mistakes, whereas the address for his mother, the formula 'dobra ytra!' (728), at best the Russian for 'good day,' represents a true puzzle both for the parents and for us today. Whereas the mother suspects that he might be a Czech or a Wend, the expression is close to the actual Russian 'dobre utra,' but not to the 'dobry' den' in Czech. The narrator, however, identifies it as Bohemian, or Czech.

The result is naturally confusion from his family:

diu hûsfrou sprach: 'herre wirt,	
wir sîn der sinne gar verirt.	Note the genitive: 'confused of the senses'.
er ist niht unser beider kint:	
er ist ein Bêheim oder ein Wint*.'	*Bohemian or Sorb'
der vater sprach: 'er ist ein Walh*.	*'foreigner, typically Romance-speaking'[16]
mîn sun, den ich got bevalh,	
der ist ez niht sicherlîche	
und ist im doch gelîche.'	
dô sprach sîn swester Gotelint:	
'er ist niht iuwer beider kint.	
er antwurt mir in der latîn:	
er mac wol ein phaffe sîn.'	

[16] This word's checkered history is clear from the meaning of the Modern English cognate, *Welsh*. It originally meant something like 'foreigner', probably connected to an old tribal name, *Volcae*, a Celtic group. In some areas, like English- and Dutch-speaking areas, it came to be applied to Celts, while in MHG and ENHG, it referred to Romance speakers, often specifically Italians, cf. *welschwîn* 'Italian wine'. We still have this in *Walloon*.

Here is more of VON TRIMBERG'S RENNER, showing regional stereotyping of speech (see the middle):

Swer wênt daz die von Âche
Reden als die von Franken,
Dem süln die miuse danken.
Ein ieglich lant hât sînen site,
Der sînem lantvolke volget mite.
An sprâche, an mâze und an gewande
Ist underscheiden lant von lande.
Der werlde dinc stêt über al
An sprâche, an mâze, an wâge, an zal.
Swâben ir wörter spaltent,
Die Franken ein teil si valtent,
Die Beier si zezerrent,
Die Düringe si ûf sperrent,
Die Sahsen si bezückent*,   *schnell wegziehen
Die Rînliute si verdrückent,
Die Wetereiber si würgent,
Die Mîsener si vol schürgent*,   *schieben, stossen, treiben
Egerlant si swenkent,
Oesterrîche si schrenkent,
Stîrlant si baz lenkent,
Kernde ein teil si senkent,
Bêheim, Ungern und Lamparten
Houwent niht mit tiutscher barten
Franzois, Walhe und Engellant,
Norweye, Yberne sint unbekant
An ir sprâche tiutschen liuten . . .

The website mediaevum.de has extensive collections online now (visit http://texte.mediaevum.de/12mhd.htm). In particular the links to the Bibliotheca Augustana are useful.

5.6 Vocabulary: lexical semantic change

One of the most immediate impressions many students have on first encountering MHG literary texts is the number of 'false friends' they find. One famous example is *arebeit,* which means something like 'Mühsal' rather than 'work'. Or take these other examples from the early lines of the Nibelungenlied:

MHG	Modern (translation from Lexer's MHG *Taschenwörterbuch*)
wunder	unbegreifliches Geschehen
vröude	Frohsinn, Freude
hôchgezîten	Feiern eines Festes
klagen	Wehgeschrei als Ausdruck eines Schmerzes
strîten	kämpfen

Our immediate concern is not with the details of each particular semantic development, but with starting to think about how meaning can change. In each chapter so far, we've talked briefly about change in vocabulary, but we haven't directly addressed how the meanings of words change. We have seen that sound change appears to be regular (largely, at least, and in most views), and we've seen clear patterns of morphological change over long spans of time in German's history (whether loss of inflectional morphology or acquisition of more grammatical forms). A long search for similar regularities in semantic change has been generally far less successful (though see Traugott & Dasher 2002 for an important recent effort). Traditional approaches focus on taxonomies of semantic change, like broadening versus narrowing or (e.g. Fritz 2006: 57–60, elsewhere, Nübling et al. 2013: 108–134, and the frontmatter to Kluge 2002). Standard examples are (1) the broadening of meaning of OHG *sahhe*, originally restricted to specifically legal matters, but now 'bleached' to mean *Sache* generally, and (2) the narrowing of OHG *faz* meaning virtually any kind of vessel, to modern *Faß*, while *Gefäß* has taken on the broader meaning.

Some recent work, like Fortson (2003), sees the value of such taxonomies as far from explanatory. He argues that there are in principle no constraints on lexical-semantic change, and that we would do better to pursue how people reanalyze word meanings, especially children during language acquisition. Eckardt (2011) provides an example of reanalysis, which should give you reason to be skeptical about the value of taxonomies of change. Taking the history of German *fast*, related to OHG *fasto* (related to *festi*, source of *fest*), she distinguishes three stages of development:

$[[\text{fast}]]_1$ = 'physically firm, fixed' (*fest*)
$[[\text{fast}]]_2$ = 'very much, intense' (obs.)
$[[\text{fast}]]_3$ = 'almost'

That is, the word initially becomes an intensifier and then moves in the opposite direction. The MHG adverb *vast* means, among other things, 'fest, stark, gewaltig, schnell, sehr', reflecting stage 2. In ENHG, we see the shift to stage 3. Eckardt sees 'precarious uses' as triggering changes like this (with a term borrowed from Diewald), where an 'utterance was not really wrong, but it was a risky way for the speaker to convey her message' (2011: 37). In this case, an intensifying meaning like *sehr, recht* can only be used to modify gradable concepts, like *groß/klein*, where the quantity can be greater or lesser. She finds, though, that users were stretching the meaning here by using it in non-gradable contexts, and in ways that would have been ambiguous to listeners:

> sei rouften laut, sei schrewend fast
> 'they called loudly, they screamed *fast*'

She lays out two quite different interpretations (2011: 42): the second half of the sentence could be interpreted as 'scream very much' or as elaborating the first: 'they cried loudly, they almost screamed'. Confronted with such examples, learners eventually reanalyzed the meaning of *fast* from intensifying to 'almost'.

Tracing meaning changes rigorously in this way has barely begun, but it should be easy to see how our initial example could be reinterpreted by learners: OHG *arabeit* 'Bedrängnis, Not' gradually yields to 'Mühsal' in the MHG period. As Schwarz (1982: 46) observes, the word could surely have been used for the hard labor of a peasant, but this isn't the common context of use in our classic literary texts from the period. Even Luther's usage is not always with the modern meaning.

We'll return to semantic change and reanalysis in the next chapter.

5.7 Conclusion

We began this chapter by problematizing the notion that there are distinct periods in the history of the language. Throughout the chapter, we've seen how tightly interconnected processes and developments are from Old High German to Middle High German and how closely Middle High German is, in various ways, to modern varieties spoken today.

The sound changes associated with this period traditionally illustrate this clearly. Morphologically, the language is by this time much closer to being readable for those who know modern German. We have many more texts from this period, and know much more about the writers, the circumstances under which they were written and the purposes for which they were written. This means that we're able to begin to get glimpses into the sociolinguistic setting of language and social variation, like in the immediately preceding section. At the same time, we have confronted modern constructs that were earlier projected back onto Middle High German, such as the notion of a standard.

With this, our focus has shifted from the relatively simple statements about OHG to patterns of variation. In many regards, exemplified especially with sound patterns in this chapter, some living Germanic languages show the absence of changes charted here. In morphology, we have seen the clear rise of plural marking, and the beginnings of morphological use of umlaut (if not yet complete in either case), along with clearing up little oddities like the *ge*-lessness of passive *worden*.

With that, we can close our survey of the High Middle Ages and move on to the early modern period. There, we will see these trends accelerating.

6

Early New High German

Richer structural evidence and socio-historical context

6.0 Introduction

One way that non-linguists (and even linguists) try to gauge roughly how familiar or different linguistic varieties may be is by thinking in terms of mutual intelligibility: can you understand some spoken or written variety? As laid out in §4.0, we often draw the line between 'dialect' and 'language' by whether a speaker of one can understand the other language written or spoken: if so, the varieties are dialects; if not, distinct languages. This is at best a rough gauge of course but it can be applied to historical stages. For example, you might hear that Icelanders can read the Old Norse sagas written in the Middle Ages, whereas no monolingual speaker of modern English can read *Beowulf* in the original. Early New High German is the stage at which German speakers will often say that they can read a historical form of the language without training—MHG is clearly too different in many ways, but ENHG is a good step closer for many contemporary German speakers. Among other things, this informal sense may be encoded in the popular (and sometimes scholarly) cliché that during this period Martin Luther (1483–1546) 'created the Modern German language' or 'was the father of the German language': his German Bible (Figure 6.1, p. 246 and Figure 7.1, p. 307) can be understood by educated modern-day readers without much difficulty.

But the same holds across the period and for work of the same era or even earlier. Consider the text below, 'The Baker', by Hans Sachs, a contemporary of Luther. (We will look at other pieces from the same series later on.) If you can read fonts from the family often known as *Fraktur* or 'Gothic', the text is readily accessible. *Fraktur* itself grew from similar 'black letter' fonts based ultimately on medieval writing styles, and Gutenberg used an early form, *textualis*, for his Bible. If you do not know these fonts, here is a transliteration:

Zu mir rein / wer hat Hungers not /
Ich hab gut Weitz und Růcken Brot /

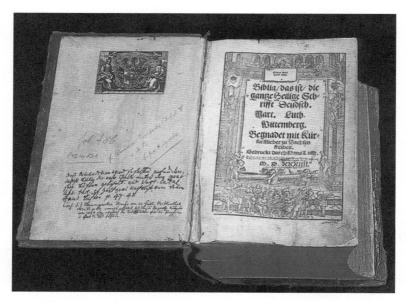

FIGURE 6.1 The Luther Bible.

Auß Korn / Weitzen und Kern bachen[1]/
Gesaltzn recht / mit allen sachen /
Ein recht gewicht / das recht wol schmeck /
Semmel / Bretzen / Laub / Spuln und Weck /
Dergleich Fladen und Eyerkuchn /
Thut man zu Ostern bey mir suchn.

In terms of the text itself, you will note a few oddities from the modern perspective, but these are not restricted to the Early New High German period: the use of 'th' for 't' (as in *thut*) remains common into the modern period, for example. Some regional vocabulary for baked goods may be unfamiliar, but both *Weck* and *Semmel* are today regional terms for *Brötchen*, in the Southwest and Southeast, respectively (see König 2007: 239, now König et al. 2015).

Our goals in this chapter parallel those of previous chapters, but they also reflect the increasing amount of written and comparative evidence available with more widespread literacy, access to writing materials and the printing

---

[1] David Fertig points out that the fricative in *bachen* reflects the original WGmc simplex *k in the past tense and participle, contrasting with the *-ck-* <WGmc *-kk-, originally restricted to the infinitive and present tense forms. The direction of leveling of the root-final consonant of *backen* (*-ck-* *vs.* *-ch-*) is indicative of the Central German vs. Upper German provenience of a text in the medieval and early modern periods (Paul 2007: 256).

Der Beck.

Zu mir rein/wer hat Hungers not/
Ich hab gut Weiß vnd Rucken Brot/
Auß Korn/Weißen vnd Kern/bachen/
Gesalßn recht / mit allen sachen/
Ein recht gewicht / das recht wol schmeck/
Semel / Breßen / Laub/Spuln vñ Weck/
Dergleich Fladen vnd Eyerkuchn/
Thut man zu Ostern bey mir suchn.

FIGURE 6.2 Der Beck (Bäcker).

press. As a result, we can talk more about sociolinguistic issues and issues of
language in use. Our goals then are these:

- Learn the key sound changes, with a focus on monophthongization/
  diphthongization and lenition.

- Take special note of patterns of diffusion (over time and space), variation and tensions between competing tendencies (e.g. unrounding of front rounded vowels versus secondary rounding).
- Be able to identify major dialect features and the dialect of texts.
- In morphology, be able to describe the kinds of regularization or leveling that we find during this period.
- Be able to talk about the solidification of plural marking on nouns, and the connection between sound changes, especially apocope, and plural marking.
- Be able to describe where the ENHG period fits into the broader morphosyntactic patterns we see ongoing, including with regard to periphrasis and word order.
- Understand the basics of pragmatic change, especially in second person pronouns.
- Be prepared to outline the path toward a unified language, including the limits on its success during this period.

In terms of periodization, it is very difficult to say exactly to what extent Early New High German is truly distinct from the modern dialects that descend from it, for the reason just noted. Even the standard handbook, Reichmann & Wegera (1993: 5), concedes this, with the authors deciding:

In der hier vorgelegten Grammatik wird der Zeitraum von der Mitte des 14. bis zur Mitte des 17. Jahrhunderts als frühneuhochdeutsch betrachtet und als eigene, dem Mittelhochdeutschen und Neuhochdeutschen gleichberechtigte Epoche des Deutschen verstanden, nicht also als Teil des Neuhochdeutschen.

In the present grammar, we take the time period from the middle of the 14th to the middle of the 17th century to be Early New High German and we see it as its own period of the German language, equal with Middle High German and New High German, that is, not as part of New High German.

Structurally, by this time most of the features of the contemporary standard language and dialects are attested, though they are virtually all limited to particular regions. This means that changes from this point in history onward must be considered in the context of which variants become part of the modern standard and which do not: many features of colloquial German have arisen in the last few centuries and not (yet) found their way into the standard, while others have. Traditionally, histories of German have focused on reinforcing the threadbare myth of an inexorable march toward the standard. This book pursues the broader and, I would argue, far more interesting goal of understanding the historical roots of the broad spectrum of 'Germans' that exist today.[2]

---

[2] The plural here may sound ironic, given the trendy use of plurals in cultural studies, but it fits here: it makes far more sense to talk about a set of Germans rather than one fictional unified 'German' with variants.

Socially, we begin to find literacy spreading during this time, so that we have writings by a broader range of society—these are still overwhelmingly people who could be considered relatively prosperous but it is now a much broader swath than in the MHG period. Famously, a technological change of this era has an impact on the language: the invention of movable type. Scholars rightly stress this as a watershed moment in terms of the surviving linguistic evidence and development of a written form of the language.

While the invention of the printing press, or rather of movable type, is rightly regarded as a revolutionary moment, there is a more significant increase in texts in this period:[3] A literate middle class wrote letters and other documents, vast numbers of which have been preserved in local archives and other places. This is, then, another 'media revolution', one no doubt larger in terms of impact on society as a whole than the initial (i.e. runic) writing of Germanic languages, or the writing in the Roman alphabet. To underscore it, several illustrations in this chapter (Figures 6.2, 6.5, 6.6, 6.7 with a note attached to the last) illustrate professions associated with printing. This availability of material naturally triggers an explosion of corpus-oriented work among contemporary scholars, now that we have the tools to aggregate such information. One notable ENHG corpus is the Historical Corpus of German Newspapers, 1650–1800, GerManC (https://www.sketchengine.co.uk/germanc-corpus); throughout this chapter we will come across other corpora developed by particular scholars for particular goals.

Chapter 4 noted that the entire surviving OHG corpus consists of some-where around 650,000 written words, including literary texts, non-literary texts, and even glosses. By comparison, an important study we'll discuss in detail in this chapter, Fertig 2000, examined a half million words written by hand in Nuremburg over about 250 years, texts for which he could identify the author's handwriting and for which he had biographical information on the author. This yielded over 85,000 verb forms for quantitative analysis. We'll deal with these issues of literacy and the rapidly increasing richness of texts and context throughout this chapter.

Understanding this historical period thus involves careful integration of structural and social factors, and reminds us that they are fundamentally intertwined in language history: we now see the real beginnings of the development of a standard language, one that really takes root and has ties to the modern standard. While traditional scholarship speaks of this as if it were a relatively short process, the actual codification, especially with regard to the

---

[3] Vast amounts of ENHG material are now available online including here: http://texte.mediaevum.de/15frnhd.htm. The Bonn project listed there is particularly noteworthy. And myriads of specialized sources are becoming available today, such as the ledgers of the Augsburger master builders from 1320 to 1466 (https://www.augsburger-baumeisterbuecher.de).

spoken language, continues well into the 20th century, and norms and expectations continue to evolve today, as we will see in the rest of this book.

6.1 Sound changes

In this section, we'll review the major sound changes in a way that will lead to a fairly simple table which you can use for recognizing dialect texts.

6.1.1 Vowels

The first four changes, or better perhaps two pairs of changes, considered here are often regarded as defining Early New High German: monophthongization and diphthongization on the one hand and open syllable lengthening and closed syllable shortening on the other. The first pair were introduced in the last chapter, but let us review them and expand on the earlier discussion.

1. Monophthongization. The—to a modern eye odd-looking—diphthongs we saw in MHG (and earlier, in part)—namely *ie*, *üe*, *uo*—disappear especially from central German dialects and do not become part of the standard. The original first elements, high vowels in all three cases, remain but the second elements, what we call 'offglides', are lost.

MHG		NHG	
ie [iə]	>	i:	*liep* > [li:p]
uo	>	u:	*bruoder* > *bruder*
üe [yə]	>	ü: [y:]	*müede* > *müde* (recall that 'y' = IPA for *ü*)

This sound change is usually dated to the 11th century, though that is uncertain. Reichmann & Wegera reasonably argue that our best evidence is finding simple <i> spellings for earlier <ie>, though that is hardly consistent. This example in modern German is still spelled *lieb*, despite being pronounced as a monophthong in the standard language. Keep in mind that these vowels remain diphthongal in Bavarian and some other dialects. This change began most likely in the West Central area, spreading especially eastward from there.

2. Diphthongization. The old long high vowels now become diphthongs in many dialects and are reflected in the modern standard language. Note that the diphthongs have a high second element but a lower first element or onset. (I leave ENHG out here, as a transition period with competition between the two forms.)

MHG		NHG			
î	>	ei	[aj]	*rîche*	> *reich*
û	>	au	[aw]	*hûs*	> *haus*
iu [y:]	>	eu	[ɔj]	*liute*	> *leute*

In particular, this process largely misses the dialects of the north and the southwest. Evidence from orthography and rhymes indicates that these three vowels did not change simultaneously, with *î* lagging behind the other two changes in some areas (see also Kranzmayer 1956: 49 for more).

The traditional mnemonics for remembering these, by the way, are these New High German phrases: *liebe gute Brüder* and *mein neues Haus*—the first set all words that once had diphthongs and the latter originally monophthongs. See Chapter 5 for Maps 12 and 13 of the spread of monophthongization and diphthongization over time. Current work is exploring the chronology of these changes, and they may have spread more slowly than those maps suggest.

Geographically, both of these changes come to be particularly characteristic of Central German, and especially East Central German. Bavarian shows diphthongization but not monophthongization; these old diphthongs are still heard there today, although otherwise much has changed in Bavarian vowel systems. Likewise, far away dialects like Alemannic and Low German typically underwent neither process. We will explore a couple of aspects of this pattern later on. First, this allows us to quickly and easily identify central versus southeastern versus southwestern texts. Second, the standard reflects especially East Central German patterns.

Step back for a moment and consider a point about the bigger picture: we've treated a lot of vowel changes already and English, Dutch, and other members of the family have undergone similarly complex vowel changes, such as the famous Great Vowel Shift. This chain shift in English, illustrated here, occurred at roughly the same time. This included changes in the long (but not the short) vowels of the language, and the diphthongization of /i:/ and /u:/ to /ai/ and /au/, as we just saw for German (and note that part of the oddity of English vowel spellings compared to spelling of vowels in many European languages reflects a pre-shift pronunciation):

The Great Vowel Shift (Early Modern English)

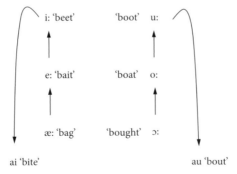

Other Germanic languages show similar patterns. Many of these are 'chain shifts', where more than one vowel changes at once, in a kind of game of vocalic musical chairs. As a result, and especially having worked through the often complex changes of earlier periods of the German language, you may be wondering: What is going on with these vowels? Why can't they just be still? In a classic paper on the Great Vowel Shift, Stockwell (1978: 337) makes a bold point:

The vowel shift occurred no more at the usually cited dates than at any other date in the documented history of English. That is, it **did** occur then, and also (equally, I believe) over the past 200 years, or over the 200 years between the birth of Alfred and the death of Aelfric, or any other period of that length. This kind of vowel shifting is a pervasive and persevering characteristic of vowel systems of a certain type.

Stockwell is arguing, in other words, that these kinds of shifts are chronic, inherent patterns of change for Germanic. This point of view has been picked up in varying form by many scholars of late, most famously Labov 1994 (and more recently Jacewicz et al. 2006), to account for changes underway today in American English. In particular, since the 19th century, people have observed a tendency for long (or tense) vowels to rise in chain shifts and for short (or lax) vowels to lower. The raising of long vowels is, for example, the very heart of the Great Vowel Shift, and with an archaic spelling system is the reason why we write a mid-vowel symbol but produce a high vowel in words like *feet* or *seed* and *boot* or *food*.

We have seen various shifts in the history of German and the *Frühneu-hochdeutsche Grammatik* (Reichmann & Wegera 1993: 37) describes a set for the ENHG period that fit into the kinds of patterns just noted, adapted in the figure below (following the original, sound changes are indicated by arrows; phonemic changes further marked with boxes).

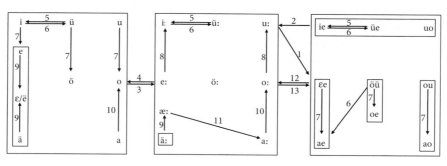

1 NHG Diphthongization	8 Raising
2 Central German Monophthongization	9 *e*-Merger
3 Lengthening	10 Near-merger of *a* and *o*
4 Shortening	11 *æ:* > *a:*
5 Unrounding	12 Monophthongization (MHG *ɛe; öü; ou*)
6 Rounding	13 Diphthongization (MHG *e:; ö:; o:*)
7 Lowering	

A full analysis of all these changes is well beyond our focus, but you can see that most of the changes with short vowels involve lowering, while almost all of the long monophthongs rise. The parallels across very different, if related, languages is remarkable, and many German and West Germanic dialects show similar patterns (Wiesinger 1970, 1983). It becomes more remarkable when we know that many Nordic languages have undergone eerily similar changes (Küspert 1988).

How is this possible? Much recent work focuses on social factors (Labov 1994), but such consistency suggests that structural factors should be at work too. A proposal for this is being developed today: we pronounce vowels differently when we emphasize them. This warping of the vowel space under more emphatic pronunciations may correlate with vowel change during cross-generational transmission. Evidence suggests that in some social contexts and in some cultural traditions, the way adults talk to young children involves realizations of vowels that parallel those found in emphatic utterances. If so, the early input to a new generation is systematically skewed in the same directions as in prosodically prominent realizations, which in turn could drive vowel changes over multiple generations, even centuries. How this may work is schematized below with an example of a lax vowel lowering, from Jacewicz et al. (2009: 100):

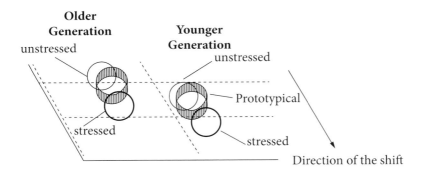

Jacewicz et al. have tested this prediction with speakers of three American English dialects, and results support the hypothesis. Shown below are forms of [ɪ], the vowel in *bit*, for three generations of western North Carolina speakers. A2 is the oldest generation (adults), A1 are young adults and A0 reflects the speech of children. Emphatic realizations (black symbols) and non-emphatic realizations (open symbols) are plotted for each generation.

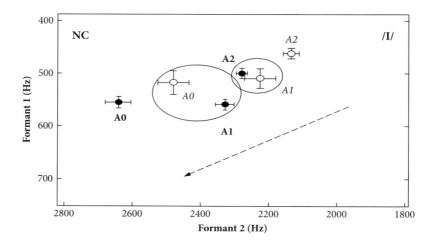

In short, a younger generation's non-emphatic vowels appear to be located very close to where an older generation's emphatic ones were.

Another factor is no doubt at work here, namely the profoundly diphthongal character that long vowels often have or develop: for almost all English speakers and a surprisingly large number of German speakers, vowels which we regard as phonologically 'long' are often actually phonetically diphthongs. That is, these vowels are distinguished (e.g. perceptually) and characterized (e.g. in syllable weight) as long, they can also show considerable movement in the vowel space. In American English and other varieties, for instance, in words like *go* and *say*, /o:/ and /e:/ are typically [ow] and [ej]. This means the transition from long vowel to monophthong or back is less dramatic than it might seem. And that could make explaining some traditionally unusual-looking changes easier to understand, like Germanic *ō > OHG *uo* > ENHG *ū*.

3. Open syllable lengthening (OSL). An open syllable is one with no conso-nant at the end of it, that is, lacking a coda.[4] Thus, the following types are open: (C)V, (C)V. In contrast, closed syllables are those with a consonant in the coda: (C)VC, (C)VCC. In ENHG, open syllables with short vowels undergo lengthening:

MHG		NHG
săgen	>	s[a:]gen
lĕben	>	l[e:]ben
hăben	>	h[a:]ben
năme	>	N[a:]me

---

[4] An alternative to this kind of analysis would involve 'syllable cut' theory, which has been applied to related patterns in the history of English; see Murray (2000).

This is a complex process, and has spread analogically in some forms, but not everywhere. Take OHG *weg* 'path' (see next paragraph). In the modern language, we have *Wege* with a long vowel in an open syllable, and today the singular is too: *Weg* [veːk], but the adverb *weg* [vɛk] 'away' is still short. While not everyone has these patterns for these words, lots of people actually do produce them that way.

4. **Closed syllable shortening (CSS)**. We also find shortening in closed syllables, especially when the syllable ends in more than one consonant, though this too is an inconsistent process:

MHG	(E)NHG
lieht	*Licht*
gienc	*ging*

Once again, as is typical throughout the last several centuries, these changes didn't affect the whole German-speaking area; they are found especially in the east central area and typically not in the south (Bavarian and Alemannic).

Both of these changes involve THE REGULATION OF WEIGHT in stressed syllables. As we discussed in Chapter 3, in earlier stages of the language, stressed syllables achieved an optimal weight, two moras, by a variety of different means. OSL fits into that same conspiratorial mode, and it happens not only in most kinds of German, but across most parts of the Germanic family OSL in particular is pervasive. OSL ensures that stressed syllables have enough weight; CSS is the other bookend, ensuring that syllables don't have too much weight. Like other conspiratorial prosodic patterns, OSL has been the focus of much important modern work (see the references for works by Kyes, Murray & Vennemann, Dresher & Lahiri, Page, Ramers, Smith).

These changes also show patterns of exceptions, as illustrated in Table 6.1, which draws its examples from Page (2007). In the first set, we have a morphological motivation for the oddities of OSL: while MHG *wec* was not an open syllable, the plural forms were, as well as the dative and genitive singular forms, where a suffix vowel followed the consonant: *wege* syllabified as *we.gə*. In this instance, different inflected forms of the word level out this difference so that all have a long vowel.

In this process, then, the singular has adjusted to match the plural and eliminated a vowel-length difference within nominal paradigms. As noted, the modern adverb *weg* 'away' is pronounced [vɛk], without lengthening. This form is attested

TABLE 6.1 **Exception 1: lengthening in monosyllables**

MHG	OSL	Leveling	NHG		gloss
wec	wec	weːc	Weg	[veːk]	'way'
weg	weːge	weːge	Wege	[veːgə]	'ways'

from the 14th century, replacing MHG *enwec* < OHG *in weg* 'auf dem Weg'.[5] During the time of OSL, it was presumably not perceived by speakers as still part of the same paradigm—rightly—and so did not participate in the process.

The second set of forms is less straightforward: OSL fails sometimes before *t* and *m*, particularly in disyllables ending in *-er*, *-el*. See Table 6.2: Here, you'll see modern spellings with double consonants PURELY to indicate

TABLE 6.2 **Exception 2: absence of lengthening before *t*, *m***

No lengthening		Lengthening	
Hammer	'hammer'	*Name*	'name'
Himmel	'sky'	*Schemel*	'stool'
kommen	'to come'	*nehmen*	'to take'
Vetter	'cousin'	*Vater*	'father'
Gatte	'husband'	*Kater*	'tomcat'

short preceding vowels, i.e. in settings where there was never any gemination.

As we've discussed earlier, these are prosodic changes, regulating weight, rather than changes to particular sounds or involving particular features. Page argues that prosodically driven changes like these are particularly prone to irregularity. While segmental sound change is expected to be regular, changes involving longer stretches of speech often show patterns of exceptionality like these.

5. Apocope. This is simply the loss of final unstressed vowels—in this case of German—and the concluding step in the Laws of Finals, the weakening and loss of endings that began in earliest Germanic. (See Lindgren 1953 for a classic study, and see the dialect map at historyofgerman.net, clicking on 'apocope' under the Dialect Map link.) Two examples show the kinds of patterns we find, first that particular suffixes show apocope and that apocope occurs in final position of monomorphemic words (often heavy stems).

MHG	NHG
Particular suffixes	
bezzerunge	*besserung*
küneginne	*königin*
vinsternisse	*finsternis*
Heavy monomorphemic words	
vorhte	*furcht*
herze	*herz*
reine	*rein*

Schwas were sometimes lost through sound change and reintroduced in written usage.

---

[5] This parallels the history of English *away*, from OE *onweg* 'on [one's] way'.

6. **Syncope.** This is the loss of (unstressed) vowels within a word. Vowels of final syllables are being lost in this period, using examples of inflectional suffixes here:

MHG	NHG
schrîbest	*schreibst*
schrîbet	*schreibt*

There is one notable exception, codified in the modern standard language: schwa typically stays after dentals, as in NHG *bittest*, *redet*, *leidet*. This reflects a common pattern across languages to avoid adjacent segments or syllables that are identical or very similar. (Consider English plurals, where we add [s] or [z] in words like *desk* or *wall* but if a noun ends in sounds like [s, z, ʃ], we retain a historical vowel: *houses* or *dishes*.)

7. **High vowel lowering.** Another dialectal process with important implications for the modern language is **lowering**, where older *i, u, ü* became *e, o, ö*:

MHG	NHG
sunne	*Sonne*
vrum	*fromm*
künec	*König*
mügen	*mögen*

High vowel lowering appears to have begun in the 12th century and early on is reportedly especially common in environments where we're now used to seeing vowel changes, most typically before nasals and before *r, l* (liquids) plus consonant. These particular sounds all have clear tendencies to obscure some acoustic characteristics of preceding vowels in the same syllable. You will recall a similar example of prenasal raising (*bend- > *bind-*), and there are various vowel changes in this environment, especially when *l* or *r* reduces or vocalizes, as discussed in the blocking of primary umlaut in Chapter 4.

This lowering is most characteristic of the central dialects, but is found beyond there as well, for example in some varieties of Swabian. As we've already seen from the Second Sound Shift, the modern standard draws particularly heavily on central German, so that this process is richly attested in the standard language today—as is the case with all the examples given so far—but many dialects have preserved the older patterns.

Just as long or tense vowels tend to rise in sound changes, especially 'chain shifts', short or lax vowels tend to lower. This looks like an example of such a development, although we will not speculate here about whether there is any plausible connection to other vocalic changes in the system during this period.

8. **Unrounding and secondary rounding.** An important dialectal process not found in the standard language is 'unrounding' or turning front-rounded or 'umlaut' vowels into front vowels that aren't rounded, so that *schön* and

grün are pronounced [e:] and [i:], so more like *Shane* and *green*. (See the dialect map at historyofgerman.net, clicking on 'unrounding' on the Dialect Map.) Judging from rhymes and spellings, this was happening in the 13th century in Bavarian and perhaps earlier. It has eventually become widespread across the German-speaking world except for the north (Low German, the Rhineland) and the southwest (parts of Alemannic).

Today, this is a very widespread phenomenon not only across dialects but also characteristic of *regionale Umgangssprachen* or colloquial regional varieties (see §6.7, ch. 7). The dialectal distribution is shown on Map 15, and it also shows the geography of apocope, *müde* versus *müd*. Note that while the standard language patterns of diphthongization and monophthongization reflect central German varieties, those varieties are mostly unrounded and overwhelmingly have apocope, while the modern standard has both.

And once again, we see parallels across the West Germanic family: the process is much like what happened far earlier in English—*king* was Old English *cyning*, where *y* represents a front rounded vowel—and we find unrounding attested from about the 13th century and spreading through the early modern period. Standard Yiddish has unrounded vowels as well, e.g. *ibər*, cognate with *über* (Jacobs 2005: 16).

In German, unrounded pronunciations were widespread among the most highly educated speakers even in the 18th and into the 19th century and in extremely formal usage, including canonical literary texts. The famous examples of this are rhyming patterns from Goethe, Schiller, and others, like *Blick* = *Glück* (so, pronounced *Glick*), *König* = *wenig*, and so on. As we'll see soon, norms for 'standard' pronunciation don't really get established until the late 19th century, so that these aren't 'non-standard' in any very real sense.[6] This is yet another example of the Frankenstein's monster that is the modern standard language, an instance where the standard incorporates a clear minority form from across the territory.

There's also a process of 'SECONDARY ROUNDING' in some areas, where etymologically FRONT vowels become ROUNDED:

MHG	NHG
helle	*Hölle*
zwelef	*zwölf*
sweren	*schwören*

---

[6] That so many German dialects spoken in the United States and Canada have unrounding is not, for the most part, due to influence from English, as many laypeople believe, but rather the pattern can be traced back to original dialects with unrounding that were imported to the Western Hemisphere. Low German dialects, for instance, did not unround and they have often retained front rounded vowels in diaspora.

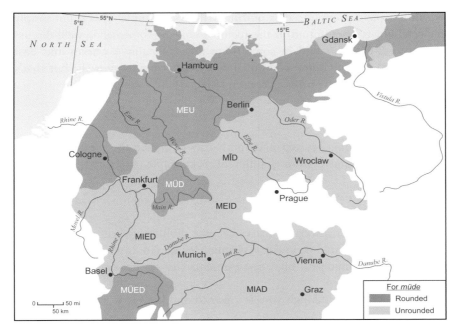

MAP 15 Unrounding.
Adapted from König et al. (2015: 148).

Historically, to underscore the point, the vowels in the left column are the older ones: we saw earlier that *hell/Hölle* comes from a form like *halja, with primary umlaut and West Germanic gemination.

This is an extremely irregular process, frequently found adjacent to labial consonants like *w*, which in many dialects long remained (and often remains to the present) a bilabial [w] rather than [v] (Schirmunski 1962: 366–369). It often occurs near [ʃ], a sound which—in contrast to the similar sound in English—often involves lip rounding and even protrusion of the lips. As in all the examples so far, secondary rounding is frequent with following *l* or *r*. In some varieties of German, /l/ in codas is velarized, and sometimes even vocalized to a *w*- or *u*-like sound. That is, in many though not all instances secondary rounding may have been phonetically motivated by neighboring sounds with lip rounding.

At the same time, it may have social motivation as an example of hypercorrection from the border areas where unrounding dialects meet dialects that keep umlauted vowels, where words like those presented on the previous page make it into the standard language. In some dialects it's very widespread, and you can get loss of *w*, cf. forms like *süster, tüschen* for *Schwester, zwischen.* In parts of central German territory (like Thuringian) and other areas, you find words like *nicht* pronounced as *nüscht* [nʏʃt], for example. This is not simply dialectal but is often found in the regional *Umgangssprache*, as we'll discuss in the next chapter. And in some other areas, notably Bavarian and East Franconian, we find some additional new front rounded vowels, but that's another story and beyond our concern here.

6.1.2 Summary of vowel changes

This summary aims to step back and draw together the various changes outlined so far above from a different perspective, to help you see new connections.

Changes involving high vowels

- Old long, high vowels (**iː, uː, üː**) become diphthongs with a high second element but a mid or low first element (**ei, au, äu**, in modern spelling).
- Old diphthongs with high first elements (**ie, uo, üe**) become long high vowels (**iː, uː, üː**).
- In many areas, old high vowels lower to mid vowels.

Prosodic changes

- Vowel length in stressed syllables adjust their quantity according to whether the syllable is open (short vowel becomes long) or closed (long becomes short).
- Unstressed vowels, now realized as schwa, continue to be lost finally or medially, especially in monomorphemic words with heavy stressed syllables.

(Un)rounding

- In central and southern dialects, front rounded vowels become unrounded.
- In some areas that maintain front rounded vowels, some front vowels become rounded, especially around labials and liquids.

6.1.3 Consonants

As noted already, a lot of regional developments take place during this period with consonants. They are mostly pretty minor, like the loss phonetic [h] between vowels (where the second vowel is a schwa) or after consonants (where the following vowel is a schwa):

sehen	*sehen*	[zeːn] or [zeːən]
bevelhen	*befehlen*	[bəfeːlən]
stahel	*Stahl*	[ʃtaːl]

Note that we still have *h* in the spelling of these words (marking vowel length in the second and third examples), but that's something about orthography, not about real pronunciation.[7]

And MHG *w* 'hardens' to a voiced stop, *b*, after *r* and *l*, but these sequences are not that common:

swalwe   *Schwalbe*
varwe   *Farbe*

6.1.4 Lenition

The most important consonantal development for our purposes is lenition, or 'weakening' (*Konsonantenschwächung*). Lenition is devilishly difficult to define precisely, but for present purposes we can see it as a loss of occlusion or constriction, that is, as movement toward greater sonority or more vowel-like sounds. This is a kind of anti-*Medienverschiebung*, where *p, t, k, s, f* > *b, d, g, z, v*. It is limited to the 'binnendeutschen Raum', not found in the far

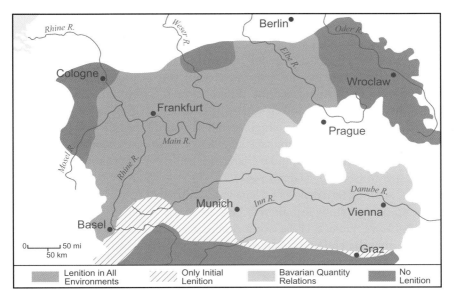

MAP 16 Lenition.
Adapted from König et al. (2015: 148).

---

[7] It is not terribly difficult to get some native speakers to produce an [h] here, in a form like [zeːhən], under extreme emphasis, like over a very bad phone connection or speaking to someone with limited knowledge of German.

south or north. There had long been variation, of course, in forms like initial *d ~ t* (even *deutsch ~ teutsch!*), and this is a big swing of the pendulum: earlier consonant changes like the First and Second Sound Shifts are often interpreted as fortitions or strengthenings (but see Honeybone 2005, forthcoming). The weakening of consonants, especially between vowels, is one of the most common types of sound change in the languages of the world, and very well attested across Germanic. (Holsinger 2000, 2008 provides a very solid theoretical and historical treatment of these issues.)

Map 16 is redone from König et al. so as to give a broad overview of the geography of this kind of weakening.

The results have massive impact on some dialects, like East Franconian, where lots of words become homophonous, because the voiceless (or fortis) and voiced (or lenis) sounds are no longer distinguished, all pronounced more like the lenis (*b, d, g*). These examples show the pattern in initial position:

> *Pass = Bass*
> *Tier = dir*
> *Karten = Garten*

You can hear these 'lenited' forms in the speech of many central and southern German speakers today.

The modern standard includes these distinctions—lacking lenition—and evidence shows that people from areas with this change, like Nuremberg, worked very hard to master the difference and use it in writing, though much more so in formal and especially professional writing and less in private writing. Important here sociolinguistically is that the people who seem most committed to a 'standard language ideology' are most successful in mastering such characteristics of a standard language which are not part of their own native speech (see Lippi-Green 1994).

In the southeastern dialects we have the 'Bavarian Quantity Relations', which show up in morphological alternations, especially singular vs. plural: [tiːʒ] ~ [tɪʃː] 'table vs. tables'. These are a different animal, where the quality of a consonant at the end of a syllable (whether it's fortis or lenis) correlates with the quality of the vowel in the syllable (whether it's tense or lax). If you have a tense vowel, you have to have a lenis consonant; if a lax vowel, a fortis consonant. Like other weight adjustments, it serves to create monosyllabic words of the same overall type.

The history is more complex and more interesting, as Fertig (2014) notes. We saw in §4.1 and §6.1 that German and other Germanic languages regulate prosodic weight, typically around a preference for bimoraic stressed syllables. In Bavarian, the modern fortis obstruents often come from old geminates or clusters. That is, they often go back to phonetically and phonologically long consonants, so that weight was already part of the equation. Fertig tells the story this way (drawing on earlier histories of Bavarian, especially Kranzmayer 1956): In monosyllables, old lenis codas correspond to tense vowels, while old fortis codas and some clusters can have either relation, for historical reasons. Before apocope, there was general lengthening (or tensing) with lenition of the consonant of the old monosyllables (as in Open Syllable Lengthening; see §4.1, §6.1.1), which created [ti:ʒ̊] in the singular from an old form like [tɪʃ]. In contrast, the old disyllables escaped that process, and hence retain their old structures, giving us, after apocope, the plural [tɪʃ:] from an old form like [tɪʃə].

6.2 Early New High German dialects

With the information you have received on sound changes, you're ready to identify ENHG dialects. (There are also morphological and syntactic differences across ENHG dialects, as you would expect.) In what follows we'll talk about the sociolinguistic importance of these dialects and how they were used.

You already understand the role of the Second Sound Shift in identifying dialects. From OHG to the modern dialects, it is your most secure starting point for determining where a text is from. For ENHG, the other key features are some of the vowel developments described in §6.1, monophthongization and diphthongization. Another useful feature is the loss of unstressed vowels, syncope (word-internal) and apocope (word-final). These are summarized here:[8]

	Second Sound Shift	Monophthong-ization	Diphthong-ization	Syncope/Apocope
Low German	–	–	–	–
East Central	+	+	+	–
Alemannic	++	–	–	+
Bavarian	++	–	+	+

You'll recall that the Second Sound Shift is partially realized in central areas, but more fully in the south, thus a difference between central '+' and southern '++'. Other dialect features we've discussed remain, as you might expect: the 3rd person singular masculine person *he* (or spelling variants) immediately signals a northern text, for instance.

---

[8] This table was developed by Rob Howell. Given the complexity of the data, there is some inevitable simplification, e.g. more complex distributions of apocope.

These patterns are dynamic, changing over the course of this period. Lindgren 1953 treats apocope in great detail, indicating that it is complete in the south only in the early 15th century. (Again, see the online dialect map at historyofgerman.net for the modern dialectal distribution.) That is, occasional final schwas still occur in southern texts during the early part of this period. In short, we must keep chronology in mind alongside region in using this table.

In addition, you can use points of reference from modern German and what you know of earlier stages. The set of ENHG texts readily available is almost limitless today, with many internet resources, which often contain images of texts as well (and see historyofgerman.net for exercises):

- http://mdz1.bib-bvb.de/~db/bsb00001078/images/index.html
- http://www.ingolstadt.de/stadtmuseum/scheuerer/museum/eck-luce.htm
- http://dewey.library.upenn.edu/sceti/printedbooksNew/index.cfm? TextID=pf_3455_i5

6.3 Morphology

In Early New High German morphology, we find some changes in what categories are marked and how, but much more movement of particular words from one category to another. So, for instance, the category of gender remains stable (i.e. nouns are still masculine, feminine, or neuter), but lots of nouns change genders, something we'll look at in some detail when we get to modern German. In general, the patterns we observed in MHG continue. This section surveys key developments in nominal and then verbal inflection, then notes one development in derivational morphology, namely how 'linking' in compounds was accomplished, that is, how modern *Fugenelemente* came into the language and how they worked in ENHG.

Nouns. The crucial development in this period for the nouns is what Wegera & Solms (2000: 1544) call the 'Profilierung der Kategorie Numerus' often called *Pluralprofilierung*. For MHG, we observed the clear emergence of plural marking, e.g. in the old masculine *a*-stems, like singular *tac* versus plural *tage* (with the one wrinkle of dative singular *tage*). In ENHG, we find the pattern of -*e*—phonetically schwa, [ə]—plural marking spreads, perhaps most notably to the old neuter *a*-stems. You already know that in OHG and MHG, words like *wort* had zero-marked plurals in the nominative and accusative cases, like English *deer* ~ *deer*. Now, *wort*, *dinc* 'thing', and many other words begin to show schwa plurals like *worte* and *dinge*. In the southern dialects, such as Bavarian, apocope eliminates final schwas, but these dialects also continue to develop distinctive plural marking, simply using other markers: *Stück* ~ *Stücker*,

Künig ~ Künigen, Tag ~ Täg (examples from Wegera & Solms 2000: 1544). Later, schwa is restored in this function in many words in many dialects.[9]

In the feminines, the *-(e)n* plural forms we find today in the standard language become widespread. Among the old ō-STEMS the singular forms ended in *-e* (or Ø, for apocopating dialects), where the *-n* that originally marked only DAT. or GEN. PL. now comes to mark all plural forms, so *sache* (or *sach*) is singular and *sachen* is plural for all four cases. That is, this *-en* presumably spread from those earlier dative/genitive forms into all plural forms. While we usually expect the most common and/or default forms (like nominative case forms) to provide a model for reshaping other parts of a paradigm, the general rise of distinctive plural marking (see also §5.3 and §8.2) may have helped yield this outcome where the dative and genitive plural form spreads to the nominative and accusative. Another piece of understanding these patterns is that the old plural (and singular oblique) marker *-en* takes on the role of plural marking specifically for feminines, as well as for some neuters.

For the OHG and MHG periods, we only briefly mentioned a tiny group of neuter nouns that in Proto-Germanic had stems in *-iz/-az*, like *lamb, kalb*, and *farh* 'piglet' (§3.4.4). For classical MHG, Wegera & Solms (2000: 1544) list only nine words in this class: *blat, ei, huon, lamp, rint, rîs, rat, tal, kalb*. With rhotacization, the old *z becomes *r* and the *-ir* form wins out over the *-ar* form, so that the reflex of the stem-class marker becomes *-er* with weakening.

In the 13th century, we start finding *-er* on masculine nouns that used to be neuter, like *got*. Among the neuters, even in the 14th and 15th centuries (according to Reichmann & Wegera's *Frühneuhochdeutsche Grammatik*), there's little spread of *-er*, but it then comes in and takes over a lot of territory in the 16th century; and by the 17th, we find a situation close to the modern one, including competition between plurals with semantic differentiation, like these pairs:

Worte ≠ Wörter
'words in some collection like a speech or phrase' VERSUS 'individual or isolated words like those making up a dictionary'

Lande ≠ Länder
'regions', often in the phrase deutsche Lande, or Niederlande VERSUS 'countries'

---

[9] This is a topic that calls out for further historical investigation; see Nübling (2008: 312–325) and Kürschner (2008a, 2008b) for some recent perspectives on the reshaping of inflectional classes in some dialects. Very recent work is also treating the importance of syncope for syntax, for instance Sapp (2009) on its role in loss of the preterit in southern dialects.

In such instances, variants in widespread use get recruited for the standard language for somewhat different purposes. People typically understand the increase in -er and umlaut as efforts to maintain and extend the singular–plural distinction in the face of changes like apocope that would eliminate the distinction.

Once more, this provides an answer to an apparent oddity in the modern language: this old zero-marking is retained for quantities, like *zwei Glas Bier* or *zwei Stück Papier*. This pattern also remains productive with currencies: *es kostet 20 Euro*. Non-linguists tend to understand this as singular today, but its roots are clearly plural in the morphological history of German.

Patterns similar to the spread of -ir occur with UMLAUT. This is most notably true for southern dialects where apocope eliminated the plural marking on words that in modern German have schwa suffixes and no umlaut: *hund, tag, tod*, and so on have from this era to the present day been formed by umlaut in many southern dialects, where you hear singular *Tag* but plural *Täg*.

Weak or *n*-stem nouns continue to dwindle in number over time. A number of old *n*-stem nouns that have taken on the *n* even in the nominative singular: earlier forms like *garte, boge, grabe, mage* become *Garten, Bogen, Graben, Magen*. With these, some have umlaut in the plural in Standard German, like *Garten*, and others vary, like *Magen* (that is, with un-umlauted plural forms used by some speakers). These nouns are inanimates, referring to things, not people or other living creatures, which leaves weak nouns in the contemporary language more and more restricted to animates: *Herr, Student, Gatte, Kollege, Löwe, Bär*, etc. Of course this is not (yet) a rigid pattern, cf. *Name*.

Adjectives. One of the most challenging patterns of German for learners and teachers (and occasionally native speakers) is the system of adjective endings in attributive usage, that is, as part of a noun phrase, as in *das brave Kind* (as opposed to predicative use, like *das Kind ist ja brav*). In Chapter 4, we briefly treated the rise of the strong versus weak systems. Early modern usage differed substantially from the current standard, though. While we use weak endings after definite articles today (*der beste Student*), Luther's usage, for instance, diverges often, e.g. *der knörrender rauher Pöbel* (Voeste 1999: 159) and *das erst Buch* (see Chapter 7).

Traditional sources see the settling out of these paradigms as happening during the ENHG period, e.g. Reichmann & Wegera (1993: 201–202) and von Polenz (1994: 258–259), who writes that the consolidation of the inflection of the noun phrase 'war bereits im Frühneuhochdt. grundsätzlich eingetreten' and he sees only 'restliche Belege' of earlier variation by the 17th and even the 18th century. Voeste provides very solid evidence that things remain far more unsettled in the first half of the 18th, in fact.

She provides evidence from a set of written sources AND grammarians of that period for ongoing competition: in the weak paradigm, for example, the nominative and accusative plural vary between *-e* and *-en*, so *die gute/ guten Leute.*

Pronouns. Throughout the book, we've spent relatively little time on pronouns, but in the ENHG period, they serve to illustrate the amount of variation we find along various parameters. Table 6.3, adapted for clarity from Howe (1996: 253), gives you an idea of the complexity of the system, especially across dialects.[10]

TABLE 6.3 **Early New High German Pronouns**

	NOM.	ACC.	DAT.	GEN.
1 S	**ich**	**mich**	**mir** (WC, Th 14, 15 also mi; C also mer; UG also mier)	**min/mein, m(e)iner** (C 14, 15 also mines; Alem 15–17 also m(e)inen)
2 S	**du** -(t)u, (-t)	**dich**	**dir** (CF, ECG, 14, 15 also di)(der; UG also dier)	**din/dein, d(e)iner** (C 14, 15 also dines; Alem 16, 17 also dinen/deinen)
3 S M	**er**, C also **he, her** (hei, hie; ECG occas. ha, har)	**in/ihn**, also **i(h)ne** (rarer inen/ihnen; C also en/on) (rare -n)	**im/ihm, i(h)me**; C esp. 14, 15 also em/om, eme/ome	**sin/sein, s(e)iner** (C 14, 15, NEU 14 also s(e)ines; Alem also s(e)inen)
3 S F	**sie/si** (14, 15 also: WU, B siu/sü/ seu, Th su) (-s)	**sie/si** (14, 15 also: WU B siu/sü/seu, Th su) (esp. acc. -s)	**ir/ihr** (also: WU i(h)ro, a esp. 16 i(h)ren; NEU 17 -o; WC, (HA, NEU) -e)	**ir/ihr** (also: C 16-er; WC 14 -s; WU 16 -en; Alem -o, HA 15 -e)
3 S N	**es/ez**, also **is/iz**; often, esp. acc. -s (-z) (CF 14, 15 also it/id (-t))	**es/ez**, also **is/iz**; often, esp. acc. -s (-z) (CF 14, 15 also it/id (-t))	**im/ihm, i(h)me**; C esp. 14, 15 also em/om, eme/om	**sin/sein** (HA 16 also sinen; rare seiner Als 16) (also es etc.)

[10] The leftmost column uses '1, 2, 3' for first, second, third person, 'S, P' for singular and plural, and 'M, F, N' for the genders (where they are relevant).

TABLE 6.3 **Continued**

1 P	wir (rarer also mir) (wier; C also wer, mer; CF, ECG 14, 15 also wi)	uns (UG also üns) (v. occas. us)	uns (UG also üns) (v. occas. us)	unser (16, 17 also uns(e) rer)(rare uns, unse, unsers)
2 P	ir/ihr (ECG 14, 15 also i/ie; C also er; CF rare dir; B also ez, es, rare -s)	üch/uch/euch (HA 14, 15, B 14–16 also iu/ew; B also enk, ench)	üch/uch/euch (UG, ECG 14, 15, B 14–16 also iu/ü/ u/ew; B also enk, ench)	üwer/uwer/e(u)wer (UG 17, C also ew(e)rer; R 14, 15 also ur(r)e, ur(e)s; B also enker)
3 P	sie/si 14, 15 UG also siu/sü/seu (Th, MF also su) (UG -s)	sie/si 14, 15 UG also siu/ sü/seu (Th, MF also su) (UG -s)	in/ihn later general ine(n)/ihne(n) (C also en, on)	ir/ihr, irer/ihrer (also: WU -en; C 14, 15 -(e)s; esp. HA -o; occas. -e; rare -a)

Numbers indicate centuries, Alem = Alemannic, Als = Alsatian, B = Bavarian, C = Central German, CF = Central Franconian, HA = High Alemannic, MF = Mosel-Franconian, NEU = Northeast Upper German, R = Ripuarian, Th = Thuringian, WC = West Central German, WU = West Upper German.

ENHG has a set of what Howe calls 'extended forms', where a second syllable has been added to an old monosyllabic pronoun (1996: 252–254). In MHG and the beginning of the ENHG period, the third person dative plural pronoun was usually a short form, *in* or *ihn*. During the period, it gains a second syllable, originally in Alemannic but spreading throughout much of the German-speaking territory and it eventually becomes part of the modern standard, of course. It is possible that this comes from the *-en* characteristic of dative plural nouns or from inflected adjectives. Taken in isolation, that might sound ad hoc, but Howe gives a set of similar developments from across Germanic (1996: 80–86). ENHG actually attests a broader set, like 3rd personal single feminine dative *iren*, *ihren*, but these have a less successful history in terms of the standard.

Numerals. In Chapter 3, we noted that the numerals 1–3 inflected for gender and, to an extent, for case. This continues to the present day in the indefinite article, forms of *ein*. In ENHG, the gender differentiation of *zwei* in the nominative and accusative continued, according to the handbooks (e.g. Reichmann & Wegera 1993: 206–207), into the 16th century, with masculine *zwen(e)*, neuter *zwei*, and feminine *zwo*. Even *drei* shows some remnant inflection early in the period.

Reality is, as so often, happily richer than the handbook presentation: various dialects continue to inflect 'two' down to the present, as these examples from an East Franconian dialect still spoken in southern Indiana (Nützel 2009):

zw**ee** weeng
'two wagons' (masc.)

zw**uu** kern
'two churches' (fem.)

zw**aa** heisa
'two houses' (neut.)

But even in colloquial German, we have an odd survival from this set: in speech where clarity is an issue, such as on the telephone, the old feminine *zwo* is still used.

Verbs. Sound changes like syncope bring us overall very close to the contemporary system (*sagete > sagte*). Analogical change (as will be discussed) also gets rid of lots of wrinkles that we've seen until now, for example:

- Verner alternations (grammatischer Wechsel) are lost save for in a few words, so MHG *verliesen* 'to lose' normally takes on the *r* of the other forms. Still, we find alternations in verbs where they are gone today: *kiesen ~ erkoren, sehen ~ gesagen.* (e.g. Moser et al. 1970–1998: IV, 520–521). For Nuremberg, Fertig (2000) shows that some writers still used *was* instead of *war* for the third singular preterit of *sein*.
- *Rückumlaut* disappears from all but a few verbs that had it. We still find forms like *mercken–marckte* and a few others in Luther. While it is often said that modern German has six of these (*brennen, kennen, nennen, rennen, senden, wenden*), the last two are often weak today and *Duden Grammatik* lists regular forms for the rest, like *nennte*, though marking them as 'selten'. After a mere 1200 or so years, this irregularity is fading away.
- Leveling removes much complexity from some of the strong verbs. For example, you'll recall that in MHG, we have *ei* in the singular preterits of class I—*treib*—but *ê* where there was monophthongization, like before *h* in *zêh*.
- The *ge-* prefix becomes more securely established as a marker of past participles. Fertig 1998 shows that early modern texts from Nuremberg still occasionally have *ge-* with *-ieren* verbs. A set of verbs still lack the prefix in this area, like *gehen, geben, kaufen, kriegen*. You'll note that these all begin with *g-* or *k-*, and it was long believed that syncope of the schwa in the prefix triggered loss of the prefix as a whole: *gegeben > ggeben = geben*. Fertig shows that it is instead a process of haplology, where in a sequence of similar or identical syllables one is omitted. (Consider the widespread English pronunciation of *library* as [laibri].)

These changes are famously complex and provide challenges and opportunities to scholars interested in how analogical change works. Crucially, in this period we have enough data for fine-grained examination. One of the best and most accessible studies of the period, in fact, is Fertig's treatment of verbs in early modern Nuremberg, mentioned repeatedly already in this chapter. While Nuremberg verb inflection looks generally like the modern standard in many respects, Fertig shows that first person singular forms in *-en* we saw in OHG and even MHG still occur occasionally. More importantly, he shows clear social variation during this period. For instance, the first and third person plural forms of *sein*, modern standard *sind*, appear as *sein* among administrators for his earliest writers, while most others prefer *sind* and a third group, mostly lay-women (as opposed to those in cloisters), uses *sin/sen*. In short, careful work can chart patterns of structural and social variation because we have enough written material surviving. We often find new features first adopted by women rather than men, and by lower middle class rather than upper or lower class speakers, for instance.

Let us consider one key pattern, the shift of strong (ablauting) verbs to weak classes. The increase in weak verbs at the expense of strong classes has happened in all Germanic languages. Linguists have long recognized that morphological change correlates with frequency. In particular irregular forms maintain themselves longer if the words are frequently used and learned early on. This is often observed about noun plurals in English, like *woman ~ women, man ~ men, child ~ children*, as well as words that were historically more common than they are today, like *ox ~ oxen, mouse ~ mice, louse ~ lice*. One recent study, Lieberman et al. 2007, argued along these lines that the rate of movement from strong to weak was inversely connected to frequency, but goes on to say that the rate is linear. They posit a 'half-life' of strong verbs: 'a verb that is 100 times less frequent regularizes 10 times as fast', even predicting that the next English verb to become weak will be *to wed*.[11] For German, though, Carroll et al. (2012) found that the rate of regularization in German changes over time: 'in the German system regularization begins later and occurs at a lower rate. From 750 until 1650 little change occurs, but large-scale regularization begins with ENHG.' The most frequent verbs—starting from *sein, geben, kommen, werden*—have all remained strong to the present, but in the least frequent class, only one (in bold) has remained strong: **genesen**, *gleißen, keimen, nagen, niesen, schaben, schwellen, walken, wallen, walzen*. The take-home point is that this process begins on a large scale during the ENHG period and continues down to the present.

---

[11] For discussion of such patterns for English verbs, Hare & Elman (1995) is a classic reference.

The process of regularization has been not only slow but complex. Any given verb follows its own chronological path, which can usually be traced using the Grimms' *Deutsches Wörterbuch*. *Snîwen*, modern *schneien*, has largely become weak by MHG, but some southern dialects continue strong forms. *Kneten* still showed lots of strong forms (*knat*, *gekneten*, and present *knitt*) in the 16th century, but it is weak in the modern standard. Many contemporary younger readers may not have known that *pflegen* was typically inflected as a strong verb almost down to the present—in fact, Duden's *Zweifelsfälle* still lists *gepflogen*, but marked as 'veraltet'.[12]

A few verbs still have two forms today, at least for some speakers:

    backen   buk vs. backte
    melken   molk vs. melkte

The 1998 edition of the *Duden Grammatik* examines such variation (§243 and elsewhere) in often great detail. In almost all cases of competition, the weak forms win out over the strong, to use an ironic formulation.

There is still much to be learned about the particular types and patterns of frequency that correlate with regularization. Dammel et al. (2010), for instance, present evidence that leveling in Swedish has followed somewhat different paths than German, English, and Dutch. Swedish preserves strong preterit forms better, with West Germanic languages seeming to keep strong forms of past participles.

Since the first edition of this book, much new work has looked at strong verb regularization, including at issues of the resilience of classes (see e.g. Carroll et al. 2012: 163–164, and especially Pijpops et al. 2015 and other work by the latter team), but much remains to be done on type frequency and other issues. We have only begun to explore parallels to such patterns in nominal morphology, for example the regularization of noun plurals in West Germanic.

Modal verbs. Finally, let us consider the modal verbs, the old preterit presents. These continue their long heritage as verbs marching to their own drummer(s) and in this period too they undergo a number of important and striking changes. Let's look briefly at two.

For one thing, as we saw in earlier chapters, they are not expected to show umlaut in present forms: present forms of the preterit presents did not have an *i* which would have triggered umlaut. These verbs did have optative or subjunctive forms that did (Schirmunski 1962: 546–547):

---

[12] The continued use of this particular form may be supported by the noun *Gepflogenheit*, a noun formed when the verb was still strong.

OHG   MHG
durfi   dürfe
kunni   künne
mugi   müge

By the ENHG period, we can clearly think of these verbs as modals. At least since Schirmunski, scholars have seen umlaut as a clear marker of modality, motivating the spread of umlaut into the infinitives. While the modern standard has umlaut in some modals—like *dürfen, können, müssen*, as just illustrated—not all modal verbs are umlauted—like *sollen* and *wollen*. Various dialects, though, do umlaut those infinitives, like Thuringian *söl* and *wöl* (where the infinitive lacks *-en*) and many Low German varieties.

For another, most modals had high vowels in MHG, so would be expected to show vowel lowering, as discussed in the previous section. Here is Fertig's (1999) summary of the traditional view of how the modals developed; look at the earlier and later forms:

	Present subj., infinitive, and plural ind.	Preterit ind.	Preterit subj.
Before	*sullen*	*sollte*	*sollte*
After	*sollen*	*sollte*	*sollte*
Before	*dürfen*	*dorfte*	*dörfte*
After	*dürfen*	*durfte*	*dürfte*
Before	*künnen*	*konnte*	*könnte*
After	*können*	*konnte*	*könnte*
Before	*mügen*	*mochte*	*möchte*
After	*mögen*	*mochte*	*möchte*
Before	*wellen*	*wollte*	*wollte*
After	*wollen*	*wollte*	*wollte*

Overview of the standard account of stem-vowel changes in the modals

The purpose of this graphic is simply to show how messy even a relatively superficial view of the modals' development is. Scholars have long attributed these changes to 'analogical leveling' which eliminated wrinkles in these verbs, but Fertig has by far the best data available, in quantity and quality, and uses databases for quantitative analysis. With that, he shows that the interplay of sound change and regional differences are at work with morphological patterns from a fuller paradigm of the modals and also from beyond the modals themselves. There's no single reason, in other words, for why the modals end up the way they do; they are the result of many competing forces.

Let's briefly look at one of the simplest of the changes, one where the regional differences are crucial—where considering detailed evidence from Central versus Upper German dialects changes the picture (again, from Fertig):

	Singular present ind.	Present subj. and plural ind.	Infinitive	Preterit
OHG	*sal*	*suln*	*soln/(suln)*	*solte*
late OHG/MHG	*sol*	*suln*	*soln/suln*	*solte*
ENHG	*sol*	*soln*	*soln*	*solte*

Actual developments in *sollen*, Upper German

	Singular present ind.	Present subj. and plural ind.	Infinitive	Preterit
OHG	*sal*	*suln*	*soln/(suln)*	*solte*
MHG	*sal*	*soln*	*soln*	*solte*
16th c.	*sol*	*soln*	*soln*	*solte*

Actual developments in *sollen*, Central German

The developments differ in how the stem vowel 'settles out' to *o*. In the south, this happens earlier in the singular present indicative, while in the central area it's the infinitive, the plural indicative, and preterit subjunctive that all change earlier. Fertig interprets these data as indicating that the central pattern reflects the sound change we discussed earlier of high-vowel lowering (the *sunne > Sonne* type). That sound change is found in these areas especially with a following *l*. Only later does the *sal* form come into line with the broader set of forms containing *o* as their stem vowel.

In almost every regard, the modal verbs present considerable challenges: their sound patterns and morphological shapes, their semantics, their syntax and how all these things change, and we will see this continue in the next chapter. As was recently concluded in a different context, 'modals are messy' (Brown & Putnam 2011).

Derivational morphology: *Fugenelemente*.[13] Throughout the book to now, we've seen examples of grammaticalization, in particular where earlier syntactic patterns become later morphological patterns. Most of our examples have been inflectional, like the development of *ge-* as a marker of past participles from an old particle or the addition of a *-t* to second person verb forms. We've also seen numerous examples of grammaticalization creating

---

[13] We have, in general, paid little attention to derivational morphology, but there is a tradition of research on the topic, e.g. Habermann et al. (2002).

individual words or small sets of words, like *ni+eo+wiht* > *nicht*, along with other negative adverbs, or words like *tagsüber*.

The same patterns are found in productive derivational morphology as well. Modern German compounds are often characterized by linking elements, called—among many other things—*Fugenelemente* in German. Consider a word like German *Bundesbank,* Bund+**es**+bank. Like in this example, the link is often transparently a genitive-like ending. In an important book about the development of noun phrases in German, Demske (2001a: 300–305) treats this as the lexicalization of certain forms, with a reinterpretation of the structure, erasing a word boundary and creating a compound:

> [[der Kirchen] Ceremonien] >   [der [Kirchen Ceremonien]]
> of the church ceremonies

The impossibility of understanding these as plural markers is underscored by a couple of examples passed along by James Cathey, where the first elements exist in the relevant sense only in the singular:

> [der sunnun]   scīn > der [Sonnenschein]
> of the sun   shine
> [der Marien]   kirche > die [Marienkirche]
> of [the] Mary   church

These elements appear to have arisen largely during ENHG and Michel shows how they have developed. Look first at how different the overall distribution of elements is, in Table 6.4, between ENHG and modern German

TABLE 6.4 **Frequency and distribution of individual *Fugenelemente***

Fugenelement	-ø-	-n-	-en-	-s-	-es-	-e-	-er-	total
ENHG dictionary	2,217	172	80	59	4	13	10	2,555
	86.8%	6.7%	3.1%	2.3%	0.2%	0.5%	0.4%	
NHG wordlist	291	45	21	127	8	6	6	504
	57.7%	8.9%	4.2%	**25.2%**	1.6%	1.2%	1.2%	

From Michel (2010: 185), corrected (with NHG data from Kürschner 2003).

The large rise in linking *-s* over time is striking, along with a considerable decline in the number of zero-marked compounds. Eventually, these patterns of linking become more abstract, that is, no longer directly based on the word's historical inflection. With this, the process comes to apply even where the element was never present in the inflection of the first noun, like the use of *-s* with feminine nouns, e.g. *Geburtstag* 'birthday' or *Arbeitszimmer* 'work room'. That is, the *s* is not paradigmatic here.

Michel establishes a set of principles, including both phonetic-phonological and morphological properties, which already correlate with the elements used in ENHG over a corpus drawn from a dictionary:

Distribution of *Fugenelemente* in ENHG after Michel (2010)

Fugenelement	phon.-phon. properties		morph. properties	
	Syllable count	final segment	gender	paradigm
-ø-	—	—	—	—
-n-	2	Vowel (ə)	Feminine	paradigmatic
-en-	1	Consonant (stop)	Masc.-Fem.	paradigmatic
-s-	1–2	Consonant (stop)	Masc.-Neut.	paradigmatic (unparadigmatic)
-es-	1	Consonant (stop)	Masc.-Neut.	paradigmatic
-e-	1	Consonant (stop)	Masc.-Neut.	paradigmatic
-er-	1	Consonant (stop)	Neuter	paradigmatic

In short, there are clear patterns already in ENHG, with *n* used for schwa-final feminines, for instance, and overwhelmingly patterns that are consistent with the inflectional paradigms of the first elements. We will return to these patterns in the next chapter, showing that they have continued to develop.

6.4 Syntax

Some broader morphosyntactic tendencies. In the big picture, we also see the continuation of processes we have already discussed, like the use of articles, pronouns, and more prepositions. All those characteristics are part of what Nichols (1986) calls a move from 'head-marking' to 'dependent marking': in a noun phrase like *das schöne Haus*, the noun can be considered in some sense the 'head' or main element of the phrase.[14] In OHG, grammatical relations (notably case) were, as we've seen, more often and clearly marked on the noun

---

[14] Today, this is no longer the usual syntactic analysis of these phrases, since the DP hypothesis, which treats the Determiner (here, *das*) as the head. While the DP hypothesis is critical to much syntactic analysis, including the work by Demske just discussed, it is not immediately relevant to Nichols' point.

itself. The marking is now increasingly on other words within the grammatical phrase and not on the noun itself but rather on articles or adjectives.

The next step in this progression is to carry out the marking using more syntactic means: prepositions. In English, we've pushed this tendency much farther, having lost much case marking on pronouns and all case marking on nouns save for genitive -s. In English we use word order more heavily for grammatical purposes, while German uses it more for pragmatic purposes, like focus or emphasis. But where even in MHG just case inflection was used, German now uses prepositions. Recall our earlier discussions of the once-widespread use of the genitive case in many functions, especially §5.4.5, like in these examples of a partitive relationship (from Paul 2007: 342):

MHG	Modern German
ich muoz wesen . . . dins gesindes	*ich muß [einer]* **von deinem Gefolge sein**
er wânde, er wære der vînde	*er glaubte, jener wäre [einer]* **von den Feinden.**

Periphrasis. We continue to find more periphrasis in this period and the developments become interesting for the modern language in new ways. Consider the use of the preterit (or simple past) vs. the perfect. Older sources like Lockwood already point out (1968: 122) that in the 12th century, epics often used perfect forms when representing spoken language, but the preterit for narrative (I've highlighted relevant forms):

der künec si GRUOZTE *schône; er sprach: sît willekomen*
wer iuch her HABE GESENDET, *des'n* HÂN *ich niht* VERNOMEN

While Luther's central-colored German continues this general pattern (as does the modern language for many speakers), the perfect comes to dominate in the south, as we have already discussed and will discuss further in later chapters.

How and why did this come about? One long if hardly universally held view is that the loss of final schwa (apocope, as already discussed) triggered the loss of the preterit or simple past. Standard German and many dialects distinguish between, for instance, 3rd person singular present *macht* 'does, makes' and 3rd person singular preterit *machte* 'did, made'. Apocope would make those homophonous, so the argument goes, leaving speakers to rely on the perfect form to make the crucial distinction between present and past: present *macht* versus past *hat gemacht*. Moreover, both apocope and preterit loss are identified with southern varieties of German. Sapp 2009 draws on a large corpus (20,000 clauses in the past tense), and confirms part of the traditional view, namely that texts showing more apocope also show more use of perfect rather than preterit. But the finding is more nuanced than this: perfect forms tend to occur not so much with third singular forms, but rather with second person forms, so that *hast gemacht* is preferred over *machtest* more than *hat gemacht* over *machte*. In those second person forms it would have been internal vowel loss (syncope) rather than apocope that triggered the change. Sapp sees this syncope as the real trigger, the initial pattern from which a large change grew. At the same time, he is careful to include the full set of factors that likely helped it spread across the broad territory where it's found today, from psycholinguistic (following Abraham 1999) to sociolinguistic (such as Drinka 2004, 2015, discussed earlier).

Fertig (2014) pushes back against this particular story, drawing on classic works such as Dal (1960) and Schirmunski (2010). He rightly notes that many southern varieties haven't actually lost preterit forms but have rather restricted them to use in the subjunctive. There is a loss of these *qua* preterits, but not a loss of the forms themselves. Vowel reductions lead to homophony, he points out, between preterit indicative and subjunctive forms, and people could employ periphrastic constructions to disambiguate, either (i) by using the preterit for past and periphrastic forms for subjunctive or (ii) by using the old preterit for subjunctive and periphrastic forms for past. When and where these developments began and how they progressed are promising avenues.

Whatever role apocope and syncope ultimately end up playing in this change, quantitative sifting and effort to integrate multiple factors into the analysis are clearly positive directions to move in. That being said, as Fertig makes clear, this work has to be done in the context of the full verbal system of the relevant varieties.

While we see dramatic changes over the period in terms of when periphrasis is used, certain aspects of the system are remarkably stable from the ENHG period to the present. You know that German perfect forms vary between taking *haben* 'to have' and *sein* 'to be' as their auxiliary, as English used to (e.g. King James' *is come*). The basic generalization about this 'split auxiliary system' is that transitive verbs take *haben* while certain kinds of intransitive verbs may take *sein*—depending on meaning. As explored by Drinka (2015), a whole set of European languages have split auxiliary systems for the perfect. Taking a gradient approach to this problem, Sorace (2000) proposes an 'Auxiliary Selection Hierarchy', where at one pole, *have* is preferably selected with certain verbs and at the other *be* is. The prototypical *have* environments, for instance, are verbs for controlled processes that do not involve motion, like *reden* or *arbeiten*. The prototypical *be* environments, in contrast, are those involving change of location or state, like *entkommen* or *wachsen*. Verbs that fit neither pattern closely,

Sorace argues, are most likely to show variation, like statal verbs (which you may recall from Chapter 3).

In some respects, the German pattern goes back to Old High German, which shows some *sein* auxiliaries, often used like modern forms:

> Druhtin was irstantan (Otfrid, cited in Lockwood 1968: 116)
> 'the Lord had arisen'

Drawing on the same corpus developed for his 2009 article just discussed, Sapp (2011b) identifies a clear set of exceptions, intransitive verbs that today would have to take *sein* but which are attested with *haben*:

> wie wir also drey Stundt vngefehr hatten gefahren
> 'when we had traveled about three hours'
>
> Sy hedden by yn getreden vnd nyet by dat banner
> 'they had stepped over to him and not to the banner'

Sapp explains such forms semantically, since the examples either specify duration of an activity ('had traveled') or manner of motion ('had stepped'). Overall, though, these are relatively few and far between, with only 10 of 467 intransitive 'change of location' verbs taking *haben*. As predicted by Sorace's model, the most variation is found with verbs indicating the existence of a state, in this case typically a physical position: *liegen, sitzen, stehen*. If those verbs lack a clear reference to time (especially duration), they tilt heavily toward *sein*, but otherwise show a mix.

For these three verbs, there is regional variation in the Early New High German period, with southern dialects preferring *sein* and northern ones showing much more use of *haben*. This is continued down to the present, with many southern speakers preferring *ist gestanden* over *hat gestanden*.

Important here is that we see an instance of stability over the modern history of German: with few exceptions, the patterns of auxiliary selection at work in ENHG are still found today and even the areas of variation seem to be chronic problems over the centuries. All this is, moreover, in sharp contrast to English, where the so-called split auxiliary system has all but disappeared in the time since the King James Bible translation.

There are other changes in auxiliary use, as well. In the next chapter, we'll discuss the use of *tun* as an auxiliary for the present indicative. It appears in the second half of the 14th century in southern Germany (*Frühneuhochdeutsche Grammatik* 1993: 395–396, for instance), though how frequent it was is the subject of some controversy (Langer 2001, Fischer 2001).

Developments of future auxiliaries are particularly complex, with *sollen, wollen, müssen* used in various regions. *Werden* had been used already in

OHG, but with inchoative meaning and in the ENHG period increasingly marks the future, especially in the 16th century, probably spreading from the east to the west. Much about the development remains uncertain, enough so that Leiss (1985) proposes that it had its source in Old Czech. As we've discussed with regard to the spread of the periphrastic perfect with *haben/sein*, contact explanations for such patterns face serious challenges, so too here. For more on future periphrasis, see Ágel (2000) and Reichmann & Wegera (1993: 390–393), and on the historical roles of *werden* in German syntax, see Kotin (2003).

The *würde* + infinitive construction, often called 'conditional', has been attested since late MHG. Durrell & Whitt (2016) trace its establishment to the second half of the 17th century. It was once argued that this construction arose as a way to avoid ambiguity where the preterit indicative and preterit subjunctive are identical (*sie machte*, 'she did', she would do', as we discussed just now, for preterit loss in southern dialects). This is not supported in their data, but Durrell & Whitt show that such ambiguity does not seem to correlate with use of the periphrastic construction historically. Again, there is promise for a new investigation of the relationships between preterit loss and periphrastic subjunctives over time and space.

This example of a periphrastic construction is most notable for the attention it has received from prescriptivists, as we will discuss in the next chapter.

Word order. In ENHG—around Luther's time—we find a powerful tendency toward clause-final verbs. We've already mentioned the *Satzrahmen* or *Satzklammer* (verbal or sentence frame), perhaps the classic characteristic of modern German word order. Recall that until not long ago, many scholars believed that Luther singlehandedly helped shape the modern standard language. It was long claimed that establishing this verbal frame was one of Luther's big structural contributions to New High German, and some examples show that he changed such patterns from the earliest to later editions of his translation, with a slight increase in the total number of verb-final structures. See Table 6.5.

TABLE 6.5 **Some data from Luther**

September Bibel 1522	1546 Bibel
..., so **wirtt** euch ewr vatter auch nitt **vergeben** ewre feyle...	..., so **wird** euch ewer Vater ewre feile auch nicht **vergeben**...
...vnnd der weg ist breitt, **der** do **abfuret** zur verdamnis:	...vnnd der weg ist breit, **der** zur Verdamnis **abfueret**...
..., **das** yhm eyn mulsteyn wurd an seynen hals gehengt,...	..., **das** jm ein muelstein an seinen Hals gehengt **wuerde**,...
Total: 78%	Total: 81%

To probe the patterns of change on this point, Ebert (1983) examined documents (including personal letters) written by 28 Nurembergers in the 16th century. He determined that almost all of these people were using the new word order more consistently than Luther, even writers of Luther's generation. Most of the texts where verb-final rates were lower than Luther's were diaries, specifically private and informal documents. Ebert concludes: 'the Luther Bible cannot be considered...to have had any significant effect on the increase in the use of full-frames in Nuremberg in the 16th century...circumstantial evidence in the form of the widespread dissemination of the Luther Bible and its importance in daily life in the 16th century is insufficient to support the assumption of linguistic influence' (1983: 154).

More generally, Sapp (2011a: ch. 3) shows that ENHG is the critical transition to the modern order. Recall from the last chapter that he used '1' for inflected verbs and '2' for non-finite forms like participles and infinitives. Figure 6.3 shows the decline of 1–2 order over the period.

Sapp's sample draws, as for MHG, from a broad set of regional varieties, and his most dramatic finding is that there were great regional differences during this period (see Table 6.6):

TABLE 6.6 **Effect of dialect on 1–2 order, MHG vs. ENHG**

Dialect (MHG/ENHG area)	% of 1–2, MHG	% of 1–2, ENHG
Cologne	46.7%	8.6%
Alsace	n/a	11.8%
Hesse	35.9%	12.4%
Thuringia	10.8%	14.8%
Switzerland	13.1%	16.2%
(Eastern) Swabia/Augsburg	12.5%	23.9%
Bavaria/Vienna	31.9%	24.3%
Saxony	n/a	31.3%
E. Franconia/Nuremberg	19.4%	35.8%
Black Forest/Swabia	81.7%	41.7%
Total	28.7%	23.1%

Note that many areas show a sharp drop in 1–2 order, like Cologne and Hesse, while Nuremberg, the topic of so many studies in ENHG, has a strikingly high percentage of 1–2 patterns. The variation between these orders continues to

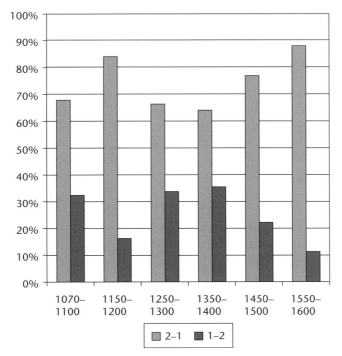

FIGURE 6.3 Overall patterns of 2–1 versus 1–2 with participle, after Sapp.

show finer-grained conditioning as discussed in the previous chapter for MHG. Two major conditioning factors are these:

- **Type of construction**. A construction with a participle is relatively likely to show 2–1 order, while modal plus infinitive constructions are more prone to have 1–2, a pattern also attested in Standard Dutch.
- **Prosodic structure**. The presence of a stressed word favors 1–2 order, as does focus, including contrastive focus.

Overall then with the Early New High German period, we have the major pieces of the modern standard language's morphology and syntax present in recognizable form, but naturally with regional variation that parallels what we tend to find in those modern dialects. With what you know now, some time with ENHG texts would allow you to recognize the broad patterns of change into the standard language and to recognize survival/loss of ENHG-period features in many or most dialects. For example, the verbal frame has come to be generally well established in the standard language, especially in writing, but not in most dialects. The genitive survives in the standard but is entirely gone from dialects and colloquial use.

6.5 Pragmatics and discourse: language in use

As our texts grow richer, we are able to glean more insights not only into language structure but also increasingly into understanding 'language as people's main instrument of "natural" and "societal" interaction', to use the description of pragmatics from the website of the *Journal of Pragmatics.* That is, pragmatics is language from the perspective of users, language use in its social context. The field is in practice vastly more complex, ranging from formal work closely tied to semantics and syntax to close connections to neighboring fields like discourse analysis, and we'll take a very broad view here and in the next chapter.

The opportunities for understanding language use for social interaction are limited in early periods, especially since the richest and most immediate patterns of interactions are found in spoken rather than written language. Still, we've noted some texts that include invented dialogue or conversation, like the Paris and Kassel 'conversations' in OHG or the *Nibelungenlied* in MHG (see Kilian 2005: 32–33 for a set of references). Even in the ENHG period, the issue of 'orality' in written texts can be daunting (see Betten 2000 for discussion and references).

Only recently have people begun to explore good tests for evaluating historical texts in terms of how close to oral language they seem to be. Koch & Oesterreicher (1985, see Figure 6.4) have developed a model for this. Starting from a distinction between *Sprache der Nähe* and *Sprache der Distanz* (in English usually rendered as 'language of immediacy' and 'language of distance'), they try to capture characteristics associated more with 'conceptually oral' and 'conceptually written' language. Below is their now famous effort to show these relationships. More immediate language is more oral-like, more distant language more written-like, so that, as we move from left to right, patterns increasingly correlate with graphic rather than with phonic representation. Characteristics of more oral language are the use of dialogue over monologue, the familiarity of the partner involved, spontaneous vs. 'reflected' language, and so on.

Linguists now often use this model to evaluate the variation they find in language from different historical texts, in intuitively appealing ways. Private personal letters, though written, often look much more like what we expect from spoken language judging from these criteria, while official documents overwhelmingly fall to the right side of the model. Given the rich set of text types available for ENHG, this helps us start to see stylistic variation of the sort more easily discussed in contemporary settings—a matter we will address briefly in the next chapter. (Schiegg 2015: 19–21 and elsewhere has also applied this to OHG.)

In the early modern period, we also begin to have extensive and explicit discussions about talk. Politeness, for example, was a sufficient concern that books were published about how to compliment people, in often remarkably

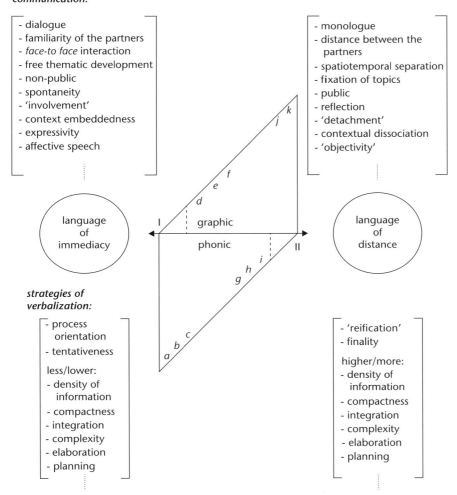

FIGURE 6.4 Koch and Oesterreicher's model.

From Koch & Oesterreicher (1985: 23) (English version from Koch & Oesterreicher 2012).

ritualized and formalized ways. Lest we be tempted to romanticize this, there's an obvious and coarsely classist structure to this, as two examples from Beetz (1990: 134) underscore:

Mit Leuten zu complimentiren, denen keine Complimente gebühren z.E. Handwercks = Leuten, Knechten, Mägden, Bettlern etc. heisset sich gemein und gering; den anderen aber hochmüthig machen....

je geringer der Stand ist, je weniger Decori ist er benöthiget.

FIGURE 6.5 Der Papyrer.

Or consider the relatively simple example of titles.[15] Terms like *Herr* and *Frau*
go back to a dramatically different societal structure, where they were reserved
for nobility. With social changes, the inventory of titles changed and their use
changed. Beetz (1990: 250, elsewhere) observes that particular titles slowly
descend the social ladder: in the mid-16th century, *Edler* was used for the
Freiherrenstand (basically a baron-like status), while by the middle of the 18th,
it was applied to craftsmen. At the same time, he traces a politically motivated
'titular inflation', as *Ehrwürdig=Hochgebohrner* (Kaiser Matthias, 1613) is
escalated to *Hochwürdig=Durchläuchtig=Hochgebohrner* (Leopold I., 1660),
which by 1711 had been elevated to *Hochwürdigst=Durchläuchtigster*.

---

[15] In the next chapter, we'll treat the related matter of pronouns of address, §7.4.

6.6 The establishment of a (more) unified language

We have already talked about speculative and largely ill-founded attempts to tease out the existence of a robust codified, supraregional linguistic norm for German during the Middle High period, and we have mentioned in passing even shakier efforts aimed at the Old High period. There was, at best, limited evidence of *koinē* formation among poets (and others) along with some additional polishing and smoothing off of distinct regional patterns during transmission. This ultimately feeds into the less than dialectal character of large collections like the poems of the Heidelberg manuscript. In the early modern period, at last, we can finally begin to talk about the first real movement toward a unified language. Langer (2014: 298) notes: 'The eighteenth century is often identified as the time when the standardization of German was completed.' More important is Langer's bigger conclusion about the social understanding of standard forms (2014: 299):

What had become ungrammatical in higher register language remained perfectly normal in everyday language, something we continue to find in the present day. The role of prescriptive grammarians—as members of the educated middle classes—was to confirm the de-selection of particular variants and to publicise such de-selections, so that speakers could identify these as shibboleths to mark particular language practices and, by implication, deduce the social status of whoever uses or doesn't use such constructions. In this way, the eighteenth century very much echoes the role of the standard language in the twenty-first century; strikingly many of the eighteenth-century shibboleths remain markers of 'good language' today.

From here forward, in other words, we have to keep in mind what kind of German we are talking about: spoken versus written, formal versus informal, and so on (see Elspaß 2014 on this issue in the 19th century).

The process of developing a unified linguistic variety involves two sides of a single coin. On the one hand, there is the positive work of forging and defining a new form of the language from the available material, here drawing from a pool of regional variants in particular. On the other, there is the suppression of particular features, features that come to be condemned as 'wrong' or 'sub-standard'. That this is an active process is neatly reflected in the apt title of Davies & Langer's 2006 volume, *The Making of Bad Language*.

Practically speaking of course, a standard variety is tremendously useful for ease of communication across geographical and social space. Developing a standard is also a profoundly political process, one sanctioning the language use—real and often imagined—of particular groups as 'right'. In the early modern era, our focus can turn increasingly to adding a metalinguistic perspective to the structural linguistic perspective we've explored until now: in addition to linguistic structures and the social history of language, we have more and better evidence about how people think about and judge language.

Structurally, the construction of a standard variety is, as we'll explore here, simply an additional layer added to the available forms of the language, and a highly artificial layer. (Langer 2007, Burke 2004, and other scholars point out how clearly this differs from the history of languages like English, Norwegian, or Russian, where a particular dialect served far more directly as a model for the standard.) That is, its existence does not replace local dialects, regional *Umgangssprachen*, or other varieties, and certainly not instantly or automatically. Nor, as we will see amply demonstrated, does the presence of a standard halt the ongoing development of real varieties. Even the best established standard continues to evolve over time, as a necessary response to how speakers use a language, often despite the resistance of some forces in society.

In short, the rest of this book will argue that the rise of a standard language is tremendously important socially and politically, not to mention of practical importance to language learners, but it must be seen in the full context of the full range of German language varieties that have been and continue to be used by many millions of speakers around the world. This view differs dramatically from the traditional historiography of German, as exemplified in this quote from Waterman (1966):

we are primarily interested in tracing the history of the standard language (*die Hochsprache* or *die Schriftsprache*).

In reaction to this traditional bias, a new generation of socio-historical linguists is pursuing what has come to be called *Sprachgeschichte von unten* (see Elspaß 2005, Elspaß et al. 2007, among many other works). This approach avoids the traditional teleological approach—that language change is of interest only as it yields the product of the standard language. Instead, this approach places the rise of standard languages into the context of written and oral use across the broadest possible range of the population.

Before we turn to some broader sociolinguistic issues, let us consider a couple of answers to one key question: What leads to the beginning of the rise of a relatively unified language? In the traditional literature, as reviewed by Hartweg & Wegera (2005: 45–58) and Sapp (2011a: ch. 6), different theories have given pride of place to three different factors and varieties:

- The influence of the Prague chancery, which was adopted by others, a view associated with the scholar Konrad Burdach.
- The leveled-out dialect of the East Middle German region, adopted by the Meissen chancery, a view associated with Theodor Frings.
- The crystallization of a supraregional compromise variety with elements from East Middle German, East Franconian, and Bavarian, a view associated with Werner Besch.

More recently, several factors have usually been considered in the early modern period, each playing a distinct role, and all ultimately working in the same direction.

1. Language of the *Kanzleien*. Royal courts had, since OHG times, chanceries, offices for producing bureaucratic documents. Over time cities and other entities also developed these administrative units. Official documents from the big chanceries were increasingly written in German from the late Middle Ages. And they showed supraregional tendencies and it is traditionally claimed that their language use, in orthography and other respects, influenced the language of the growing middle class and especially business people. (For a brief introduction, see Benzinger 2000.)

Two chanceries are often noted in this regard:

BÖHMISCHE KANZLEI: Prague (considered relatively progressive in linguistic matters). Under the Lützelburgers: 1347–1437, Karl der IV. 1347–1378. In terms of dialect, it had generally Central German character, so showing ENHG diphthongization and such features. The chancery's writings were known for relatively consistent orthography.

HABSBURGISCHE KANZLEI: Vienna (in the 14th century, the language is Bavarian-looking). From 1438, under Maximilian I. 1493–1519. This is often called 'gemeines Teutsch'. (Note the meaning, where *gemein* = modern German *allgemein*.)

The most famous reference to chancery language comes from Martin Luther, in a Latin-German bilingual quotation from his *Tischreden*:[16]

ich rede nach DER SECHSISCHEN CANZLEY, quam imitantur omnes duces et reges Germaniae [which is imitated by all dukes and kings of Germany]; alle reichstette, fürstenhöfe schreiben nach der Sechsischen cantzeleien vnser churfürsten. Ideo est communissima lingua Germaniae. [This is the most common language of the Germans.]

Not everybody places great positive value on the language of the chanceries. Straßner writes (1995: 35), for example, about the Latin used there and its influence on German, which he traces to the universities:

Die Kanzleisprache entwickelte sich zu einer unglücklichen Mischung aus jener lateinisch deutschen Juristensprache und der halbfranzösischen Hofsprache. Schon Mitte des 16. Jahrhunderts wurde Kritik an diesem 'Küchenlatein' laut. Noch im heutigen Amtsdeutsch ist der Einfluss des Latein deutlich zu spüren.

---

[16] These 'table talks' were comments recorded by a student and others. The mixing or codeswitching between Latin and German we see here is a famous characteristic of these texts. This kind of codeswitching would provide one of the best scenarios for how Latin syntactic patterns might have been transferred into German, but such evidence, to my knowledge, has not (yet) been presented and would still leave large questions of how patterns would have been disseminated from the always-small Latin-German bilingual community to the full set of German speakers. Appeals to 'prestige' are not helpful in that regard (Milroy 1992a, 1992b).

Der Buchdrücker.

Ich bin geschicket mit der preß
So ich aufftrag den Firniß reß/
So bald mein dienr den bengel zuckt/
So ist ein bogn papyrs gedruckt.
Da durch kombt manche Kunst an tag/
Die man leichtlich bekommen mag.
Vor zeiten hat man die bücher gschribn/
Zu Meintz die Kunst ward erstlich triebn.

F iij   Der

FIGURE 6.6 Der Buchdrücker.

Der Schriftgiesser.

Page from the *Eygentliche Beschreibung aller Stände auff Erden, hoher und nidriger, geistlicher und weltlicher, aller Kunsten, Handwercken und Händeln: Durch d. weitberumpten Hans Sachs gantz fleissig beschrieben u. in teutsche Reimen gefasset* published in 1568. The author is THE Hans Sachs, and the woodcuts were done by Jost Amman. (The image is from here: http://de.wikisource.org/wiki/Eygentliche_Beschr eibung_Aller_Stände_auff_Erden:Der_S chrifftgiesser.)

Wissmat = bismuth (a metal used in making alloys)
Versal = capital

Ich grüß die Schrifft zu der Druckrey
Gemacht auß Wißmat/ Zin vnd Bley/
Die kan ich auch gerecht justiern/
Die Buchstaben zusammn ordniern
Lateinisch vnd Teutscher Geschrifft
Was auch die Griechisch Sprach antrifft
Mit Versalen/ Puncten vnd Zügn
Daß sie zu der Truckrey sich fügen.

E   iij   Der

FIGURE 6.7 Der Schrifftgiesser.

Aside from the oddly evaluative aspect of this passage (in what sense was it 'unglücklich'? Perhaps according to his aesthetic sense?), these comments turn out to be historically unsupported for the most part. Notably, the notion that modern bureaucratic German is so heavily influenced by Latin is questionable. This continues the old bias toward Latin as an elite language which mutates into a tool for explaining how German developed. Of course, Latin does contribute some words to German, including during this period.

But it's also important to note that local officials produced their own documents in German as well, like land titles, and land and tax registers (*Urbare, Rodel*). These too came to be written in German from the 13th century onward. On some key matters, evidence suggests that chancery style spreads across regions. Work from Ebert (1981) to Sapp (2011a) supports this for word order in subordinate clauses. The use of the finite verb after the non-finite verb shows no clear regional basis (see Chapter 5), for instance.

In the end, current scholars are inclined to agree that the *Kanzleisprachen* came to be very similar to one another and in this way they help create a 'framework' for the standard language in morphology and spelling (see Benzinger 2000 for references).

2. Printers' language. This period also sees an interlocking set of technological innovations that tremendously increases the amount of written material that could be produced. Parchment was made from animal skin, and a small sheep could yield a piece of parchment ca. 50×35 centimeters large. Producing a single Bible required the skins of alarmingly large numbers of sheep, each subject to a long and labor-intensive process of preparation for use as a writing surface. (See Schneider 2009: 105–109 for fuller discussion.) Material came to be produced relatively inexpensively thanks first to the increasing availability of paper, which arrived in Europe from Asia during the Middle Ages. Germany's first paper mill was founded in Nuremburg in 1389. (Again, see Schneider 2009: 110–112 for details and references.)

More famous though is the invention of mobile type and the printing press. Around the same time, we find *Blockbücher* beginning to be produced, books consisting of woodcuts. People often and with some justification talk about this as the beginning of mass media. Early printing was often in Latin, but German is found too from the very beginning. (For a broad survey of German book publishing and sales, see Wittmann 1999; specifically on a key piece of the process, binding, see https://travelingscriptorium.library.yale.edu/binding-models/medieval-manuscripts-bookbinding-terms-materials-methods-and-models.)

The proportion of printing swings away from Latin toward local vernaculars like German quickly. A split evolves in what language is used when, with Latin typically for older texts, while German works were often written specifically for the printer, *Flugblätter, Volksbücher, Schmäh- und Streitschriften.* Keller (1978: 360, 485) sketches the early history of predominately Latin book printing, with a majority of books printed in German only in 1681 and German slowly becoming 'dominant' after that, though even in 1740 a quarter of all books published were in Latin and 5% in 1799.

As we'll soon see, these new technologies quickly came to be exploited in the brutal political and religious struggles of the day, reaching broad audiences.

3. So, what was Martin Luther's role? It is a cliché—widespread in the older scholarly literature and still heard from non-linguists—that Luther was 'the father of the Modern German language'.[17] In their widely used book, Priebsch

---

[17] Unsurprisingly, such views seem to be more widespread in Protestant than in Catholic communities.

& Collinson wrote, for example, that Luther came along at the time of the various other developments discussed here and 'consolidated into a single aim all the separate tendencies' (1938: 344). They continue in this way (345):

This 'Luther-Deutsch' based on Middle German thus became the foundation of the modern literary language, though much time was required to complete the superstructure. We find that his influence did not permeate the whole region with equal rapidity. (p. 345)

Non-linguists still continue to make similar proclamations, occasionally even in scholarly publications. Sanders treats his work as 'a "people's" Bible translation that gave shape to a standard language' (2010: 5), and that 'In one stroke, the Luther Bible advanced the goal of a universal German language further than the chancery efforts had' (2010: 138).[18] Luther laid out his own approach to translation in his famous *Sendbrief von Dolmetschen* (*Open letter on translating*) from 1530, now available in a new edition (Jones 2017, available for download).

Certainly, Luther's Bible translation contributed various idioms which are common down to the present, and he influenced word choices in the modern standard, but in terms of the bigger picture evaluation, differences remain. I'm inclined to think that König et al. (2015: 97) are right that:

Luther schafft keine neue Sprache (in grammatikalischer Hinsicht), auch kein neues Schreibsystem; in dieser Beziehung nimmt er das bereits Vorhandene auf und führt es in Richtung von schon länger wirksamen Tendenzen weiter. Bei Luther lassen sich keine syntaktischen Fügungen nachweisen, die nicht auch schon im Sprachgebrauch seiner Zeitgenossen vorhanden sind.

Luther does not create a new language, grammatically speaking, nor a new orthography. In this regard, he takes up material already at hand and takes it farther in directions of tendencies already at work for a long time. With Luther, we do not see new syntactic configurations which were not already present in the language of his contemporaries.

At the same time, Besch (2000: 1740) stresses the contributions of the translation in this way:

Der Lutherbibel verdankt das große dialektal extrem untergliederte dt. Sprachgebiet letztlich die Einheit der Schriftsprache. Kein anderer Text hat zudem mit seiner Sprache so intensiv auf die Literatur eingewirkt wie Luthers Bibeldeutsch. Dies bezeugen Dichter und Denker unserer Geistesgeschichte in vielen Äußerungen. Das ist das große Erbe bis heute.

---

[18] The most striking statement on the subject in the book is on the inner front flap, namely that Luther's translation 'in effect forged from a dozen spoken dialects a single German language'. I know of no contemporary specialists who would accept such a statement, nor that there were a dozen spoken dialects of German.

The unity of the written language can be attributed to the Luther Bible in the large and dialectally extremely divided German language area. No other text has moreover had such an intensive effect on the literature as Luther's Bible German. Poets and thinkers of our intellectual tradition attest to this in many statements. That is the great inheritance down to today.

The German-speaking lands were deeply divided along religious lines during this period, and this is reflected in the emerging standard. As we will see, the influence of East Central German, Luther's variety, was most clearly felt in Protestant areas, where his Bible and catechism were often the only books found in many homes into the 18th and even 19th centuries. (You can see contemporary anti-clerical images of Martin Luther here: http://www.payer.de/religionskritik/karikaturen17.htm.)

While Luther's influence has sometimes been considered strong in the lexical realm, even there the picture is mixed (examples from Keller 1978):

Luther (East Central)	Johann Eck (Upper German)
Antlitz	Angesicht
bang	Angst haben, betrübt
Ekel	Greuel, Abscheu
Fliege	Mucke
tauchen	eintunken
Ziege	Geiß
Topf	Hafen
Lippe	Lefze (now 'flews' of a hound)
fett	feist (now negative, esp. fingers, face)
Hülfe	Hilfe
harren	warten
flugs	bald

In some cases, that is, Luther's lexical choices have won out in the modern standard but in others, they have not.

4. Population movements. Populations were moving eastward in the Middle High German period; those continue and then pick up in the early modern period. In particular, settlers from a wide range of areas move to East Central Germany, to Thuringia, Upper Saxony, and points east. Permanent movement of large numbers of people creates far better circumstances for the rise of a stable *koinē*-type variety than we saw in MHG. But we also see more general increases in movement of people. Traditional sources stress the role of commercial traffic along particular routes (*Handelstraßen*), but at the same time, we see urbanization taking hold, with people beginning to flood into cities from surrounding countryside. This inevitably brings speakers of different varieties of German into contact with each other, and drives the formation of urban dialects (*Stadtsprachen*).

Of course, just as with Straßner (1995) placing great stress on the role of Latin, historiography of many sorts has traditionally shown massive bias toward the roles of the elite, especially elite men, so that the profound effects of such movements have long stood in the shadows of what Luther did, what the most influential men at the most influential chanceries did, and what the most famous printers did.

At the same time, Davies & Langer emphasize that modern Standard German did not evolve from a single geographical variety to nearly the extent that English did from London speech, what they term monocentric developments—see also France and Spain. Davies & Langer see things as follows (2006: 62):

> Generally speaking, E[ast] C[entral] G[erman] was used in the Protestant territories whilst E[ast] U[pper] G[erman] became the language of the German Catholic territories, a norm dualism that continued well into the eighteenth century.... The status of these two norms was not equal with EUG constantly incorporating ECG features but not vice versa.

5. Other factors. While traditional overviews of the history of German rightly stress the importance of the just-mentioned movements and their changing and conflicting political and social roles, another kind of population movement was taking place across Europe: urbanization. Work like de Vries 1984 charts this process quantitatively across western Europe. From 1600 to 1800, England, for instance, shows massive movement to cities, especially to London. Schilling (1993: 11–12) provides extensive data on cities in German-speaking areas of Europe during the period (drawing often on de Vries). Table 6.7 gives selected cities from their longer table to give you an idea of the growth of cities, but also of the sometimes dramatic contractions they suffered:

TABLE 6.7 **City populations, in thousands ('—' = unknown)**

	1500	1550	1600	1650	1700	1750	1800
Ansbach	0	0	0	0	4	6	12
Augsburg	20	45	48	21	21	–	28
Berlin	12	–	25	12	55	90	150
Breslau	25	35	30	–	–	55	54
Chemnitz	0	1	2	0	4	11	11
Dresden	5	8	12	15	40	52	55

TABLE 6.7 **Continued**

Düsseldorf	2	0	0	5	5	–	20
Erfurt	15	18	19	15	17	17	17
Flensburg	0	0	0	0	0	–	13
Frankfurt a.M.	12	12	18	17	28	32	35
Hamburg	14	29	40	75	70	75	100
Köln	30	35	40	45	42	43	42
Leipzig	10	10	14	11	20	35	32
Mainz	6	–	20	10	20	24	22
Mannheim	0	0	0	1	13	20	22
München	13	16	20	10	21	32	34
Nürnberg	36	40	40	25	40	30	27
Soest	12	15	10	5	5	5	5
Stettin	9	13	12	6	6	12	23
Ulm	17	19	21	14	–	15	13
Graz	5	0	8	–	–	20	31
Wien	20	–	50	60	114	175	231

As we've observed several times now, Germans were long regarded as a relatively rural population. The German-speaking lands 'possessed a large number of regional centres, but no city to integrate these centres either politically or economically' (de Vries 1984: 115). Still, during this period, de Vries observes the emergence of 'a well-ordered urban hierarchy in the absence of a unified state' (1984: 116), where growth in cities like Hamburg stands out (153–154). These effects cross what are now national boundaries, sometimes in surprising ways. As Howell shows (2006, with references to earlier work), the modern Dutch third person plural reflexive pronoun almost surely has its origins in the movement of many German speakers to the Low Countries in this period. Hamburg and Berlin in particular stand out (153–154). But note that there's broad general growth in the population. Table 6.8 gives a general idea of population development.

To conclude this section, political and social factors in the early modern period foster the rise of a more unified variety of German, beginning a process

TABLE 6.8 **Population development in Germany**

Year	Est. pop., millions	Event
ca. 1340	16.0	Plague
ca. 1360	8.5	
ca. 1500	16.0	
ca. 1620	26.0	Thirty Years War
ca. 1650	16.5	
ca. 1750	20.5	

which continues for centuries. It also becomes possible in this period to begin to trace language use among a broader slice of society:

- Printing makes books more widely available, especially as prices drop.
- The rising middle class sends its children to *teutsche Schulen*, to learn to read and write German (see more on this later in the chapter).
- We increasingly see private correspondence and other less formal uses of written German, showing a fuller range of styles.
- Some evidence is very consistent with the view that writers are adopting supraregional norms, including those of the chanceries.
- Population movements, eastward and toward urban areas, help along the process of leveling out more local dialectal differences.

Like the complex patterns of generalization we see in sound change, where acoustics, perception, phonology, sociolinguistics, and language acquisition all work together in shaping change, the beginning of a unified German language is a process where multiple factors were involved. And like with sound change, our challenge is determining which factors played what roles. As so often, the foundations laid to date provide us now with great opportunities for future progress.

6.7 Prescriptivism

In Chapter 5, we introduced and defined the notion of '**standard language ideology**'. This kind of ideology helped fuel the development of standard languages and it remains a potent force in German-speaking societies today. This general pattern is found across Europe and beyond, of course, often in closely parallel ways—we will see perhaps surprising similarities between how this plays out in German and English, for instance.

After introducing the notion of prescriptivism and giving a couple of recent German examples of it, this section sketches key areas, first the rise of written grammars, as an example of standardization, then French influence, and moving into the broader question of purism. It concludes with a few words on contemporary norms and the standardization of pronunciation.

An important but often overlooked point about standardization is that the rise of a relatively unified variety of German and then the creation of what we now call a 'standard' language SUPPLEMENTS existing varieties. It does NOT REPLACE local dialects, regional colloquial varieties and so on, at least not for significant numbers of people and not for centuries after its creation. While today we find large numbers of people in German-speaking countries who basically speak (and write) 'Standard German' with some regional characteristics, this is a recent development, and dialects remain very much alive in many German-speaking regions of Europe.

We cannot talk about standardization without attention to the attitudes connected with standard languages and it is important to consider the real-world political consequences of such views:

Linguistic conventions are quite possibly the last repository of unquestioned authority for educated people in secular society.... [T]he social function of [grammatical rules] is not arbitrary. Like other superficially innocuous 'customs', 'conventions' and 'traditions' (dress codes included), rules of language use often contribute to a circle of exclusion and intimidation.... Within the privileged space of the academy, for example, where it is normally a sign of intellectual competence to broach the question 'why?', questioning the minutiae of linguistic conventions is a sign of incomplete or faulty socialization.

Deborah Cameron (1995: 12)

Like I did earlier in this chapter, linguists generally acknowledge the great practical value of having standard languages, but abhor prescriptivism and other linguistically based prejudices—these are typically based more on what we might think of as hallucinations rather than data, and not infrequently used covertly or even for overtly racist ends. Cameron argues that we should see 'language mavens' and prescriptive efforts as:

the popular culture of language; as with all popular culture studies, the study of verbal hygiene must enquire into the sources of interest and pleasure that make something 'popular'. (1995: 31)

She makes this point, one echoed in Figure 6.8:

conservatives use 'grammar' as the metaphorical correlate for a cluster of related political and moral terms: order, tradition, authority, hierarchy and rules.... A panic about grammar is...interpretable as the metaphorical expression of persistent conservative fears that we are losing the values that underpin civilization and sliding into chaos.

FIGURE 6.8 Fashion police and grammar police.
Source: https://xkcd.com/1735. © xkcd. Used with permission.

Studies of this type on the German language from the 16th century to the present could yield a rich harvest with real social value. Especially in the context of German culture and recent history, the uncritical acceptance of authority in any sphere is worth investigating.

Until recently, a fair number of linguists in German-speaking countries have embraced standard language ideology in ways that I find troublingly value-laden for scientific researchers. For instance, in his *Deutsche Sprach-kultur*, Erich Straßner regularly expresses concern about a linguistic decline, picking this up on the last page of the text in a discussion of current language use (p. 437):

Sicher ist aber, daß ein gefestigtes Sprachgefühl und Normempfinden immer seltener anzutreffen sind, auch bei Berufsschreibern, etwa Journalisten und Schriftstellern.

But it is certain that a firm feel for the language and sense of norms are less common today, even among professional writers, such as journalists and literary authors.

In bemoaning the decline of our linguistic civilization, Straßner provides no clear evidence for such decay, but only a catalogue of historical value judgments. He never really develops a real argument about how it is that speakers today lack 'ein gefestigtes Sprachgefühl und Normempfinden' or exactly what that means.

And we see this bias toward standardized language shaping scholarship on the history of German. Consider this fuller version of a quote noted above (p. 286) from Waterman's *A History of the German Language* (1966: 162, still in use today as a textbook in a 1991 edition):

> The history of the German language during the 17th and 18th centuries is essentially a history of the *Schriftsprache*... during the time the language underwent none of the profound changes in phonology and morphology that had marked its evolution in the 15th and 16th centuries.

This quote seems to imply that the rise of a *Schriftsprache* somehow halted real structural change. Standardization hardly stops the change we see in languages, even German, although some of the interesting developments simply are not taken up quickly in the most formal written language. The rise of a written standard may allow some people heavily invested in standard language ideology to ignore other varieties, and miss a lot of interesting changes.

Standardization. A vast literature has grown up about how standards arise, with much work specifically on the German language and in Germany. For our purposes, a key is to recognize that there's a structural aspect to this—a relatively unified variety of the language needs to be established, forms selected and codified in ways accessible to speakers—and a social-political aspect—that variety has to be accepted, promulgated, and used. The structural standardization of written German for official and other purposes was largely accomplished by the 17th and 18th centuries, though vernacular writing remains vigorously more diverse into the 21st century. With regard to the social and political aspects, Mattheier (2000) is rightly cautious:

> Die dt. Hochsprache als Standardvarietät innerhalb der (historischen) Gesamtsprache Deutsch hatte jedoch zu Beginn des 19. Jhs. nur eine minimal soziolinguistische Realität. Damit ist gemeint, daß es um 1800 nur eine soziologisch sehr kleine Gruppe von Verwendern dieser Varietäten gegeben hat.

> The German language as standard variety within the full (historical) total German language had, though, at the beginning of the 19th century only a minimal sociolinguistic reality. By that I mean that around 1800 there was only a sociologically very small group of users of these varieties.

During the course of the 19th century, Mattheier argues, this variety comes to be widely known and used across a broad range of society, including parts of the working class, when instruction in the standard language achieves status in schools, and when knowledge of standard comes to be highly valued in society.

This is a tremendously important change for individuals in those groups and the whole society. Let's look briefly now at how the structural prerequisites for that were created.

Schools and grammars. In the 16th century, many manuals for spelling German were produced (like Valentin Ickelsamer's), and these were used in schools where German literacy was taught. Lippi-Green (1994: 26–29) aptly describes an educational system as 'a system with its own networks and status hierarchies'. In her study of early modern Nuremberg, she sketches the city's full array, including the *Stadt-* or *Ratschule*, run by the Church and overseen by city officials, aimed at preparing the elite for universities and taught in Latin. There were also *Rechenschulen* for German-based training of merchants. Growing during the 16th century were the *teutsche Schulen*, 'where the only goal was the acquisition of reading and writing skills' (1994: 27).

In that same century, we find some more complete descriptions of German grammar, albeit written in Latin. The 17th century sees the emergence of German grammars in German, among them:

Justus Georg Schottelius. 1663. Ausführliche Arbeit von der Teutschen HaubtSprache.

Schottelius pushes *Kulturpatriotismus*, and he appeals to Karl der Große, Martin Luther, and others for historical justification of the importance of German and German grammar. To give an example particularly important from a contemporary perspective, being very concerned with '*Reinligkeit*' or *puritas*, he cites Tacitus' claim that the Germanic 'tribes' were 'not mixed', a view long since no longer tenable, as discussed in Chapter 3. Like most people of his day, he is very directly oriented toward written language rather than the spoken and openly prefers the usage of the elite, *die Meister* and *die gelehrten Männer*, over *mancherley Landarten* (see von Polenz 1994: 111–112, and now McLelland 2011 for a full study of this book). Hundt (2000) explores how Schottelius, Harsdörffer, and others of the time engaged in *Spracharbeit*, a set of activities ranging from philosophical to description efforts, rich in language ideology and political implications, as just described.

Other historically important grammars were published by Gottsched (1748) and Adelung (1774–1786) and their numbers ballooned: by 1800 about 120 had been published. Dictionaries were being published in this same era, with similar attitudes, and using the example of one dictionary:

Die kulturpatriotische Motivation bestand für den Lexico-graphus *(Kramer) darin, die Vorzüge, ja die Überlegenheit der* teutschen HaubtSprache *gegenüber anderen Sprachen, vor allem den damaligen Prestigesprachen Latein, Italienisch und Französisch nachzuweisen.* (von Polenz 1994: 182)

The cultural–patriotic motivation for the lexicographer (Kramer) lay in showing the advantages, even the superiority, of the German language as opposed to other languages, above all, the prestige languages of the time, Latin, Italian and French.

These works created codified norms for the written language to a considerable extent. They are also infused with political views that come along with a standard, with regard to social class and status, nation, and even 'race'. As the last quote above underscores, all this reflects (and in turn helps shape) attitudes about neighboring languages and contact with them.

One way of legitimizing German was to argue that it was 'an ancient and venerable language', as Davies & Langer (2006: 70–71) put it. A language that after Babel 'would still have been a divinely inspired, very regular and inherently valuable language' was naturally a highly diverse set of varieties by this period, leaving grammarians the problem of which form to use as the standard. This divided opinions into two camps. One favored using 'the best current language use' (*anomalia*) as the model, incorporating the irregularities it had. As we'll discuss, this often meant the speech of Meissen and surrounding areas. The other pursued an approach of *analogia*, that is, aiming to iron out the wrinkles of the language in an effort to create a standard closer to the variety spoken at Babel, i.e. one without irregularities.

French influence. During and especially after the Thirty Years War (i.e. after 1648), French influence becomes important for German, and intense contact leads to considerable bilingualism among the elite in German-speaking lands. As a result, a notable amount of lexical borrowing took place in commerce, architecture, military, the arts, etc. One study by William Jones found from 3.1% French loans (and 2.2% loans from other languages) in Chemnitz's history of the Thirty Years War to upwards of a third French loans in a language parody called the *Alamodischer Brief*. (While that text consciously exaggerated French influence, most of the loans in it are attested elsewhere.)

More interesting for us are the more systemic effects of this language contact.

- A whole set of familiar derivational affixes came into the language in this period, such as *-ade, -age, -är, -elle*, which have spread from direct French loans (*Volontär, Militär*) to novel German forms (*Funktionär*).
- Such words typically have final stress, rather than the kind of Germanic stress we discussed in earlier chapters. Speyer (2009) goes as far as arguing that German has, on the whole, adopted a Latinate stress pattern based on the borrowing in this period.
- In inflectional morphology, French loans are generally well integrated. We do find the plural marker *-s*, but that is widespread in Low German

and Dutch and occurs with loans from those languages as well as French and English. That is, French does not have a unique role in the spread of -s plurals in German, a topic we'll return to in the coming chapter.

- These loans had some impact on the sounds of German: we find nasal vowels in modern Standard German *Balkon, Bonbon, Restaurant, Parfum*, although many German speakers substitute sequences of vowel plus velar nasal (or labial in the last item). The fricative [ʒ] is found in *Journalist, Genre, beige*, etc., but in some areas it, too, is replaced, usually by [ʃ].
- As in English, French stress patterns (together with Latin) have left some traces, where instead of the usual initial stress, we find the last heavy syllable stressed: *Amnes'tie, Hori'zont*.
- While many people still believe that German uvular variants of *r* (the so-called *Zäpfchen-r*) came into German from French, this view lacks significant support, since uvular *r* appears to be quite old in German and is found in dialects without significant French influence; see Howell 1991 and other works. One of the most compelling arguments against a French source is King & Beach (1998), drawing on Yiddish evidence. Still, the French /r/ may have supported existing uvular pronunciations in Germany.

On the last bullet point, note the complex geographical distribution of uvular rhotics across western Europe, shown in Map 17.

This map shows that a broad swath of central and northern Europe has adopted the uvular /r/, covering Romance- and Germanic-speaking territory. While the geographical distribution is intriguing, the variants of German /r/ are many, and the sound remains highly variable in the contemporary spoken language, even in formal speech, as we'll see in the next chapter.

Overall, this kind of French influence is broad in terms of vocabulary and it reaches beyond just vocabulary. Compared to many contact settings from around the world, it ultimately proves to be a modest instance of contact-related change. That outcome was to be expected, given the limits of bilingualism—a language that is used in limited (if elite) parts of the population typically serves as a source for vocabulary, and perhaps some elements of derivational morphology. The examples of apparent impact on structure are mostly limited to loanwords themselves and haven't spread to native vocabulary, such as nasalized vowels or /ʒ/, and not all speakers of German actively produce those features at all.

Still, the influence was very salient, and it proved to be enough to help prompt a strong social and political reaction, namely purism.

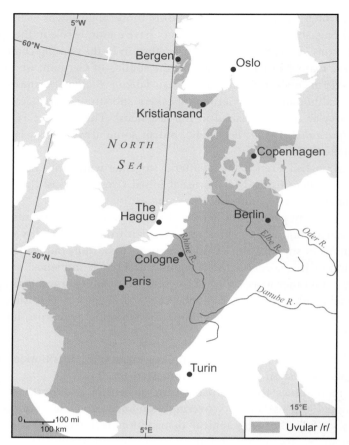

MAP 17 Uvular /r/ in Europe.
Adapted from Chambers & Trudgill (1986: 186).

Purism. We can see two somewhat different trends in German 'verbal hygiene':

(1) purism, often directed against 'foreign influences', but also regional and other forms.
(2) efforts to regulate the language orthographically, morphologically, and so on.

These threads are not always distinct. The *Sprachgesellschaften* played prominent roles here, most notably probably the *Fruchtbringende Gesellschaft*, 1617 (see Figure 6.9). Opitz, Gryphius, Schottelius, and Zesen were associated one way or another with this group, which included mostly nobles, but also

FIGURE 6.9 Die Fruchtbringende Gesellschaft.

scholars and literary figures. Other groups included the *Deutschgesinnte Genossenschaft*, *Elbschwanenorden*, and *Aufrichtige Tannengesellschaft*.

Traditionally given considerable attention in histories of the language, these societies become far less important when our focus is the language as used in the society rather than a march toward an invariable standard. The rest of the way, our focus will thus fall far more heavily on standardization, standard language ideology and such issues.

6.8 Vocabulary

Vocabulary is a relatively volatile part of human language—at an age in adulthood when it has become impossible or close to impossible to master new linguistic structures, from pronunciation to morphological systems, we still readily adapt to the ever-changing vocabulary of everyday life. It's no surprise that the ENHG lexicon differs considerably from today's, to the extent that dictionaries exist for the period. Götze (1967), for instance, was compiled for theologians, historians, and others who need to read materials from the period with accuracy. Often, the changes are focused semantic ones, like *genieß* meaning modern *Nutzen, Unterhalt,* or *genug tun* for modern *Ehre machen.*

At the same time, as hinted at above (p. 300), many are loanwords from other languages that are no longer current, like these (from Götze):

liberei, library	*Bibliothek*
bateilie	*Schlacht(ordnung), Schlachtheer*
triangle	*Dreieck*
passato	*im vergangen Monat*
akkord(o)	*Vergleich, Vertrag*
doul	*Pfennig* (Rotwelsch 'thieves' argot')

But the kinds of organizations described here did strive to 'purify' German of foreign elements. Those efforts and modern research on them often focused on vocabulary. (See Jones 1999, Kirkness 1975 for more, and Kilian 2003 for a kind of contemporary update.) One of the easiest places for officialdom to actually effect real change in language is in vocabulary, though the prescribers usually lose there too. The effort to create German equivalents for foreign borrowings, *Verdeutschungen,* yielded numerous invented words we still know and use today, usually alongside the borrowed form, and sometimes with semantic differentiation. These examples were invented by Zesen (here from von Polenz 1994: 121; see Blume 1967 for an analysis of the morphology of Zesen's creations):

Abstand	*Distanz*
Anschrift	*Adresse*
Augenblick	*Moment*
Entwurf	*Projekt*
Mundart	*Dialekt*
Verfasser	*Autor*

Many more such forms failed, like *Jungfernzwinger* for *Kloster.* The *Parade-beispiel* of a failed form, though, turns out to be a piece of linguistic mythology:

it is claimed in many sources (e.g. Schwarz 1967: 99) that Zesen mistook *Nase* for a loanword and proposed replacing it with *Gesichtserker*, creating a compound with an architectural term (English *oriel*) and having the effect of something like 'bay window of the face'. However, it appears that Zesen never used the word in his writings and it first appears in print much later, and it could well have been created as a satirical proposal rather than a serious effort at a *Verdeutschung*.[19]

It's hardly the case that all lexical change in this (or any other period) was driven by contact or language ideology, and one area subject to constant change, it seems, is that of intensifiers. English speakers have long used *very* (well, since it was borrowed from Anglo-Norman), and *terribly* almost as long (the OED gives 'It raines and snowes terribly' from 1606), and UrbanDictionary. com lists a seemingly endless supply, like *squared* ('that test was hard squared'), along with many that would offend some readers. Like many of these, contemporary German intensifiers like *brutall* and *tierisch* may turn out to have short lifespans. But the development of new intensifiers is hardly new and some still-current ones have long histories. The modern intensifier *sehr* developed from the meaning 'painful' and has broadened since MHG (Kluge), though *versehren* provides a link to the earlier meaning. Fritz (2006: 144) provides examples of intensifiers that were well enough known to be condemned by Schottel in the ENHG period, like *schrecklich lustig* and *grausam froh*. *Ungeheuer* and *saumäßig* are attested from the 19th century, while forms like *feierlich häßlich* and *häßlich schön* have faded away, to my knowledge, over the last 100 years.

6.9 Conclusion

We have seen in this chapter the emergence of what is unquestionably something close to the modern language, if not yet the contemporary one. And the rapidly increasing richness of data for this period has allowed us to see the social and political parameters of variation far better than we could for earlier periods.

That is, while the structural linguistic changes under discussion are largely very familiar—continued unfolding of changes in pronunciation, word forms, and sentence structures—we can now see how they were used, by whom, and in what circumstances. And we begin to gain some insight into the history of language in use. In this last section, on the development of a standard, we have

---

[19] A 2011 query by Nils Langer to the Forum for Germanic Language Studies mailing list yielded many responses about this, and Simon Pickl provided the earliest attestation, from Heinrich von Braun's *Anleitung zur deutschen Sprachkunst*, 1768.

moved even beyond the period in order to see the first serious efforts at standardizing pronunciation, tangled with political and social issues that shadow us today.

Our aim of using German's linguistic past to understand its present occasionally means simply seeing how some unusual or even unnatural system came about, in this case shaped in part by standardizers. So it is with the history of adjective endings and also with the reactions to borrowed vocabulary which created lexical doublets still in use.

Let us now finally turn to the contemporary language and the perhaps surprising amount of change happening even today in structure, variation, and attitudes.

7

New High German

Recent and ongoing change

7.0 Introduction

We've begun our surveys of periods of German with sample texts. But for
the modern language, consider how you would translate the Early New High
German text, from the 1534 Luther Bible, into modern German (Figure 7.1):[1]

FIGURE 7.1 Am Anfang...

Photo by Charles J. James.

---

[1] This is one of those instances where the internet is not reliable: if you Google 'Lutherbibel',
you'll find quite different versions given as the 1545 edition, Luther's *Ausgabe letzter Hand*.

Das Erſt Buch Moſe.

1. Am anfang ſchuff Gott himel vnd erden. 2. Und die erde war wüſt vnd leer / vnd es war finster auff der tieffe / und der Geist Gottes ſchwebet auff dem waſſer. 3. Vnd Gott ſprach / Es werde liecht / Vnd es ward liecht.

The point is simple: there's little actual translating to do, though note that some passages are more difficult. *Ward* has been replaced by *wurde*, but that is readily recognizable for the modern eye, likewise the *-n* on *Erde* and a lacking schwa on the adjective in the title (see the discussion of adjective endings in Chapter 6). The use of *auff* sounds unidiomatic, but again is easily understood. The text is otherwise unremarkable for a formal, written text, save for some (considerable) spelling oddities.

Perhaps connected to this closeness between the eras, there exists today a widely held popular opinion that change in the German language has been stopped by the creation and establishment of a standard language. This chapter demonstrates that this view is false: like all human languages, German continues to change steadily, and the changes follow the lines of development we've seen over the last two millennia.[2] In fact, patterns of change have no doubt become more complex and variegated with the rise of standard languages and formal education, something we'll discuss in this chapter.

There is a vast and growing literature on contemporary German from a dizzying array of perspectives. Despite this, the study of language change in progress is still relatively underrepresented (though see work like Elspaß 2015). In the Anglophone world, that has become a major subfield, often referred to as 'language variation and change'. In the German-speaking world, there was a wave of activity a couple of decades ago, known often as 'Tendenzen der Gegenwartssprache'.[3]

Where change is recognized as happening, it is often interpreted as the language collapsing due to 'bad grammar', much as in the English-speaking world. A recent survey shows this clearly among Germans today (Hoberg 2009: 155, see also Hoberg et al. 2008):

Ein großer Teil der Bevölkerung und besonders der Älteren glaubt, dass die deutsche Sprache immer mehr verkomme, dass die heutigen Jugendlichen die Sprache schlechter beherrschten als frühere Generationen, und das wird darauf zurückgeführt, dass heute weniger gelesen und mehr ferngesehen werde, dass beim Austausch von E-Mails

---

[2] You may hear it asserted that dead languages don't change, but even this has its complications. Latin, for instance, is really not dead, and its speakers continue to develop new words. Even a language not spoken by anyone, like Runic or Old High German, changes in a sense as new materials are found, giving us more data.

[3] At the same time, the English-speaking world lags far behind the German-speaking world (and Europe more generally) in terms of research into linguistic geography, as illustrated by Auer & Schmidt (2010).

und SMS zu wenig auf eine gute Ausdrucksweise geachtet werde und dass in den Medien, aber auch in der Schule nicht genügend Wert auf die Sprache gelegt werde.

Hoberg goes on to argue in interpreting these results, in some sense, that the German language today is a particularly rich and supple instrument for communication, and that changes have nothing to do with degrading or damaging the language. (We'll return to more of Hoberg's comments later on, and also discuss whether the media play a role in structural change.)

At the same time, the actual linguistic impact of the most notable events in recent German history on the German language itself have been surprisingly limited. We have some coincidences, of course: the events leading to the establishment of the German Empire in 1871 correlate roughly with key pieces in the codification of Standard German spelling, such as the 1880 publication of Konrad Duden's *Vollständiges Orthographisches Wörterbuch der deutschen Sprache*. (See http://www.duden.de/ueber_duden for details, and Wurzel 1998 for a biography of Duden.) We'll see, building on the discussion in the last chapter, that pronunciation is standardized only much later.

But it is important to keep in mind that Duden was and remains a basically independent entity, not a governmental language agency. More importantly, and as we'll discuss soon, German is a pluricentric language: while foreigners tend to learn the German of Germany, or rather a particular mostly invented variety of German associated with Germany, other German-speaking countries have their own traditions. These include extensive and systematic lexical differences—see Ebner's Austrian dictionary (1998) for instance, or the fact that Microsoft Word's spellchecker has long had an option for 'Swiss German' under 'language'.

As was sketched at the beginning of Chapter 5, new periods in the history of German have traditionally been posited for every 300 years, with the beginning of Early New High German marked at 1350, and the dawn of New High German at 1650. Elspaß (2007) notes that we are due for a new era after 1950. He labels the period just past 'Mittelneuhochdeutsch' and the post-1950 era 'Gegenwartsdeutsch'. He brings both language-internal and language-external arguments for this view. In language-internal terms, Elspaß (2007: 8–12) calls attention to many of the structures we'll treat in this chapter, including the movement of strong verbs to weak, decline of genitive as an *Objektkasus*. Bridging internal and external factors, Elspaß makes the important (and I think novel) point that we have in this period important 'Sprachnormwandel', including changes in prescribed norms of usage, attitudes toward varieties of spoken and written language, the role of regional speech, and so on.

Second, a key principle in the language-external side of periodization is a connection to major historical events. For this era, the events often discussed are the Nazi period and the Cold War era, and these provide a convenient time to place a caesura (like Wells 1985). These events obviously reshaped the linguistic map of Europe in many ways, through the systematic destruction of vast Yiddish-speaking communities in the former case and the creation of new linguistic diasporas in both cases. For the German language, the large population movements after the war promoted the shift away from dialect in some areas, such as Schleswig-Holstein, where refugees at a point reached nearly half the population or perhaps more.

Beyond that, the direct structural impact on the German language in both instances was overwhelmingly limited to specialized vocabulary. With the social and especially institutional changes in the post-World War II era and the reunification era, most of those lexical items have simply faded or become historical curiosities, while some once-unproblematic words have essentially been lost due to the taint of Nazi ideology. (See Sternberger et al.'s *Aus dem Wörterbuch des Unmenschen* for the classic contemporary discussion.)

In the case of National Socialism, a whole post-war wave of scholarship explored the issue of the nature of 'Nazi language', but more recent work has, quite rightly as far as I can see, acknowledged that the language use of the Nazis was in almost no important way original—mostly continuing familiar trends, even employing mostly familiar rhetorical strategies. Young & Gloning conclude (2004: 301) that one ...

reason why it is inaccurate to speak of Nazi language is that the regime had no coherent linguistic policy and acted in the arbitrary fashion typical of many dictatorships. . . . Instead, the regime was obsessed with the control of propaganda.

And they were indeed arbitrary and inconsistent: where one would probably expect vehement opposition to foreign words from these nationalists, they actually opposed many efforts at purism. In the end, ideology and propaganda were presented in the German language, but the Nazis had little impact on the language itself. A leading scholar of this question, the linguist Ruth Römer (often quoted, including by Young & Gloning) summarizes this point by arguing that 'there can be no "Mißbrauch der Sprache" only "Mißbrauch mit der Sprache"'. Recent work has, in that spirit, undertaken discourse analysis of Nazi language (such as Horan 2007).

Textbooks and even technical works covering the most recent period of history often have little to say about basic structures of the language (aside from the 'Tendenzen der Gegenwartssprache' discussions). This has been in part due to a sometimes near-obsessive focus on the standard, where the establishment of norms has almost teleological value, and seems at times to function as a license to ignore any changes going on elsewhere in the language. As Davies & Langer (2006: 118) observe about the situation since the early 20th century:

One finds very few voices questioning the necessity of a relatively uniform standard-ized variety. Nearly all the literature in German seems to assume that imparting competence in (written and spoken) standard is or should be one aim, if not the major aim of German teachers.

Instead, focus often goes to language and politics and purism, rather than phonetics, phonology, morphology and syntax. We'll continue our focus on core structural matters in their social context. As we'll see, real and important progress has come in a recent movement already mentioned, namely 'Sprach-geschichte von unten', especially in the study of colloquial varieties. Many millions of speakers use some regional dialect of German on a daily basis, of course, but virtually all use some kind of regionally colored variety all the time.

In the rest of this chapter, we'll look at numerous changes underway which seem to go beyond the standard language—innovations in phonetics and phonology, morphology, syntax, and pragmatics, along with the current state of attitudes toward language and language in use. Some of the changes may surprise students of the language—and even shock you, if you're still invested in the standard language—but they call for much more work, as we'll see. In particular, we'll see some examples where it is not entirely clear WHETHER language change is happening.

7.1 Sound change in contemporary German: still going

Courses on the History of the English Language in the United States have the opportunity to end with a bang on sound change: there are massive and salient ongoing vowel changes underway in American dialects today like these: the Midwestern *hackey* pronunciation for the finest sport on ice and the more widespread raising of [æ], the Southern change including *bit* being pro-nounced like *bee-it*, and the rapidly spreading merger of the vowels in *cot–caught*. But in the history of German, 'sound change in progress' is not usually a topic for language histories. As discussed already, the main issue in modern pronunciation is the standardization, around the turn of the 20th century, that Siebs undertook in his famous *Bühnenaussprache*. While the kind of pronun-ciation you'd want on stage may differ from how you'd talk on the radio or TV, this guide evolved into what has come to be called *Hochlautung* instead of stage language. As Besch (2003: 15) points out, 'nobody follows the strict rules of Siebs or other pronunciations; there are regional markers involved'.

Just as in other areas of grammar, standardization has not halted sound change in German, even among those most invested in standard language ideology. Below we treat four simple examples of important recent sound changes. The first is a change that has probably spread in part as a result of standardization, and the second is a recent innovation that is spreading rapidly through the *Umgangssprache*. That is, in one case, pronunciation is moving away from prescribed standard and in the other, toward it. The third example is one where the standard language itself has changed and the fourth is a possible, perhaps probable, change in progress.

1. **Auslautverhärtung.** We have discussed the fact that differences of 'voicing' (or in line with traditional and many newer views, lenis ~ fortis) between sounds like those below are eliminated at the ends of words.

$p \sim b \rightarrow$ [p]   lo[b]en but Lo[p]
$t \sim d \rightarrow$ [t]   Rä[d]er but Ra[t]
$k \sim g \rightarrow$ [k]   Ta[g]e but Ta[k]
$s \sim z \rightarrow$ [s]   Glä[z]er but Gla[s]
$f \sim v \rightarrow$ [f]   bra[v]e but bra[f]

This process is found not only at the ends of words (*Hund*, *Tag*, etc.), but also in the codas of word-internal syllables for many speakers (*Wagner*, *abgeben*).

We think today of this 'final fortition' as a highly consistent and salient part of German, and it's so ingrained in native speakers of German that many have difficulty overcoming it in learning a language like English, where we distinguish pairs such as *bat* ~ *bad* and *hiss* ~ *his*. As we've seen, spellings that look like they indicate final fortition were found in OHG and were the norm in MHG. In ENHG, things get more complex. Here's a brief summary from the Reichmann & Wegera (1993: 23):

Im Konsonantenbereich hat die Nichtkennzeichnung der Auslautverhärtung etymologischer *b, d, g* morphologische Gründe. Es handelt sich dabei um eine Erscheinung, die bereits in den Handschriften des Mhd. (nicht dagegen in normalisierten Textausgaben) begegnete, im 14. Jh. eine deutliche Tendenz zur Regelhaftigkeit erkennen lässt und sich bis ins 16. Jh. als Regel durchsetzt.

That is, in this period people gave up the MHG tradition of spelling fortition (MHG *lop* ~ *lobes*), and they instead adopted—so we normally assume—a spelling based not on the actual (or surface) pronunciation, but rather one that reflects the abstract character of the sound: you spell 'advice' *Rat* with *t* because that *t* never varies; you spell *Rad* with *d* because that *d* does show up whenever a vowel is added in alternations, such as in *Rade, Rades, Räder, Rädern, radeln.*

Even if we assume that this development from MHG to ENHG and beyond was a spelling change and not a phonological one, modern German final fortition is no straightforward continuation of an ancient tradition.[4] There

---

[4] The following paragraphs are adapted from Iverson & Salmons (2007).

are at least three different systems of word-final laryngeal phonology across the German-speaking world. The most notable and widespread was obstruent lenition in medial and final position in Upper and Central German dialects. As Mihm argues (2004: 176), early modern poets (with his examples from Upper Saxony) rhymed pairs such as *Kleid ~ weit* and *Berg ~ Werk*, but crucially, he argues, by means of neutralization to the lenis member of the pair, via final lenition rather than fortition.[5] As with historical patterns of final fortition, some modern dialects, especially central German ones, continue the pattern of final lenition. For the Hessian dialect of the Odenwald, Holsinger (2008) summarizes the relevant facts as follows:

As in the majority of German dialects, it has a fortis/lenis distinction in stops, but in this dialect, the fortis realization is present only in prevocalic onsets and neutralized elsewhere to a lenis (phonologically unmarked) stop—final fortition is not present, and coda laryngeal oppositions are fully neutralized.

In other words, Odenwald distinguishes aspirated or 'fortis' *p, t, k, s,* etc. from 'lenis' *b, d, g, z,* etc. only at the beginning of syllables. Otherwise, we have the 'weak' forms, such as *b, d, g, z.*

In the southeast, we find another change in the so-called 'Bavarian Quantity Relations'. As discussed in the last chapter, in this system the laryngeal quality of a final obstruent associates with vowel quality. In this prosodic reorganiza-tion of the syllable rhyme, a long or tense nucleus requires a lax or lenis coda obstruent, while a short or lax nucleus correlates with a tense or fortis coda obstruent.

Unexpectedly, a third system is also attested, viz. retention of final contrast. Mihm (2004) gives evidence that the prestige model for spoken German in the 18th century, Meißen (Saxony), actively distinguished lenis from fortis in word-final position, and that neutralization was regarded as a 'provincialism'. As Mihm illustrates, some notable figures, including Goethe, actually insisted that actors should produce laryngeal distinctions in final position. This advice, in fact, was often prescribed as standard until the end of the 19th century.

Two of these patterns—final lenition and renegotiation in terms of overall syllable structure—reflect later developments, dating from the late medi-eval and early modern periods. The history of the third, retention of laryngeal distinctions in final position, is perhaps less clear. The relevant point, however,

---

[5] This follows, he maintains, from the medial loss of the distinction, as in *Kleider* vs. *weiter*, which can only be understood in terms of lenition. As Andrea Menz rightly points out, final fortition and medial lenition are both very plausible processes here and would represent two different ways of neutralizing in two different environments.

is that by the time a written standard began to emerge for modern German, the spoken language included all three phonological patterns.

No systematic attempt to regularize Standard German pronunciation took hold until the turn of the 20th century, but prior to this, pronouncements of various kinds can be found, including on the subject under discussion. The social process of language standardization is most often ultimately about choosing between available and structurally viable options, and in this case standardizers pushed hard for the variant (final fortition) that happened to serve another role—signaling boundaries of particular units of speech.

Compare this to the requirement in a number of editions of the (now superseded) prescriptive Siebs pronunciation manual (*Bühnenaussprache*) that *p* and *t* should be aspirated after <s>, so that *Stadt* should be pronounced with both *t*'s aspirated, as [ʃtʰatʰ] (cf. Siebs 1944: 80).[6] While this might be helpful from the stage for listeners in the back rows, no dialect shows this pattern to my knowledge and no historical evidence suggests that it ever existed beyond social affect (notably as upper-class Northern pronunciation). Few languages have aspiration here and it seems to be pretty hard to produce. In this case, then, efforts at prescribing pronunciation have failed, in the absence of the pressures favoring aspiration that we saw for final fortition.

In fact, it seems safe to assert here that both pronunciations with and without neutralization were widespread in particular dialects (something Mihm downplays) and that this debate was over a choice between two available options. This distinction is actually difficult to produce phonetically (various dialects of American English may be beginning to lose it now, in fact) and having *Auslautverhärtung* actually plays a helpful role in decoding what you hear: it helps you recognize the ends of words clearly, which is useful in parsing longer phrases—little mile markers that tell you where you are along the route of spoken discourse. This is called 'edge marking'—the tendency to identify where words begin or end.

The difference is also often difficult to hear, and many languages neutralize these distinctions in final position (Dutch, Polish, some dialects of Yiddish, etc.), perhaps driven by this. German speakers do this widely, in fact, often with emphatic release of final stops. König (1989, vol. II: 82) shows that in formal interviews across West Germany, people aspirated final <b, d, g> about 60% of the time.[7] Educated German speakers are aware of the distinction of course—in part just from spelling—and although they normally neutralize this distinction entirely (Fourakis & Iverson 1984, Jessen 1998), if you give them

---

[6] Sound recordings of Siebs himself (see p. 364) show that he did not follow his own stage norms.

[7] Final fortition is not, however, considered part of Austrian German; see Moosmüller (1991).

minimal pairs such as *Rat* vs. *Rad* to produce, they can and will make a distinction pretty often.

2. mich = misch: [ç]→ [ɕ], [ʃ]. People from western areas of Germany—from the Palatinate area up through the Rhineland—as well as in eastern areas including much of Saxony, and other places pronounce the *ich*-Laut [ç] as a voiceless alveolo-palatal fricative [ɕ], which merges with *isch*, a process called coronalization. (The [ɕ] sounds to many ears, of German and English L1 listeners, like [ʃ].) Map 18 is adapted from the new *Atlas zur deutschen Alltagssprache*, using the word *zwanzig* as an example (see also Auer 1997):

For such people, pairs such as *mich* and *misch* or *welch* and *Welsch* are pronounced identically or very similarly. This change, at least in central Germany, is remarkably recent, according to the best available evidence

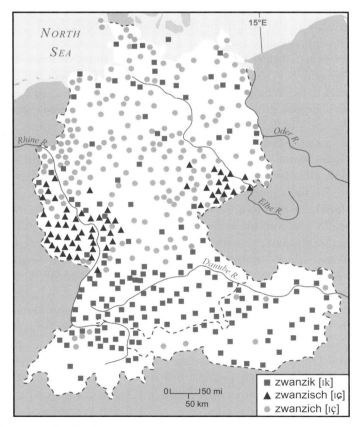

MAP 18 g-spirantization in contemporary German.
Adapted from *Atlas zur deutscher Alltagssprache* at www.atlas-alltagssprache.de.

having started in the mid-19th century in and around cities. As argued by Herrgen (1986, 2010: 678–680) and expanded on considerably by Robinson (2001), this change was characteristic of neither dialects nor *Hochsprache* originally, but spread up and down the register from a regional *Umgangssprache*. That is, for instance, there are communities in which the local dialect has [ç] and speakers use [ç] in standard speech, but the local colloquial variety has [ɕ]. From there it has spread into increasingly standard speech, so that we hear highly educated people, including in the media, using this. For Berlin, it seems that the pronunciation was first noted by Lasch (1928). This innovation is readily recognized by listeners as emphatically not standard, yet increasing numbers of speakers are pronouncing German in their daily lives in a way that differs from the prescriptive norm.

Robinson shows how this development can be motivated in terms of articulatory and perceptual phonetics and in terms of phonology—there is a reason beginners often find [ç] hard to produce. For one thing, these two sounds are acoustically similar, so that learners, whether L1 or L2, may have difficulty hearing the difference.

What we hear is tightly bound up with what we think we know about the speakers. Jannedy & Weirich (2014) got important results about this particular sound change in Berlin by playing recorderd speech to Berliners and asking what they heard. They took pronunciations of *fischte* 'I fished' and *Fichte* 'spruce tree', manipulated the sounds [ʃ] and [ç] to create a continuum from one sound to the other, and asked listeners which sound they heard—a common technique today. Where sounds vary along a continuum, as here, or between two vowel sounds, this shows us where the perceptual boundary is between the categories. Speakers heard a sound and clicked a box next to a picture of someone fishing or next to a picture of a spruce tree, according to what word they heard. In addition, for some listeners, the paper with the pictures had 'Kreuzberg', 'Zehlendorf', or nothing written on them, and the same words on the information sheet the listeners filled out. Kreuzberg is a neighborhood famously associated with migration in Berlin, while Zehlendorf is not. That simple association with a particular part of Berlin was enough to trigger significantly different interpretations of the same sounds. Middle-aged listeners were more likely to hear [ʃ] when it was connected with Kreuzberg, which suggests that they associated this pronunciation with the neighborhood. But younger listeners heard the sound as [ʃ] across the board, which suggests that, for them, these new forms had already become their new standard (Jannedy & Weirich 2014: 114). The study reinforces the view that this sound change is progressing in Berlin and that this feature is being 'de-ethnicized', that is, associated with place rather with than some social group.

From many perspectives then, *ich* to *isch* provides us a striking case of a change moving away from standard pronunciation, and it is further connected to the complex and highly artificial patterns developed in the 19th century. In the standard, variation in the pronunciation of the *-ig* suffix was resolved toward [-ɪç], but Viëtor 1904 (quoted here in Robinson's translation) writes that:

The stage conference has decided that *-ig, -igs* should be pronounced with a fricative [ç], except for *-ig* before *-lich* (which should be pronounced with a [k], since the twofold [iç] is thought to sound unpleasant), and that *-ige*, etc. should have a stop [g]. . . .

All of this leads Robinson to challenge the notion of 'standard' in some sense, as his title suggests: *Whose German?* Namely, to understand German speech, we need to understand precisely this kind of colloquial pattern alongside the construct we call 'Hochlautung'—illustrating, I think, precisely what Besch was getting at in the passage just quoted. Indeed Herrgen (2010) provides evidence of other movement away from the standard in the pronunciation of the West Central region, namely the voicing of intervocalic /s/, so that *reisen* and *reißen* are both pronounced with [z].

3. Rhotics. As Howell (1991 and elsewhere) has clearly shown, German has long had a wide range of *r* sounds used in different regions and by different social groups. That is, *rot* can be pronounced, among other ways, as an apical trill (as in Spanish), [r], or as a uvular, the so-called *Zäpfchen-r*. Map 19 shows the major variants, with the apical across the north and southeast, English-like retroflex forms attested in some areas and so on. (And recall the map on the distribution of uvular *r* from the last chapter, which shows a vastly coarser picture than the still simple one here.)

The uvular trill [ʀ] can be regarded as 'stiff' today, but the uvular fricative [ʁ] is widespread and appears to be spreading. Wiese (2003: 29) writes about the recent history of rhotics in Standard German:

In Standard German as the system prescribed by norm, a change in the r-sound from a trilled alveolar [r] to a uvular approximant [ʁ] is arguably the only sound change that many present-day German speakers are aware of within their own lifetime exposure to their language: pre-war actors use the former, post-war actors, within a short period of transition, use the latter variant in movies and other recordings. The written norm for speaking on stage, called 'Deutsche Bühnenaussprache' ('German stage pronunciation') since THEODOR SIEBS (1900), required a trilled [r] until 1957 (the 16th ed. of this work), when both versions (alveolar and uvular) were accepted reluctantly, and has changed its prescribed pronunciation almost completely towards a uvular variant since then.

Here then we have a rapid and dramatic change in the standard pronunciation. Broader changes are probably also underway beyond the prescribed pronunciation: some argue that the velar pronunciation of *r* is spreading among younger people at the expense of the apical trill. In some areas, it seems to be increasingly pronounced like a voiced version of the *ach*-Laut or [ɣ] (like a northern Dutch *g* sound in *goed* 'good'). This is clearly documented

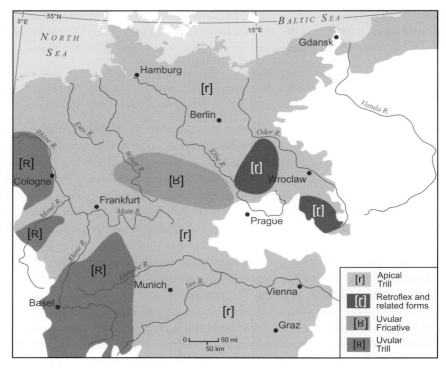

MAP 19 Major variants of /r/.
Adapted from Göschel (1971: 94) and Wiese (2003).

again in the *Atlas zur deutschen Alltagssprache* (see Map 20), using the word *Sport* as an example.

Note once again that this particular pattern is a national one: the apical trill is alive and well in Switzerland and Austria.

4. [ɪ] > [ʏ]? There is a reasonably widespread impression, including by some linguists, that younger speakers in Germany often pronounce words such as *nicht* and *wird* with a centralized-sounding vowel, which is often represented in writing as *nücht*, *würd*, and transcribed phonetically as a front-rounded [ʏ], though it can be heard sometimes at least as more centralized than rounded. Unfortunately, to my knowledge, no good empirical work has demonstrated that the pronunciation is spreading today. While we wait for that, two notes are still relevant about the pattern.

First, it is something that has been known in German pronunciation for decades and something that corrective phonetic texts (aimed at native speakers, that is) have railed about. Martens & Martens (1961: 52) list as the first 'Hauptfehler' involving the pronunciation of [ɪ]: 'Das kurze, offene [ɪ] wird mit

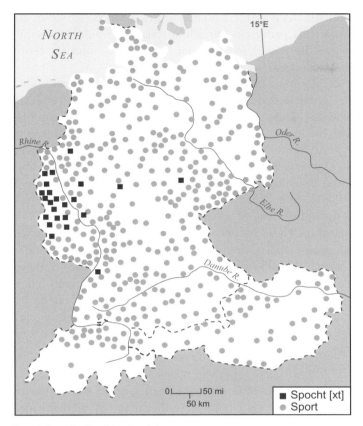

MAP 20 Devoicing of velar fricative /r/.

Adapted from *Atlas zur deutscher Alltagssprache* at www.atlas-alltagssprache.de.

Lippenrundung gesprochen, wie das kurze, offene [ɪ]. Dies geschieht häufig vor [ʃ] »sch«, [r] und [rʃ] »rsch«.' (The short, open [ɪ] is spoken with lip rounding, like the short, lax [ʏ]. This happens frequently before [ʃ] 'sch', [r] and [rʃ] 'rsch'.) That is, if this form is spreading, it is another instance of the spread of a feature away from the standard, an innovation being actively decried by prescriptivists.

Second, as we saw in the last chapter, these variants have been around for at least half a millennium, and were widespread enough that the modern stand-ard language has incorporated many rounded forms that have historical front unrounded vowels, see high-vowel forms such as *fünf, Würde*, as well as mid *zwölf* and *schwören*, with occasional doublets/near-doublets. That is, these go back to historical forms such as *finf, wirde, zwelf*, etc. and never had, in most cases, the original *i/j* 'trigger' for umlaut (*fünf* < Old High German *fimf* < Germanic *femf), or had no relevant back vowel (*schwören* < *swerian* < *swar-jan). If this pattern is spreading today, it would represent a sound change where the underlying variation has been around for centuries, but which for some reason has become dynamic today.

Above all, the importance of this example is underscoring how little we really know about sound change in progress in the German-speaking world, especially where it cuts against prescribed norms. In fact, human beings often end up with the impression that something we've just noticed is new when in fact it has been around for a long time but gone unnoticed, by some people or generally. This is a pervasive pattern with language, dubbed the 'recency illusion' (and described by Arnold Zwicky and others on the blog *Language Log*, see here: http://itre.cis.upenn.edu/~myl/languagelog/archives/002386. html). As we will see later, it is hardly limited to pronunciation.

5. Conclusion. These are only examples, and more is bubbling with regard to German pronunciation at present, colloquial and standard. Still, relatively little systematic, scientific attention has as yet been devoted to these matters. Beyond the point about *r* (pp. 294–296), von Polenz gives only a few pages to pronunciation in his 757-page volume on the history of German in the 19th and 20th century. Drawing from other sources, he cites (1999: 342) as 'Entwicklungstendenzen der deutschen Lautungspraxis' a few patterns which may reflect changes in progress, or may simply reflect variation that suggests changes in progress, for instance:

- Reduction of schwa in unstressed syllables, of the *haben* [habm] type.
- Pronunciation of long <ä> as [e:] rather than [ɛ:], so that *gäbe* and *gebe* are pronounced the same.
- 'Normwidrige' initial stress of polysyllabic words, both loans (*Attentat, finanziell, Motor*) and indigenous words (*Bewässerung, Entsorgung*).

Without solid data on how widespread these forms are today and how widespread they were at some point in the past, it is impossible to be sure that we have changes in progress. For the related example of syllabic nasals (of the *habm* sort), variation of the sort he notes has surely been around for quite a while. While we can assume that the more reduced variant arose by sound change, I'm aware of no particular reason to believe that it is spreading at present. In the second example, many dialects have (presumably) lacked [ɛ:] for many centuries, so that its absence naturally results from continuation of local speech patterns: it's not that people have lost this distinction, but rather that they never acquired it. Still, there is clear evidence for some patterns of change that are what Herrgen (2010) calls 'standard-divergent', like coronalization and intervocalic /s/ voicing in the Middle Rhine area.

In short, there is tremendous and important work to be done to answer the question of what is actual change in progress and what is recency illusion, from the just-discussed issue of *nicht/nücht* or whether there is ongoing change in nasalized vowels versus realization with a velar nasal, [baĺkɔŋ] versus [baĺkɔ]. New online corpora like those of the Institut für Deutsche Sprache make this more easily doable than it once was.

7.2 Morphological change at present

This section begins with summarizing familiar findings and claims in the realm of morphology, with a heavy focus on the more complex patterns underway in the nominal system and a brief note on the verbal system. These phenomena are interesting for two reasons, both of which we have already discussed: First, they provide barometers of interest in what counts as 'proper', 'standard', or 'correct' German. Second, they tie in directly to patterns of variation, often reaching back centuries.

A recent study by Wegener (2007) carries this subtitle: *Wird Deutsch einfacher?* She argues, by and large, that German today is indeed simplifying in an important sense. In the broader perspective of the history of German, these individual changes are much more the continuation of old trends, of course.

7.2.1 The nominal system

Let us turn to the steady forward march of reduction of inflectional morphology on nouns. Consider these continuing patterns of change in nominal morphology, drawn from a set of books about tendencies in the contemporary language (Braun 1987, Hotz 1977, Sommerfeldt 1989, Drosdowski & Henne 1980):

7.2.2 Reduction of case marking

1. GEN.SG. is often no longer marked with -*s*, especially on proper names:
   • des Vatikans → 'ein hoher Vertreter des Vatikan'
   • des Barocks → 'die Musik des Barock'.
   Drosdowski & Henne give examples of how this has continued to progress beyond just proper names:
   • 'Erfinder des Radar'
   • 'Geruch des Thymian'.
2. Sommerfeldt notes double marking of genitive on weak nouns, what is usually called the 'mixed declension'-*en* > -*ens*:
   • des Herzen → 'des Herzens'
   • des Namen → 'des Namens'.

This is another step in the ongoing erosion of the old -*n* stem nouns. That is, in MHG and ENHG, weak nouns had very simple inflection, -*e* in the nominative singular and -*n* elsewhere. Adding the -*s* in the genitive brings it into line with other masculine and neuter nouns, though forms like *herzens* go back at least to ENHG.

Note that this isn't strictly a reduction of case marking but an increase in distinctiveness of a case form, a leveling that makes the genitive -*s* marking more consistent.

3. Genitive → prep.; genitive with verbs and adjectives has retreated, cf. also *wegen, während*.
   - die Farbe des Hauses → die Farbe vom Haus
   - Ich freue mich des Sommers → Ich freue mich **über** den Sommer (König)

Especially the second example here has become pretty marginal today, and the genitive is retreating increasingly to particular idioms or limited constructions, like expressions of indefinite time like *eines Tages* or *meines Wissens* while Duden notes that a 'small and steadily decreasing number of adjectives and verbs require the genitive, in constructions like *bewußt* "aware of"' (*Duden* 2016, §1534, with more at 917–918). And the genitive is also still alive in relatively formal speech (though yielding ground) in *wegen des Wetters* ~ *wegen dem Wetter*.

4. Marking of Dat.Sg. in masculine or neuter nouns by -*e* increasingly only in idiomatic or fixed phrases. But note that this has shown regional and other restrictions for centuries. Still, the change appears to be real rather than illusory: Ziegler (2007) analyzes 60 *Schulaufsätze* covering the century from 1821 until 1920. In those written before 1871, she finds -*e* in 92% of the instances where it was prescribed. In those written later, it occurs in 81% of forms.

This is increasingly limited to fixed phrases, with forms like these still being widely used even in colloquial speech:
   - 'im Jahre'
   - 'nach/zu Hause'

Less common, though, are forms like this, which may not even sound natural to some speakers:
   - 'auf dem Tische'

Wegener notes (2007: 48) the increasing use of (case-marked) articles in place of case marking here:
   - zu Grab**e** tragen → zu**m** Grab tragen

Again, we're seeing the last remnants of what was once utterly regular morphology increasingly just in fixed expressions. More importantly, the actual sound change happened centuries ago—schwa apocope—and the contemporary change is the creeping of this *e*-less pattern into formal writing. We might think of this as the (very slow) failure of the effort to impose the 'Lutheran *e*' as part of the standard, the effort centuries ago to preserve an inflectional final schwa at a time when many dialects were undergoing apocope.

5. Non-marking of Dat.Pl. with *-n*, esp. with *-el*, *-er*:
   - 'mit sieben Siegel'
   - 'Hunderte von Interbau-Besucher' (Sommerfeldt)
6. Move from weak to strong noun inflection:
   - den Spezialist<u>en</u> → 'den Spezialist'
   - den Präsident<u>en</u> → 'den Präsident'.

7.2.3 Extension of number marking

Duden's 8th edition (2009: 222 ff.) gives for examples of general variation in plural and other nominal inflection.

1. Replacement of ø-plural marking with *-s*:
   - zwei Kumpel → 'Kumpels'
   - zwei Fräulein → 'Fräuleins'.
   As Davies & Langer show (2006: 135–142), this form plays no role in grammars of the Baroque period, and gets occasional mention in the 18th century, mostly for Low German loanwords (*Wrack* ~ *Wracks*) and French loanwords (*Wagon* ~ *Wagons*). In the 19th century, though, it is widely discussed and seen as bad usage in grammars. Today, it is increasingly seen as colloquial.
2. Increase in umlaut plurals:
   - die Boden > die Böden
   - die Kasten > die Kästen
3. Increase in inflectional plurals, replacing older derivational ways of marking number. For instance plurals occur for words that earlier were not considered 'pluralfähig'. That is, 'mass nouns' (things you can't count, like *milk, honey, brandy*) are becoming 'count nouns'. See Duden (2009: 173) on the issue of *Sortenplural*.
   - Weinbrandsorten, etc. → 'Weinbrände'
   - 'Honige', 'Zemente', 'Rotweine'.
   We saw the opposite development in American youth language a while back, where the suffix *-age* was used to turn count nouns into mass nouns, *(potato) chips* → *chippage*, as in this question from a host at a party: *how are we doing on chippage?*

Overall, then, the effect of these changes is toward firming up the restructuring we've seen since the beginning in the history of the German language, a shift from suffixes on nouns marking class, case, number together to straightforward plural marking. On the one hand, these changes continue reducing the case inflection directly on nouns—with the retreat of DAT.SG. -e, DAT.PL. -n, and the retreat of the genitive case generally. These last really salient pieces of case-related inflectional marking on nouns in German are retreating. On the other hand, we find more salient and more consistent plural marking. Let's turn now to how these interact with gender assignment, which has evolved as well.

As with the phonetic and phonological discussions in the preceding section, these patterns have often been surmised rather than rigorously demonstrated, so you're urged to keep the recency illusion in mind.

7.2.4 The continuing evolution of gender assignment and plural marking

A good example of ongoing morphological change in contemporary German is the constant renegotiation of gender in nouns, which interacts with how plurals have developed and are changing today. You know the historical core of this story: in early Germanic, nouns were organized into classes, but sound changes have eroded class marking since Proto-Germanic, typically beginning with the sounds that we still use to identify the classes, like the *n* of *n*-stems and the *a* of *a*-stems. But then, much more slowly, the distinctive case and number marking associated with those classes has also disappeared. For example, in OHG, the dative plural endings were distinct in the prototypical or 'handbook' forms of paradigms for the biggest classes (although already weakening, of course, even then), but they have become indistinguishable today:

	Old High German	Modern German
a-stems	*tagum, wortum*	*Tagen, Wörtern/Worten*
ō-stems	*gebōm*	*Gaben*
i-stems	*gastim*	*Gästen*

The two distinct traces of this heritage visible today are gender, where we still have the three traditional classes, and plurals, where German has been very conservative in maintaining a famously complex mass of different ways of marking plurality. Almost all other Germanic languages have leveled plural forms out—English largely to -s, Danish to -er, Dutch and Frisian to -en or -s, etc.[8]

For gender, it's far more complicated: not only do learners think of German gender as virtually arbitrary, but also many linguists have said that gender

---

[8] Yiddish has a system much like German in its basic structure for straightforward historical reasons. Icelandic and Faroese are generally very conservative, including in nominal inflection.

must be learned with each word: Chomsky (1965: 170–177), Maratsos (1979: 235), de Bleser & Bayer (1988: 51). The usual claim under such views is that gender has to be learned—and stored in your mental lexicon—with every individual word. But there are important and profound regularities buried in the system, and this section sketches them with an aim at connecting history to the contemporary facts. It may also help you figure out German nominal morphology as you continue to learn the finer points of the language.

First, the easy part: plurals. At the same time as these historical developments take place, the number distinction (i.e. singular ≠ plural) has come to be increasingly clearly marked, as we've discussed particularly for the example of umlaut.[9] Different plural markers reflect, sometimes indirectly, the old nominal classes, and they remain closely connected to gender. Consider these correlations, which leave aside umlaut, drawn from Augst (1975: 5–71) and Köpcke (1989: 307), see also *Duden-Grammatik* (1998: 236–237):

Gender	Plural class		Percent
masculine	*-e*	ca.	90% (inanimates only; see p. 68, p. 266)
feminine	*-(e)*	over	70% (*-(e)n*, no umlaut)
	n		
neuter	*-e*	over	70%
	-er	over	20% (essentially always with umlaut)

In some classes, the correlation is powerful (inanimate masculines), while in others, it's weak, like neuter nouns with *-er* plurals. These reflect the old classes listed just above, with changes we've already discussed—*a*-stem patterns for the masculines and neuters, and feminines ultimately from the old ō-stems, but with the generalization of the *-n*. Note the remarkable growth of the tiny class of *-iz/-az*-stems (that is, plurals with umlaut + *-er*).

But let's think more broadly for a moment about the organization of nominal inflection and its connection to gender. For contemporary German, Nübling 2008 begins from a very simple three-way system, based on the genitive singular form and the plural form of a noun:

Weak inflection: genitive singular and plural both with *-(e)n*: *der Herr*
Strong inflection: neither genitive singular nor plural with *-(e)n*: *das Buch*, *der Tisch*, *die Wand*
Mixed inflection: plural with *-(e)n* and genitive singular not with *-(e)n*: *die Frau*, *der Kunde*

---

[9] In fact, Wurzel (1984) surveys the full range of functions that umlaut carries today in German and concludes that it has become a *Markiertheitsmarker*, a marker of markedness.

For MHG, she builds on that to propose the following inflectional class system (which I have rearranged somewhat from her presentation):

	Earlier class	gen.sg.	/ nom.pl.	fem.	masc.	neuter
1	n-stem	–n	/ –n	zunge	bote	herze
2	i-stem	uml. + –e	/ uml. + –e	kraft		
3	i-stem	–(e)s	/ uml. +–e		gast	
4	a-stem	–(e)s	/ –e		tac	
5	a-stem	–(e)s	/ Ø			wort
6	iz/az-stem	–(e)s	/ uml. + –er			kalp
7	'mixed'	Ø	/ Ø (dat/gen.pl. –n)	gebe		
8	root nouns	Ø	/ Ø		man (rare)	

Note that there's no strong connection between her inflectional classes and gender yet. In fact, if you leave aside the weak nouns in the top row, MHG shows each gender having distinct inflectional patterns, where feminine = 2 or 7, masculine 3 or 4 (plus the few in 8), and neuter 5 or 6.

Take a quick look at a few of the key changes she charts to NHG (drawing on the work of earlier scholars as well), for the feminine and the masculine classes.

The old feminine *n*-stems move into class 7, so that once-weak *zunge* inflects like *gebe*—modern German *die Zunge, die Gabe,* PL. *Zungen, Gaben.* The feminine *i*-stems today are often recognizable as a group: they have umlautable vowels (back vowels), are monosyllabic, and often complex codas, like *Kraft, Kunst, Wand, Wurst,* plus a few members that aren't prototypical members: *Kuh, Maus.*

In the masculines, the once-large class of weak nouns shows complex changes:

- Some become feminine, like *Hefe* and *Schlange* (recognizably weak in OHG *hevo, slango*).
- Inanimate weak nouns may take on the *-n* in the stem, like *der schade > der Schaden.*
- A few create a new 'mixed' class—like *Name, Wille, Gedanke*—with GEN.SG. *-s*, and plural *-n*.

In the transition to NHG, two broader generalizations stand out. First, null plurals decline, as neuter *a*-stems move into other classes, for instance. Second, there is considerable movement within each gender (shown with vertical lines), and movements between masculine and neuter classes, but none between feminine and the other two genders. That is, the nominal inflection system looks like it is organized to an extent around ±feminine.

Today, the relationship between gender and plural has been described in terms of complementarity: gender characterizes singular forms, namely marked by determiners. The earlier scheme relying on genitive singular forms is now hardly relevant, as genitive singular inflection is virtually gone in the spoken language, replaced by *von* + dative (*das Halsband vom Hund*) or other means, like *dem Hund sein Halsband* (Nübling 2008: 308). Today, we can best classify nouns by gender in the singular, while the plural form shows inflectional class. Nübling captures the overall development this way:

Number	Gender	Inflect. class
Sing.	3 gender	(found in Gmc and OHG)
Plural	found in OHG (adjectives, pronouns)	Plural allomorphy: Blume-n Kränz-e Bänd-er

⟹

Number	Class
Singular contains gender	die Blume der Kranz das Band
Plural contains inflectional class	Multiple classes Blume-n Kränz-e Bänd-er

Turning now back to gender, animacy—whether a noun refers to a living creature or not—has come over time to play a role in plurals in addition to gender assignment. Animate masculine nouns have often remained weak, or at least continue to show an *-en* plural form, while the inanimates have often moved into other classes (see Curme 1922: 87–88, Wegener 2007: 42–43 and elsewhere):

der Lappe 'Sami' [person], Lappen
der Lappen 'cloth, rag'

der Franke 'Frank, Franconian', Franken
der Franken 'franc'

der Tor 'fool', Toren
das Tor 'gate', Tore

The class continues to be productive, with words that weren't created until the 19th or 20th centuries:

der Mormone, Mormonen

This in turn fits with a well-established pattern in many languages, 'differential object marking' (or DOM, Bossong 1985 and much work since) captures the tendency to show case marking preferentially on animate over inanimate nouns, on pronouns over nouns, on definites over indefinites, and so on. Here German is showing distinct inflection only on animates, as most nominal inflection (like the 'Lutheran e') is in retreat. Yager et al. (2015) show that some heritage German varieties appear to have innovative DOM effects quite different from these, where dative marking is more likely to survive on pronouns over nouns and on definite over indefinite noun phrases.

But the most robust generalization about Standard German plurals is this: except for -s plurals, they show a remarkably consistent pattern (described in detail by Wiese 2000 and Menz & Ruf manuscript):

- Nouns with one syllable take a plural that adds a second syllable:
    Tisch (e), Wand ("e), Buch ("er), Frau (en), etc.
- Nouns with two syllables take a plural form that does not add an extra syllable:
    Vater ("), Segel (Ø), Auge (n—but note that it adds no syllable)

For longer nouns or nouns with (derivational) suffixes on them, the question is whether the final syllable contains a schwa or a full vowel. These two suffixes, for example, both contain a full vowel, and so are followed by a schwa-adding plural marker:

-ung   -en
-nis   -e

This has been traced to the preference in German (and Germanic generally) for words that end in a sequence of a stressed plus an unstressed syllable, or a trochaic foot: if the noun already ends in that structure (basically where the second syllable has a schwa or schwa-like vowel, as in *Vater, Segel, Auge*), you don't need another syllable. If it ends in a stressed syllable, adding a schwa syllable (*-e, -en, -er*) creates that structure. (A regular alternation of stressed and unstressed syllables is called a 'perfect grid' in phonology.)

A remarkable thing about this system is that it does not appear widely in the modern or historical dialects, nor does it reflect a direct continuation of any obvious historical trends—some dialects, including the East Central area—had patterns like this, but they were hardly without exception. Menz & Ruf argue that the early grammarians, who were intensely interested in poetics and metrics in addition to grammar writing, found this pattern appealing, and so encoded this already-existing pattern in their grammars and pushed it. As they conclude:

18th and 19th century grammarians, due to various aesthetic, cultural, political and other considerations, incorporated what was previously a more or less robust

(depending on historical and regional variety), but by no means exceptionless, prosodic pattern in Germanic into the standard form of the language, thus [promoting the
spread and adoption of] a phonological rule that is exceptionless today in standard
language dictionaries, but almost nowhere else.

Just how much of a role grammarians and standardizers played still requires
considerable exploration, but this would fit a broader pattern. Much like we
saw in the development of final fortition, this is a common recipe for success
of a given feature establishing itself during the social and political process of
language standardization:

- Some phenomenon exists (if inconsistently) in key dialects: tendency
  toward trochaic plurals in East Central area.
- It has a structure that is regular and coherent in ways that are easily
  learned: plural nouns end with a stressed plus an unstressed syllable.
- Grammarians pick up on it for some reason. In this case, metrics surely
  play a role, or the alternation of stressed and unstressed syllables, 'perfect
  grid'.

The interesting structural fact here is that Germanic, and especially West
Germanic, repeatedly shows a preference for certain 'prosodic templates'
('prosodic' here just meaning with reference to units bigger than a single
sound). The relevant template, of course, is the trochaic foot, especially
where the second syllable has a schwa or schwa-like vowel—called a *schwallable* by some phonologists. (Recall that in Chapter 3 we used the notion of
'template' to capture the general structures of strong verbs. We'll explore
briefly a far broader notion of templatic structure in the next chapter.)

The practical point is obvious: together with this template, if you know the
plural **or** the gender of a noun, you have a good shot at guessing the other. But
increasingly, the set of distinct plural markers are the last and fading remnants
of the old class system and even those connections are often very indirect, as
with the *-er* or umlaut, both of which have spread very far beyond their
original territory.

**The harder part: How is gender of a noun determined in the contempo-
rary language?** As just illustrated by the discussion of Nübling's work on
inflectional classes, it's important to keep in mind that in some cases, old
stem-types and/or genders match up relatively well with some common
phonological shapes: *-er*, *-e*, etc. In those cases the reshuffling is less radical,
since the shape of the word is still related to its gender and/or class
assignment. That is, a broad variety of endings which have long been
preponderantly feminine—going back to the Germanic ō-stems—reduce to
word-final schwa in modern German. For instance, the following items are

feminine from OHG to NHG with final vowels which have all reduced to schwa:

stunta	*Stunde*	'hour'
thek(k)ī	*Decke*	'cover', etc.
lēre/lēra	*Lehre*	'teaching', etc.

While word-final schwa represents a reduction of mostly old feminines, it (and its less reduced antecedents) would have been a salient marker of feminine far back into the history of Germanic.

Beyond that, things are obviously complex. Today, there are, as students learn from early on, some **absolute** rules:

- *-ung, -heit, -keit* > feminine
- *-chen/-lein* > neuter
- *-ment* > neuter
- Ø-derived nouns from verbs: *Essen, Trinken, Schlafen* > neuter

Almost everything else is simply TENDENTIAL, e.g.:

- Natural gender doesn't always hold, even in monomorphemic words:
  - *das Weib*
  - *das Ding* in the meaning 'girl'
  - *die Wache* 'sentry, guard', from the days when they were by definition male.

But some of these tendencies are surprisingly strong, with few exceptions, and some are probably not familiar to you, like those involving prefixes:

Prefixes (on monosyllabic nouns)
Be-, Ver-	→	masc
Ge-	→	neuter (also semantics: superordinates are neuter)

Suffixes
-er	→	masc

These can naturally be overridden by the categorical suffixes: *Betrieb* and *Verkehr* are expected to be masculine but *Bekehrung* and *Beziehung* are naturally feminine. Generally, when various factors come into conflict, there is a hierarchy of what outranks what.

Be + monosyllable	-ung	Noun< Verb
Bezug	*Beziehung*	*Beziehen*
Beruf	*Berufung*	*Berufen*
Masculine	**Feminine**	**Neuter**

Frequency is widely mentioned as a reason why some nouns resist tendencies as well, and it probably plays a role. German has a set of monosyllabic nouns that begin with *Kn-* and all but one are masculine, as in these few examples:

Knecht
Knast
Knopf
Knall
Knirps
Knie (das)

The exception may be pretty resilient because it's frequent—core vocabulary learned early by children, etc. How such correlations developed isn't obvious, but most of these were always masculine and some of them may well have arisen as historical accidents.

How can such a complicated system exist? It appears that our mental lexicon allows us to access or associate words along many dimensions, like these for the word *Hut*:

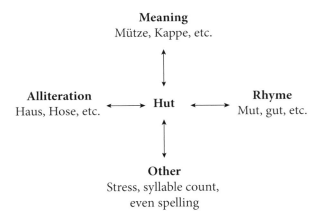

That is, gender assignment seems to parallel what words are associated with each other in our mental lexicon. I have argued (1993) that this structure helps to determine gender assignment today—nouns change gender over time to fit with those they're most closely associated with in the mental lexicon. We don't really understand the structure of the lexicon very well yet (although things are infinitely more advanced than you would see from my 1993 article), but this has got to be part of the puzzle.

Over time, meaning has come to correlate better and better with gender. Zubin & Köpcke (1984 and elsewhere) give examples of such semantic correlates of gender:

power, strength	→	feminine	die Kraft, Macht, Gewalt, List
garbage, waste	→	masculine	der Dreck, Müll, Abfall, Schund, etc.
games	→	neuter	das Poker
pointed objects	→	feminine	die Spitze, Klinge, Nadel

In some cases, such words have sound shapes that would point toward a particular gender, like *-er* = masc., *Ge-* = neuter, etc. But the semantic factor wins, overriding other, non-semantic factors.

A detailed case study of how semantic factors figure in gender assignment. Zubin and Köpcke (1984 and elsewhere) examine nouns reflecting introversion vs. extroversion, a pair of characteristics which they refer to as 'affect'. 'Extroversion' is conduct or attitudes which are 'directed toward controlling the outside world or view it as controllable, or which protect the self from outside control', such as *Hochmut*, while 'introversion' is the opposite, e.g. *Wehmut* (1984: 51). Introversion correlates with feminine gender and extroversion with masculine, based on data from dictionaries and their own experimental work. Over time, gender has often changed to reflect meaning: *Qual* 'torture', an introverted item, is solely feminine in NHG but alternated between masculine and feminine in MHG, as did *Reue, Gunst*, etc.

Of 81 OHG items in their corpus, 41 showed conflict between affect and gender assignment, while in NHG only 12 conflicts remain. Zubin and Köpcke also apply this analysis to *-mut, -sal*, and *-nis* suffixes, which show similar patterns.

Perhaps upwards of 20% of the changes listed in old work on the subject (Florer, Polzin, Michels) bring individual lexical items into line with (or create) the semantic categories established for modern German by Zubin and Köpcke. For instance, NHG words like *List* and *Gewalt* have shifted from masculine/feminine to exclusively feminine, reflecting the semantic field of 'knowledge/skill' or 'power' which correlates with feminine. *Kot* shifts from masculine/neuter to simply masculine, in line with the tendency for the semantic field 'waste' to show masculine gender. *Spelt* 'spelt' shifts from feminine to masculine in line with other grain names (*Roggen, Weizen, Hafer*, etc.). Surveying such forms reveals only a few counterexamples, e.g. OHG *der asco* 'ash', which might seem to fit the category of 'waste', becomes MHG *diu asche*.

An equally important body of work on gender is by Steinmetz (2006 and earlier papers) and Rice (2006 and earlier papers). Steinmetz's research is especially important for its explorations of competing tensions in gender assignment, and his work in ways anticipated the constraint-based approaches to phonology and morphology made popular in Optimality Theory.

7.2.5 Derivational morphology

I noted already in the Preface and Introduction that diachronic work on word formation is relatively limited, generally and within Germanic, which was noted by Trips (2014: 385), Hartmann (2016: 1), and Bousquette & Salmons (2017: 403–405). The situation is improving now and I will say a little about linking elements and note progress in understanding the history of nominalizations.

In the last chapter we dealt with *Fugenelemente* or 'linking elements', segments inserted between the pieces of compounds. Even for ENHG, we talked about this in terms of grammaticalization of once inflectional pieces that come to appear in new places, conditioned in part still morphologically (gender, noun class), but in part phonologically (final segment, syllable count). Nübling & Szczepaniak (2008: 1) argue that these

are hybrid elements situated between morphology and phonology. On the one hand, they have a clear morphological status since they occur only within compounds (and before a very small set of suffixes) and support the listener in decoding them. On the other hand, they also have to be analysed on the phonological level. . . . Thus, they are marginal morphological units on the pathway to phonology (including prosodics).

Particularly with regard to -*s*-, as in *Seminararbeit* > *Seminarsarbeit*, Nübling & Szczepaniak (2010) show that its addition is, increasingly, prosodically conditioned, more likely to be used the further the first element is from being the preferred disyllabic trochee with a 'schwallable'.

We have here a pretty normal-looking grammaticalization story, but one involving the rise of a new derviational pattern. Moveover, the resulting pattern ties in to prosodic templates related to those we have seen elsewhere.

Consider also the formation of new nouns with -*ung*. Modern German is famous—for many people, more accurately infamous—for its use of complex nominal forms, up to and including so-called *Nominalstil*, basically the packing of maximal information into nouns rather than verbs in clauses (see *Duden* 2016 for some discussion). This widely criticized style includes use of prepositional phrases, often in strings; and it is associated with bureaucratic style, in this example specifically with the GDR (a stereotypical association; the example comes from https://de.wikipedia.org/wiki/Nominalstil):

Stellvertreter des Vorsitzenden des Komitees antifaschistischer Widerstandskämpfer der DDR
'deputy of the chair of the committee of antifascist resistance fighters of the GDR'

Because of this, even though the processes are broadly similar to those in other Germanic languages, forming new nouns may have interest beyond

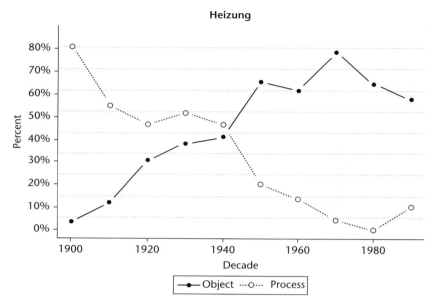

FIGURE 7.2 Change in use of *Heizung* from 'process of heating' to 'heater' over time. From Hartmann (2016: 280).

derivational morphology. Hartmann (2016) provides a richly documented study of nouns from infinitives (*essen* > *das Essen*) and especially -*ung* nouns, of the type *heizen* > *Heizung* (see Figure 7.2). In ENHG and well into NHG, he shows that these still tend to have meanings close to the verbal meaning, as for instance *Heizung* in the sense of 'process of heating'. Only in the 20th century does his corpus show the extension of this noun to the meaning of 'object for heating, heater'. With corpus data, he tracks the shift in those two meanings over time:

The direction of development of the meanings is probably unsurprising, but we have barely begun to look at enough of this kind of data to make broad, empirically sound generalizations about how common such patterns are.

7.2.6 The verbal system

In the verbal system, we can talk more straightforwardly about simplification—the number of weak verbs far exceeds that of strong verbs, and new verbs are (almost) always weak in German.[10]

---

[10] 'Simplification', though, hardly captures the full set of changes in verbal conjugation. Dammel (2011) provides a fuller analysis of types of changes in terms of reduction, restructuring, and expansion.

1. Strong verbs continue to become weak:
    *   triefen, küren, gären, melken, backen.
    *   In the *Umgangssprache* we find forms like: 'scheinte, gescheint'

In the time of Jacob Grimm (1871, quoted in Wegener 2007: 37), we saw intuitions that differ dramatically from those of even the very most conservative, prescriptively oriented speaker today:

Fühlt man aber nicht, daß es schöner und deutscher klinge, zu sagen *buk, wob, boll*...als *backte, webte, bellte* und daß zu jener Form die Partizipia *gebacken, gewoben, gebollen* stimmen?

What's most remarkable here is the broad swath of uncertainty even among reference works about what counts as the norm today. The *Oxford Duden German Dictionary* gives the following (among many others) as strong verbs, but notes that they show weak forms: *bleichen, dünken, gären, senden, spalten, stecken*. Far more striking is the 'complete' list of strong verbs in the 6th edition of the *Duden Grammatik* (1998: 134–144) which contains 56 footnotes clarifying wrinkles in addition to dozens of variants noted directly in the paradigms. (Mercifully, that presentation format is gone in the newer editions.) A couple of examples are reproduced here in adapted form:

Infinitive	Preterit	Subjunctive	Participle
heben	hob/hub (archaic)	höbe/hübe (archaic)	gehoben
helfen	half	hülfe/hälfe (rare)	geholfen
küren	kor	köre	hat gekoren

The last carries a footnote that the regular forms *kürte* and *gekürt* are 'heute üblicher'.

2. A pattern of change between *e* vocalism in infinitive and *i* in 2nd/3rd PERS.SG. (including imperative) appears to be losing ground, mostly in spoken language for now:
    *   'werf!', 'sprech!' for prescribed *wirf! sprich!*
    *   'Helfe auch Du!' (on a poster) for prescribed *hilf!*

These patterns are old, far advanced and well established in many regional varieties (like Hessian) but appear to be becoming more common in more formal contexts, including in writing.

In the realm of morphology, then, we see clearly that change in German, colloquial spoken to formal written, continues apace. The examples above are continuations of old patterns, often leveling or simplifications in some sense, or the solidification of some familiar trend. Let us close this section with a more dramatic change that appears to loom on the horizon: the use of *nen* ('einen') with neuter accusative nouns or even nominatives. Vogel (2006) gives a set of examples like these, from chats and other informal sources:

ich hab da nen kleines Problem
willst du nen image voner CD mit Bewerbungen?

nen lesezeichen wär nicht schlecht gewesen
dat war nen Bier.

She describes this as 'vor allem eine Erscheinung der überregionalen Umgangssprache' (2006: 190), one without a clear geographical center. While a full explanation is not obvious at this point, Vogel suggests that the reduced form of *ein*—often spelled *n*—has come to be perceived as too short, and that this form added needed phonetic/phonological heft to the form. (Recall the discussion of negative *ni* two chapters ago, and the process of adding new material to the negative known as Jespersen's cycle, as well as the discussion of 'extended' pronouns in §6.3.) Whatever the reason, we have here yet another standard-divergent development, this time in inflectional morphology, and one that cuts against a long historical tradition: neuter nouns have never shown a nominative/accusative distinction.

7.2.7 Complementizer agreement: dramatically non-standard new inflection

Recent innovations, or at least innovations that haven't been documented into deep prehistory, include perhaps more surprising changes to German. In Chapter 4, in our earliest substantial discussion of syntax, we looked at constituency and observed that relations among clauses changed in OHG with the development of a complementizer, conjunctions like *dass* that mark a following clause as a complement of the main clause. The position after a complementizer has proven to be a site of syntactic innovation, a place where new things happen (including some examples we've treated, like Somers (2011) on -*st*).

In varieties of West Germanic, complementizers like *wenn, dass, ob* take suffixes that, like verbal endings, agree with the subject. In recent years, a large literature has grown up around this phenomenon, called 'complementizer agreement' (Weiss 2005, Bousquette 2013, 2014). This example (from Nützel 2009) is from an East Franconian dialect spoken in Indiana:

> **East Franconian**
> ich wass nett **wustu** bist
> I know not where-2SG-you are-2SG
> I don't know where you (sing.) are

That is, *wo* (*wu* in the dialect) has not only the second person pronoun (*tu*, cf. *du*), but also the -*st*. This pattern has tremendous implications for synchronic and diachronic syntactic theory, but we do not yet know its history in any detail, its distribution across space, nor its social parameters—it is found in dialects and to some extent now in colloquial varieties. Here are a couple of additional examples (from Weiss 2005) to give you an idea of how widespread it is in dialects of central European German, though it occurs in a set of West Germanic languages, from Dutch and West Frisian on down to Cimbrian, spoken in northern Italy.

Thuringian:
obs du willst
'whether-2SG you want'

Central Bavarian:
das**ma** mia aaf Minga fahrn
'that-1PL we to Munich go'

Pfalz:
wei**ts** iwet pruk khumt, sea**tses** wīetshaus
'when-2PL over-the bridge come, see-2PL-the pub'

Beyond the novelty of such an innovation—verbal suffixes appearing on a complementizer—popping up all over the territory in recent centuries, there are larger points for our purposes: first, we have spent much time looking at the loss of inflectional material since IE. While we've seen grammaticalization, it has not by and large created new kinds of inflection. Second, it shows how murky language history can be even when we have some written texts: the phenomenon is first well attested in 13th century Dutch (Goeman 1997), but it is not yet documented in early German. Joshua Bousquette aptly describes the robust attestations of complementizer agreement as coming from 'the time when we get a lot of people writing, and writing how they talk'.

This development already bridges from morphology to syntax, but there are other syntactic patterns of interest under discussion in contemporary German.

7.3 Syntactic change today

As with sound change and morphology, contemporary German offers abundant examples of recent syntactic change and changes underway at present. Here too, current trends continue the familiar lines of development we've seen unfold through the course of this text. But perhaps even more than with those areas, contemporary syntactic change is closely tied to standardness, and prescriptions about 'proper' usage. But how that's happening may surprise you if you still think in terms of the ongoing acceptance of an unchanging, rigidly codified standard language.

Here, we'll concentrate on verbal syntax, and two kinds of issues. We'll first briefly review three different examples of the fate of increasingly periphrastic structure—the perseverance of *würde*-subjunctives in *wenn*-clauses, the use of *tun* as an auxiliary, and the rise of the *am* + infinitive + *sein* construction. Next we will discuss the possible rise of a new modal verb, a new grammatical category—evidentiality—and patterns of doubling. Then we'll turn to word order—first with a few words about order in so-called 'verb clusters', followed by a slightly more detailed treatment of verb-final versus verb-second order in *weil* clauses and concluding with notes on existential ('there is') constructions.

1. Prescriptivism and the struggle over periphrasis. Through over a thousand years of German texts, we've traced the steady creation of an increasing range of periphrastic verb constructions for tense, mood, aspect, and voice. Most of these have become part of the contemporary standard language of course and in the south, simple preterit structures have essentially disappeared for many speakers in favor of the perfect. Nonetheless, there seems to be a deep-seated feeling among prescriptivists that inflection-heavy forms are somehow better than more syntactically oriented periphrastic ones. This bias is old and deep-seated and may well have roots in part due to implicit or explicit comparison to Latin or classical Greek, both far more inflected than German. Or it may be explainable by fundamental conservatism, since earlier forms of modern German had these patterns and their retreat triggers some sense of loss. We'll deal with three such examples that have been controversial, and whose success has been variable.

Wenn-Sätze sind würde-los* or *Deutsch ist eine würdelose Sprache. We mentioned in the last chapter the spread of the *würde* + infinitive construction in the ENHG period. More recently, in the literature on 'Tendenzen der Gegenwartssprache', one can read that the subjunctive with *würde* has increased over time at the expense of directly marked subjunctive forms. So, sentences like the first example below are less used, and those like the second and third are increasingly used:[11]

Wenn du ihn **einlüdest**, käme er bestimmt.
Wenn du ihn **einladen würdest**, käme er bestimmt.
'Wenn du ihn **einladen würdest**, **würde** er bestimmt **kommen**.'

It is surely safe to say that subjunctive forms like *gösse* from *giessen*, *schöbe* from *schieben*, or *verdürbe* from *verderben* occur rarely, and will sound odd to

---

[11] The status of *würde*-forms in the second clause of such sentences is quite different—they have not been traditionally stigmatized.

many native speakers of German, though *Duden* continues to faithfully list them. Related to this is the old schoolmaster's cliché that 'Wenn-Sätze sind würde-los', that is, the prescription that the first type is 'proper' and the second and third are not. That is, the first just-cited form is regarded by some speakers as the 'correct' one in clauses introduced by *wenn*.

Durrell (2007) traces the history of this prescription, which arose relatively late, in the 19th century. It became 'one of the central shibboleths of "good" German'. It was defended vigorously by enforcers of the standard language up until past the middle of the 20th century, when the battle died down. Some still speak for the use of *gewönne, hülfe, stürbe*. Usage, Durrell shows, never really matched the prescription, and this particular prescription has since been entirely abandoned.

Durrell concludes (2007: 255; and see now Durrell & Whitt 2016 for elaboration and refinement of these views):

> In practice, the prescription seems to have existed primarily in school grammar books and the imagination of those guardians.... Ultimately, it did not prove possible to uphold a prescriptive rule which was confusing and inconsistent, and at variance not only with common spoken usage, but also—and probably far more importantly—with the written usage of the educated literary elite...

Sometimes, in short, the authorities do not win, although in this case the deck was stacked against success on virtually every front.

tun + infinitive. In earlier periods, *tun* is found in many texts as an auxiliary verb, attested back to OHG (see Chapter 6 and the Grimms' *Deutsches Wörterbuch* under *thun*). Lockwood notes for the ENHG period that 'Hans Sachs makes great play of it; Luther, on the other hand, eschews it...' (1968: 157).[12] The precise meaning of this auxiliary is complex—some have traditionally treated it as a tool for 'emphasis', but it often is connected to aspectual distinctions, like habituality, durativity, and so on. Some others see it as semantically empty, allowing speakers to avoid difficult ablaut patterns (see the subjunctive forms earlier on this page), or allowing more word order flexibility (see Langer 2007).

Over time, Davies & Langer show (2006: 211–224, building on Langer 2001) show how the construction moves from carrying no stigma to being stigmatized only in poetry, and then coming to be regarded as regional (southern) and spoken rather than written. From the mid-18th century until the 20th, it is condemned as *Pöbelsprache*, while it continues to be pretty widely attested, even in prestigious literature:

ob er mit einer gleichgesinnten
sich thut bei tisch und bette finden.

Faust, 57, 258

---

[12] The *Deutsches Wörterbuch* does give an example from Luther.

Today, Davies & Langer observe that some make an exception for *tun* when used to allow topicalization of a verb (that is, used to allow moving the verb to the initial position in a clause), so that the first form below is acceptable to such authorities (including *Duden* 2016: §594), while the second one is not:

> Singen tut er gerne.
> *Er tut gerne singen.

In fact, Abraham & Fischer (1998: 45, elsewhere) argue that this kind of topicalization is so basic to German that if no other auxiliary is available (like a modal verb, a perfect auxiliary, etc.), that *tun* creates a structure that allows such forms to surface, a kind of functional explanation. This goes hand in hand with arguments that use of an auxiliary may have some advantages for psycholinguistic processing (see Fischer 2001, Langer 2001).

Elspaß (2005a, 2005b) finds a robust pattern of the construction in his extensive corpus of 19th-century German letters, with the regional distribution shown in his schematic dialect map. He concludes that:

> Das auxiliäre tun ist im 19. Jahrhundert in allen Funktionen und in allen Schreib-regionen lebendig und findet sich sogar in solchen Regionen, in denen es durch den Dialekt offenbar nicht gestützt ist. Die tun-Fügung ist daher als autonome Fügung der geschriebenen Alltagssprache des 19. Jahrhunderts zu bewerten.

The numbers in Map 21 show how many times auxiliary *tun* was attested in Elspaß's corpus.

In this instance, a form widely attested in the 19th century has retreated from 'standard' usage in the face of stigmatization. At the same time, as Elspaß observes (2005b: 21), the construction continues to be used, including in new contexts/media, as illustrated by a 'ready-made text message' from T-Mobile: *tu mich nicht vergessen.* Exiled from standard written usage, at least in most forms and according to most sources, *tun* continues to swim below the surface. Still, it is a form not taught and most non-native speakers are unaware of it until they encounter it 'in the wild'.

An emerging modal verb: *brauchen*. We've talked since Chapter 3 about the ongoing development of modal verbs in the language. Even today, the class continues to change.[13] One important example is *brauchen*, which is today widely used with a bare infinitive, that is, without *zu*, except in formal writing (Duden 2009: 415–426), especially in negative contexts, like in these examples:

---

[13] See the chapters in Müller & Reis (2001) for a survey of some key historical issues on modals generally.

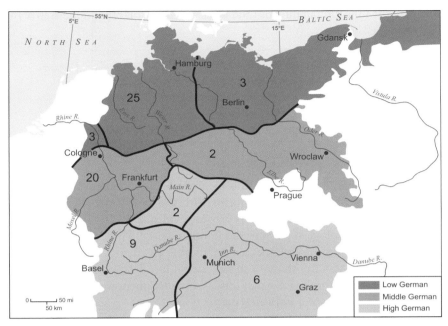

MAP 21 Distribution of auxiliary *tun* in 19th-century letters.
Adapted from a line drawing in Elspaß (2005b).

Du brauchst Dich nicht kümmern.
Du brauchst nichts [zu] sagen.

The most recent edition of Duden simply notes that usage is variable, the *zu* being far more common in writing (*Duden* 2016: §591). The full historical unfolding of these patterns is not yet clear, so that we do not know the extent to which we may have recency illusions here (cf. Freywald 2010).

   While the absence of the *zu* yields a syntactic pattern like traditional modals, morphological changes bring it more tightly into the fold. Moreover, *brauchen* is an otherwise weak verb in the modern language (though OE has a strong cognate and there were wrinkles in OHG *bruhhan*), in contemporary spoken German, it has the subjunctive form quite often with umlaut: 'Man bräuchte mehr Zeit'. In the last chapter, we saw that the modals had also developed along similar lines.

   Girnth (2000) documents an increasing use of the third person singular of the verb without the inflectional -*t* in some West Central areas (see also Duden 2009: 458 for written examples). Together with the fact that first person singular -*e* is often lost in colloquial German, this brings the new modal into line with the inflection of modals (and *wissen*), which still echo the IE stative in key respects:

	Lexical verb	Modal verb	
Inf.	legen	sollen	brauchen
1st sg.	leg(e)	soll-Ø	brauch-Ø
2nd sg.	legst	sollst	brauchst
3rd sg.	legt	soll-Ø	brauch-Ø

Girnth and others have regarded this as an analogical change, and Diewald (1997: 116) asserts that other full forms with the same final cluster do not simplify, but Maitz & Tronka (2009) provide evidence that final -*t* is likewise often lost for phonological reasons and in other words. Thus, this appears not to be a particular feature of *brauchen*. In another frequent verb, for example, Herrgen (2010: 680–681) shows a steady spread in *t*-deletion in *hast*, providing further support for the view that this is a broader phenomenon, not simply the grammaticalization of *brauchen* per se.

While *Duden* now reckons *brauchen* among the modal verbs, the grammar describes some other patterns of grammaticalization in verbal syntax in terms of *Modalitätsverben*, or semi- or quasi-modals. Let us look briefly at a key type.

Evidentiality: new grammatical constructions. In some languages of the world, statements are encoded for the source of the evidence the speaker has for something, for instance, whether it's been directly observed (sometimes specifically whether it was seen or heard etc.) or has been reported to them by someone else. In Quechua, for example, clitics convey this information (from Aikhenvald 2004: 68–69):

huk-**si**   ka-sqa huk   machucha-piwan payacha
once-REPORTED be-SUDDEN DISCOVERY one old.man-WITH woman
'Once there were an old man and an old woman.'

Pidru kunan-**mi**   wasi-ta   tuwa-shan-n
Pedro now-DIRECT EVIDENCE   house-ACC   build-PROG-3SG
'It is now that Pedro is building the house'.

In early Germanic texts, it's sometimes made clear in a poetic first line what source of evidence the storyteller has, like in the OHG *Hildebrandslied* or the MHG *Nibelungenlied*, where in Quechua, an enclitic could have done the job:

Hildebrandslied
ik gihôrta đat seggen
'I have heard it told…'

Nibelungenlied

uns ist in alten mæren   wunders vîl geseit

'In old stories, we are told much of amazing things...'

Diewald & Smirnova (2010) develop a detailed argument that four verbs in German have grammaticalized into markers of evidentiality—*werden, scheinen, drohen,* and *versprechen,* still used today with *zu* + infinitive. In the case of *drohen,* for instance, it began as a speech act verb—a role it still has today, of course—as in this example from Tatian (Diewald & Smirnova 2010: 272):

Threuuita ín	ther heilant	quedanti...
threatened them	the savior	saying...

'The savior threatened them saying...'

The subject must be an agent (typically a person) and it is the subject who will carry out the undesirable consequences being threatened. At this stage, the verb can take a dative object. During the medieval period, they report that the meaning broadens to cover any 'action or behavior which is characterized by a negative impact on the undergoer', a more abstract kind of threat. By the 18th century, we see it used with non-agents as subjects, as in this example from Tatian (Diewald & Smirnova 2010: 277):

Eine gefährliche Trennung **drohte** dem ganzen protestantischen Bunde den Untergang.

And it begins to appear with infinitives (with *zu*) and accusative objects, like in this 19th-century example from the same source (2010: 282):

...aber die Sonnenhitze brennt gar zu stark, daß mir das zarte Kraut zu welken droht.

The key to the distinction between the lexical verb *drohen* and evidential *drohen* is that the subject is no longer the threat, but rather that the speaker has some information indicating that there is a threat, in this case the heat of the sun. All of these verbs have come to signal what is called 'indirect inferential evidentiality'. The changes happen along somewhat different paths (starting from a visual verb with *scheinen* but speech act verbs with *drohen*) and at somewhat different times (earlier with *werden* than with *drohen*) and to somewhat different degrees (greater grammaticalization with *scheinen* than with *drohen*).

Note that the system is hardly developed to a Quechua-like level—these are still verbs that require *zu* + infinitive, for instance, and nothing has reduced to clitic or affix as we see in full-blown grammaticalization. Some may find the connection to more explicitly marked evidentiality to sound like exoticizing German, while others will appreciate the connection to broader cross-linguistic patterns. However that may be, Diewald and Smirnova argue, these verbs form an identifiable, tight-knit, and coherent system (2010: 325).

Verbal aspect: *am* + infinitive. In English, we distinguish sentences like the following two, where the first indicates a general point or typical state, while the second indicates that it's now in progress:

She works hard.
She is working hard.

German has traditionally lacked a clear equivalent to this 'progressive' form and this is reflected in difficulties German speakers have with the English distinction, e.g. in the use of the second for future action—as in *I go home now for *I'm going home now* (see §3.5). In German, this would traditionally be expressed with an adverbial construction. Contemporary German has developed forms that are parallel, though, namely with *am/im/beim* + nominalized Inf. + *sein*, such as (Reimann 1999):

Hier *ist* immer etwas *am Wachsen*.

In sharp contrast to the *tun*-construction, the *Duden Grammatik* (1998: 91) now accepts these forms as standard:

Die Verwendung von *beim* und *im* ist, neben der mit *am*, nicht nur landschaftlich, sondern schon auch standardsprachlich, besonders in der gesprochenen Sprache, möglich.

In his 19th-century corpus of letters written by ordinary speakers, Elspaß (2005a: 269) finds only 15 examples of this construction, all from writers from Westphalia or the Rhineland, leaving aside 15 occurrences of the fixed phrase *am Leben sein*. In surveying 'classical literary' texts, Van Pottelberge (2004: 231–239, elsewhere) finds it used by an array of notable authors, from Goethe to Büchner and Heine to Kafka, and as far back as the early 16th century (2004: 233), from the *Tagebuch des Lucas Rem*:

Fand wir king Philips, der *am herausreitten* was.

Canonical literary attestations appear at least from 1778, with multiple examples in the work of J. H. Jung-Stilling, like this:

Es *waren* just sechs Taglöhner *am Dreschen*.

Elspaß quite reasonably treats this as a straightforward case of grammaticalization—the rise of new aspectual marking—in the spread of the regional form into supraregional usage. Sociolinguistically, he argues, it was motivated by the just-discussed stigmatization of *tun* + infinitive constructions, which served (and serve) a similar function. This new syntactic form, in short, appears to have arisen without significant resistance from prescriptivists. In other words, a significant syntactic change has taken place without the harsh condemnation of language authorities.[14] Still, there is of course more complexity, for instance regionally. Elspaß (in correspondence) gives an assessment of the regional situation: 'In Switzerland, it is far more accepted than in Austria. In the West of Germany, it is more accepted than in the East or in Bavaria. It's far more grammaticalized in Switzerland and the West in Germany than elsewhere.'

Verb and other doubling in Swiss German. Across spoken Swiss German, certain verbs can be, very roughly speaking, 'doubled' to signal movement or the initiation of an action. The doubled form is an uninflected particle, reduced from the relevant verb but still recognizably related to it. I am drawing here on Christen et al. (2013: 333–335), and reproducing the forms they give:

Verb	Particle form	Gloss
gaa	*go*	'to go'
laa	*la*	'to let'
choo	*cho*	'to come'
aafaa	*afa*	'to begin'

The doubling yields sentences like these (for the Standard German 'er lässt den Schreiner kommen'):

Er laat de Schriiner la choo
He lets the carpenter let come
'he has a carpenter come'

The construction is not brand new—it is attested in the early modern period—but it has clearly spread in the past fifty years, according to Christen and her colleagues. And the verbs show different geographical distributions, *go* being the most widespread form, found north of Switzerland and used obligatorily, while the others are found only in Swiss varieties.

Informally, this feels like a kind of hyper-periphrasis in some ways... maybe even one reminiscent of the rise of new negations with Jespersen's cycle. More importantly, it is another example of the striking divergence from standard forms, here involving a set of verbs with related but partially independent paths of development.

---

[14] See also Van Pottelberge (2004), who puts this German construction in the context of the many other West Germanic languages that have parallel structures—Dutch, West Frisian, and Pennsylvania German. In Dutch at least, it seems to be attested earlier than in German.

Indeed, Swiss German shows a much broader set of doubling phenomena—negation, wh-words, determiners, and some pronominal constructions. Glaser & Frey (2006: 2, 8 and passim) give examples like the following, the first one reported among two-thirds of respondents:

Determiner doubling
Ä ganz ä liebi frau.
a really a lovely wife
'A really lovely wife.'

Wh-word doubling
Wer isch da gsi wer?
who AUX there been who
'Who was there?'

That is, Swiss German shows a rich range of doubling, but—and this is the punchline—Glaser & Frey (2006: 11) conclude that 'this survey seems to show that Swiss German dialects do not demonstrate a particularly high number of doubling phenomena when compared to e.g. Dutch dialects. As far as we know there are e.g. no cases of subject pronoun doubling or subject agreement doubling, which is common in other European areas.' In short, doubling is found across the Swiss German grammar and across other West Germanic varieties. For colloquial German, these include what Duden calls the *doppelte Perfektbildung*, of the type *dann hab ich ihm mal eine tablette gegeben gehabt*, which the editorial team associates with the spoken language (Duden 2016: 1258–1259 and elsewhere).

2. Word order. Much research in the historical syntax of ENHG focused, as we saw, on the fixing of verb-final order, creating the sentence 'frame'. By that period, the basic syntax of subordinate clauses was already verb final, in some sense, yet new research continues to trace the slow and variable fixing of that pattern. Let us look at the simplest of examples of this process. Recall that the finite verb is labeled '1' and the non-finite (infinitive or participial) form '2', so that 'verb-final' order is called '2–1' and its opposite '1–2', while additional, non-verbal elements can be labeled 'X'.[15] Consider sentences like these, from Sapp (2011a):

(1) das er in kainer sund *verczweiffeln sol* 2–1
      that he in no sin despair$_2$ shall$_1$
      'that he shall not despair in any sin' (*Pillenreuth* 161)

---

[15] These patterns often involve other elements, such as a third verb (of the *hätte machen müssen* type). We leave them aside here.

(2) das der mensch alle sein lebttag nicht anders *scholt thun* 1–2
    that the person all his life.days nothing else should₁ do₂
    'that man should do nothing else all the days of his life'
                                                    (*Pillenreuth* 206)

(3) das der mensche nicht *scholt* sein rew sparen an das todpett 1–X–2
    that the person not should₁ his regret save₂ on the deathbed
    'that one should not hold back his repentance on his deathbed'
                                                    (*Pillenreuth* 212)

A whole set of structural factors correlate with how quickly verb-final order emerges, including the particular verb constructions involved and the non-verbal elements present. But of course this change proceeds across space as well, as summarized in Figures 7.3 and 7.4 (Sapp 2011a).

In the end, again, Sapp (2011a: 210) provides support for the view that this fixing was not a feature of East Central German that was adopted as standard, but more likely that the increasingly fixed verb-final order was supraregional. Even late, in the 16th century, he argues, areas like German-speaking Switzerland, where the modern standard order is not required in the dialects, showed surprising adherence to the emerging norm.

As with so many other features, many dialects and even colloquial varieties spoken today do not follow the standard, but continue old patterns. Dubenion-Smith (2007, 2010) finds no evidence for change in these aspects of dialect syntax across two generations of speakers, so that dialect usage appears stable even at present in the face of pressure from the standard variety. What is perhaps most remarkable here, though, is that the standardizers of German have invested so much energy over so many centuries in codifying and enforcing this norm. In Dutch, by contrast, the standard language freely allows a range of options. This simple example comes from De Schutter (1994: 466):

... dat ze het **gezegd had**
... that she it said had

... dat ze het **had gezegd**
... that she it had said
'... that she had said it'.

Dialect group	1350–99	1450–99	1550–99	Total
West (Col., Hes., Als., Zur.)	12%	15%	7%	12%
Central (Swabia, Nuremb.)	61%	28%	28%	38%
EMG (Saxony, Thuringia)	43%	27%	9%	24%
Bavarian-Austrian	46%	21%	3%	24%

FIGURE 7.3 1–2 order over time by dialect, after Sapp.

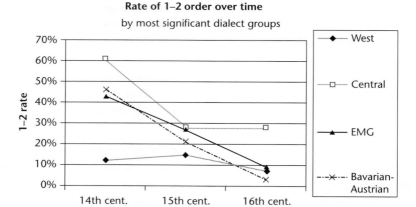

FIGURE 7.4 Frequency of the 1–2 order by dialect and century, after Sapp.

In fact, De Schutter argues, the latter order appears 'to be gaining ground in the modern language, especially in writing'. Standard Dutch seems to have admitted variable patterns over time, while German prescriptive grammarians have rigidly codified the language.

weil + verb second. The popular press and many linguistically observant (or, often, prescriptively obsessed) people in Germany are convinced that *weil* is increasingly being used with V2 (verb-second) word order rather than the prescribed verb-final order:

> Ich komme erst jetzt, weil ich **hab** noch gearbeitet.
> Wir müssen unbedingt dahin gehen, weil die **machen** jetzt bald zu.

The usual view is that this occurs only in spoken language, and some find it not just with *weil*, but clauses with *während*, *obschon*, and *wenn*.

> So hat er die Situation beschrieben, obwohl so schlimm **war's** auch nicht.

> Ich weiss, daß ihr recht habt / ihr habt recht.

Certainly the form is widely used today, not just in spoken language but also in styles close to the spoken today, like on the web: a Google search for the exact string 'weil ich hab' got about 132,000 hits in December of 2007, from a wide variety of text types.

While the synchronic analysis of those patterns is beyond our immediate concern, there's a growing literature on that, see Günthner (1993) and Antomo & Steinbach (2010).

But the recency illusion, discussed throughout this chapter, can rear its ugly head in syntactic change too: it is not entirely clear whether this in fact represents change in usage, or just increased awareness of a usage that has been around for a long time. Farrar (1999) examines two large sets of recorded German speech (the Freiburger corpus [1968–1974] and the Utah corpus [1989–1994]). She concludes, among other things, that there is indeed change happening. In the older Freiburg corpus, V2 is rare (2.4%), in the Utah corpus, it's just over 31%. Elspaß (2005a), on the other hand, is able to securely document *weil* plus verb-second word order to at least the middle of the 19th century (with a couple of early 19th-century examples), so that this is hardly a 20th-century pattern. Happily Freywald (2010) does us the service of collecting descriptions of the history of *weil* with V2, some of which, all published since 1991, are given here without attributions (which are in the original):

- in der letzten Dekade
- during the last ten to fifteen years
- in jüngster Zeit
- at least since the early 1970s
- seit den 1920er Jahren
- since Old High German
- mit Unterbrechung seit dem Althochdeutschen
- bekanntlich das im Substandard immer bewahrte ältere Muster

Far more importantly, she questions whether there is anything special about *weil*, and gives quantitative corpus evidence showing that in spoken German, *obwohl* and *während* in fact pattern like *weil*, all showing roughly 10% V2 and 90% verb-final order, and she gives evidence for *daß* + V2 as well (Figure 7.5).

For some sociolinguistically salient patterns, 10% occurrence of a marked form is enough to trigger listener sensitivity. Labov et al. (2006: 15) and Purnell et al. (2009: 335) discuss this with regard to so-called 'g-dropping' in American English, where roughly 10% use of forms like *talkin'* [-n] rather than *talking* [-ŋ] may trigger an impression that the speaker is doing this while a lower rate goes less noticed. So speakers may be using *weil* + V2 just often enough for listeners to catch it and hear the pattern. She reasonably suggests that we may be more aware of the *weil* pattern in part due to its much higher frequency.

Before we move on, consider another example—one not really widely discussed in the historical linguistic literature (to my knowledge)—which involves ES GIBT, the existential or 'there is' construction. Since at least Old High German, ES has been used as an expletive subject, which is the linguistic

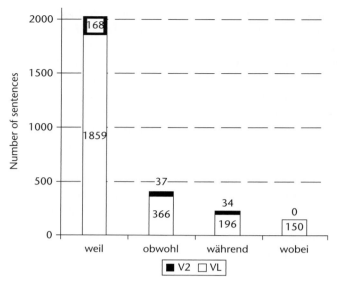

FIGURE 7.5 Verb second vs. verb last for *weil* vs. other subordinating conjunctions, after Freywald (2010).

name of what many students of German learn of as a 'dummy' or 'placeholder' (see Lockwood 1968: 55–56 or Lenerz 1985: 104–109 for more examples):

uuanda iz tenne filo regenot
'because it rains a lot'

iz ist giscrîban
'it is written'

Recall from the last chapter that V1 declarative sentences have been permitted at various historical stages of German, and we saw examples from OHG where the modern language requires an ES or a different order. English speakers can use *there* or *it* and Gothic used nothing, but there is real complexity across the family (see Harbert 2007: 224–236.)

In OHG, this pronoun was not required but could occur, with considerable differentiation according to the kind of verb involved. For instance, verbs with a dative or accusative object seldom use it, and impersonal verbs do show it (both examples from Notker, quoted in Lenerz 1985: 105):

únde dúnchet mir reht
'and it seems right to me'

iz nahtet
'it becomes night'

The arguments go beyond our current concerns, but note that Lenerz argues that there are two distinct forms of *es*: one is a subject and the other marks topics.

The pronoun clearly becomes more common over time; early on it occurs famously in the *Nibelungenlied*:

> *Ez wuohs in Búrgónden ein vil édel magedîn,*
> 'a very noble young woman grew up in Burgundy'

The existential *es gibt* appears only in late MHG/early ENHG, but there are suggestive parallel constructions that might point to a West Germanic construction, and even to similar constructions in Old Irish and Latin (see Joseph 2000 for full discussion and further references).

Wiese (2013), drawing examples from internet forums, notes that contemporary usage includes examples like these (and they are easy to find with any search today, also spelled *es gibs, es gibt's*):

> **Es** gibts nicht zum Anziehen für den Schulanfang!

Wiese sees this as a case of 'univerbation', where an enclitic *-s* eventually becomes part of the verb, so that *gibts* is a single morpheme. This is something we've seen repeatedly—recall how *-t* came to be added to second person singular verb forms; or recall the rise of complementizer agreement just discussed.

She finds a further striking development in *Kiezdeutsch*, the urban multi-ethnolect discussed a few pages later (see pp. 360–361 in this chapter):

> Guck ma was hier alles noch gibs...
> Ich weiß wo die gibs...

Here *gibs* occurs without the subject *es*. She sees it now as a particle taking the position of a verb. Note that her examples are in subordinate clauses, where the word order reveals that we don't have the usual existential construction (*die gibt's* etc.), but the construction is otherwise well integrated into German syntax.

Let us look at the history of *es* and of the existential construction. First, the development of *gibs* to a verbal particle is surely recent, but the *es gibts* construction it expands from does not appear to be. A search in Grimms' online dictionary yields early examples, the first from the 16th century:

> ach **es** gibts podagram!
> (Fischart)[16]

---

[16] *Podagra* is the Latin word for 'gout' and, like German *Gicht*, it is a feminine noun, so that the *-s* should not be a reduced form of *das*.

es gibts die vernunft, dasz *u.s.w.*

(Olearius)

How could this have come about? Curme (1922: 335) writes about *es gibt*: 'The real nature of this construction is sometimes little felt, as in dialect the object of *geben* sometimes becomes the subject and this incorrect usage appears occasionally in the literary language.' He gives this example from Goethe's *Urfaust*, where the verb form shows a plural subject, *mehr*, rather than singular *es*:

Es ist ein Kauz, wie's mehr noch geben.

Parallel to what happens with the rise of complementizer agreement, for speakers, such ambiguity could promote the development of *es gibts*.

In short, if this analysis pans out, we would have another significant syntactic development flying under the radar of grammarians and linguists for centuries, made possible perhaps by opportunities for reanalysis by speakers.

7.4 Pragmatics

Returning to language in social interaction, this section is a chance to note briefly two areas where German makes distinctions that English in some sense lacks, pronouns of address and modal particles.

First, consider one instance where the modern language has added a distinction, and one with a relatively complex history: the creation of a formal pronoun.

Originally, Germanic only had singular and plural forms for second person, *du* and *ihr* basically. Already by OHG, we find a handful of apparently clear examples of the use of *ir* for a single person (Simon 2003a, 2003b, Hickey 2003, and many earlier works), including also in the *Pariser Gespräche*. Simon (2003b: 94) cites Otfrid's letter to Salomo, Bishop of Constance, as the earliest, including this line:

Oba **ir** hiar findet iawiht thés   thaz wirdig ist dhes lésannes
whether **you** find something here worthy of reading

MHG similarly uses a courtly *ihr* for singular, though Simon and others show that there is considerable variability in the system, e.g. across manuscripts of the *Nibelungenlied*. The use of plural forms for politeness is found in other languages, including European languages. Later, third person singular *er* and *sie* (with the obvious gender correlation), arise in ENHG, after earlier use of nouns and third person forms for address ('Gebe der Herr mir den Rock...'). They form another layer of distinction, and survive into the 19th century and beyond. (Whatever the explanation of the particular event, I was once addressed with *Er* while doing fieldwork with some Texas German speakers in the late 1970s.) This establishes itself to a degree in the 18th century, while formal *Ihr* continues to have a regional/dialectal presence (Besch 1996, von Polenz 1999: 383–386). Howe (1996: 97–98) treats this as 'functional reinterpretation', where second person or third person singular pronouns are repurposed as formal second person forms. He observed that 'such usage can be explained by indirectness'. In the Early New High German period, *Sie* comes into vogue, taking now the third person plural form and creating yet more distance from the addressee. The pinnacle of respect-inflation is the use of *dieselben*, referring to an earlier plural form of address like *Eure Fürstliche Gnaden* (Behaghel 1923: 324–325, also in Simon 2003b: 115), as in this 1632 quote: 'daß Ew. fürstl. gn. ankomnes schreiben alsbald gelifert worden, werden **dieselben** aus meinem bericht verstanden haben.' For this baroque (in two senses of the word) system, Simon (2003b: 116) gives Gottsched's 'five levels of politeness' from 1762 as follows:

natürlich	ich	bitte	dich
althöflich	ich	bitte	euch
mittelhöflich	ich	bitte	ihn
neuhöflich	ich	bitte	Sie
überhöflich	ich	bitte	dieselben

Of course formality is a fundamentally social and political notion, and usage has varied and changed with social and political changes, and the system has today sorted itself out into a simpler one again. Notable during the 1960s and since has been a trend toward use of *du* in broader social circumstances.

Simon (2003b: 93, with related versions elsewhere) graphically represents the fuller development of terms of address in German (the version below is considerably adapted):

				dieselben	dieselben	
				Sie	Sie	
			er/sie	er/sie	ihr	
	ihr (rare)	ihr (variable)	ihr	ihr	er/sie	Sie
du	du	du	du	du	du	du
Germanic	OHG	MHG	17th c.	18th c.	early 19th c.	Contemporary standard
I	II		III	IV	V	VI

Politeness is an important part of pragmatics generally, and the case has been made that German has developed a grammatical category for 'respect', parallel to the way that honorifics in languages like Japanese have been treated (Simon 2003b).

Second, languages have various ways for speakers to signal aspects of their intent in or attitudes toward utterances. One option open to German speakers but not, at least not in the same way, to English speakers is the use of modal particles like *doch, ja, schon, mal*. Contrast a sentence like *komm her!* with *komm mal her!* To capture the (relatively softened) sense of the second, English speakers often use questions instead, like *why don't you just come over here?* or something, in line with the occasional German term for the particles, *Abtönungspartikel*.

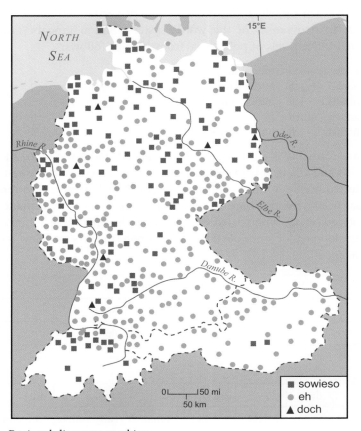

MAP 22 Regional discourse marking.

Adapted from *Atlas zur deutscher Alltagssprache*, http://www.philhist.uni-augsburg.de/Lehrstuele/germanistik/sprachwissenschaft/ada/runde_1/f16a_b/.

Modal particles are an established part of contemporary German and their history is a long one. *Thoh*, the ancestor of modern *doch*, for example, is well known from major OHG texts (see Fritz 2006: 158–161, examples and translations from there):

> thaz ist **thoh** arunti min (Otfrid)
> das ist doch mein Auftrag

> **Ia** negedenchent ir gold ufen dien boumen zesuochenne (Notker)
> Ihr denkt doch nicht daran, Gold auf den Bäumen zu suchen . . .

The set of particles has since steadily expanded in German (Fritz posits *thoh* 'doch', *thanne* 'denn', and *ia* 'ja' as an initial set, but I treated OHG *nu* as part of the group in Chapter 4).

They haven't always been well received: we should remember Luther's quip that modal particles were 'lice in the fur of the language', *Läuse im Pelz der Sprache*. They have, obviously, persisted and today show some clear regional uses, as shown by Map 22.

A growing body of work covers the history of particles, such as Auer & Günthner (2005), Autenrieth (2002), Burkhardt (1994), and most recently Diewald (2011). Some of this work is now framed in terms of grammaticalization. (I argued in Chapter 4 that there are some respects in which the modal particles exemplify degrammaticalization over the centuries, which is not necessarily at odds with those views.)

7.5 The sociolinguistics of contemporary German

In this section, let us briefly note a couple of areas where language and society intersect today in ways that are informed by history and that themselves, in some sense can help inform history themselves. Those are the many forms of the language which are neither dialect nor standard but rather somewhere in between, the modern tradition of bilingualism and multilingualism, the pluricentric character of German as an international language, changing attitudes about regional varieties, and finally attitudes about foreign, especially (American) English, influence. The most important point may perhaps be one made by Schmidt (2010: 218–219):

By the end of the twentieth century, all German dialect speakers had acquired active bivarietal competence (in dialect and regiolect) and at least passive competence in the standard spoken language. The comprehensive regionalization of communication had decisively reshaped all interaction.

That is, in contemporary German-speaking society, speakers now have command of varieties that were forged in and since the Early Modern period—the standard language—and varieties that are still emerging—regional, non-dialectal varieties which have come to be called 'regiolects'.

A dialect-standard continuum and discontinuity. It is important to keep in mind that there's a continuum in most of the German-speaking world, where truly Standard German shades into *regionale Hochsprache*. Traditionally, in German linguistics, people talk about intermediate stages in terms of *dialektnahe Umgangssprache*, and so on. König et al. (2015: 135) gives a set of forms on a continuum for the Meißen area, originally reported from R. Grosse, all variants of the sentence *es wird bald anfangen zu regnen* (and following the orthography in the original):

(1) s ward bāe uanfang mid rāin
(2) s ward bāle ānfang mit rān
(3) s wärd balde ānfang mit rächn
(4) s werd balde anfang dse rächn
(5) s wird bald anfang dsu rēchnen

Similar, sometimes longer and more dramatic sets, have been compiled for various parts of Germany—Bavaria, Swabia, etc. The main point from the perspective of the history of German is perhaps that we have seen how such a continuum arose: the basilectal (most dialectal) patterns follow a relatively more linear development from the earliest texts, while forms closer to the standard have been negotiated by speakers through education and institutional use. Particularly striking is the emergence of broad colloquial patterns of speech that conform neither to traditional dialectal speech nor to the standard, as we've seen with new forms like the *isch* pronunciation and the *nen* neuter forms above (pp. 335–336).

The shading between standard and dialect ultimately does not lead upward (to follow the usual metaphorical direction) to a single norm. And the difficulties of tracing the rapidly changing patterns are not to be underestimated, as shown by Lenz (2003).

Instead, German must be understood as a pluricentric language. That is, as argued in recent work (especially by Michael Clyne, but also others, and introduced nicely in Russ 1994), German has multiple centers and thus, to an extent, different 'standards' and national variants even in their most formal/standard form. Consider these variants reported from Swiss German:[17]

---

[17] Elspaß & Kleiner (forthcoming) will provide rich detail on the state of areal variation in Standard German.

- Stress: Fábrik, Nótiz (further examples in Kleiner 2011–)
- Lexicon: *Nachtessen, aper (schneefrei), sturm (schwindlig)* (and see Bickel & Landolt 2012 for many examples).
- Morphology:
  - Word formation: *Zugmitte*, without a linking *s*, vs. German German *Zugsmitte* (http://www.atlas-alltagssprache.de/runde-3/f01a-d)
  - Gender: *der Couch, die Koffer*, etc.

Why do we care about contemporary variation in the context of language history, especially things like stylistic and 'register' differences? Here are some reasons:

- Variation at a single point in time is a key indicator of either change in progress or areas of potential future change. This is the foundation for much modern sociolinguistic work (like Labov, the Milroys, and others).
- Very recent studies are showing a tremendous amount of change along these lines (including standard vs. dialect) in the life of a single individual. Wagener (1997) finds, for example, that the very same speakers recorded in the 1950s speak very differently in re-interviews from recent years. Some speakers have moved toward dialect, others away from it, etc. One West-phalian farmer had 91% unshifted stops (i.e. Low German forms) in 1957 but only 67% in 1993.
- While we're starting to figure out a lot about this kind of variation today, almost no work has gone into reconstructing similar patterns historically. Romaine (1989: 373–374) calls on historical linguists to 'reconstruct prior stages with possibly richer morphophonemic alternation and variability differentiated to a number of social parameters, such as style, ethnicity, age, sex, etc.' Surprisingly little such historical sociolinguistic work has been done, and that provides a healthy challenge to the next generation of historical linguists working on German.

But a far more fundamental difference between standard and dialect has been proposed. We've noted repeatedly that standard languages are constructed entities acquired in school or other settings, whereas ordinary varieties of languages are acquired 'naturally'. In a set of works, Weiß (2001, 2004, elsewhere) has argued that this has consequences for language change. Early language acquisition, as noted at the beginning of Chapter 2 and several times since, is critical in shaping our grammar. Standard German is now being acquired as a first language today, a process he calls 'renaturalization'. Because standard languages have not been naturally acquired first languages, they are not reliable data for linguistic theorizing. This view is not uncontroversial (see Simon 2004), but the differences in how standard languages and other languages have been acquired is something to keep in mind, and we'll return to it briefly in what follows.

Dialects and discontinuity in diaspora. German in many forms has been spoken in Wisconsin for well over a century and a half now; and, over the generations, speakers have constantly renegotiated their position within the German-speaking and English-speaking world they live in. This is closely paralleled by changes in their language. Today almost everybody in those communities is now an English speaker, but fourth- and fifth-generation bilinguals are still not hard to find.

If you look back to Chapter 4 (especially §4.5), you'll be reminded of the complex and perplexing patterns of 'dialect mixing' found in Old High German manuscripts. The present helps us understand the past (Labov 1975), and in this section I will draw on contemporary patterns of 'dialect mixing' in German spoken by third- to fifth-generation Wisconsinites, in order to advance our understanding of those Old High German texts that show disparate regional features. A surprising number of OHG texts show features from across various OHG dialects and from other West Germanic languages, for example Old Saxon. The famously mixed Hildebrandslied includes forms like *ik* 'I' (OHG *ih*) and *dat* ~ *ðat* 'that' (OHG *daȝ*) next to unambiguously southern-looking forms, for instance with shifted initial *k*, as in *chind in chunincrîche* 'child in the kingdom'; and single words show mixes such as *chud* with shifted *k* (German *kund*) *and* nasal loss (English *(un)couth*).

Such combinations of features make the impression of a crazy quilt where random pieces of cloth are sown into it without following a clear pattern (for an image, see https://en.wikipedia.org/wiki/Crazy_quilting). They seem like implausible reflections of spoken language, and I did not suggest that our OHG texts reflect anybody's normal speech patterns; but ongoing work on Wisconsin Heritage German (Litty et al. 2015) shows parallel patterns. Litty et al. investigated communities where American-born German speakers have overwhelmingly northeastern German ancestry, typically from Pomerania. And they show some expected feature, for example northern or western gliding of *g* (*je-* for Standard German *ge-*). Yet in the very same sentences these speakers may have shibilization of /st/ and /rst/ (*mescht,* *Wurscht* for German *meist, Wurst*). (See the dialect maps at historyofger-man.net for the geographical distributions.) And these speakers show wide ranges of standard-like features; indeed what they speak is, overwhelmingly, a kind of colloquial German that shows contact with English, not with any kind of Low German. These patterns are unexpected in *koinē* formation settings where salient regional markers tend to disappear and appear alongside broader patterns of *koinē* formation. It looks as if in these communities inherited regional markers have remained in the grammar but have lost their earlier social and regional meanings.

We know little about the scribes who wrote most OHG manuscripts, and their linguistic biographies were clearly quite different from those of Wisconsin German speakers. Still, as I argued in Chapter 4, scriptoria provided environmental similarities that suggest that we should expect to find extensive 'dialect mixing'.

The particular set of forms found in the Hildebrandslied are forms that likely did not exist as single grammars in OHG—though I imagine there was somebody who, in speaking to some other individual, codeswitched in roughly those ways between varieties roughly that distant from one another. Strikingly, our modern Wisconsin Heritage German data show that such crazy quilt variation can exist.[18]

Bilingualism and multilingualism. Today we recognize that the German-speaking lands are multilingual, in large part thanks to the movement of speakers, especially of languages ranging from Turkish and Greek to Russian, Somali, and Arabic, into urban areas since the mid-20th century. But these regions and, in modern times, the relevant nation-states have always had significant bilingual and multilingual populations, presumably from the period when Germanic speakers arrived and Germanic varieties developed. As we have discussed, some varieties traditionally called 'dialects' are sufficiently distinct to count as different languages according to the usual definitions of linguists; certainly Low German, various southern varieties, and ultimately various others fall into this category. Even leaving aside multilingual Switzerland and the Austro-Hungarian Empire, other languages have been spoken for many centuries in what is now Germany, in some cases having arisen there, as did East and North Frisian (West Germanic), Danish (North Germanic), and Sorbian (Slavic). A map by Bennet Schulte shows areas that had more than 5% speakers of languages other than German in 1900 (https://de.wikipedia.org/wiki/Deutsches_Kaiserreich#/media/File:Sprachen_-Deutsches_Reich_1900.png). The appearance of many of these populations naturally reflects the broad borders of the Reich at that time (they encompassed areas that are now in Poland, France, and so on), but we also see the presence of immigrant Polish speakers in the west. On a now widespread current view, it is no accident that people tend to forget about the presence of these languages. In

---

[18] Schirmunski (1930: 118) has insightful discussions of what features survive in these kinds of settings; see especially his obsevations on 'primary' vs. 'secondary' dialect features, where the former are more local and the latter more regional. Primary features, he argues, tend to be replaced, while secondary ones persist.

some sense, they have been 'invisibilized', in contrast to the highly visible language(s) used in writing and education, for instance, in this case mostly Standard German.

Sociolects: Kiezdeutsch.[19] We've focused overwhelmingly on regional variation and standard language throughout this book, but social groups also develop specific varieties. Some, like student language, have proven relatively stable over long periods of time, though they dwell in remarkably specific niches. As just noted, the late 20th century brought large immigration to Germany from Turkey and many other places, especially to urban areas. While early linguistic interest in these communities focused on the acquisition of German, including educational challenges and loss/maintenance of native tongues, these areas have now begun to develop distinct patterns of speech, known now as *Kiezdeutsch*, shared not only by immigrant children but by co-territorial children whose families have long been German. *Kiez* means roughly the same as contemporary American English *'hood*. While such varieties are still nascent and may prove to be transitional, Wiese (2009, 2012, 2013), Wiese et al. (2009), and others have been able to identify clear structural characteristics, with similar work being done in similar settings across western and northern Europe.[20]

The patterns found are consistent with what we expect in settings of complex language contact. They include some lexical borrowings, like Turkish *lan* 'man, guy (with pejorative connotations)'. Structural features often parallel developments in other varieties of German, such as coronalization of [ç] to [ɕ] (see the first section of this chapter). Like in other contact settings, speakers appear to show some morphological reductions (like the schwa-less *mein Schwester*) and non-adherence to V2 (*morgen ich geh...*). At the same time, Wiese (2009) shows that Kiezdeutsch includes complex innovations, like the development of new particles *musstu* (from *mußt du*) and *lassma* (from *lass uns mal*), both now sentence-initial particles introducing directives: '*musstu* is speaker-exclusive and indicates a suggestion to the hearer (using *p* as some action: "You should do p."/"You have to do p in order to achieve your goal."), while *lassma* is speaker-inclusive and introduces a proposal for an action performed by speaker and hearer(s) ("Let us do p")' (2009: 799):

musstu lampe reinmachen
you have to put a lamp in.

---

[19] The first major work on this area in English, to my knowledge, is Stevenson (2017), focusing on Berlin as a multilingual city; this work appeared too late to be treated here. Kern (2015) provides a brief and accessible overview of the 'Turkish German' in English.

[20] This is also the relatively uncommon situation where scholarly linguistic research draws the attention of the popular press; see here: http://www.welt.de/kultur/article12538546/Sprichst-Du-Kiezdeutsch-Abu-gib-mal-Handy.html.

As Wiese shows, these patterns have strong affinity to longstanding colloquial patterns of usage, like verb-initial structures of the type *musst du einfach mal hingehen* 'you just have to go there some time'. Kiezdeutsch then shows deeper connections to German than may be obvious to many (including in the media), and the overall characteristics look very consistent with what we find under similar contact settings elsewhere.

One of the most important books about language in Germany in recent years, Heike Wiese's (2012) *Kiezdeutsch: Ein neuer Dialekt entsteht*, develops this line of thought, revealing its main argument in the subtitle (see also Wiese 2013 and other work by her and co-authors). German, like any living language, continues to develop, including through the creation of new social and other varieties. Kiezdeutsch is just such a developing variety; and for this reason it is 'typically German' in its structural patterns thoroughly and prototypically German. More detailed comparison to established German dialects over the course of the book drives this idea home:

- Kiezdeutsch is not 'broken German' any more than Swabian is a failed attempt to speak Standard German.
- Kiezdeutsch is no more a reflection of 'insufficient intregration' into German society than Bavarian. Speakers of both have those varieties as part of a broader repertoire.
- Kiezdeutsch is no more of a threat to German than Saxon or any other traditional dialect.

The ultimate conclusion is on the mark linguistically, and it is a socially important conclusion for German society today: Kiezdeutsch is a *sprachliche Bereichung* (linguistic enrichment).

Modern norms. Germany never really established a language academy or commission—like France, Italy, Spain, Iceland, and so on, but instead has accepted the norm established by one publisher as authoritative.[21] Let us now look at the person behind that modern authority briefly, Konrad Duden (see Figure 7.6).

Over time, a kind of consensus slowly developed around many features that we find in the modern language today. Consider the ways of spelling long vowels (drawing here on von Polenz 1994: 246 ff.). During the 16th century, East Central German printers abandoned the use of diacritics for length, and during the 17th, we see the development of modern spellings for this feature, such as an <h> after the vowel (*Höhle, stehlen*, etc.), as well as the use of <e> after <i> to mark length—in forms where MHG had a diphthong, like *hier*,

---

[21] There were such efforts, including the *Berliner Akademie* in the late 17th century, aimed at protecting the German language, but conducting business in French.

FIGURE 7.6 Konrad Duden statue, Bad Hersfeld.

Bier, etc., but also in words like *Riese*, cf. MHG *rise*. The percentage of spellings matching modern norms rises from 56.7% in 1569 to 76% in 1626 and then 92.2% by 1694. Some other features, like the capitalization of nouns, were established somewhat earlier (see von Polenz 1994: 248 for discussion and references).

Konrad Duden (1829–1911) published an orthographic guide in 1880 and by 1903 this was accepted as defining Standard German. Russ (1994: 5) writes that '... the authority of Duden as representing the orthographic norm for German has been extended, by unofficial implication, to other areas of language such as grammar and word formation, although Duden is at pains to deny this.' (See also Sauer 1988 for an extensive history of Duden.)

Unlike more narrowly prescriptive grammar traditions in some countries, and even in the earlier history of German, *Duden*[22] has a refreshingly descriptive tone on many points (but see Langer 2007). Take these two examples, first case use with 'wegen' from *Duden*'s *Zweifelsfälle* (but note changes in the *Duden Grammatik* discussed earlier in this chapter):

---

[22] *Duden* here refers not to the person, but rather to the multi-volume collection of reference works on the language now updated and edited by a small army of professionals.

1. **Kasus** (*wegen des Hundes/wegen dem Hund · wegen Umbaus/wegen Umbau...*):
Nach der Präposition 'wegen' steht hochsprachlich der Genitiv: *wegen des schlechten Wetters, wegen Mangels an Beweisen....* Umgangssprachlich und landschaftlich wird 'wegen' häufig mit dem Dativ verbunden: *wegen dem Hund fuhr er nicht in Urlaub....* Dieser Gebrauch gilt nicht als korrekt. Dagegen wird 'wegen' bei stark gebeugten Substantiven im Plural auch hochsprachlich mit dem Dativ verbunden, wenn der Genitiv formal nicht zu erkennen ist: Wegen Geschäften verreist sein.... Steht nach 'wegen' ein stark zu beugendes Substantiv im Singular ohne Artikel und ohne Attribut, dann wird in der Alltagssprache die Genitivendung häufig weggelassen: Wegen Umbau (statt: wegen Umbaus).... Tritt die Präposition 'wegen' zu einem Personalpronomen, dann werden die Zusammensetzungen *meinetwegen, deinetwegen...* gebraucht. 'Wegen mir', 'wegen uns', usw. gelten als umgangssprachlich. 'Wegen meiner' ist veraltet und kommt nur noch landschaftlich vor (Bayern, Schwaben, Niederrhein).

While *Duden* clearly insists on genitive in most instances for the standard, the authors readily note the colloquial pattern, and yield much of the gray zone here to the dative forms. Note especially how many shades of register are distinguished here.

Even less prescriptive is the treatment of our second example, *brauchen* + infinitive with or without *zu*:

In der Alltagssprache—weniger in der geschriebenen als in der gesprochenen—wird das 'zu' vor dem Infinitiv oft weggelassen. Diese scheinbare Nachlässigkeit ist in Wirklichkeit das Zeichen einer sprachlichen Entwicklung. Denn 'brauchen' schließt sich damit an die Reihe der Modalverben...an.... Die Verwendung von 'brauchen' mit dem reinen Infinitiv wird auch heute noch von vielen als umgangssprachlich angesehen und gilt besonders in der Schule als nicht korrekt.... Wer aber die oben angedeuteten Zusammenhänge beachtet... wird erkennen, daß hier eine Entwicklung im Gange ist, die auf die Dauer nicht unterbunden werden kann. Es ist daher eine gewisse Toleranz gegenüber dem reinen Infinitiv angebracht, wenigstens für den außerschulischen Bereich.

Finally, keep in mind that what particular linguistic structures are sanctioned or not sanctioned is really socially and politically determined, and has nothing to do with linguistic structure per se. Consider negative concord (traditionally called 'double negation'). This is a truly ancient pattern across Germanic and widely used in older literature (i.e. *Belletristik*); today it is surely one of the most harshly condemned syntactic structures in English in the UK and North America. Still, the construction is alive and well in virtually all vernacular varieties of English. In many other languages (like in Slavic ones), multiple negation is firmly established in even formal standard language. German on this point takes an intermediate position: it remains common in dialects, to an extent in colloquial speech, and it survived long in the literary language (examples from Lockwood 1968: 210–211):

... nirgends war keine Seele zu sehen (Goethe)
... das disputiert ihm niemand nicht (Schiller)

Even today, this construction does not seem to be subject to the constant and salient disdain that it carries in English.

Davies & Langer (2006: 241–260) provide a detailed survey of such forms over time, showing that until the 1750s the construction served simply to emphasize a negative interpretation, without stigma. After that, they point to increasingly sharp condemnations of negative concord as 'lower-class language', while in the 20th century we find a 'unanimous verdict by grammarians that poly-negation is non-standard', though that position has eased in some recent works, including *Duden*.

Vorbilder, linguistic models to be followed, have historically played a role in determining what's 'good German'. If the usage of Goethe and Schiller were enough to define 'good German', then negative concord would be fine usage today. Nonetheless, of course, most of us do not use these constructions regularly and we don't teach them to our students in beginning classes.

Standardization of pronunciation. The standardization of spoken German pronunciation lagged far behind the regularization of spelling, vocabulary and grammar in most respects. The central figure in this process, in some respects, is Theodor Siebs.[23]

Consider this quote from the 'Vorwort zur amerikanischen Ausgabe' of Siebs *Deutsche Bühnenaussprache—Hochsprache* (1944):

Martin Luther schuf die 'neuhochdeutsche Schriftsprache', indem er die sächsische Kanzleisprache mit dem lebendigen Wortschatz seiner heimatlichen Mundart erfüllte.... Erst die Klassiker des 18. Jahrhunderts schreiben die gleiche Sprache, ob sie Schwaben, Franken, Preußen oder Oesterreicher sind.

Aber sie schreiben sie nur. Luther sprach weiter seine mansfeldische Mundart; der unreine Reim *Waffen—betroffen* in der Hymne 'Ein' feste Burg ist unser Gott' ist nur dadurch zu erklären, daß er eben *Woffen* hörte und sprach. Schiller schwäbelte; er sagte: *meischterhaft* und *so ischt's recht*. Grillparzer sprach wienerisch. Sogar Goethe konnte sich zeitlebens von seinem Frankfurter Dialekt, der ihn *neige* und *Schmerzensreiche* reimen läßt, nicht freimachen....

In diesem Babel wollte trotzdem die Frage nach dem richtigen, dem 'besten' Deutsch nicht verstummen, und tatsächlich kam bald diese, bald jene Landschaft in den Ruf der Musteraussprache. Wie Hannover dieser Ehre teilhaftig wurde, ist nicht ganz erfindlich.

So, Luther pronounced the /a/ of *Waffen* as a rounded vowel, and Goethe produced intervocalic /g/ as a fricative. Both these forms and many similar ones are widely used today, but marked as non-standard.

The contemporary view of the development of the standard language is profoundly different on many counts from that—in terms of Luther's role, the importance given to classical literature, and implied negative reaction to

---

[23] You can hear Siebs pronouncing some words and giving advice on pronunciation generally here: http://www.humboldt-forum.de/objekt/?month=200507.

linguistic variation ('Babel'). And here we can see dramatic examples of how people's language attitudes differed from their own behavior: Goethe did indeed have clear regional rhymes, but he also wrote *Regeln für Schauspieler*, intended to free them from 'allen Fehlern des Dialekts', where he prescribes pronunciation patterns that he didn't have and which are not part of the modern language, like that there should be no *Auslautverhärtung* or final fortition (Mihm 2004: 178, and see §5.2.3).

While final fortition becomes part of the modern standard—and it is something many native speakers of German have trouble overcoming in English—Siebs and some other pronunciation guides give us some surprising advice (single quote mark = aspiration), as already noted (1944 edition; with an apostrophe representing aspiration) above:

p. 79: Der gutterale stimmlose Verschlußlaut k ist stets gehaucht zu sprechen, z.B. K'ind, Ack'er, Lak'en, Dreck', Spuk'.

The guttural [velar] voiceless stop k is always to be pronounced aspiration, for example. *K'ind, Ack'er, Lak'en, Dreck', Spuk'*.

German speakers certainly can and often do release final stops in this way, but it's hardly a consistent feature of even careful speech. But the amazing thing is that this extends even to s + stop clusters, such as *St'adt'* on p. 78. To my knowledge, no variety of German as spoken natively shows this pattern. Aspiration of stops after *s* is extremely rare in the world's languages (but found in Sanskrit and Ancient Greek), even though a huge number of languages have aspirated stops.

How prescriptively and aesthetically oriented Siebs was becomes very clear at times:

p. 82: Man hüte sich Schlag, Tag wie Schlack, Tack zu sprechen—hierzu neigen besonders die Schlesier; auch die allzu schwache Aussprache des auslautenden g nach langen Vokalen, wie sie in süddeutschen Gegenden üblich ist, muß vermieden werden. Vor allem aber beachte man, daß keine Reibelaute ... gesprochen werden dürfen: nicht Tach ...; sonst entsteht jener häßliche, leider selbst auf guten Bühnen im ernsten Drama vorkommende Zwiespalt, wie er auf Seite 4 gerügt worden ist.

One should take care to pronounce *Schlag, Tag as Schlack, Tack*—especially the Silesians tend to this; also the all too weak pronunciation of the final *g* after long vowels, as is usual in southern German regions, must be avoided. But above all one should pay attention that no fricatives ... may be pronounced here: not *Tach* ...; otherwise that ugly split arises, unfortunately even on good stages during serious drama, as was criticized on p. 4.

At the outset of the book (p. 4), he calls variation between [g] and [x] 'für den feiner Empfindenen unerträglich'. And, as we'll discuss, the resolution of particular points of standard pronunciation often hinged on such questions of taste.

An excellent case study of when *g* is to be pronounced as [k] (like in *Tag)* versus [ç] (as in *mächtig* or *König*) is presented in Orrin Robinson's *Whose German?*

Attitudes. Much sociolinguistic work aims at capturing structural variation and change of the sort discussed in this chapter, but attitudes toward language are important and they too change over time. In the last chapter, I noted that the speech of the East Central region (such as that of Upper Saxony) was regarded by many as a model for developing the modern standard. It was praised specifically for its pleasant sound. As Hollmach (2009) shows, the reputation of *Sächsisch* within Germany has suffered over time. In a survey asking Germans which broad regional dialects they found most or least likable (i.e. *sympathisch, unsympathisch*), the East Central area fares worst, by quite a margin and the southeast fares the best, as shown in Figure 7.8. Similar but far more detailed findings are presented in Gärtig et al. (2010), where North German speech is judged the most likable, above Bavarian, and Saxon the least likable. Unsurprisingly they find that respondents tended to judge their own regional varieties more positively. In general, regional- or dialect-colored speech was rated as likable or very likable by almost two-thirds.

Gärtig and her colleagues provide a remarkable catalogue of language attitudes, from showing that people consider attention to spelling rules (*Rechtschreibung*) to be virtually as important as the care paid to speaking or writing (2010: 171–178) for evaluating the German skills of non-native speakers (over 55% 'good' and almost a further quarter 'very good', 2010: 240). In the context of multilingualism and migration, their results for the likability of different foreign accents are notable; they are partially reproduced in the two graphs in Figure 7.7. (2010: 244, 247).

Familiar languages from European countries nearby are rated most likable: French, Italian, English. (Note that 'American' is rated far lower than 'English'.) Least likable are the languages spoken by large groups of recent arrivals: Russian, Turkish, Polish, followed at some distance by 'American'.

The role of the media in language change? The quote from Hoberg at the beginning of this chapter shows that many Germans blame television—along with texting and email and so on—for the decline of the quality of German used by young people. Internationally, the view is widespread among non-specialists that the broadcast media are influencing how we speak. Serious research to systematically investigate whether this is true or how it would work is only now beginning. It is widely claimed by North American sociolinguists that only superficial features, like words or expressions, are prone to transmission in this way, while fundamental structure of languages are picked up during acquisition and/or through face-to-face contact (Labov 2001). Let us look at one attempt to connect language change in Austrian German with television.

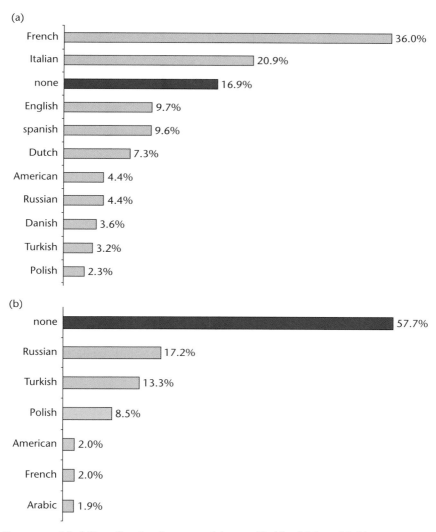

FIGURE 7.7 Likability of regional accents: (a) most likable; (b) least likable.

Muhr devotes an article to 'media-induced language change in Austrian German (AG) which is caused by language contact with German German (GG) as presented in television programs broadcast via satellite' (2003: 103). Muhr presents much evidence for a recent and sharp increase in viewing of broadcasting from Germany especially among Austrian youth. He then shows that a number of features of German German increased in usage among young

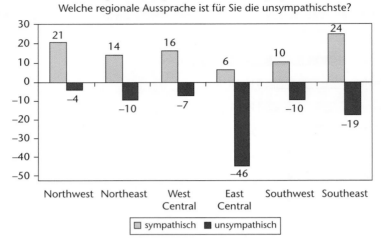

Welche regionale Aussprache ist für Sie die sympathischste?
Welche regionale Aussprache ist für Sie die unsympathischste?

FIGURE 7.8 Likability of regional accents, after Hollmach.

Austrians in the same period, such as more frequent occurrence of the modal particle *mal*, where Austrian German has *einmal* and other examples like these, where the Austrian form appears to be receding while the German appears to be spreading:

Austrian form	German form	
jmd pflanzen	jmd verarschen	'to ridicule somebody'
Verkühlung	Erkältung	'cold', noun
in der Früh,	morgens,	'in the morning'
die Früh	am Morgen	

Recall our discussion in Chapter 6 about variation between *haben* and *sein* as auxiliaries for the perfect. These appear to be changing in Austria and he sees the increased usage of auxiliary verb *haben* compared to *sein* with a set of verbs: Austrian German uses the former with present perfects of *sitzen, liegen, stehen* and a few other verbs. He asserts that constructions like *hat gestanden* are displacing these increasingly in Austria. He attributes all this to the 'prestige' of media from Germany, which leads to the restriction of traditional Austrian forms to 'the spoken language of the older generation, socially powerless groups and/or regional varieties' (2003: 124).

Muhr certainly shows a clear correlation: broadcasting from Germany has increased at about the same time as linguistic features from Germany among a population that watches a lot of television. Unfortunately, there is no rigorous way to make the leap from correlation to actual causation.

As tempting as German German influence is here, it is thoroughly possible that it plays only a minor role in a far more complex set of factors. For the most promising effort at overcoming this thorny issue, see Stuart-Smith (2014).

Appeals to prestige are classic moves in explaining language change, such as Bonfante's (1947: 357) stark claim:

The main factor in the triumph of a language or of a linguistic innovation (which is the same thing) is its prestige. This is not only military, political, or commercial; it is also, and much more, literary, artistic, religious, philosophical.

However, as already noted earlier, Milroy (1992a, 1992b) and others have shown for various cases that the notion of 'prestige' collapses on closer analysis. We may adopt forms because we hear them from people we want to be like, for instance, but we lack rigorous empirical demonstration that political or artistic prestige leads us to adopt different forms, such as *hat gestanden* over *ist gestanden*.

That is, if we are to establish media influence on spoken German, we will need a more nuanced account of what's going on; and, since Muhr's article, such work has begun. Specifically with regard to television, Stuart-Smith (2007: 141) considers that the traditional view in the English-speaking world is that television is able 'to influence systemic language change, but indirectly through changes in attitudes toward linguistic varieties'. In contrast, in the German-speaking world, scholars have tended to take it as uncontroversial that the media have real influence on language, even as an agent of change. Stuart-Smith notes that Brandt (2000: 2164) declares broadcast media influence to be 'uncontroversial' (*unumstritten*). It is easy to read into Brandt's work some discomfort with media influence (on language and elsewhere), but he ultimately concedes that concrete proof of real effects runs into great difficulties (*stößt... auf erhebliche Schwierigkeiten*). So what does the evidence really show?

On the one hand, in the American context, many of the most influential statements about media influence are concerned less with whether viewers adopt pronunciation features from broadcast media than with whether media are leading to a loss of linguistic diversity. Labov & Ash (1997: 508) regard one 'main finding' of their broader research on this point as expressly counterintuitive—a finding that 'violates the most commonsense expectation of how language works and is supposed to work':

In spite of the intense exposure of the American population to a national media with a convergent network standard of pronunciation, sound change continues actively in all urban dialects that have been studied, so that the local accents of Boston, New York, Philadelphia, Atlanta, Buffalo, Detroit, Chicago, and San Francisco are more different from each other than at any time in the past.

On the basis of current evidence this claim seems uncontroversially true, but leaves untouched whether we might adopt certain forms or features from the media beyond catchphrases and new vocabulary. In contrast, Androutsopoulos (2014: 13) observes that German research (using Holly & Püschel 1993 as his example) 'casts the net widely [sic]: television influence encompasses here standardization (in the sense of dialect leveling), an impact on language attitudes, and the spread of neologisms and vogue words.'

While the two traditions have to a large extent been asking different questions, key work on English by Stuart-Smith (2014, with references to earlier works) has shown clearly that Glasgow speakers who follow the TV show *East Enders* are in fact adopting pronunciations typical of that show but very foreign to Glasgow, including *th*-fronting, *think* > [f]*ink* mentioned early in this book in another context (p. 90).

The key result emerging from this body of work is that the relationship between structural language change and media—in matters that go beyond vocabulary and catchphrases—is real but very indirect, and far more so than people think.

7.6 Vocabulary: fear of an Anglophone planet

Anxieties about the future of German abound today, and we can note two varieties here, one about the displacement of German from international usage and even in certain domains within Germany and the other about the use of English loanwords in German.[24]

On the first point, consider once more the quote from Hoberg (2009: 155) at the beginning of the chapter about the widespread fear among Germans today that their language is in decline. The quoted passage followed the phrase 'zum Einen', and he actually laid out two major concerns, here now the second:

Zum anderen macht man sich Sorgen um den englischen Einfluss, darüber dass immer mehr Anglizismen ins Deutsche eindringen und die deutsche Sprache durch die englische immer stärker verdrängt wird, nicht nur beim Fremdsprachenlernen im Ausland, sondern auch im Inland. Man fürchtet, dass vieles von dem, was die deutsche Sprache auszeichnet, verloren geht.

On the first point, Hoberg concludes, as noted, that German is not actually going to hell in a handbasket, but on the second (and see Hoberg 2004 for additional discussion), he is far less optimistic. His immediate concern is not that of lexical borrowings (on which more in a moment), but of the loss of

---

[24] In keeping with the discussions of vocabulary throughout, this section is brief but there's a massive literature for those interested. Glahn (2002) and Onysko (2007) are two places to start.

German as a language of international science and scholarship, that the domains of usage of English are displacing German. Such fears are remarkably widespread among certain groups of German academics. Meyer (2004) entitles an essay 'Global English—A new lingua franca or a new imperial culture?', concluding this (2004: 82):

It is not the bizarre mixture of German and English into so-called 'Denglish' that really threatens the future of German. It is the wide-spread contempt for our own mother tongue which makes us an object of scientific curiosity.... Nobody can predict the further course of history and of course I do not want to accept that German is seriously endangered. But if the rise of English to the position of the leading language in the emerging global society should seal the fate of German as the language of a living culture, this would not be the fault of the Americans or of the English-speaking world. It would be a self-inflicted tragedy.

Other scholars are far blunter, like Braselmann (2004), who talks at length about 'the "killer language" English', without any discernible irony, concluding about 'the American Virus' that in western Europe 'the "allergy" to English is pronounced; it is the single linguistic and cultural "enemy"' (2004: 112). To be clear, English has displaced, or is rapidly displacing, many languages around the world, but German is surely not one of them, in any of the relevant senses. The term 'killer language' is in fact widely attributed to Anne Pakir (who apparently did use it in print; see Mühlhäusler 2002: 20); it is a term similar to what Mühlhäusler calls 'imperial languages'—languages 'such as Mandarin, Spanish, French, and Indonesian'. This notion is predicated on connections between nationhood and a single language. Mühlhäusler traces the phenomenon to France, 'where the idea of central government was shaped by the insistence on having one language spoken by everyone in the nation'. The term hardly fits, then, the relationship between English and German.

Tensions between German and 'alien' tongues of course go back to the beginnings of German and far beyond: Indo-European was surely a killer language in prehistoric western Europe (see the contributions to Olsen et al. 2015). Though the basis of the new culture was necessarily Latin, Charles understood the value of local institutions and of the native language' (Bostock 1976: 116). Clearly, for centuries German was not the language of writing, nor the language of religious and political institutions. We have seen a succession of 'killer languages'—or rather 'killer cultures', since languages in and of themselves are relatively harmless in this sense—and the influence of English will surely wane in the future, perhaps far faster than that of Latin has.[25] Suffice it to say

---

[25] The languages actually being displaced by English are co-territorial ones, such as the indigenous languages across the United States. Close parallels make clear that it's not something about English that leads to such displacement; see situations with Spanish and Portuguese in the

that compared to half the world's languages which are thought to be on the verge of extinction today, German's future does not seem in doubt.

The second concern, English loanwords and the creation of a bastardized *Denglisch*, is much more the domain of popular writers. (For older but accessible scholarly overviews, see von Polenz 1999: 391–412 or Clyne 1984.)These concerns have certainly intensified in the last half century, but are hardly new, like this example from 1897:

- Sagt man noch Déjeuner a la fourchette?
- Kaum, Papa. Wie du weißt, es ist jetzt alles englisch.

Theodor Fontane, *Der Stechlin* (quoted by Hoberg 2000: 306)

In fact, English borrowings go back a long way, and American borrowings (some but not all directly from English) come in as soon as German-speaking people learned of the western hemisphere, both points illustrated with these examples, given with earliest known date of attestation:

From the so-called 'new world' (Palmer 1939):

Yam	1534
Batate	1534 'potato'
Moskito	1575
Hickory	1697
Skalp	1735
Yankee	1792
Rancho	1809
Prärie	1826

From England (Ganz 1957):

die Jury	18th c.
der Clerk	18th c.
der Farmer	18th c. (but marginal until 19th c. < America)

But it is the post-World War II era that has provoked great fears about English. Websites like http://www.kauderwelschseite.de/ and that of the Verein Deutsche Sprache http://www.vds-ev.de/are good examples. The former advertises itself this way:

Denglisch breitet sich in Deutschland, Österreich und der Schweiz immer weiter aus. Diese Seiten wenden sich gegen den unnötigen Gebrauch von Anglizismen in der deutschen Sprache.

Americas, French in West Africa, and minority languages of Russia and China. For a grounded treatment of English as an international language today, see Kachru et al. (2006).

The latter announced 'Wir schätzen unsere deutsche Muttersprache, die "Orgel unter den Sprachen", wie Jean Paul sie nannte' and the VDS has as its goal German 'als eigenständige Kultur- und Wissenschaftssprache zu erhalten und vor dem Verdrängen durch das Englische zu schützen' (October 9, 2009). Later (February 1, 2012), the campaign turned to *Fetzenliteratur*, like tweets and text messages, leading to this conclusion:

'Jeder Journalist, jeder Lehrer und jeder Sprachwissenschaftler weiß, dass die Sprachkompetenz in Deutschland in den vergangenen Jahrzehnten nachgelassen hat', sagte der Vorsitzende des VDS, Professor Walter Krämer.

We've noted through the previous chapters the existence of mixed-language Latin-Old High German texts (Chapter 4) and high rates of French loanwords in use in the early modern period (Chapter 6), and a count of word histories in an English dictionary will show a remarkable percentage of words of Romance origin. Controversy over borrowing, too, then, turns out not to be a new topic in German culture, even if it bubbles through highbrow strata of German society: one of Germany's leading newspapers, *Die Zeit*, ran a long article called 'Ist Deutsch noch zu retten?' in July of 2010, and see now Eisenberg (2013) for a leading linguist's view of Anglicisms.

In the longer view, these are variations on an old theme. Like in so many other cases, a historical perspective turns out to be a valuable one.

7.7 Conclusion

We see here a *bunte Mischung* with regard to syntactic changes and prescriptive approval in contemporary German. Just consider a few of the syntactic and pragmatic patterns we've treated in this chapter.

Wenn-Sätze were never *würde-los* and prescriptivists seem to have abandoned the battle. They've had more success at suppressing *tun* + infinitive in formal writing. In terms of word order, the establishment of verb-final order, even in printed texts, proves to have come to completion later and in more complex ways than scholars believed not that many years ago.

In many other cases, robust change is going on, often along the lines described as grammaticalization. The construction *am Xen sein* has come to take a place in expressing durativity, without a strong reaction, e.g. from Duden. A relatively new modal, *brauchen*, appears to be arising long after the system might have seemed stable, and whole new categories have come to be increasingly encoded grammatically, like evidentiality and politeness.

The most important pattern we've seen may be a caveat, how careful we have to be in assuming that a pattern has changed, whether [ɪ] to [ʏ] is a recent development, how new complementizer agreement is and how much of the modal behavior of *brauchen* is contemporary. In the last example, *weil*, even if it's not a modern innovation, it has firmly established itself in spoken usage, as part of a broader pattern.

Sociolinguistically, we now have a more firmly established standard language as a point of reference and in some sense as a native tongue for many speakers, with potential implications for language change. Some regional dialects are changing dramatically, even disappearing, but we have evidence for the rise of new regional patterns, often as *Umgangssprache* rather than traditional dialect.

At the same time, attitudes remain volatile, of course, whether with regard to the aesthetic value of particular regional dialects or which alien language is regarded as currently the most immediate threat to the future of German. But while the characters have changed, the basic storyline has not.

In large part, this chapter has begun to probe the seam that runs between historical linguistics in one traditional sense (in particular the study of earlier forms of language) and the new field of language change in progress. Even more than in the material covered in earlier chapters, the opportunities for immediate research progress in the recent history of German are immense and readily realizable.

8

Conclusion

Interpreting the significance of the past for us

8.0 Introduction

At the outset, I expressed the goal that through the course of this book, a reader should have the chance to understand contemporary German in new ways by learning something of the language's history. I hope to have delivered on that, from what history shows us about the basic characteristics of German dialects to the vagaries of how 'Standard German' came to be the Frankenstein's monster it is today, assembled from different regional, historical, and stylistic parts, with made-up-out-of-thin-air rules thrown in for good measure. You have now seen how the kinds of wrinkles and exceptions Mark Twain once complained about arose and survived. You now know that they often form part of some formerly highly regular system, like the beautiful regularity of ablaut in early Germanic. In other examples, the messiness reflects some still-emerging system, like the increasingly semantic basis of gender assignment. And the repeated rounds of borrowings from and contact with other languages still echo today in the final pages of the previous chapter.

Let us close by drawing together some of the threads we've woven in throughout the book. The first is one last reminder of what the past can tell us about the present. The second is a note about some of the overarching patterns we observe in the wide-lens view of the history of German and Germanic. The third is a note on how linguistic theories have helped us advance our understanding of the historical development of German and how I have understood theory in writing this book.

8.1 Historical developments on today's map

To the first point, you are now familiar with the basic map of German dialects. The first paragraph of Chapter 1 noted that a group of economists (Falck et al. 2010) have argued that 'language variation is probably the best measurable

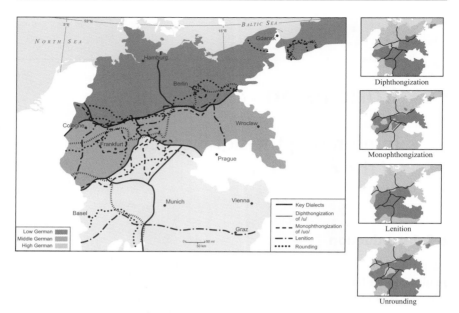

MAP 23 Key isoglosses in Modern German dialects.
Adapted from König et al. (2015: 230–231).

indicator of cultural differences'. And the basic dialect map (see Map 23) surely shows some clear examples of 'history scattered across a map', most obviously perhaps political history in the linguistic boundaries or the many *Sprachinseln* scattered across the east (many of which are now gone).

You know the most basic dialectal divisions are some of the most familiar historical features of the language. This begins of course with the Second Sound Shift, used to encode the fundamental splits between Low, Middle, and High German dialects. At the same time, we've followed more recent areal patterns like these, shown in Map 23:

- Lenition
- Syncope and apocope
- Monophthongization and diphthongization
- Unrounding.

You have in the course of the book seen maps of all those features and more, and each feature is a historical development we've treated. Together they provide a good set of diagnostics for contemporary dialects. This alone is enough to identify many dialect samples with some accuracy.

At the same time, in other cases—illustrated on the clickable dialect map at historyofgerman.net—we see dialectal extensions of familiar patterns. For instance, in our discussion of Middle High German sound changes, we briefly treated the shibilization, or change from /s/ to /ʃ/, in clusters with another consonant in word-initial position—*sp-*, *st-*, *sl-*, *sr-*, etc. You'll recall that the change appears to have spread from shibilization before *l* to gradually involve more and more sounds, and it eventually generalized beyond initial clusters as well. The map shows across the Southwest the *fest/fescht* boundary, which delineates the areas that carried the shibilization of /st/ clusters beyond word-initial position. We have seen repeatedly how sound changes begin very locally and get generalized further and further over time and space.

Similarly, we noted nasal loss with compensatory lengthening as a process back in Chapter 3, with a note that English shows the pattern broadly (*fünf* ≠ *five*, *Mund* ≠ *mouth*, *Gans* ≠ *goose*). The geographical pattern is complex, obviously. The northwest area is likely related to the English process—as part of an ancient grouping of coastal dialects—and the northeastern area includes many colonists from that area. The Alemannic area was an independent parallel development.

History also anchors our understanding of German regional morphology and syntax. Especially in the north, but across many areas, we find case

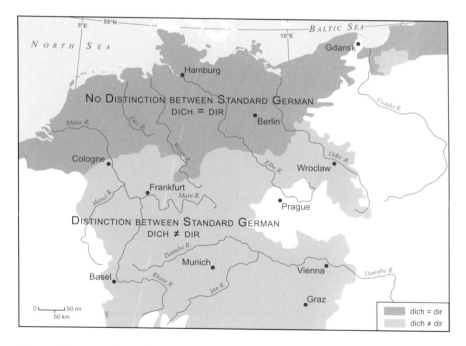

MAP 24 Retention/loss of dative/accusative distinction, illustrated by the 2nd person singular pronoun.

Adapted from König et al. (2015: 160).

reductions more extreme than the ongoing retreat of the genitive, such as the merger of dative and accusative. Many dialects have merged the two, as shown in Map 24.

The spread of periphrasis is likewise advanced far beyond the state of the standard language, notably thanks to *Präteritumschwund*. Map 25 indicates the presence of simple past forms (in the north) and the prevalence of preterit-only farther south. The map is a classic one, from Wenker's atlas (see also Sapp 2009), showing the distribution of *kam* versus *ist gekommen*.

The next map, Map 26, redrawn from Sperschneider, gives a more detailed snapshot of how a set of verbs do or do not have simple past forms across Thuringian: the darkened part of the circles reflects the percentage of preterit forms. Instead of a simple isogloss that reflects patterns of one verb, we get an idea of the number of verbs that show simple past forms. Still, our understanding of the regional distribution of syntactic variation and innovation is not yet well developed.

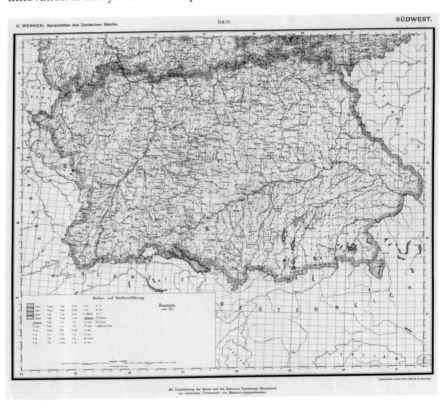

MAP 25 *kam* (northern) vs. *ist gekommen* (southern).

From *Digitaler Wenker-Atlas* (Map 474).

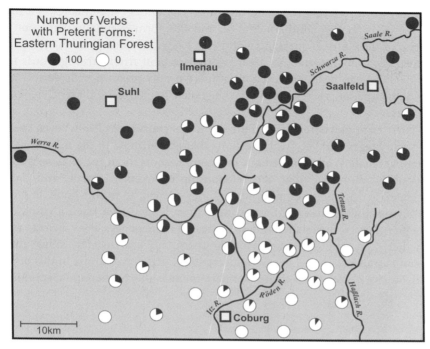

MAP 26 Verbs with preterit forms in the eastern Thuringian forest.
Adapted from Sperschneider (1959: 90–91, Map 18; see also the version in König et al. 2015: 162).

Of course these are hardly the only features that distinguish regional varieties. Speakers often notice and call attention to lexical differences. Maps 27 and 28 show two quite different examples, words for 'to speak' and 'potato'.

In our various if always brief discussions of vocabulary, we have not treated these particular terms but these too are historically instructive. The first map contains a set of words that speakers of the standard language know and use, but with different meanings. *Plaudern* means 'to chat' for speakers of Standard German, but is the default word for 'to speak' for some central German dialects. *Schwätzen* has negative connotations for most speakers, as in 'to prattle, blab, etc.', but neutral ones for speakers in a broad area of the west and southwest. The map then shows some lexical semantic reorganization within the 'field' of verbs for speaking.

While many of the words for 'to speak' have long Germanic and Indo-European histories, 'potato' is a new word, after the plant was brought from the western hemisphere. But we see a rich set of strategies for vocabulary development. The standard word is a borrowing from Italian, *tartuficolo*, from a Latin word referring to a kind of truffle. The initial *t* dissimilates, not first in Germany but in southern France, and this form eventually wins out in much of the German-speaking world (see Kluge's etymology of the term for references). Other terms not treated here are built from existing words for foods, like pear, bean, and even chestnut, typically prefixed with 'earth'. We see similar patterns across Europe, as suggested by *Erdäpfel* and French *pomme de terre*.

These examples barely scratch the surface, of course, and I won't even speak to some bigger and very real questions that are encoded in the maps you've seen: As Sheila Watts pointed out in a conversation about regional variation, specialists all realize that the relationship between 'German' and 'Low German' is extremely complex (something touched on in this book, in fact) but maps obscure many of those complexities. This is true when it comes to whether these varieties should best be treated as languages or as dialects and whether such attitudes have changed, structurally and socially. While they essentially always show Low German territory, maps, even those in this book and on the associated website, variably include the Netherlandic-speaking territories.

8.2 The broad swath of German linguistic history

What we have seen for the history of German holds in many instances for English and Dutch and the rest of the family as well. Like English, many of German's continental cousins and its own constituent dialects show fuller developments of trends we have treated throughout the book. We can even sketch the broad paths of development in the family in those terms (see also Salmons 2016a, Bousquette & Salmons 2017). That is, compared to Proto-Germanic and more so to Indo-European, modern Germanic languages and dialects share characteristics like these:

Phonetics and phonology
- We see chain shifts, in both vowels and consonants, as chronic and defining features of the family itself (Grimm's Law) and dialects (the Second Sound Shift).
- Assimilatory processes are particularly widespread. For instance, all Germanic varieties show conditioned changes in vowel height, and all save Gothic show forms of the regressive vocalic assimilation processes known as umlaut.
- Unstressed vowels are inevitably reduced, even at the earliest stage of attestation, compared to reconstructed ancestors.

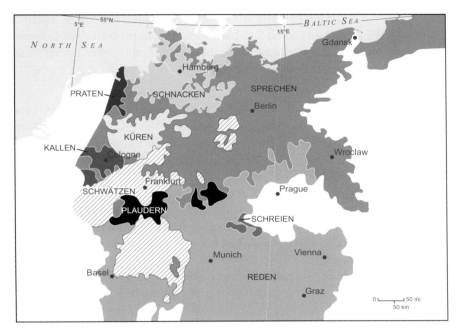

MAP 27 Verbs for 'to speak'.

Adapted from König et al. (2015: 176).

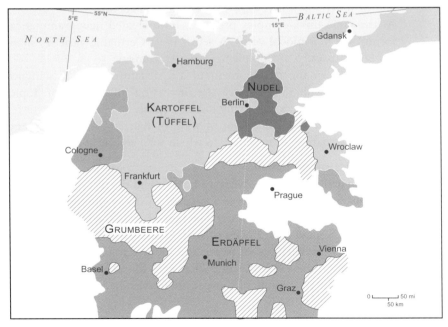

MAP 28 Words for 'potato'.

Adapted from König, et al. (2015: 206).

- We've observed patterns of weight regulation, like Open Syllable Lengthening and Closed Syllable Shortening, in the history of German. Such prosodic patterns are robust across the family, often taking eerily similar forms of development.

Morphology

- Every modern variety of German and Germanic has eliminated some overtly marked morphological categories in the historical period. Even Icelandic, regarded as particularly conservative in its morphology, has seen considerable change, as described in detail in Axelsdóttir (2014).
- At the same time, we see the expansion or solidification of some categories, like plurality on nouns.
- Germanic varieties have expanded sets of 'weak' or dental preterit verbs at the expense of 'strong' or ablauting verbs. Along with such regularization, we also find less common but persistent patterns of irregularization (see p. 384).
- More generally, we see movement from synthetic to analytic, that is, from more morphological marking of grammatical relations to more syntactic marking.

Syntax

- Building on the preceding point, all Germanic languages have increased the use of periphrastic constructions to convey meanings and/or functions which were once marked inflectionally.
- At the same time, complex processes have created new grammatical forms, like new modal verbs. A set of West Germanic varieties share the salient pattern of Complementizer Agreement.
- We have seen the development of V2 structures, and a 'sentence frame', and with that, we see the increasing importance of 'topic' position, though it is essentially lost in English.
- We've watched the emergence of ways of marking definiteness and systematic changes in negation, to which we'll return in a moment.

Sociolinguistics and pragmatics

- Fundamentally, we can see what we know about the history of German and how we know it in terms of a series of 'media revolutions': it began with the advent of runic writing, then moved on to the introduction of Latin writing, and then finally to writing and glossing in indigenous varieties. The availability of paper and the invention of the printing press expand things dramatically, while with sound recording we have fundamentally new kinds of sources, followed now by material of all sorts available online.

- Over time, this means that our sources of evidence have changed dramatically, time and time again, and the question of who is writing and how and why has informed and often restricted what we can and cannot know about language in a given period.
- Across the family, like around the world, the modern era has seen the development of standard varieties, including norms for spelling, pronunciation, etc.
- Along with that, standard language ideology brings efforts to 'protect' languages from 'foreign influence', 'media', 'technology'. Often, much blame goes to 'the youth'.
- We find the rise of colloquial (not always regional) varieties alongside 'dialects', including the innovation of distinctly non-standard forms, or 'standard-divergent' forms.
- How speakers interact using language, e.g. how they show politeness and deference, has changed as well, and continues to.

One of the most promising opportunities we have today is to begin to explore how some of these patterns interact with each other. For instance, we talked briefly in Chapter 5 about possible connections between the loss of inflection and syntactic changes. Finer-grained connections are being productively explored today. Consider two of the morphological phenomena examined throughout the inflectional morphology sections of this whole book: loss of overtly marked categories and consolidation of plural marking. Kürschner & Nübling (2011) establish a typology of Germanic languages in terms of gender and declension, two different criteria by which we can categorize nouns. Chapter 4 described some of the relatively complex ties between gender and declensional class—the $\bar{o}$-stems all feminine, the i-stems masculine or feminine, and at least some nouns of all genders in the n-stem class. In Chapters 5 through 7 we watched steady changes in declension, while all three genders are maintained in Standard German; yet many dialects and other Germanic languages have reduced to two genders or lost morphological gender of this type entirely. The associations have been maintained and reshaped in some varieties or weakened or lost in others, but Kürschner & Nübling (2011: 381) reach a striking conclusion:

Gender is historically less and less marked in the plural paradigms of associated words, but retained in the singular paradigms. Declension, on the other hand, is reduced in the singular and profiled in the plural. Both classification systems are thus used complementarily for number marking.

In Chapter 6 we talked about so-called *Pluralprofilierung*, an increasingly clear marking of plural forms of nouns that draws on old declensional patterns. Kürschner & Nübling's findings suggest that gender has become the main classification system in the singular, declension the main classification system in the plural. These systems are complementary but not completely independent of each other, as we saw in the associations between gender and plural form in §7.2.

At the same time, morphology has been traditionally seen as an area prone to heavy regularization through analogy and to simplification through loss of inflectional categories, along the lines of Sturtevant's Paradox discussed briefly in Chapter 5. Yet throughout this book we have repeatedly seen instances of irregularization. Nübling (2011) argues convincingly against the notion that irregular morphological forms are merely residues that haven't been cleaned up. Yes, as we have seen, sound changes lead to morphological complexity and eventually to pretty irregular looking forms; just recall how simple the early Germanic ablaut series were before sound changes disturbed the patterns. But Nübling shows three other paths to irregularity that have all been illustrated here:

- 'Accelerated sound changes' happen, in other words highly frequent forms can come to show particular patterns of reduction, which split them from originally closely related forms. We saw this in Chapter 5 with the splitting off of the reduced form of *haben*, namely *han* or *hân*.
- Morphological changes themselves can lead to disorder rather than to order, through interference across paradigms. The messiness of developments in the modal verbs discussed in Chapter 6 looks like an example of this.
- Different lexemes can be reassembled as parts of a single paradigm, creating dramatically suppletive forms and patterns. We saw this in the contributions of three IE verbs to Germanic paradigms of 'to be' in Chapter 3.

A full understanding of how irregularization functions and how it interacts with regularization would be most welcome.

All of these features have been central points in this book, both as type and as token. That is, even our relatively superficial introduction to the history of German prepares you for understanding the broader patterns in the Germanic family and in language and language change generally. Just look at how many times the contrast between German and English has been informative: numerous shared sound changes that have unfolded in different ways (umlaut, for instance), instances where English has moved farther along the paths that German takes (loss of morphology, periphrasis), and places where the paths have diverged sharply (basic loss of V2, lack of modal particles, and lack of a formal/informal pronoun distinction in contemporary English).

In fact, these patterns are in many cases characteristic of Indo-European as a whole—Romance languages, Bulgarian (a Slavic language), and Hindi (an Indic one) have all seen case syncretism, for instance. And the patterns are found beyond Indo-European as well. At the same time, some of these features may be more common in western Europe than other parts of the world. McWhorter (2011), for example, notes that in Australian languages and in the Algonquian family, richly inflected morphological systems appear to be have been highly stable for thousands of years.

8.3 The theoretical basis of this book[1]

Textbook histories of a language sometimes pass themselves off, implicitly or explicitly, as atheoretical or theoretically neutral. Any scientific work, though, makes fundamental theoretical assumptions and uses particular theoretical perspectives, methods, and tools. Previous histories of German have often been done within the general framework of structuralism—an approach famously associated with Ferdinand de Saussure, and one that has contributed to our understanding of how the pieces of language fit together, among other areas; but this approach is often problematic when it comes to the relationship between synchrony and diachrony.[2] All histories of languages, I think, draw on other theories and views, such as today an increasingly sociolinguistic orientation. It is inevitable that any detailed treatment of linguistic material will use insights and theories from dialectology, philology, and other perspectives from other disciplines as well: archeology, social history, demography, geography, and so on. So, what theories have actually been used in this book and how? The answer is simple: all that I am familiar with and which I think provide potentially valuable insights into the data and processes we see.[3]

Let us consider linguistic theory in a pretty basic sense. In recent decades, linguistics—and perhaps especially historical linguistics—has been seen as divided between 'formal' (often specifically 'Chomskyan') and 'functional' approaches. The former anchors the study of language in the human cognitive ability to learn and use language, Universal Grammar. On this view, much or

---

[1] The idea for this section came from discussion with Elly van Gelderen, and it follows the model of the last chapter of her 2006 book.

[2] See Weinreich et al. (1968) for a classic account of how synchronic structural theories long hamstrung our understanding of language change.

[3] One of the things that strikes me most as I finish this book is how different and distinct the German-speaking and English-speaking worlds remain in terms of theoretical frameworks. I have tried to bring some of the former to an English-speaking audience in this volume, and also to use insights from the latter to probe German historical developments.

even all of core linguistic change is found in acquisition, how children make different generalizations and build different grammars based on the primary linguistic data they receive (see Lightfoot 1991, 2003, for example). The latter is a very heterogeneous set of approaches, typically focused on how language use (rather than the language faculty) shapes language, or what the broad typological patterns found in human language can tell us about language. In some cases, proponents dismiss or tremendously reduce the role of abstract synchronic structure, like Bybee (2001) for phonology. Today, happily, many scholars anchored in one or the other stream actively pay attention to work in the other. To a surprising extent, analyses across the two are today being made more compatible, and analyses in one are often readily adaptable to the other.

Grammaticalization is a notion which we've drawn on repeatedly here, if somewhat critically in places (Joseph 2003, for instance, recasts the discussion in terms of 'morphologization from syntax'), and it's the topic of a tremendous amount of research in German-speaking Europe today. It has been traditionally rooted in an emphatically functionalist mindset but more recently formally oriented linguists have treated the same phenomena from a different perspective. Let's contextualize briefly how some German facts fit and don't fit with these approaches.

Functionalists have often argued that the 'paths' of development described in grammaticalization are unidirectional. That is, independent words weaken, cliticize, and become inflection, but we never (or in some formulations, ALMOST never) see the reverse direction of change. Along these lines, we have considered most often the path from syntax to morphology. At the same time, recall that in Chapter 4, we saw how OHG authors like Tatian cliticized modal particles onto verbs, as in *seno* or *senu* 'see+now'. This pattern has apparently been lost over time. Just as importantly, many patterns associated with grammaticalization have been remarkably stable over a millennium or more, like the encliticization of subject pronouns of the *haste* 'have+you' type. What this shows, as I understand the data, is that there is not inevitability to movement along this cline. This too is a contested matter: Is language change teleological, moving toward some goal or end, or not? I am not convinced that change serves a purpose, improves anything, or drives toward any goal. (See Luraghi 2010b: 364–366 for more on teleology in language change.) At any rate, I haven't generally contested such points of theory, but have tried to present the patterns found in the data informed by current theory.

My personal view, put dangerously briefly and very informally, is that the functionalist tradition has made important observations about tendencies of language change, observations that historical linguists need to interpret and explain. But I am not convinced, at least yet, that grammaticalization has actual status as a type of language change or that those paths can be unidirectional, in a narrow sense. Instead, the observed patterns seem more likely to be the result of ultimately independent processes that often co-occur: unstressed forms tend to show phonetic reduction, and new generations of learners can interpret those forms eventually as being part of the words they have come to lean on. The effects we call grammaticalization may be, in other words, epiphenomenal.

But for present purposes at least, this hardly means that they are uninteresting or not of value for linguistics. In both Chapters 4 and 7, for instance, we noted apparent 'cycles of renewal', instances where elements that were reduced over time came to be reinforced by new phonetic material—the replacement of *ni* by *nicht*, or the apparent bulking up of neuter *'n* from *ein* to *'nen*. As we saw, *ni* was the typical negative element in OHG, while in MHG it co-occurs with another element, like *niht*, and eventually independent *ni* disappears, leaving *nicht*, *nie*, *niemand*, etc. Van Gelderen (2007, 2011) presents evidence for a whole set of other cycles and analyzes them in Chomskyan terms, concluding that cycles are driven by cognitive features which are part of our linguistic capacity, especially principles of Economy (2011). This is a promising path forward in this area. That is, there may be a fundamental sense in which certain kinds of grammaticalizations are driven by a single mechanism.

One of the reasons we haven't dealt with lexical semantic change in more detail is, in fact, that it seems far less regular than sound change and subject to fewer clear 'rules' of development (see Fortson 2003, and Chapter 5). That said, work in grammaticalization is ultimately rooted in part in efforts to find patterns of semantic change. Sweetser (1990) and many others have observed that the patterns of semantic generalization, often called 'bleaching', help move grammaticalization along: 'to go' may lend itself semantically in some ways to becoming a marker of futurity, as in English *gonna*. The status of bleaching is, though, contentious: along the lines of our discussion in Chapter 5, Fortson (2003: 658; and see now also Urban 2014) finds it to be an overvalued tendency and epiphenomenal, though he of course notes that 'basic metaphorical extensions' are found repeatedly across languages.

An issue treated briefly (in Chapters 3 and 7) was that of 'templates', traditionally used to refer to some kind of abstract structure with set elements, ordering, or length. As Good (2011: 731, also 2016) justifiably quips, this notion is 'often invoked but undertheorized', and its status has indeed been unclear. Aiming to capture the broadest set of patterns possible, he defines the term this way (Good 2016: 7, but see the whole book for intense discussion of the notion):

Template: An analytical device used to characterize the linear realization of a linguistic constituent whose linear stipulations are unexpected from the point of view of a given linguist's approach to linguistic analysis.

This is broadly in line with how I have used the term to talk about various patterns—such as final fortition (a way of marking right edges of words), the shapes of strong verb class membership since OHG, plural forms since ENHG, and also linking elements in NHG. For plurals, German allows many kinds of syllables and feet, but we can consider it surprising that plurals are so overwhelmingly trochaic, with the second syllable a reduced one or 'schwallable'. Good is, however, interested especially in syntactic templates and sees a 'topological' approach to the German clause as one of the 'clearest examples of a class of analyses involving a syntactic template' (2016: 17). The verbal 'frame' we discussed for modern German word order in the last chapter has been expanded by people like Kathol (see Kathol 2000), to a full picture of word order in clauses, including First Position, Second Position, Middlefield, Verb Cluster, and Postverbal Field. Together, these are strikingly unexpected patterns: 'their linearization patterns do not appear to be straightforwardly analyzable in terms of linear ordering constraints on "natural" syntactic classes like subject but, rather, require the use of "unnatural" categories like either finite verb or complementizer' (2016: 18).

The place of templates in most current linguistic theories is still less than fully worked out—what status do they have in a grammar, for instance?—but German is rich in these patterns across its phonology, morphology, and syntax. It may be a fruitful area in the coming years.

The preceding brief discussion suggests, I think, one key to thinking about and maybe beginning to explain language change. It is not only understanding the individual components of grammar, what we usually call 'modules', but understanding how they work together. Especially in changes that require multiple generations to reach completion, the complexity of possible interactions are vast. Pursuing this means following the principle dubbed 'informational maximalism' by Janda & Joseph (2003: 37 and mentioned in ch. 1, above), which they define as 'the utilization of all reasonable means to extend our knowledge'. To understand the examples just treated requires command of not only phonology and morphology and syntax, but also philology (to determine what has been written as separate words versus parts of the same, see Somers Wicka 2009), corpus linguistics (to survey a broad set of data), and instrumental phonetics (to understand how reduction works). We have good tools for all of these, but often less good ways of understanding how these aspects fit together in the bigger picture of change.

Indeed, how the pieces of grammar *sensu lato* fit together is one of the key current themes of linguistic research generally, and in historical linguistics particularly. As noted earlier, these seams between grammatical components are called 'interfaces' (German *Schnittstellen*).[4] We have seen examples throughout the book.[5] Just take the example of umlaut. We introduced it as a directly phonetically motivated pattern, actually an apparently universal pattern: the tendency of vowels produced in different parts of the mouth to assimilate (if only ever so slightly) to vowels in a neighboring syllable: [a] was raised and fronted before /i, j/ in a word like *gasti*. At some point and for reasons we do not yet understand, this grew into a phonological pattern, creating new vowels, like *sc[o:]no* versus *sc[ø:]ni*, which come to contrast with the weakening of final unstressed vowels, and umlaut then becomes a marker of myriad morphological categories and distinctions. The interactions between morphology and syntax are equally tight and equally important, as in the development of periphrastic forms and loss of synthetic/inflectional forms, whatever the actual relationship between such changes may have been. Such chains of change have long been framed in terms of a 'lifecycle of language change' (see Iverson & Salmons 2009 for discussion of Germanic, and now Bermúdez-Otero 2015 and Ramsammy 2015 for more general theoretical perspectives).

It is critical to stress that notions of the life cycle of language change are metaphorical. That is, a life cycle is not necessarily an inevitable or unidirectional path of change—though, again, van Gelderen is today making forceful arguments for a more fundamental way of motivating cyclicity in change. Nor are such changes types or mechanisms of change, rather descriptions of patterns that we often observe and ones which can be helpful in seeing the bigger picture of how small changes ultimately fit together in a full grammatical system.

One of the implications of informational maximalism is that we should avoid false dichotomies. For instance, even today it is easy to find discussions of how to distinguish 'internal' from 'external' factors in language change, that is, to work out what is structural versus what is social. When I took History of the German Language as an introductory course with Edgar Polomé (see the preface), I did not realize how unusual his approach was in seeing these as intimately connected rather than competing factors: all language change has

---

[4] I hasten to note that this is a 'modular' view of grammar, something not everyone accepts.
[5] Within our limited space, though, I have simply not dealt with others. For instance, almost no attention has gone to the relationship between prosody and syntax, save for passing mention. See Betten (1987), Sapp (2011a,) and many earlier works on this.

social and structural aspects. This book tries hard to assemble these as integral pieces of a larger puzzle, woefully incomplete though that effort is.

Think, before we leave the topic, about how surprising the connections can be between the social and the structural. We talked in §7.3 about 'prescriptivism and the struggle over periphrasis', where I noted a prescriptivist and/or standardizer preference for more over less inflected forms. A value-laden, ideological view of morphological inflection goes back a long ways in our field. As Koerner (1995: 213) observes about the beginnings of linguistic typology in the early 19th century (and this includes people like the Schlegels and von Humboldt):

The high degree of fusion of morphological information into single markers, noticed especially in the classical Indo-European languages, Greek, Latin, and Sanskrit, was taken as a sign of linguistic sophistication that was reason enough to accord the so-called 'flectional' or inflective languages the highest point on the evolutionary ladder.

This echoes down to the recent past in scholarship on various languages. Roberge (1990: 140) shows that early discussions about Afrikaans suggest 'widespread insecurity' over its lack of inflectional morphology; he draws comparisons with English, a 'relative' with little inflection: 'Clearly, it was felt to be important that Afrikaans was in acceptable company as concerns the stripping of inflections.' A powerfully ideological association with a purely structural typological characteristic of human language—use of inflectional morphology—took root early and has in some sense not yet been extirpated today.

This goes to another, broader issue, balancing the often invoked problem of 'making the best use of bad data' (Labov 1994: 11) with full exploitation of informational maximalism.[6] Early in my career I heard philology being derided, among other reasons, for being a *'Hilfswissenschaft'* (translatable, less pejoratively, as 'ancillary science'). But philology has now become a hip area of research, thanks in part to fresh connections to and anchoring in various subfields of linguistics, from historical phonology to historical sociolinguistics, both neatly illustrated by Seiler's (2014) study of OHG orthography. At the same time, philology helps us secure a more solid empirical foundation for historical linguistic research. Informational maximalism fundamentally involves using all the available data, even data as tenuous and difficult to interpret as OHG glosses. Schiegg shows that making the most of these particular 'bad' data is more doable and more profitable than it seemed even in the recent past: along the way this attempt yields rich insights into OHG philology, linguistic structure, and sociolinguistics. Rather than out-of-context lexical items serving as cheat sheets for monastic learners, he shows us glosses as

---

[6] This paragraph draws from my review of Schiegg (2015); see Salmons (2016b).

complex and multilayered parts of the texts and contexts where we find them. In terms of language structure, quantitative work on sound change and on morphological changes can be transformed through the inclusion of gloss data; tremendous amounts of sociolinguistic information about reading and teaching cultures can be gleaned from gloss data.

The biggest point of theory in the book, though, is hidden in plain sight: the subtitle of this book implies that diachronic development informs our understanding of synchronic structure. It is valuable not just for language learners and teachers to know the history of a language but for linguists seeking to understand the current structure of that language. Some current approaches, like that of Evolutionary Phonology (Blevins 2004), give history THE central role, as in its central premise (2004: 23) that:

Principled diachronic explanations for sound patterns have priority over competing synchronic explanations unless independent evidence demonstrates, beyond reasonable doubt, that a synchronic account is warranted.

Many others would not go so far and prefer a robust role for both diachrony and synchrony. I would again stress that exploring what those precise roles are and how they fit together is among the most central tasks for not only historical linguistics but linguistics in the broadest sense.

Let us close with one broader point: even the best theory is dependent on a solid empirical basis and reliable analysis of that data. We have seen throughout that theories have been proposed without examining the full available data. Ignoring Netherlandic data on the unfolding of umlaut is such a case and it is clearly fatal to classic American structuralist views of *i*-umlaut. In morphology, we saw repeatedly that quantitative examination of morphological evidence is fundamentally improving how we see OHG, MHG, and ENHG paradigms and inflectional classes. A set of University of Wisconsin graduate students, in working on exactly that issue (Luiten et al. 2013), adopted as an informal motto 'Data is nice'. Such empirical shortcomings undermine some significant arguments made in Natural Morphology in particular—though they do not undermine the value of the theory per se. In the last chapter, we saw a surprising number of examples of the recency illusion, where claims have been made about language change without actual solid evidence that change is occurring or has (recently) occurred. In short, while we push hard to develop better theories of language structure and language in its social context and so on, we are also pushing equally hard to exploit all available data as best we can, a key aspect of informational maximalism.

Still, we have not directly answered the most basic question, posed in the introduction to Chapter 2: how and why does language change? Fundamentally, we are only uncovering pieces of an answer today. What you have seen are some critical parts of the answer: a variety of patterns are always present in a linguistic community, whether it's *schnacken* vs. *sprechen*, *Adresse* vs. *Anschrift*, [nɪçt] vs. [nɪɡt], or *melkte* vs. *molk*. The origins of those are varied, as you know: earlier speech patterns in the community, like the earlier community language (the Low German word for 'to speak'), or the result of foreign borrowing (and nationalistic reaction to that), low-level variation in pronunciation that gets adopted by speakers, or extension of patterns already present in the grammar. But the presence of variants, even new variants, doesn't represent change. Variants must be transmitted through the speech community, learned by children as native forms. We've seen this again through language contact as well as dialect contact (*koinē* formation) and it surely often happens as people align themselves socially with others, adjusting to the others' speech as part of that process. At the same time, we've seen it happen due to social changes, like the rise of formal education and the adoption of supraregional or standard forms of speech by parents, learned natively by their offspring.

8.4 Conclusion

So, we are now at the end of our survey. Take a particularly tired cliché: 'Give somebody a fish and you feed them for a day; teach them to fish and you feed them forever.' While the examples above illustrate some morsels I hope you've enjoyed, you should also have gotten insight into how we go about the business of reckoning relationships among languages, both genetic and contact relationships, tracing language change in many domains of language structure and language use, and how we're beginning to understand the roles played by social relations and attitudes in language change.

The study of language change, in fact, is today more tightly integrated into the full range of linguistic subfields than it has been for a long time. Theoreticians working on synchronic syntax and phonology, for instance, currently pay attention to historical data and diachronic analysis.

One of the perennial questions about language change is whether we can predict in any sense how languages will change (see Janda & Joseph 2003: 179–180, for instance). The obvious and safe position is that we cannot predict it, but it's worth stressing that we see clear and consistent directions of change over time from prehistory to the present day. This is not the place for a discourse on philosophy, but in fact, 'prediction' in historical and social sciences is a famously thorny matter among philosophers of science. Karl Popper argues for real limits on the possibility of predictions of this sort (see Thornton 2017), though his body of work makes room for a notion of 'retrodiction'.

One obvious example is the steady movement from ablaut to 'weak' inflection of verbs or the erosion of case in the nominal system, as well as the broad tendency toward more syntactically oriented analytic constructions, like periphrasis in the verb system. This particular change seems more clearly structured than many, as individual verbs change type, just as it seems like that verbal inflection has sometimes been more stable over time than nominal inflection, e.g. for instance with the retention of a robust strong verb system even in a language like English.

From the prescriptivist perspective, the future almost inevitably seems to be worrisome, with grave threats to the language. Today, this is often expressed as the fear of German being overrun by English—as illustrated by Hoberg's 2000 title 'Sprechen wir bald alle Denglisch oder Germeng?'[7] And the concerns are hardly limited to language: German Transportation Minister Peter Ramsauer made news with efforts to replace common loanwords with German forms, like *Klapprechner* for *Laptop*, and pushing for older forms like *Fahrschein* over *Ticket*. In December 2010, he was quoted in *Spiegel* (http://www.spiegel.de/politik/deutschland/0,1518,736912,00.html):

Dem Volk aufs Maul geschaut! Und schon weiß ich, was die Nöte, Sorgen und Probleme der Menschen sind. Und vor allen Dingen, was ich zu tun habe, um Abhilfe zu schaffen.

I've looked the people right in the mouth. And I already know what the needs, worries and problems of people are. And above all, what I have to do to provide a remedy.

Typically, as we've seen, purist and prescriptivist efforts are framed in nationalist or other political terms. Here, it becomes a struggle to solve humanity's problems.

And the steady march of the standard language leads to another fear, anxiety about the death of dialects. As far back as 1959, Leopold wrote an essay called 'The Decline of German Dialects'—and more recently the same perspective is illustrated by Eichhoff's essay in the same (2000) volume as Hoberg's: 'Sterben die Dialekte aus?' Eichhoff concludes:

Als Fazit bleibt festzuhalten, dass die Dialekte im traditionellen Sinne, die Basis- und die Verkehrsdialekte, mehr und mehr an dialektaler Substanz und an Verbreitung verlieren werden.

Perhaps, but Leopold's earlier essay closed on a more interesting note, with a stress on the continuing rise of colloquial varieties. As we've seen, these continue to develop and innovate. Dialects are passing out of use in some areas, certainly, but linguistic variety continues and is growing in other ways. The wild dialect mixing in OHG texts and von Trimburg's admonition to focus on variation in MHG (look back to Chapter 5) echo loudly today.

---

[7] The title illustrates the point at hand, but I should note that his answer in the essay is more nuanced in some ways.

That said, whether you are interested in the prehistory of Germanic, texts written in medieval forms of the language, or the rise of the standard and modern colloquial varieties, there is only one point to close with: we are in a period of tremendous progress in understanding this language's history, and work on German will contribute to our understanding of language change generally. As I prepare to send this book off for editing within the next day, I'm both daunted by what we need to do and excited about how doable it is. One thing is clear: the real work remains to be done.

References

Abraham, Werner. 1997. 'The interdependence of case, aspect and referentiality in the history of German: The case of the verbal genitive'. *Parameters of Morphosyntactic Change*, ed. by Ans van Kemenade & Nigel Vincent, 29–61. Cambridge: Cambridge University Press.

Abraham, Werner. 1999. '*Präteritumschwund* in German: The parsing trigger'. *Folia Linguisica Europaea* 33.39–58.

Abraham, Werner & Annette Fischer. 1998. 'Das grammatische Optimalisierungsszenario von *tun* als Hilfsverb'. *Deutsche Grammatik—Thema in Variationen: Festschrift für Hans-Werner Eroms zum 60. Geburtstag*, ed. by Karin Donhauser & Ludwig M. Eichinger, 35–47. Heidelberg: Carl Winter.

Adams, James N. 2003. *Bilingualism and the Latin Language*. Cambridge: Cambridge University Press.

Admoni, Wladimir G. 1990. *Historische Syntax des Deutschen*. Tübingen: Niemeyer.

Ágel, Vilmos. 2000. 'Syntax des Neuhochdeutschen bis zur Mitte des 20. Jahrhunderts'. *Sprachgeschichte: Ein Handbuch zur Geschichte der deutschen Sprache und ihrer Erforschung*, ed. by Werner Besch et al., 1855–1902. Berlin: de Gruyter.

Aikhenvald, Alexandra Y. 2004. *Evidentiality*. Oxford: Oxford University Press.

Androutsopoulos, Jannis. 2014. 'Mediatization and sociolinguistic change: Key concepts, research traditions, open issues'. *Mediatization and Sociolinguistic Change*, ed. by Jannis Androutsopoulos, 3–48. Berlin: Walter de Gruyter.

Anthony, David W. 2007. *The Horse, the Wheel, and Language: How Bronze-Age riders from the Eurasian steppes shaped the modern world*. Princeton: Princeton University Press.

Antomo, Mailin & Markus Steinbach. 2010. 'Desintegration und Interpretation: *Weil*-V2-Sätze an der Schnittstelle zwischen Syntax, Semantik und Pragmatik'. *Zeitschrift für Sprachwissenschaft* 29.1–37.

Antonsen, Elmer H. 1969. 'Zur Umlautfeindlichkeit des Oberdeutschen'. *Zeitschrift für Dialektologie und Linguistik* 36.201–207.

Antonsen, Elmer H. 1975. *A Concise Grammar of the Older Runic Inscriptions*. Tübingen: Niemeyer.

Antonsen, Elmer H. 2002. *Runes and Germanic Linguistics*. Berlin: Mouton de Gruyter.

Antonsen, Elmer H. 2003. '"Weil die Schrift immer strebt...": On phonological reconstruction'. *NOWELE* 43.2–20.

Auer, Anita & Michiel de Vaan, eds. 2016. *Le palimpseste gotique de Bologne: Études philologiques et linguistiques / The Gothic Palimpsest from Bologna: Philological and linguistic studies*. (Cahiers de l'ILSL 50.) Lausanne: Centre de Linguistique et des Sciences du Langage de l'Université de Lausanne (Suisse). http://www.unil.ch/clsl/home/menuinst/publications/pour-commander.html.

Auer, Peter. 1997. 'Führt Dialektabbau zur Stärkung oder Schwächung der Standardvarietät? Zwei phonologische Fallstudien'. *Standardisierung und Destandardisierung europäischer Nationalsprachen*, ed. by Klaus J. Mattheier & Edgar Radtke, 129–162. Frankfurt: Peter Lang.

Auer, Peter & Susanne Günthner. 2005. 'Die Entstehung von Diskursmarkern im Deutschen—ein Fall von Grammatikalisierung?'. *Grammatikalisierung im Deutschen* (Linguistik—Impulse & Tendenzen 9), ed. by Torsten Leuschner & Tanja Mortelmans, 335–362. Berlin: Mouton de Gruyter.

Auer, Peter & Jürgen Erich Schmidt, eds. 2010. *Language and Space: An international handbook of linguistic variation. Theories and methods.* Berlin: Mouton de Gruyter.

Augst, Gerhard. 1975. *Untersuchungen zum Morpheminventar der deutschen Gegenwartssprache.* Tübingen: Gunter Narr.

Autenrieth, Tanja. 2002. *Heterosemie und Grammatikalisierung bei Modalpartikeln. Eine synchrone und diachrone Studie anhand von* eben, halt, e(cher)t, einfach, schlicht *und* glatt. Tübingen: Niemeyer.

Axel, Katrin. 2007. *Studies on Old High German Syntax.* Amsterdam: John Benjamins.

Axel, Katrin. 2009. 'The verb-second property in Old High German: Different ways of filling the prefield'. *Information Structure and Language Change: New approaches to word order variation in Germanic*, ed. by Roland Hinterhölzl & Svetlana Petrova, 17–43. Berlin: Mouton de Gruyter.

Axelsdóttir, Katrín. 2014. *Sögur af orðum: Sex athuganir á beygingarþróun í íslendsku.* Reykjavík: Háskólaútgáfan.

Baković, Eric. 2000. 'The conspiracy of Turkish vowel harmony'. *Jorge Hankamer WebFest.* http://ling.ucsc.edu/Jorge/bakovic.html.

Baldi, Philip & Richard Page. 2006. Review of Theo Vennemann, 2003, *Europa Vasconica–Europa Semitica. Lingua* 116.2183–2220.

Balter, Michael. 2004. 'In search of the Indo-Europeans'. *Science* 303.1323–1326.

Bammesberger, Alfred. 1986. *Der Aufbau des germanischen Verbalsystems.* Heidelberg: Carl Winter.

Bammesberger, Alfred. 1990. *Die Morphologie des urgermanischen Nomens.* Heidelberg: Carl Winter.

Barbour, Stephen & Patrick Stevenson. 1990. *Variation in German: A critical approach to German sociolinguistics.* Cambridge: Cambridge University Press.

Barðdal, Jóhanna. 2009. 'The development of case in Germanic'. *The Role of Semantic, Pragmatic and Discourse Factors in the Development of Case*, ed. by Jóhanna Barðdal & Siobhan Chelliah, 123–160. Amsterdam: John Benjamins.

Beekes, Robert R. S. 2011. *Comparative Indo-European Linguistics: An introduction.* 2nd edn., rev. and corr. by Michiel de Vaan. Amsterdam: John Benjamins.

Beetz, Manfred. 1990. *Frühmoderne Höflichkeit: Komplimentierkunst und Gesellschaftsrituale im altdeutschen Sprachraum.* Stuttgart: Metzler.

Behaghel, Otto. 1909. 'Beziehungen zwischen Umfang und Reihenfolge von Satzgliedern'. *Indogermanische Forschungen* 25.110–142.

Behaghel, Otto. 1923–1932. *Syntax: Eine geschichtliche Darstellung.* Heidelberg: Carl Winter. 4 vols.

Benware, Wilbur A. 1996. 'Processual change and phonetic analogy: Early New High German <s> > <sch>'. *American Journal of Germanic Linguistics and Literatures* 8.265–287.

Benzinger, Rudolf. 2000. 'Die Kanzleisprachen'. *Sprachgeschichte: Ein Handbuch zur Geschichte der deutschen Sprache und ihrer Erforschung*, ed. by Werner Besch et al., 1665–1673. Berlin: de Gruyter.

Bergmann, Rolf & Stefanie Stricker. 2009. *Die althochdeutsche und altsächsische Glossographie: Ein Handbuch*. Berlin: Walter de Gruyter. 2 vols.

Bergmann, Rolf, Heinrich Tiefenbach, & Lothar Voetz, eds., in association with Herbert Kolb, Klaus Matzel, & Karl Stackmann. 1988. *Althochdeutsch*. Heidelberg: Carl Winter. 2 vols.

Bermúdez-Otero, Ricardo. 2015. 'Amphichronic explanation and the life cycle of phonological processes'. *The Oxford Handbook of Historical Phonology*, ed. by Patrick Honeybone & Joseph Salmons, 374–399. Oxford: Oxford University Press.

Bertelsmeier-Kierst, Christa. 2000. 'Aufbruch in die Schriftlichkeit: Zur volkssprachlichen Überlieferung im 12. Jahrhundert'. *Wolfram-Studien* 16. 157–174. (*Aspekte des 12. Jahrhunderts* ed. by Wolfgang Haubrichs, Eckart Conrad Lutz, & Gisela Vollmann-Profe.)

Bertelsmeier-Kierst, Christa & Jürgen Wolf. 2000. 'Man schreibt Deutsch. Volkssprachliche Literalität im 13. Jahrhundert'. *Jahrbuch der Oswald von Wolkenstein-Gesellschaft* 12.21–34.

Besch, Werner. 1996. *Duzen, Siezen, Titulieren: Zur Anrede im Deutschen heute und gestern*. Göttingen: Vandenhoeck & Ruprecht.

Besch, Werner. 2000. 'Die Rolle Luthers für die deutsche Sprachgeschichte'. *Sprachgeschichte: Ein Handbuch zur Geschichte der deutschen Sprache und ihrer Erforschung*, ed. by Werner Besch et al., 1713–1745. Berlin: de Gruyter.

Besch, Werner. 2003. 'Aussprache-Standardisierung am grünen Tisch? Der "Siebs" nach 100 Jahren'. *'Standardfragen'*, ed. by Jannis K. Androutsopoulos & Evelyn Ziegler, 15–26. Frankfurt: Peter Lang.

Besch, Werner & Norbert Richard Wolf. 2009. *Geschichte der deutschen Sprache: Längsschnitte—Zeitstufen—Linguistische Studien*. Berlin: Erich Schmidt.

Besch, Werner et al., eds. 2000. *Sprachgeschichte: Ein Handbuch zur Geschichte der deutschen Sprache und ihrer Erforschung*. Berlin: de Gruyter.

Betten, Anne. 1987. *Grundzüge der Prosasyntax: Stilprägende Entwicklungen vom Althochdeutschen zum Neuhochdeutschen*. Tübingen: Niemeyer.

Betten, Anne. 2000. 'Zum Verhältnis von geschriebener und gesprochener Sprache im Frühneuhochdeutschen'. *Sprachgeschichte: Ein Handbuch zur Geschichte der deutschen Sprache und ihrer Erforschung*, ed. by Werner Besch et al., 1646–1664. Berlin: de Gruyter.

Betz, Werner. 1974. 'Lehnwörter und Lehnprägungen im Vor- und Frühdeutschen'. *Deutsche Wortgeschichte*, ed. by Friedrich Mauerer & Heinz Rupp, 135–163. Berlin: de Gruyter.

Bickel, Hans & Christoph Landolt. 2012. *Schweizerhochdeutsch: Wörterbuch der Standardsprache in der deutschen Schweiz*. Mannheim: Bibliographisches Institut.

Birkmann, Thomas. 1987. *Präteritopräsentia*. Tübingen: Niemeyer.

Bittner, Andreas. 1996. *Starke 'schwache' Verben / schwache 'starke' Verben: Deutsche Verbflexion und Natürlichkeit*. (Studien zur deutschen Grammatik 51.) Tübingen: Stauffenburg.

Blevins, Juliette. 2004. *Evolutionary Phonology*. Cambridge: Cambridge University Press.

Blume, Herbert. 1967. *Die Morphologie von Zesens Wortneubildungen*. Ph.D. dissertation, Universität Gießen.

Boersma, Paul & David Weenink. 2010. Praat: Doing phonetics by computer. http://www.fon.hum.uva.nl/praat.

Bonfante, Giuliano. 1947. 'The neolinguistic position'. *Language* 23.344–375.

de Boor, Helmut, ed. 1988. *Das Nibelungenlied*. Wiesbaden: Brockhaus. 22nd edn., ed. by Roswitha Wiesniewski, based on the edition by Karl Bartsch.

Bossong, Georg. 1985. *Empirische Universalienforschung: Differentielle Objektmarkierung in den neuiranischen Sprachen*. Tübingen: Narr.

Bostock, J. Knight. 1976. *A Handbook on Old High German Literature*. 2nd edn., rev. by K. C. King & D. R. McLintock. Oxford: Clarendon.

Bousquette, Joshua. 2013. *Complementizer Agreement in Modern Varieties of West Germanic: A model of reanalysis and renewal*. Ph.D. dissertation, University of Wisconsin–Madison.

Bousquette, Joshua. 2014. 'Complementizer agreement in eastern Wisconsin: (Central) Franconian features in an American heritage language community'. *Sprachtypologie und Universalienforschung / Language Typology and Universals* 67.561–588.

Bousquette, Joshua & Joseph Salmons. 2017. 'The Germanic languages'. *The Indo-European Languages*, ed. by Mate Kapović, 387–420. London: Routledge.

Boutkan, Dirk. 1995. *The Germanic 'Auslautgesetze'*. (Leiden Studies in Indo-European 4.) Amsterdam: Rodopi.

Bowern, Claire & Bethwyn Evans, eds. 2015. *The Routledge Handbook of Historical Linguistics*. London: Routledge.

Brandt, Wolfgang. 2000. 'Sprache in Hörfunk und Fernsehen'. *Sprachgeschichte: Ein Handbuch zur Geschichte der deutschen Sprache und ihrer Erforschung*, ed. by Werner Besch et al., 2159–2168. Berlin: de Gruyter.

Braselmann, Petra. 2004. 'Language policies in East and West: National language policies as a response to the pressures of globalization'. *Globalization and the Future of German*, ed. by Andreas Gardt & Bernd Hüppauf, 99–117. Berlin: Mouton de Gruyter.

Braun, Peter. 1987. *Tendenzen in der deutschen Gegenwartssprache*. Stuttgart: Kohlhammer.

Braune, Wilhelm. 1994. *Althochdeutsches Lesebuch*. 17th edn., ed. by Ernst Ebbinghaus. Tübingen: Niemeyer.

Braune, Wilhelm & Ingo Reiffenstein. 2004. *Althochdeutsche Grammatik I: Laut- und Formenlehre*, 15th edn. Tübingen: Max Niemeyer.

Bremmer, Rolf H. 2009. *An Introduction to Old Frisian: History, grammar, reader, glossary*. Amsterdam: John Benjamins.

Brown, Joshua R. & Michael T. Putnam. 2011. 'Functional convergence and extension in contact: Syntactic and semantic attributes of the progressive aspect in Pennsylvania Dutch'. Paper presented at the Second Workshop on Immigrant Languages in America. Fefor, Norway, September 21–24.

Brugmann, Karl. 1904. *Kurze vergleichende Grammatik der indogermanischen Sprachen*. Strassburg: Karl Trübner. (Reprinted 1970, Walter de Gruyter, Berlin.)

Brugmann, Karl & Berthold Delbrück. 1886–1900. *Grundriss der vergleichenden Grammatik der indogermanischen Sprache.* Leipzig: Teubner.

Buccini, Anthony F. 1992. *The Development of Umlaut and the Dialectal Position of Dutch in Germanic.* Ph.D. dissertation, Cornell University.

Buccini, Anthony F. 1995. 'Ontstaan en vroegste ontwikkeling van het Nederlandse taallandschap'. *Taal en Tongval* 48.8–66.

Burke, Peter. 2004. *Languages and Communities in Early Modern Europe.* Cambridge: Cambridge University Press.

Burkhardt, Armin. 1994. 'Abtönungspartikeln im Deutschen: Bedeutung und Genese'. *Zeitschrift für Germanistische Linguistik.* 2.129–151.

Bybee, Joan. 2001. *Phonology and Language Use.* Cambridge: Cambridge University Press.

Cairns, Charles E. & Eric Raimy, eds. 2011. *Handbook of the Syllable.* Leiden: Brill.

Calabrese, Andrea. 2011. 'Metaphony in Romance'. *The Blackwell Companion to Phonology*, ed. by Marc van Oostendorp, Colin J. Ewen, Elizabeth Hume, & Keren Rice. Oxford: Blackwell Publishing. Blackwell Reference Online. http://www.companiontophonology.com/subscriber/tocnode?id=g9781405184236_chunk_g978140 5184236112.

Cameron, Deborah. 1995. *Verbal Hygiene.* London: Routledge.

Campbell, Lyle. 1988. Review article on Greenberg 1987. *Language* 64.591–615.

Campbell, Lyle & Alice C. Harris. 2002. 'Syntactic reconstruction and demythologizing "Myths and the prehistory of grammars"'. *Journal of Linguistics* 38.599–618.

Campbell, Lyle & Mauricio J. Mixco. 2007. *A Glossary of Historical Linguistics.* Edinburgh: Edinburgh University Press.

Campbell, Lyle & William J. Poser. 2008. *Language Classification: History and method.* Cambridge: Cambridge University Press.

Carroll, Ryan, Ragnar Svare & Joseph Salmons. 2012. 'Quantifying the evolutionary dynamics of German verbs'. *Journal of Historical Linguistics* 2.153–172.

Catford, J. C. 2001. 'On Rs, rhotacism and paleophony'. *Journal of the International Phonetic Association* 31:2.171–185.

Chambers, J. K. & Peter Trudgill. 1986. *Dialectology.* Cambridge: Cambridge University Press.

Chang, Will, Chundra Carhcart, David Hall, & Andrew Garrett. 2015. 'Ancestry-constrained phylogenetic analysis supports the Indo-European steppe hypothesis'. *Language* 91.194–244.

Chinca, Mark & Christopher Young, eds. 2017. *Digital Philology and Medieval Studies in the German-Speaking World.* Special issue of *Digital Philology.*

Christen, Helen, Elvira Glaser, & Matthias Friedli, eds. 2013. *Kleiner Sprachatlas der deutschen Schweiz.* 5th edn. Frauenfeld: Huber.

Cichosz, Anna. 2010. *The Influence of Text Type on Word Order of Old German Languages: A corpus-based contrastive study of Old English and Old High German.* Frankfurt: Peter Lang.

Chomsky, Noam. 1965. *Aspects of the Theory of Syntax.* Cambridge, Mass.: MIT Press.

Clackson, James. 2007. *Indo-European Linguistics.* Cambridge: Cambridge University Press.

Classen, Albrecht. 2007. 'Polyglots in medieval German literature: Outsiders, critics or revolutionaries?' *Neophilologus* 91.101–115.

Clyne, Michael. 1984. *Language and Society in the German-speaking Countries.* Cambridge: Cambridge University Press.

Clyne, Michael. 1992. 'Pluricentric languages: Introduction'. *Pluricentric Languages: Differing norms in different nations*, ed. by Michael Clyne, 1–9. Berlin: Mouton de Gruyter.

Collinge, N. E. 1985. *The Laws of Indo-European.* Amsterdam: John Benjamins.

Coniglio, Marco. 2012. 'On V1 declarative clauses in Middle High German'. *Linguistische Berichte* 229.5–37.

Crystal, David. 2008. *A Dictionary of Linguistics and Phonetics.* 6th edn. Oxford: Wiley Blackwell.

Curme, George O. 1922. *A Grammar of the German Language, Designed for a Thoro and Practical Study of the Language as Spoken and Written to-day.* 2nd edn. New York: MacMillan.

Dal, Ingrid. 1960. 'Zur Frage des südeutschen Präteritumschwundes'. *Indogermanica: Festschrift für Wolfgang Krause zum 65. Geburtstage am 18. September 1960 von Fachgenossen und Freunden gezusammengebracht*, 1–7. Heidelberg: Winter.

Dammel, Antje. 2011. *Konjugationsklassenwandel: Prinzipien des Ab-, Um- und Ausbaus verbalflexivischer Allomorphie in germanischen Sprachen.* Berlin: Walter de Gruyter.

Dammel, Antje, Jessica Nowak, & Mirjam Schmuck. 2010. 'Strong-verb paradigm leveling in four Germanic languages: A category frequency approach'. *Journal of Germanic Linguistics* 22.337–359.

Davies, Winifred V. & Nils Langer. 2006. *The Making of Bad Language: Lay linguistic stigmatizations in German—Past and present.* Frankfurt: Peter Lang.

Davis, Garry W. & Gregory K. Iverson. 1995. 'Segment organization in the High German consonant shift'. *Beiträge zur Geschichte der deutschen Sprache under Literatur* 121:2.177–200.

Davis, Garry W., Gregory K. Iverson, & Joseph C. Salmons. 1999. 'Peripherality and markedness in the spread of the Old High German consonant shift'. *Beiträge zur Geschichte der deutschen Sprache und Literatur* 118:1.69–86.

de Bleser, Ria & Josef Bayer. 1988. 'On the role of inflectional morphology in agrammatism', *Theoretical Morphology: Approaches in modern linguistics*, ed. by Michael Hammond & Michael Noonan, 45–70. New York: Academic Press.

De Schutter, Georges. 1994. 'Dutch'. *The Germanic Languages*, ed. by Ekkehard König & Johan van der Auwera, 439–477. London: Routledge.

Delbrück, Berthold. 1900. *Vergleichende Syntax der germanischen Sprachen*, III. (Grundriß der vergleichenden Grammatik der indogermanischen Sprachen 5.) Strassburg: Trübner.

Demske, Ulrike. 2001a. *Merkmale und Relationen: Diachrone Studien zur Nominalphrase des Deutschen.* Berlin: Mouton de Gruyter.

Demske, Ulrike. 2001b. 'Zur Distribution von Infinitivkomplementen im Althochdeutschen'. *Modalität und Modalverben im Deutschen* (Linguistische Berichte Sonderheft 9), ed. by Reimar Müller & Marga Reis, 61–86. Hamburg: Helmut Buske.

Demske, Ulrike. 2008. 'Raising patterns in Old High German'. *Grammatical Change and Linguistic Theory: The Rosendal papers*, ed. by Thórhallur Etyhórsson, 143–172. Amsterdam: John Benjamins.

Denton, Jeannette. 1998. 'Phonetic perspectives on West Germanic consonant gemination'. *The American Journal of Germanic Linguistics and Literatures* 10.201–235.

Denton, Jeannette. 1999. 'Phonetic motivation for consonant gemination: Evidence from Greek, Romance, and Germanic'. *Proceedings of the XIVth International Congress of the Phonetic Sciences (ICPhS)*, 325–328.

Denton, Jeannette. 2002. 'Rhotic articulation and the Early Upper German gemination of *r'. *Beiträge zur Geschichte der deutschen Sprache und Literatur* 124.385–410.

Denton, Jeannette Marshall. 2003. 'Reconstructing the articulation of Early Germanic *r'. *Diachronica* 20.11–42.

Deutsch Digital Diachron. n.d. http://www.deutschdiachrondigital.de. (Project conducted by Karin Donhauser, Jost Gippert, Rosemarie Lühr in Berlin.)

Dewey, Tonya Kim. 2006. *The Origins and Development of Germanic V2: Evidence from alliterative verse*. Ph.D. dissertation, University of California, Berkeley.

Diewald, Gabriele. 1997. *Grammatikalisierung: Eine Einführung in Sein und Werden grammatischer Formen*. Tübingen: Niemeyer.

Diewald, Gabriele. 1999. *Die Modalverben im Deutschen: Grammatikalisierung und Polyfunktionalität*. Tübingen: Niemeyer.

Diewald, Gabriele. 2011. 'Pragmaticalization (defined) as grammaticalization of discourse functions'. *Linguistics* 49.365–390.

Diewald, Gabriele & Elena Smirnova. 2010. *Evidentiality in German: Linguistic realization and regularities in grammaticalization*. Berlin: Mouton de Gruyter.

Donhauser, Karin. 1998. 'Negationssyntax im Althochdeutschen: Ein sprachhistorisches Rätsel und der Weg zu seiner Lösung'. *Deutsche Grammatik—Thema in Variationen: Festschrift für Hans-Werner Eroms zum 60. Geburtstag*, ed. by Karin Donhauser & Ludwig M. Eichinger, 283–298. Heidelberg: Carl Winter.

Donhauser, Karin, Annette Fischer, & Lars Mecklenburg. 2007. *Moutons interaktive Einführung in die historische Linguistik des Deutschen / The Mouton Interactive Introduction to Historical Linguistics of German* (CD-ROM). Berlin: Mouton de Gruyter.

Dresher, B. Elan & Aditi Lahiri. 1991. 'The Germanic foot: Metrical coherence in Old English'. *Linguistic Inquiry* 22.251–286.

Dresher, B. Elan & Aditi Lahiri. 1999. 'Open syllable lengthening in West Germanic'. *Language* 75.678–719.

Drinka, Bridget. 2004. 'Präteritumschwund: Evidence for areal diffusion'. *Focus on Germanic Typology*, ed. by Werner Abraham, 211–240. Berlin: Akademie.

Drinka, Bridget. 2015. *Language Contact in Europe: The periphrastic perfect through history*. Cambridge: Cambridge University Press.

Drosdowski, Günter & Helmut Henne. 1980. 'Tendenzen der deutschen Gegenwartssprache'. *Lexikon der germanistischen Linguistik*, ed. by P.-H. Althaus, H. Henne, & H. E. Wiegand, 619–632. Tübingen: Niemeyer.

Dubenion-Smith, Shannon A. 2007. *Verbal Complex Phenomena in the West Central German Dialects*. Ph.D. dissertation, University of Wisconsin–Madison.

Dubenion-Smith, Shannon A. 2010. 'Verbal complex phenomena in West Central German: Empirical domain and multi-causal account'. *Journal of Germanic Linguistics* 22.99–191.

Duden: Die Grammatik. 2016. 9th edn. Berlin: Dudenverlag. (Also cited: 8th edn. 2009, 6th edn. 1998.)

Durrell, Martin. 2007. 'Deutsch ist eine *würde*-lose Sprache: On the history of a failed prescription'. *Germanic Language Histories 'from Below' (1700–2000)*, ed. by Stephan Elspaß, Nils Langer, Joachim Scharloth, & Wim Vandenbussche, 243–258. Berlin: de Gruyter.

Durrell, Martin & Richard J. Whitt. 2016. 'The development of the *würde* + infinitive construction in Early Modern German (1650–1800)'. *Beiträge zur Geschichte der deutschen Sprache und Literatur* 138.325–364.

Ebert, Robert P. 1978. *Historische Syntax des Deutschen.* Stuttgart: Metzler.

Ebert, Robert P. 1983. 'Verb position in Luther's Bible translation and the usage of his contemporaries'. *Monatshefte* 75.147–155.

Ebner, Jakob. 1998. *Wie sagt man in Österreich? Wörterbuch des Österreichischen Deutsch.* 3rd edn. Mannheim & Vienna: Duden.

Eckardt, Regine. 2011. 'Semantic reanalysis and language change'. *Language and Linguistics Compass* 5:1.33–46. DOI: 10.1111/j.1749-818X.2010.00260.x.

Eggenberger, Jakob. 1961. *Das Subjektpronomen im Althochdeutschen: Ein syntaktischer Beitrag zur Frühgeschichte des deutschen Schrifttums.* Grabs: Selbstverlag.

Eichhoff, Jürgen. 2000. 'Sterben die Dialekte aus?' *Die deutsche Sprache zur Jahrtausendwende*, ed. by Karin Eichhoff-Cyrus & Rudolf Hoberg, 80–88. Mannheim: Dudenverlag.

Eichler, Ernst, Gerold Hilty, Heinrich Löffler, Hugo Steger, & Ladislav Zgusta, eds. 1995. *Namenforschung / Name Studies / Les Noms Propres: Ein internationales Handbuch zur Onomastik.* Berlin: de Gruyter.

Eisenberg, Peter. 2013. 'Anglizismen im Deutschen'. *Reichtum und Armut der deutschen Sprache. Erster Bericht zur Lage der deutschen Sprache*, ed. by the Deutschen Akademie für Sprache und Dichtung and the Union der deutschen Akademien der Wissenschaften, 57–119. Berlin: de Gruyter.

Elspaß, Stephan. 2005a. *Sprachgeschichte von unten: Untersuchungen zum geschriebenen Alltagsdeutsch im 19. Jahrhundert.* Tübingen: Niemeyer.

Elspaß, Stephan. 2005b. 'Language norm and language reality: Effectiveness and limits of prescriptivism in New High German'. *Linguistic Purism in the Germanic Languages*, ed. by Nils Langer & Winifred V. Davies, 20–45. Berlin: de Gruyter.

Elspaß, Stephan. 2007. 'A twofold view "from below": New perspectives on language histories and language historiographies'. *Germanic Language Histories 'from Below' (1700–2000)*, ed. by Stephan Elspaß, Nils Langer, Joachim Scharloth, & Wim Vandenbussche, 4–9. Berlin: de Gruyter.

Elspaß, Stephan. 2007. 'Vom Mittelneuhochdeutschen (bis ca. 1950) zum Gegenwartsdeutsch'. *Zeitschrift für Dialektologie und Linguistik* 75.1–20.

Elspaß, Stephan. 2014. 'Prescriptive norms and norms of usage in nineteenth-century German'. *Norms and Usage in Language History, 1600–1900: A sociolinguistic and comparative perspective*, ed. by Gijsbert Rutten, Rik Vosters, & Wim Vandenbussche, 303–320. Amsterdam: John Benjamins.

Elspaß, Stephan. 2015. 'Grammatischer Wandel im (Mittel-)Neuhochdeutschen—von oben und von unten: Perspektiven einer historischen Soziolinguistik des Deutschen'. *Zeitschrift für germanistische Linguistik* 43.387–420.

Elspaß, Stephan & Stefan Kleiner. Forthcoming. 'Forschungsergebnisse zur arealen Variation im Standard-deutschen'. *Language and Space*, vol. 4: *Deutsch*, ed. by Joachim Herrgen and Jürgen Erich Schmidt. Berlin: de Gruyter.

Emonds, Joseph & Jan Terje Faarlund. 2014. *English: The Language of the Vikings*. Olomouc: Palacký University Press. http://anglistika.upol.cz/vikings2014.

Enger, Hans-Olav. 2013. 'Sound laws, inflectional change and the autonomy of morphology: The case of Scandinavian case (and gender)'. *Diachronica* 30.1–26.

Erdmann, Oskar. 1886. *Grundzüge der deutschen Syntax nach ihrer geschichtlichen Entwicklung*, vol. 1. Stuttgart: Cotta.

Ernst, Peter. 2005. *Deutsche Sprachgeschichte*. Vienna: WUV/UTB Basics.

Etymologisches Wörterbuch des Althochdeutschen. 1988–. Göttingen: Vandenhoeck & Ruprecht. (To date, six volumes appeared, from *a-pûzza*.)

Faarlund, Jan Terje. 2004. *The Syntax of Old Norse*. Oxford: Oxford University Press.

Faarlund, Jan Terje. 2010. 'Word order'. *The Continuum Companion to Historical Linguistics*, ed. by Silvia Lurgahi & Vit Bubenik, 201–211. London: Continuum.

Falck, Oliver, Stephan Heblich, Alfred Lameli, & Jens Südekum. 2010. 'Dialects, cultural identity, and economic exchange'. *Forschungsinstitut zur Zukunft der Arbeit*, Discussion Paper No. 4743. http://ideas.repec.org/s/iza/izadps.html.

Farrar, Kimberley. 1999. 'Explanations for word order change in modern German'. *Zeitschrift für Dialektologie und Linguistik* 61.1–30.

Ferraresi, Gisella & Maria Goldbach, eds. 2008. *Principles of Syntactic Reconstruction*. Amsterdam: John Benjamins.

Fertig, David. 1996. 'Orthography, phonology and the umlaut puzzle'. *Syntactic and Diachronic Studies in Germanic Linguistics*, ed. by Rosina Lippi-Green & Joseph C. Salmons, 169–184. Amsterdam: John Benjamins.

Fertig, David. 1998. 'The *ge-* participle prefix in ENHG and the modern dialects'. *American Journal of Germanic Linguistics and Literatures* 10.237–278.

Fertig, David. 1999. 'Analogical "leveling" from outside the paradigm: Stem-vowel changes in the Germanic modals'. *Diachronica* 16.233–260.

Fertig, David. 2000. *Morphological Change Up Close: Two and a half centuries of verbal inflection in Nuremberg*. Tübingen: Niemeyer.

Fertig, David. 2013. *Analogy and Morphological Change*. Edinburgh: Edinburgh University Press.

Fertig, David. 2014. Review of *A History of German*, by Joseph Salmons, 2012. *Language* 90.548–551.

Fischer, Annette. 2001. 'Diachronie und Synchronie von auxiliarem *tun* im Deutschen'. *Zur Verbmorphologie germanischer Sprachen*, ed. by Sheila Watts, Jonathan West, & Hans-Joachim Solms, 137–154. Tübingen: Niemeyer.

Fleischer, Jürg, Roland Hinterhölzl, & Michael Solf. 2008. 'Zum Quellenwert des althochdeutschen Tatian für die Syntaxforschung'. *Zeitschrift für germanistische Linguistik* 17.211–239.

Fleischer, Jürg & Oliver Schallert. 2011. *Historische Syntax des Deutschen: Eine Einführung*. Tübingen: Gunter Narr.

Florer, W. 1900. 'Gender change from Middle High German to Luther, as seen in the 1545 edition of the Bible'. *Publications of the MLA* 15.442–491.

Font-Santiago, Cristopher & Joseph Salmons. 2016. 'The descent of English: West Germanic, any way you slice it'. *Language Dynamics & Change* 6.37–41.

Forster, Peter, Valentino Romano, Francesco Calì, Arne Röhl & Matthew Hurles. 2004. 'MtDNA markers for Celtic and Germanic language areas in the British Isles'. *Traces of Ancestry: Studies in honour of Colin Renfrew*, ed. by Martin Jones, 99–114. Cambridge: McDonald Institute.

Forster Peter, Tobias Polzin, & Arne Röhl. 2006. 'Evolution of English basic vocabulary within the network of Germanic languages'. *Phylogenetic Methods and the Prehistory of Languages*, ed. by Peter Forster & Colin Renfrew, 131–138. Cambridge: McDonald Institute.

Fortson, Benjamin W. 2003. 'An approach to semantic change'. *The Handbook of Historical Linguistics*, ed. by Brian D. Joseph & Richard D. Janda, 648–666. Oxford: Blackwell.

Fortson, Benjamin W. 2010. *Indo-European Language & Culture*. 2nd edn. Oxford: Wiley Blackwell.

Fourakis, Marios & Gregory K. Iverson. 1984. 'On the "incomplete neutralization" of German final obstruents'. *Phonetica* 41.140–149.

Fox, Anthony. 1995. *Linguistic Reconstruction: An introduction to theory and method*. Oxford: Oxford University Press.

Fox, Anthony. 2015. 'Phonological reconstruction'. *Oxford Handbook of Historical Phonology*, ed. by Patrick Honeybone & Joseph Salmons, 49–71. Oxford: Oxford University Press.

Frey, Benjamin E. & Joseph Salmons. 2012. 'Dialect and language contact in emerging Germanic'. *Archaeology and Language: Indo-European studies presented to James P. Mallory* (Journal of Indo-European Studies Monograph 60), ed. by Martin E. Huld, Karlene Jones-Bley, & Dean Miller, 95–120.

Frey, Evelyn. 1994. *Einführung in die Historische Sprachwissenschaft des Deutschen*. Heidelberg: Julius Groos.

Freywald, Ulrike. 2010. 'Obwohl vielleicht war es ganz anders: Vorüberlegungen zum Alter der Verbzweitstellung nach subordinierenden Konjunktionen'. *Historische Textgrammatik und Historische Syntax des Deutschen*, ed. by Arne Ziegler, 55–84. Berlin: de Gruyter.

Fritz, Gerd. 2006. *Einführung in die historische Semantik*. 2nd edn. Tübingen: Metzler.

Froschauer, Regine. 2003. *Genus im Althochdeutschen: Eine funktionale Analyse des Mehrfachgenus althochdeutscher Substantive*. Heidelberg: Winter.

Fuß, Eric. 2005. *The Rise of Agreement: A formal approach to the syntax and grammaticalization of verbal inflection*. Amsterdam: John Benjamins.

Gamkrelidze, Thomas V. & Vjačeslav V. Ivanov. 1995. *Indo-European and the Indo-Europeans*. Berlin: Mouton de Gruyter. Translated from the Russian by Johanna Nichols. 2 vols.

Ganz, Peter F. 1957. *Der Einfluß des Englischen auf den deutschen Wortschatz, 1640–1815*. Berlin: Erich Schmidt.

Gärtig, Anna-Kathrin, Albrecht Plewnia, & Astrid Rothe. 2010. *Wie Menschen in Deutschland über Sprache denken: Ergebnisse einer bundesweiten Repräsentativerhebung zu aktuellen Spracheinstellungen*. Mannheim: Institut für Deutsche Sprache.

Gelderen, Elly van. 2006. *A History of the English Language*. Amsterdam: John Benjamins.

Gelderen, Elly van. 2007. 'The definiteness cycle in Germanic'. *Journal of Germanic Linguistics* 19.275–308.

Gelderen, Elly van. 2011. *The Linguistic Cycle: Language change and the language faculty*. Oxford: Oxford University Press.

Girnth, Heiko. 2000. *Untersuchungen zur Theorie der Grammatikalisierung am Beispiel des Westmitteldeutschen*. Tübingen: Niemeyer.

Givón, Talmy. 1971. 'Historical syntax and synchronic morphology: An archaeologist's fieldtrip'. *Papers from the Seventh Regional Meeting of the Chicago Linguistic Society*, 394–415. Chicago, Ill.: Chicago Linguistic Society.

Glahn, Richard. 2002. *Der Einfluss des Englischen auf gesprochene deutsche Gegenwartssprache: Eine Analyse öffentlich gesprochener Sprache am Beispiel von 'Fernsehdeutsch'*. 2nd edn. Frankfurt: Peter Lang.

Glaser, Elvira. 1996. *Frühe Griffelglossierung aus Freising: Ein Beitrag zu den Anfängen althochdeutscher Schriftlichkeit*. Göttingen: Vandenhoeck & Ruprecht.

Glaser, Elvira & Natascha Frey. 2006. 'Doubling phenomena in Swiss German dialects'. Paper presented at the workshop 'Syntactic Doubling in European Dialects', March 16–18. http://www.meertens.knaw.nl/projecten/edisyn/Online_proceedings/Paper_Glaser-Frey.pdf.

Glover, Justin & Tracy Alan Hall. 2009. 'The historical development of /g/ and /b/ in a German dialect'. *Folia Linguistica Historica* 30.219–245.

Goeman, Ton. 1997. 'De zeldzaamheid van Comp–agreement in taaltypologisch en historisch opzicht: Voorkomen buiten de Germania en datering van voegwoordcongruentie–vormen in het Nederlands'. *Vervoegde voegwoorden*, ed. by Eric Hoekstra & Caroline Smits, 87–111. Amsterdam: P. J. Meertens Instituut.

Good, Jeff. 2011. 'The typology of templates'. *Language and Linguistics Compass* 5.731–747.

Good, Jeff. 2016. *The Linguistic Typology of Templates*. Cambridge: Cambridge University Press.

Göschel, Joachim. 1971. 'Artikulation und Distribution der sogenannten Liquida *r* in den europäischen Sprachen'. *Indogermanische Forschungen* 76.84–126.

Götze, Alfred. 1967. *Frühneuhochdeutsches Glossar*. 7th edn. Berlin: Walter de Gruyter.

Gray, Russell D. & Quentin D. Atkinson. 2003. 'Language-tree divergence times support the Anatolian theory of Indo-European origin'. *Nature* 426.435–439.

Green, D. H. 2000. *Language and History in the Early Germanic World*. Cambridge: Cambridge University Press.

Greenberg, Joseph H. 1987. *Language in the Americas*. Stanford, Calif.: Stanford University Press.

Gress-Wright, Jonathan. 2010. *Opacity and Transparency in Phonological Change*. Ph.D. dissertation, University of Pennsylvania.

Grimm, Jakob & Wilhelm Grimm. 1845–1971. *Deutsches Wörterbuch*. Leipzig: Hirzel. 16 vols. http://dwb.uni-trier.de/Projekte/WBB2009/DWB/wbgui_py?lemid=GA00001.

Grotans, Anna. 2006. *Reading in Medieval St. Gall*. Cambridge: Cambridge University Press.

Günthner, Susanne. 1993. '"...weil—man kann es ja wissenschaftlich untersuchen": Diskurspragmatische Aspekte der Wortstellung in WEIL-Sätzen'. *Linguistische Berichte* 143.37–59.

Gütter, Adolf. 2011. 'Frühe Belege für den Umlaut von ahd. /u/, /ō/, /ū/'. *Beiträge zur Geschichte der deutschen Sprache und Literatur* 133.1–13.

Haak, Wolfgang, Iosif Lazaridis, Nick Patterson, Nadin Rohland, Swapan Mallick, Bastien Llamas, Guido Brandt, E. Nordenfelt, E. Harney, K. Stewardson, & Q. Fu. 2015. 'Massive migration from the steppe was a source for Indo-European languages in Europe'. *Nature* 522.207–211.

Habermann, Mechthild, Horst Haider Munske, & Peter O. Müller. 2002. *Historische Wortbildung des Deutschen*. Tübingen: Niemeyer.

Hall, T. Alan. 1993. 'The phonology of German /R/'. *Phonology* 10.83–105.

Hall, T. Alan. 2000. *Phonologie: Eine Einführung*. Berlin: de Gruyter. (2nd edn., 2011.)

Hall, T. Alan. 2008. 'Middle High German rs > rʃ as height dissimilation'. *Journal of Comparative Germanic Linguistics* 11.213–248.

Hall, T. Allan. 2014. 'The analysis of Westphalian German Spirantization'. *Diachronica* 31.223–266.

Halle, Morris. 1997. 'On stress and accent in Indo-European'. *Language* 73.275–313.

Handbook of the International Phonetic Association: A guide to the use of the International Phonetic Alphabet. 1999. Cambridge: Cambridge University Press.

Harbert, Wayne. 2007. *The Germanic Languages*. Cambridge: Cambridge University Press.

Hare, Mary & Jeff Elman. 1995. 'Learning and morphological change'. *Cognition* 56.61–98.

Harnisch, Rüdiger. 2001. *Grundform- und Stamm-Prinzip in der Substantivmorphologie des Deutschen. Synchronische und diachronische Untersuchung eines typologischen Parameters*. Heidelberg: Carl Winter.

Harris, Alice C. & Lyle Campbell. 1995. *Historical Syntax in Cross-linguistic Perspective*. Cambridge: Cambridge University Press.

Hartmann, Stefan. 2016. *Wortbildungswandel: Eine diachrone Studie zu deutschen Nominalisierungsmustern*. Berlin: de Gruyter.

Hartweg, Frédéric & Klaus-Peter Wegera. 1995. *Frühneuhochdeutsch: Eine Einführung in die deutsche Sprache des Spätmittelalters und der frühen Neuzeit*. Tübingen: Niemeyer.

Havinga, Anna & Nils Langer, eds. 2015. *Invisible Languages in the Nineteenth Century*. Oxford: Peter Lang.

Hawkins, John A. 1986. *A Comparative Typology of English and German: Unifying the contrasts*. Austin: University of Texas Press.

Heather, Peter. 2010. *Empires and Barbarians: The fall of Rome and the birth of Europe*. Oxford: Oxford University Press.

Herrgen, Joachim. 1986. *Koronalisierung und Hyperkorrektion: Das palatale Allophon des /ch/-Phonemes und seine Variation im Westmitteldeutschen*. Wiesbaden: Steiner.

Herrgen, Joachim. 2010. 'The *Linguistic Atlas of the Middle Rhine (MRhSA)*: A study on the emergence and spread of regional dialects'. *Language and Space: An international handbook of linguistic variation—Theories and methods*, ed. by Peter Auer & Jürgen Erich Schmidt, 668–686. Berlin: Mouton de Gruyter.

Hewson, John. 2006. 'From ancient to modern Germanic'. *From Case to Adposition: The development of configurational syntax in Indo-European languages*, ed. by John Hewson & Vit Bubenik, 274–303. Amsterdam: John Benjamins.

Hickey, Raymond. 2002. 'Ebb and flow: A cautionary tale of language change'. *Sounds, Words, Texts, Change: Selected papers from the Eleventh International Conference on English Historical Linguistics (11 ICEHL)*, ed. by Teresa Fanego, Belén Mendez-Naya, & Elena Seoane, 105–128. Amsterdam: John Benjamins.

Hickey, Raymond. 2003. 'The German address system: Binary and scalar at once'. *Origin and Development of Address Terms in European Languages*, ed. by Andreas H. Jucker & Irma Taavitsainen, 401–425. Amsterdam: John Benjamins.

Hickey, Raymond. Forthcoming. 'Language contact in Celtic and Early Irish'. *Oxford Handbook of Language Contact*, ed. by Anthony Grant. Oxford: Oxford University Press.

Hill, Eugen. 2004. 'Das germanische Verb für "tun" und die Ausgänge des germanischen schwachen Präteritums'. *Sprachwissenschaft* 29.257–303.

Hill, Eugen. 2010. 'A case study in grammaticalized inflectional morphology: Tracing back the Germanic weak preterite'. *Diachronica* 27.411–458.

Hinterhölzl, Roland & Svetlana Petrova. 2009. 'Introduction'. *Information Structure and Language Change: New approaches to word order variation in Germanic*, ed. by Roland Hinterhölzl & Svetlana Petrova, 1–17. Berlin: Mouton de Gruyter.

Hoberg, Rudolf. 2000. 'Sprechen wir bald alle Denglisch oder Germeng?' *Die deutsche Sprache zur Jahrtausendwende* ed. by Karin Eichhoff-Cyrus & Rudolf Hoberg, 303–316. Mannheim: Dudenverlag.

Hoberg, Rudolf. 2004. 'English rules the world: What will become of German?' *Globalization and the Future of German*, ed. by Andreas Gardt & Bernd Hüppauf, 85–97. Berlin: Mouton de Gruyter.

Hoberg, Rudolf. 2009. 'Ist unsere Sprachidentität gefährdet?' *Der Sprachdienst* 53.155–157.

Hoberg, Rudolf, Karin Eichhoff-Cyrus, & Rüdiger Schulz, eds. 2008. *Wie denken die Deutschen über ihre Muttersprache und über Fremdsprachen?* Eine repräsentative Umfrage der Gesellschaft für deutsche Sprache in Zusammenarbeit mit dem Deutschen Sprachrat. Wiesbaden: Gesellschaft für deutsche Sprache.

Hock, Hans Henrich. 1990. 'On the origin and development of relative clauses in early Germanic, with special emphasis on Beowulf'. *Stæfcræft: Studies in Germanic linguistics* (Current Issues in Linguistic Theory 79), ed. by Elmer Antonsen & Hans Henrich Hock, 55–89. Amsterdam: John Benjamins.

Hock, Hans Henrich. 2013. 'Proto-Indo-European verb-finality: Reconstruction, typology, validation'. *Journal of Historical Linguistics* 3.49–76.

Hodge, Carleton T. 1970. 'The linguistic cycle'. *Language Sciences* 13.1–7.

Hollmach, Uwe. 2009. 'Das Verhältnis der Deutschen zu ihren Dialekten'. *Der Sprachdienst* 53.54–62.

Holly, Werner & Ulrich Püschel. 1993. 'Sprache und Fernsehen in der Bundesrepublik Deutschland'. *Sprache in den Medien nach 1945* ed. by Bernd U. Biere & Helmut Henne, 128–157. Tübingen: Niemeyer.

Holsinger, David J. 2000. *Lenition in Germanic: Prosodic templates in sound change*. Ph.D. dissertation, University of Wisconsin–Madison.

Holsinger, David J. 2008. Germanic prosody and consonantal strength. *Lenition and Fortition*, ed. by Joaquim Brandão de Carvalho, Tobias Scheer, & Philippe Ségéral, 273–300. Berlin: Mouton de Gruyter.

Holsinger, David J. & Joseph C. Salmons. 1999. 'Toward "a complete analysis of the residues": On regular vs. morpholexical approaches to Old High German umlaut'. *The Emergence of the Modern Language Sciences: Studies on the transition from historical–comparative to structural linguistics in honour of E. F. Konrad Koerner*, vol. 2, ed. by Sheila Embleton, John E. Joseph, & Hans-Josef Niederehe, 239–253. Amsterdam: John Benjamins.

Honeybone, Patrick. 2016. 'Are there impossible changes? θ > f but f ≯ θ'. *Papers in Historical Phonology* 1.316–358.

Honeybone, Patrick. Forthcoming. *Diachronic Evidence in Segmental Phonology: The case of obstruent laryngeal specifications.* Oxford: Oxford University Press.

Hopper, Paul J. & Elizabeth Closs Traugott. 2003. *Grammaticalization.* 2nd edn. Cambridge: Cambridge University Press.

Horan, Geraldine. 2007. " 'Er zog sich die 'neue Sprache' des 'Dritten Reiches' über wie ein Kleidungsstück": Communities of Practice and Performativity in National Socialist Discourse'. *Linguistik Online* 30. http://www.linguistik-online.de/30_07/horan.html.

Hotz, Karl, ed. 1977. *Deutsche Sprache der Gegenwart: Entwicklungen und Tendenzen.* Stuttgart: Reclam.

Hotzan, Jürgen. 1997. *dtv-Atlas Stadt: Von den ersten Gründungen bis zur modernen Stadtplanung.* 2nd edn. Munich: dtv.

Howe, Steven. 1996. *The Personal Pronouns in the Germanic Languages: A study of personal pronoun morphology and change in the Germanic languages from the first records to the present day.* Berlin: Mouton de Gruyter.

Howell, Robert B. 1991. *Old English Breaking and Its Germanic Analogues.* Tübingen: Max Niemeyer.

Howell, Robert B. 2006. 'Immigration and koineisation: The formation of early modern Dutch urban vernaculars'. *Transactions of the Philological Society* 104.207–227.

Howell, Robert B. 2017. 'What do we really know about Gothic breaking? On the problem of consonantally conditioned sound changes'. Paper presented at the 23rd Germanic Linguistics Annual Conference, University of Texas at Austin.

Howell, Robert B. & Joseph C. Salmons. 1997. 'Umlautless residues in Germanic'. *American Journal of Germanic Linguistics & Literatures* 9.83–111.

Howell, Robert B., Paul T. Roberge, & Joseph C. Salmons. Forthcoming. *The Cambridge History of the Germanic Languages.* Cambridge: Cambridge University Press.

Hundt, Markus. 2000. *'Spracharbeit' im 17. Jahrhundert.* Berlin: Walter de Gruyter.

Hüpper, Dagmar. 1988. '*Apud Thiudiscos*: Zu frühen Selbstzeugnissen einer Sprachgesellschaft'. *Althochdeutsch*, ed. by Rolf Bergmann, Heinrich Tiefenbach, & Lothar Voetz, in association with Herbert Kolb, Klaus Matzel, & Karl Stackmann, 1059–1081. Heidelberg: Carl Winter. 2 vols.

Hyman, Larry M. 2006. 'Word-prosodic typology'. *Phonology* 23.225–257.

Ickelsamer, Valentin. 1534. *Ein Teutsche Grammatica.* Erfurt.

Iverson, Gregory K., Garry W. Davis, & Joseph C. Salmons. 1994. 'Umlaut blocking environments in Old High German'. *Folia Linguistica Historica* 15.131–148.

Iverson, Gregory K., Garry W. Davis, & Joseph C. Salmons. 1996. 'The primacy of primary umlaut'. *Beiträge zur Geschichte der deutschen Sprache und Literatur (PBB)* 118.69–86.

Iverson, Gregory K. & Joseph C. Salmons. 1995. 'Aspiration and laryngeal representation in Germanic'. *Phonology* 12.369–396.

Iverson, Gregory K. & Joseph C. Salmons. 1999. 'Glottal spreading bias in Germanic'. *Linguistische Berichte* 178.135–151.

Iverson, Gregory K. & Joseph C. Salmons. 2003a. 'The ingenerate motivation of sound change'. *Motives for Language Change*, ed. by Raymond Hickey, 199–212. Cambridge: Cambridge University Press.

Iverson, Gregory K. & Joseph C. Salmons. 2003b. 'Laryngeal enhancement in Early Germanic'. *Phonology* 20.43–72.

Iverson, Gregory K. & Joseph C. Salmons. 2005. 'Filling the gap: English tense vowel plus final /š/'. *Journal of English Linguistics* 33.207–221.

Iverson, Gregory K. & Joseph C. Salmons. 2006. 'On the typology of final laryngeal neutralization: Evolutionary phonology and laryngeal realism'. *Theoretical Linguistics* 32:2.205–216.

Iverson, Gregory K. & Joseph C. Salmons. 2007. 'Domains and directionality in the evolution of German final fortition'. *Phonology* 24.1–25.

Iverson, Gregory K. & Joseph C. Salmons. 2008. 'Germanic aspiration: Phonetic enhancement and language contact'. *Sprachwissenschaft* 33.257–278.

Iverson, Gregory K. & Joseph C. Salmons. 2009. 'Naturalness and the lifecycle of sound change'. *On Inflection: In memory of Wolfgang U. Wurzel*, ed. by Patrick Steinkrüger & Manfred Krifka, 89–105. Berlin: Mouton de Gruyter.

Iverson, Gregory K. & Joseph C. Salmons. 2011. 'Final devoicing and final laryngeal neutralization'. *Companion to Phonology*, ed. by Marc van Oostendorp, Colin Ewen, Beth Hume, & Keren Rice, vol. 3, 1622–1643. Oxford: Wiley Blackwell. Blackwell Reference Online. http://www.companiontophonology.com/subscriber/tocnode?id=g9781405184236_chunk_g978140518423671.

Jacewicz, Ewa, Joseph Salmons, & Robert Fox. 2006. 'Prosodic prominence effects on vowels in chain shifts'. *Language Variation & Change* 18:3.285–316.

Jacewicz, Ewa, Robert Fox, & Joseph Salmons. 2009. 'Prosodic conditioning, vowel dynamics and sound change'. *Variation in Phonetics and Phonology*, ed. by Caroline Féry, Jörg Mayer, Frank Kügler, & Ruben van de Vijver, 100–124. Berlin: Mouton de Gruyter.

Jacobs, Neil G. 2005. *Yiddish: A linguistic introduction*. Cambridge: Cambridge University Press.

Jäger, Agnes. 2008. *History of German Negation*. (Linguistik Aktuell/Linguistics Today 118.) Amsterdam: John Benjamins.

Janda, Richard D. & Brian D. Joseph. 2003. 'On language, change, and language change'. *Handbook of Historical Linguistics*, ed. by Richard D. Janda & Brian D. Joseph, 3–180. Oxford: Blackwell.

Jannedy, Stefanie & Melanie Weirich. 2014. 'Sound change in an urban setting: Category instability of the palatal fricative in Berlin'. *Laboratory Phonology* 5.91–122.

Jessen, Michael. 1998. *Phonetics and Phonology of Tense and Lax Obstruents in German*. Amsterdam: John Benjamins.

Jones, Howard. 2009. Aktionsart *in the Old High German Passive*. Hamburg: Buske.

Jones, Howard, trans. 2017. *Martin Luther: Ein Sendbrief vom Dolmetschen / An open letter on translating*. (Treasures of the Taylorian, Series One: Reformation

Pamphlets.) Oxford: Taylorian Institution Library. https://ora.ox.ac.uk/objects/uuid:61dd3bfe-bd7d-48a2-adca-79e28d5cc63d.

Jones, Howard & Martin Jones. Forthcoming. *The Oxford Guide to Middle High German*. Oxford: Oxford University Press.

Jones, William Jervis. 1995. *Sprachhelden und Sprachverderber: Dokumente zur Erforschung des Fremdwortpurismus (1478–1750)*. Berlin: de Gruyter.

Jones, William Jervis. 1999. *Images of Language*. Amsterdam: John Benjamins.

Joseph, Brian D. 2000. 'What gives with es gibt? Typological and comparative perspectives on existentials in German, Germanic, and Indo-European'. *American Journal of Germanic Linguistics and Literatures* 12.187–200.

Joseph, Brian D. 2003. 'Morphologization from syntax'. *The Handbook of Historical Linguistics*, ed. by Brian D. Joseph & Richard D. Janda, 472–492. Oxford: Blackwell.

Joseph, Brian D. & Joseph C. Salmons, eds. 1998. *Nostratic: Sifting the evidence*. Amsterdam: John Benjamins.

Kabak, Barış. 2011. 'Turkish vowel harmony'. *The Blackwell Companion to Phonology*, ed. by Marc van Oostendorp, Colin J. Ewen, Elizabeth Hume, & Keren Rice. Oxford: Wiley Blackwell. Blackwell Reference Online. http://www.companiontophonology.com/subscriber/tocnode?id=g9781405184236_chunk_g9781405184236120.

Kachru, Braj B., Yamuna, Kachru, & Cecil L. Nelson, eds. 2006. *The Handbook of World Englishes*. Oxford: Wiley Blackwell.

Kapović, Mate, ed. 2017. *The Indo-European Languages*. 2nd edn. London: Routledge.

Kallio, Petri. 2012. 'The prehistorical Germanic loanword strata in Finnic'. *A Linguistic Map of Prehistoric Northern Europe*, ed. by Riho Grünthal & Petri Kallio, 225–238. (Mémoires de la Société Finno-Ougrienne 266). Helsinki: Suomalais-Ugrilaisen Seuran Toimituksia.

Kathol, Andreas. 2000. *Linear Syntax*. Oxford: Oxford University Press.

Keller, R. E. 1978. *The German Language*. London: Faber & Faber.

Kern, Friederike. 2015. 'Turkish German'. *Language and Linguistics Compass* 9.219–233.

Kerswill, Paul. 2002. 'Koineization and accommodation'. *The Handbook of Language Variation and Change*, ed. by J. K. Chambers, Peter Trudgill, & Natalie Schilling-Estes, 669–702. Oxford: Blackwell.

Kerswill, Paul & Peter Trudgill. 2005. 'The birth of new dialects'. *Dialect Change: Convergence and divergence in European languages*, ed. by Peter Auer, Frans Hinskens, & Paul Kerswill, 196–220. Cambridge: Cambridge University Press.

Kienle, Richard von. 1960. *Historische Laut- und Formenlehre des Deutschen*. Tübingen: Niemeyer.

Kilian, Jörg. 2003. 'Zum Artikel "Sprachkritik und Sprachwissenschaft—Anmerkungen zu einer komplizierten Beziehung"'. *Sprachreport* 19.3–11.

Kilian, Jörg. 2005. *Historische Dialogforschung: Eine Einführung*. Tübingen: Niemeyer.

Kim, Ronald. 2002. *Topics in the Reconstruction and Development of Indo-European Accent*. Ph.D. dissertation, University of Pennsylvania.

King, Robert D. & Stephanie A. Beach. 1998. 'On the origins of German uvular [R]: The Yiddish evidence'. *Journal of Germanic Linguistics* 10.279–290.

Kiparsky, Paul. 1973. 'The inflectional accent in Indo-European'. *Language* 49.794–849.

Kiparsky, Paul. 1995. 'Indo-European origins of Germanic syntax'. *Clause Structure and Language Change*, ed. by Adrian Battye, & Ian Roberts, 140–169. New York & Oxford: Oxford University Press.

Kiparsky, Paul. 1996. 'The shift to head-initial VP in Germanic'. *Comparative Germanic Syntax*, ed. by H. Thrainsson, J. Peter, & S. Epstein, 140–179. Dordrecht: Kluwer. http://www.stanford.edu/~kiparsky.

Kiparsky, Paul. 1997. 'The rise of positional licensing'. *Parameters of Morphosyntactic Change*, ed. by Ans van Kemenade & Nigel Vincent, 460–494. Cambridge: Cambridge University Press. https://web.stanford.edu/~kiparsky/Papers/kemenade.new.pdf.

Kirkness, Alan. 1975. *Zur Sprachreinigung im Deutschen 1789–1871*. Tübingen: Gunter Narr.

Kisseberth, Charles W. 1970. 'On the functional unity of phonological rules'. *Linguistic Inquiry* 1.291–306.

Klein, Thomas. 1994a. 'Althochdeutsch *diutsch* und die Adjektiva auf *–isk* im Alt- und Mittelhochdeutschen'. *Studien zum Altgermanischen: Festschrift für Heinrich Beck*, ed. by E. Schadel & U. Voigt, 381–410. Berlin: de Gruyter.

Klein, Thomas. 1994b. 'Zum Alter des Wortes *Deutsch*'. *Zeitschrift für Literaturwissenschaft und Linguistik* 24.12–25.

Klein, Thomas. 2000. 'Zur Sprache der Pariser Gespräche'. *Theodisca: Beiträge zur althochdeutschen und altniederdeutschen Sprache und Literatur in der Kultur des frühen Mittelalters*, ed. by Wolfgang Haubrichs et al., 38–59. Berlin: de Gruyter.

Kleiner, Stefan, with the cooperation of Ralf Knöbl. 2011–. *Atlas zur Aussprache des deutschen Gebrauchsstandards (AADG)*. Mannheim: Institut für Deutsche Sprache.

Kluge, Friedrich. 2002. *Etymologisches Wörterbuch der deutschen Sprache*, ed. by Elmar Seebold. 24th edn. Berlin: de Gruyter.

Koch, Peter & Wulf Oesterreicher. 1985. 'Sprache der Nähe, Sprache der Distanz: Mündlichkeit und Schriftlichkeit im Spannungsfeld von Sprachtheorie und Sprachgeschichte / Langage de la proximité, langage de la distance: L'oralité et la scripturalité entre la théorie linguistique et l'histoire de la langue'. *Romanistisches Jahrbuch* 36.15–43.

Koch, Peter & Wulf Oesterreicher. 2012. 'Language of immediacy, language of distance: Orality and literacy from the perspective of language theory and linguistic history'. *Communicative Spaces: Variation, contact, and change—Papers in honour of Ursula Schaefer*, ed. by Claudia Lange, Beatrix Weber, & Göran Wolf, 441–473. Frankfurt: Peter Lang.

Koerner, E. F. K. 1995. 'History of typology and classification'. *Concise History of the Language Sciences: From the Sumerians to the cognitivists*, ed. by E. F. K. Koerner & R. E. Asher, 212–217. Oxford: Pergamon.

Koivulehto, Jorma. 1999. *Verba mutuata: Quae vestigia antiquissimi cum Germanis aliisque Indo-Europaeis contactus in linguis Fennicis reliquerint* (Suomalais–Ugrilaisen Seuran Toimituksia/Mémoires de la Société Finno-Ourgrienne 237), ed. by Klaas Ruppel. Helsinki: Finnisch–Ugrische Gesellschaft.

Koivulehto, Jorma. 2001. 'Etymologie und Lehnwortforschung: Ein Überblick um 2000'. *Finnischugrische Forschungen* 56.42–78.

König, Werner. 1989. *Atlas zur Aussprache des Schriftdeutschen in der Bundesrepublik Deutschland*. Ismaning: Hueber Verlag. 2 vols.

König, Werner, Stephan Elspaß, & Robert Möller. 2015. *dtv-Atlas zur deutschen Sprache*. 18th edn. Munich: Deutscher Taschenbuch Verlag.

Köpcke, Klaus-Michael. 1989. 'Schemas in German plural formation'. *Lingua* 74.303–335.

Kotin, Michail. 1998. *Die Herausbildung der grammatischen Kategorie des Genus Verbi im Deutschen: Eine historische Studie zu den Vorstufen und zur Entstehung des deutschen Passiv-Paradigmas*. Tübingen: Buske.

Kotin, Michail. 2003. *Die* werden-*Perspektive und die* werden-*Periphrasen im Deutschen: Historische Entwicklung und Funktionen in der Gegenwartssprache*. Frankfurt: Peter Lang.

Kranzmayer, Eberhard. 1956. *Historische Lautgeographie des gesamtbairischen Dialektraumes*. Vienna: H. Böhlau.

Kroonen, Guus. 2013. *Etymological Dictionary of Proto-Germanic*. Leiden: E. J. Brill.

Krüger, Bruno et al., eds. 1983. *Die Germanen—Geschichte und Kultur der germanischen Stämme in Mitteleuropa: Ein Handbuch in zwei Bänden*, vol. 2. 4th edn. Berlin: Akademie Verlag.

Kufner, Herbert L. 1972. 'The grouping and separation of the Germanic languages'. *Toward a Grammar of Proto-Germanic*, ed. by Frans van Coetsem & Herbert L. Kufner, 71–98. Tübingen: Niemeyer.

Kümmel, Martin. 2015. 'The role of typology in historical phonology'. *Oxford Handbook of Historical Phonology*, ed. by Patrick Honeybone & Joseph Salmons, 121–132. Oxford: Oxford University Press.

Kuroda, Susumu. 2007. Zur valenzmodifizierenden Funktion der Verbalpräfixe im Althochdeutschen und Gegenwartsdeutschen. *Sprachwissenschaft* 32.29–75.

Kürschner, Sebastian. 2003. *Von* Volk-s-musik *und* Sport-Ø-geist *im* Lemming-Ø-land—*af* folk-e-musik *og* sport-s-ånd *i* lemming-e-landet: *Fugenelemente im Deutschen und Dänischen: Eine kontrastive Studie zu einem Grenzfall der Morphologie*. Freiburg: FreiDok.

Kürschner, Sebastian. 2008a. 'Semantische Konditionierung in der Pluralallomorphie deutscher Dialekte'. *Dialektale Morphologie, dialektale Syntax. Beiträge zum 2. Kongress der Internationalen Gesellschaft für Dialektologie des Deutschen, Wien, 20–23. September 2006*, ed. by Franz Patocka & Guido Seiler, 141–156. Vienna: Praesens.

Kürschner, Sebastian. 2008b. *Deklinationsklassen-Wandel: Eine diachron-kontrastive Studie zur Entwicklung der Pluralallomorphie im Deutschen, Niederländischen, Schwedischen und Dänischen* (Studia Linguistica Germanica 92.) Berlin: de Gruyter.

Kürschner, Sebastian & Damaris Nübling. 2011. 'The interaction of gender and declension in Germanic languages'. *Folia linguistica* 45.355–388.

Küspert, Klaus-Christian. 1988. *Vokalsysteme im Westnordischen: Isländisch, Färöisch, Westnorwegisch: Prinzipien der Differenzierung* (Linguistische Arbeiten 198.) Tübingen: Niemeyer.

Kyes, Robert L. 1967. 'The evidence for *i*-umlaut in Old Low Franconian'. *Language* 43.666–673.

Kyes, Robert L. 1989. 'German vowel lengthening: Causes and conditions'. *American Journal of Germanic Linguistics and Literatures* 1.153–176.

Kylstra, A. D. 1991–96. *Lexikon der älteren germanischen Lehnworter in den ostseefinnischen Sprachen*. Amsterdam: Rodopi. (Continued by Sirkka-Liisa Hahmo, Tette Hafstra, & Osmo Nikkilä.)

Labov, William. 1975. 'On the use of the present to explain the past'. *Proceedings of the 11th International Congress of Linguists*, ed. by Luigi Heilmann, 825–851. Bologna: Il Mulino. (Reprinted in *Linguistics at the Crossroads*, 1977, ed. by Adam Makkai, Valerie Becker Makkai, & Luigi Heilmann, pp. 226–261. Padova, Italy: Liviana and Lake Bluff, Ill.: Jupiter Press.)

Labov, William. 1994. *Principles of Linguistic Change*, vol. 1: *Internal Factors*. Oxford: Blackwell.

Labov, William. 2001. *Principles of Linguistic Change*, vol. 2: *Social Factors*. Oxford: Blackwell.

Labov, William. 2007. 'Transmission and diffusion'. *Language* 83.344–387.

Labov, William & Sharon Ash. 1997. 'Understanding Birmingham'. *Language Variety in the South Revisited*, ed. by Cynthia Bernstein, Thomas Nunnally, & Robin Sabino, 508–573. Tuscaloosa: University of Alabama Press.

Labov, William, Sharon Ash, & Charles Boberg. 2006. *Atlas of North American English: Phonetics, phonology, and sound change*. Berlin: Mouton de Gruyter.

Langer, Nils. 2001. *Linguistic Purism in Action: How auxiliary* tun *was stigmatized in Early New High German*. Berlin: de Gruyter.

Langer, Nils. 2007. 'Finding Standard German: Thoughts on Linguistic Codification'. *Standard, Variation und Sprachwandel in germanischen Sprachen*, ed. by Christian Fandrych & Reinier Salverda, 217–214. Tübingen: Gunter Narr.

Langer, Nils. 2014. 'Standard German in the eighteenth century'. *Norms and Usage in Language History, 1600–1900: A sociolinguistic and comparative perspective*, ed. by Gijsbert Rutten, Rik Vosters, & Wim Vandenbussche, 277–302. Amsterdam: John Benjamins.

Lasch, Agathe. 1928. *Berlinisch: Eine berlinische Sprachgeschichte*. Berlin: Reimar Hobbing.

Lass, Roger. 1994. *Old English: A historical linguistic companion*. Cambridge: Cambridge University Press.

Lehmann, Christian. 1985. 'Grammaticalization: Synchronic variation and diachronic change'. *Lingua e Stile* 20.303–318.

Lehmann, Winfred P., ed. 1967. *A Reader in Nineteenth Century Historical Indo-European Linguistics*. Bloomington: Indiana University Press. http://www.utexas.edu/cola/centers/lrc/books/readT.html.

Lehmann, Winfred P. 1972. 'Proto-Germanic syntax'. *Toward a Grammar of Proto-Germanic*, ed. by Frans van Coetsem & Herbert L. Kufner, 239–268. Tübingen: Max Niemeyer.

Lehmann, Winfred P. 1986. *A Gothic Etymological Dictionary*. Leiden: E. J. Brill.

Lehmann, Winfred P. 1994. 'Gothic and the reconstruction of Proto-Germanic'. *The Germanic Languages*, ed. by Ekkehard König & Johan van der Auwera, 19–37. London: Routledge.

Leiss, Elisabeth. 1985. 'Zur Entstehung des neuhochdeutschen analytischen Futurs'. *Sprachwissenschaft* 10.250–273.

Leiss, Elisabeth. 2000. *Artikel und Aspekt: Die grammatischen Muster von Definitheit* (Studia Linguistica Germanica 55). Berlin: Walter de Gruyter.

Lenerz, Jürgen. 1985. 'Zur Theorie syntaktischen Wandels: Das expletive *es* in der Geschichte des Deutschen'. *Erklärende Syntax des Deutschen*, ed. by Werner Abraham, 99–136. Tübingen: Narr.

Lenz, Alexandra. 2003. *Struktur und Dynamik des Substandards: Eine Studie zum Westmitteldeutschen (Wittlich/Eifel)*. Stuttgart: Steiner.

Leopold, Werner F. 1959. 'The decline of German dialects'. *WORD* 15.130–153. (Reprinted in *Readings in the Sociology of Language*, 1972, ed. by Joshua Fishman, 340–364. Berlin: Mouton de Gruyter).

Leuschner, Torsten, Tanja Mortelmans, & Sarah De Groodt, eds. 2005. *Grammatikalisierung im Deutschen*. Berlin: De Gruyter.

Lhuyd, Eduard. 1707. *Archaeologia Britannica*. Oxford: Printed at the Theater.

Lieberman, Erez, Jean-Baptiste Michel, Joe Jackson, Tina Tang, & Martin A. Nowak. 2007. 'Quantifying the evolutionary dynamics of language'. *Nature* 449.713–716.

Lightfoot, David. 1991. *How to Set Parameters: Arguments from language change*. Cambridge, Mass.: MIT Press.

Lightfoot, David. 2002. 'Myths and the prehistory of grammars'. *Journal of Linguistics* 38.113–136.

Lightfoot, David. 2003. 'Grammatical approaches to syntactic change'. *The Handbook of Historical Linguistics*, ed. by Brian D. Joseph & Richard D. Janda, 495–508. Oxford: Blackwell.

Lindeman, Fredrik Otto. 1987. *Introduction to the 'Laryngeal Theory'*. Oslo: Norwegian University Press.

Lindgren, Kaj. 1953. *Die Apokope des mittelhochdeutschen -e in seinen verschiedenen Funktionen*. Helsinki: Annales Academiae Scientiarum Fennicae.

Lippi-Green, Rosina L. 1994. *Language Ideology and Language Change in Early Modern German: A sociolinguistic study of the consonantal system of Nuremberg*. Amsterdam: John Benjamins.

Lippi-Green, Rosina L. 1997. *English with an Accent: Language, ideology and discrimination in the United States*. London: Routledge. (2nd edn., 2012.)

Litty, Samantha, Christine Evans, & Joseph Salmons. 2015. 'Gray zones: The fluidity of Wisconsin German language and identification'. *Linguistic Construction of Ethnic Borders*, ed. by Peter Rosenberg, 183–205. Frankfurt: Peter Lang.

Lockwood, W. B. 1965. *An Informal History of the German Language*. London: Deutsch.

Lockwood, W. B. 1968. *Historical German Syntax*. Oxford: Clarendon.

Luiten, Tyler. 2011. *Old High German Nominal Morphology Revisited: A fresh look at old paradigms*. Ph.D. dissertation, University of Wisconsin–Madison.

Luiten, Tyler, Andrea Menz, Angela Bagwell, Benjamin Frey, John Lindner, Mike Olson, Kristin Speth, & Joseph Salmons. 2013. 'Beyond the handbooks: A quantitative approach to analysis of Old High German phonology and morphology'. *Beiträge zur Geschichte der deutschen Sprache und Literatur (PBB)*. 135.1–18.

Luraghi, Silvia. 2010a. 'The rise (and possible downfall) of configurationality'. *The Continuum Companion to Historical Linguistics*, ed. by Silvia Luraghi & Vit Bubenik, 212–229. London: Continuum.

Luraghi, Silvia. 2010b. 'Causes of language change'. *The Continuum Companion to Historical Linguistics*, ed. by Silvia Luraghi & Vit Bubenik, 358–370. London: Continuum.

Mailhammer, Robert. 2007a. 'Islands of resilience: The history of the verbs from a systemic point of view'. *Morphology* 17.77–108.

Mailhammer, Robert. 2007b. *The Germanic Strong Verbs: Foundations and development of a new system.* Berlin: Mouton de Gruyter.

Mailhammer, Robert. 2008. 'Ablaut variation in the Proto-Germanic noun: The long arm of the strong verbs'. *Sprachwissenschaft* 33.279–300.

Maitz, Péter & Krisztián Tronka. 2009. '*Brauchen*: Phonologische Aspekte der Auxiliarisierung'. *Zeitschrift für Dialektologie und Linguistik* 76.189–202.

Mallory, J. P. 1989. *In Search of the Indo-Europeans: Language, archaeology and myth.* London: Thames & Hudson.

Mallory, J. P. & Douglas Q. Adams, eds. 1997. *Encyclopedia of Indo-European Culture.* London: Fitzroy Dearborn.

Mallory, J. P. & Douglas Q. Adams. 2006. *The Oxford Introduction to Proto-Indo-European and the Proto-Indo-European World.* Oxford: Oxford University Press.

Maratsos, M. P. 1979. 'Learning how and when to use pronouns and determiners'. *Language Acquisition: Studies in first language development*, ed. by P. Fletcher & M. Garman, 225–240. Cambridge: Cambridge University Press.

Martens, Carl & Peter Martens. 1961. *Phonetik der deutschen Sprache: Praktische Aussprachelehre.* Munich: Max Hueber.

Masalon, Kevin Ch. 2010. 'Sprachgeschichte im Internet'. *Zeitschrift für germanistische Linguistik* 38.150–152.

McKitterick, Rosamond. 1989. *The Carolingians and the Written Word.* Cambridge: Cambridge University Press.

McLelland, Nicola. 2011. *J. G. Schottelius's* Ausführliche Arbeit von der Teutschen HaubtSprache *(1663) and Its Place in Early Modern European Vernacular Language Study.* (Publications of the Philological Society 44.) Oxford: Wiley Blackwell.

McWhorter, John. 2011. 'Tying up loose ends: The creole prototype after all'. *Diachronica* 28.89–117.

Meineke, Eckhard & Judith Schwerdt. 2001. *Einführung in das Althochdeutsche.* Paderborn: Verlag Ferdinand Schöningh.

Menz, Andrea. 2010. *Accent Type and Language Change in Germanic and Baltic-Finnic.* Ph.D. dissertation, University of Wisconsin–Madison.

Menz, Andrea & Helena Ruf. Manuscript. 'The bisyllabic trochaic foot in German plural nouns: An "evolutionary" account'.

Meyer, Hans Joachim. 2004. 'Global English: A new lingua franca or a new imperial culture?'. *Globalization and the Future of German*, ed. by Andreas Gardt & Bernd Hüppauf, 65–84. Berlin: Mouton de Gruyter.

Meyer-Benfey, Heinrich. 1901. 'Über den Ursprung der germanischen Lautverschiebung'. *Zeitschrift für Deutsches Altertum* 45.101–128.

Michel, Sascha. 2010. '*OR + EN + WURM, TAG+S+BRIEF, KELB+ER+ARZET*: Fugenelemente in N+N Komposita des Frühneuhochdeutschen'. *Beiträge zur Geschichte der deutschen Sprache und Literatur* 132.177–199.

Michels, Victor. 1889. *Zum Wechsel des Nominalgeschlechts im Deutschen.* Strassburg: Grübner.

Mihm, Arend. 2004. 'Zur Geschichte der Auslautverhärtung und ihrer Erforschung'. *Sprachwissenschaft* 29.133–206.

Miller, D. Gary. Forthcoming. *The Oxford Gothic Grammar.* Oxford: Oxford University Press.

Milroy, James. 1992a. *Linguistic Variation & Change: On the historical sociolinguistics of English*. Oxford: Oxford University Press.

Milroy, James. 1992b. 'Social network and prestige arguments in sociolinguistics'. *Sociolinguistics Today: International perspectives*, ed. by K. Bolton & H. Kwok, 146–162. London: Kingsley Bolton.

Minkova, Donka. 2003. *Alliteration and Sound Change in Early English*. Cambridge: Cambridge University Press.

Minkova, Donka. 2014. *A Historical Phonology of English*. Edinburgh: Edinburgh University Press.

Mladenova, Olga M. 2009. 'On morphosyntactic change in Bulgarian: Case and definiteness'. *Diachronica* 26.408–436.

Moosmüller, Sylvia. 1991. *Hochsprache und Dialekt in Österreich: Soziophonologische Untersuchungen zu ihrer Abgrenzung in Wien, Graz, Salzburg und Innsbruck*. Vienna: Böhlau.

Morpurgo Davies, Anna. 1975. 'Language classification in the nineteenth century'. *Historiography of Linguistics,* ed. by Thomas A. Sebeok, 607–717. The Hague: Mouton de Gruyter.

Mortensen, David. 2012. 'The Emergence of Obstruents after High Vowels'. *Diachronica* 29.434–470.

Moser, Hugo, Hugo Stopp, Werner Besch, et al. 1970–1988. *Grammatik des Frühneuhochdeutschen*. Heidelberg: Carl Winter. 7 vols.

Mühlhäusler, Peter. 2002. *Linguistic Ecology: Language change and linguistic imperialism in the Pacific region*. London: Routledge.

Muhr, Rudolf. 2003. 'Language change via satellite: The influence of German television broadcasting on Austrian German'. *Journal of Historical Pragmatics* 4.103–127.

Müller, Reimar & Marga Reis, eds. 2001. *Modalität und Modalverben im Deutschen*. Hamburg: Buske.

Müller, Stephan. 2007. *Althochdeutsche Literatur: Eine kommentierte Anthologie. Althochdeutsch/Neuhochdeutsch/Altniederdeutsch/Neuhochdeutsch: Eine kommentierte Anthologie. Neuübersetzung*. Stuttgart: Reklam.

Munske, Horst Haider, ed. 2001. *Handbuch des Friesischen / Handbook of Frisian Studies*. Produced in collaboration with Nils Århammar, Volkert F. Faltings, Jarich Hoekstra, Oebele Vries, Alastair G. H. Walker, & Ommo Wilts. Tübingen: Max Niemeyer.

Murray, Robert W. 1988. *Phonological Strength and Early Germanic Syllable Structure*. Munich: Fink.

Murray, Robert W. 2000. 'Syllable cut prosody in Early Middle English'. *Language* 76.617–654.

Murray, Robert W. & Theo Vennemann. 1983. 'Sound change and syllable structure in Germanic phonology'. *Language* 59.514–528.

Neckel, Gustav. 1900. *Über die altgermanischen relativsätze*. Berlin: Mayer & Müller.

Nichols, Johanna. 1986. 'Head-marking and dependent-marking grammar'. *Language* 62.56–119.

Nichols, Stephen G. 1990. 'Introduction: Philology in a manuscript culture'. *Speculum* 65.1–10. (Special issue *The New Philology*.)

Nielsen, Hans Frede. 1989. *The Germanic Languages: Origins and early dialectal interactions.* Tuscaloosa, Ala.: University of Alabama Press. (Updated translation of his 1979 *De germanske sprog.*)

Nielsen, Hans Frede. 2000. *The Early Runic Language of Scandinavia.* Heidelberg: Carl Winter.

Niepokuj, Mary. 1997. *The Development of Verbal Reduplication in Indo-European* (Journal of Indo-European Studies Monograph 27.) Washington: Institute for the Study of Man.

Nübling, Damaris. 2000. *Prinzipien der Irregularisierung: Eine kontrastive Analyse von zehn Verben in zehn germanischen Sprachen* (Linguistische Arbeiten 415.) Tübingen: Niemeyer.

Nübling, Damaris. 2008. 'Was tun mit Flexionsklassen? Deklinationsklassen und ihr Wandel im Deutschen und seinen Dialekten'. *Zeitschrift für Dialektologie und Linguistik* 75.282–331.

Nübling, Damaris. 2011. 'How do exceptions arise? On different paths to morphological irregularity'. *Expecting the Unexpected: Exceptions in grammar,* ed. by Horst Simon & Heike Wiese, 139–162. Berlin: Walter de Gruyter.

Nübling, Damaris, Antje Dammel, Janet Duke, & Renata Szczepaniak. 2013. *Historische Sprachwissenschaft des Deutschen: Eine Einführung in die Prinzipien des Sprachwandels.* 4th edn. Tübingen: Gunter Narr.

Nübling, Damaris & Renata Szczepaniak. 2008. 'On the way from morphology to phonology: German linking elements and the role of the phonological word'. *Morphology* 18.1–25.

Nübling, Damaris & Renata Szczepaniak. 2010. 'Was erklärt die Diachronie für die Synchronie der deutschen Gegenwartssprache? Am Beispiel schwankender Fugenelemente'. *Jahrbuch für germanistische Sprachgeschichte: GGSG; Perspektiven der germanistischen Sprachgeschichtsforschung,* 205–224. https://www.germanistik.uni-mainz.de/files/2015/03/Nubling_Szczepaniak_2010-GGSG-Fugen.pdf.

Nützel, Daniel. 2009. *The East Franconian Dialect of Haysville, Indiana: A study in language death / Die ostfränkische Mundart von Haysville, Indiana: Eine Untersuchung mit ausgewählten morphologischen und syntaktischen Phänomenen.* (Regensburger Dialektforum 15.) Regensburg: Edition Vulpes.

Olsen, Birgit Annette, Robert Mailhammer, & Theo Vennemann, eds. 2015. *Die sprachlichen Wurzeln Europas – Linguistic roots of Europe: Ursprung und Entwicklung – Origin and development.* Copenhagen: Tusculanum Press.

Olson, Mike & Shannon Dubenion-Smith. 2007. 'Towards a typology of relativization strategies in Old Saxon'. Paper presented at the 18th International Conference on Historical Linguistics, Montreal.

Önnersfors, Olaf. 1997. *Verb-erst-Deklarativsätze: Grammatik und Pragmatik* (Lunder germanistische Forschungen 60.) Stockholm: Almqvist & Wiksell International.

Onysko, Alexander. 2007. *Anglicisms in German: Borrowing, lexical productivity and written codeswitching.* Berlin: de Gruyter.

Oxford Duden German Dictionary. 2005. 3rd edn., ed. by Michael Clark & Olaf Thyen. Oxford: Oxford University Press.

Page, B. Richard. 1997. 'Verner's Law'. *Beiträge zur Geschichte der deutschen Sprache und Literatur* 120.175–193.

Page, B. Richard. 1999. 'The Germanic *Verschärfung* and prosodic change'. *Diachronica* 16. 297–334.

Page, B. Richard. 2007. 'On the irregularity of open syllable lengthening in German'. *Historical Linguistics 2005*, ed. by Joseph Salmons & Shannon Dubenion-Smith, 337–350. Amsterdam: John Benjamins.

Palmer, Philip M. 1939. *Neuweltwörter im Deutschen*. Heidelberg: Carl Winter.

Paul, Hermann. 2007. *Mittelhochdeutsche Grammatik*. 25th edn., ed. by Thomas Klein, Hans-Joachim Solms, & Klaus-Peter Wegera. Syntax section by Ingeborg Schöbler, reworked by Heinz-Peter Prell. Tübingen: Max Niemeyer.

Pelkey, Jamin. 2015. 'Reconstructing phylogeny from linkage diffusion: Evidence for cladistic hinge variation'. *Diachronica* 31.397–433.

Penzl, Herbert. 1949. 'Umlaut and secondary umlaut in Old High German'. *Language* 25.223–240.

Penzl, Herbert. 1964. 'Die Phasen der althochdeutschen Lautverschiebung'. *Taylor Starck Festschrift*, ed. by Werner Betz et al., 27–41. The Hague: Mouton.

Penzl, Herbert. 1984. '"Gimer min ros": How German was taught in the ninth and eleventh centuries'. *German Quarterly* 57.392–401.

Penzl, Herbert. 1994. 'Historiographie und Sprachgeschichte: Zur Beschreibung des althochdeutschen i-Umlauts'. *American Journal of Germanic Linguistics & Literatures* 6.51–62.

Philippi, Julia. 1997. 'The rise of the article in the Germanic languages'. *Parameters of Morphosyntactic Change*, ed. by Ans van Kemenade & Nigel Vincent, 62–93. Cambridge: Cambridge University Press.

Pickl, Simon. 2017. 'Neues zur Entwicklung der Negation im Mittelhochdeutschen: Grammatikalisierung und Variation in oberdeutschen Predigten'. *Beiträge zur Geschichte der deutschen Sprache und Literatur* 139.1–46.

Pijpops, Dirk, Katrien Beuls, & Freek Van de Velde. 2015. 'The rise of the verbal weak inflection in Germanic: An agent-based model'. *Computational Linguistics in the Netherlands Journal* 5.81–102.

Pokorny, Julius. 1959. *Indogermanisches etymologisches Wörterbuch*. Bern: Francke.

Polomé, Edgar C. 1986. 'The Non-Indo-European Component of the Germanic Lexicon'. *o-o-pe-ro-si: Festschrift für Ernst Risch zum 75. Geburtstag*, ed. by Annemarie Etter, 661–672. Berlin: de Gruyter.

Polomé, Edgar C. 1983. 'The linguistic situation in the Western provinces of the Roman Empire'. *Aufstieg und Niedergang der römischen Welt: Geschichte und Kultur Roms im Spiegel der neueren Forschung*, ed. by Hildegard Temporini & Wolfgang Haase, 509–533. Berlin: Walter de Gruyter.

Polomé, Edgar C. 1989. 'Substrate lexicon in Germanic'. *NOWELE* 14.53–73.

Polomé, Edgar C. 1996. 'Germanic in early Roman times'. *Germanic Linguistics: Syntactic and diachronic*, ed. by Rosina Lippi-Green & Joseph C. Salmons, 137–147. Amsterdam: John Benjamins.

Polomé, Edgar C. 1988. 'Sprachzustände in den westlichen Provinzen des römischen Kaiserreichs'. *Sociolinguistica* 2.52–72.

Polzin, Albert 1903. *Geschlechtswandel der Substantiva im Deutschen (mit Einschluss der Lehn- und Fremdworte)*. Hildesheim: Gerstenberg.

Priebsch, Robert & William E. Collinson. 1938. *The German Language.* New York: Macmillan.

Prokosch, Eduard. 1917. 'Die deutsche Lautverschiebung und die Völkerwanderung'. *Journal of English and Germanic Philology* 16.1–26.

Prokosch, Eduard. 1938. *A Comparative Germanic Grammar* (William Dwight Whitney Linguistics Series.) Baltimore, Md.: Linguistic Society of America.

Purnell, Thomas, Eric Raimy, & Joseph Salmons. 2009. 'Defining dialect, perceiving dialect and new dialect formation: Sarah Palin's speech'. *Journal of English Linguistics* 37.331–355.

Purnell, Thomas, Joseph Salmons, Dilara Tepeli, & Jennifer Mercer. 2005. 'Structured heterogeneity and change in laryngeal phonetics: Upper Midwestern final obstruents'. *Journal of English Linguistics* 33:4.307–338.

Purnell, Thomas, Dilara Tepeli, & Joseph Salmons. 2005. 'German substrate effects in Wisconsin English: Evidence for final fortition'. *American Speech* 80.135–164.

Ramat, Paolo. 1981. *Einführung in das Germanische.* Tübingen: Niemeyer.

Ramers, Karl Heinz. 1994. 'Verners Gesetz: Ein Beispiel für die Interdependenz segmentaler und prosodischer Faktoren des Lautwandels'. *Sprachwissenschaft* 19.271–306.

Ramers, Karl Heinz. 1999. *Historische Veränderungen prosodischer Strukturen* (Linguistische Arbeiten 400.) Tübingen: Max Niemeyer.

Ramsammy, Michael. 2015. 'The life cycle of phonological processes: Accounting for dialectal microtypologies'. *Language & Linguistics Compass* 9.33–54.

Randall, William & Howard Jones. 2015. 'On the early origins of the Germanic preterite presents'. *Transactions of the Philological Society* 113.137–176.

Ratkus, Artūras. 2018. 'Greek ἀρχιερεύς in Gothic translation. *NOWELE* 71. 3–34.

Referenzkorpus Mittelhochdeutsch (1050–1350). n.d. Website. Bochum: Sprachwissenschaftliches Institut. https://www.linguistics.rub.de/rem.

Reichmann, Oskar & Klaus-Peter Wegera, eds. 1993. *Frühneuhochdeutsche Grammatik,* ed. by R. Ebert, O. Reichmann, H.-J. Solms, & K.-P. Wegera. Tübingen: Niemeyer.

Reimann, Ariane. 1999. *Die Verlaufsform im Deutschen: Entwickelt das Deutsche eine Aspektkorrelation?* Ph.D. dissertation, Universität Bamberg.

Renfrew, Colin. 1987. *Archaeology and Language: The puzzle of the Indo-European origins.* London: Jonathan Cape.

Renn, Manfred & Werner König. 2006. *Kleiner Bayerischer Sprachatlas.* Munich: Deutscher Taschenbuch Verlag.

Riad, Tomas. 1988. 'Tracing the Foot: A metrical analysis of change in Nordic languages'. *Arkiv för Nordisk Filologi* 103.1–35.

Riad, Tomas. 1992. *Structures in Germanic Prosody: A diachronic study with special reference to the Nordic languages.* Ph.D. dissertation, Stockholm University.

Rice, Curt. 2006. 'Optimizing gender'. *Lingua* 116.1394–1417.

Ringe, Donald A. 1992. *On Calculating the Factor of Chance in Language Comparison* (Transactions of the American Philosophical Society 82.1.) Philadelphia, Pa.: American Philosophical Society.

Ringe, Don. 2006. *From Proto-Indo-European to Proto-Germanic.* Oxford: Oxford University Press.

Ringe, Don & Joseph F. Eska. 2013. *Historical Linguistics: Toward a twenty-first century reintegration.* Cambridge: Cambridge University Press.

Ringe, Don, Tandy Warnow, & Anne Taylor. 2002. 'Indo-European and computational cladistics'. *Transactions of the Philological Society* 100.59–129.

Rix, Helmut et al., eds. 2001. *Lexikon der indogermanischen Verben.* 2nd edn. Wiesbaden: Reichert.

Roberge, Paul T. 1990. 'The ideological profile of Afrikaans historical linguistics'. *Ideologies of Language*, ed. by John E. Joseph & Talbot J. Taylor, 131–149. London: Routledge.

Roberge, Paul T. 2010. 'Contact and the history of the Germanic languages'. *The Handbook of Language Contact*, ed. by Raymond Hickey, 406–431. Oxford: Blackwell.

Robinson, Orrin W. 1975. 'Abstract phonology and the history of umlaut'. *Lingua* 37.1–29.

Robinson, Orrin W. 1980. 'An exception to Old High German umlaut'. *American Indian and Indoeuropean Studies: Papers in honor of Madison S. Beeler*, ed. by K. Klar, M. Langdon, & S. Silver, 449–460. The Hague: Mouton.

Robinson, Orrin W. 1992. *Old English and Its Closest Relatives: A survey of the earliest Germanic languages.* Stanford, Calif.: Stanford University Press.

Robinson, Orrin W. 2001. *Whose German? The ich/ach alternation and related phenomena in 'standard' and 'colloquial'.* Amsterdam: John Benjamins.

Roelcke, Thorsten. 1995. *Periodisierung der deutschen Sprachgeschichte.* Berlin: de Gruyter.

Rögnvaldsson, Eiríkur. 1995. 'Old Icelandic: A non-configurational language?'. *North-Western European Language Evolution* 26.3–29.

Romaine, Suzanne. 1989. 'Pidgins, creoles, immigrant, and dying languages'. *Investigating obsolescence: Studies in language contraction and death*, ed. by Nancy C. Dorian, 369–383. Cambridge: Cambridge University Press.

Ruhlen, Merritt. 1987. *A Guide to the World's Languages.* Stanford, Calif.: Stanford University Press.

Russ, Charles V. J. 1994. *The German Language Today: A linguistic introduction.* London: Routledge.

Salmons, Joseph. 1992a. *Accentual Change and Language Contact: Comparative survey and case study of early northern Europe.* Stanford, Calif.: Stanford University Press/ London: Routledge.

Salmons, Joseph. 1992b. 'The evolution of gender assignment rules from OHG to NHG'. *Recent Developments in Germanic Linguistics*, ed. by Rosina Lippi-Green, 81–95. Amsterdam: John Benjamins.

Salmons, Joseph. 1992c. *The Glottalic Theory: Survey and synthesis* (Journal of Indo-European Studies Monographs 10.) Washington, DC: Institute for the Study of Man.

Salmons, Joseph. 1992d. 'Northwest Indo-European vocabulary and substrate phonology'. *Perspectives on Indo-European Language, Culture and Religion: Studies in honor of Edgar C. Polomé* (Journal of Indo-European Studies Monographs 9), vol. 2, 265–279. Washington, DC: Institute for the Study of Man.

Salmons, Joseph. 1992e. 'A look at the data for a global etymology: *tik "finger"'. *Explanation in Historical Linguistics*, ed. by Garry W. Davis & Gregory K. Iverson, 207–228. Amsterdam: John Benjamins.

Salmons, Joseph. 1993. 'The structure of the lexicon: Evidence from German gender assignment rules'. *studies in language* 17.411–435.

Salmons, Joseph. 1994. 'Umlaut and plurality in Old High German: Some problems with a Natural Morphology account'. *Diachronica* 11.213–229.

Salmons, Joseph. 2004. 'How (non-)Indo-European is the Germanic lexicon? . . . And what does that mean?' *Etymologie, Entlehnungen und Entwicklungen: Festschrift für Jorma Koivulehto zum 70. Geburtstag* (Mémoires de la Société Néophilologique 63), ed. by Irma Hyvärinen, Petri Kallio, & Jarmo Korhonen, 311–321. Helsinki: Société Néophilologique.

Salmons, Joseph. 2015. 'Language shift and the Indo-Europeanization of Europe'. *Die sprachlichen Wurzeln Europas / Linguistic roots of Europe: Ursprung und Entwicklung / Origin and development*, ed. by Birgit Annette Olsen, Robert Mailhammer, & Theo Vennemann, 103–125. Copenhagen: Tusculanum Press.

Salmons, Joseph. 2016a. 'The evolution of Germanic'. *Comparative Indo-European Linguistics: An international handbook of language comparison and the reconstruction of Indo-European*, ed. by Jared Klein, Brian Joseph, & Matthias Fritz, 129–153. Berlin: Mouton de Gruyter.

Salmons, Joseph. 2016b. Review of *Frühmittelalterliche Glossen: Ein Beitrag zur Funktionalität und Kontextualität mittelalterlicher Schriftlichkeit* by Markus Schiegg, 2015. *Diachronica* 33.417–422.

Salmons, Joseph. Forthcoming. 'The larynx and Indo-European obstruent phonology and phonetics'. *Historische Sprachforschung / Historical Linguistics*.

Salmons, Joseph & Thomas Purnell. 2010. 'Language contact and the development of American English'. *The Handbook of Language Contact*, ed. by Raymond Hickey, 454–477. Oxford: Blackwell.

Sanders, Ruth H. 2010. *German: Biography of a language.* Oxford: Oxford University Press.

Sapp, Christopher D. 2009. 'Syncope as the cause of *Präteritumschwund*: New Data from an Early New High German corpus'. *Journal of Germanic Linguistics* 21.419–450.

Sapp, Christopher D. 2011a. *The Verbal Complex in Subordinate Clauses from Medieval to Modern German.* Amsterdam: John Benjamins.

Sapp, Christopher D. 2011b. 'Auxiliary selection in the Early New High German perfect tenses'. *Groninger Arbeiten zur germanistischen Linguistik* 52.29–43.

Sauer, Wolfgang Werner. 1988. *Der 'Duden': Geschichte und Aktualität eines 'Volkswörterbuchs'.* Stuttgart: Metzler.

Schaffner, Stefan. 2001. *Das Vernersche Gesetz und der innerparadigmatische grammatische Wechsel des Urgermanischen Nominalbereich.* Innsbruck: Innsbrucker Beiträge zur Sprachwissenschaft.

Schiegg, Markus. 2015. *Frühmittelalterliche Glossen: Ein Beitrag zur Funktionalität und Kontextualität mittelalterlicher Schriftlichkeit.* Heidelberg: Winter.

Schilling, Heinz. 1993. *Die Stadt in der frühen Neuzeit.* Munich: Oldenbourg.

Schirmunski, Viktor M. 1930. *Sprachgeschichte und Siedlungsmundarten.* Heidelberg: Carl Winter.

Schirmunski, Viktor M. 2010. *Deutsche Mundartforschung: Vergleichende Laut- und Formenlehre der deutschen Mundarten,* ed. by Larissa Naiditch. Frankfurt: Peter Lang. (Original edition, 1962. Berlin: Akademie Verlag.)

Schlosser, Horst Dieter. 2004. *Althochdeutsche Literatur*. Berlin: Erich Schmidt.

Schmidt, Jürgen Erich. 2010. 'Language and space: The linguistic dynamics approach'. *Language and Space: An international handbook of linguistic variation. Theories and methods*, ed. by Peter Auer & Jürgen Erich Schmidt, 201–225. Berlin: Mouton de Gruyter.

Schmidt, Wihlelm et al. 2007. *Geschichte der deutschen Sprache: Ein Lehrbuch für das germanistische Studium*. 9th edn. Stuttgart: Hirzel.

Schneider, Karin. 2009. *Paläolographie/Handschriftenkunde: Eine Einführung*. 2nd edn. Tübingen: Niemeyer.

Schrodt, Richard. 1974. *Die germanische Lautverschiebung und ihre Stellung im Kreise der indogermanischen Sprachen* (Wiener Arbeiten zur germanischen Altertumskunde und Philologie 1.) Vienna: Halosar.

Schrodt, Richard. 2004. *Althochdeutsche Grammatik II: Syntax*. Tübingen: Max Niemeyer.

Schuhmann, Roland. 2017. 'A new Abrogans fragment'. *Altgermanistik* (blog). http://altgermanistik.blogspot.com/2017/05/a-new-abrogans-fragment.html.

Schulte, Michael. 2006. 'Oral traces in Runic epigraphy: Evidence from older and younger inscriptions'. *Journal of Germanic Linguistics* 18.117–151.

Schulte, Michael. 2013. 'The Norwegian Hogganvik stone as an emblem of social status and identity'. *Across the Sólundarhaf: Connections between Scotland and the Nordic world—Selected papers from the inaugural St. Magnus conference 2011*, ed. by Alexandra Sanmark & Angus Somerville. Special issue of *Journal of the North Atlantic* 4.120–128.

Schulte, Michael. 2017. 'When did Nordic become Nordic?' Paper presented at the 23rd Germanic Linguistics Annual Conference, University of Texas at Austin.

Schulze, Jan Henning. 2010. *Der i-Umlaut im Althochdeutschen. Theorie, Phonetik und Typologie sowie eine optimalitätstheoretische Analyse*. Bamberg: University of Bamberg Press.

Schwarz, Ernst. 1982. *Kurze Deutsche Wortgeschichte*. 2nd edn. Darmstadt: Wissenschaftliche Buchgesellschaft.

Schweikle, Günther. 1986. *Germanisch-deutsche Sprachgeschichte im Überblick*. Stuttgart: Metzler.

Schwink, Frederick W. 2004. *The Third Gender: Studies in the origin and history of Germanic grammatical gender*. (Indogermanische Bibliothek.) Heidelberg: Winter.

Seiler, Annina. 2014. *The Scripting of the Germanic Languages: A comparative study of 'spelling difficulties' in Old English, Old High German and Old Saxon*. Zürich: Chronos.

Selkirk, Elisabeth O. 1995. 'The prosodic structure of function words'. *Papers in Optimality Theory*, ed. by Jill N. Beckman, Laura Walsh Dickey, & Suzanne Urbanczyk, 439–469. (UMOP 18.) Amherst: GLSA.

Siebs, Theodor. *Deutsche Bühnenaussprache*. Berlin: de Gruyter. (Many editions, with varying titles; American edition, 1944, New York: Frederick Ungar.)

Sihler, Andrew. 1995. *New Comparative Greek and Latin Grammar*. Oxford: Oxford University Press.

Simon, Horst J. 2003a. 'From pragmatics to grammar: Tracing the development of respect in the history of the German pronouns of address'. *Diachronic Perspectives on Address Term Systems*, ed. by Irma Taavitsainen & Andreas H. Jucker, 85–123. Amsterdam: John Benjamins.

Trips, Carola. 2014. 'Derivation and historical change'. *Oxford Handbook of Derivational Morphology*, ed. Rochelle Lieber & Pavol Stekauer, 284–406. Oxford: Oxford University Press.

Trudgill, Peter. 1983. 'Acts of conflicting identity: The sociolinguistics of British popsong pronunciation'. *On Dialect: Social and geographical perspectives*, 141–160. Oxford: Blackwell.

Trudgill, Peter. 2010. *Investigations in Sociohistorical Linguistics*. Cambridge: Cambridge University Press.

Tschirsch, Fritz. 1983. *Geschichte der deutschen Sprache*. Berlin: Erich Schmidt. 2 vols.

Twaddell, W. Freeman. 1938. 'A note on OHG umlaut'. *Monatshefte* 30.177–181.

Urban, Matthias. 2014. 'Lexical semantic change and semantic reconstruction'. *The Routledge Handbook of Historical Linguistics*, ed. by Claire Bowern & Bethwyn Evans, 362–392. London: Routledge.

Van Coetsem, Frans. 1994. *The Vocalism of the Germanic Parent Language: Systemic evolution and sociohistorical context*. Heidelberg: Winter.

Van Coetsem, Frans, Ronald Hendricks, & Susan McCormick. 1981. 'Accent typology and sound change'. *Lingua* 53.295–315.

Van Pottelberge, Jeroen. 2004. *Der am-Progressiv: Struktur und parallele Entwicklung in den kontinentalwestgermanischen Sprachen*. (Tübinger Beiträge zur Linguistik 456.) Tübingen: Gunter Narr.

Vaught, George Mason. 1977. *A Study of 'Auslautsverhärtung' in Old High German*. Ph.D. dissertation, University of Massachusetts, Amherst.

Vennemann, Theo. 1984. 'Hochgermanisch und Niedergermanisch: Die Verzweigungstheorie der germanisch-deutschen Lautverschiebung'. *Beiträge zur Geschichte der deutschen Sprache und Literatur* 106.1–45.

Vennemann, Theo. 1985. 'The bifurcation theory of the Germanic and German consonant shifts: Synopsis and some further thoughts'. *Papers from the Sixth International Conference on Historical Linguistics*, ed. by Jacek Fisiak, 527–547. Amsterdam: John Benjamins.

Vennemann, Theo. 1988. *Preference Laws for Syllable Structure and the Explanation of Sound Change, with Special Reference to German, Germanic, Italian, and Latin*. Berlin: Mouton de Gruyter.

Vennemann, Theo. 2003. *Europa Vasconica—Europa Semitica* (Trends in Linguistics Studies and Monographs 138), ed. by Patrizia Noel Aziz Hanna. Berlin & New York: Mouton de Gruyter.

Vennemann, Theo. 2007. 'Rome, Etruria, Carthage? Origins of the Germanic runes'. Plenary paper presented at the 18th International Conference on Historical Linguistics, Montreal.

Verner, Karl. 1875. 'Eine Ausnahme der ersten Lautverschiebung'. *Zeitschrift für vergleichende Sprachforschung* 23.97–130.

Viëtor, Wilhelm. 1904. *Elemente der Phonetik des Deutschen, Englischen und Französischen*. 5th edn. Leipzig: O. R. Reisland.

Voeste, Anja. 1999. *Varianz und Vertikalisierung: Zur Normierung der Adjektivdeklination in der ersten Hälfte des 18. Jahrhunderts*. Amsterdam: Rodopi.

Vogel, Petra. 2006. '"Ich hab da nen kleines Problem!": Zur neuen Kurzform des indefiniten Artikels im Deutschen'. *Zeitschrift für Dialektologie und Linguistik* 73.176–193.

von Polenz, Peter. 1994. *Deutsche Sprachgeschichte*, II: *17. und 18. Jahrhundert*. Berlin: de Gruyter. (2nd edn., 2013.)

von Polenz, Peter. 1999. *Deutsche Sprachgeschichte*, III: *19. und 20. Jahrhundert*. Berlin: de Gruyter.

Voyles, Joseph B. 1991. 'A history of OHG *i*-umlaut'. *Beiträge zur Geschichte der deutschen Sprache und Literatur* 113.159–195.

Vries, Jan de. 1984. *European Urbanization 1500–1800*. Cambridge, Mass.: Harvard University Press.

Vries, Jan P. de. 1962. *Altnordisches etymologisches Wörterbuch*. 2nd edn. Leiden: Brill.

Vries, Jan P. de. 1971. *Nederlands etymologisch woordenboek*. Leiden: Brill.

Wagener, Peter. 1997. 'Nach 40 Jahren: Zu individuellen Veränderungen der gesprochenen Sprache'. *Varietäten des Deutschen: Regional- und Umgangssprachen*, ed. by Gerhard Stickel, 291–307. Berlin: de Gruyter.

Walkden, George. 2013. 'The correspondence problem in syntactic reconstruction'. *Diachronica* 30.95–122.

Walkden, George. 2014. *Syntactic Reconstruction and Proto-Germanic*. Oxford: Oxford University Press.

Walker, Rachel. 2011. *Vowel Patterns in Language*. Cambridge: Cambridge University Press.

Waterman, John T. 1966. *A History of the German Language, with Special Reference to the Cultural and Social Forces that Shaped the Standard Literary Language*. Seattle: University of Washington Press.

Watkins, Calvert. 2011. *The American Heritage Dictionary of Indo-European Roots*. 3rd edn. Boston: Houghton Mifflin.

Wauchope, Mary Michele. 1992. 'Old High German *nu*'. *Recent Developments in Germanic Linguistics*, ed. by Rosina Lippi-Green, 57–68. Amsterdam: John Benjamins.

Weddige, Hilkert. 2008. *Einführung in die germanistische Mediävistik*. 7th edn. Munich: C. H. Beck.

Weerman, Fred. 1986. *The V2 Conspiracy: A synchronic and diachronic analysis of verbal positions in the Germanic languages* (Publications in Language Sciences 31.) Dordrecht: Foris.

Wegener, Heide. 1993. '*weil—das hat schon seinen Grund*. Zur Verbstellung in Kausalsätzen mit *weil* im gegenwärtigen Deutsch'. *Deutsche Sprache* 21.289–305.

Wegener, Heide. 1999. 'Syntaxwandel und Degrammatikalisierung im heutigen Deutsch? Noch einmal zu *weil*-Verbzweit'. *Deutsche Sprache* 27.3–26.

Wegener, Heide. 2007. 'Entwicklungen im heutigen Deutsch—Wird Deutsch einfacher?' *Deutsche Sprache* 35.35–62.

Wegera, Klaus-Peter & Hans-Joachim Solms. 2000. 'Morphologie des Frühneuhochdeutschen'. *Sprachgeschichte: Ein Handbuch zur Geschichte der deutschen Sprache und ihrer Erforschung*, ed. by Werner Besch et al. Part 2: *1542–1554*. Berlin: de Gruyter.

Weinreich, Max. 2008. *History of the Yiddish Language*. New Haven, Conn: Yale University Press, ed. by Paul Glasser, trans. by Shlomo Noble with the assistance of Joshua A. Fishman. 2 vols. (Originally published in 1973 as *Geshikhte fun der yidisher shprakh*, by the Yivo Institute for Jewish Research.)

Weinreich, Uriel, William Labov, & Marvin I. Herzog. 1968. 'Empirical foundations for a theory of language change'. *Directions for Historical Linguistics: A symposium*, ed. by Winfred P. Lehmann & Yakov Malkiel, 97–195. Austin: University of Texas Press.

Weiß, Helmut. 2001. 'On two types of natural languages: Some consequences for linguistics'. *Theoretical Linguistics* 27.87–103.

Weiß, Helmut. 2004. 'A question of relevance: Some remarks on standard languages'. *Studies in Language* 28.648–674.

Weiß, Helmut. 2005. 'Inflected Complementizers in Continental West Germanic Dialects'. *Zeitschrift für Dialektologie und Linguistik* 72.148–166.

Wells, Christopher J. 1985. *German: A linguistic history to 1945*. Oxford: Clarendon.

Wenker, Georg. 1926ff. *Deutscher Sprachatlas auf Grund des von Georg Wenker begründeten Sprachatlas des Deutschen Reiches*. Marburg: Elwert (= *Der Digitale Wenker Atlas*, http://www.diwa.info.).

Wiese, Heike. 2009. 'Grammatical innovation in multiethnic urban Europe: New linguistic practices among adolescents'. *Lingua* 119.782–806.

Wiese, Heike. 2012. *Kiezdeutsch: Ein neuer Dialekt entsteht*. Munich: C. H. Beck.

Wiese, Heike. 2013. 'Das Potential multiethnischer Sprechergemeinschaften'. *Das Deutsch der Migranten*, ed. by Arnulf Deppermann, 41–58. Berlin: de Gruyter.

Wiese, Heike, Ulrike Freywald, & Katharina Mayr. 2009. *Kiezdeutsch as a Test Case for the Interaction between Grammar and Information Structure* (= *Interdisciplinary Studies on Information Structure*, 12, Universität Potsdam: kobv.de/ubp/volltexte/2009/3837).

Wiese, Richard. 2000. *The Phonology of German*. 2nd edn. Cambridge: Cambridge University Press.

Wiese, Richard. 2003. 'The unity and variation of (German) /r/'. *Zeitschrift für Dialektologie und Linguistik* 70.25–43.

Wiesinger, Peter. 1970. *Phonetisch–phonologische Untersuchungen zur Vokalentwicklung in den deutschen Dialekten*, vol. 1: *Langvokale im Hochdeutschen*; vol. 2: *Diphthonge im Hochdeutschen*. Berlin: de Gruyter.

Wiesinger, Peter. 1983. 'Phonologische Vokalsystem deutscher Dialekte: Ein synchronischer und diachronischer Überblick'. *Dialektologie: Ein Handbuch zur deutschen und allgemeinen Dialektforschung*, ed. by Werner Besch et al., vol. 1, 1042–1076. Berlin: de Gruyter.

Wiesinger, Peter. 1989. *Die Flexionsmorphologie des Verbum im Bairischen*. Wien: Verlag der österreichischen Akademie der Wissenschaften.

Wipf, Karl A. 1992. *Althochdeutsche poetische Texte: Althochdeutsch/Neuhochdeutsch*. Stuttgart: Reklam.

Wittmann, Reinhard. 1999. *Geschichte des deutschen Buchhandels*. 2nd edn. Munich: C. H. Beck.

Wodtko, Dagmar S., Britta Irslinger, & Carolin Schneider. 2008. *Nomina im Indogermanischen Lexikon*. Heidelberg: Carl Winter.

Wolf, Norbert Richard. 2000. 'Syntax des Mittelhochdeutschen'. *Sprachgeschichte: Ein Handbuch zur Geschichte der deutschen Sprache und ihrer Erforschung*, ed. by Werner Besch et al., 1385–1391. Berlin: de Gruyter.

Wolff, Gerhart. 1990. *Deutsche Sprachgeschichte*. Tübingen: UTB/Francke.

Wright, Joseph. 1907. *Historical German Grammar*, vol. 1: *Phonology, Word-Formation and Accidence*. Oxford: Oxford University Press.

Wurzel, Wolfgang Ullrich. 1980. 'Ways of morphologizing phonological rules'. *Historical Morphology*, ed. by Jacek Fisiak, 443–462. The Hague: Mouton.

Wurzel, Wolfgang Ullrich. 1984. 'Was bezeichnet der Umlaut im Deutschen?' *Zeitschrift für Phonetik, Sprachwissenschaft und Kommunikationsforschung* 37.647–663.

Wurzel, Wolfgang Ullrich. 1989. *Inflectional Morphology and Naturalness*. Dordrecht: Kluwer.

Wurzel, Wolfgang Ullrich. 1992. 'Morphologische Reanalysen in der Geschichte der deutschen Substantivflexion'. *Folia Linguistica Historica* 13.279–307.

Wurzel, Wolfgang Ullrich. 1998. *Konrad Duden: Leben und Werk*. Mannheim: Dudenverlag.

Yager, Lisa, Nora Hellmold, Hyoun-A Joo, Michael T. Putnam, Eleonora Rossi, Catherine Stafford, & Joseph Salmons. 2015. 'New Structural Patterns in Moribund Grammar: Case Marking in Heritage German'. *Frontiers in Psychology* 6. http://journal.frontiersin.org/article/10.3389/fpsyg.2015.01716/full.

Young, Christopher & Thomas Gloning. 2004. *A History of the German Language through Texts*. London: Routledge.

Ziegler, Evelyn. 2007. 'Putting Standard German to the test'. *Germanic Language Histories 'from Below' (1700–2000)*, ed. by Stephan Elspaß, Nils Langer, Joachim Scharloth, & Wim Vandenbussche, 309–329. Berlin: de Gruyter.

Zubin, David & Klaus-Michael Köpcke. 1984. 'Affect classification in the German gender system'. *Lingua* 63.41–96.

Zwicky, Arnold. 'Clitics and particles'. *Language* 61.283–305.

Index of languages, language families, and dialects

Index of authors

Subject index

a-group 76–8
ablative 67
ablaut 74, 78–80, 115, 153–4, 211–13, 219, 270, 339, 375, 382, 384, 392
Abrogans 6
abstractionist (in reconstruction) 41
accent (accentual system) xxii, 6, 33, 37, 55, 78
accidental similarities 14
accusative 67, 171, 232, 336, 377–8
ach-Laut 42, 204
acquisition, language 13, 195, 216, 242, 295, 320, 355, 357, 360, 366, 386
address, pronouns of 284
adjectives 115, 143, 162, 167, 224, 266
adverb 171
affricate 119, 122
agglutination 65
allative 67
alliteration 164, 331
analogy (analogical change) 64, 212, 214, 217, 272, 300, 342, 384
analytic 65, 164, 382
anaptyxis 61, 128
Anatolian homeland 20
animate/inanimate 68, 233, 325–8
apocope 248, 256, 263–4, 266, 276–7, 376
Arme Heinrich, Der 234
articulation, manner and place 39
aspect 71, 73, 339, 344
aspiration 50–1, 117, 314, 365
athematic 66, 73, 82, 155
attitudes 5, 7, 239, 296, 300, 306, 309, 311, 354–5, 365–6, 369–70, 374, 380, 392
Ausgliederung (breakup, Germanic) 82–3, 92
auxiliary verb, auxiliation 80, 154, 166, 168, 225, 277–8, 339–41
Avars 95

Bavarian Quantity Relations 262, 313
Behaghel's Law 222
bible 93–4, 245–6, 280, 290–2, 307
bilingualism 95, 168, 287, 300–1, 355, 359
Bindevokal (linking vowel) 154, 214
Beowulf 245

borrowing 20, 223, 372–3, 375, 379
Bühnenaussprache 311, 314, 317
Bunny Conundrum 52

case 67–9, 168, 171, 212, 215, 231, 276, 321, 328, 385, 392
causative 81
chain shift 251–2, 257, 380
chanceries 229, 286–7, 289, 291, 293, 295
chronology (absolute and relative) 63, 98, 123, 133, 163, 199, 251
cladistics 22
clitic (cliticization) 49, 100, 150, 164, 172–4, 230–1, 342–3, 386
Closed Syllable Shortening (CSS) 210, 250, 255, 382
cluster (consonant) 50–1, 138–9, 201, 203, 210, 262, 365
Codex Argenteus 93–4
cognate 25
colonization, *Ostkolonisation* 194, 196, 238
comparative method 17, 102
compensatory lengthening 59, 87, 126, 236, 377
complementizer (agreement) 165, 336–7, 351–2, 373, 382
configurationality 221, 233
conjunction 165
conspiracy (in language change) 80, 138, 255
contact (language, dialect) 20, 84, 96, 116, 124, 168, 223, 301, 305, 360, 367, 375, 392
constituent, constituency 164
contraction (of medial stops) 201, 210
corded ware 20, 24, 83
correspondences, systematic sound 16–17, 20, 41, 45
coronal, coronalization 69, 315, 320, 360
corpus, corpora 249, 275, 278, 332, 340, 388
courts (medieval) 23, 193, 236
Crusades 195
cycle, Jespersen's cycle 336, 345

dative 67, 69, 159, 200, 231–3, 265, 268, 363, 377–8
definiteness 170–2, 223, 231, 266, 328, 382